HOSPITALITY INDUSTRY MANAGERIAL ACCOUNTING

Educational Institute Books

HOSPITALITY FOR SALE
C. DeWitt Coffman

UNIFORM SYSTEM OF ACCOUNTS AND EXPENSE DICTIONARY FOR SMALL HOTELS, MOTELS, AND MOTOR HOTELS
Fourth Edition

RESORT DEVELOPMENT AND MANAGEMENT
Second Edition
Chuck Y. Gee

PLANNING AND CONTROL FOR FOOD AND BEVERAGE OPERATIONS
Third Edition
Jack D. Ninemeier

STRATEGIC MARKETING PLANNING IN THE HOSPITALITY INDUSTRY: A BOOK OF READINGS
Edited by Robert L. Blomstrom

TRAINING FOR THE HOSPITALITY INDUSTRY
Second Edition
Lewis C. Forrest, Jr.

UNDERSTANDING HOSPITALITY LAW
Second Edition
Jack P. Jefferies

SUPERVISION IN THE HOSPITALITY INDUSTRY
Second Edition
Raphael R. Kavanaugh/Jack D. Ninemeier

SANITATION MANAGEMENT: STRATEGIES FOR SUCCESS
Ronald F. Cichy

ENERGY AND WATER RESOURCE MANAGEMENT
Second Edition
Robert E. Aulbach

MANAGEMENT OF FOOD AND BEVERAGE OPERATIONS
Second Edition
Jack D. Ninemeier

MANAGING FRONT OFFICE OPERATIONS
Second Edition
Charles E. Steadmon/Michael L. Kasavana

STRATEGIC HOTEL/MOTEL MARKETING
Revised Edition
Christopher W. L. Hart/David A. Troy

MANAGING SERVICE IN FOOD AND BEVERAGE OPERATIONS
Anthony M. Rey/Ferdinand Wieland

THE LODGING AND FOOD SERVICE INDUSTRY
Second Edition
Gerald W. Lattin

SECURITY AND LOSS PREVENTION MANAGEMENT
Raymond C. Ellis, Jr., & the Security Committee of AH&MA

HOSPITALITY INDUSTRY MANAGERIAL ACCOUNTING
Second Edition
Raymond S. Schmidgall

PURCHASING FOR HOSPITALITY OPERATIONS
William B. Virts

THE ART AND SCIENCE OF HOSPITALITY MANAGEMENT
Jerome J. Vallen/James R. Abbey

MANAGING COMPUTERS IN THE HOSPITALITY INDUSTRY
Michael L. Kasavana/John J. Cahill

MANAGING HOSPITALITY ENGINEERING SYSTEMS
Michael H. Redlin/David M. Stipanuk

UNDERSTANDING HOSPITALITY ACCOUNTING I
Second Edition
Raymond Cote

UNDERSTANDING HOSPITALITY ACCOUNTING II
Second Edition
Raymond Cote

MANAGING QUALITY SERVICES
Stephen J. Shriver

MANAGING CONVENTIONS AND GROUP BUSINESS
Leonard H. Hoyle/David C. Dorf/Thomas J. A. Jones

HOSPITALITY SALES AND ADVERTISING
James R. Abbey

MANAGING HUMAN RESOURCES IN THE HOSPITALITY INDUSTRY
David Wheelhouse

MANAGING HOUSEKEEPING OPERATIONS
Margaret M. Kappa/Aleta Nitschke/Patricia B. Schappert

CONVENTION SALES: A BOOK OF READINGS
Margaret Shaw

DIMENSIONS OF TOURISM
Joseph D. Fridgen

HOSPITALITY TODAY: AN INTRODUCTION
Rocco M. Angelo/Andrew N. Vladimir

MANAGING BAR AND BEVERAGE OPERATIONS
Lendal H. Kotschevar/Mary L. Tanke

POWERHOUSE CONFERENCES: ELIMINATING AUDIENCE BOREDOM
Coleman Lee Finkel

HOSPITALITY INDUSTRY MANAGERIAL ACCOUNTING

Second Edition

Raymond S. Schmidgall, Ph.D., CPA

A nonprofit educational foundation

Disclaimer

This publication is designed to provide accurate and authoritative information in regard to the subject matter covered. It is sold with the understanding that the publisher is not engaged in rendering legal, accounting, or other professional service. If legal advice or other expert assistance is required, the services of a competent professional person should be sought.

—From the Declaration of Principles jointly adopted by the American Bar Association and a Committee of Publishers and Associations.

The author, Raymond S. Schmidgall, is solely responsible for the contents of this publication. All views expressed herein are solely those of the author and do not necessarily reflect the views of the Educational Institute of the American Hotel & Motel Association (the Institute) or the American Hotel & Motel Association (AH&MA).

Nothing contained in this publication shall constitute a standard, an endorsement, or a recommendation of the Institute or AH&MA. The Institute and AH&MA disclaim any liability with respect to the use of any information, procedure, or product, or reliance thereon by any member of the hospitality industry.

©Copyright 1990
By the EDUCATIONAL INSTITUTE of the
AMERICAN HOTEL & MOTEL ASSOCIATION
1407 South Harrison Road
P.O. Box 1240
East Lansing, Michigan 48826

The Educational Institute of the American
Hotel & Motel Association is a nonprofit
educational foundation.

Printed in the United States of America
    4 5 6 7 8 9 10 94 93 92 91

Library of Congress Cataloging-in-Publication Data
Schmidgall, Raymond S., 1945–
    Hospitality industry managerial accounting.

    Includes bibliographical references.
    1. Hospitality industry—Accounting.
2. Managerial accounting. I. Title.
HF5686H75S34   1990   647.94'068'1   90-3983
ISBN O-86612-058-0

Editors: Timothy J. Eaton
             Lisa A. Kloack

Contents

Preface

Hospitality Industry Managerial Accounting presents managerial accounting concepts and explains how they apply to specific operations within the hospitality industry. This book is written not only for managers in the hospitality industry, but also for hospitality students at both the two-year and four-year college levels. Readers of this textbook should already be familiar with basic accounting concepts and procedures, or have taken an introductory course in basic accounting.

Each chapter begins by posing a number of questions that managers in the hospitality industry may have regarding accounting concepts which will be developed within the chapter. At the close of each chapter, there are a number of discussion questions and problems designed to test the reader's understanding of the concepts covered within that chapter. Some chapters are followed by supplemental readings which present more detailed approaches to concepts mentioned in the text. In addition, computer applications of managerial accounting concepts appear throughout the text. Readers who are unfamiliar with fundamental computer terminology may find it helpful to read Appendix B, "Essentials of Computer Systems."

The text consists of 15 chapters and begins with an overview of accounting in Chapter 1. Chapters 2 through 4 cover the three basic financial statements—the balance sheet, the income statement, and the statement of cash flows, respectively. While the presentations of the balance sheet and the statement of cash flows are similar to the coverage found in most financial accounting texts, the presentation of the income statement is based on various schedules from the *Uniform System of Accounts and Expense Dictionary for Small Hotels, Motels, and Motor Hotels.*

Chapter 5 focuses on ratio analysis as a means of interpreting information reported on financial statements. For each ratio presented, the chapter outlines its purpose, the sources of data needed for the ratio's calculation, the formula by which it is calculated, and the interpretation of the ratio results from the varying viewpoints of owners, creditors, and managers.

Chapters 6, 7, and 8 cover basic cost concepts, cost-volume-profit analysis, and cost approaches to pricing. Chapter 6 presents the various types of costs and how managers can identify the relevant costs in particular decision-making situations. Chapter 7's discussion of cost-volume-profit analysis is presented in both equation and graphic form. In addition, this chapter discusses and illustrates the determination of each breakeven point. Chapter 8 takes a cost approach to pricing and includes pricing examples for food, beverages, and rooms.

Forecasting methods and operations budgeting are the subjects of Chapters 9 and 10, respectively. Chapter 9 focuses on basic mathematical models for forecasting sales. This chapter also presents hospitality industry examples of sales forecasting procedures at Stouffer Hotels and Resorts, Canteen Corporation, and Pizza Hut. The operations budgeting chapter discusses how budgets are prepared, how budgets are used for controlling operations, and how the operations budgeting process may take different forms at multi-unit hospitality enterprises as compared with single properties.

Chapter 11 covers cash management and includes sections on cash budgeting and managing working capital. Chapter 12 presents basic requirements of internal accounting control for various accounting functions including cash receipts, cash disbursements, accounts receivable, accounts payable, inventories, payroll, fixed assets, and marketable securities. Capital budgeting is the subject of Chapter 13. The capital budgeting models presented include payback, accounting rate of return, net present value, and internal rate of return.

The final two chapters deal with lease accounting and income taxes. Although both of these topics are generally found in financial accounting texts, they are addressed here because managers of hospitality operations should have some knowledge in each of these areas. The chapter on lease accounting includes illustrations of accounting for various types of leases, and the Supplemental Reading to the chapter provides a sample lease. The chapter on income taxes does not dwell on tax details. Instead, it provides an overview of the elements of taxes, discusses tax avoidance, and presents the advantages and disadvantages of various forms of business organization from a tax point of view.

Writing this textbook has been a most challenging experience, and I could not have completed it without the assistance of many industry personnel and several of my colleagues—including Michael Kasavana, John Tarras, and Jack Ninemeier—at the School of Hotel, Restaurant, and Institutional Management at Michigan State University. I am most indebted to Joseph F. Cotter, former Vice President of Development of The Sheraton Corporation, for his assistance in reviewing the manuscript, submitting outlines for several chapters, and supplying several exhibits for the first edition of this text. Other Sheraton personnel who assisted in the development of the first edition were Brian Baker, Joseph Beatty, Peter Johnson, William Dewhurst, Jose Fardullia, Edward Gremlich, John Pignataro, and Ronald Sawyer.

Richard Brooks of Stouffer Hotels and Resorts provided the primary input for the computerization sections of most chapters. Michael Kasavana provided Appendix B, "Essentials of Computer Systems." Julie Smith, my former graduate assistant and now a management consultant with Arthur Anderson & Co., was most helpful with reviewing the entire manuscript and providing several of the computerization illustrations.

Special thanks are in order for A. Paul Matteucci, former Director of Internal Audits for Westin Hotel & Resorts, who supplied the internal questionnaire forms appended to Chapter 12.

The industry examples of sales forecasting were provided by Raymond Holmes, John Coonce and Alex Wilson of Stouffer Hotels and Resorts; Donald Finger of Canteen Corporation; and Pat Johns of Pizza Hut, Inc.

Wesley Byloff, while financial controller of Metro Hotels Corporation, reviewed the entire manuscript for the first edition and provided several useful suggestions for improvement.

For this second edition, a review committee provided useful insights and invaluable suggestions. The committee consisted of: Lance Crocker, Chairman, Business/Economics Department, Hotel/Hospitality Management, Johnson State College; James W. Damitio, Assistant Professor of Accounting, Central Michigan University; Michael Flannery, Coordinator and Associate Professor, Restaurant, Hotel, and Institutional Management, Behavioral Science Department, Purdue University—Calumet; Audrey McCool, Professor and Michael D. Rose Chair, William F. Harrah College of Hotel Administration, Department of Hospitality Administration and Tourism, University of Nevada, Las Vegas; Kathleen R. McIntee, Vice President of Corporate Accounting, AIRCOA; Lyell E. Metcalf, Associate Professor, William F. Harrah College of Hotel Administration, Department of Hospitality Administration and Tourism, University of Nevada, Las Vegas; Douglas B. Rusth, Assistant Professor, Conrad Hilton College of Hotel and Restaurant Management, University of Houston; and Kathy Savage, Instructor, School of Hotel, Restaurant and Institutional Management, Pennsylvania State University.

My wife, Barbara, spent hundreds of hours typing, editing, and retyping the original manuscript and again spent many hours assisting with the preparation of the second edition. Her patience and dedication to this project are largely responsible for its completion.

Dedication

In memory of Raymond Klein Schmidgall,
loving father, entrepreneur, and leader of people by example.

1 Introduction to Managerial Accounting

Hospitality is a huge and growing industry. A property manager needs more knowledge today than ever before and will need even more tomorrow. Managerial accounting focuses upon those aspects of accounting which concern hospitality managers most. These aspects include internal financial statements, budgeting, internal control, and costs. This introductory chapter will provide answers to many questions, including the following:

1. How does the hospitality industry differ from many other industries?

2. Why are food and beverage inventories relatively low in hospitality operations?

3. What are three aspects of seasonality in lodging properties?

4. What is the scope of the accounting function in hotels?

5. What are the major principles of accounting?

6. What are the various branches of accounting?

7. Why are rooms, in essence, perishable inventory?

8. What are the three forms of business organization?

This chapter will present an overview of the hospitality industry and then focus on the accounting function within the industry. We will briefly review the principles, branches, and mechanics of accounting, discuss the accounting cycle, and describe the three forms of business organization.

Overview of the Hospitality Industry

The hospitality industry consists of several different types of operations providing both products and services to its clients or guests. It includes hotels, motels, motor hotels, inns, quick-service restaurants, fine dining restaurants, cafeterias, resorts, country clubs, and city clubs, to mention a few. These hospitality operations serve both the traveling public and local residents. While this is particularly true of food and beverage operations, many lodging properties also market their accommodations to local residents by promoting "weekend escape" packages.

Properties in the lodging segment of the hospitality industry range from single-unit operations of fewer than 10 rooms to Holiday Inns, the largest chain operation in the United States, with over 1,500 hotels and 310,000 rooms. In 1990, there were over 60 mega-hotels—hotels with 1,000 or more rooms—in the United States.[1] Smith Travel Research estimates that there were 3,040,000 rooms in 44,100 establishments in 1990 and predicts that in 1995 there will be 3.34 million rooms.[2] The differences among lodging operations are vast. At one extreme, there are budget hotels and motels providing only rooms, and at the other, luxury properties providing nearly every imaginable service a guest might desire.

There are also many different types of food service operations. Properties in the food and beverage segment of the hospitality industry range from the single-unit operation with only window service to the McDonald's Corporation with over 11,000 restaurants throughout the world. In the club segment of the hospitality industry, there are some operations with fewer than 200 members and others with over 15,000 members.

Lodging facilities in the United States took in $50 billion in a recent year, while food service establishments took in approximately $227 billion in revenues. The total revenues of these two segments of the hospitality industry approximated 5% of the U.S. gross national product.[3]

Exhibits 1.1 and 1.2 provide further insights into financial aspects of the hospitality industry. Exhibit 1.1 illustrates what happens to the average revenue dollar in the lodging industry—where it comes from and where it goes. Exhibit 1.2 illustrates this for the average revenue dollar in four segments of the food service industry. Notice that in the lodging industry, food sales are the second largest source of total revenues. Also notice that the largest category of expense for lodging operations is payroll and related expenses, while for the restaurant industry, payroll costs are generally second only to the cost of food. Finally, note that for food service operations, net income before taxes represents a relatively small percentage of total revenues while, for the average lodging operation, net income before taxes shows a *loss*.

Seasonality of Business

Although both manufacturing firms and hospitality operations frequently experience "seasonal" fluctuations in sales volume, hospitality operations also deal with activity variations throughout the day. Check-in times vary, but many hotels are busiest with check-ins between 3 and 5 p.m. Check-out at many hotels is extremely busy between 7 and 9 a.m. and between 11 a.m. and 1 p.m. Similarly, some food service operations may be full from 7:30 to 8:30 a.m., 11:30 a.m. to 1:30 p.m., and 6 to 8 p.m., and nearly empty during other hours of the day. Hospitality business may also vary during the week.

A common measure of activity for lodging operations is paid occupancy percentage. Paid occupancy percentage indicates what percentage of the rooms available for sale are actually sold. It is calculated by dividing the number of rooms sold by the number of rooms available. Transient hotels—that is, hotels catering primarily to business people—may experience 100% occupancy Monday through Thursday and 30% occupancy Friday through Sunday, averaging 70% for the week. Weekly seasonality for many resort hotels results in the opposite distribution; their busiest

Exhibit 1.1   U.S. Lodging Industry Dollar

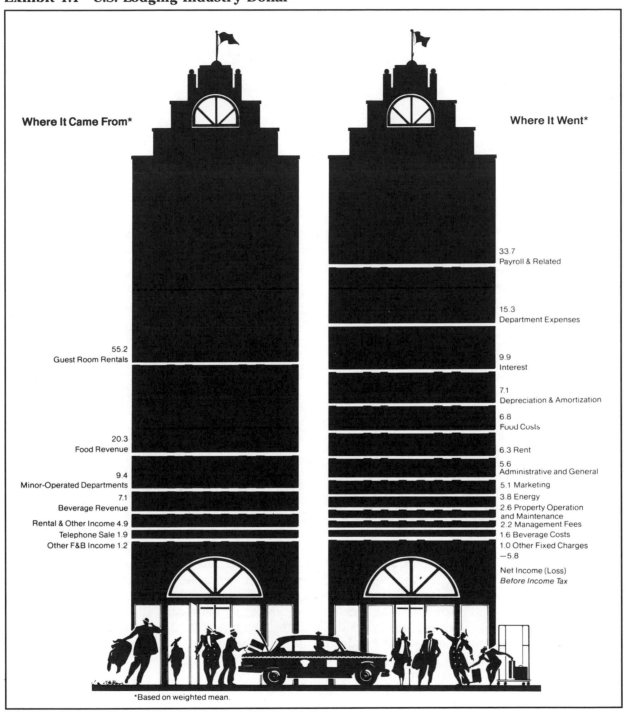

Where It Came From*

55.2
Guest Room Rentals

20.3
Food Revenue

9.4
Minor-Operated Departments

7.1
Beverage Revenue

Rental & Other Income 4.9
Telephone Sale 1.9
Other F&B Income 1.2

Where It Went*

33.7
Payroll & Related

15.3
Department Expenses

9.9
Interest

7.1
Depreciation & Amortization

6.8
Food Costs

6.3 Rent

5.6
Administrative and General

5.1 Marketing

3.8 Energy

2.6 Property Operation
and Maintenance

2.2 Management Fees

1.6 Beverage Costs

1.0 Other Fixed Charges

−5.8

Net Income (Loss)
Before Income Tax

*Based on weighted mean.

Source: Laventhol & Horwath, *U.S. Lodging Industry 1989* (Philadelphia: Laventhol & Horwath, 1989), p. 14. Reprinted by permission.

periods are usually weekends rather than weekdays. In addition, their multiple occupancy, determined by dividing the number of rooms with more than one guest by the total number of rooms occupied, is higher than that of transient hotels. In a recent year, the multiple occupancy was

Exhibit 1.2 U.S. Restaurant Industry Dollar

	Full-Menu Tableservice	Limited-Menu Tableservice	Limited-Menu No Tableservice	Cafeteria
Where It Came From*				
Food Sales	81.3	83.5	98.1	97.1
Beverage Sales	16.8	14.6	1.6	1.2
Other Income	1.9	1.9	0.3	1.7
Where It Went*				
Cost of Food Sold	29.5	28.3	31.1	36.9
Cost of Beverage Sold	4.6	3.9	0.4	0.4
Payroll	26.9	28.9	23.5	25.4
Employee Benefits	2.6	4.5	3.1	4.1
Direct Operating Expenses	6.9	6.4	5.7	4.2
Music and Entertainment	1.0	0.5	0.3	0.1
Advertising and Promotion	2.6	2.6	4.8	1.3
Utilities	2.8	3.0	2.9	2.7
Administrative and General	3.8	4.3	4.4	3.7
Repairs and Maintenance	1.9	1.7	2.1	1.3
Rent	4.7	3.7	6.8	6.4
Property Taxes	0.6	0.7	0.7	0.5
Other Taxes	1.3	0.5	0.4	0.6
Property Insurance	1.3	1.2	0.9	0.8
Interest	1.1	1.1	0.6	0.8
Depreciation	2.9	2.9	3.0	3.6
Other Deductions	0.5	0.5	0.4	0.6
Net Income Before Income Taxes	5.0	5.3	8.9	6.6

*All figures are weighted averages.
**Based on 1988 data.

Source: National Restaurant Association and Laventhol & Horwath, *Restaurant Industry Operations Report '89*, p.9.

40.3% for transient hotels and 81.5% for resort hotels.[4] (Occupancy percentages are discussed further in Chapter 5.)

Seasonality throughout the year is a serious factor for many hotels. Many resorts are open for only one season of the year. Other lodging establishments, although open all year, have much more sales activity during certain times of the year. For example, the occupancy of many Florida hotels is higher during the winter months as vacationers from the north descend on Florida to enjoy its warmth and sunshine.

Exhibit 1.3 shows the monthly occupancy rates in selected U.S. cities and states for 1988. Boston hotels registered 89% occupancy in October and 48% in December, while Miami hotels registered a high of 85% in February and a low of 60% in June. Thus, Exhibit 1.3 reveals both seasonal fluctuations and large differences among cities and states.

Short Distribution Chain and Time Span

In a food service operation, there is a relatively fast conversion of raw materials into a finished product and of the product into cash. Like manufacturing operations, food service operations must offer products that meet the consumer's expectations. However, the distribution chain and time span is considerably shorter for hospitality "products" than for most consumer goods.

Exhibit 1.3 Monthly Occupancy Rates

	1st Half 1989	Average for Year 1988	1988											
			Dec.	Nov.	Oct.	Sept.	Aug.	July	June	May	April	Mar.	Feb.	Jan.
Albuquerque	61 %	62 %	42 %	58 %	72 %	67 %	73 %	72 %	70 %	67 %	63 %	62 %	49 %	49 %
Atlanta	58	60	42	55	62	56	66	65	61	62	59	64	65	60
Austin	67	55	36	55	58	53	60	54	62	62	59	60	48	47
Boston	67	72	48	71	89	85	87	79	84	65	73	69	58	51
Chattanooga	57	57	38	45	66	61	66	69	66	58	62	54	63	54
Chicago	63	55	49	69	77	75	73	66	78	72	69	64	54	47
Colorado Springs	48	55	31	40	51	67	84	83	79	61	49	45	40	38
Corpus Christi	58	51	38	43	27	45	63	73	66	58	58	57	55	44
Dallas/Fort Worth	60	55	42	53	62	53	57	55	54	53	53	58	58	65
Denver	52	55	36	46	52	54	64	62	63	49	48	51	48	47
Fort Lauderdale	71	68	63	72	59	52	54	56	58	69	74	79	86	71
Houston	60	55	43	57	62	47	60	57	60	54	55	58	60	54
Kansas City	56	62	49	65	67	62	76	66	65	66	67	59	55	50
Knoxville	64	65	50	61	74	66	75	75	71	66	67	58	49	45
Little Rock	66	62	48	55	68	68	74	75	59	61	61	59	60	47
Los Angeles	71	70	57	67	74	72	80	74	74	70	70	75	69	66
Memphis	61	58	47	60	64	61	68	65	61	58	55	55	56	49
Miami	74	69	65	70	66	61	65	64	60	71	69	78	85	82
Minneapolis	62	62	48	61	67	67	71	66	65	58	58	56	59	52
Nashville	68	69	53	63	78	73	74	79	82	74	69	65	59	51
New Orleans	67	65	44	67	81	59	67	65	64	70	73	64	72	80
New York City	72	77	70	82	89	79	79	69	81	82	74	74	69	61
Orange County, CA	75	68	54	62	69	64	81	76	76	69	72	78	67	57
Orlando Area:														
Disney/Kissimmee	89	82	60	76	83	69	93	95	91	87	92	90	84	66
International Drive	86	77	57	69	79	70	86	91	80	74	88	88	82	69
City of Orlando	76	65	52	55	59	54	70	73	64	61	74	81	78	59
Palm Beach	75	67	59	59	59	57	69	61	59	65	79	87	87	73
Philadelphia	71	72	53	73	84	72	72	64	77	83	80	70	69	58
Phoenix	69	57	47	57	57	50	46	40	47	58	68	83	76	62
St. Louis	59	62	47	59	70	68	73	71	74	65	62	63	46	45
St. Paul	56	57	41	46	62	58	62	63	68	60	57	64	59	41
San Antonio	69	67	53	58	68	63	80	85	79	63	64	66	61	48
San Diego County	68	69	51	58	69	72	84	79	69	70	73	77	72	60
San Francisco	72	73	61	69	90	76	79	82	79	77	68	74	64	55
Scottsdale	72	59	43	56	60	52	43	38	44	64	76	87	80	67
Tampa Bay	75	68	51	66	68	55	71	67	60	68	74	87	83	63
Tucson	72	63	52	57	65	59	51	53	75	59	64	80	84	60
Washington, D.C.	71	68	45	60	79	72	70	69	81	85	82	78	58	42
Alabama	64	63	49	62	67	66	67	72	69	66	63	66	60	54
Arizona	69	59	47	56	60	54	50	47	55	58	67	81	76	60
Arkansas	63	62	46	55	69	66	73	73	68	60	59	59	57	48
Colorado	52	54	37	41	49	54	66	65	61	48	46	55	50	46
Florida	77	69	55	64	65	59	68	73	68	69	77	83	80	66
Georgia	64	60	43	55	64	61	62	67	65	61	68	66	57	47
Hawaii	80	79	71	75	80	76	87	81	78	73	74	82	87	76
Illinois	63	58	45	61	66	68	76	69	70	63	63	53	53	46
Minnesota	60	60	45	53	63	65	72	68	66	60	59	58	58	49
Mississippi	58	57	39	54	58	59	60	61	63	58	62	63	50	41
New Mexico	64	64	46	55	72	71	78	77	74	68	61	63	49	45
New York State	70	74	64	77	85	77	79	70	80	79	71	71	65	58
Northern California	68	68	57	64	79	73	77	75	75	72	67	67	61	53
Oklahoma	55	45	37	52	49	52	53	53	53	44	47	47	41	38
South Carolina	57	56	37	46	58	61	67	72	67	62	65	57	45	37
Tennessee	62	62	47	57	72	65	72	73	71	63	61	56	55	48
Texas	61	57	44	54	59	53	62	61	61	55	56	58	57	55
Utah	66	66	54	53	62	67	78	70	70	61	61	71	62	54
Virginia	61	65	40	57	74	68	78	77	76	73	73	64	59	43
Wyoming/Montana	55	56	37	44	55	68	81	76	67	54	52	54	49	40

Reprinted from *Trends in the Hotel Industry, U.S.A. Edition,* ©1989 Pannell Kerr Forster.

For example, a new automobile purchased from a dealer may have been assembled several months before the sale, thousands of miles away, by a different company using finished parts supplied by more than 50 companies. In hospitality operations, inventory is often purchased one day and sold the next. The product is produced, sold, and consumed at the same location, often in less than two hours, sometimes within minutes. The food service "manufacturer" purchases the raw ingredients, prepares them to suit the consumer's tastes, and serves the finished product on the premises. The food service operator will in many cases receive immediate feedback on the quality of the food and service product, especially if it failed to meet the consumers' expectations.

As a result of this short distribution chain and time span, hospitality operations do little advance production. Thus, they maintain a minimal inventory of the goods they provide. This is reflected by the fact that major operations in the hospitality industry generally have less than 5% of their total assets invested in inventory of goods for resale. In contrast, the inventory of many major manufacturing firms equals at least 30% of their total assets.

A Labor-Intensive Industry

There is another important difference between the hospitality and manufacturing industries. In the manufacturing sector, automatic equipment has reduced the need for labor. This is not the case in the hospitality industry. As we have already seen, payroll expense is a major element in the cost of sales for both the lodging and food service segments of the hospitality industry. The seasonality of hospitality sales also contributes to the labor intensity of the industry. The busy check-in and check-out times during daily hotel operations require much labor to provide quality service. Similarly, food service operations have increased labor needs for spurts of activity throughout the day. Scheduling personnel for busy times is important if a hospitality operation is to generate profits while meeting guests' needs and wants.

Another important dimension of food and beverage operations in lodging facilities is the need to provide service even when it may not be profitable. For example, food service must be provided to guests even on low-occupancy days, and room service must always be available in first-class properties.

The short distribution chain and time span characteristic of the delivery and consumption of hospitality products and services also contributes to the industry's labor intensity. Personnel must prepare, produce, sell, and serve the operation's offerings. Labor must be available to prepare food when a guest wants it. Some food service operations promise the finished product within minutes after the guest's order is taken. Such prompt guest-oriented service can only be provided by a large and efficient staff. The total labor cost may be as low as 20% of the total revenue dollar at a quick-service restaurant or over 50% at a private club. Controlling labor costs while satisfying the needs and wants of guests is crucial to the success of any hospitality operation.

Major Investment in Fixed Assets

In addition to being labor-intensive, hospitality properties are also, for the most part, fixed-asset-intensive as well. Lodging facilities provide rooms for guests to relax, rest, entertain, and conduct business in. The room as a product is carried as a fixed asset, and its cost is written off (depreciated) over time. The basic cost of the room is the same whether or not it is occupied. In this sense, a room is the most perishable product a lodging operation has, because the revenue lost from an unsold room can never be regained. The construction cost of lodging facilities, including

Exhibit 1.4   Responsibilities of Hotel Controllers

Area	Percentage Reporting Responsibility
General Accounting	92%
Accounts Payable	92%
Accounts Receivable	91%
Computer System Accounting	88%
Payroll	87%
Night Audits	80%
Cash Management	77%
Beverage Controls	67%
Food Controls	65%
Cashiers	64%
Tax Returns	61%
Purchasing	60%
Computer System Front Office Reservations	58%
Receiving	52%
Storage	52%
Investments	42%
Security	22%

the furniture and fixtures, may vary between $10,000 and $400,000 per room. The cost of rooms represents a major investment by lodging operations, and the fixed assets of major hotels range between 55% and 85% of their total assets. In contrast, the fixed assets of many manufacturing companies approximate only 30% of their total assets.

This overview of the hospitality industry has described many of the different types of hospitality operations and indicated the impressive dimensions of the industry. As we have seen, the hospitality industry is greatly affected by seasonal (daily, weekly, monthly, and yearly) sales fluctuations, by the short distribution chain and quick consumption of its offerings, by the need for a large, efficient work force, and by large investment in fixed assets. These characteristics of hospitality operations give shape to the challenges which the accounting function must face within the industry.

The Accounting Function in the Hospitality Industry

The accounting function in hospitality industry properties is performed by a group of specialists ranging from bookkeepers to executives with such titles as Executive Vice-President and Controller (or Comptroller). Chief accounting executives are responsible for typical accounting functions such as receivables, payables, payroll, and, in some cases, storage and security. Exhibit 1.4 summarizes the results of a recent survey of 278 hotel *property* (as opposed to *corporate*) controllers and shows a wide range of reported responsibilities.

The size of an accounting staff may vary widely—from a part-time bookkeeper in a 10-room motel to several hundred people in a large hotel or restaurant chain. The size of the accounting staff at an individual property varies with the size and diversity of the hotel's operations. The accounting staff at hotels with more than 1,000 rooms ranges from 30 to

Exhibit 1.5 Controller's Department Organization Chart

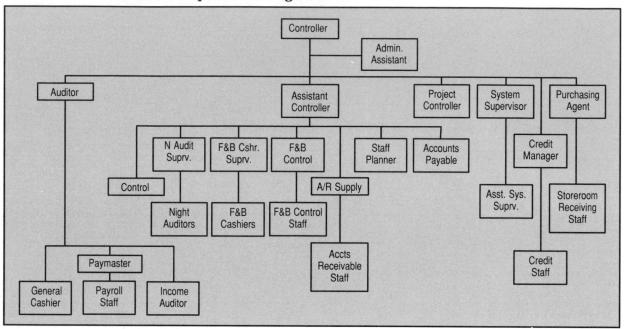

50 people. The accounting staff at one major worldwide hotel firm totals approximately 250, while the corporate accounting staff (A/P, payroll, internal audit, tax, and so forth) at a major food service headquarters totals 150. Exhibit 1.5 is a sample organization chart for the accounting function at a large hotel.

The accounting function within a lodging property is information-oriented—that is, its major role is providing information to users. For external users such as financial institutions, accounting usually communicates through financial statements. Internally, accounting provides a wide variety of financial reports, including operating statements. (Exhibit 3.3 in Chapter 3 lists various management reports generally prepared by accounting department personnel.) The operating statements are formatted to reflect revenues and related expenses by areas of responsibility. In addition to the income statement of the property as a whole, departmental statements are prepared for each department generating revenues and incurring expenses, such as rooms, food and beverage, and telephone. Service centers such as marketing and property operation and maintenance also provide separate statements. (These statements are discussed in greater detail in Chapter 3.)

Regardless of the size of an operation's accounting department, the diversity of its responsibilities, or the number and types of reports produced, the accounting staff is responsible for providing *service*. The accounting staff must work closely with operating management and other service departments in order for the hospitality property to meet its objectives. Exhibit 1.6, an organization chart of a major hotel, reflects the relative position of the controller and his/her staff within the hotel's organization.

Exhibit 1.6 Organization Chart for a Large Lodging Establishment

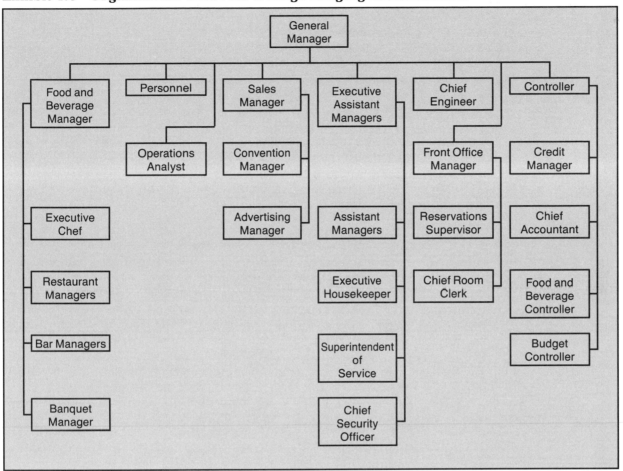

		Uniform Systems of Accounts

Uniform Systems of Accounts

For internal purposes (that is, for management use), uniform accounting systems, commonly called *uniform systems of accounts*, have been developed. These systems are popular among hospitality organizations because they provide a turnkey accounting system. Uniform systems have been tested over time and refined to meet the ever-changing needs of management. We will refer to several uniform systems throughout this text. Uniform systems are discussed in greater detail in Chapter 3.

Principles of Accounting

In order to understand accounting methods, you must understand basic accounting principles. These **generally accepted accounting principles** (often referred to by the acronym *GAAP*) provide a uniform basis for preparing financial statements. Although not "etched in stone," accounting principles have become accepted over time through common usage and also through the work of such major accounting bodies as the American Institute of Certified Public Accountants, the American Accounting Association, and the Financial Accounting Standards Board (FASB).

Students of hospitality accounting may often wonder why an accounting transaction is recorded in a particular way at a particular time or why some asset value is not changed at some point. Generally, the reasons relate to accounting principles. For example, a fixed asset may have cost $10,000 in 19X1 but has a market value of $15,000 in 19X5. The *cost principle* dictates that the fixed asset is retained on the books at its cost of $10,000 rather than being increased to its market value of $15,000. A second example is the accrual of payroll at the end of the month. Assume that employees have worked the last few days of the month and the next pay date falls in the following month. The *matching principle* dictates that the unpaid payroll for the period be recognized both as an expense and as a liability.

The following sections briefly discuss several generally accepted accounting principles.

The Cost Principle

The **cost principle** states that when a transaction is recorded, it is the transaction price or cost that establishes the accounting value for the product or service purchased. For example, if a restaurateur buys a dishwasher, the agreed-upon price between the restaurant and the supplier determines the amount to be recorded. If the agreed-upon price is $5,000, then the dishwasher is initially valued at $5,000 in the restaurant's accounting records. The supplier may have acquired the dishwasher from the manufacturer for $4,000 and the restaurant may receive an offer of $5,500 for it the day it is purchased; however, it is the actual cost which establishes the amount to be recorded. If amounts other than cost (such as estimates or appraisals) were used to record transactions, then accounting records would lose their usefulness. When cost is the basis for recording a transaction, the buyer and seller determine the amount to be recorded. This amount is generally an objective and fair measure of the value of the goods or services purchased.

When the value of *current* assets is clearly less than the cost recorded on the books, this decline in value must be recognized. Thus, the *conservatism principle* (to be discussed later) overrides the cost principle. For example, many properties carry inventory at the lower of cost or current market value. On the other hand, property and equipment (also frequently called fixed assets) are normally carried at cost less the depreciated amounts and are not reduced to market value as long as management plans to retain them for their useful life. This treatment of property and equipment is based on the *going-concern principle* (also discussed later).

Business Entity

Accounting and financial statements are based on the concepts that (1) each business is a **business entity** that maintains its own set of accounts and (2) these accounts are separate from the other financial interests of the owners. For example, if a hotel owner decides to take some food home from the hotel for personal use, it should be properly charged to the owner's account. Recording business activity separately from the owner's personal affairs allows a reasonable determination of the property's profitability. Not only does separate recording provide excellent information for managing the business, it is also necessary for properly filing tax returns.

Continuity of the Business Unit (Going Concern)

According to the **continuity of the business unit principle**, in preparing the accounting records and reports, it is assumed that the business will continue indefinitely and that liquidation is not in prospect—in other words, the business is a **going concern**. This assumption is based on the concept that the real value of the hotel or motel is its ability to earn a profit, rather than the value its assets would bring in liquidation. According to this concept, the market value of the property and equipment need not appear on the financial statements, and prepaid expenses are considered assets. If there is a reasonable chance the hospitality property may be unable to continue operations in the near future, allowance for this future event should be reflected in the financial statements. This may be best accomplished by reducing asset values to their market values.

Unit of Measurement

The financial statements are based on transactions expressed in monetary terms. The monetary unit is assumed to represent a stable unit of value so that transactions from past periods and the current period can be included on the same statement.

In the late 1970s and early 1980s, inflation (as measured by the Consumer Price Index) exceeded 10%. The FASB responded by requiring large hospitality firms to show current replacement cost of their property and equipment in footnotes to their financial statements. For some lodging properties, the current values of property and equipment exceeded twice the amount of the fixed assets carried on the books. Since inflation has been relatively low for the past several years, the FASB has rescinded this reporting requirement.

Some hospitality businesses, such as Hilton Hotels Corporation, throughout the 1980s provided financial information in addition to that required by the FASB. Hilton not only provided the traditional financial statements based on historical cost, as well as certain figures to reflect current replacement cost. It also provided certain figures based on the present value of income streams from their fixed assets.

Objective Evidence

Accounting transactions and the resulting accounting records should be based as much as possible on **objective evidence**. Generally, this evidence is an invoice and/or a canceled check. However, estimates must be assumed in the absence of such objective evidence. For example, suppose that the owner of a restaurant contributes equipment, purchased several years ago for personal use, to a restaurant corporation in exchange for 100 shares of stock. Further assume that there is no known market value for the restaurant corporation's stock. The owner may believe the equipment is worth $1,200, while the original catalog shows the cost several years ago of $1,400, and an appraiser appraises the equipment at $850. In this example, the most objective estimate of its value today would be the appraiser's estimate of $850.

Full Disclosure

The financial statements must provide information on all the facts pertinent to the interpretation of the financial statements. This **full disclosure** is accomplished either by reporting the information in the body of the financial statements or in footnotes to the financial statements. Footnote disclosures might include the accounting methods used, changes in the accounting methods, contingent liabilities, events occurring after the

Exhibit 1.7 Types of Disclosure

Type of Disclosure	Example
Accounting methods used	Straight-line method of depreciation
Change in the accounting methods	A change from depreciating a fixed asset using the straight-line method to using the double declining balance method
Contingent liability	A lawsuit against the company for alleged failure to provide adequate security for a guest who suffered personal injury
Events occurring after the financial statement date	A fire destroys significant uninsured assets of the hotel company one week after the end of the year
Unusual and non-recurring items	A hotel firm in Michigan suffers significant losses due to an earthquake

financial statement date, and unusual and non-recurring items. An example of each type of disclosure is presented in Exhibit 1.7.

Consistency
Several accounting methods are often available for reporting a specific kind of activity. Management chooses the method most appropriate under the circumstances. For example, there are several ways to determine inventory values, and there are several methods of depreciating fixed assets. The **consistency principle** requires that, once an accounting method has been adopted, it should be followed from period to period unless a change is warranted and disclosed. The consistency principle allows a user of financial information to make reasonable comparisons between periods. Without consistent accounting, trends indicated by supposedly comparable financial statements might be misleading. When it becomes necessary to change to another method, the change must be disclosed and the dollar effect on earnings and/or the balance sheet must be reported.

The consistency principle does *not* dictate that an operation must or even should use the same accounting methods for preparing tax returns that it uses to prepare financial statements for external users. The principle does not even require that a method selected for one element of a company be used for all similar elements. For example, the straight-line method of depreciation may be used to depreciate one hotel and an accelerated method of depreciation may be used to depreciate another hotel owned by the same company.

Matching
The **matching principle** refers to relating expenses to revenues. For example, suppose that a hotel purchases a computerized reservations system which will benefit the hotel for several years. The cost is therefore recorded as a fixed asset and the cost of the system is written off over the system's life. The result is a partial write-off of the fixed asset each year against the revenues generated in part by using the system. This process is referred to as matching and is the basis for adjusting entries at the end

of each accounting period. The matching principle is used when transactions are recorded on an accrual rather than cash basis. The accrual basis and cash basis of accounting are discussed later in this chapter.

Conservatism

The **conservatism principle** calls for recognizing expenses as soon as possible, but delaying the recognition of revenues until they are ensured. The practical result is to be conservative (low) in recognizing net income for the current year. It is not proper to deliberately understate net income; however, many accountants wish to be cautious in recognizing revenues and "generous" in recognizing expenses.

A good example of this is the accounting treatment of lawsuits. If a hotel is a plaintiff in a lawsuit and its legal counsel indicates the case will be won and estimates the amount of settlement, the amount is not recorded as revenue until a judgment is rendered. On the other hand, if the same hotel is a defendant in a lawsuit and its legal counsel indicates the hotel will lose the lawsuit and most likely will pay a stated amount, this "expense" is recognized immediately.

Conservatism is apparent in the valuation of inventory at the lower of cost or current market value and the recognition of non-refundable deposits for future banquets as a liability until the banquet is catered.

Materiality

According to the **materiality principle**, events or information must be accounted for if they "make a difference" to the user of the financial information. An item is material in comparison to a standard. Some accountants have attempted to establish materiality by rules of thumb; for example, an item may be recognized if it exceeds a certain percentage of total assets or total income. However, this approach fails to address an item's relative importance over time. In addition, several immaterial items may be material when viewed collectively.

The materiality principle is often applied to fixed assets. Tangible items with useful lives beyond one year are commonly recorded as fixed assets. However, when such items cost less than a certain amount (specified by the board of directors of the purchasing organization), they are expensed because the cost is considered immaterial. An example would be a wastebasket. A $39 wastebasket might have a useful life of ten years, but since it cost less than the (for example) $100 limit for recording expenditures as fixed assets, it is expensed. In this case, the expenditure was immaterial to record as a fixed asset.

When a hospitality property provides footnotes to supplement its financial statement, only material or potentially material items are presented.

Cash Versus Accrual Accounting

The cash and accrual bases of accounting are two methods of determining when to record a transaction.

Cash basis accounting recognizes an accounting transaction at the point of cash inflow or outflow. For example, cash received in 19X2 for rooms sold in 19X1 would be treated as 19X2 revenues. Likewise, expenses incurred in 19X1 for which cash was disbursed in 19X2 would be treated as 19X2 expenses. Because of these improper assignments of revenues and expenses, cash basis accounting is generally not a fair reflection of business operations. Cash basis accounting usually violates the generally accepted accounting principles discussed earlier. However, using this method is acceptable if the results do not differ *materially* from those that accrual basis accounting would produce. This method is used only by very small hospitality operations.

The more commonly used **accrual basis accounting** recognizes revenues when earned (regardless of when cash is received) and expenses when incurred (regardless of when cash is disbursed). For example, suppose that a hotel room is sold for the period of December 30, 19X1, through January 2, 19X2, and the hotel guest pays the bill of $240 ($60 per night for four nights) on the morning of January 3, 19X2. Under accrual basis accounting, two days of rooms revenue are recorded in December and two days of rooms revenue are recorded in January.

Expenses must be recognized periodically (because of the matching principle) even when no transaction has occurred. Examples of non-transaction expense recognition include depreciation of property and equipment, reduction of prepaid insurance, accrual of payroll, and provisions of an allowance for uncollectible receivables. For example, insurance coverage may be purchased twelve months in advance. Accrual basis accounting would recognize insurance expense over the 12-month period rather than when the cash is disbursed. The vehicle for this recognition is *adjusting entries*, which are briefly discussed later in this chapter.

Branches of Accounting

Accountants classify accounting activities in a variety of ways. However, most agree that there are distinct (though overlapping) branches. These branches are financial accounting, cost accounting, managerial accounting, tax accounting, auditing, and accounting systems.

Financial accounting refers to accounting for revenues, expenses, assets, and liabilities. It involves the basic accounting processes of recording, classifying, and summarizing transactions. This area is often limited to the accounting necessary to prepare and distribute financial reports. Financial accounting is historical in nature; that is, it deals with past events. Managerial accounting, on the other hand, deals with proposed events.

Cost accounting is the branch of accounting dealing with the recording, classification, allocation, and reporting of current and prospective costs. Cost accountants determine costs by departments, functions, responsibilities, and products and services. The chief purpose of cost accounting is to help operations personnel control operations.

Managerial accounting is the branch of accounting designed to provide information to various management levels in the hospitality operation for the purpose of enhancing controls. Management accountants prepare performance reports, including comparisons to the budget. One major purpose of these reports is to provide in-depth information as a basis for management decisions. Although managerial accounting may vary among segments of the hospitality industry and certainly among different establishments, many management accountants use various management science techniques.

Tax accounting is the branch of accounting relating to the preparation and filing of tax forms with governmental agencies. Tax planning to minimize tax payments is a significant part of the tax accountant's work. Tax accounting usually focuses on income tax at the federal, state, and local levels, but may also include sales, excise, payroll, and property taxes. Many hospitality operations employ tax accountants. Some operations contract the services of tax accountants employed by certified public accounting firms.

Auditing is the branch of accounting involved with reviewing and evaluating documents, records, and control systems. Auditing may be either external or internal. It is most often associated with the independent, external audit called a **financial audit**. The external auditor reviews the financial statements of the hospitality operation, its underlying internal control system, and its accounting records (journals, vouchers, invoices, checks, bank statements, and so forth) in order to render an opinion of the financial statements. The auditor usually then provides recommendations for strengthening the operation's internal controls. Financial audits may only be conducted by certified public accounting firms.

Over the past several years, hospitality operations have increasingly employed internal auditors, whose primary purpose is to review and evaluate internal control systems. Many large hospitality firms have a full staff of internal auditors who conduct audits at individual properties to help management maintain the internal control system.

The final branch of accounting is accounting systems. Accounting systems personnel review the information systems of hospitality organizations. Information systems include not only the accounting system but other elements such as reservations. Because many hospitality operations are now computerized, many accounting systems experts are electronic data processing specialists, such as programmers and systems analysts. The trend toward larger accounting systems staffs in hospitality organizations will continue as the information revolution extends into the twenty-first century.

Review of Accounting Mechanics

Introductory accounting textbooks use several chapters to cover the mechanics of accounting, from the fundamental accounting equation to the preparation of the financial statements. Let us briefly review these topics.[5]

The **fundamental accounting equation** is simply *assets equal liabilities plus owners' equity*. The equation is a balance to be tested and proven, not a formula to be calculated. This equality is reflected in the balance sheet prepared at the end of each accounting period. **Assets**, simply defined, are things owned by the hospitality operation, including cash, inventory, accounts receivable, land, buildings, and equipment. **Liabilities**, simply stated, are obligations to outside parties and include accounts payable, notes payable, income tax payable, long-term debt payable, and accrued payroll. **Owners' equity** is the residual claims owners have on assets. In other words, assets less liabilities equals owners' equity. After each business transaction is recorded, the total assets must equal the total of liabilities and owners' equity.

There are two major sub-classifications of owners' equity— **permanent accounts** and **temporary accounts**. An **account** is simply a device for showing increases and/or decreases in an individual asset, liability, or owners' equity item. For example, a hospitality operation would have an account for cash in its bank account called "cash in bank." Permanent owners' equity accounts are not closed at the end of an accounting period. They include accounts for recording capital stock and retained earnings. Temporary owners' equity accounts are closed out at the end of each fiscal year and include all revenue and expense accounts. Revenues increase owners' equity, while expenses decrease owners' equity.

The fundamental accounting equation can now be expanded as follows:

Assets (A) =   Liabilities (L)
+ Permanent Owners' Equity Accounts (POEA)
+ Temporary Owners' Equity Accounts (TOEA)

Revenues (R) and expenses (E) can be substituted for the TOEA, producing the following equation:

$$A = L + POEA + R - E$$

Debit and Credit

The left side of any account is called the **debit** side and the right side is the **credit** side. To debit an account means to record an amount on the left side, while to credit an account means to record an amount on the right side. The difference between the total debits and total credits of an account is called the **balance**. The normal balance of an account is the kind of balance, either debit or credit, which the account generally shows. The major classes of accounts have normal balances as follows:

Type of Account	Normal Balance
Asset	Debit
Liability	Credit
Owners' Equity:	
Permanent	Credit
Revenue	Credit
Expense	Debit

Each transaction is recorded with equal dollar amounts of debits and credits in **ledger accounts**. This equality of debits and credits in ledger accounts is tested by preparing a **trial balance**, which will be discussed later.

Debits (dr) and credits (cr) increase (+) and decrease (−) the various classes of accounts as follows:

Assets	=	Liabilities	+	Owners' Equity
+ | −		− | +		− | +
dr | cr		dr | cr		dr | cr

Revenues	Expenses
− | +	+ | −
dr | cr	dr | cr

Exhibit 1.8 Documents and Transactions

	Documents	
Type of Transaction	Prepared by Firm	Prepared Outside of Firm
Sales of products and services	Food guest check Telephone voucher Laundry voucher	—
Cash receipts	Cash Register tape	Checks
Purchases of products and services	Purchase order	Suppliers' invoices
Payroll	Time cards Payroll checks	—
Cash disbursements	Check	—

The Accounting Cycle

In every accounting period (generally one year), an **accounting cycle** begins, starting with recording transactions and ending with a post-closing trial balance. Each step in the cycle will be defined and discussed briefly.

There are five common transactions in a hospitality operation:

1. Sales of products and services
2. Cash receipts
3. Purchases of products and services
4. Payroll
5. Cash disbursements

With each transaction, documents are prepared and/or received from which bookkeepers record the transaction. Exhibit 1.8 lists a few key documents for each type of transaction.

Step 1 in the accounting cycle is recording the transactions in journals. Journals are simply books used for initially recording individual transactions. There is generally a separate journal (generically called a **specialized journal**) for each type of transaction. In addition, each establishment maintains a **general journal** for recording entries not recorded in specialized journals. The process of recording requires that each transaction be analyzed and that a minimum of two accounts be affected. For example, a cash sales transaction results in increases to the cash account and the sales account.

Step 2 in the accounting cycle is transferring the amounts from the journals to the ledger accounts. This process, called **posting**, tracks individual accounts. For example, assume that cash at the beginning of the period is $1,000, cash receipts for the month total $50,000 (per the cash receipts journal), and cash disbursements equal $45,000 (per the cash disbursements journal). The cash account after these postings would show the following:

CASH

Date	P/R	Debit	Credit	Balance
Bal.		1,000		1,000
EOM	CR	50,000		51,000
EOM	CD		45,000	6,000

Normally, the columns of each specialized journal are totaled and these totals are posted to the proper accounts at the end of the month (EOM). Amounts recorded in the general journal, however, are posted individually. The example shows posting references (P/R) of CR for the cash receipts journal and CD for the cash disbursements journal. The beginning cash balance of $1,000 increased to $6,000 by the end of the month because $50,000 was received and $45,000 disbursed.

Step 3 in the accounting cycle is preparing a trial balance. The trial balance is simply a listing of all account balances, with debit balance accounts and credit balance accounts in separate columns. The totals of each column should be equal and prove the equality of debits and credits. Exhibit 1.9 presents the Manson Motel's trial balance for the month ended December 31, 19X1. Notice that the debit and credit columns both total $488,000.

Step 4 in the accounting cycle is preparing **adjusting entries**. Adjusting entries are required to adjust accounts to reflect the proper account balances. The adjusting entries are recorded in the general journal at the end of the accounting period. The major categories of adjusting entries, along with examples, are shown in Exhibit 1.10.

Step 5 is posting the adjusting entries. All adjusting entries are posted individually from the general journal. All adjustments are different, so there are no common accounts affected by the adjustments (in contrast to the entries recorded in specialized journals).

Step 6 in the accounting cycle is preparing an adjusted trial balance. After the adjusting entries are posted to the accounts, an adjusted trial balance is prepared to once again test the equality of debit and credit accounts. This process may be facilitated by using a worksheet (see Exhibit 1.11).

Step 7 is the preparation of the financial statements. Using a worksheet approach, the accountant simply extends all figures from the adjusted trial balance to the proper income statement and balance sheet columns. Exhibit 1.11 reveals that the difference between the debit and credit columns under the "income statement" results in net income. For the Manson Motel, revenues of $150,000 exceeded expenses of $105,350, resulting in net income of $44,650. Net income of $44,650 added to the total credits of $353,150 (balance sheet columns) equals total debits of $397,800 (balance sheet columns).

The accountant then prepares a formal income statement and balance sheet in accordance with generally accepted accounting principles

Exhibit 1.9   Manson Motel Trial Balance

Manson Motel Trial Balance December 31, 19X1		
	Debits	**Credits**
Cash	$ 5,000	
Marketable Securities	10,000	
Accounts Receivable	8,000	
Cleaning Supplies	2,500	
Prepaid Insurance	4,500	
Furniture	40,000	
Accumulated Depreciation, Furniture		$ 20,000
Equipment	10,000	
Accumulated Depreciation, Equipment		5,000
Building	300,000	
Accumulated Depreciation, Building		100,000
Land	20,000	
Accounts Payable		5,000
Notes Payable		5,000
Mortgage Payable		100,000
Melvin Manson, Capital		103,000
Room Revenue		150,000
Manager's Salary	15,000	
Assistant Manager's Salary	7,500	
Maids' Wages	15,000	
Payroll Taxes	3,000	
Cleaning Supplies Expense	2,000	
Office Supplies	1,000	
Utilities	5,000	
Advertising	500	
Repairs and Maintenance	9,000	
Property Taxes	22,000	
Interest Expense	8,000	
Total	**$488,000**	**$488,000**

Source: Clifford T. Fay, Jr., Raymond S. Schmidgall, and Stanley B. Tarr, *Basic Financial Accounting for the Hospitality Industry* (East Lansing, Mich.: Educational Institute of the American Hotel & Motel Association, 1982), p. 55.

(especially the full disclosure principle). This process may include footnotes to the statements and additional financial statements, such as the statement of cash flows.

In Step 8, after preparation of the financial statements, the revenue and expense accounts are closed. These temporary owners' equity accounts are closed into retained earnings. The closing entries either increase retained earnings (if the hospitality operation earned a profit) or decrease retained earnings (if a loss was suffered). The closing entries result in zero balances in all revenue and expense accounts. The closing entries are recorded in the general journal and posted to the proper accounts.

Step 9, the final step in the accounting cycle, is the preparation of a post-closing trial balance. This balance is prepared to prove once again the equality of debits and credits.

Exhibit 1.10 Major Categories for Adjusting Entries

		Accounts	
Category	Examples	Debited	Credited
1. Prepaid expense	a. Reduction of prepaid insurance	Insurance Expense	Prepaid Insurance
	b. Reduction of prepaid rent	Rent Expense	Prepaid Rent
2. Accrued expense	a. Accrual of payroll	Payroll Expense	Accrued Payroll
	b. Accrual of interest expense on a note payable	Interest Expense	Interest Payable
3. Unearned revenue	Reduction of unearned rent	Unearned Rent	Rental Revenue
4. Accrued revenue	Accrual of interest earned on note receivable	Interest Receivable	Interest Income
5. Estimated items	Depreciation expense	Depreciation Expense	Accumulated Depreciation, Fixed Assets
6. Inventory adjustment	Recording of ending inventory from physical inventory. (Note: other account balances such as Purchases are also transferred to the Cost of Goods Sold account.)	Inventory end of month	Cost of Goods Sold

Forms of Business Organization

There are three basic forms of business organization: the sole proprietorship, the partnership, and the corporation. The business entity principle applies to all businesses. That is, all three forms of business organization are separate from other business entities and separate from their owners for accounting purposes.

A **sole proprietorship** is a business owned by a single person who generally (but not necessarily) manages the business. Many small lodging and food service businesses are organized as sole proprietorships. There are no legal formalities in organizing these businesses; thus, formation is quick and easy. The owner is held legally responsible for all debts of the business. However, the operation is, for accounting purposes, a separate business entity.

A **partnership** is a business owned by two or more people who often manage the business. Partnerships are created by either an oral or written agreement. The written agreement is preferable, as it provides a permanent record of the terms of the partnership. The written agreement includes the duties and initial investment of each partner and the sharing of profits and losses. Each partner is responsible for the debts of the business. As with the sole proprietorship, for accounting purposes, the partnership is a separate business entity.

A **limited partnership** is a form of partnership that offers the protection of limited liability to its **limited partners**. In order to have limited liability, limited partners may not actively participate in managing the business. A limited partnership must have at least one **general partner**

Exhibit 1.11 Manson Motel Worksheet

Manson Motel
Work Sheet
For the year ended December 31, 19X1

Account Title	Trial Balance Debit	Trial Balance Credit	Adjustments Debit	Adjustments Credit	Adjusted Trial Balance Debit	Adjusted Trial Balance Credit	Income Statement Debit	Income Statement Credit	Balance Sheet Debit	Balance Sheet Credit
Cash	5000				5000				5000	
Marketable Securities	10000				10000				10000	
Accounts Receivable	8000				8000				8000	
Cleaning Supplies	2500			(b) 700	1800				1800	
Prepaid Insurance	4500			(a) 1500	3000				3000	
Furniture	40000				40000				40000	
Accumulated Depreciation, Furniture		20000		(c) 4000		24000				24000
Equipment	10000				10000				10000	
Accumulated Depreciation, Equipment		5000		(d) 1000		6000				6000
Building	300000				300000				300000	
Accumulated Depreciation, Building		100000		(e) 10000		110000				110000
Land	20000				20000				20000	
Accounts Payable		5000				5000				5000
Notes Payable		5000				5000				5000
Mortgage Payable		100000				100000				100000
Melvin Manson, Capital		103000				103000				103000
Room Revenue		150000				150000		150000		
Managers Salary	15000				15000		15000			
Assistant Managers Salary	7500				7500		7500			
Maids' Wages	15000		(f) 150		15150		15150			
Payroll Taxes	3000				3000		3000			
Cleaning Supplies Expense	2000		(b) 700		2700		2700			
Office Supplies	1000				1000		1000			
Utilities	5000				5000		5000			
Advertising	500				500		500			
Repairs & Maintenance	9000				9000		9000			
Property Taxes	22000				22000		22000			
Interest Expense	8000				8000		8000			
	488000	488000								
Insurance Expense			(a) 1500		1500		1500			
Depreciation Expense, Furniture			(c) 4000		4000		4000			
Depreciation Expense, Equipment			(d) 1000		1000		1000			
Depreciation Expense, Building			(e) 10000		10000		10000			
Accrued Wages				(f) 150		150				150
			17350	17350	503150	503150	105350	150000	397800	353150
Net Income							44650			44650
							150000	150000	397800	397800

Source: *Basic Financial Accounting*, pp. 68-69.

who is responsible for the debts of the partnership—that is, the general partner has unlimited liability.

A **corporation** is a form of business organization owned by any number of people. It is incorporated under the laws of one of the United States. The corporation differs from the other forms of business organization because it is a *legal* business entity. Its continued existence depends on its charter from the state, not the lives of its owners.

The owners of the corporation are stockholders who buy shares of stock in the corporation. The stockholders are not responsible for the debts of the corporation, and, should the corporation fail, the stockholders lose only the amount they have paid for their shares. In contrast to the personal assets of sole proprietors and partners (or general partners in limited partnerships), the stockholders' personal assets are protected from the corporation's creditors.

The stockholders do not directly manage the lodging corporation, but rather elect a board of directors to represent their interests. The board selects officers (such as president and vice-president) who manage the corporation. Payments to the stockholders from the corporation's profits are called **dividends**. Once the board of directors declares dividends, the dividends are legal liabilities of the corporation and must be paid.

The forms of business organization are discussed further in Chapter 15, specifically with regard to the tax ramifications for each form.

Computer Applications

Less than 15 years ago, computers were almost unknown in the hospitality industry, usually found only at corporate headquarters. Now, they are increasingly common even in the smallest hospitality operations. Originally used to process accounts payable, accounts receivable, and general ledger transactions, computers are now used to process payroll, make reservations, post charges to guest accounts, and even report rooms ready for occupancy. Restaurants are using computers to record reservations, control food costs, and even notify the maître d' when a table is ready.

Most of the chapters which follow will include a section discussing typical computer applications for the chapter subject. In these discussions, two types of computers will be referred to—the minicomputer and the personal computer (PC). Larger computers, or mainframe computers, can also be used for most of the applications discussed. However, they are expensive to own and operate and are still not common in most hotel properties. Minicomputers and personal computers generally do not require a data processing staff to operate them. In fact, the personal computer is so sophisticated it often allows the user, without any knowledge of computer programming, to make the machine do what is needed. For example, the user simply instructs the computer in easily understood commands to add, subtract, or calculate the present value and the machine does the rest.

A word of caution is appropriate, however. If the user does not understand the principles of accounting, a computer can provide incorrect results. It is critical that management understand the principles of accounting and what the machine should be doing. Without this knowledge, inaccurate financial results can be reported. In addition, employees who understand what the machine should be doing may be able to commit fraud. The computer must be considered a management tool. If management does not know how to use the tool properly, it may be useless or even harmful.

Summary

The major objectives of this chapter have been to provide a brief overview of the hospitality industry and a review of basic accounting procedures and concepts. Businesses in the hospitality industry, although different in several respects from firms in many other industries, maintain their accounts according to the same basic principles. A hospitality manager should therefore be well versed in general accounting and the special accounting considerations of a hospitality operation.

Hotels and restaurants may experience large fluctuations in demand and often maintain very perishable products. Although a manufacturing firm's inventory may have a shelf life of several years, a restaurant's inventory will perish after a few days and an unsold hotel room night can never be recovered. Hospitality operations do not maintain extensive inventories, so labor must be readily available to prepare and serve food and other products. This labor force must be able to satisfy many ranges of seasonality; different times of the day, days of the week, and seasons of the year will generate different levels of sales.

In order to reflect accurately the operations of these businesses and to ensure consistent recording between periods and properties, hospitality accountants follow generally accepted accounting principles. The cost principle stipulates that items be recorded at the amount for which they are purchased. The continuity of the business unit principle assumes that the organization is a going concern which is not threatened by having to liquidate immediately. The property must be treated as an entity separate from its owners according to the business entity principle. Other requirements are that accountants use objective evidence whenever possible and fully disclose financial items of significance to the users of the financial statements. If these principles are adhered to, the resultant statements will more accurately report the property's operations and financial position.

This chapter also provided a brief overview of basic accounting mechanics. Assets are items owned by the property and have debit balances; liabilities are amounts the property owes and have credit balances. The difference between assets and liabilities is owners' equity—the amount of residual claims owners have on assets. The final section of this chapter included a brief description of the three types of business organization: sole proprietorships, partnerships, and corporations.

Endnotes

1. *1990 Directory of Hotel & Motel Systems,* 59th Ed. (Washington, D.C.: American Hotel & Motel Association, 1990).

2. Telephone interview with Randy Smith of Smith Travel Research, 9 May 1990.

3. National Restaurant Association and Laventhol & Horwath, *Restaurant Industry Operations Report '89* (Washington, D.C.: National Restaurant Association; Philadelphia: Laventhol & Horwath, 1989).

4. Pannell Kerr Forster, *Trends in the Hotel Industry 1989* (New York: Pannell Kerr Forster, 1989).

5. This text assumes that the reader has read an introductory accounting text or has access to one. *Basic Financial Accounting for the Hospitality Industry* by Clifford T. Fay, Jr., Raymond S. Schmidgall, and Stanley B. Tarr (East Lansing, Mich.: Educational Institute of the American Hotel & Motel Association, 1982) contains several chapters which provide detailed coverage of the concepts in this section. Another appropriate text is Raymond Cote's *Understanding Hospitality Accounting I* (East Lansing, Mich.: Educational Institute of the American Hotel & Motel Association, 1987).

Key Terms

account
accounting cycle
accrual basis accounting
adjusting entries
assets
balance
business entity principle
cash basis accounting
conservatism principle
consistency principle
continuity of the business unit principle
corporation
cost principle
credit
debit
dividends
financial audit
full disclosure principle
fundamental accounting equation
general journal

general partner
generally accepted accounting principles
going concern principle
journals
ledger account
liabilities
limited partner
limited partnership
matching principle
materiality principle
objective evidence
owners' equity
partnership
permanent account
posting
sole proprietorship
specialized journal
temporary account
trial balance
unit of measurement principle

Discussion Questions

1. What are some differences between hospitality operations and manufacturing firms?

2. What types of seasonality would a transient hotel most likely experience?

3. Approximately what percentage of total revenues is labor cost in the hospitality industry?

4. What is the matching principle?

5. How does inflation affect the unit of measurement principle?

6. What accounts are included in the Temporary Owners' Equity Accounts?

7. What is posting?

8. What are the five types of accounts which are included in the general ledger of all hospitality firms?

9. What is the concept of materiality?

10. What are the six branches of accounting and the major responsibilities of each?

Problems

Problem 1.1

Fill in the blanks below with the accounting principle which best applies.

A. Cost principle

B. Business entity

C. Continuity of the business unit

D. Unit of measurement

E. Objective evidence

F. Full disclosure

G. Consistency

H. Matching

I. Conservatism

1. A fire occurred in your hotel during the previous year. The estimated loss due to a pending lawsuit is recorded because of the _____ principle.

2. You purchased a new dishwasher from Mike's Machines for $1,250, and, because of the _____ principle, it is recorded at $1,250, even though you could now sell it for $1,500.

3. Although the last biweekly pay period ended December 26, your employees have worked through the end of December. The unpaid salaries and wages are accrued as of December 31 because of the _____ principle.

4. Your firm is the defendant in a major lawsuit. Your attorney believes you may lose. Although the attorney is unable to estimate the potential loss, the lawsuit is briefly mentioned in a footnote to the financial statements because of the _____ principle.

5. You went to a bankruptcy auction yesterday and china, almost identical to that used in your restaurant, was selling for $.20 a piece. Yours is on the books for $1.00 a piece. You do not reduce the carrying cost of your china to $.20 a piece because of the _____ principle.

6. You have historically depreciated furniture in your hospitality firm by the straight-line method. You are going to change to an accelerated method, even for the furniture you previously depreciated using the straight-line method. This violates the _____ principle.

Problem 1.2

Fill in the blanks below with the accounting principle which best applies.

A. Cost principle
B. Business entity
C. Continuity of the business unit
D. Unit of measurement
E. Objective evidence

F. Full disclosure
G. Consistency
H. Matching
I. Conservatism
J. Materiality

1. A lodging company pays a fire insurance premium of $40,000. The policy covers a two-year period. The $40,000 cash disbursement is recorded as insurance expense. This violates the _____ principle.

2. A wastebasket costing $20 for a guestroom is expensed when it is purchased. The wastebasket should have a five-year life. This is probably acceptable accounting because of the _____ principle.

3. The food inventory is generally valued at its cost at the end of each year. However, this year it is written down to its market value because the market value is less than cost. The valuing of food inventory at the lower of cost or market is according to the _____ principle.

4. A. Smith, the proprietor of Smith's Dining, takes a few steaks home from his business. He records the cost of the steaks taken for personal use as "A. Smith—Drawing" in accordance with the _____ principle.

5. The Yorkshire Hotel, in addition to including its depreciation expense on the income statement, mentions its method of depreciation and the estimated lives of its property and equipment in a footnote. This is based on the _____ principle.

6. A hotel corporation owns a property with a market value of only 80% of its net book value. The hotel corporation plans to keep the hotel over its remaining life of ten years. It will probably not be reduced to its market value because of the _____ principle.

Problem 1.3

You have been hired as an accountant by Holly Hibble, the owner of Holly's Hideaway. During your first day on the job, the following transactions occur:

1. Ms. Hibble purchases a new microcomputer to be used at the front desk. It costs $5,000 and was purchased on account.

2. The pay period ended, and the motel's employees received salaries/wages of $2,000 (ignore any tax withholdings or deductions). They will receive cash today.

3. This is also the final day of the accounting period (one month), and the depreciation expense must be recorded. The fixed assets total $1,000,000 and should be depreciated over 20 years using the straight-line method. Assume that the salvage value is zero.

4. Cash sales for today totaled $3,000.

5. Ms. Hibble lends $20,000 to the business in the form of a two-year note.

Required:

Prepare the necessary journal entries showing debits and credits and provide a brief explanation of each entry.

Problem 1.4

Mr. Gregory Vain is a successful business person who does not fully understand the fundamental accounting equation and how various transactions affect it. You have been hired to share your knowledge with him.

Required:

1. State the basic equation and briefly explain each element of it.

2. Explain how each type of account could be increased and illustrate with examples. Be sure to describe all the effects of your examples.

   Example: Asset accounts would increase when a new hotel is purchased. However, in order to remain in equilibrium, another asset account, "cash," would decrease if the hotel is purchased with cash.

3. State how temporary accounts relate to the fundamental accounting equation.

Problem 1.5

Browny Brad's Beach Motel (BBBM's), a 40-room lodging facility, has operated for the past three years. BBBM's night auditor has kept accurate records over the past year but has not analyzed any of these data. The following is a summary of the rooms sold by month:

Rooms sold:

January	400	May	960	September	800
February	600	June	980	October	705
March	700	July	992	November	650
April	840	August	973	December	500

Assume there are 365 days in the year and that the summer months include May, June, July, and August. The off-season comprises all other months.

Required:

Determine the paid occupancy percentage for the summer months, the off-season, and the entire year.

Problem 1.6

Below is a list of the 19X3 activities/transactions for Emily's Eatery.

1. A fire insurance policy for July 1, 19X3, through June 30, 19X4, was purchased on May 15, 19X3. The premium paid totaled $24,000 and was recorded as prepaid insurance.

2. The operation purchased a new cash register costing $12,000 on September 1, 19X3, and recorded it in the equipment account. The cash register is expected to have a useful life of seven years and a salvage value of $1,000. No depreciation has been recorded. Emily's uses the straight-line method of depreciation.

3. The employees were paid for their work through December 26. They worked 300 hours for the period of December 27–31, 19X3, and will be

paid on January 10, 19X4. The average hourly wage is $6.00.

4. Sales for the year totaled $800,000. The allowance for doubtful accounts has a December 31 balance of $1,000. The allowance should be adjusted at year-end to 1/2% of sales for the year.

5. The electric bill for the period of December 5, 19X3, through January 4, 19X4, totaled $620. It has not been recorded and will be paid on January 10, 19X4.

Required:

For each situation, prepare the adjusting entry to record the proper expense for 19X3.

Problem 1.7

The following balance sheet for the Sundowner Motel has several accounts that require adjusting before preparation of the December 31, 19X5, financial statements.

Balance Sheet
The Sundowner Motel
November 30, 19X5

Assets

Current Assets:

Cash	$ 15,000
Accounts Receivable	108,000
Allowance for Doubtful Accounts	(6,000)
Food Inventory	4,000
Prepaid Insurance	3,000
Total Current Assets	124,000

Property and Equipment:

Land	50,000
Building	1,440,000
Equipment	400,000
Accumulated Depreciation	(490,000)
Total Property and Equipment	1,400,000

Total Assets	$1,524,000

Liabilities and Owners' Equity

Current Liabilities:

Notes Payable	$ 5,000
Accounts Payable	10,000
Wages Payable	12,000
Taxes Payable	17,000
Total Current Liabilities	44,000

Long-term Liabilities:

Mortgage Payable	600,000

Owners' Equity:
   James Sun, Capital   880,000

   Total Liabilities and Owners' Equity $1,524,000

Additional information:

1. The allowance for doubtful accounts is calculated as 5.5% of the total accounts receivable and then rounded to the next $100. The accounts receivable at December 31, 19X5, totaled $123,200.

2. The annual insurance premium of $6,000 was paid on May 15 for the period of June 1, 19X5, through May 31, 19X6.

3. The physical food inventory at December 31, 19X5, totaled $3,800.

4. The building is depreciated over 30 years using the straight-line (SL) method (assume a salvage value of $100,000). The equipment is depreciated over five years using the SL method (assume a salvage value of zero). For purposes of depreciation calculation, assume that the equipment was purchased on January 1, 19X3. Calculate depreciation expense for the month of December only.

Required:

Prepare the adjusting entries for The Sundowner Motel.

Problem 1.8

Robbie Hanson owns a resort on an excellent fishing lake. Her busy season begins May 15 and extends through mid-fall. During the winter, she engaged a contractor to build a boat house and dock for a total price of $25,000. The contract called for completion by May 15 because the resort was completely booked for the week of May 15 to 22, the opening week of the fishing season. Because the completion date was so important to Hanson, she specified in the contract that if the construction was not completed by May 15, the price would be reduced by $100 per day until completion.

The construction was not completed until June 9, at which time Hanson paid the contract price of $22,500, deducting $100 for each day's delay. Hanson is convinced that she lost goodwill because the resort's facilities were inadequate and that several of her guests shortened their stays because the facilities were still under construction.

Hanson included the boat house and dock as assets valued at $25,000 on the balance sheet prepared on September 30, the end of her fiscal year. Included in her revenues was an item "Penalty payments received in lieu of lost revenue—$2,500."

The auditor who examined Hanson's report objected to this treatment and insisted that the facilities be recorded at their actual cost, $22,500. Hanson stated that she could not understand the logic of this position. "Accounting principles are out of tune with reality," she complained. "What if the contract had been 250 days late and the boat house and dock had cost me nothing; would you record on my balance sheet that I had no asset? I lost at least $100 per day in revenues because of the construction delay."

<u>Required:</u>

At what amount should these facilities be reported on the balance sheet of September 30? (You may ignore depreciation from June 9 to September 30.) Explain your position in terms of accounting principles.

2 Balance Sheet

The **balance sheet** is a major financial statement prepared at the end of each accounting period. It reflects a balance between an organization's assets and claims to its assets called liabilities and owners' equity. This statement is also referred to as a statement of financial position. It contains answers to many questions that managers, owners (investors), and creditors may have, such as:

1. How much cash was on hand at the end of the period?
2. What was the total debt of the hospitality operation?
3. What was the mix of internal and external financing at the end of the period?
4. How much was owed to the hotel by guests?
5. What amount of taxes was owed to the various governmental tax agencies?
6. What was the operation's ability to pay its current debt?
7. What was the financial strength of the operation?
8. How much interest do stockholders have in the operation's assets?

This chapter addresses the purposes and limitations of the balance sheet. We will also consider the formats and contents of balance sheets with special attention to the suggested balance sheet from the *Uniform System of Accounts and Expense Dictionary for Small Hotels, Motels, and Motor Hotels* (*USASH*).[1] In addition, we will discuss the kinds and purposes of footnotes attached to balance sheets. Finally, we will consider techniques for analyzing the financial information contained in a balance sheet. The Supplemental Reading at the end of this chapter includes the financial statements and the accompanying footnotes for the Hilton Hotels Corporation from its 1989 annual report.

Purposes of the Balance Sheet

Other major financial statements—the income statement, the statement of retained earnings, and the statement of cash flows—pertain to a period of time. The balance sheet reflects the financial position of the hospitality operation—its assets, liabilities, and owners' equity—at a given date.

Management, although generally more interested in the income statement and related department operations statements, will find balance sheets useful for conveying financial information to creditors and investors. In addition, management must determine if the balance sheet reflects to the best extent possible the financial position of the hospitality operation. For example, many long-term loans specify a required **current ratio** (which is current assets divided by current liabilities). Failure to meet the requirement may result in all long-term debt being reclassified as current and thus due immediately. Since few operations could raise large sums of cash quickly, bankruptcy could result. Therefore, management must carefully review the balance sheet to determine that the operation is in compliance. For example, assume that at December 31, 19X1 (year-end), a hotel has $500,000 of current assets and $260,000 of current liabilities. Further assume that the current ratio requirement in a bank's loan agreement with the hotel is 2 to 1. The required current ratio can be attained simply by taking the appropriate action. In this case, the payment of $20,000 of current liabilities with cash of $20,000 results in current assets of $480,000 and current liabilities of $240,000, resulting in a current ratio of 2 to 1.

Creditors are interested in the hospitality operation's ability to pay its current and future obligations. The ability to pay its current obligations is shown, in part, by a comparison of current assets and current liabilities. The ability to pay its future obligations depends, in part, on the relative amounts of long-term financing by owners and creditors. Everything else being the same, the greater the financing from investors, the higher the probability that long-term creditors will be paid and the lower the risk that these creditors take in "investing" in the enterprise.

Investors are most often interested in earnings which lead to dividends. To maximize earnings, an organization should have financial flexibility, which is the operation's ability to change its cash flows to meet unexpected needs and take advantage of opportunities. Everything else being the same, the greater the financial flexibility of the hospitality operation, the greater its opportunities to take advantage of new profitable investments, thus increasing net income and, ultimately, cash dividends for investors.

In addition, the balance sheet reveals the liquidity of the hospitality operation. **Liquidity** measures the operation's ability to convert assets to cash. Even though a property's past earnings have been substantial, this does not in itself guarantee that the operation will be able to meet its obligations as they become due. The hospitality operation should have sufficient liquidity not only to pay its bills, but also to provide its owners with adequate dividends.

Analysis of several balance sheets for several periods will yield trend information which is more valuable than single period figures. In addition, comparison of balance sheet information with projected balance sheet numbers (when available) will reveal management's ability to meet various financial goals.

Limitations of the Balance Sheet

As useful as the balance sheet is, it is generally considered less useful than the income statement to investors, long-term creditors, and especially to management. Since the balance sheet is based on the cost principle, it often does not reflect current values of some assets, such as property and equipment. For hospitality operations whose assets are appreciating rather than depreciating, this difference may be significant. Hilton Hotels Corporation may be a fair reflection of this difference. In its 1988 annual report, it revealed the current value of its assets (footnote disclosure only) to be $4,027,000,000, while its balance sheet showed the book value of its assets to be $1,892,500,000. The difference between current value and book value was $2,134,500,000. The assets reflected in the balance sheet for Hilton were only 47% of their current value.[2] This "understatement," if unknown or ignored by management, investors, and creditors, could lead to less than optimal use of Hilton's assets.

Another limitation of balance sheets is that they fail to reflect many elements of value to hospitality operations. Most important to hotels, motels, restaurants, clubs, and other sectors of the hospitality industry are people. Nowhere in the balance sheet is there a reflection of the human resource investment. Millions of dollars are spent in recruiting and training to achieve an efficient and highly motivated work force, yet this essential ingredient for successful hospitality operations is not shown as an asset. Other valuable elements not directly shown on the balance sheet include such things as goodwill, superior location, loyal customers, and so on.[3] Understandably, it may be difficult to assign an objective value to these elements. Nevertheless, they are not only critical to an operation's success, they are also of significant value.

Balance sheets are limited by their static nature; that is, they reflect the financial position for only a moment. Thereafter, they are less useful because they become outdated. Thus, the user of the balance sheet must be aware that the financial position reflected at year-end may be quite different one month later. For example, a hospitality operation with $1,000,000 of cash may seem financially strong at year-end, but if it invests most of this cash in fixed assets two weeks later, its financial flexibility and liquidity are greatly reduced. This situation would generally only be known to the user of financial documents if a balance sheet and/or other financial statements were available for a date after this investment has occurred.

Finally, the balance sheet, like much of accounting, is based on judgments; that is, it is *not* exact. Certainly, assets equal liabilities plus owners' equity. However, several balance sheet items are based on estimates. The amounts shown as accounts receivable (net) reflect the estimated amounts to be collected. The amounts shown as inventory reflect the lower of the cost or market (that is, the lower of its original cost and its current replacement cost) of the items expected to be sold, and the amount shown as property and equipment reflects the cost less estimated depreciation. In each case, accountants use estimates to arrive at "values." To the degree that these estimates are in error, the balance sheet items will be wrong.

Exhibit 2.1   Balance Sheet Account Format

<table>
<tr><td colspan="4" align="center">**Manson Motel**
Balance Sheet
December 31, 19X1</td></tr>
<tr><td align="center">**ASSETS**</td><td></td><td align="center">**LIABILITIES AND OWNERS' EQUITY**</td><td></td></tr>
<tr><td>Current Assets:</td><td></td><td>Current Liabilities:</td><td></td></tr>
<tr><td> Cash</td><td>$ 2,500</td><td> Notes Payable</td><td>$ 23,700</td></tr>
<tr><td> Accounts Receivable</td><td>5,000</td><td> Accounts Payable</td><td>8,000</td></tr>
<tr><td> Cleaning Supplies</td><td>2,500</td><td> Wages Payable</td><td>300</td></tr>
<tr><td>   Total</td><td>10,000</td><td>   Total</td><td>32,000</td></tr>
<tr><td>Property & Equipment:</td><td></td><td>Long-term Liabilities:</td><td></td></tr>
<tr><td> Land</td><td>20,000</td><td> Mortgage Payable</td><td>120,000</td></tr>
<tr><td> Building</td><td>300,000</td><td>   Total Liabilities</td><td>152,000</td></tr>
<tr><td> Furnishings and Equipment</td><td>50,000</td><td></td><td></td></tr>
<tr><td></td><td>370,000</td><td>Melvin Manson, Capital at
  January 1, 19X1</td><td>64,500</td></tr>
<tr><td> Less Accumulated</td><td></td><td>Net Income for 19X1</td><td>38,500</td></tr>
<tr><td> Depreciation</td><td>125,000</td><td>Melvin Manson, Capital at</td><td></td></tr>
<tr><td> Net Property &</td><td></td><td> December 31, 19X1</td><td>103,000</td></tr>
<tr><td> Equipment</td><td>245,000</td><td></td><td></td></tr>
<tr><td>**Total Assets**</td><td>**$255,000**</td><td>**Total Liabilities**
  and Owners' Equity</td><td>**$255,000**</td></tr>
</table>

Balance Sheet Formats

The balance sheet can be arranged in either the account or report format. The **account format** lists the asset accounts on the left side of the page and the liability and owners' equity accounts on the right side. Exhibit 2.1 illustrates this arrangement.

The **report format** shows assets first, followed by liabilities and owners' equity. The group totals on the report form can show either that assets equal liabilities and owners' equity or that assets minus liabilities equal owners' equity. Exhibit 2.2 illustrates the report format.

Content of the Balance Sheet

The balance sheet consists of assets, liabilities, and owners' equity. Simply stated, assets are things owned by the firm, liabilities are claims of outsiders to assets, and owners' equity is claims of owners to assets. Thus, assets must equal (balance) liabilities and owners' equity. Assets include various accounts such as cash, inventory for resale, buildings, and accounts receivable. Liabilities include accounts such as accounts payable, wages payable, and mortgage payable. Owners' equity includes capital stock and retained earnings. These major elements are generally divided into various classes as shown in Exhibit 2.3. While balance sheets may be organized differently, most hospitality operations follow the order shown in Exhibit 2.3.

Exhibit 2.2 Balance Sheet Report Format

Manson Motel
Balance Sheet
December 31, 19X1

ASSETS

Current Assets:

Cash		$ 2,500
Accounts Receivable		5,000
Cleaning Supplies		2,500
Total Current Assets		10,000
Property and Equipment:		
Land	$ 20,000	
Building	300,000	
Furnishings and Equipment	50,000	
Less Accumulated Depreciation	125,000	
Net Property Equipment		245,000
Total Assets		**$255,000**

LIABILITIES AND OWNERS' EQUITY

Current Liabilities:		
Notes Payable	23,700	
Accounts Payable	8,000	
Wages Payable	300	$ 32,000
Long-term Liabilities:		
Mortgage Payable		120,000
Total Liabilities		152,000
Owners' Equity:		
Melvin Manson, Capital at January 1, 19X1	64,500	
Net Income for 19X1	38,500	
Melvin Manson, Capital at		
December 31, 19X1		103,000
Total Liabilities and Owners' Equity		**$255,000**

Current Accounts

Under both "assets" and "liabilities and owners' equity" is a current classification. **Current assets** normally refer to items to be converted to cash or used in operations within one year or in a normal operating cycle. **Current liabilities** are obligations that are expected to be satisfied either by using current assets or by creating other current liabilities within one year or a normal operating cycle.

Exhibit 2.4 reflects a normal operating cycle which includes (1) the purchase of inventory for resale and labor to produce goods and services, (2) the sale of goods and services, and (3) the collection of accounts receivable from the sale of goods and services.

Exhibit 2.3 Major Elements of the Balance Sheet

Assets	Liabilities and Owners' Equity
Current Assets	Current Liabilities
Noncurrent Assets:	Long-term Liabilities
Noncurrent Receivables	Owners' Equity
Investments	
Property and Equipment	
Other Assets	

Exhibit 2.4 Normal Operating Cycle

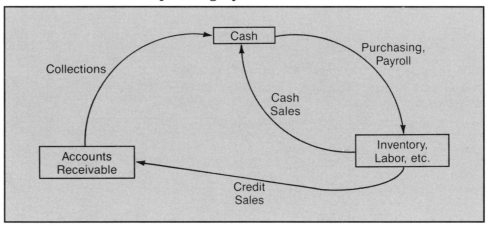

A normal operating cycle may be as short as a few days, as is common for many quick-service restaurants, or it may extend over several months for some hospitality operations. It is common in the hospitality industry to classify assets as current/noncurrent on the basis of one year rather than on the basis of the normal operating cycle.

Current Assets. Current assets, listed in the order of liquidity, generally consist of cash, marketable securities, receivables, inventories, and prepaid expenses. Cash consists of cash in house banks, cash in checking and savings accounts, and certificates of deposit. The exception is cash restricted for retiring long-term debt, which should be shown under other assets. Cash is shown in the balance sheet at its face value.

Marketable securities are shown as current assets when they are available for conversion to cash. Marketable securities which are not available for conversion to cash are considered investments. Generally, the critical factor in making this current/noncurrent decision is management's intent. Marketable equity securities—that is, temporary investments in capital stock of other companies—are usually valued at the lower of cost or market. Marketable debt securities, such as temporary investments in bonds of other companies, are carried at cost for balance sheet purposes.

The current asset category of receivables consists of accounts receivable—trade and notes receivable. Accounts receivable—trade are open accounts carried by a hotel or motel on the guest, city, or rent ledgers. Notes receivable due within one year are also listed, except for notes from affiliated companies, which should be shown under "Investments." Receivables should be stated at the amount estimated to be collectible. An allowance for doubtful accounts, the amount of receivables estimated to be uncollectible, should be subtracted from receivables to provide a net receivables amount.

Inventories of a hospitality operation consist of merchandise held for resale. Inventories are generally an insignificant percentage of the total assets of a hospitality operation and may be valued at cost. If the amount of inventory is material and the difference between cost and market is significant, then the inventory should be stated at the lower of cost or market.

The final current asset category is prepaid expenses. Prepaid expenses represent purchased goods and services to be used by the hospitality operation within one year. For example, assume that a fire insurance premium of $6,000 affords insurance protection for one year after the transaction. At the date of the expenditure, the $6,000 is classified as prepaid insurance and, thereafter, is amortized by a monthly reduction of $500 ($1/12$ of $6,000) which is shown on the income statement as insurance expense. Other prepaid expenses include prepaid rent, prepaid property taxes, prepaid interest, and prepaid maintenance and service contracts.

Prepaid expenses which will benefit the operation beyond one year from the balance sheet date should be classified as other assets. For example, assume that a three-year fire insurance policy costs $18,000. The entry to record the cash disbursement would be to debit prepaid insurance for $6,000 (the cost of coverage for the next 12 months) and to debit deferred charges—insurance for $12,000 (the cost of insurance coverage paid that benefits the operation for periods beyond 12 months from the balance sheet date).

Current Liabilities. Current liabilities are obligations at the balance sheet date which are expected to be paid by converting current assets within one year. They generally consist of one of the four following types:

1. Payables resulting from the purchase of goods, services, and labor and from the applicable payroll taxes

2. Amounts received in advance of the delivery of goods and services, such as advance deposits on rooms and banquet deposits

3. Obligations to be paid in the current period relating to fixed asset purchases or to reclassification of long-term debt as current

4. Dividends payable and income taxes payable

The major classifications of current liabilities according to the *USASH* are notes payable, current maturities of long-term debt, federal, state, and city income taxes, deferred income taxes, accrued expenses, and advance deposits. Notes payable include short-term notes which are due within 12 months. Current maturities of long-term debt include the principal payments of long-term debt such as notes and similar liabilities, sinking fund obligations, and the principal portion of capitalized leases due within 12 months. Accounts payable include amounts due to creditors for merchandise, services, equipment, or other purchases. Deferred income taxes—

current include amounts which represent the tax effects of timing differences attributable to current assets and current liabilities which are accounted for differently for financial and income tax reporting purposes. Accrued expenses are expenses incurred before the balance sheet date which are not due until after the balance sheet date. Advance deposits include amounts received for services which have not been provided as of the balance sheet date.

Obligations to be paid with **restricted cash** (that is, cash that has been deposited in separate accounts, often for the purpose of retiring long-term debt) should not be classified as current, but rather as long-term.

Current liabilities are often compared with current assets. The difference between the two is commonly called **working capital**. The current ratio results from dividing current assets by current liabilities. Many hospitality properties operate successfully with a current ratio approximating 1 to 1, compared with a reasonable current ratio for many other industries of 2 to 1. The major reason for this difference lies with the relatively low amount of inventories required and relatively high turnover of receivables by hospitality operations as compared with many other industries.

Noncurrent Receivables

Noncurrent receivables include both accounts and notes receivable which are not expected to be collected within one year from the balance sheet date. If any collectibility is uncertain regarding noncurrent receivables, an allowance for doubtful noncurrent receivables should be used (similar to the allowance account for current receivables) and subtracted from total noncurrent receivables to provide net noncurrent receivables.

In the balance sheet based on the *USASH*, noncurrent receivables are divided between noncurrent receivables from "owners and officers" and "others."

Investments

Investments consist of long-term investments to be held for more than one year. Included as investments are investments in securities (capital stock and debt instruments), cash advances to affiliated companies, and investments in property not currently used in operations. For example, a hotel company may have invested in center city land with the expectation of constructing a hotel in the future. The land purchase should be shown as an investment and not listed under property and equipment on the balance sheet. Investments and advances should generally be stated on the balance sheet at the lower of cost or market.

Property and Equipment

Property and equipment consists of fixed assets including land, buildings, furnishings and equipment, construction in progress, leasehold improvements, and china, glassware, silver, linens, and uniforms.[4] Property and equipment under capital leases should also be shown in this section of the balance sheet. With the exception of land, the cost of all property and equipment is written off to expense over time due to the matching principle discussed in Chapter 1. Depreciation methods used should be disclosed in a footnote to the balance sheet. The depreciation method used for financial reporting to outsiders and that used for tax purposes may differ, resulting in deferred income taxes. Deferred income taxes are generally a liability and will be discussed later in the chapter. On the balance sheet, fixed assets are shown at cost and are reduced by the related accumulated depreciation and amortization, except for china, glassware, silver, linen, and uniforms, which are simply shown at their net amount.

Other Assets   Other assets consist of all noncurrent assets not included in the afore-mentioned categories. Other assets include:

1. Preopening expenses—including amounts expended for advertising and promotion, training, and salaries, wages, and related costs. All these costs are expended before a hotel's opening and will benefit the lodging operation for several future accounting periods. Preopening expenses are amortized over a relatively short time, generally three to five years.

2. Deferred charges—charges for services received but which should benefit future periods, such as advertising and maintenance. Deferred expenses also include financing costs related to long-term debt.

3. Security deposits—funds deposited with public utility companies and similar types of deposits.

Other assets also include the costs to organize the hospitality operation (organization costs), cash surrender value of life insurance policies, and unamortized franchise costs. The initial franchise fee paid by the franchisee should be recorded as an other asset and amortized against revenue over the life of the franchise agreement.

Long-Term Liabilities   **Long-term liabilities** are obligations at the balance sheet date which are expected to be paid beyond the next 12 months or, if paid in the current year, will be paid from restricted funds. Common long-term liabilities consist of notes payable, mortgages payable, bonds payable, capitalized lease obligations, and deferred income taxes. Any long-term debt to be paid with current assets within the next year is reclassified as current liabilities. Still, long-term debt per the *USASH* is reported on the balance sheet in total with the amount due within 12 months subtracted as "Less Current Maturities."

Lease obligations reported as long-term liabilities generally cover several years, while short-term leases are usually expensed when paid. (Chapter 14 presents detailed discussion of lease accounting.) Deferred income taxes result from timing differences in reporting for financial and income tax purposes—that is, the accounting treatment of an item for financial reporting purposes results in a different amount of expense (or revenue) than that used for tax purposes. Generally, the most significant timing difference for hotels and motels relates to depreciation, since many operations use the straight-line method for financial reporting purposes and an accelerated method for income tax purposes.

For example, suppose a hotel decides to depreciate a fixed asset on a straight-line basis at $15,000 a year for reporting purposes, and depreciate the same asset $25,000 for the year using an accelerated method for tax purposes. If the firm's marginal tax rate is 25%, then the difference in depreciation expense of $10,000 ($25,000 – $15,000) times 25% results in $2,500 cash saved and reported as a noncurrent liability. The book entry to record this savings is as follows:

Income tax expense	$2,500	
Deferred income taxes		$2,500

Owners' Equity

The **owners' equity** section of the balance sheet reflects the owner's interest in the operation's assets. The detail of the owners' equity section is a function of the organization of the business. The three major types of business organization, as discussed in Chapter 1, are sole proprietorships, partnerships, and corporations. The owners' equity section of a corporation includes capital stock, additional paid-in capital, retained earnings, and treasury stock. **Capital stock** for most hospitality operations is **common stock**; however, a few operations have also issued **preferred stock**. When more than one type of stock has been issued, each should be reported separately. Capital stock is the product of the number of shares outstanding and the par value of the shares.

The additional paid-in capital category consists of payments for capital stock in excess of the stated and/or par value of the capital stock. For example, cash of $50 received from the sale of common stock with a par value of $10 would be recorded as $10 to the common stock account and the remainder ($40) as "paid-in capital in excess of par."

Retained earnings reflect earnings generated but not distributed as dividends. Changes in this account during the year are commonly shown on a statement of retained earnings.

Treasury stock represents the property's own capital stock which has been repurchased but not retired. The cost of the treasury shares is shown as a reduction of owners' equity.

Exhibits 2.5 and 2.6 are the prescribed formats of the assets section and the liabilities and owners' equity section of the balance sheet from the *USASH*. Note that the owners' equity section of the balance sheet pertains to a lodging operation organized as a corporation.

When a lodging operation is organized as a sole proprietorship, all the owners' equity is reflected in one account as illustrated in Exhibit 2.1, Melvin Manson, Capital. The $103,000 of capital of Melvin Manson would have been spread across at least two accounts, capital stock and retained earnings, if the Manson Motel had been incorporated.

Finally, many lodging businesses are organized as partnerships. The owners' equity section of a partnership should reflect each partner's equity. The balance sheet for a partnership with many partners simply will refer to a supplementary schedule showing each partner's share. The owners' equity section of a business organized as a partnership by its three owners is illustrated as follows:

M.	Kass, Capital	$ 50,000
J.	Ninety, Capital	25,000
R.	Chicklets, Capital	25,000
	Total Owners' Equity	$100,000

Footnotes

The balance sheets of hospitality operations, although packed with considerable financial information, are not complete without the other financial statements and footnotes. The income statement and statement of cash flows are the subjects of Chapters 3 and 4, while footnotes are discussed below.

The full disclosure principle (discussed in Chapter 1) requires that financial information be sufficient to inform the users—creditors, owners, and others. This can only be accomplished by providing footnote disclosure in addition to the financial statements. Thus, footnotes are an integral part of the financial statements of a hospitality operation. They should contain additional information not presented in the body of the financial statements. They should not contradict or soften the disclosure of the financial statements, but rather provide needed explanations. Hilton Hotels Corporation's 1989 financial statements, found in the Supplemental Reading to this chapter, include the following footnotes:

1. Summary of Significant Accounting Policies
2. Accounts and Notes Receivable
3. Inventories
4. Investments
5. Property and Equipment
6. Current Liabilities
7. Long-term Debt
8. Income Taxes
9. Capital Stock
10. Employee Benefit Plans
11. Leases
12. Segments of Business
13. Supplementary Financial Information
14. Commitments and Contingent Liabilities

Consolidated Financial Statements

Many major hospitality companies consist of several corporations. For example, the hypothetical XYZ Hotel Company consists of a parent corporation, XYZ Hotel Company, and three separately incorporated hotels—Hotel X, Hotel Y, and Hotel Z. The XYZ Hotel Company owns 100% of the capital stock of each of the three hotels. Each hotel has its own set of financial statements, but for purposes of financial reporting, they are combined with the parent's financial statements. The combined statements are referred to as **consolidated financial statements**. Generally, the first footnote includes a brief description of the principles of consolidation used to combine the statements of a parent corporation and its subsidiary corporations.

Hilton Hotels Corporation's financial statements in the Supplemental Reading to this chapter are consolidated financial statements, and the basis of consolidation is described in footnote #1.

In effect, consolidated financial statements reflect a single economic unit rather than the legal separate entities resulting from separate corporations. Generally, more than 50% of the voting stock of a subsidiary should

Exhibit 2.5   Balance Sheet—Assets

BALANCE SHEET

Assets

	Date	
	19___	19___
CURRENT ASSETS		
Cash		
House Banks	$	$
Demand Deposits		
Temporary Cash Investments		
Total Cash		
Marketable Securities		
Receivables		
Accounts Receivable—Trade		
Notes Receivable		
Other		
Total Receivables		
Less Allowance for Doubtful Accounts		
Net Receivables		
Inventories		
Prepaid Expenses		
Other		
Total Current Assets		
NONCURRENT RECEIVABLES		
Owners and Officers		
Other		
Total Noncurrent Receivables		
INVESTMENTS		
PROPERTY AND EQUIPMENT		
Land		
Buildings		
Leaseholds and Leasehold Improvements		
Construction in Progress		
Furnishings and Equipment		
China, Glassware, Silver, Linen, and Uniforms		
Less Accumulated Depreciation and Amortization		
Net Property and Equipment		
OTHER ASSETS		
Security Deposits		
Preopening Expenses		
Deferred Charges		
Other		
Total Other Assets		
	$	$
TOTAL ASSETS		

Exhibit 2.6   Balance Sheet—Liabilities and Owners' Equity

BALANCE SHEET (continued)

Liabilities and Owners' Equity

CURRENT LIABILITIES
Notes Payable $ $
Current Maturities of Long-Term Debt
Accounts Payable
Federal, State, and City Income Taxes
Deferred Income Taxes
Accrued Expenses
Advance Deposits
Other   _____   _____
        Total Current Liabilities   _____   _____

LONG-TERM DEBT
Notes and Other Similar Liabilities
Obligations Under Capital Leases   _____   _____

Less Current Maturities   _____   _____
        Total Long-Term Debt   _____   _____

OTHER LONG-TERM LIABILITIES

DEFERRED INCOME TAXES

COMMITMENTS AND CONTINGENCIES

*OWNERS' EQUITY
Preferred Stock, Par Value $_____
    Authorized _____ Shares
    Issued _____ Shares
Common Stock, Par Value $_____
    Authorized _____ Shares
    Issued _____ Shares
Additional Paid-In Capital
Retained Earnings   _____   _____
        Total Owners' Equity   _____   _____

TOTAL LIABILITIES AND OWNERS' EQUITY $_____ $_____

See the accompanying notes to financial statements.

*The line items of this section reflect a corporate form of business organization. For line items appropriate to proprietorships and partnerships, see the explanatory notes for this section.

be owned by the holding company or by the same interests if the associated companies' financial statements are to be combined. Accounting procedures related to financial statement consolidations are covered in advanced accounting textbooks. They are beyond the scope of this text.

Balance Sheet Analysis

The information shown on the balance sheet is most useful when it is properly analyzed. The analysis of a balance sheet may include the following:

1. Horizontal analysis (**comparative statements**)
2. Vertical analysis (**common-size statements**)
3. Ratio analysis

In the remainder of this chapter, the first two techniques will be discussed. The third, ratio analysis, will be discussed in detail in Chapter 5.

Horizontal Analysis

Horizontal analysis compares two balance sheets—the current balance sheet and the balance sheet of the previous period. In this analysis, the two balance sheets are often referred to as **comparative balance sheets**. This represents the simplest approach to analysis and is essential to the fair reporting of the financial information. Often included for management's analysis are the two sets of figures with the changes from one period to the next expressed both in absolute and relative terms.

Absolute changes show the change in dollars between two periods. For example, assume that cash was $10,000 at the end of year 19X1 and $15,000 at the end of year 19X2. The absolute change is the difference of $5,000.

The relative change (also called the percentage change) is found by dividing the absolute change by the amount for the previous period. The relative change, using the cash example above, is 50% ($5,000 ÷ $10,000). The $5,000 absolute change may not seem significant by itself, but viewed as a relative change, it is a 50% increase over the previous year.

Examine the comparative balance sheets for the Stratford Hotel found in Exhibit 2.7. Comparative analysis shows that marketable securities increased by $629,222 in absolute terms and 404.7% in relative terms. The increase is substantial. In light of these figures, a manager would desire answers to several questions, including the following:

1. Are the marketable securities readily convertible to cash?
2. Is the amount invested in marketable securities adequate for cash needs in the next few months?
3. Should some of the dollars invested in marketable securities be moved to less liquid, but higher rate-of-return investments?

Significant changes in other accounts should be similarly investigated.

To explain the drastic change in some balance sheet items, a **fluctuation explanation** may be prepared. This explanation provides detail not available on the balance sheet. Exhibit 2.8 illustrates a fluctuation explanation of marketable securities for the Stratford Hotel.

Vertical Analysis

Another approach to analyzing balance sheets is to reduce them to percentages. This **vertical analysis**, often referred to as common-size statement analysis, is accomplished by having total assets equal 100% and individual asset categories equal percentages of the total 100%. Likewise,

Exhibit 2.7 Comparative Balance Sheets

	Comparative Balance Sheets Stratford Hotel			
	December 31		**Change from 19X1 to 19X2**	
ASSETS	19X2	19X1	Amount	Percentage
Current Assets:				
Cash	$ 104,625	$ 85,600	$ 19,025	22.2%
Marketable Securities	784,687	155,465	629,222	404.7
Accounts Receivable (net)	1,615,488	1,336,750	278,738	20.9
Inventories	98,350	92,540	5,810	6.3
Other	12,475	11,300	1,175	10.4
Total	2,615,625	1,681,655	933,970	55.5
Property and Equipment:				
Land	905,700	905,700	0	0
Buildings	5,434,200	5,434,200	0	0
Furnishings and Equipment	2,617,125	2,650,500	(33,375)	(1.3)
Less: Accumulated Depreciation	1,221,490	749,915	471,575	62.9
Total	7,735,535	8,240,485	(504,950)	(6.1)
Other Assets	58,350	65,360	(7,010)	(10.7)
Total Assets	$10,409,510	$ 9,987,500	$ 422,010	4.2%
LIABILITIES				
Current Liabilities:				
Accounts Payable	$ 1,145,000	$ 838,000	$ 307,000	36.6%
Current maturities of long-term debt	275,000	275,000	0	0
Income taxes payable	273,750	356,000	(82,250)	(23.1)
Total	1,693,750	1,469,000	224,750	15.3
Long-term Debt				
Notes Payable	50,000	0	50,000	N.M.
Mortgage payable	1,500,000	1,775,000	(275,000)	(15.5)
Less: Current maturities	275,000	275,000	0	0
Total	1,275,000	1,500,000	(225,000)	(15.0)
Total Liabilities	2,968,750	2,969,000	(250)	0
OWNERS' EQUITY				
Common stock	1,750,000	1,750,000	0	0
Additional paid-in capital	250,000	250,000	0	0
Retained earnings	5,440,760	5,018,500	422,260	8.4
Total	7,440,760	7,018,500	422,260	6.0
Total Liabilities and Owners' Equity	$10,409,510	$ 9,987,500	$ 422,010	4.2%

N.M. = not meaningful

total liabilities and owners' equity equal 100% and individual categories equal percentages of 100%.

Exhibit 2.8   Fluctuation Explanation

		Balance at Dec. 31		Increase
		19X2	19X1	(Decrease)
Marketable Securities				
Commercial Paper		$240,000	$ 90,000	$150,000
Bank Repurchase Agreements		44,687	15,465	29,222
Treasury Bills		150,000	25,000	125,000
Treasury Bonds		150,000	25,000	125,000
Corporate Stocks & Bonds		200,000	0	200,000
		$784,687	$155,465	$629,222

Fluctuation Explanation – Marketable Securities
Stratford Hotel

Common-size balance sheets permit a comparison of amounts relative to a base within each period. For example, assume that cash at the end of year 19X1 is $10,000 and total assets are $100,000. At the end of year 19X2, assume that cash is $15,000 and total assets are $150,000. A horizontal analysis shows a $5,000/50% increase. But cash at the end of each year is 10% of the total assets ($10,000 divided by $100,000 equals 10%; $15,000 divided by $150,000 equals 10%). What first appears to be excessive cash at the end of year 19X2 ($5,000) may not be excessive since cash is 10% of total assets in both cases. However, only a detailed investigation would resolve whether cash equal to 10% of total assets is required in each case.

Examine the Stratford Hotel's common-size balance sheets (Exhibit 2.9). Notable changes include marketable securities (1.6% to 7.5%), total current assets (16.9% to 25.1%), accumulated depreciation (–7.5% to –11.7%), and accounts payable (8.4% to 11.0%). Management should investigate significant changes such as these to determine if they are reasonable. If the changes are found to be unreasonable, management should attempt to remedy the situation.

Common-size statement comparisons are not limited strictly to internal use. Comparisons may also be made against other operations' financial statements and against industry averages. Common-size figures are helpful in comparing hospitality operations which differ materially in size. For example, assume that a large hospitality operation has current assets of $500,000, while a much smaller operation's current assets are $50,000 and that both figures are for the same period. If total assets equal $1,500,000 for the large operation and $150,000 for the small enterprise, then both operations have current assets equaling 33.3% of total assets. These percentages provide a more meaningful comparison than the dollar amount of the current assets when comparing financial statements of the two companies.

Computerization

The balance sheet preparation was one of the first activities to be computerized. There are software programs (general ledger packages)

Exhibit 2.9 Common-Size Balance Sheets

Common-Size Balance Sheets **Stratford Hotel**					
		December 31		Common Size	
ASSETS		19X2	19X1	19X2	19X1
Current Assets:					
Cash	$	104,625	$ 85,600	1.0%	0.9%
Marketable Securities		784,687	155,465	7.5	1.6
Accounts Receivable (net)		1,615,488	1,336,750	15.5	13.4
Inventories		98,350	92,540	1.0	0.9
Other		12,475	11,300	0.1	0.1
Total		2,615,625	1,681,655	25.1	16.9
Property and Equipment:					
Land		905,700	905,700	8.7	9.1
Buildings		5,434,200	5,434,200	52.2	54.4
Furnishings and Equipment		2,617,125	2,650,500	25.1	26.5
Less: Accumulated Depreciation		1,221,490	749,915	(11.7)	(7.5)
Total		7,735,535	8,240,485	74.3	82.5
Other Assets		58,350	65,360	0.6	0.6
Total Assets		$10,409,510	$ 9,987,500	100.0%	100.0%
LIABILITIES					
Current Liabilities:					
Accounts Payable	$	1,145,000	$ 838,000	11.0%	8.4%
Current maturities of long-term debt		275,000	275,000	2.6	2.8
Income taxes payable		273,750	356,000	2.6	3.6
Total		1,693,750	1,469,000	16.2	14.8
Long-term Debt					
Notes Payable		50,000	0	0.5	0
Mortgage payable		1,500,000	1,775,000	14.4	17.8
Less: Current maturities		275,000	275,000	(2.6)	(2.8)
Total		1,275,000	1,500,000	12.3	15.0
Total Liabilities		2,968,750	2,969,000	28.5	29.8
OWNERS' EQUITY					
Common stock		1,750,000	1,750,000	16.8	17.5
Additional paid-in capital		250,000	250,000	2.4	2.5
Retained earnings		5,440,760	5,018,500	52.3	50.2
Total		7,440,760	7,018,500	71.5	70.2
Total Liabilities and Owners' Equity		$10,409,510	$ 9,987,500	100.0%	100.0%

available which require that the bookkeeper enter all of the journal entries as they occur, and which use this information to generate the financial statements at the end of the period. Many of these packages require sophisticated hardware to operate. However, in recent years, more packages for minicomputers and personal computers have been developed.

Even if a general ledger package is not used by a hospitality operation, the computer can be used as a tool in the balance sheet preparation. For example, a property's fixed assets can be maintained on the computer and the depreciation expense calculated with a spreadsheet program. Exhibit 2.10 is a partial listing of the Lincoln Motel's fixed assets. Using this spreadsheet, an accountant could merely enter the fixed asset's name, cost, purchase date, and expected life, and the computer could then generate the depreciation amounts (straight-line with no salvage value) in the following years. The sum of each individual asset's depreciation is automatically calculated for the income statement's depreciation expense. With a more sophisticated spreadsheet, the user could record accumulated depreciation, make use of salvage values, and even calculate depreciation using different methods such as double declining balance or sum-of-the-years' digits.

Summary

Although the balance sheet may not play the vital role in management decision-making that other financial statements play, it is still an important tool. By examining it, managers, investors, and creditors may determine the financial position of the hospitality operation at a given point in time. It is used to help determine an operation's ability to pay its debts, offer dividends, and purchase fixed assets.

The balance sheet is divided into three major categories: assets, liabilities, and owners' equity. Assets are the items owned by the operation, while liabilities and owners' equity represent claims to the operation's assets. Liabilities are amounts owed to creditors. Owners' equity represents the residual interest in assets for investors. Both assets and liabilities are divided into current and noncurrent sections. Current assets are cash and other assets which will be converted to cash or used in the property's operations within the next year. Current liabilities represent present obligations which will be paid within one year. The major categories of noncurrent assets include noncurrent receivables, investments, property and equipment, and other assets. Long-term liabilities are present obligations expected to be paid beyond the next 12 months from the date of the balance sheet.

Owners' equity generally includes common stock, paid-in capital in excess of par, and retained earnings. Common stock is the product of the number of shares outstanding and the par value of the shares. Paid-in capital in excess of par is the amount over the par value paid by investors when they purchased the stock from the hospitality property. Retained earnings are the past earnings generated by the operation but not distributed to the stockholders in the form of dividends.

As assets are the items owned by the property, and liabilities and owners' equity are claims to the assets, the relationship involving the three is stated as follows: Assets = Liabilities + Owners' Equity. The balance sheet is prepared with either assets on one side of the page and liabilities and owners' equity on the other (account format) or with the three sections in one column (report format).

Exhibit 2.10   Lincoln Motel's Computerized Depreciation Schedule

	Cost	Year Purchased	Year Life	XX XX XX	Year's Depreciation			
					19X1	19X2	19X3	19X4
Building	$1,000,000	19X1	40	XX	$25,000	$25,000	$25,000	$25,000
Furniture	200,000	19X1	10	XX	20,000	20,000	20,000	20,000
Truck	15,000	19X2	3	XX		5,000	5,000	5,000
				XX				
				XX				
				XX				
				XX				
				XX				
				XX				
				XX				
				XX				
Total F/A	$1,215,000			XX				
				XX				
				XX				
TOTAL DEPRECIATION EXPENSE:					**$45,000**	**$50,000**	**$50,000**	**$50,000**

In order to gain more information from the balance sheet, it is frequently compared to the balance sheet prepared at the end of the previous period. One tool used is horizontal analysis, which presents not only the current year's data, but also the data from the prior period, and calculates absolute and relative differences between the two periods. Significant differences are generally analyzed. Another type of analysis is vertical analysis, which states all accounts as percentages of either total assets or total liabilities and owners' equity. Differences between the end results of two periods can then be examined. A final analysis is the comparison of the balance sheet figures for the particular hospitality operation with data from other properties or with averages for the hospitality industry as a whole. These comparisons can highlight differences and help management identify areas of concern.

Endnotes

1. *Uniform System of Accounts and Expense Dictionary for Small Hotels, Motels, and Motor Hotels,* Fourth edition (East Lansing, Mich.: Educational Institute of the American Hotel & Motel Association, 1987).

2. *Hilton Hotels Corporation 1988 Annual Report* (Beverly Hills, Calif.: Hilton Hotels Corp., 1989), pp. 32, 44.

3. The exception is that **purchased goodwill** is shown on the balance sheet. This goodwill results when a purchaser of a hospitality operation is unable to assign the entire purchase price to the operation's individual assets. The excess of the purchase price over the dollars assigned to the individual assets is labeled goodwill. Self-generated goodwill, which for many hospitality operations is significant, is not shown on the balance sheet.

4. The detailed accounting for these items (capitalization, depreciation, amortization) is covered in Clifford T. Fay, Jr., Raymond S. Schmidgall, and Stanley B. Tarr, *Basic Financial Accounting for the Hospitality Industry* (East Lansing, Mich.: Educational Institute of the American Hotel & Motel Association, 1982).

Key Terms

account format	horizontal analysis
balance sheet	liquidity
capital stock	long-term liabilities
common stock	noncurrent receivables
common-size balance sheets	owners' equity
common-size statements	preferred stock
comparative balance sheets	purchased goodwill
comparative statements	report format
consolidated financial statements	restricted cash
current assets	retained earnings
current liabilities	treasury stock
current ratio	vertical analysis
fluctuation explanation	working capital

Discussion Questions

1. How do creditors and investors use the balance sheet?

2. What are some of the limitations of the balance sheet?

3. What are the differences and similarities between the account and report formats of the balance sheet?

4. What are assets, liabilities, and owners' equity? What is the relationship among the three?

5. What is meant by the phrase "the lower of cost or market"? When is it used?

6. What are deferred income taxes? Where are they recorded on the balance sheet?

7. What are the differences between a comparative balance sheet and a common-size balance sheet?

8. What is the order of liquidity for the following accounts (most liquid first): marketable securities, prepaid expenses, cash, inventories, and receivables?

9. How do the terms "current" and "long-term" relate to the balance sheet?

10. How is the current ratio determined? What does it reflect?

Problems

Problem 2.1

Using major classifications from the *USASH* balance sheet (see Exhibits 2.5 and 2.6), classify each account below:

Food inventory	Banquet deposits
Front office computer	James Smith, Capital
Utility deposits	Goodwill
State income taxes payable	Deferred insurance
Bonds payable	Investment in GM stock
Treasury stock	(100 shares)
Prepaid insurance	Loan to James Smith (owner)
Leased equipment under	Land (10 acres—undeveloped)
capital leases	Accrued payroll
Petty cash	Deferred income taxes
Kitchen utensils	Cash—First National Bank
Paid-in capital in excess of par	Retained earnings

Problem 2.2

Listed below are asset, liability, and owners' equity accounts for Sue & Jerry's Sleepy Hollow as of December 31, 19X1.

Common Stock	$ 44,600
Inventories	23,241
Treasury Stock	7,278
Land	111,158
House Banks	11,738
Deferred Income Taxes (noncurrent/credit balance)	190,038
Paid-in Capital in Excess of Par	115,501
Notes Payable	42,611
Retained Earnings	327,137
Demand Deposit	8,803
Dividend Payable	21,246
Accounts Receivable	128,179
Accrued Salaries	78,293
Certificates of Deposit	2,934
Prepaid Expenses	13,499
Notes Receivable	22,420
Building	682,093
Marketable Securities	134,634
Long-Term Debt	262,930
Investments	30,049

Accounts Payable	58,690
Allowance for Doubtful Accounts	16,316
Deferred Expenses	12,794
Advance Deposits—Banquets	14,203
Current Maturities on Long-Term Debt	25,824
Security Deposits	8,569

Required:

Prepare the current assets section of the balance sheet for Sue & Jerry's Sleepy Hollow in accordance with the *USASH* (see Exhibit 2.5).

Problem 2.3

Using the data from Problem 2.2:

1. Prepare the liabilities section of the balance sheet in accordance with the *USASH* (see Exhibit 2.6).

2. Determine the current ratio.

Problem 2.4

The Spartan Inn, a sole proprietorship, has several accounts as follows:

Room sales	$1,000,000
Land	80,000
Cash	5,000
Accounts payable	20,000
Inventories	15,000
Accounts Receivable	80,000
Bonds payable (long-term)	300,000
Jerry Spartan, Capital (1/1/19X4)	300,000
Accrued expenses	10,000
Prepaid expenses	8,000
Temporary investments	25,000
Building	500,000
Equipment and furnishings	200,000
Franchise fees (deferred)	15,000
Accumulated depreciation	150,000
Income tax payable	10,000
Deferred income taxes (long-term)	20,000
Interest expense	25,000

Other information is as follows:

The Spartan Inn's net income for 19X4 was $145,000, and Jerry Spartan withdrew $27,000 for personal use during 19X4.

Required:

Prepare a balance sheet for the Spartan Inn as of December 31, 19X4 in accordance with the *USASH* (see Exhibits 2.5 and 2.6).

Problem 2.5

The following information is KRS, Inc.'s balance sheet account balances as of December 31, 19X1 and 19X2. You have been hired by Kermit Smith, the owner, to prepare a financial package for a bank loan including comparative balance sheets.

Assets	19X1	19X2
Cash	$ 16,634	$ 20,768
Accounts Receivable	16,105	11,618
Marketable Securities	10,396	10,496
Inventories	14,554	18,554
Prepaid Expenses	4,158	3,874
Land	116,435	116,435
Building	1,007,090	1,007,090
China, Glass, etc.	269,255	284,934
Accumulated Depreciation	453,263	537,849

Liabilities & Owners' Equity		
Accounts Payable	13,265	12,945
Accrued Expenses	2,047	1,039
Deferred Income Taxes	8,163	7,927
Current Portion of Long-Term Debt	20,407	20,060
Long-Term Debt	553,429	533,369
Retained Earnings	192,853	149,380
Common Stock	211,200	211,200

Required:

Prepare comparative balance sheets for December 31, 19X1 and 19X2, in accordance with the *USASH*. Note: the comparative approach is shown in Exhibit 2.7.

Problem 2.6

Noreen Bayley, the owner/manager of Winkie's Motel, has come to you with some accounting questions. As a result of a fire at the motel, many of the records as of December 31, 19X2, were either burned or soaked by the sprinkler system. You are to help her determine the following balances:

1. In one report, the current ratio for the motel is 1.2 to 1. In addition, you have determined the amount of current liabilities (including $14,736 of current portion of long-term debt) to be $105,380 and long-term debt to be $60,000. What is the amount of current assets for Winkie's Motel?

2. Ms. Bayley has her December 31, 19X2 bank statement which says she has $49,765 in her savings account and $36,072 in her checking account. She has a copy of the inventory sheet which states total inventory on December 31, 19X2, of $15,491. Assuming that the only current assets are cash, inventory, and accounts receivable, what is the total accounts receivable owed to Ms. Bayley?

3. Ms. Bayley has a copy of the balance sheet from November 30, 19X2, which states that current assets were 30% of the total assets. Assuming this relationship is the same at December 31, 19X2, what are the total assets as of December 31, 19X2?

4. Based on the information in parts 1 through 3, what is the Owners' Equity as of December 31, 19X2?

Problem 2.7

Wayne Smith is the new owner of the Mobley Hotel in Wilmington, Delaware. However, he has no experience in the hospitality industry and has hired you to help the hotel's newest employee, Carol Zink, computerize the back office operations. The first job you must tackle is teaching her about the balance sheet. The following is a list of selected account balances in the General Ledger on December 31, 19X1, and also some additional information.

Bank Balance	$ 141,022
Marketable Securities	532,000
Accounts Payable	1,530,761
Land	3,861,725
Retained Earnings	3,462,476
Current Portion Long-Term Debt	392,000
Building	4,768,333
Accounts Receivable	1,843,999
Furniture & Equipment	2,000,741
Paid-In Capital in Excess of Par	1,795,463
Prepaid Insurance	??
Accumulated Depreciation	847,937
Long-Term Debt	??
Capital Stock	??

Additional Information:

1. The market value of the marketable securities as of December 31, 19X1, is $575,998.

2. On January 1, 19X1, the previous owner purchased a two-year insurance policy for $40,000 to cover the years of 19X1–19X2.

3. On December 31, 19X1, there were 50,000 shares of stock issued and outstanding with a par value of $10/share. The 50,000 shares were sold for $2,295,463.

4. Long-term debt is the difference between total assets and owners' equity plus liabilities other than long-term debt.

Required:

1. Prepare the balance sheet in accordance with the *USASH* (see Exhibits 2.5 and 2.6).

2. Calculate the common-size percentages for the December 31, 19X1, balance sheet.

Problem 2.8

The trial balance of balance sheet accounts of Lancer's, a popular casual dining spot, as of December 31, 19X3, is as follows:

	Debits	Credits
Cash	$ 5,000	
Marketable securities	10,000	
Accounts receivable	100,000	
Allowance for doubtful accounts		$ 5,000
Food inventory	15,000	
Prepaid rent	5,000	
Prepaid insurance	8,000	
Investments	50,000	
Land	80,000	
Building	420,000	
Equipment	100,000	
Accumulated depreciation		100,000
Accounts payable		15,000
Income taxes payable		–0–
Accrued expenses		25,000
Dividends payable		–0–
Long-term debt		300,000
Capital stock		89,000
Paid-in capital in excess of par		68,000
Retained earnings (1/1/X3)		61,000

Additional information:

1. Dividends declared during 19X3 totaled $30,000. Only $20,000 of the dividends declared in 19X3 have been paid as of December 31, 19X3. The unpaid dividends have not been recorded.

2. Operations generated $800,000 of revenue for 19X3. Expenses recorded totaled $650,000. Additional adjustments required are as follows:

   A. The allowance for doubtful accounts should be adjusted to 10% of accounts receivable.

   B. Prepaid insurance of $8,000 is the premium paid for insurance coverage for July 1, 19X3, through June 30, 19X4.

   C. Unrecorded depreciation expense for 19X3 totals $41,000.

   D. Income taxes have not been recorded. Lancer's average rate is 20%.

3. The long-term debt account includes $50,000 which must be paid on June 30, 19X4.

Required:

Prepare a balance sheet according to *USASH* (see Exhibits 2.5 and 2.6).

Problem 2.9

Below is selected information from the comparative and common-size asset portion of balance sheets for Martin's Motel.

Martin's Motel

	December 31		Dollar	Common-Size
	19X1	19X2	Difference	(Dec.31, 19X2)
Current Assets				
Cash				
House Bank	$ _____	$ _____	$ (10)	_____%
Demand Deposit	10,000	60	9,940	.6
Total Cash	1000	990	(10)	1.0
Accounts Receivable	1,241	1414.7	173.7	14.0
Inventories	-822	-784.7	-37.3	_____
Total Current Assets	1419	1,620	201	_____
Investments	1,250	1,275	25	2.0
Property & Equipment(net)				
Land	957	1,030	73	7.6
Building	4,350			
Furniture	300	375	(75)	25.0
Other Assets	49	49.25	.25	.5
Total Assets	$_____	$_____	$_____	_____%

Required:

Fill in the blanks above. Round all amounts to the nearest dollar.

Problem 2.10

Below is selected information from the comparative and common-size liabilities and owners' equity sections of balance sheets of December 31, 19X1 and 19X2, of Lengal's Motel.

	December 31		%	Common-Size
	19X1	19X2	Difference	(Dec.31, 19X2)
Current Liabilities				
Accounts payable	$ 10,000	$ 12,000	_____%	_____%
Notes payable	_____	25,000	50.0	_____
Wages payable	_____	10,000	_____	_____
Accrued expenses	_____	_____	(10.0)	_____
Total Current Liabilities	_____	_____	_____	15.0
Long-Term Debt	_____	_____	(10.0)	25.0
Deferred income taxes	_____	_____	10.0	5.0
Total Liabilities	_____	_____	0.0	_____

Owners' Equity
  Capital stock   _____   150,000   _____   _____
  Retained earnings   60,000   _____   25.0   _____
  Treasury stock   _____   5,000   0.0   _____
    Total Owners' Equity   _____   _____   _____   _____

Total Liabilities and
  Owners' Equity $_____ $ 400,000   10.0%   _____

Required:

Fill in the blanks above. Round all amounts to the nearest dollar.

Supplemental Reading

Hilton Hotels Corporation
and Subsidiaries

CONSOLIDATED STATEMENTS OF INCOME
(In millions, except per share amounts)

Year Ended December 31,		1989	1988	1987
Revenue	Rooms	$335.8	302.8	272.1
	Food and beverage	216.8	207.4	197.0
	Casino	311.4	319.8	265.3
	Casino promotional allowances	(42.5)	(38.3)	(34.9)
	Management and franchise fees	74.1	72.1	66.5
	Other	58.5	51.6	49.4
	Operating income from unconsolidated affiliates	44.1	38.2	28.4
		998.2	953.6	843.8
Expenses	Rooms	106.1	95.6	85.4
	Food and beverage	171.2	158.0	149.8
	Casino	130.0	127.6	94.6
	Other costs and expenses	359.0	328.7	305.6
		766.3	709.9	635.4
		231.9	243.7	208.4
	Gain (loss) from property transactions	(3.7)	—	43.8
Operating Income		228.2	243.7	252.2
	Interest and dividend income	44.0	32.6	22.9
	Interest expense	(62.0)	(48.9)	(29.1)
	Interest expense, net, from unconsolidated affiliates	(25.8)	(21.8)	(15.8)
	Corporate expense	(25.6)	(20.8)	(18.3)
Income before Income Taxes		158.8	184.8	211.9
	Provision for income taxes	48.7	53.9	72.0
Net Income		$110.1	130.9	139.9
Net Income per Share		$ 2.27	2.72	2.80

See notes to consolidated financial statements

Hilton Hotels Corporation and Subsidiaries	CONSOLIDATED BALANCE SHEETS *(In millions)*		

	Assets December 31,	1989	1988
Current Assets	Cash and equivalents	$ 316.1	313.7
	Temporary investments	129.1	120.6
	Other current assets	164.6	151.9
	Total current assets	609.8	586.2
Investments, Property and Other Assets	Investments in and notes from unconsolidated affiliates	252.2	216.2
	Other investments	46.0	43.0
	Restricted securities	—	16.9
	Property and equipment, net	1,255.9	1,001.8
	Other assets	52.1	28.4
	Total investments, property and other assets	1,606.2	1,306.3
Total Assets		$2,216.0	1,892.5
	Liabilities and Stockholders' Equity		
Liabilities	Current liabilities	$ 586.9	306.7
	Long-term debt	487.1	568.5
	Deferred income taxes	184.5	179.1
	Insurance reserves and other	74.5	24.1
	Total liabilities	1,333.0	1,078.4
Stockholders' Equity	Preferred stock, none outstanding	—	—
	Common stock, 48.0 million and 47.8 million shares outstanding, respectively	127.6	127.6
	Additional paid-in capital	12.9	18.5
	Retained earnings	917.5	855.4
		1,058.0	1,001.5
	Less treasury shares	175.0	187.4
	Total stockholders' equity	883.0	814.1
Total Liabilities and Stockholders' Equity		$2,216.0	1,892.5

See notes to consolidated financial statements

Hilton Hotels Corporation
and Subsidiaries

CONSOLIDATED STATEMENTS OF CASH FLOWS
(In millions)

Year Ended December 31,	1989	1988	1987
Operating Activities			
Net income	$110.1	130.9	139.9
Adjustments to reconcile net income to net cash provided by operating activities:			
Depreciation and amortization	80.8	63.6	57.0
Change in working capital components:			
Inventories	(.4)	(.8)	(1.0)
Accounts receivable	(11.0)	(27.3)	.8
Other current assets	(1.6)	(7.3)	.6
Accounts payable and accrued expenses	6.4	32.1	1.5
Income taxes payable	(2.7)	22.8	8.4
Change in deferred income taxes	5.4	5.3	14.7
Change in other liabilities	39.4	(15.5)	17.0
Unconsolidated affiliates' distributions in excess of earnings	5.7	4.2	2.1
(Gain) loss from property transactions	3.7	—	(43.8)
Other	(18.8)	(13.5)	(6.0)
Net cash provided by operating activities	217.0	194.5	191.2
Investing Activities			
Capital expenditures	(329.3)	(287.1)	(108.3)
Additional investments	(45.3)	(23.4)	(39.8)
Payments on notes receivable	3.8	2.7	5.3
Reduction of restricted securities	16.9	53.0	8.3
Change in temporary investments	(8.5)	(49.2)	(71.4)
Proceeds from property transactions	—	—	55.8
Other	(3.2)	15.6	(15.2)
Net cash used by investing activities	(365.6)	(288.4)	(165.3)
Financing Activities			
Short-term borrowings	187.5	81.8	18.0
Long-term borrowings	31.2	248.0	5.0
Reduction of long-term debt	(26.5)	(2.2)	(4.5)
Net proceeds from joint venture financing	—	—	16.1
Issuance of common stock	6.8	3.6	4.0
Cash dividends	(48.0)	(46.4)	(44.8)
Treasury stock purchases	—	(46.8)	(33.6)
Net cash provided (used) by financing activities	151.0	238.0	(39.8)
Increase (decrease) in cash and equivalents	2.4	144.1	(13.9)
Cash and equivalents at beginning of year	313.7	169.6	183.5
Cash and equivalents at end of year	$316.1	313.7	169.6

See notes to consolidated financial statements

Hilton Hotels Corporation and Subsidiaries

CONSOLIDATED STATEMENTS OF STOCKHOLDERS' EQUITY
(In millions, except per share amounts)

	Number of Shares Outstanding	Common Stock	Additional Paid-in Capital	Retained Earnings	Treasury Shares	Total Stockholders' Equity
Balance, December 31, 1986	49.7	$127.3	15.7	675.8	(111.5)	707.3
Exercise of stock options	.2	.2	3.8	—	—	4.0
Treasury stock acquired	(1.0)	—	—	—	(33.6)	(33.6)
Net income	—	—	—	139.9	—	139.9
Dividends ($.90 per share)	—	—	—	(44.8)	—	(44.8)
Balance, December 31, 1987	48.9	127.5	19.5	770.9	(145.1)	772.8
Exercise of stock options	.1	.1	(1.0)	—	4.5	3.6
Treasury stock acquired	(1.2)	—	—	—	(46.8)	(46.8)
Net income	—	—	—	130.9	—	130.9
Dividends ($.95 per share)	—	—	—	(46.4)	—	(46.4)
Balance, December 31, 1988	47.8	127.6	18.5	855.4	(187.4)	814.1
Exercise of stock options	.2	—	(5.6)	—	12.4	6.8
Net income	—	—	—	110.1	—	110.1
Dividends ($1.00 per share)	—	—	—	(48.0)	—	(48.0)
Balance, December 31, 1989	48.0	$127.6	12.9	917.5	(175.0)	883.0

See notes to consolidated financial statements

Hilton Hotels Corporation
and Subsidiaries

NOTES TO CONSOLIDATED FINANCIAL STATEMENTS
December 31, 1989

Summary of significant accounting policies

PRINCIPLES OF CONSOLIDATION

The consolidated financial statements include the accounts of Hilton Hotels Corporation and its majority and wholly-owned subsidiaries (the Company). All material intercompany transactions are eliminated. There are no significant restrictions on the transfer of funds from the Company's wholly-owned subsidiaries to Hilton Hotels Corporation.

Investments in unconsolidated affiliates are stated at cost adjusted by equity in undistributed earnings.

CASH AND EQUIVALENTS/TEMPORARY INVESTMENTS

Cash and equivalents include investments with initial maturities or put options of three months or less. Temporary investments include items with terms between three months and one year.

CASINO REVENUES/PROMOTIONAL ALLOWANCES

Casino revenues are the aggregate of gaming wins and losses. Promotional allowances consist of complimentary food, beverage and accommodations.

PROPERTY, EQUIPMENT AND DEPRECIATION

Property and equipment are stated at cost. Interest incurred during construction of facilities is capitalized and amortized over the life of the asset.

Costs of improvements are capitalized. Costs of normal repairs and maintenance are charged to expense as incurred. Upon the sale or retirement of property and equipment, the cost and related accumulated depreciation are removed from the respective accounts, and the resulting gain or loss, if any, is included in income.

Depreciation has been computed using the straight-line method over the estimated useful lives of the assets. Leasehold improvements are amortized over the shorter of the asset life or lease term.

PRE-OPENING COSTS

Operating costs and expenses associated with the opening of hotels or major additions to hotels are deferred and charged to income over a three year period after the opening date.

UNAMORTIZED LOAN COSTS

Debt discount and issuance costs incurred in connection with long-term debt are capitalized and amortized by charges to expense, principally on the bonds outstanding method.

SELF-INSURANCE

The Company is self-insured for various levels of general liability, workers' compensation and employee medical coverage. Insurance reserves include the present values of projected settlements for claims.

INCOME TAXES

The provisions for deferred income taxes reflect the results of timing differences in recognizing income or deductions for financial reporting and income tax purposes.

STOCK OPTION PLANS

No charges or credits to income are made with regard to the options granted under the Company's stock option plans.

NET INCOME PER SHARE

Net income per share is based on the weighted average number of common shares outstanding plus the common share equivalents which arise from the assumed exercise of stock options.

RECLASSIFICATIONS

The consolidated financial statements for prior years reflect certain reclassifications to conform with classifications adopted in 1989. These reclassifications have no effect on net income.

Hilton Hotels Corporation
and Subsidiaries

NOTES TO CONSOLIDATED FINANCIAL STATEMENTS
(continued)

Accounts and Notes Receivable

Included in other current assets at December 31, 1989 and 1988 are accounts and notes receivable as follows:

(In millions)	1989	1988
Hotel accounts and notes receivable	$102.5	88.4
Less allowance for doubtful accounts	8.3	7.9
	94.2	80.5
Casino accounts receivable	43.4	47.9
Less allowance for doubtful accounts	7.6	9.1
	35.8	38.8
Federal tax refund receivable	2.0	2.0
Total	$132.0	121.3

Based primarily on historical trends, an allowance for estimated uncollectible casino receivables is provided to reduce casino accounts receivable to amounts anticipated to be collected within twelve months of the date credit was granted. Such allowances are included in casino expenses in the amount of $9.3 million, $11.9 million and $5.5 million in 1989, 1988 and 1987, respectively.

Inventories

Included in other current assets at December 31, 1989 and 1988 are inventories of $10.7 million and $10.3 million, respectively, determined on a first-in, first-out basis.

Investments

The composition of the Company's total investments in and notes from unconsolidated affiliates at December 31, 1989 and 1988 is as follows:

(In millions)	1989	1988
Equity investments		
50% owned affiliates		
Hotel partnership joint ventures (eight in 1989 and 1988)	$172.6	175.3
Other	11.4	10.2
Less than 50% owned affiliates		
Hotel partnership joint ventures (ten in 1989, nine in 1988)	35.7	24.7
Other	11.6	2.0
Total equity investments	231.3	212.2
Notes receivable (net of current maturities of $.3 in 1988)	20.9	4.0
Total	$252.2	216.2

The changes in the Company's equity investments in such affiliates are as follows:

(In millions)	1989	1988
Investments, January 1	$212.2	199.1
Earnings	18.3	16.4
Distributions received	(24.0)	(20.6)
Additional investments	24.8	21.9
Transfer of assets	—	(4.6)
Investments, December 31	$231.3	212.2

Two unconsolidated affiliates have limitations on distributions of earnings under certain circumstances. At December 31, 1989 neither affiliate had restrictions on such distributions.

Management fees totaling $23.5 million, $20.2 million and $17.2 million were charged by the Company to its unconsolidated affiliates in 1989, 1988 and 1987, respectively. Other group services were provided to unconsolidated affiliates with no significant element of profit.

Summarized balance sheet information of the 50% owned affiliates at December 31, 1989 and 1988 is as follows:

(In millions)	1989	1988
Current assets	$146.0	90.0
Property and other assets, net	773.8	770.5
Current liabilities	92.5	56.7
Long-term debt and other	430.0	402.5
Equity	397.3	401.3

Summarized balance sheet information of the less than 50% owned affiliates at December 31, 1989 and 1988 is as follows:

(In millions)	1989	1988
Current assets	$ 95.6	58.0
Property and other assets, net	475.3	511.0
Current liabilities	80.0	175.9
Long-term debt and other	350.2	292.0
Equity	140.7	101.1

Hilton Hotels Corporation and Subsidiaries   NOTES TO CONSOLIDATED FINANCIAL STATEMENTS *(continued)*

Of total long-term unconsolidated affiliate obligations totaling $780.2 million at December 31, 1989, $767.6 million is secured solely by venture assets or is guaranteed by other venture partners without recourse to the Company.

The Company's proportionate share of equity as reflected in the unconsolidated affiliates' financial statements is $20.6 million and $22.2 million in excess of the Company's cost in 1989 and 1988, respectively, and is being amortized over the estimated useful lives of the underlying assets. Such amortization amounted to $1.6 million in 1989 and 1988, and $1.9 million in 1987.

The Company's proportionate shares of capital expenditures and depreciation expense of unconsolidated affiliates were $34.9 million and $30.9 million, respectively, in 1989, $42.1 million and $28.1 million, respectively, in 1988, and $99.3 million and $24.3 million, respectively, in 1987.

Summarized results of operations of the 50% owned affiliates for the three years ended December 31, 1989 are as follows:

(In millions)	1989	1988	1987
Revenue	$509.8	460.7	435.5
Expenses	471.6	425.5	401.5
Net income	35.8	32.3	31.9

Summarized results of operations of the less than 50% owned affiliates for the three years ended December 31, 1989 are as follows:

(In millions)	1989	1988	1987
Revenue	$345.2	346.4	291.0
Expenses	341.8	344.6	312.2
Net income (loss)	3.4	1.8	(21.2)

The proportionate taxable income or loss of all partnership joint ventures is included in the taxable income of their respective partners. Therefore, no provisions for income taxes on such entities, except for certain local taxes on income of partnership joint ventures in the District of Columbia and the Federal income tax of a corporate joint venture, are included in the above statements.

Other investments at December 31, 1989 and 1988 consist of:

(In millions)	1989	1988
Safe harbor tax lease benefits	$ 9.8	10.7
Other notes and investments	36.2	32.3
Total	$46.0	43.0

Property and Equipment

Property and equipment at December 31, 1989 and 1988 are as follows:

(In millions)	1989	1988
Land	$ 99.4	87.9
Buildings and leasehold improvements	904.9	735.1
Furniture and equipment	341.0	283.0
Property held for sale or development	6.4	6.4
Construction in progress	268.4	212.7
	1,620.1	1,325.1
Less accumulated depreciation	364.2	323.3
Total	$ 1,255.9	1,001.8

Purchases of property and equipment with assumed long-term debt or financed with construction payables totaled $21.7 million, $59.0 million and $1.4 million in 1989, 1988 and 1987, respectively.

Current Liabilities

Current liabilities at December 31, 1989 and 1988 are as follows:

(In millions)	1989	1988
Accounts payable and accrued expenses	$174.7	165.4
Short-term borrowings	287.3	99.8
Current maturities of long-term debt	89.1	3.0
Income taxes payable	35.8	38.5
Total	$586.9	306.7

Long-Term Debt

Long-term debt at December 31, 1989 and 1988 is as follows:

(In millions)	1989	1988
Collateral trust bonds, 8% due 1990 to 1993	$ 6.8	7.8
Industrial development revenue bonds at adjustable rates, due 2015	82.0	82.0
Mortgage bonds and notes, 9.25% to 12%, due 1990 to 2003	86.0	56.9
Senior notes, 9.3% to 9.95%, due 1991 to 1998	199.2	199.2
Senior debentures, 11.375%, due 1992	74.8	74.8
Senior debentures, 10.625%, due 1994	75.0	75.0
Other	52.4	75.8
	576.2	571.5
Less current maturities	89.1	3.0
Net long-term debt	$487.1	568.5

Hilton Hotels Corporation   NOTES TO CONSOLIDATED FINANCIAL STATEMENTS
and Subsidiaries   *(continued)*

Cash interest paid, net of amounts capitalized, were $59.6 million, $45.2 million and $29.1 million in 1989, 1988 and 1987, respectively. Capitalized interest amounted to $19.2 million, $9.8 million and $6.6 million, respectively.

Debt maturities during the next five years are as follows:

	(In millions)
1990	$89.1
1991	16.8
1992	7.4
1993	97.7
1994	88.4

Secured debt obligations of $176.8 million at December 31, 1989 are collateralized by property with a net book value of $484.9 million and are payable over remaining terms ranging to 25 years.

The Company has on file shelf registration statements whereby it could offer up to $600 million in senior debentures or senior and subordinated debentures totaling $600 million, with the subordinated debentures comprising not more than $300 million.

The Company has issued $199.2 million in fixed rate senior notes under these registration statements at December 31, 1989. Of this amount, $100 million is due in 1998 and is redeemable at par plus accrued interest on or after June 1, 1995.

The 10.625% senior debentures due in 1994 are redeemable by the Company, in whole or from time to time in part, at 100% of the principal amount plus accrued interest to the date of redemption on or after January 15, 1991. Subsequent to December 31, 1989 the Company exercised its option to call, in March 1990, the 11.375% senior debentures due in 1992. Accordingly, such amounts are included in current maturities as of December 31, 1989.

During 1989, 1988 and 1987 the Company issued and renewed commercial paper and private notes for varying periods with interest at market rates. The Company had $287.3 million, $99.8 million and $18.0 million in commercial paper and private notes outstanding at December 31, 1989, 1988 and 1987, respectively. In 1989, 1988 and 1987 average amounts of commercial paper and private notes outstanding were $240.8 million, $307.9 million and $140.5 million, respectively,

with the largest amounts outstanding at any one time being $287.3 million, $411.9 million and $194.3 million, respectively. Weighted average interest rates were 9.26%, 7.63% and 6.72%, respectively.

Lines of credit available include $460 million in money-market facilities with interest and maturity terms as quoted by the participating banks at the time of any borrowing thereunder. The money-market facilities carry no commitment fees and may be withdrawn at the discretion of the participating banks. There were no borrowings under these facilities in 1989 and 1988.

The Company is limited under its most restrictive debt covenant as to the amount of retained earnings available for payment of cash dividends and acquisition of the Company's stock. At December 31, 1989, $737.9 million of retained earnings was unrestricted.

Income Taxes

The provisions for income taxes for the three years ended December 31, 1989 are as follows:

(In millions)	1989	1988	1987
Current			
Federal	$ 32.6	39.8	46.8
Investment and other tax credits	(1.2)	(.3)	(2.5)
State and local	5.3	2.1	6.2
	36.7	41.6	50.5
Deferred	12.0	12.3	21.5
Total	$ 48.7	53.9	72.0

During 1989, 1988 and 1987 the Company paid income taxes of $40.1 million, $25.6 million and $29.5 million, respectively.

Deferred income taxes arise from timing differences in the recognition of revenue and expense for tax and financial reporting purposes. Tax effects of these differences are:

(In millions)	1989	1988	1987
Depreciation	$ 8.4	7.7	8.6
Joint venture interests	3.4	6.0	4.3
Allowance for doubtful accounts	—	(4.2)	—
Asset dispositions	—	—	10.8
Self-insurance reserves	(3.7)	.6	(1.0)
Benefit plans	4.6	.9	(2.9)
Other, net	(.7)	1.3	1.7
Total	$ 12.0	12.3	21.5

Hilton Hotels Corporation and Subsidiaries

NOTES TO CONSOLIDATED FINANCIAL STATEMENTS *(continued)*

Deferred taxes arising from a safe harbor leasing transaction are charged or credited directly to deferred income tax liabilities.

The Deficit Reduction Act of 1984 provided certain tax benefits to corporations established by the Alaskan Native Claims Settlement Act known as Alaskan Native Corporations (ANCs). The Tax Reform Act of 1986 clarified the availability of these tax benefits. Accordingly, during 1989, 1988 and 1987 the Company entered into transactions with various ANCs resulting in reductions of $.3 million, $2.4 million and $3.9 million, respectively, in the Company's provision for income taxes.

The Financial Accounting Standards Board has issued a new accounting standard for income taxes. The Company must adopt the accounting and disclosure requirements of the standard no later than 1992. Based on existing conditions and a preliminary review, the Company expects a favorable effect on its financial position when the new standard is adopted.

Reconciliation of the Federal income tax rate and the Company's effective tax rate is as follows:

	1989	1988	1987
Federal income tax rate	34.0%	34.0	40.0
Increase (reduction) in taxes:			
State income tax (net of Federal tax benefit)	2.1	.8	1.7
Benefit of dividend and municipal bond income	(3.6)	(3.7)	(2.7)
Investment and other tax credits	(.5)	—	(1.1)
ANC tax benefits	(.1)	(1.3)	(1.8)
Benefit of capital gains rate	—	—	(1.4)
Other	(1.2)	(.6)	(.7)
Effective tax rate	30.7%	29.2	34.0

Capital Stock

Ninety million shares of common stock with a par value of $2.50 per share are authorized, of which 51.0 million were issued at December 31, 1989 and 1988, including treasury shares of 3.0 million and 3.2 million in 1989 and 1988, respectively.

Ten million shares of preferred stock with a par value of $1.00 per share are authorized. The shares are issuable in series. No shares were outstanding in 1989 or 1988.

The Company has a Share Purchase Rights Plan, under which a right is attached to each share of the Company's common stock. The rights may only become exercisable under certain circumstances involving actual or potential acquisitions of the Company's common stock by a specified person or affiliated group. Depending on the circumstances, if the rights become exercisable, the holder may be entitled to purchase units of the Company's junior participating preferred stock, shares of the Company's common stock or shares of common stock of the acquiror. The rights remain in existence until July 25, 1998 unless they are terminated, exercised or redeemed.

In 1988 the Company's Board of Directors authorized a 2-for-1 stock split in the form of a 100 percent stock distribution. All share and per share data in the consolidated financial statements and notes for 1988 and prior years were adjusted accordingly.

At December 31, 1989, 1.2 million shares of common stock were reserved for the exercise of options under the Company's stock option plans. Options may be granted to salaried officers and other key employees of the Company to purchase common stock at not less than fair market value at the date of grant.

Options may be exercised in installments commencing one year after date of grant and expire either five or ten years after date of grant. The plan also permits the granting of Stock Appreciation Rights (SARs). There were no SARs outstanding at December 31, 1989 or 1988.

Changes in stock options during 1989 were as follows:

	Options Price Range (Per Share)	Options Outstanding	Available for Grant
Balance at January 1	$13.81- 44.38	1,000,785	452,624
Granted	53.19-111.63	204,500	(204,500)
Exercised	13.81- 44.38	(207,743)	—
Cancelled	14.16- 53.19	(23,244)	23,244
Balance at December 31	14.16-111.63	974,298	271,368
Exercisable at December 31	$14.16- 44.38	533,776	

Under provisions of Nevada gaming laws and the Company's certificate of incorporation, certain securities of the Company are subject to restrictions on ownership which may be imposed by specified governmental commissions. Such restrictions may require the holder to dispose of the securities or, if the holder refuses to make such disposition, the Company may be obligated to repurchase the securities.

Hilton Hotels Corporation and Subsidiaries

NOTES TO CONSOLIDATED FINANCIAL STATEMENTS *(continued)*

Employee Benefit Plans

The Company has a non-contributory retirement plan (Basic Plan) covering substantially all regular full-time, non-union employees. The Company also has plans covering qualifying officers and non-officer directors (Supplemental Plans). Benefits for all plans are based upon years of service and compensation, as defined.

The Company's funding policy is to contribute annually the minimum amount deductible under Federal guidelines. Contributions are intended to provide not only for benefits attributed to service to date, but also for benefits expected to be earned in the future.

The following sets forth the funded status for the Basic Plan as of December 31, 1989 and 1988:

(In millions)	1989	1988
Actuarial present value of benefit obligations:		
Accumulated benefit obligation, including vested benefits of $(77.7) and $(52.7), respectively	$(81.4)	(64.5)
Projected benefit obligation for service rendered to date	$(98.2)	(78.9)
Plan assets at fair value, primarily listed securities and temporary investments	115.0	94.1
Plan assets in excess of projected benefit obligation	16.8	15.2
Unrecognized net loss from changes in assumptions	.7	5.5
Unrecognized net asset as of January 1, 1986	(14.6)	(16.0)
Prepaid pension cost	$ 2.9	4.7
Pension cost includes the following components:		
Service cost	$ 4.0	3.5
Interest cost on projected benefit obligation	7.5	6.3
Actual return on plan assets	(20.9)	(9.5)
Net amortization and deferral	11.3	.9
Net periodic cost before allocation	1.9	1.2
Cost allocated to managed properties	.7	.5
Net periodic pension cost	$ 1.2	.7

Included in plan assets at fair value are securities of the Company of $24.7 million and $15.9 million at December 31, 1989 and 1988, respectively.

The following sets forth the funded status for the Supplemental Plans as of December 31, 1989 and 1988:

(In millions)	1989	1988
Actuarial present value of benefit obligations:		
Accumulated benefit obligation, including vested benefits of $(2.2) and $(4.4), respectively	$ (2.3)	(7.0)
Projected benefit obligation for service rendered to date	$ (7.7)	(11.1)
Plan assets	11.9	—
Plan asset (unrecognized obligation)	4.2	(11.1)
Unrecognized net loss from changes in assumptions	3.9	3.2
Unrecognized obligation as of January 1, 1986	4.7	4.2
Prepaid cost (accrued liability)	$ 12.8	(3.7)
Pension cost includes the following components:		
Service cost	$ .2	.1
Interest cost on projected benefit obligation	.9	.9
Actual return on plan assets	(.3)	—
Net amortization and deferral	.8	.6
Net periodic pension cost	$ 1.6	1.6

The discount rates used in determining the actuarial present values of the projected benefit obligations were 8.25% and 8.50% in 1989 and 1988, respectively, with the rate of increase in future compensation projected at five percent in each year. The expected long-term rate of return on assets is nine percent. The unrecognized net (asset) obligation is being amortized over a 15 year period.

A significant number of the Company's employees are covered by union sponsored, collectively bargained multi-employer pension plans. The Company contributed and charged to expense $8.0 million, $6.8 million and $7.1 million in 1989, 1988 and 1987, respectively, for such plans. Information from the plans' administrators is not sufficient to permit the Company to determine its share of unfunded vested benefits, if any.

The Company also has an employee investment plan whereby the Company contributes certain percentages of employee contributions. The cost of the plan is not significant.

Hilton Hotels Corporation
and Subsidiaries

NOTES TO CONSOLIDATED FINANCIAL STATEMENTS
(continued)

Leases

The Company operates six properties under non-cancellable operating leases, all of which are for land only, having remaining terms up to 44 years. Upon expiration of three of the leases, the Company has renewal options of 25, 30 and 40 years. Five leases require the payment of additional rentals based on varying percentages of revenue or income.

Minimum lease commitments under non-cancellable operating leases are as follows:

Year ending December 31,	(In millions)
1990	$ 4.7
1991	4.2
1992	3.5
1993	3.1
1994	2.9
1995 to 2033	4.9
Total	$23.3

Total lease rental expense for all operating leases is composed of:

(In millions)	1989	1988	1987
Minimum rentals	$5.2	6.7	8.3
Additional rentals	3.8	2.9	1.9
Total	$9.0	9.6	10.2

Segments of Business

Financial data of the Company's business segments for the years ended December 31, 1989, 1988 and 1987 are as follows:

(In millions)	1989	1988	1987
Depreciation (1)			
Hotels	$ 68.1	58.9	51.3
Gaming	33.6	28.9	28.2
Corporate	3.1	1.7	1.0
Total	$ 104.8	89.5	80.5
Capital Expenditures (1)			
Hotels	$ 142.5	242.0	172.7
Gaming	222.3	87.5	32.3
Corporate	2.3	57.3	.6
Total	$ 367.1	386.8	205.6
Assets			
Hotels (2)	$ 908.6	800.0	739.1
Gaming (2)	745.1	558.0	444.4
Corporate	562.3	534.5	240.1
Total	$2,216.0	1,892.5	1,423.6

(1) Includes Hilton's proportionate share of unconsolidated affiliates.
(2) Includes investments in unconsolidated affiliates.

Supplemental hotels segment operating data for the three years ended December 31, 1989 are as follows:

(In millions)	1989	1988	1987
Revenue			
Rooms	$ 202.0	172.5	151.1
Food and beverage	105.1	93.8	87.1
Other products and services	36.2	32.4	26.5
Management and franchise fees	68.6	66.8	63.2
Operating income from unconsolidated affiliates	41.3	35.7	27.3
	453.2	401.2	355.2
Costs and expenses			
Departmental direct costs			
Rooms	60.4	51.1	44.8
Food and beverage	83.2	73.9	69.2
Other costs and expenses	180.3	161.1	140.5
	323.9	286.1	254.5
Hotels income contribution	$ 129.3	115.1	100.7

Supplemental gaming segment operating data for the three years ended December 31, 1989 are as follows:

(In millions)	1989	1988	1987
Revenue			
Rooms	$ 133.8	130.3	121.0
Food and beverage	111.7	113.6	109.9
Casino	311.4	319.8	265.3
Casino promotional allowances	(42.5)	(38.3)	(34.9)
Other products and services	30.6	27.0	27.3
	545.0	552.4	488.6
Costs and expenses			
Departmental direct costs			
Rooms	45.7	44.5	40.6
Food and beverage	88.0	84.1	80.6
Casino	130.0	127.6	94.6
Other costs and expenses	178.7	167.6	165.1
	442.4	423.8	380.9
Gaming income contribution	$ 102.6	128.6	107.7

Hilton Hotels Corporation and Subsidiaries

NOTES TO CONSOLIDATED FINANCIAL STATEMENTS *(continued)*

Supplementary Financial Information (unaudited)

Quarterly Financial Data *(In millions, except per share amounts, stock prices and percentages)*

1989	Occupancy (1) Hotels	Gaming	Revenue	Income Contribution	Income Before Income Taxes	Net Income	Earnings Per Share	Dividends Per Share	High/Low Stock Price
1st Quarter	67%	86	$225.1	36.6	19.2	13.1	.27	.25	59.25/48.38
2nd Quarter	73	86	265.0	80.4	62.6	42.0	.87	.25	106.50/55.50
3rd Quarter	71	87	248.5	58.2	38.1	28.1	.58	.25	115.50/95.25
4th Quarter	67	87	259.6	56.7	38.9	26.9	.55	.25	110.25/81.25
Year	69%	86	$998.2	231.9	158.8	110.1	2.27	1.00	115.50/48.38
1988									
1st Quarter	66%	85	$214.2	52.3	40.5	27.6	.57	.225	47.38/34.00
2nd Quarter	73	87	248.9	74.5	60.5	40.8	.85	.225	50.88/42.63
3rd Quarter	71	91	236.1	54.1	38.5	27.3	.57	.25	50.75/42.25
4th Quarter	68	85	254.4	62.8	45.3	35.2	.73	.25	55.25/45.50
Year	70%	87	$953.6	243.7	184.8	130.9	2.72	.95	55.25/34.00

(1) Properties owned or managed.

As of December 31, 1989 there were approximately 5,200 stockholders of record.

Commitments and Contingent Liabilities

At December 31, 1989 the Company had contractual commitments at its wholly-owned or leased properties for major expansion and rehabilitation projects of approximately $139.9 million. There were also entertainer and sporting event commitments of $3.9 million. Additionally, the Company is committed, under certain conditions, to invest or loan up to $56.9 million to entities developing hotel properties.

In 1984 a lawsuit was initiated by 37 former casino employees of the Las Vegas Hilton. In March 1989 a jury awarded the plaintiffs $38.0 million, including $30.0 million in punitive damages. On February 1, 1990 a final judgment of $45.0 million was entered, which includes the plaintiffs' attorneys fees and interest on the jury award. The Company believes the verdict and judgment are contrary to the facts and law and intends to file an appeal.

In management's opinion, disposition of this matter, and various other lawsuits pending against the Company, is not expected to have a material effect on the Company's financial position.

Hilton Hotels Corporation and Subsidiaries   TEN YEAR SUMMARY

	(Dollars in millions, except per share amounts)	1989	1988	1987
Operating Data For Years Ended December 31	Revenue			
	Hotels [1]	$1,500.6	1,395.2	1,279.4
	Management fees	34.4	33.3	31.3
	Franchise fees	34.2	33.5	31.9
	Total hotels	1,569.2	1,462.0	1,342.6
	Gaming [1]	694.3	695.3	589.7
	Total	2,263.5	2,157.3	1,932.3
	Less non-consolidated managed	1,309.4	1,241.9	1,116.9
	Total revenue from consolidated operations	$ 954.1	915.4	815.4
	Income contribution [2]			
	Hotels	$ 129.3	115.1	100.7
	Gaming	102.6	128.6	107.7
	Total	231.9	243.7	208.4
	Net interest and dividend income (expense) [2]	(43.8)	(38.1)	(22.0)
	Corporate expense	(25.6)	(20.8)	(18.3)
	Property transactions	(3.7)	—	43.8
	Provision for income taxes	(48.7)	(53.9)	(72.0)
	Net income	$ 110.1	130.9	139.9
	Funds provided from operations [3]	199.5	207.0	219.6
	Depreciation [2]	104.8	89.5	80.5
	Capital expenditures [2]	367.1	386.8	205.6
Stockholder Data	Net income per share	$ 2.27	2.72	2.80
	Average common and equivalent shares	48.5	48.1	50.0
	Stockholders' equity	$ 883.0	814.1	772.8
	Stockholders' equity per share	18.40	17.03	15.80
	Return on average stockholders' equity	13.0%	16.5	18.9
	Dividends per share	$ 1.00	.95	.90
	Market price per share — high/low	116/48	55/34	46/28
Financial Position at Year End	Working capital	$ 22.9	279.5	206.9
	Assets	2,216.0	1,892.5	1,423.6
	Long-term debt	487.1	568.5	283.7
	Ratio of long-term debt to total capital [4]	.30	.36	.22
General Information	Percentage of occupancy [1]			
	Hotels	69	70	68
	Gaming	86	87	84
	Number of properties at year end			
	Wholly-owned or leased	13	9	8
	Partially owned	14	12	13
	Managed	22	21	22
	Franchised	214	225	224
	Gaming	4	4	4
	Total	267	271	271
	Available rooms at year end			
	Wholly-owned or leased	7,739	6,494	6,027
	Partially owned	13,750	13,409	13,528
	Managed	13,518	13,383	14,183
	Franchised	52,612	54,876	55,641
	Gaming	7,411	7,326	7,318
	Total	95,030	95,488	96,697

(1) Includes properties owned or managed.
(2) Includes Hilton's proportionate share of unconsolidated affiliates.
(3) Net income plus depreciation, net deferred income taxes from operations and distributions from affiliates in excess of (less than) earnings.
(4) Total capital represents total assets less current liabilities.
* Average annual return.

1986	1985	1984	1983	1982	1981	1980	Ten Year Compound Growth Rate
1,228.3	1,138.8	1,086.3	978.0	909.0	892.0	832.7	6.9%
28.8	28.2	25.4	20.5	17.7	17.1	15.9	9.4
30.7	28.2	26.2	23.1	19.5	17.5	14.3	12.1
1,287.8	1,195.2	1,137.9	1,021.6	946.2	926.6	862.9	7.0
483.7	366.7	341.0	323.8	291.4	269.1	251.6	11.6
1,771.5	1,561.9	1,478.9	1,345.4	1,237.6	1,195.7	1,114.5	8.2
1,052.5	877.5	831.6	696.1	638.1	610.5	560.2	9.8
719.0	684.4	647.3	649.3	599.5	585.2	554.3	6.4
83.6	90.5	107.8	101.0	92.6	113.8	114.5	2.1
88.1	76.4	69.7	68.6	52.2	79.1	80.0	3.9
171.7	166.9	177.5	169.6	144.8	192.9	194.5	2.8
(22.1)	(11.7)	(3.2)	(8.0)	3.9	12.6	8.6	
(17.6)	(15.0)	(10.7)	(10.5)	(10.0)	(9.0)	(7.8)	15.4
(2.5)	3.1	27.9	37.6	2.8	—	—	
(31.7)	(43.1)	(77.5)	(76.1)	(58.1)	(83.9)	(89.2)	
97.8	100.2	114.0	112.6	83.4	112.6	106.1	1.0
160.0	155.1	148.6	164.9	134.4	141.9	132.1	
71.3	65.4	58.9	56.7	51.1	40.2	36.1	
240.7	293.1	261.4	99.5	131.9	178.7	92.8	
1.96	2.01	2.16	2.10	1.56	2.11	2.00	1.9
49.9	49.8	52.7	53.7	53.5	53.4	53.1	
707.3	651.4	592.8	634.3	568.5	532.6	458.9	
14.23	13.16	12.00	11.87	10.66	9.99	8.70	
14.4	16.1	18.6	18.7	15.1	22.7	25.1	17.9*
.90	.90	.90	.90	.90	.83	.71	6.3
40/30	37/28	29/23	30/20	26/14	26/17	24/13	
173.4	259.3	125.7	165.7	99.7	109.1	132.1	
1,302.3	1,225.6	1,163.8	1,099.2	938.3	816.5	696.8	
280.9	284.3	275.6	242.2	179.6	119.5	120.6	
.24	.26	.27	.24	.21	.17	.19	
65	64	64	60	61	65	69	
84	86	84	80	72	81	81	
8	11	11	13	14	14	15	
14	14	13	13	14	15	14	
22	23	22	23	19	16	15	
223	218	204	194	188	171	163	
4	4	3	3	3	3	2	
271	270	253	246	238	219	209	
6,085	7,399	7,580	10,464	10,909	11,072	11,737	
14,350	14,123	12,904	13,430	14,152	13,235	12,887	
13,425	13,692	13,258	12,031	8,852	7,977	7,454	
55,602	54,285	49,543	46,914	44,877	39,630	36,877	
7,318	6,602	6,025	6,025	6,025	5,523	4,539	
96,780	96,101	89,310	88,864	84,815	77,437	73,494	

REPORT OF INDEPENDENT PUBLIC ACCOUNTANTS

To the Board of Directors and Stockholders of Hilton Hotels Corporation:

We have audited the accompanying consolidated balance sheets of Hilton Hotels Corporation (a Delaware corporation) and subsidiaries as of December 31, 1989 and 1988, and the related consolidated statements of income, stockholders' equity and cash flows for each of the three years in the period ended December 31, 1989. These financial statements are the responsibility of the Company's management. Our responsibility is to express an opinion on these financial statements based on our audits.

We conducted our audits in accordance with generally accepted auditing standards. Those standards require that we plan and perform the audit to obtain reasonable assurance about whether the financial statements are free of material misstatement. An audit includes examining, on a test basis, evidence supporting the amounts and disclosures in the financial statements. An audit also includes assessing the accounting principles used and significant estimates made by management, as well as evaluating the overall financial statement presentation. We believe that our audits provide a reasonable basis for our opinion.

In our opinion, the financial statements referred to above present fairly, in all material respects, the financial position of Hilton Hotels Corporation and subsidiaries as of December 31, 1989 and 1988 and the results of their operations and their cash flows for each of the three years in the period ended December 31, 1989, in conformity with generally accepted accounting principles.

ARTHUR ANDERSEN & CO.

Los Angeles, California
February 2, 1990

3 Income Statement

The **income statement**, also called the statement of earnings, the profit and loss statement, the statement of operations, and various other titles, reports the success of the hospitality property's operations for a period of time. This statement may be prepared on a weekly or monthly basis for management's use and quarterly or annually for outsiders such as owners, creditors, and governmental agencies.

Users of financial statements examine an operation's income statements for answers to many questions, such as:

1. How profitable was the hospitality operation during the period?

2. What were the total sales for the period?

3. How much was paid for labor?

4. What is the relationship between sales and cost of sales?

5. How much have sales increased over last year?

6. What is the utilities expense for the year and how does it compare with the expense of a year ago?

7. How much was spent to market the hospitality operation's services?

8. How does net income compare with total sales for the period?

These and many more questions can be answered by reviewing the income statements that cover several periods of time. Income statements, including statements by individual departments called **departmental income statements**, are generally considered to be the most useful financial statements for management's review of operations. Owners and creditors, especially long-term creditors, find that the income statement yields significant information for determining investment value and credit worthiness. However, when analyzing the operating results of any entity, an income statement should be considered in conjunction with other financial statements as well as with the footnotes to those financial statements.

In this chapter, we will address the major elements of the income statement and consider its relationship with the balance sheet. We will also note the differences between income statements prepared for internal users and those for external users. The uniform system of accounts and the general approach to income statements in the hospitality industry will also be discussed. We will provide an in-depth discussion of the contents of the income statement, consider the uses of departmental statements and industry operating statistics, and discuss guidelines and techniques for analyzing income statements. Finally, a brief overview of the income statement based on the *Uniform System of Accounts for Restaurants* (*USAR*) will be presented.

Major Elements of the Income Statement

The income statement reflects the revenues, expenses, gains, and losses for a period of time. **Revenues** represent the inflow of assets, reduction of liabilities, or a combination of both resulting from the sale of goods or services. For a hospitality operation, revenues generally include food sales, beverage sales, room sales, interest and dividends from investments, and rents received from lessees of retail space.

Expenses are defined as the outflow of assets, increase in liabilities, or a combination of both in the production and rendering of goods and services. Expenses of a hospitality operation generally include cost of goods sold (for example, food and beverages), labor, utilities, advertising, depreciation, and taxes, to list a few.

Gains are defined as increases in assets, reductions in liabilities, or a combination of both resulting from a hospitality operation's incidental transactions and from all other transactions and events affecting the operation during the period, except those that count as revenues or investments by owners. For example, there may be a gain on the sale of equipment. Equipment is used by the business to provide goods and services and, when sold, only the excess proceeds over its net book value (purchase price less accumulated depreciation) is recognized as gain.

Finally, **losses** are defined as decreases in assets, increases in liabilities, or a combination of both resulting from a hospitality operation's incidental transactions and from other transactions and events affecting the operation during a period, except those that count as expenses or distributions to owners. In the equipment example above, if the proceeds were less than the net book value, a loss would occur and would be recorded as "loss on sale of equipment." Another example would be a loss from an "act of nature," such as a tornado or hurricane. The loss reported is the reduction of assets less insurance proceeds received.

In the income statement for hospitality operations, revenues are reported separately from gains, and expenses are distinguished from losses. These distinctions are important in determining management's success in operating the hospitality property. Management is held accountable primarily for operations (revenues and expenses) and only secondarily (if at all) for gains and losses. Generally, gains and losses are shown near the bottom of the income statement before income taxes.

Relationship with the Balance Sheet

The income statement covers a period of time, while the balance sheet is prepared as of the last day of the accounting period. Thus, the income statement reflects operations of the hospitality property for the period between balance sheet dates. The result of operations—net income or loss for the period—is added to the proper equity account and shown on the balance sheet at the end of the accounting period.

Income Statements for Internal and External Users

Hospitality properties prepare income statements for both internal users (management) and external users (creditors, owners, and so forth). These statements differ substantially, as the income statements provided to external users are relatively brief, providing only summary detail about the results of operations. Income statements for external users are often called **summary income statements**, even though the word "summary" does not usually appear on the form. Exhibit 3.1 is the income statement presentation of Marriott Corporation and Subsidiaries from a recent annual report. Marriott's income statement shows the following:

- Sales by segment
- Operating expenses by segment
- Operating income by segment (sales less operating expenses)
- Interest expense
- Interest income
- Corporate expense
- Income taxes
- Income from discontinued operations
- Net income
- Earnings per share

We have already stated that footnotes, which generally appear after the financial statements in the financial report, are critical to interpreting the numbers reported on the income statement. Note that The Marriott Corporation notifies readers of the importance of footnotes on the same page as the income statement.

Although the amount of operating information shown in the income statement and accompanying footnotes may be adequate for external users to evaluate the hospitality property's operations, management requires considerably more information. Management also needs this information more frequently than outsiders. In general, the more frequent the need to make decisions, the more frequent the need for financial information. Management's information needs are met, in part, by detailed monthly income statements which reflect budget numbers and report performance for the most recent period, the same period a year ago, and year-to-date numbers for both the current and past year.

If any difference between the year-to-date numbers and the originally budgeted numbers is expected, the income statements of many firms in the hospitality industry also show the latest forecast of results (reforecasting). Management is then able to compare actual results against the most recent forecasts. (We will discuss reforecasting in Chapter 9.)

Exhibit 3.1   Sample Income Statement

Marriott Corporation and Subsidiaries Fiscal years ended December 29, 1989, December 30, 1988 and January 1, 1988	**1989**	1988	1987
	(in millions, except per share amounts)		
SALES			
Lodging			
Rooms	**$2,093**	$1,815	$1,536
Food and beverage	**1,082**	997	875
Other	**371**	328	262
	3,546	3,140	2,673
Contract Services	**3,990**	3,484	3,173
	7,536	6,624	5,846
OPERATING COSTS AND EXPENSES			
Lodging			
Departmental direct costs			
Rooms	**481**	404	338
Food and beverage	**816**	745	646
Other operating expenses, including payments to hotel owners and, in 1989, restructuring costs of $194 million	**2,117**	1,693	1,425
Contract Services, including $51 million of restructuring costs in 1989	**3,818**	3,281	2,984
	7,232	6,123	5,393
OPERATING INCOME			
Lodging	**132**	298	264
Contract Services, including $231 million gain on divestiture of the airline catering division in 1989	**403**	203	189
	535	501	453
Corporate expenses, including $11 million of restructuring costs in 1989	**(107)**	(93)	(75)
Interest expense	**(185)**	(136)	(90)
Interest income	**55**	40	47
INCOME FROM CONTINUING OPERATIONS BEFORE INCOME TAXES	**298**	312	335
Provision for income taxes	**117**	123	148
INCOME FROM CONTINUING OPERATIONS	**181**	189	187
DISCONTINUED OPERATIONS, net of income taxes			
Income from discontinued operations	**35**	43	36
Provision for loss on disposal	**(39)**	—	—
	(4)	43	36
NET INCOME	**$ 177**	$ 232	$ 223
EARNINGS (LOSS) PER SHARE:			
Continuing operations	**$ 1.62**	$ 1.59	$ 1.40
Discontinued operations	**(.04)**	.36	.27
	$ 1.58	$ 1.95	$ 1.67

Courtesy of Marriott Corporation, Washington, D.C.

Management's need for financial information on a monthly basis may be met, to a large degree, by using an income statement and accompanying departmental statements that are contained in the various uniform systems of accounts. In addition to the monthly income statement, a more frequent major report prepared for management is the **daily report of operations**.

Ultimately, however, hospitality managers require even more information than is provided by daily reports and monthly statements. Exhibit 3.2 lists various management reports and the frequency, content, comparisons, intended readers, and purpose of each report. Even this list does not include all reports required by the various levels of management in a hospitality operation. For example, two major financial statements included in this text, the balance sheet and the statement of cash flows, are absent from the list.

Uniform Systems of Accounts

The **uniform systems of accounts** are standardized accounting systems prepared by various segments of the hospitality industry.[1] A uniform system of accounts provides a turnkey system for new entrants into the hospitality industry by offering detailed information about accounts, classifications, formats, and the different kinds, contents, and uses of financial statements and reports. For example, the *Uniform System of Accounts and Expense Dictionary for Small Hotels, Motels, and Motor Hotels* (*USASH*) contains not only the basic financial statements, but also over 20 supplementary departmental operating statements and appendices covering budgeting and forecasting, a discussion of compiling revenues by market source, forms of statements, break-even analysis, and a uniform account numbering system.

The uniform system of accounts also allows for a more reasonable comparison of the operational results of similar hospitality properties. When various establishments follow a uniform system of accounts, the differences in accounting among these hospitality properties are minimized, thus ensuring comparability.

A uniform system of accounts is a time-tested system. The *Uniform System of Accounts for Hotels* (*USAH*) was first produced in 1925–26 by a designated group of accountants for the Hotel Association of New York City. Since then, the *USAH* has been revised many times by committees, beginning with New York City accountants and, most recently, by accountants from across the United States. The eighth revised edition of the *USAH* was prepared in 1986 by a select committee of the International Association of Hospitality Accountants. During the work on the eighth revision, consultations on changes were made with various other accounting groups including the British Association of Hospitality Accountants. The *USASH* has also been revised a number of times, the fourth edition having come out in 1987.

Finally, the uniform system of accounts can be adapted for use by large and small hospitality operations. The uniform system of accounts illustrated in this chapter is the *USASH*. The *USAH* is similar to the *USASH* and differs primarily by including more profit centers on the summary income statement. The *USASH* contains many more accounts and classifications than will generally be used by a single hotel or motel. Therefore, each facility simply selects the schedules and accounts that are required for its use and ignores the others.

Exhibit 3.2 Management Reports

Report	Frequency	Content	Comparisons	Who Gets It	Purpose
Daily Report of Operations	Daily, on a cumulative basis for the month, the year to date.	Occupancy, average rate, revenue by outlet, and pertinent statistics.	To operating plan for current period and to prior year results.	Top management and supervisors responsible for day to day operation.	Basis for evaluating the current health of the enterprise.
Weekly Forecasts	Weekly.	Volume in covers, occupancy.	Previous periods.	Top management and supervisory personnel.	Staffing and scheduling; promotion.
Summary Report — Flash	Monthly at end of month (prior to monthly financial statement).	Known elements of revenue and direct costs; estimated departmental indirect costs.	To operating plan; to prior year results.	Top management and supervisory personnel responsible for function reported.	Provides immediate information on financial results for rooms, food and beverages, and other.
Cash Flow Analysis	Monthly (and on a revolving 12-month basis.)	Receipts and disbursements by time periods.	With cash flow plan for month and for year to date.	Top management.	Predicts availability of cash for operating needs. Provides information on interim financing requirements.
Labor Productivity Analysis	Daily Weekly Monthly	Dollar cost; manpower hours expended; hours as related to sales and services (covers, rooms occupied, etc.)	To committed hours in the operating plan (standards for amount of work to prior year statistics).	Top management and supervisory personnel.	Labor cost control through informed staffing and scheduling. Helps refine forecasting.
Departmental Analysis	Monthly (early in following month.)	Details on main categories of income; same on expense.	To operating plan (month and year to date) and to prior year.	Top management and supervisors by function (e.g., rooms, each food and beverage outlet, laundry, telephone, other profit centers.	Knowing where business stands, and immediate corrective actions.
Room Rate Analysis	Daily, monthly, year to date.	Actual rates compared to rack rates by rate category or type of room.	To operating plan and to prior year results.	Top management and supervisors of sales and front office operations.	If goal is not being achieved, analysis of strengths and weaknesses is prompted.
Return on Investment	Actual computation, at least twice a year. Computation based on forecast, immediately prior to plan for year ahead.	Earnings as a percentage rate of return on average investment or equity committed.	To plan for operation and to prior periods.	Top management.	If goal is not being achieved, prompt assessment of strengths and weaknesses.
Long-Range Planning	Annually.	5-year projections of revenue and expenses. Operating plan expressed in financial terms.	Prior years.	Top management.	Involves staff in success or failure of enterprise. Injects more realism into plans for property and service modifications.
Exception Reporting	Concurrent with monthly reports and financial statements.	Summary listing of line item variances from predetermined norm.	With operating budgets.	Top management and supervisors responsible for function reported.	Immediate focusing on problem before more detailed statement analysis can be made.
Guest History Analysis	At least semi-annually; quarterly or monthly is recommended.	Historical records of corporate business, travel agencies, group bookings.	With previous reports.	Top management and sales.	Give direction to marketing efforts.
Future Bookings Report	Monthly.	Analysis of reservations and bookings.	With several prior years.	Top management, sales and marketing, department management.	Provides information on changing guest profile. Exposes strong and weak points of facility. Guides (1) sales planning and (2) expansion plans.

Source: *Lodging*, July 1979, pp. 40–41.

The *USASH* is designed to be used at the property level rather than the corporate level of a hotel. The format of the income statement is based on **responsibility accounting**. That is, the presentation is organized to focus attention on departmental results such as the rooms and food and beverage departments. The income statements prepared at the corporate level, where more than one lodging property is owned by the lodging corporation, would probably be considerably different and would include sale of properties, corporate overhead expenses, and so on, not necessarily shown on an individual lodging property's income statement. Our discussion of income statements for management in this text will focus primarily on the *USASH*, although, as stated earlier, the *USAR* will also be presented near the end of this chapter.

Approach to Hospitality Industry Income Statements

In many industries, the basic income statement format consists of the following:

	Revenues
Less:	Cost of goods sold
Equals:	Gross profit
Less:	Overhead expenses
Equals:	Net income

Revenues less cost of goods sold equals gross profit. The cost of goods sold is the cost of the product sold. For wholesale and retail firms, it is the cost of goods purchased for resale, while for manufacturers, it is a combination of labor, raw materials, and overhead expenses incurred in the manufacturing process. The expenses subtracted from gross profit to equal net income consist of all other expenses such as administration and selling expenses, depreciation, and income taxes.

By contrast, the income statement format in the *USASH* approach consists of the following:

	Revenues
Less:	Direct operating expenses
Equals:	Departmental operating income
Less:	Overhead expenses
Equals:	Net income

Revenues less direct operating expenses equals departmental operating income. Departmental operating income less overhead expenses equals net income. Direct operating expenses include not only the cost of goods sold, but also the direct labor expense and other direct expenses. Direct labor expense is the expense of personnel working in the profit centers, such as the rooms department and the food and beverage department. Other direct expenses include supplies used by these revenue-producing departments. Therefore, everything else being the same, gross profit would exceed departmental operating income, since direct operating expenses include direct labor and other direct expenses in addition to cost of goods sold.

The income statements based on the *USASH* provide separate line reporting by profit center, that is, sales and direct expenses are shown separately for the rooms department, the food and beverage department, the telephone department, and so forth. In addition, the overhead expenses are divided among undistributed operating expenses, management fees, and fixed charges. The undistributed operating expenses are further detailed on the income statement by major service centers such as marketing and data processing. The detail provided by both profit centers and service centers reflects reporting by areas of responsibility and is commonly referred to as responsibility accounting.

Thus, the *USASH* income statement is useful to managers in the hospitality industry because it is designed to provide the information necessary to evaluate the performance of managers of the lodging facility by area of responsibility.

Contents of the Income Statement

The income statement per the *USASH* (illustrated in Exhibit 3.3) is divided into three major sections—operated departments, undistributed operating expenses, and the final section which includes management fees, fixed charges, gain or loss on sale of property, and income tax.

The first section, operated departments, reports net revenue by department for every major revenue-producing department. Net revenue is the result of subtracting allowances from related revenues. Allowances include refunds and overcharges at the time of sale which are subsequently adjusted. For example, hotel guests may have been charged $100 (rack rate) for their rooms when they should have been charged the group rate of $80. The subsequent adjustment of $20 the following day is treated as an allowance. Revenues earned from non-operating activities such as investments are shown with rentals. If these amounts are significant, they should be reported separately.

For each department generating revenues, direct expenses are reported. These expenses relate directly to the department incurring them and consist of three major categories: cost of sales, payroll and related expenses, and other expenses. Cost of sales is normally determined as follows:

	Beginning inventory
Plus:	Inventory purchases
Equals:	Goods available for sale
Less:	Ending inventory
Equals:	Cost of goods consumed
Less:	Goods used internally
Equals:	Cost of goods sold

Cost of sales is determined by starting first with beginning inventory. The beginning inventory is the value of the inventory at the start of the accounting period. Inventory purchases include the purchase cost of goods for sale plus the related shipping cost. An important, but relatively small, category of direct expense is "goods used internally" and may best be illustrated by the following example. Food may be provided free of

Exhibit 3.3   Income Statement

STATEMENT OF INCOME

	Schedule	Current Period				
		Net Revenue	Cost of Sales	Payroll and Related Expenses	Other Expenses	Income (Loss)
OPERATED DEPARTMENTS						
Rooms	1	$	$	$	$	$
Food and Beverage	2					
Telephone	3					
Gift Shop	4					
Garage and Parking	5					
Other Operated Departments						
Rentals and Other Income	6	——	——	——	——	——
Total Operated Departments		——	——	——	——	——
UNDISTRIBUTED OPERATING EXPENSES						
Administrative and General	7					
Data Processing	8					
Human Resources	9					
Transportation	10					
Marketing	11					
Property Operation and Maintenance	12					
Energy Costs	13				——	——
Total Undistributed Operating Expenses					——	
INCOME BEFORE MANAGEMENT FEES AND FIXED CHARGES		$ ——	$ ——	$ ——	$ ——	
Management Fees						
Rent, Property Taxes, and Insurance	14					
Interest Expense	14					
Depreciation and Amortization	14					——
INCOME BEFORE INCOME TAXES AND GAIN OR LOSS ON SALE OF PROPERTY						
Gain or Loss on Sale of Property	14					——
INCOME BEFORE INCOME TAXES						
Income Taxes	15					——
NET INCOME						$ ——

charge to employees (employee meals), to entertainers (entertainers–complimentary food), to guests for promotional purposes (promotion–food), or to other departments (transfers to the beverage department). In each case, the cost of food transferred must be charged to the proper account of the benefiting department and subtracted in the calculation of cost of food sold. For example, cost of employee meals for the rooms department is subtracted to determine cost of food sold. The cost of employee meals for rooms department employees is shown as an expense in the rooms department.

The second major direct expense category of operated departments is "payroll and related expenses." This category includes the salaries and wages of employees working in the designated operated departments, for example, servers in the food and beverage department. Salaries, wages, and related expenses of departments not generating revenues but providing service, such as marketing, are recorded by service departments. The category of "related expenses" includes all payroll taxes and fringe benefits relating to employees of each operated department. For example, in the rooms department, the front office manager's salary and related payroll taxes and fringe benefits would be included in the "payroll and related expenses" of the rooms department.

The final major expense category for the operated departments is "other expenses." This category includes only other direct expenses. For example, the nine major other expense categories for the rooms department (per the *USASH*) are commissions, contract cleaning, guest transportation, laundry and dry cleaning, linen, operating supplies, reservation expense, uniforms, and other. Expenses such as marketing, administration, and transportation are recorded as expenses of service departments. They benefit the rooms department and other profit centers but only on an indirect basis.

Net revenue less the sum of cost of sales, payroll and related expenses, and other expenses results in departmental income or loss. The departmental income or loss is shown on the income statement (Exhibit 3.3) for each operated department.

The second major section of the income statement is undistributed operating expenses. This section includes the seven general categories of administrative and general expenses, data processing, human resources, transportation, marketing, property operation and maintenance, and energy costs. These expense categories are related to the various service departments. In the income statement, two of the expense elements—payroll and related expenses, and other expenses—are shown for each category. The administrative and general expense category includes service departments such as the general manager's office and the accounting office. In addition to salaries, wages, and related expenses of service department personnel covered by administrative and general, other expenses include, but are not limited to, insurance—general, professional fees, and provision for doubtful accounts. Appendix A at the end of this text presents *USASH*'s recommended schedule for administrative and general expenses which details the several expense categories for administrative and general expenses.

The *USASH* recommends a separate departmental accounting of data processing expenses for those lodging operations with significant investments in data processing. (This recommended schedule is also shown in Appendix A.) As with most other service centers, the two major sections of expense are payroll and related expenses, and other expenses. If data processing expenses are not considered significant, then the *USASH* recommends data processing expenses be included as part of administrative and general expenses.

Another service center for which the *USASH* recommends separate departmental accounting is the human resources department. This schedule includes labor cost of departmental personnel and other expenses such as employee housing, recruiting expenses, cost of relocating employees, and training costs. The recommended schedule is shown in Appendix A.

The fourth service department is transportation. The purpose of this service department is to provide transportation services for lodging guests, such as transportation to and from the airport. The expenses to be included on the transportation department schedule (see the recommended schedule in Appendix A) include payroll and related expenses, and other expenses such as fuel, operating supplies, and repairs and maintenance. If guest transportation expenses are not considered significant, then the *USASH* recommends transportation expenses be included as part of the rooms department expenses.

Marketing expenses include costs relating to personnel working in marketing areas of sales, advertising, and merchandising. In addition, other marketing expenses include advertising and merchandising expenses such as direct mail, in-house graphics, point-of-sale materials, and print, radio, and television advertising. Agency fees, franchising fees, and other fees and commissions are also included as marketing expenses.

The sixth major category of undistributed operating expenses is property operation and maintenance. Included in property operation and maintenance are salaries and related payroll costs of the property operation and maintenance personnel and the various supplies used to maintain the buildings, grounds, furniture, fixtures, and equipment.

The final category of undistributed operating expenses is energy costs. The recommended schedule includes separate listings of the various utilities, such as electricity and water. Sales by the hotel to tenants and charges to other departments are subtracted in determining net energy costs.

Subtracting the total undistributed operating expenses from the total operated departments income results in income before management fees and fixed charges. Many industry personnel continue to refer to this difference between operating revenue and expense as gross operating profit, or simply GOP, but this is terminology from an earlier edition of *USASH*'s format for the income statement.

Operating management is considered fully responsible for all revenues and expenses reported to this point on the income statement, as they generally have the authority to exercise their judgment to affect all these items. However, the management fees and the fixed charges which follow in the next major section of the income statement are the responsibility primarily of the hospitality property's board of directors. The expenses listed on this part of the statement generally relate directly to decisions by the board, rather than to management decisions.

Management fees are the cost of using an independent management company to operate the hotel/motel. The fixed charges are also referred to as **capacity costs**, as they relate to the physical plant or the capacity to provide goods and services to guests.

The fixed charges include rent, property taxes, insurance, interest, and depreciation and amortization. Rent includes the cost of renting real estate, computer equipment, and other major items that, if they had been purchased, would have been recorded as fixed assets. Rental of miscellaneous equipment for specific functions such as banquets is to be shown as a direct expense of the food and beverage department.

Property taxes include real estate taxes, personal property taxes, taxes assessed by utilities, and other taxes (but not income and payroll taxes) which cannot be charged to guests. Insurance expense is the cost of insuring the facilities including contents for damage caused by fire or other catastrophes.

Interest expense is the cost of borrowing money and is based on the amounts borrowed, the interest rate, and the length of time for which the funds are borrowed. Generally, loans are approved by the operation's board of directors, as most relate to the physical plant. Thus, interest expense is considered to be a fixed charge.

Depreciation of fixed assets and amortization of other assets are shown on the income statement as fixed charges. The depreciation methods and useful lives of fixed assets are normally disclosed in footnotes.[2]

The income statement per the *USASH* then shows gains or losses on the sale of property and equipment. A gain or loss on sale of property results from a difference between the proceeds from the sale and the carrying value (net book value) of the fixed asset. For example, a 15-unit motel which cost $300,000 and was depreciated by $150,000 was sold for $200,000. The gain in this case is determined as follows:

$$\text{where NBV} = \text{Cost} - \text{Accumulated Depreciation}$$
$$= \$300,000 - \$150,000$$
$$= \underline{\underline{\$150,000}}$$

$$\text{where Gain} = \text{Proceeds} - \text{NBV}$$
$$= \$200,000 - \$150,000$$
$$= \underline{\underline{\$50,000}}$$

In the *USASH*'s income statement, gains are added while losses are subtracted in determining income before income taxes.

Finally, income taxes are subtracted from income before income taxes to determine net income.

Departmental Statements

Departmental statements, supplementary to the income statement and referred to as **schedules**, provide management with detailed information by operated departments and service centers. The classifications listed in the income statement suggest up to 15 schedules. Each of these schedules is included in Appendix A of this text.

Exhibit 3.4 illustrates an operated department schedule using the rooms department of the Vacation Inn. The operated department schedule reflects both revenues and direct expenses.

The expenses are subdivided on the rooms department schedule between "payroll and related expenses" and "other expenses." Under payroll and related, salaries and wages and employee benefits are shown. Employee benefits include both payroll taxes and fringe benefits, such as

Exhibit 3.4 Rooms Department Schedule

Schedule 1

Vacation Inn
Rooms
For the year ended December 31, 19X1

Revenue	
Transient—Regular	$543,900
Transient—Group	450,000
Permanent	48,000
Other	2,000
Allowances	2,700
Net Revenue	1,041,200
Expenses	
Salaries and Wages	159,304
Employee Benefits	26,030
Total Payroll and Related Expenses	185,334
Other Expenses	
Commissions	5,124
Contract Cleaning	3,200
Laundry and Drycleaning	20,706
Linen	9,494
Operating Supplies	21,742
Reservations	9,288
Uniforms	1,400
Other	8,126
Total Other Expenses	79,080
Total Expenses	264,414
Departmental Income	$ 776,786

cost of health insurance paid by the lodging operation and similar benefits.

Other expenses include direct expenses of the rooms department. According to the *USASH*, nine expense categories are shown under other expenses of the rooms department. All other room department expenses should be classified in these nine categories if the *USASH* is to be followed. When a classification is not used, it should not be shown on the rooms department schedule. Exhibit 3.4 does not include the "guest transportation" category (as shown in the rooms department statement in Appendix A) because transportation is treated as a separate department as reflected on the income statement in Exhibit 3.5.

Totals from the rooms department schedule and other operated department schedules are reflected on the income statement. In the rooms department illustration in Exhibit 3.4, the following totals are carried from the department statement to the property's income statement:

- Net Revenue $1,041,200

Exhibit 3.5   Income Statement—Vacation Inn

	Schedules	Net Revenues	Cost of Sales	Payroll and Related Expenses	Other Expense	Income (Loss)
Operated Departments						
Rooms	1	$1,041,200	$ 0	$ 185,334	$ 79,080	$ 776,786
Food and Beverage	2	626,165	208,448	218,532	66,513	132,672
Telephone	3	52,028	46,505	14,317	6,816	(15,610)
Total Operated Departments		1,719,393	254,953	418,183	152,409	893,848
Undistributed Operating Expenses						
Administrative and General	7			47,787	24,934	72,721
Data Processing	8			20,421	11,622	32,043
Human Resources	9			22,625	4,193	26,818
Transportation	10			13,411	7,460	20,871
Marketing	11			33,231	33,585	66,816
Property Operation and Maintenance	12			31,652	49,312	80,964
Energy Costs	13			0	88,752	88,752
Total Undistributed Operating Expenses				169,127	219,858	388,985
Income Before Fixed Charges		$1,719,393	$ 254,953	$ 587,310	$ 372,267	504,863
Rent, Property Taxes, and Insurance	14					200,861
Interest	14					52,148
Depreciation and Amortization	14					115,860
Income Before Income Taxes						135,994
Income Tax	15					48,707
Net Income						$ 87,287

- Payroll and Related Expenses $ 185,334
- Other Expenses $ 79,080
- Departmental Income $ 776,786

Exhibit 3.5 is the Vacation Inn's income statement. The above figures from the rooms department schedule are reflected in the top row of figures on the income statement.

In contrast to the profit center schedules prepared by the revenue-producing operated departments of a hospitality operation, a service center schedule reports only expenses by area of responsibility. Although these activity areas do not generate revenues, they do provide service to the operated departments and, in some cases, to other service centers.

Exhibit 3.6   Property Operation and Maintenance Schedule

Schedule 12

Vacation Inn
Property Operation and Maintenance
For the year ended December 31, 19X1

Salaries and Wages	$27,790
Employee Benefits	3,862
Total Payroll and Related Expenses	31,652
Other Expenses	
Building Supplies	8,900
Electrical and Mechanical Equipment	8,761
Engineering Supplies	1,981
Furniture, Fixtures, Equipment, and Decor	14,322
Grounds and Landscaping	6,241
Operating Supplies	2,651
Removal of Waste Matter	2,499
Swimming Pool	2,624
Uniforms	652
Other	681
Total	49,312
Total Property Operation and	
Maintenance	**$80,964**

Exhibit 3.6 illustrates a service center departmental schedule by using the property operation and maintenance schedule of the Vacation Inn. The three numbers which are carried over to Vacation Inn's income statement (Exhibit 3.5) for this department are total payroll and related expenses of $31,652, other expenses of $49,312, and total expenses of $80,964. Notice that the total expenses of service departments are shown on the income statement under the Income (Loss) column.

The number and nature of the supporting schedules reported in a lodging facility depends on the size and organization of the establishment. A small lodging property which provides very limited guest transportation services would not have a separate transportation department (as does the Vacation Inn in Exhibit 3.5). In this case, the relatively minor transportation expenses would be shown in the rooms department schedule (see the rooms department schedule in Appendix A). For large hotels, *USAH* may be an appropriate alternative.

Lodging Industry Operating Statistics

A sale of $x by any operated department increases total revenues by that amount, but the increase in the total operated department *income* from additional sales of $x depends on the operated department making the sale. The different effects on this bottom line are caused by the direct expenses of the operated department generating the sale.

The difference between an operated department's revenues and direct expenses is referred to as departmental income. The operated department contributing most to the lodging property's ability to pay overhead costs and generate profit is the one which has the greatest departmental income.

Pannell Kerr Forster (PKF), an international accounting firm providing specialized services to establishments in the hospitality industry, recently released figures showing that the average hotel reports rooms departmental income of 72.7% of total room revenues, while the food and beverage departmental income is only approximately 23.3% of total food and beverage revenues.[3] Historically, the telephone departments of most hotels have experienced losses from operations, although recently they have shown relatively minor profits from operations. Therefore, all things being the same, a manager would rather have an additional sale of $x made in the rooms department than in any other operated department, because the contribution toward overhead costs and profit would be greater than from any other operated department. That is, based on PKF's figures, a sale of $100 in the rooms department would result in a departmental income of approximately $72.70. A similar sale in the food and beverage department would result in a departmental income of only approximately $23.30.

Within the food and beverage department, the gross profit (sales less cost of sales) generally differs substantially between food sales and beverages sales. According to PKF's statistics, the **contribution margin** of food sales is 68% compared to 78.5% for beverage sales.[4] PKF does not separate payroll and related expenses nor other direct expenses of the food and beverage department between food operations and beverage operations as it does cost of sales. However, if we assume that these expenses relate proportionately to sales, then from a profit perspective, increased beverage sales are more desirable than increased food sales. For example, $100 of food sales and $100 of beverage sales result in a food contribution margin of $68.00 and a beverage contribution margin of $78.50—a difference of $10.50 per $100 of sales.

Exhibit 3.7 provides statistics revealing the percentage distribution of revenues and expenses for the average hotel/motel. These statistics support the preceding discussion of the greater desirability of beverage sales compared with food sales, and the increased desirability of rooms sales compared with sales in any other department. However, do not consider these averages to be the norm. They are only averages and are based on lodging establishments which PKF selected on a judgmental, not random, basis. The operated departments of a particular hotel will most likely produce different percentages. However, of 1,000 hotels and motels in the PKF study, significant numbers noted in Exhibit 3.7 include:

- Rooms revenues approximate 61.6% of total revenues

- Food revenues approximate 23.6% of total revenues

- Beverage revenues approximate 7.6% of total revenues

- Total operated department income approximates 53.4% of total revenues

Exhibit 3.7   Comparative Results of Operations

	1988	1987		1988	1987
Revenues:			**Rooms Department:**		
Rooms	61.6 %	61.6 %	Rooms Net Revenue	100.0 %	100.0 %
Food—Including Other Income	23.6	23.6			
Beverages	7.6	7.9	**Departmental Expenses:**		
Telephone	2.4	2.4	Salaries and Wages Including Vacation	13.2 %	13.4 %
Other Operated Departments	2.7	2.5	Payroll Taxes and Employee Benefits	4.5	4.1
Rentals and Other Income	2.1	2.0	Subtotal	17.7 %	17.5 %
Total Revenues	100.0 %	100.0 %	Laundry, Linen, and Guest Supplies	3.8	3.6
			Commissions and Reservation Expenses	2.9	2.8
Departmental Costs and Expenses:			All Other Expenses	2.9	3.5
Rooms	16.9 %	16.8 %	Total Rooms Expense	27.3 %	27.4 %
Food and Beverages	25.6	25.9	Rooms Departmental Income	72.7 %	72.6 %
Telephone	2.0	2.1			
Other Operated Departments	2.1	2.0	**Food and Beverage Department:**		
Total Costs and Expenses	46.6 %	46.8 %	Food Net Revenue	100.0 %	100.0 %
Total Operated Departmental Income	53.4 %	53.2 %	Cost of Food Consumed	34.2 %	35.6 %
			Less: Cost of Employees' Meals	2.2	2.5
Undistributed Operating Expenses:			Net Cost of Food Sales	32.0 %	33.1 %
Administrative and General	9.5 %	9.8 %	Food Gross Profit	68.0 %	66.9 %
Management Fees*	2.7	2.6			
Marketing and Guest Entertainment*	6.8	6.7	Beverage Net Revenue	100.0 %	100.0 %
Property Operation and Maintenance	5.6	5.6	Cost of Beverage Sales	21.5	21.9
Energy Costs	4.5	4.6	Beverage Gross Profit	78.5 %	78.1 %
Other Unallocated			Food and Beverage Revenue	100.0 %	100.0 %
Operated Departments*	0.5	0.5	Net Cost of Food and Beverage Sales	29.3 %	30.2 %
Total Undistributed Expenses	29.6 %	29.8 %	Gross Profit on Combined Sales	70.7 %	69.8 %
Income before Fixed Charges	23.8 %	23.4 %	Public Room Rentals	2.5	2.0
			Other Income	2.1	1.6
Property Taxes and Insurance:			Gross Profit and Other Income	75.3 %	73.4 %
Property Taxes and Other Municipal					
Charges	3.1 %	3.0 %	**Departmental Expenses:**		
Insurance on Building and Contents	0.8	1.1	Salaries and Wages Including Vacation	30.8 %	31.1 %
Total Property Taxes and Insurance	3.9 %	4.1 %	Payroll Taxes and Employee Benefits	10.6	9.8
Income before Other Fixed Charges**	19.9 %	19.3 %	Subtotal	41.4 %	40.9 %
			Laundry and Dry Cleaning	1.1	1.0
Percentage of Occupancy	66.3 %	65.8 %	China, Glassware, Silver, and Linen	1.6	1.6
			Contract Cleaning	0.4	0.4
Average Daily Rate per Occupied Room	$ 72.67	$ 69.52	All Other Expenses	7.5	7.8
			Total Food and Beverage Expenses	52.0 %	51.7 %
Average Daily Room Rate per Guest	$ 49.88	$ 47.98	Food and Beverage Departmental Income	23.3 %	21.7 %
Percentage of Double Occupancy	45.7 %	44.9 %			
Average Size (Rooms)	243	243			

*Averages based on total groups although not all establishments reported data.
**Income before deducting Depreciation, Rent, Interest, Amortization, and Income Taxes.
NOTE: Payroll Taxes and Employee Benefits distributed to each department. See Figure No. 6 on Page 35 for Payroll Cost Data.

Reprinted from *Trends in the Hotel Industry, U.S.A. Edition*, ©1989 Pannell Kerr Forster.

- Undistributed operating expenses approximate 29.6% of total revenues

Finally, industry averages vary widely by type of lodging establishment. Exhibit 3.8 is a comparison of statistics from three Laventhol & Horwath (L&H) publications which cover the economy/limited-service and all-suites segments, as well as the U.S. lodging industry as a whole. Again, the reader is cautioned that the percentages shown are not norms

Exhibit 3.8 Sales and Expenses as a Percentage of Total Sales for the U.S. Lodging Industry and Two Selected Segments

	All Lodging Properties[1]	Economy/ Limited-Service Properties[2]	Suites[3]
Revenues:			
Rooms	64.3%	97.9%	92.9%
Food	23.7	—	11.9
Beverage	7.4	—	4.5
Other Food & Beverage	1.4	—	1.0
Telephone	2.3	2.3	3.0
Other	3.0	1.4	3.4
Total	100.0%	100.0%	100.0%
Department Expenses:			
Rooms	17.6	23.9	23.0
Food & Beverage	27.3	—	16.9
Telephone	1.9	0.7	2.2
Other	2.5	1.9	1.7
Total	43.2	26.0	25.6
Total Operated Department Profit	56.8	73.9	74.4
Undistributed Operating Expenses:			
Administrative & General	10.2	7.9	9.5
Marketing	6.6	4.0	7.6
Energy Costs	5.0	4.1	4.9
Property Operations & Maintenance	5.4	8.3	4.9
Total	27.4	26.6	28.7
Income Before Management Fees	29.3	46.6	44.0
Management Fees	3.4	4.9	3.0
Income Before Fixed Charges	26.0	42.4	39.4
Fixed Charges	31.2	39.6	10.9
Income Before Income Taxes	(2.7%)	3.4%	(2.1%)

All numbers are medians and do not necessarily add to totals shown.
[1]*U.S. Lodging Industry 1989* (Laventhol & Horwath, 1989)
[2]*U.S. Economy/Limited Service Lodging Industry 1989* (Laventhol & Horwath, 1989)
[3]*U.S. All-Suite Lodging Industry 1988* (Laventhol & Horwath, 1989)

or standards but statistics based on a judgmental sample selected in this case by L&H.

Hospitality industry statistics for the various segments of the industry are published annually by PKF and L&H, and are listed in Exhibit 3.9. These publications are generally available upon request.

Analysis of Income Statements

The analysis of income statements enhances the user's knowledge of the hospitality property's operations. This can be accomplished by

Exhibit 3.9   Major Hospitality Statistical Publications

Publication	Industry Segment	Firm
Trends in the Hotel Industry—Worldwide	Lodging	PKF
Trends in the Hotel Industry—USA	Lodging	PKF
Clubs in Town and Country	Clubs	PKF
Worldwide Hotel Industry	Lodging	L&H
U.S. Lodging Industry	Lodging	L&H
U.S. Economy/Limited-Service Lodging Industry	Lodging	L&H
U.S. All-Suites Lodging Industry	Lodging	L&H
Restaurant Industry Operations Report	Restaurant	NRA/L&H

horizontal analysis, vertical analysis, and ratio analysis. Since much less financial information is available to owners (stockholders and partners who are not active in the operation) and creditors than is available to management, their analytical approaches will generally differ.

Horizontal analysis compares income statements for two accounting periods in terms of both absolute and relative variances for each line item in a way similar to the analysis of comparative balance sheets discussed in Chapter 2. Any significant differences are investigated by the user. Another common comparative analysis approach is to compare the most recent period's operating results with the budget by determining absolute and relative variances.

Exhibit 3.10 illustrates the horizontal analysis of operating results of the Vacation Inn for years 19X1 and 19X2. In this comparative analysis, 19X1 is considered the base. Because the revenues for 19X2 exceed revenues for 19X1, the dollar difference is shown as positive. On the other hand, if 19X2 revenues had been less than 19X1 revenues, the difference would have been shown as negative. Actual 19X2 expenses increased compared to 19X1, resulting in a positive difference. This should be expected, since as revenues increase, expenses should also increase. If actual 19X2 expenses had decreased compared to 19X1, the differences would have been shown as negative. The percentage differences in this statement are determined by dividing the dollar difference by the base (that is, the 19X1 numbers).

Another approach in analyzing income statements is vertical analysis. The product of this analysis is also referred to as common-size statements. These statements result from reducing all amounts to percentages using total sales as a common denominator. Exhibit 3.11 illustrates two **common-size income statements** for the Vacation Inn.

Vertical analysis allows for more reasonable comparisons of two or more periods when the activity for the two periods was at different levels. For example, assume the following:

	19X1	19X2
Food sales	$500,000	$750,000
Cost of food sales	150,000	225,000

Exhibit 3.10 Comparative Income Statements

Vacation Inn
Comparative Income Statements

	19X1	19X2	Difference $	Difference %
Total Revenue	$1,719,393	$1,883,482	$164,089	9.54%
Rooms – Revenue	1,041,200	1,124,300	83,100	7.98
Payroll & Related Expenses	185,334	192,428	7,094	3.83
Other Expense	79,080	84,624	5,544	7.01
Department Income	776,786	847,248	70,462	9.07
Food & Beverage – Revenue	626,165	697,241	71,076	11.35
Cost of Sales	208,448	235,431	26,983	12.94
Payroll & Related Expenses	218,532	249,620	31,088	14.23
Other Expense	66,513	76,675	10,162	15.28
Department Income	132,672	135,515	2,843	2.14
Telephone – Revenue	52,028	61,941	9,913	19.05
Cost of Sales	46,505	50,321	3,816	8.21
Payroll & Related Expenses	14,317	16,289	1,972	13.77
Other Expense	6,816	7,561	745	10.93
Department Income	(15,610)	(12,230)	3,380	21.65
Total Operated Department Income	893,848	970,533	76,685	8.58
Undistributed Operating Expenses				
Administrative and General	72,721	79,421	6,700	9.21
Data Processing	32,043	35,213	3,170	9.89
Human Resources	26,818	28,942	2,124	7.92
Transportation	20,871	21,555	684	3.28
Marketing	66,816	79,760	12,944	19.37
Property Operation and Maintenance	80,964	84,465	3,501	4.32
Energy Costs	88,752	96,911	8,159	9.19
Total Undistributed Operating Expenses	388,985	426,267	37,282	9.58
Income Before Fixed Charges	504,863	544,266	39,403	7.80
Rent, Property Taxes, and Insurance	200,861	210,932	10,071	5.01
Interest	52,148	61,841	9,693	18.59
Depreciation and Amortization	115,860	118,942	3,082	2.66
Income Before Income Taxes	135,994	152,551	16,557	12.17
Income Taxes	48,707	57,969	9,262	19.02
Net Income	$ 87,287	$ 94,582	$ 7,295	8.36%

A $75,000 increase in cost of sales may at first appear to be excessive. However, vertical analysis reveals the following:

	19X1	19X2
Food sales	100%	100%
Cost of food sales	30%	30%

Exhibit 3.11 Common-Size Income Statements

Vacation Inn
Common-Size Income Statements

	19X1	19X2	Percentages 19X1	19X2
Total Revenue	$1,719,393	$1,883,482	100.0%	100.0%
Rooms – Revenue	1,041,200	1,124,300	60.6	59.7
Payroll & Related Expenses	185,334	192,428	10.8	10.2
Other Expense	79,080	84,624	4.6	4.5
Department Income	776,786	847,248	45.2	45.0
Food & Beverage – Revenue	626,165	697,241	36.4	37.0
Cost of Sales	208,448	235,431	12.1	12.5
Payroll & Related Expenses	218,532	249,620	12.7	13.3
Other Expense	66,513	76,675	3.9	4.1
Department Income	132,672	135,515	7.7	7.2
Telephone – Revenue	52,028	61,941	3.0	3.3
Cost of Sales	46,505	50,321	2.7	2.7
Payroll & Related Expenses	14,317	16,289	0.8	0.9
Other Expense	6,816	7,561	0.4	0.4
Department Income	(15,610)	(12,230)	(0.9)	(0.7)
Total Operated Department Income	893,848	970,533	52.0	51.5
Undistributed Operating Expenses				
Administrative and General	72,721	79,421	4.2	4.2
Data Processing	32,043	35,213	1.9	1.9
Human Resources	26,818	28,942	1.6	1.5
Transportation	20,871	21,555	1.2	1.1
Marketing	66,816	79,760	3.9	4.2
Property Operation and Maintenance	80,964	84,465	4.7	4.5
Energy Costs	88,752	96,911	5.1	5.1
Total Undistributed Operating Expenses	388,985	426,267	22.6	22.6
Income Before Fixed Charges	504,863	544,266	29.4	28.9
Rent, Property Taxes, and Insurance	200,861	210,932	11.7	11.2
Interest	52,148	61,841	3.0	3.3
Depreciation and Amortization	115,860	118,942	6.7	6.3
Income Before Income Taxes	135,994	152,551	8.0	8.1
Income Taxes	48,707	57,969	2.8	3.1
Net Income	$ 87,287	$ 94,582	5.1%	5.0%

In this example, vertical analysis suggests that despite the absolute increase in cost of sales from 19X1 to 19X2, the cost of food sales has remained constant at 30% of sales for both years. The relatively large increase, in terms of absolute dollars, from 19X1 to 19X2 can be attributed to the higher level of activity during the 19X2 period rather than to unreasonable increases in the cost of sales.

Vertical analysis allows more meaningful comparisons among hospitality operations in the same industry segment but differing substantially in size. This common-size analysis also allows comparisons to industry standards, as discussed previously. However, a note of caution is offered at this point. Industry averages are simply that—averages. They include firms of all sizes from vastly different locations operating in entirely different markets. The industry averages reflect neither any particular operation nor an average operation, and they certainly do not depict an ideal operation.

A third approach to analyzing income statements is ratio analysis. Since vertical analysis is a subset of ratio analysis, there is considerable overlap between these two approaches. We will provide an extensive discussion of ratio analysis in Chapter 5 of this text.

Uniform System of Accounts for Restaurants

Operations of a commercial food service operation differ from operations of a lodging business or a club, and therefore, the financial information as presented in financial statements also differs. The income statement recommended for commercial food service operations is prescribed in the *Uniform System of Accounts for Restaurants* (*USAR*) published by the National Restaurant Association.

The benefits of the *USAR* are similar to those of the *USASH*. That is, the *USAR*:

- Provides for uniform classification and presentation of operating results.

- Allows for easier comparisons to food service industry statistics.

- Provides a turnkey accounting system.

- Is a time-tested system prepared by some of the food service industry's best accounting minds.

Exhibit 3.12 is the Summary Statement of Income for the hypothetical Steak-Plus Restaurant. As with the *USASH*'s income statement, there are several recommended subsidiary schedules to this Summary Statement of Income. Although they are not shown in this text, they provide supplementary information, as do the subsidiary schedules for the *USASH*'s income statement.

The basic similarities and differences between the *USAR*'s and *USASH*'s income statement formats are as follows:

	USASH	USAR
Sales segmented	yes	yes
Cost of sales segmented	yes	yes
Payroll and related costs segmented	yes	no
Other direct costs segmented	yes	no
Controllable expenses separated from fixed charges	yes	yes
Fixed charges segmented	yes	yes

Exhibit 3.12 *USAR* Summary Statement of Income

Summary Statement of Income
Steak-Plus Restaurant
For the year ended December 31, 19X1

	Schedule Numbers	Amounts	Percentages
Revenue			
Food	D–1	$1,045,800	75.8%
Beverage	D–2	333,000	24.2
Total Revenue		1,378,800	100.0
Cost of Sales			
Food		448,000	42.8
Beverage		85,200	25.6
Total Cost of Sales		533,200	38.7
Gross Profit		845,600	61.3
Other Income	D–3	5,400	.4
Total Income		851,000	61.7
Controllable Expenses			
Salaries and Wages	D–4	332,200	24.1
Employee Benefits	D–5	57,440	4.2
Direct Operating Expenses	D–6	88,400	6.4
Music and Entertainment	D–7	14,200	1.0
Marketing	D–8	30,000	2.2
Energy and Utility Services	D–9	37,560	2.7
Administrative and General Expenses	D–10	56,400	4.1
Repairs and Maintenance	D–11	28,600	2.1
Total Controllable Expenses		644,800	46.7
Income Before Rent and Other Occupation Costs, Interest and Depreciation		206,200	15.0
Rent and Other Occupation Costs	D–12	82,200	6.0
Income Before Interest, Depreciation, and Income Taxes		124,000	9.0
Interest		21,600	1.5
Depreciation		31,200	2.3
Total		52,800	3.8
Net Income Before Income Taxes		71,200	5.2
Income Taxes		14,240	1.0
Net Income		$56,960	4.2%

Computerization

As they do with the balance sheet, larger hospitality operations often produce the income statement using a general ledger package. As personal computers become more sophisticated, smaller operations will also be able to use these packages.

In the meantime, there are many computer applications for the income statement. For example, Exhibit 3.13 was produced by a spreadsheet program which helps prepare the amounts for common-size statements. The user only had to enter the separate revenue and expense amounts; the computer calculated all totals (such as Department Income) and all percentages.

In addition, many software packages have extensive graphics capabilities. The phrase "a picture is worth a thousand words" applies here. Although graphs do not usually provide detail, managers can more easily track recent performance trends by showing results in line graphs. Exhibit 3.14 is a line graph which highlights a rooms department's revenues over a four-year period. The trend is obvious. Departmental expenses can be shown using pie charts. Departmental revenues for several years can be shown using bar charts. These charts are easy to understand, and they can be used as management tools to show employees the operation's results more effectively than the traditional financial statements which sometimes seem like a confusing list of numbers.

Summary

The income statement, complete with all departmental statements, is generally considered the most useful financial statement for management. It highlights the important financial aspects of the property's operations over a period of time.

The income statement shows four major elements: revenues, expenses, gains, and losses. Revenues (increases in assets or decreases in liability accounts) and expenses (decreases in assets or increases in liability accounts) are directly related to operations, while gains and losses result from transactions incidental to the property's major operations.

In order to standardize income statements within the hospitality industry, the original *Uniform System of Accounts for Hotels* was written in 1925–26. Since then, there have been changes and revisions, the most recent being the eighth edition published in 1986. By using an accounting system based on a uniform system of accounts, the management of a new hotel has a turnkey accounting system for a complete and systematic accounting for the hotel's operations. The various uniform systems also facilitate comparison among operations of varying sizes in the hospitality industry.

In order to enhance the usefulness of the income statement, the format set up by the *USASH* includes statements of departmental income showing the revenues produced by each profit center (operated department) and subtracting from each the corresponding direct operating expenses. Included in the direct operating expenses are not only the cost of goods sold, but also the direct payroll and other direct expenses. Next, undistributed operating expenses which consist of seven major service

Exhibit 3.13 Sample Spreadsheet Printout

```
                              VACATION INN

                     COMMON-SIZE INCOME STATEMENTS


                          D O L L A R S          P E R C E N T A G E S
                     ---------------------------    ---------------------------
                         19X1        19X2            19X1         19X2

TOTAL REVENUE        $1,719,393  $1,883,482        100.00%       100.00%
                     ===========================================================

Rooms Revenue        $1,041,200  $1,124,300         60.56%        59.69%
  Payroll & Related     185,334     192,428         10.78         10.22
  Other Expense          79,080      84,624          4.60          4.49

Department Income       776,786     847,248         45.18         44.98

Food & Beverage Revenue 626,165     697,241         36.42         37.02
  Cost of Sales         208,448     235,431         12.12         12.50
  Payroll & Related     218,532     249,620         12.71         13.25
  Other Expense          66,513      76,675          3.87          4.07

Department Income       132,672     135,515          7.72          7.19

Telephone Revenue        52,028      61,941          3.03          3.29
  Cost of Sales          46,505      50,321          2.70          2.67
  Payroll & Related      14,317      16,289          0.83          0.86
  Other Expense           6,816       7,561          0.40          0.40

Department Income       (15,610)    (12,230)        (0.91)        (0.65)

Total Operated Depart-
  ment Income           893,848     970,533         51.99         51.53

Undistributed Operating
  Expenses:
  Administrative &
    General              72,721      79,421          4.23          4.22
  Data Processing        32,043      35,213          1.86          1.87
  Human Resources        26,818      28,942          1.56          1.54
  Transportation         20,871      21,555          1.21          1.14
  Marketing              66,816      79,760          3.89          4.23
  Property Operation &
    Maintenance          80,964      84,465          4.71          4.48
  Energy Costs           88,752      96,911          5.16          5.15

Total Undistributed
  Operating Expenses    388,985     426,267         22.62         22.63
Income Before Fixed
  Charges               504,863     544,266         29.36         28.90
Rent, Property Taxes,
  and Insurance         200,861     210,932         11.68         11.20
Interest                 52,148      61,841          3.03          3.28
Depreciation & Amort-
  ization               115,860     118,942          6.74          6.32

Income Before In-
  come Taxes            135,994     152,551          7.91          8.10

Income Taxes             48,707      57,969          2.83          3.08

Net Income             $87,287     $94,582          5.08%         5.02%
                     ===========================================================
```

Exhibit 3.14 Sample Graphics

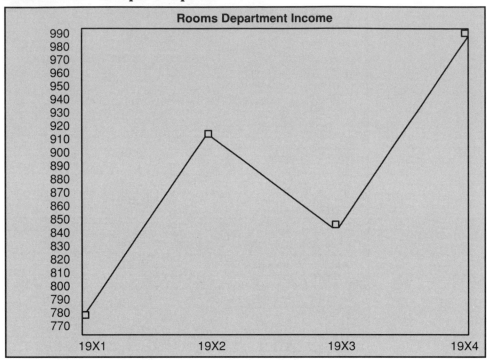

center categories—administrative and general expenses, data processing, human resources, transportation, marketing, property operation and maintenance, and energy costs—must be subtracted to determine "income before management fees and fixed charges." This is followed by management fees and fixed charges which include rent, property taxes, fire insurance, interest, depreciation, and amortization. Next, gain (loss) on sale of property and equipment is added (subtracted) to determine income before income taxes. Finally, income taxes are subtracted resulting in net income.

As a supplement to the income statement, several departmental income statements should be presented. These offer management additional insight into the operation of each department. The number of schedules necessary depends on the complexity of the lodging facility; the more cost and profit centers operated, the more supplemental statements should be presented. These departmental statements can be very useful for management. First, they can be used to compare the hotel's operations with industry averages, prior performance, and, most important, budgeted standards or goals. Also, the relative profitability of various departments can be compared.

There are three major methods management can use to analyze the income statement. The first method is horizontal analysis, which considers both the relative and absolute changes in the income statement between two periods and/or between the budgeted and actual figures. Any major variances exceeding levels predefined by management can be further investigated to determine their causes. The next type of analysis is the vertical analysis, which reduces all items to a percentage of sales.

These percentages, often referred to as common-size statements, can then be used to compare the results of the property's operations with either those of other lodging facilities or with industry standards. Again, any significant differences should be studied. The final method, ratio analysis, will be more thoroughly discussed in Chapter 5.

Endnotes

1. Uniform systems of accounts are available as follows:
    Uniform System of Accounts and Expense Dictionary for Small Hotels, Motels, and Motor Hotels, Fourth Ed. (East Lansing, Mich.: Educational Institute of the American Hotel & Motel Association, 1987).
    Uniform System of Accounts for Hotels, 8th rev. ed. (New York: Hotel Association of New York City, 1986).
    Uniform System of Accounts for Clubs (Washington, D.C.: Club Managers Association of America, 1982).
    Uniform System of Accounts for Restaurants, 5th rev. ed. (Washington, D.C.: National Restaurant Association, 1983).

2. Clifford T. Fay, Jr., Raymond S. Schmidgall, and Stanley B. Tarr, *Basic Financial Accounting for the Hospitality Industry* (East Lansing, Mich.: Educational Institute of the American Hotel & Motel Association, 1982).

3. *Trends in the Hotel Industry—USA Edition 1989* (Houston, Tex.: Pannell Kerr Forster, 1989).

4. *Trends.*

Key Terms

capacity costs
common-size income statements
comparative income statements
contribution margin
daily report of operations
departmental income statement

departmental schedule
income statement
responsibility accounting
summary income statement
uniform systems of accounts

Discussion Questions

1. What are the major differences between the balance sheet and the income statement?
2. Why are creditors interested in the income statement?
3. What are the major differences between a revenue and a gain?
4. What are three examples of direct operating expenses for the rooms department?
5. What is the difference between the income statement used in many non-hospitality industries and one prepared by a lodging facility?
6. How is the cost of food sold determined?
7. What are the advantages of the uniform system of accounts?

8. What detailed expenses are included in the property operation, maintenance, and energy costs of the income statement?

9. Why are supplemental statements valuable to management?

10. What are the different techniques of income statement analysis?

11. How is the Summary Statement of Income per the *USAR* similar to and different from the *USASH's* income statement?

Problems

Problem 3.1

As the controller for Kelly's, a hotel with a large restaurant operation, you are responsible for monitoring costs. You have collected the following information concerning the food inventory and need to calculate the cost of food sold for the month of December.

Inventory, December 1, 19X1	$12,376
Inventory, December 31, 19X1	15,845
Purchases	76,840
Employee Meals:	
A. General Manager	85
B. Food Department	648
Transfers from the Bar to Kitchen	46
Promotional Meals	256

Required:

1. Calculate the cost of food sold for December 19X1.

2. To which departments would each expense be charged?

Expense	Department
1. Cost of food sold	_____
2. Employee meals – general manager	_____
3. Employee meals – food department	_____
4. Promotional meals	_____

Problem 3.2

Several accounts from the Hilltop Motel's general ledger that pertain to the rooms department are listed below. The accounts are in random order as follows:

Sales – transient – regular	$ 100,000
Salaries	10,000
Commissions	1,000
Uniforms	500
Linen expense	1,000

Sales – transient – groups	50,000
Wages	15,000
Payroll taxes	2,000
Operating supplies	1,500
Contract cleaning	1,800
Dry cleaning	1,200
Fringe benefits	3,000
Other revenues	2,000
Allowances – rooms	500
Laundry	3,000
Other expenses	1,800

Required:

Prepare a rooms department schedule following the *USASH*. Use only classifications as shown on the prescribed schedule.

Problem 3.3

The Midnight Inn's general ledger contains several food and beverage accounts for the year ended December 31, 19X2, as follows:

Food sales	$ 800,000
Beverage sales	300,000
Cover charges (beverage)	6,000
Miscellaneous other income (food)	3,000
Uniforms	2,000
Operating supplies	10,000
Food purchases	300,000
Beverage purchases	75,000
Candy/gum purchases	1,000
Salaries – food	100,000
Wages – food	120,000
Payroll taxes – food	15,000
Fringe benefits – food (excludes employee meals)	20,000
Kitchen fuel	4,000
Laundry	7,000
Contract cleaning	8,000
China	2,000
Linen	1,500
Silver	2,000
Glassware	2,500
Licenses	2,000
Music	10,000
Employee meals – food	3,000
Employee meals – beverage	1,000
Salaries – beverage	50,000
Wages – beverage	70,000
Payroll taxes – beverage	9,000
Fringe benefits – beverage (excludes employee meals)	12,000

Other information is as follows:

Inventories	1/1/X2	12/31/X2
Food	$10,000	$12,000
Beverages	6,000	5,000
Candy/gum	500	400

Required:

Prepare a food and beverage schedule in accordance with the *USASH*.

Problem 3.4

Ron Curcio, the owner of Ron's Resort, has hired you to prepare the Resort's income statement for the year ending December 31, 19X1. He has provided you with the balances of each of the general ledger accounts, and has requested that you follow the format established in the *USASH*.

Vending Machine Revenues	$	819
Employee Meals, Food Department		443
Cost of Calls, Telephone		22,820
Ending Inventory, Food		15,386
Liability Insurance		3,000
Concessions – Revenues		1,473
Outdoor Advertising		12,121
Grounds and Landscaping		12,000
Purchases – Food and Beverage		134,999
Depreciation		76,366
Other Selling Expenses		17,868
Other Operating Expenses – Food		60,002
Other Operating Expenses – Rooms		151,123
Electric Expense		33,583
Rent Expense		75,000
Water Expense		26,859
Other Operating Expenses – Telephone		1,647
Interest Expense		42,833
Revenues:		
Rooms		1,075,475
Food and Beverage		418,076
Telephone		53,898
Salaries and Related Expenses:		
Rooms		178,461
Food and Beverage		105,519
Marketing		24,000
Property Operation and Maintenance		20,170
Energy Costs		18,700
Telephone		20,000
Data Processing		25,000
Transportation		10,000
Administrative and General		55,000
Other Departmental Expenses:		
Administrative and General		30,000
Transportation		15,000
Data Processing		15,000
Tax Rate		38%

Required:

Prepare the summary income statement in accordance with the *USASH*. Note: The beginning inventory of food was $18,795. The schedules in Appendix A at the end of the text may be helpful in determining how some of the above expenses should be categorized for income statement purposes.

Problem 3.5

The general ledger of Ramsey's, a 100-seat restaurant, as of December 31, 19X3, includes revenue and expense accounts as follows:

Salaries	$ 150,000
Wages	280,000
Payroll taxes	30,000
Fringe benefits (excludes employee meals)	50,000
Employee meals	5,000
Food sales	1,200,000
Beverage sales	500,000
Food purchases	460,000
Beverage purchases	130,000
Other sales	20,000
Direct operating expenses	100,000
Music	20,000
Marketing	30,000
Heat, light and power	35,000
Rent	152,000
Interest expense	20,000
Depreciation	50,000
Repairs	30,000
Administrative & general	92,000

Other information is as follows:

Income tax rate—30% on pre-tax income

Inventories	1/1/X3	12/31/X3
Food	$20,000	$22,000
Beverage	15,000	17,000

Required:

Prepare Ramsey's statement of income for 19X3 in accordance with the *USAR*.

Problem 3.6

The Wilson Motel has two major operated departments—rooms and food. The following information is supplied to you as of December 31, 19X6:

Account	Account Balance
Insurance (fire)	$ 5,000
Rooms department	80,000
Food department—salaries and wages	60,000

Supplies—food department	20,000
Food purchases	55,000
Room sales	380,000
Interest income	1,000
Interest expense	?
Cost of food sold	?
Food sales	180,000
A & G—wages	50,000
Advertising	10,000
Maintenance—contract	30,000
Depreciation	50,000
Heat	15,000
Power and lights	12,000
Amortization of franchise fee	2,000
Supplies and other—rooms department	30,000
Property taxes	12,000
A & G—other expense	10,000

Other information is as follows:

1. The Wilson Motel borrowed $50,000 two years ago from the Wilmore Savings and Loan. On June 30, 19X6, the first non-interest payment is made to Wilmore of $10,000. The funds were borrowed at an interest rate of 10%.

2. The beginning and ending inventories of food were $2,000 and $3,000 respectively. Food consumed by the food and rooms department employees during the year (free of charge) totaled $500 and $300, respectively.

3. Fringe benefits and payroll taxes for all employees, excluding free food, are 20% of gross salaries and wages.

4. The Wilson Motel pays an average of 25% of its pre-tax income to the various governmental units in the form of income taxes.

5. The management fee to be paid to the management company is 3% of room sales and 10% of total income before management fees and fixed charges.

Required:

Prepare an income statement for the Wilson Motel based on the *USASH*.

Problem 3.7

Tim's Tasty Tidbits' August and September 19X1 condensed income statements are as follows:

	August	September
Food Sales	$45,000	$48,000
Beverage Sales	40,000	42,000
Total Sales	85,000	90,000
Cost of Food Sales	15,300	15,840
Cost of Beverage Sales	8,000	9,240
Labor	25,500	28,800
Laundry	4,000	4,200
China, glass, silver	1,000	1,100
Other	16,000	15,500
Total Expenses	69,800	74,680

Net Income	$15,200	$15,320
Customers were served as follows:		
Food	10,000	12,000
Beverage	25,000	24,000

Required:

1. Convert the two income statements to common-size income statements.

2. Based on the information provided (including customer information), comment regarding the operating performance of Tim's Tasty Tidbits for the two months.

Problem 3.8

Pat Mulhurn, the founder of Pat's Place, wants to analyze 19X2 year's operations by comparing them with the 19X1 results. To aid him, prepare a comparative income statement using the 19X1 and 19X2 information available.

Pat's Place
Income Statement
For the years ending December 31, 19X1 and 19X2

	19X1	19X2
Revenues		
Rooms	$ 976,000	$1,041,000
Food and Beverage	604,000	626,000
Telephone	50,000	52,000
Total	1,630,000	1,719,000
Direct Expenses		
Rooms	250,000	264,000
Food and Beverage	476,000	507,000
Telephones	68,000	68,000
Total Operational Department Income	836,000	880,000
Undistributed Operating Expenses		
Administrative and General	195,000	206,000
Marketing	65,000	68,000
Property Operation and Maintenance	69,000	68,000
Energy Costs	101,000	102,000
Income Before Fixed Charges	406,000	436,000
Rent, Property Taxes, and Insurance	200,000	201,000
Interest	55,000	52,000
Depreciation and Amortization	116,000	116,000
Income Before Income Taxes	35,000	67,000
Income Taxes	7,000	17,000
Net Income	$ 28,000	$ 50,000

Required:

Prepare the comparative income statement for Pat's Place. Note: Rearrange the income statement to conform to the *USASH* format as reflected in Exhibit 3.10.

Problem 3.9

The Wilkin Inn's partially completed condensed comparative income statements are as follows:

			Difference	
	19X1	19X2	$	%
Total Revenues	$1,000,000	$1,200,000		
Rooms—Revenues	600,000			25.0
Payroll & Related Expenses		100,000	10,000	
Other Expense	50,000			10.0
Department Income				
Food & Beverage—Revenues	350,000			
Cost of Sales		130,000	15,000	
Payroll & Related Expenses	75,000			10.0
Other Expense			3,500	10.0
Department Income				
Telephone–Revenues		60,000		
Cost of Sales	40,000			12.0
Payroll & Related Expenses			2,000	14.0
Other Expense		8,000	1,000	
Department Income				
Total Operated Department Income				
Undistributed Operating Expenses:				
Administrative & General	100,000			11.0
Marketing		60,000	5,000	
Property Operation and Maintenance			10,000	
Energy Costs				12.0
Total Undistributed Operating Expenses	250,000		32,000	
Income Before Fixed Charges & Management Fees				
Management Fees		30,000	3,000	
Income Before Fixed Charges				
Rent, Property Taxes, and Insurance	100,000			6.0

Interest	_____	80,000	20,000	____
Depreciation	_____	_____	5,000	20.0
Income Before Income Taxes	_____	_____	_____	____
Income Taxes	_____	_____	6,000	10.0
Net Income	======	======	======	====

Required:

Complete the above comparative income statements.

Problem 3.10

Listed below is financial information for the Harby Hotel for the year ended December 31, 19X2.

Account	Account Balance
Commissions—Rooms Department	$ 23,500
Marketing Expense	111,800
Ending Food and Beverage Inventory	53,000
Depreciation and Amortization Expense	91,000
Net Room Revenue	1,560,000
Cost of Sales—Rental and Other Income	9,360
Rent Expense	148,200
Reservation Expense	13,500
Fire Insurance Expense	10,400
Income Taxes—40% pre-tax rate	?
Employee Benefits—Rooms Department	51,000
Food and Beverage Revenues	858,000
Proceeds from Sale of Equipment*	10,000
Other Expense—Telephone Department	6,240
Contract Cleaning—Rooms Department	5,800
Administrative and General Expenses (total)	270,400
Property Taxes	70,200
Food and Beverage Purchases	328,400
Payroll—Telephone Department	15,600
Linen Expense—Rooms Department	8,600
Other Expense—Rental and Other Income	9,360
Beginning Food and Beverage Inventory	38,900
Revenues—Rental and Other Income	119,600
Revenues—Telephone Department	62,400
Data Processing Expenses (total)	34,320
Human Resources Expenses (total)	32,614
Salaries and Wages—Rooms Department	209,000
Interest Expenses	98,800
Payroll—Rental and Other income	20,800
Free Food and Beverage—Employees**	12,300
Laundry and Drycleaning—Rooms Department	24,800
Other Expenses—Food and Beverage Department	93,600
Other Expenses—Rooms Department	130,000
Property Operation and Maintenance (total)	112,200

Cost of Sales—Telephone Department	46,800
Payroll—Food and Beverage Department	93,600
Energy costs (total)	159,500

*Equipment sold cost $15,000 and had been depreciated by $8,000.

**This has already been recorded as expense in the appropriate departments, except in the determination of the cost of food sold.

Required:

1. Prepare a rooms departmental statement in accordance with the *USASH*.
2. Determine the cost of food and beverage sold.
3. Prepare a summary income statement following the *USASH*.

4 Statement of Cash Flows

Traditionally, the principal financial statements used by hospitality operations have been the income statement and the balance sheet. The balance sheet shows the financial position of the business at the end of the accounting period. The income statement reflects the results of operations for the accounting period. Although these statements provide extensive financial information, they do not provide answers to such questions as:

1. How much cash was provided by operations?
2. What amount of property and equipment was purchased during the year?
3. How much long-term debt was borrowed during the year?
4. What amount of funds was raised through the sale of capital stock?
5. What amount of dividends was paid during the year?
6. How much was invested in long-term investments during the year?

The **statement of cash flows (SCF)** is designed to answer these questions and many more. The Financial Accounting Standards Board (FASB), which is the current accounting rule-making body, has mandated that the SCF be included with the other financial statements issued to external users only since 1988. It replaces the infamous statement of changes in financial position, which generally focused on working capital rather than cash.

Our discussion of this most recent addition to the collection of major financial statements will address the definition of cash, the relationship of the SCF to other financial statements, the purposes and uses of the SCF, a classification of cash flows, alternative formats which may be used for the SCF, a four step approach for preparing the SCF, and a comprehensive illustration of the preparation of the statement.

The Purpose of the Statement of Cash Flows

The statement of cash flows shows the effects on cash of a business's operating, investing, and financing activities for the accounting period. It explains the change in cash for the accounting period; that is, if cash increases by $5,000 from January 1, 19X1 (the beginning of the accounting period) to December 31, 19X1 (the end of the accounting period), the SCF will reflect the increase in the sum of cash from the firm's various activities.

For purposes of this statement, cash is defined to include both cash and cash equivalents. **Cash equivalents** are short-term, highly liquid investments such as U.S. Treasury Bills and money market accounts. Firms use cash equivalents for investing funds temporarily not needed for operating purposes. Generally, these short-term investments are made for 90 days or less. Since cash and cash equivalents are considered to be the same, transfers between cash and cash equivalents are not considered to be cash receipts or cash disbursements for SCF purposes.

The major purpose of the SCF is to provide relevant information regarding the cash receipts and disbursements of a hospitality business to help users (investors, creditors, managers, and others) to:

1. Assess the organization's ability to generate positive future net cash flows. Although users of financial statements are less interested in the past than in the future, many users, especially external users, must rely on historical financial information to assess an operation's future abilities. Thus, the investor interested in future cash dividends will review the SCF to determine past sources and uses of cash to evaluate the firm's ability to pay future dividends.

2. Assess the firm's ability to meet its obligations. Users of financial statements want to determine the firm's ability to pay its bills as they come due. If a firm has little likelihood of being able to pay its bills, then suppliers will most likely not be interested in selling the firm their goods and services.

3. Assess the difference between the enterprise's net income and cash receipts and disbursements. The SCF allows a user to quickly determine the major net sources of cash and how much relates to the enterprise's operations. Investors, creditors, and other users generally prefer enterprises which are able to generate cash from operations (that is, from their primary purpose for being in business), as opposed to those generating cash solely from financing and investing activities (that is, activities which are incidental to the primary purpose).

4. Assess the effect of both cash and noncash investing and financing during the accounting period. Investing activities relate to the acquisition and disposition of noncurrent assets, such as property and equipment. Financing activities relate to the borrowing and payment of long-term debt and sale and purchase of capital stock. Noncash activities (that is, transactions involving no cash) include such transactions as the acquisition of a hotel in exchange for stock or long-term debt.

The three major user groups of the SCF are management (internal) and investors and creditors (external). Management may use the SCF to

Exhibit 4.1   Relationship of SCF to Other Financial Statements

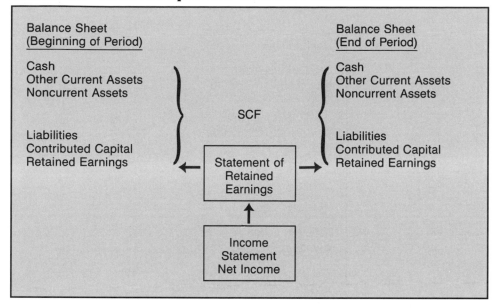

(1) assess the firm's liquidity, (2) assess its financial flexibility, (3) determine its dividend policy, and (4) plan investing and financing needs. Investors and creditors will most likely use the SCF to assess the firm's (1) ability to pay its bills as they come due, (2) ability to pay dividends, and (3) need for additional financing, including borrowing debt and selling capital stock.

The SCF in Relation to Other Financial Statements

The relationship of the SCF to other financial statements is shown in Exhibit 4.1. The statement of retained earnings, mentioned in Exhibit 4.1, reflects results of operations and dividends declared, and reconciles the retained earnings accounts of two successive balance sheets. Net income from the income statement is transferred to the retained earnings account when the temporary accounts (revenues and expenses) are closed at the end of the accounting period. In addition, net income is shown on the SCF when the SCF is prepared using the indirect approach (which is discussed later in this chapter). Finally, the SCF indirectly reconciles most accounts other than cash on the balance sheet by showing the sources and uses of cash.

Classification of Cash Flows

The SCF classifies cash receipts and disbursements as operating, investing, and financing activities. Both **cash inflows** and **cash outflows** are included within each category. Exhibit 4.2 presents classifications of cash flows under the various activities, which are further described below:

- **Operating Activities:** This category includes cash transactions related to revenues and expenses. Revenues (cash inflows) include

Exhibit 4.2   Classification of Cash Flows

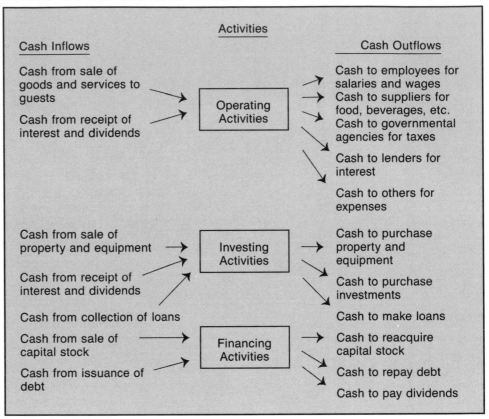

sales of food, beverages, other goods and services to lodging guests, as well as interest and dividend income. Expenses (cash outflows) are for operational cash expenditures, including payments for salaries, wages, taxes, supplies, and so forth. Interest expense is also included as an operations cash outflow.

- **Investing Activities:** These activities relate primarily to cash flows from the acquisition and disposal of all noncurrent assets, especially property, equipment, and investments. Also included are cash flows from the purchase and disposal of marketable securities (short-term investments).

- **Financing Activities:** These activities relate to cash flows from the issuance and retirement of debt and the issuance and re-purchase of capital stock. Cash inflows include cash received from issues of stock and both short-term and long-term borrowing. Cash outflows include repayments of loans (although the interest expense portion of the debt payment is an operating activity) and payments to owners for both dividends and any re-purchase of stocks. Payments of accounts payable, taxes payable, and the various accrued expenses, such as wages payable, are not payments of loans under financing activities, but they are classified as cash outflows under operating activities.

Exhibit 4.3 Schedule of Noncash Investing and Financing Activities—Gateway Inn

Common stock exchanged for long-term debt		$100,000
Capital lease obligations incurred for use of equipment		50,000
	Total	$150,000

Exhibit 4.4 Basic Format of the SCF

Cash Flows from Operating Activities (direct or indirect approaches may be used)	$XX
Cash Flows from Investing Activities (list cash inflows and outflows)	XX
Cash Flows from Financing Activities (list cash inflows and outflows)	XX
Net Increase (Decrease) in Cash	XX
Cash at the beginning of the period	XX
Cash at the end of the period	$XX
Schedule of Noncash Investing and Financing Transactions	
List individual transactions	$XX

Finally, hospitality enterprises engage in noncash investing and financing activities, such as the exchange of capital stock for a hotel building. Since this represents only an exchange, no cash transaction has occurred. Therefore, these noncash activities are not shown on the SCF. However, since a major purpose of the SCF is to include financing and investing activities, and since these activities will affect future cash flows, they must be disclosed on a separate schedule to the SCF. Thus, the user of financial information is provided with a complete presentation of investing and financing activities. Exhibit 4.3 is an example of a supplementary schedule of noncash investing and financing activities of the Gateway Inn.

The basic format of the SCF is shown in Exhibit 4.4. Generally, cash flows from operating activities are shown first. The indirect or direct approaches (to be discussed later) may be used to show cash flows from operating activities. Cash flows from investing and financing activities follow. Individual cash outflows and inflows are shown in each section. For example, long-term debt may increase by $100,000 due to the payment of $50,000 and subsequent borrowing of $150,000. Each cash flow should be shown rather than netting the two flows. Finally, as stated above, a supplementary schedule of noncash investing and financing activities to the SCF must be included.

Conversion of Accrual Income to Net Cash Flows from Operations

A major purpose of the SCF is to show net cash flows from operations. The income statement (discussed in Chapter 3) is prepared on an **accrual basis**; that is, revenues are recorded when earned, not when cash is received from guests, and expenses are recorded when incurred, not necessarily when cash is disbursed. Consequently, there may be little correlation between net income and cash flow. Consider the hypothetical Wales Inn which had $2,000,000 sales for 19X1. Its accounts receivable (AR) from guests totaled $100,000 at the beginning of the year and $110,000 at the end of the year. The cash received from sales during 19X1 is determined as follows:

$$\text{Cash receipts for sales} = \text{Sales} - \text{increase in AR}$$
$$OR \ + \text{decrease in AR}$$
$$= \$2,000,000 - \$10,000$$
$$= \underline{\$1,990,000}$$

Thus, even though the Wales Inn had sales of $2,000,000 as reported on its income statement, it would show cash receipts from sales on its SCF as $1,990,000.

Direct and Indirect Methods

There are two methods for converting net income to net cash flow from operations—the direct and the indirect methods. The **direct method** shows cash receipts from sales and cash disbursements for expenses. This method requires that each item on the income statement be converted from an accrual basis to a cash basis, as were the sales of the Wales Inn above. Another example of this conversion process for the Wales Inn is payroll expense. Assume that the Wales Inn reported $700,000 as payroll expense for 19X1, and its balance sheet's accrued payroll account at the beginning of the year showed $15,000 and at the end of the year showed $20,000. Its cash disbursements for payroll for 19X1 is determined as follows:

$$\text{Cash Disbursement for Payroll Expense} = \text{Payroll Expense} - \text{increase in Accrued Payroll}$$
$$OR \ + \text{decrease in Accrued Payroll}$$
$$= \$700,000 - \$5,000$$
$$= \underline{\$695,000}$$

So, even though payroll expense for the year totaled $700,000 as shown on the income statement, only $695,000 was disbursed during the year.

Some expenses shown on the income statement do not involve any direct cash disbursement and are simply ignored when using the direct method. For example, depreciation expense is only an adjustment to help

Exhibit 4.5   Basic Formats of the Net Cash Flow from Operating Activities Sections

Operating Activities		
Direct Method		
Cash Flows from Operating Activities:		
Cash receipts from sales		$XXX
Interest and dividends received		XXX
Total		XXX
Cash Disbursements for:		
Payroll	$XXX	
Purchases of inventory	XXX	
Other expenses	XXX	
Interest expense	XXX	
Income taxes	XXX	XXX
Net Cash Flows from Operating Activities		$XXX
Indirect Method		
Cash Flows from Operating Activities:		
Net Income		$XXX
Adjustments to reconcile net income to net cash		
flows from operating activities:		
Depreciation expense	$ XXX	
Gain on sale of property	(XXX)	
Loss on sale of investments	XXX	
Increase in accounts receivable	(XXX)	
Decrease in inventories	XXX	
.		
.		
.		
Increase in accrued payroll	XXX	XXX
Net Cash Flows from Operating Activities		$XXX

match expenses to revenues. Depreciation does not entail any cash, so it is ignored when using the direct method. The same approach is taken for amortization expense and gains and losses on the sale of property and equipment. The basic formats of cash flows from the operating activities section of the SCF for both the direct and indirect methods are shown in Exhibit 4.5.

The FASB prefers the direct approach. However, most hospitality businesses use the indirect method because the information needed to prepare it is more readily available than that needed for using the direct method. For that reason, the major focus in this chapter will be the indirect method.

The **indirect method** for determining net cash flows from operations starts with net income. Net income is then adjusted for noncash items included on the income statement. The commonest noncash expense deducted to determine net income is depreciation. Therefore, since depreciation is subtracted to compute net income on the income statement, it is added back to net income to compute net cash flows from operating activities. Other items on the income statement that must be added or subtracted include amortization expense and gains and losses on the sale of noncurrent assets and marketable securities.

To illustrate the addback of a loss on the sale of investments, assume that the Wales Inn sold a parcel of undeveloped land (an investment) in 19X1 for $200,000 which originally cost $250,000. The journal entry to record the sale was as follows:

Cash	$200,000	
Loss on sale of investments	50,000	
Investment in land		$250,000

The $200,000 of cash inflow will be shown as an investing activity on the SCF; however, the loss on sale of investments of $50,000 was included on the income statement in determining net income. Since it was subtracted in determining the Wales Inn's net income and it did not use cash, it must be added back to net income to determine the net cash flows from operating activities for the SCF.

In addition, in order to determine the net cash flows from operating activities using the indirect method, the Wales Inn's net income must be adjusted for sales that were recorded but which guests did not pay for during 19X1. This adjustment is accomplished by subtracting the increase in accounts receivable of $10,000 from net income on the SCF. There are several similar adjustments that must be made using the indirect method. These will be discussed in detail and illustrated in the next section of this chapter.

Regardless of the method used, the result will show the same amount of net cash provided by operating activities. The FASB requires that firms using the indirect method record the amount of interest expense and taxes paid in separate disclosures.

Preparing the SCF

The principal sources of information needed for preparing the SCF are the income statement, the statement of retained earnings, and two successive balance sheets from the beginning and end of the accounting period. In addition, details of transactions affecting any change in noncurrent balance sheet accounts must be reviewed. For example, if a comparison of two successive balance sheets shows the building account has increased by $5,000,000, the account must be analyzed to determine the reason(s) for the changes. Simply reflecting the net change of $5,000,000 on the SCF is generally not acceptable.

A four step approach for preparing the SCF is as follows:

1. Determine the net cash flows from operating activities.

2. Determine the net cash flows from investing activities.

3. Determine the net cash flows from financing activities.

4. Present the cash flows by activity on the SCF.

Exhibit 4.6 Balance Sheets for the Simple Hotel

Simple Hotel
Balance Sheets
December 31, 19X1 and 19X2

	19X1	19X2
Assets		
Current Assets:		
Cash	$ 5,000	$ 10,000
Accounts Receivable	30,000	26,000
Inventory	10,000	12,000
Total	45,000	48,000
Investments	50,000	300,000
Property and Equipment:		
Land	200,000	200,000
Building	10,000,000	10,000,000
Equipment	1,000,000	1,100,000
Less: Accum. Depreciation	(5,000,000)	(5,500,000)
Total	6,200,000	5,800,000
Total Assets	$ 6,295,000	$ 6,148,000
Liabilities and Owners' Equity		
Current Liabilities:		
Accounts Payable	$ 6,000	$ 6,500
Accrued Payroll	4,000	4,500
Income Taxes Payable	7,000	6,000
Dividends Payable	10,000	15,000
Total	27,000	32,000
Long-Term Debt	4,500,000	3,750,000
Owners' Equity:		
Capital Stock	1,000,000	1,250,000
Retained Earnings	768,000	1,116,000
Total	1,768,000	2,366,000
Total Liabilities and Owners' Equity	$ 6,295,000	$ 6,148,000

Exhibits 4.6 and 4.7 contain balance sheets and a condensed income statement and statement of retained earnings for the Simple Hotel. These will be used to illustrate this four step approach. (A more comprehensive illustration will be shown later in the chapter.) The preparation of the SCF is illustrated using the indirect method for showing net cash flows from operating activities.

Exhibit 4.7   Income Statement and Statement of Retained Earnings for the Simple Hotel

Simple Hotel
Condensed Income Statement and Statement of Retained Earnings
For the Year Ended December 31, 19X2

Sales	$7,000,000
Cost of Goods Sold	1,000,000
Payroll Expenses	2,450,000
Other Operating Expenses	2,400,000
Income Taxes	250,000
Depreciation Expense	500,000
Gain on the Sale of Investments	100,000
Net Income	500,000
Retained Earnings—12/31/X1	768,000
Dividends Declared	152,000
Retained Earnings—12/31/X2	$1,116,000

Other Information:

1. No property and equipment were disposed of during 19X2.

2. Investment and equipment purchases during 19X2 were made with cash. No funds were borrowed.

3. Investments costing $50,000 were sold for $150,000, resulting in a $100,000 gain on the sale of investments during 19X2.

4. Long-term debt of $250,000 was converted to capital stock in a noncash transaction during 19X2. No other capital stock was issued, and there were no repurchases of capital stock.

5. Interest expense paid during the year totaled $400,000.

Step 1: Determining Net Cash Flows from Operating Activities

To determine the net cash flow from operating activities using the indirect method, we focus first on the income statement by starting with net income of $500,000. Next, we need to adjust net income for items on the income statement which did not provide or use cash. In particular, depreciation expense and the gain on the sale of the investment are considered. Since depreciation was subtracted on the income statement to determine net income, it must be added to net income on the SCF to determine net cash flow from operating activities. Since the gain on the sale of investments is not a cash flow (the proceeds from the sale of investments of $150,000 are an investing activity on the SCF and will be discussed later), the gain of $100,000 must be subtracted from net income on the SCF. Thus, the net cash flows from operating activities are determined at this point as follows:

Net cash flows from operating activities:
    Net income $500,000
        Adjustments to Reconcile Net
            Income to Net Cash Flows
            from Operating Activities:

Depreciation expense	$500,000	
Gain on sale of investments	(100,000)	400,000
Partial net cash flows from operating activities		$900,000

The second type of adjustment includes changes in current accounts from the balance sheet. The cash account is not considered, since we are essentially looking at all other balance sheet accounts to determine what caused the change in cash for purposes of the SCF. In addition, the current liability account dividends payable is not considered in determining cash flows from operating activities, as dividends payable relate to financing activities and will be considered later. The change in the remaining five current accounts is fully considered as follows:

	Balances—December 31		Change in
Account	19X1	19X2	Account Balance
Current Assets:			
Accounts Receivable	$30,000	$26,000	$4,000 (dec.)
Inventory	$10,000	$12,000	$2,000 (inc.)
Current Liabilities:			
Accounts Payable	$6,000	$6,500	$500 (inc.)
Accrued Payroll	$4,000	$4,500	$500 (inc.)
Income Taxes Payable	$7,000	$6,000	$1,000 (dec.)

A brief explanation follows for each of the above current accounts, including how the change affects net cash flow from operating activities.

Accounts receivable relate directly to sales, which were $7,000,000 for the Simple Hotel for 19X2. Sales on account result in cash inflows when the hotel guests pay their bills. However, under accrual accounting, the sale is recorded when services are provided. Most of the sales during 19X2 resulted in cash as the guests paid their accounts, but at year end, the accounts receivable account balance was $26,000. Analysis of the account will reveal how much cash resulted from sales as follows:

Accounts Receivable			
12/31/X1 Balance	30,000	Cash received	7,004,000
Sales to hotel guests	7,000,000		
12/31/X2 Balance	26,000		

Alternatively, the cash receipts from hotel guests could be determined as follows:

$$\text{Cash Receipts from Hotel Guests} = \text{AR Beginning Balance} + \text{Sales} - \text{AR Ending Balance}$$

$$= 30,000 + 7,000,000 - 26,000$$

$$= \$7,004,000$$

In preparing the SCF, we need to show a decrease in accounts receivable of $4,000, which is added to net income as an increase in cash to determine net cash flows from operating activities.

The change in the balances of the inventory account is an increase of $2,000. Inventory relates to the purchases and cost of goods sold (food and beverages) accounts. Remember, cost of goods sold is the cost of food and beverage inventory sold, not the cash disbursed for purchases. Therefore, we need to determine the purchases for the year as follows:

	Ending inventory	$ 12,000
+	Cost of goods sold	1,000,000
	Goods available for sale	1,012,000
−	Beginning inventory	10,000
	Purchases	$1,002,000

The $2,000 increase in inventory causes the accrual-basis cost of goods sold to be $2,000 less than purchases. By assuming that purchases is the cash amount paid for purchases, we must show a decrease in cash flows from operating activities of $2,000.

However, not all purchases were made for cash. The $500 increase in accounts payable represents the difference between purchases on account and cash paid to suppliers during 19X2. An increase in accounts payable means the amount of cash paid was less than the amount of purchases. Thus, the $500 increase in accounts payable must be added back to the accrual-basis net income to determine net cash flows from operating activities. An analysis of the accounts payable account shows this as follows:

Accounts Payable			
		1/1/X2 Balance	6,000
		Purchases	1,002,000
Payments to suppliers	1,001,500		
		12/31/X2 Balance	6,500

The increase in the accrued payroll account of $500 represents the difference between the accrual basis payroll costs of $2,450,000 and the cash payments to personnel of $2,449,500. This determination is apparent in the analysis of the accrued payroll account as follows:

Accrued Payroll			
		12/31/X1 Balance	4,000
		Payroll expense	2,450,000
Payments for payroll	2,449,500		
		12/31/X2 Balance	4,500

Since the payroll payments were $500 less than the payroll expense, the $500 increase in accrued payroll is added back to the accrual-basis net income to determine net cash flows from operations.

Finally, the decrease of $1,000 in income taxes payable represents the difference between the accrual basis income taxes of $250,000, shown on the condensed income statement of the Simple Hotel, and the $251,000 paid, as determined by the analysis of the income taxes payable account as follows:

Income Taxes Payable

		12/31/X1 Balance	7,000
Income taxes paid	251,000	Income tax expense	250,000
		12/31/X2 Balance	6,000

In reality, the $7,000 of income taxes due at the beginning of 19X1 were paid along with $244,000 of income taxes for 19X2. The remaining $6,000 of taxes for 19X2 will be paid in early 19X3. However, since income taxes paid during 19X2 exceed income tax expenses for 19X2 by $1,000, the $1,000 must be subtracted from the accrual-basis net income to determine the net cash flows from operations.

In addition to differences from year to year in the payment of income taxes, a hospitality enterprise may have deferred income taxes over several years. The details of the account for deferred income taxes are beyond the scope of this text.

The Simple Hotel's SCF's net cash flows from operating activities based on the above would reflect the following:

Net Cash Flows Provided by Operating Activities:		
Net income		$500,000
Adjustments to Reconcile Net Income to Net Cash Flows from Operating Activities:		
Depreciation expense	$500,000	
Gain on sale of investments	(100,000)	
Decrease in accounts receivable	4,000	
Increase in inventory	(2,000)	
Increase in accounts payable	500	
Increase in accrued payroll	500	
Decrease in income taxes payable	(1,000)	402,000
Net Cash Flows from Operating Activities		$902,000

In general, the rules for accounting for changes in current accounts in determining net cash flows provided by operating activities are as follows:

- A decrease in a current asset is added to net income.

- An increase in a current asset is deducted from net income.

- A decrease in a current liability is deducted from net income.

- An increase in a current liability is added to net income.

Step 2: Determining Net Cash Flows from Investing Activities

Step 2 of the four step approach to preparing an SCF focuses on investing activities. In general, attention must be directed to noncurrent assets of the Simple Hotel.

The investment account increased by $250,000. Further analysis of this account is as follows:

Investments			
12/31/X1 Balance	50,000	Sale of investments	50,000
Purchase of investments	300,000		
12/31/X2 Balance	300,000		

The analysis reveals both a sale of $50,000 of investments and a purchase of investments of $300,000. Thus, cash of $300,000 was used to purchase investments, which is a use of cash in the investing activities section of the SCF. However, further analysis of the sale of investments shows the journal entry to record this transaction as follows:

Cash	$150,000
Investments	$ 50,000
Gain on sale of investments	100,000

The entry clearly shows a cash inflow of $150,000. Thus, this source of cash should be shown as an investing activity. Notice that the cost of investments sold ($50,000) and the gain on the sale of investments ($100,000) has no impact on net cash flow from investing activities.

There were no changes in the land and building accounts, as no purchases or sales were made during 19X2. Therefore, cash was not affected.

We will look next at the equipment account. According to note #1 under other information, no equipment was disposed of during 19X2. Thus, the $100,000 difference must be due to purchases of equipment. The $100,000 of equipment is shown as a use of cash in determining net cash flows from investing activities.

The Simple Hotel's final noncurrent account is accumulated depreciation, which increased by $500,000, the exact amount of depreciation expense for the year. Because depreciation does not affect cash, under the indirect method the $500,000 is added back to the accrual-basis net income as discussed under Step 1. The change in no way affects investing activities of the Simple Hotel.

Now that the noncurrent asset accounts of the Simple Hotel have been analyzed, the investing activities section of the SCF would reflect the following:

Net Cash Flows from Investing Activities:

Proceeds from sale of investments	$ 150,000
Purchase of investments	(300,000)
Purchase of equipment	(100,000)
Net cash flow from investing activities	$(250,000)

**Step 3:
Determining
Net Cash
Flows from
Financing
Activities**

To determine the net cash flows from financing activities, we must turn our attention to the noncurrent liabilities and owners' equity accounts. First, the change in the long-term debt account is a decrease of $750,000. The analysis of the long-term debt is as follows:

Long-Term Debt (LTD)			
		12/31/X1 Balance	4,500,000
Conversion to Common Stock	250,000		
Payment of LTD	500,000		
		12/31/X2 Balance	3,750,000

The above analysis is based on notes #2 and #4 under other information. Note #4 reveals that $250,000 of LTD was converted to capital stock. This is a noncash transaction and will be shown only in a supplementary schedule to the SCF. Note #2 indicates no funds were borrowed; therefore, the remaining $500,000 reduction in LTD had to be due to payment of LTD. The $500,000 payment is a cash outflow from financing activities.

The next account to be analyzed is capital stock. The increase for 19X2 is $250,000, which is due to the exchange of capital stock for LTD, as discussed above. According to the note #4 under other information, there were no other capital stock transactions. Since this change in capital stock did not involve cash, it is not shown on the SCF. However, since it is a financing activity, it is shown on a supplementary schedule as mentioned above.

The final account to be analyzed is retained earnings. The statement of retained earnings at the bottom of the income statement reflects the detailed changes in this account as follows:

Retained Earnings			
		12/31/X1 Balance	768,000
		Net income	500,000
Dividends declared	152,000		
		12/31/X2 Balance	1,116,000

The net income has already been accounted for in the SCF as an operating activity. The declaration of $152,000 of dividends is not a cash activity by itself. For the SCF, the focus is on dividend payments, not dividend declaration. When dividends are declared, they are recorded as a reduction in retained earnings and as an increase in dividends payable, a current liability account. Therefore, to determine the amount of dividends paid during 19X2, we analyze the dividends payable account as follows:

Dividends Payable			
		12/31/X1 Balance	10,000
		Dividends declared	152,000
Dividends paid	147,000		
		12/31/X2 Balance	15,000

Effectively, the $5,000 increase in the dividends payable account results in dividends declared during 19X2 exceeding dividends paid by $5,000. The $147,000 of dividends paid is shown in the SCF as a financing activity.

The Simple Hotel's SCF financing activity section would show the following:

Net Cash Flows from Financing Activities:

Payment of long-term debt	$(500,000)
Payment of cash dividends	(147,000)
Net cash flows from financing activities	$(647,000)

Step 4: Presenting Cash Flows by Activity on the SCF

We now are ready to prepare the SCF based on the analysis in Steps 1–3. The SCF for the Simple Hotel is shown in Exhibit 4.8. The three activities show cash flows as follows:

Operating activities provided cash	$902,000
Investing activities used cash	(250,000)
Financing activities used cash	(647,000)
Total	$ 5,000

The result is a bottom line of $5,000 cash inflow. The Simple Hotel's operating activities provided large enough cash inflows to cover the outflows for investing and financing.

In the preparation of the SCF, the net increase in cash of the Simple Hotel per the SCF is added to the Simple Hotel's cash at the beginning of 19X2 to equal the cash at the end of 19X2. The $5,000 net increase in cash per the SCF equals the $5,000 increase in cash per the Simple Hotel's successive balance sheets (Exhibit 4.6). This does not *prove* that the SCF is prepared correctly; however, if the $5,000 increase per the SCF had *not* been equal to the change per the successive balance sheets, we would know that we had improperly prepared the SCF. We would then need to locate our mistake and make the correction. Thus, this is at least a partial check on the SCF's accuracy.

Further, notice the supplementary schedule to the SCF which shows the noncash exchange of capital stock of $250,000 for long-term debt and the supplementary disclosure of the amounts of interest and income taxes paid during 19X2.

Analyzing the SCF

The SCF is not analyzed in the same ways that the balance sheet and the income statement are analyzed—that is, no vertical or horizontal analysis is conducted. However, financial ratios involving various figures, such as net cash flow from operating activities, are computed. Financial ratios are the topic of Chapter 5, so no further discussion is provided at this time.

Exhibit 4.8   SCF for the Simple Hotel

Simple Hotel
Statement of Cash Flow
For the Year Ended December 31, 19X2

Net Cash Flow From Operating Activities:

Net income		$500,000
Adjustments to reconcile net income to net cash flows from operating activities:		
Depreciation	$500,000	
Gain on sale of investments	(100,000)	
Decrease in accounts receivable	4,000	
Increase in inventory	(2,000)	
Increase in accounts payable	500	
Increase in accrued payroll	500	
Decrease in income taxes payable	(1,000)	402,000
Net cash flow from operating activities		902,000
Net Cash Flow From Investing Activities:		
Sale of investments	$150,000	
Purchase of investments	(300,000)	
Purchase of equipment	(100,000)	
Net cash from investing activities		(250,000)
Net Cash Flow From Financing Activities:		
Payment of long-term debt	$(500,000)	
Dividends paid	(147,000)	
Net cash from financing activities		(647,000)
Net Increase in Cash During 19X2		5,000
Cash at the beginning of 19X2		5,000
Cash at the end of 19X2		$ 10,000

Supplementary Schedule of Noncash Financing and Investing Activities

Exchange of capital stock for long-term debt	$250,000

Supplementary Disclosure of Cash Flow Information

Cash paid during the year for:	
Interest	$400,000
Income taxes	$251,000

Exhibit 4.9   Evangel Inn Balance Sheets

Evangel Inn
Balance Sheets
December 31, 19X6 and 19X7

	19X6	19X7
Assets		
Current Assets:		
Cash	$ 20,000	$ 60,000
Marketable Securities	20,000	25,000
Accounts Receivable	90,000	115,000
Inventory	15,000	20,000
Prepaid Expenses	15,000	5,000
Total Current Assets	160,000	225,000
Investments	150,000	450,000
Property and Equipment:		
Land	450,000	450,000
Buildings	2,000,000	2,000,000
Equipment	500,000	610,000
Less: Accum. Depr.	(1,000,000)	(1,300,000)
Net Property and Equipment	1,950,000	1,760,000
Other Assets—Franchise Fees	100,000	90,000
Total Assets	$2,360,000	$2,525,000
Liabilities and Owners' Equity		
Current Liabilities:		
Accounts Payable	$ 25,000	$ 35,000
Current Maturities of Long-Term Debt	50,000	50,000
Wages Payable	15,000	15,000
Dividends Payable	20,000	15,000
Total Current Liabilities	110,000	115,000
Long-Term Debt	1,000,000	1,050,000
Owners' Equity:		
Common Stock	1,160,000	1,285,000
Retained Earnings	100,000	225,000
Less: Treasury Stock	(10,000)	(150,000)
Total Owners' Equity	1,250,000	1,360,000
Total Liabilities and Owners' Equity	$2,360,000	$2,525,000

A Comprehensive Illustration

To provide a comprehensive illustration of the preparation of an SCF with accompanying explanations, the Evangel Inn's financial statements,

Exhibit 4.10 Evangel Inn Income Statement

Evangel Inn
Condensed Income Statement
For the Year Ended 19X7

Revenues:		
Sales		$2,700,000
Interest Income		80,000
Total Revenues		2,780,000
Expenses:		
Salaries and Wages		750,000
Depreciation		340,000
Amortization (franchise fees)		10,000
Interest Expense		100,000
Other Expenses		1,140,000
Income Before Gain and Losses and Income Taxes		440,000
Gain on Sale of Equipment		20,000
Loss on Sale of Investments		(50,000)
Income Taxes		80,000
Net Income		$ 330,000

Other Information:

1. Equipment costing $100,000 was sold for $80,000 during 19X7.

2. Investments costing $100,000 were sold during 19X7 for a loss of $50,000.

3. Dividends of $205,000 were declared during 19X7.

4. Treasury stock of $140,000 was purchased during 19X7.

5. Long-term debt of $100,000 was converted to common stock during 19X7.

6. Common stock of $25,000 was sold during 19X7.

7. Long-term debt of $200,000 was borrowed during 19X7.

8. Marketable securities of $5,000 were purchased during 19X7.

as shown in Exhibits 4.9 and 4.10, will be used. The Evangel Inn's SCF for 19X7 is shown in Exhibit 4.11.

The net cash flows provided by operating activities for the Evangel Inn for 19X7 are $700,000. The explanation and/or source is as follows:

Item	Explanation and/or Source
1. Net income $330,000	From 19X7 income statement.
2. Depreciation expense $340,000	Depreciation is a noncash flow shown on the income statement. It must be added back to net income, as it was subtracted from revenues

Exhibit 4.11   Evangel Inn SCF

Evangel Inn
Statement of Cash Flows
For the Year of 19X7

Cash Flow Provided by Operating Activities:		
Net Income		$330,000
Adjustments to Reconcile Net		
Income to Net Cash Flows		
Provided by Operating Activities:		
Depreciation expense	$340,000	
Amortization expense	10,000	
Gain on sale of equipment	(20,000)	
Loss on sale of investments	50,000	
Increase in accounts receivable	(25,000)	
Increase in inventory	(5,000)	
Decrease in prepaid expenses	10,000	
Increase in accounts payable	10,000	370,000
Net Cash Flows from Operating		
Activities		700,000
Cash Flow Provided by Investing Activities:		
Proceeds from sale of equipment	$ 80,000	
Proceeds from sale of investment	50,000	
Purchase of marketable securities	(5,000)	
Purchase of equipment	(210,000)	
Purchase of investments	(400,000)	
Net Cash Flows from Investing		
Activities		(485,000)
Cash Flow Provided by Financing Activities:		
Payment of long-term debt	$ (50,000)	
Borrowing—long-term debt	200,000	
Purchase of treasury stock	(140,000)	
Proceeds from sale of common		
stock	25,000	
Payment of dividends	(210,000)	
Net Cash Flows from Financing		
Activities		(175,000)
Increase in Cash		40,000
Cash at the beginning of 19X7		20,000
Cash at the end of 19X7		$ 60,000

Supplementary Schedule of Noncash Investing and Financing Activities

Exchange of Common Stock for	
Long-Term Debt	$100,000

Supplementary Disclosures of Cash Flow Information

Cash paid during the year for:	
Interest expense	$100,000
Income taxes	$ 80,000

to determine net income. To confirm this amount, the accumulated depreciation account is analyzed as follows:

Accumulated Depreciation

		12/31/X6 Balance	1,000,000
Accumulated Depreciation written off with sale of equipment	40,000	Depreciation expense	340,000
		12/31/X7 Balance	1,300,000

3. Amortization expense $10,000

The amortization expense relates to write-off of franchise fees recorded originally as an other asset. Like depreciation, it is a non-cash expense subtracted to determine net income; therefore, it must be added back to net income to determine net cash flows provided by operating activities.

4. Gain on sale of equipment $20,000

The sale of equipment resulted in a gain of $20,000, as shown on the income statement. The $80,000 received per note #1 is shown as an investing activity. The gain shown on the income statement is not a cash figure, so the $20,000 must be subtracted from net income in the SCF.

5. Loss on sale of investments $50,000

The loss on the sale of investments is shown as an investing activity. The loss shown is not a cash figure, so the $50,000 must be added to net income in the SCF.

6. Changes in current assets and liabilities: Increase in accounts receivable $25,000; increase in inventory $5,000; decrease in prepaid expenses $10,000; increase in accounts payable $10,000.

The changes in the current accounts are added or subtracted from net income as follows:

1) *increases* in current assets and *decreases* in current liabilities are *subtracted*;

2) *decreases* in current assets and *increases* in current liabilities are *added*. The marketable securities current asset accounts, current maturities of long-term debt, and dividends payable are considered in preparing the investing and financing activity sections of the SCF, as these accounts do not relate to operating activities.

The investing activities section of the SCF relates to investment and property and equipment for the Evangel Inn. The activity to be shown in the SCF relates to investment and equipment transactions as follows:

Item	Discussion
1. Proceeds from sale of equipment	According to note #1, equipment was sold for $80,000.
2. Purchase of equipment	The equipment account, as shown on the successive balance sheets for 19X6 and 19X7, shows a $110,000 increase in 19X7. However, since equipment costing $100,000 was sold during 19X7, then $210,000 was purchased in 19X7. Analysis of the equipment account below supports this conclusion.

Equipment

Balance 12/31/X6	500,000	Cost of equipment sold	100,000
Purchases during 19X7	210,000		
Balance 12/31/X7	610,000		

Item	Discussion
3. Proceeds from sale of investments $50,000	According to note #2, $100,000 of investments were sold at a loss of $50,000. Therefore, the proceeds are determined by subtracting the loss from the cost as follows:

Cost of investments sold	$100,000
Loss on sale of investments	(50,000)
Proceeds from sale	$ 50,000

Item	Discussion
4. Purchase of investments $400,000	Investments, according to the 19X6 and 19X7 balance sheets, increased by $300,000; however, during 19X7, $100,000 of investments were sold. Thus, purchases were $400,000, based on the analysis of the investment account as follows:

Investments

Balance 12/31/X6	150,000		
Purchase of investments	400,000	Sale of investments	100,000
Balance 12/31/X7	450,000		

Item	Discussion
5. Purchase of marketable securities	According to note #8, marketable securities of $5,000 were purchased in 19X7.

The financing activities of the Evangel Inn during 19X7 resulted in a net cash outflow of $175,000, as well as the noncash exchange of $100,000 of Evangel's common stock for long-term debt as shown on the Supplementary Schedule of Noncash Investing and Financing Activities at the bottom of Exhibit 4.11. The individual sources and uses of cash flows in the financing activities section of the Evangel Inn's SCF are explained as follows:

Item	Discussion
1. Payment of long-term debt $50,000	The payment of debt is determined by analyzing both the LTD and current maturities of LTD accounts as follows:

Current Maturities of LTD

		12/31/X6 Balance	50,000
Payment of LTD	50,000	Reclassification of LTD	50,000
		12/31/X7 Balance	50,000

Long-Term Debt

		12/31/X6 Balance	1,000,000
Reclassification of LTD	50,000	Borrowing during 19X7	200,000
Converted to common stock	100,000		
		12/31/X7 Balance	1,050,000

The current maturities of LTD account showed $50,000 payable on December 31, 19X6. By definition, current liabilities must be paid within one year; therefore, we can safely assume that the $50,000 balance at December 31, 19X6, was paid in 19X7. The balance at the end of 19X7 is a $50,000 reclassification of LTD which occurred during 19X7. In other words, the $50,000 of LTD due in 19X8 is shown as current maturities of LTD on December 31, 19X7.

Item	Discussion
2. Borrowed long-term debt $200,000	Note #7 reports $200,000 was borrowed during 19X7. The analysis of the long-term debt above confirms the $200,000 of new debt.
3. Purchase of treasury stock $140,000	The analysis of the treasury stock account confirms the purchase, according to note #4, of $140,000 as follows:

Treasury Stock

	12/31/X6 Balance	10,000
	Purchase	140,000
	12/31/X7 Balance	150,000

Item	Discussion
4. Proceeds from sale of common stock $25,000	Note #6 reveals $25,000 of common stock was sold during 19X7. This is confirmed by analyzing the common stock account as follows:

Common Stock

		12/31/X6 Balance	1,160,000
		Issued to retire LTD	100,000
		Issued for cash	25,000
		12/31/X7 Balance	1,285,000

The $100,000 of common stock issued for debt is a noncash transaction and is reported on the Schedule of Noncash Investing and Financing Activities shown at the bottom of Exhibit 4.11.

5. Payment of dividends $210,000

During 19X7, $205,000 of dividends were declared; however, for SCF purposes, the $210,000 amount paid must be determined and shown. Analysis of the dividends payable account reveals that $210,000 was paid as follows:

Dividends Payable

		12/31/X6 Balance	20,000
		Dividends declared	205,000
Dividends paid	210,000		
		12/31/X7 Balance	15,000

In essence, the dividends declared in 19X6 and payable at the end of 19X6 of $20,000 were paid in 19X7. In addition, $190,000 of the $205,000 of dividends declared in 19X7 were paid in 19X7, leaving $15,000 dividends to be paid in 19X8 and shown as a current liability on Evangel Inn's balance sheet at the end of 19X7.

Thus, the net total of cash flows for operating, investing, and financing activities for the Evangel Inn for 19X7 is $40,000, which equals the increase in cash of $40,000 as reflected on the Evangel Inn's 19X6 and 19X7 balance sheets.

Interpreting the Results

The Evangel Inn's SCF lends insight to the user as follows:

- While net income increased by $330,000, cash flows from operations increased by $700,000. The major difference as shown on the SCF is depreciation expense of $340,000.

- Cash flows from operations were sufficient to allow the Evangel Inn to (1) use $485,000 in net investing activities, (2) use $175,000 in net financing activities, and (3) provide an increase in cash of $40,000 during 19X7.

- In addition, noncash activities occurred in the noncash exchange of $100,000 of common stock for $100,000 of long-term debt.

Summary

The SCF is an FASB-mandated financial statement that must be issued with other financial statements released to external users. It reflects the inflow and outflow of cash for a period of time.

The SCF must show operating, investing, and financing activities. Operating activities reflect cash flows as they relate to revenues and expenses. Investing activities relate to changes in marketable securities and noncurrent asset accounts. Commonly included in these activities are the purchase and sale of property and equipment. Financing activities relate to changes in dividends payable, current maturities of long-term debt, long-term debt, and equity accounts. The sale of common stock and payment of long-term debt are two examples of financing activities. The net sum of the three activities shown on the SCF must equal the change in the cash amount shown on the two successive balance sheets.

There are two basic approaches to preparing the SCF—the direct and indirect methods. The difference between the two approaches is reflected only in the operating activities section of the SCF. The indirect approach starts with net income and includes various adjustments made to determine net income which did not affect cash. Other adjustments for the indirect approach are the changes in current accounts related to operations. The direct approach shows the direct sources of cash, such as cash receipts from sales, and direct uses of cash, such as disbursements for payroll. Most hospitality firms use the indirect approach because it is easier to prepare.

Key Terms

accrual basis	direct method
cash equivalents	indirect method
cash inflows	statement of cash flows
cash outflows	

Discussion Questions

1. What is the major purpose of the SCF?

2. How do different users of the SCF use this statement?

3. What are the three major classifications of cash flows in the SCF?

4. What are the two alternative approaches to preparing the SCF?

5. How do the two methods of preparing the SCF differ?

6. What supplementary information must be provided when the indirect approach is used in preparing the SCF?

7. How are changes in the various current balance sheet accounts shown on an SCF prepared using the indirect approach?

8. Where is the $10,000 loss on the sale of an investment shown on the SCF prepared using the indirect approach?

9. How does the sum of the cash flows from the three major classifications on the SCF relate to the change in balance sheet accounts from two successive balance sheets?

10. How is the exchange of common stock for long-term debt shown on the SCF?

Problems

Problem 4.1

The Spartan Corporation has engaged in several transactions listed below:

1. Sold food and beverages for cash
2. Purchased investments
3. Exchanged its common stock for long-term bonds
4. Sold common stock
5. Issued a stock dividend
6. Paid salaries and wages
7. Sold investments at a loss
8. Paid a cash dividend
9. Purchased a 60-day treasury bill
10. Sold land for a gain
11. Paid interest
12. Received dividends from an investment
13. Paid for food and beverage supplies
14. Paid long-term debt
15. Purchased equipment

Required:

Identify each transaction as (1) an operating activity, (2) an investing activity, (3) a financing activity, (4) a noncash transaction, or (5) none of the above.

Problem 4.2

The Eppley Hotel has incurred various activities as described in each situation below:

1. During 19X3, the Eppley Hotel had cash sales of $800,000 and sales on account of $2,540,000. During the same year, accounts receivable—hotel guests increased by $10,000. Determine the cash received from hotel guests during 19X3.

2. During 19X3, the Eppley Hotel's Board of Directors declared cash dividends of $120,000. The dividends payable account was $10,000 at the beginning of the year and $15,000 at the end of the year. Determine the dividends paid by the Eppley Hotel during 19X3.

3. During 19X3, the Eppley Hotel had cost of food used of $400,000. During the year, food inventory increased by $8,000 and the related suppliers payable accounts decreased by $5,000. Determine the cash payments for food purchases during 19X3.

4. During the year, the Eppley Hotel's long-term debt of $1,000,000 on January 1, 19X3, increased by $500,000 to $1,500,000 on December 31, 19X3. Also during 19X3, $200,000 of long-term debt was converted to common stock, and $50,000 of long-term debt was reclassified as current debt. Determine the amount of cash that was borrowed and recorded as long-term debt during 19X3.

5. The Eppley Hotel's income tax expense for 19X3 was $25,000. Its income taxes payable account on the balance sheet was $4,000 at the beginning of the year and $5,000 at the end of the year. Determine the amount of income taxes paid during 19X3.

Problem 4.3

During 19X4, the Kellogg Inn had net income of $50,000. Included on its income statement for 19X4 was depreciation expense of $100,000 and amortization expense of $5,000. Current accounts changed during 19X4 as follows:

Cash	$ 5,000	increase
Marketable securities	30,000	decrease
Accounts receivable	10,000	increase
Inventory	5,000	decrease
Prepaid expenses	4,000	increase
Accounts payable	10,000	increase
Accrued payroll	2,000	increase
Income taxes payable	3,000	decrease
Dividends payable	5,000	decrease

In addition, sales of equipment, marketable securities, and investments during 19X4 were as follows:

1. Equipment costing $100,000 with accumulated depreciation of $80,000 was sold for $25,000.

2. Investments which cost $150,000 were sold for $200,000.

3. Marketable securities of $30,000 were sold for $25,000.

Required:
Prepare the schedule of cash flows from operating activities using the indirect method.

Problem 4.4

The Owen Resort had several transactions as shown below. In the columns to the right, describe the type of activity for each transaction and what amount (if any) would be shown on the SCF prepared according to the indirect method. (For example, the payment of utilities is not shown on the SCF because it is subtracted from sales to determine net income which is shown on the SCF.)

Transaction			Type of Activity	Amount Shown on SCF
1. Cash	$125,000			
Common stock		$100,000		
Paid-in capital in excess of par		25,000	_____	_____
2. Cash	$ 25,000			
Accum. Depr.	60,000			
Equipment		$ 80,000		
Gain on sale of equipment		5,000	_____	_____
3. Cash	$125,000			
Treasury stock		$100,000		
Retained earnings		25,000	_____	_____
4. Notes payable	$ 75,000			
Common stock		$ 60,000		
Paid-in capital in excess of par		15,000	_____	_____
5. Notes payable	$100,000			
Interest expense	20,000			
Cash		$120,000	_____	_____
6. Cash	$ 10,000			
Accounts Receivable	30,000			
Sales		$ 40,000	_____	_____
7. Salaries and wages	$ 20,000			
Cash		$ 20,000	_____	_____
8. Cash	$ 5,000			
Dividend income		$ 5,000	_____	_____
9. Cash	$ 40,000			
Loss on sale of investments	10,000			
Investments		$ 50,000	_____	_____
10. Equipment	$ 15,000			
Notes payable		$ 15,000	_____	_____

Problem 4.5

You have been hired by D. Smith, a successful entrepreneur, to prepare a statement of cash flows for his two-year-old hotel, the Illini Inn. The following are copies of the condensed balance sheets and the income statement of the Illini Inn.

Illini Inn
Condensed Balance Sheets
December 31, 19X1 and 19X2

	19X1	19X2
Cash	$ 30,000	$ 40,000
Accounts Receivable	190,000	225,000
Inventory	30,000	35,000
Property and Equipment (net)	1,400,000	1,500,000
Other Assets (Pre-opening Expenses)	200,000	100,000
Total Assets	$1,850,000	$1,900,000

Accounts Payable	$ 140,000	$ 185,000
Wages Payable	10,000	15,000
Current Maturities–LTD	50,000	50,000
Long-Term Debt	1,000,000	950,000
Total Liabilities	1,200,000	1,200,000
Owners' Equity	650,000	700,000
Total Liabilities and Owners' Equity	$1,850,000	$1,900,000

Illini Inn
Condensed Income Statement
For the year ended December 31, 19X2

Sales	$1,600,000
Cost of Goods Sold	200,000
Contribution Margin	1,400,000
Undistributed Operating Expenses	950,000
Income Before Fixed Charges	450,000
Depreciation Expense	200,000
Amortization of Pre-opening Expenses	100,000
Income Before Tax	150,000
Income Tax	50,000
Net Income	$ 100,000

Additional Information:

1. Equipment was purchased for $300,000.

2. Dividends of $50,000 were declared and paid during 19X2.

3. Long-term debt of $50,000 was reclassified as current at the end of 19X2.

Required:

Prepare the SCF, with supplementary disclosures, for the Illini Inn using the indirect method.

Problem 4.6

The operations of The Freida, a small lodging operation, are becoming more complex. Ms. Martin, the owner, has asked for your help in preparing her statement of cash flows. She is able to present you with condensed balance sheets and some additional information.

The Freida
Condensed Balance Sheets
December 31, 19X1 and 19X2

	19X1	19X2
Cash	$ 10,000	$ 6,000
Accounts Receivable	26,500	25,500
Investments	10,000	5,000
Equipment	200,000	325,000
Accumulated Depreciation	(20,000)	(40,000)
Total Assets	$226,500	$321,500

Current Liabilities:		
Accounts Payable	$ 18,000	$ 21,000
Mortgage Payable (current)	5,000	5,000
Dividends Payable	5,000	5,000
Noncurrent Liabilities:		
Mortgage Payable	75,000	70,000
Notes Payable	–0–	40,000
Common Stock	50,000	100,000
Retained Earnings	73,500	80,500
Total Liabilities and Owners' Equity	$226,500	$321,500

Additional Information:

1. Equipment costing $20,000, depreciated to one half its cost, was sold for $8,000.

2. Common stock, purchased as a long-term investment for $5,000, was sold for $8,000.

3. Dividends declared during 19X2 totaled $7,000.

4. Equipment costing $145,000 was purchased during 19X2.

5. Depreciation expense for 19X2 totaled $30,000.

6. Long-term debt of $5,000 was reclassified as current at the end of 19X2.

7. Common stock of $50,000 was sold and long-term debt of $40,000 (note payable) was borrowed during 19X2.

8. The Freida generated net income of $14,000 during 19X2.

Required:

Prepare the SCF as requested by Ms. Martin using the indirect method.

Problem 4.7

The condensed balance sheets of the Spartan Inn are as follows:

Spartan Inn
Condensed Balance Sheets
December 31, 19X1 and 19X2

	19X1	19X2
Assets		
Current Assets:		
Cash	$ 30,000	$ 40,000
Marketable Securities	50,000	50,000
Accounts Receivable	100,000	95,000
Inventory	20,000	25,000
Total Current Assets	200,000	210,000

Property and Equipment:		
Land	500,000	500,000
Building	5,000,000	6,000,000
Equipment	1,000,000	1,100,000
Accumulated Depreciation	(1,600,000)	(2,000,000)
Net Property and Equipment	4,900,000	5,600,000
Investments	100,000	60,000
Total Assets	$5,000,000	$5,670,000

Liabilities and Owners' Equity

Current Liabilities:		
Accounts Payable	$ 60,000	$ 70,000
Dividends Payable	30,000	50,000
Current Portion of LTD	100,000	130,000
Total	190,000	250,000
Long-Term Debt	4,000,000	4,370,000
Capital Stock	500,000	500,000
Retained Earnings	310,000	550,000
Total Liabilities and Owners' Equity	$5,000,000	$5,670,000

Spartan Inn
Condensed Income Statement
For the year ended December 31, 19X2

Sales	$6,000,000
Cost of Sales	1,000,000
Gross Profit	5,000,000
Depreciation	400,000
Other Expenses (except depreciation)	4,500,000
Net Operating Income	100,000
Gain on Sales of Investments	300,000
Income Taxes	110,000
Net Income	$ 290,000

Additional Information:

1. Dividends declared during 19X2 totaled $50,000.

2. No investments were purchased during 19X2.

3. The current portion of long-term debt at the end of 19X2 was reclassified from noncurrent during 19X2.

4. No equipment or buildings were sold during 19X2.

5. Long-term debt was borrowed to partially finance the building purchase.

Required:

Prepare the Spartan Inn's SCF for 19X2 using the indirect method.

Problem 4.8

Below are the Badger Motel's balance sheets for the years ended December 31, 19X1 and 19X2, and the abbreviated income statements for 19X1 and 19X2.

Badger Motel
Balance Sheets
December 31, 19X1 and 19X2

	19X1	19X2
Current Assets:		
Cash	$ 10,000	$ 15,000
Accounts Receivable (net)	25,000	25,000
Marketable Securities	15,000	15,000
Inventory	8,000	10,000
Total Current Assets	58,000	65,000
Investments	60,000	50,000
Property and Equipment:		
Land	50,000	105,000
Buildings	1,000,000	1,000,000
Equipment	100,000	120,000
Less: Accum. Depreciation	(470,000)	(525,000)
Net Property and Equipment	630,000	700,000
Total Assets	$ 798,000	$ 815,000
Current Liabilities:		
Accounts Payable	$ 12,000	$ 8,000
Current Maturities of LTD	14,000	5,000
Dividends Payable	10,000	7,000
Total Current Liabilities	36,000	20,000
Long-Term Debt	200,000	205,000
Owners' Equity:		
Capital Stock	100,000	100,000
Retained Earnings	462,000	490,000
Total Liabilities and Owners' Equity	$ 798,000	$ 815,000

Badger Motel
Condensed Income Statements
For the years ended December 31, 19X1 and 19X2

	19X1	19X2
Department Income	$1,800,000	$2,000,000
Unallocable Expenses (except depr.)	1,695,000	1,850,000
Depreciation	50,000	61,000
Net Operating Income*	$ 55,000	$ 89,000

*Prior to any gains or losses from sale of investments and equipment and income taxes.

Additional Information:

1. Equipment costing $10,000, with a net book value of $4,000, was sold for a gain of $2,000 during 19X2.

2. Investments costing $10,000 were sold for $5,000 during 19X2.

3. Dividends of $36,500 were declared during 19X2.

4. The Badger Motel is subject to income taxes at 25% of pretax income.

5. The only items affecting retained earnings were net income and dividends declared.

6. The $5,000 of current maturities of LTD was reclassified from long-term debt during 19X2.

Required:

Prepare an SCF for the Badger Motel for 19X2 using the indirect method. Provide any supplementary schedules.

Problem 4.9

Below are the Hoosier Hotel's balance sheets for the years ended December 31, 19X1 and 19X2, and the abbreviated income statements for 19X1 and 19X2.

Hoosier Hotel
Balance Sheets
December 31, 19X1 and 19X2

	19X1	19X2
Current Assets:		
Cash	$ 10,000	$ 15,000
Accounts Receivable (net)	25,000	25,000
Marketable Securities	15,000	15,000
Inventory	8,000	10,000
Total Current Assets	58,000	65,000
Investments	60,000	50,000
Property and Equipment:		
Land	50,000	80,000
Buildings	1,000,000	1,000,000
Equipment	110,000	120,000
Less Accumulated Depreciation	(480,000)	(525,000)
Net Property and Equipment	620,000	675,000
Total Assets	$ 798,000	$ 790,000

Current Liabilities:		
Accounts Payable	$ 12,000	$ 8,000
Current Maturities of LTD	14,000	12,000
Dividends Payable	10,000	-0-
Total Current Liabilities	36,000	20,000
Long-Term Debt	200,000	150,000
Owners' Equity:		
Capital Stock	100,000	130,000
Retained Earnings	462,000	490,000
Total Liabilities and Owners' Equity	$ 798,000	$ 790,000

Hoosier Hotel
Condensed Income Statements
For the years ended December 31, 19X1 and 19X2

	19X1	19X2
Departmental Income	$1,800,000	$2,000,000
Unallocable Expenses Except Depr.	1,695,000	1,900,000
Depreciation	50,000	55,000
Gain from Sale of Investments	-0-	5,000
Loss from Sale of Equipment	5,000	4,000
Income Taxes	12,500	11,500
Net Income	$ 37,500	$ 34,500

Additional Information:

1. Equipment costing $30,000 with a net book value of $20,000 was sold for $16,000 during 19X2.

2. Investments costing $10,000 were sold for $15,000 during 19X2.

3. Dividends declared during 19X2 totaled $6,500.

4. Capital stock of $20,000 was retired for $20,000 during 19X2.

5. The only items affecting retained earnings were net income and dividends declared.

6. During 19X2, $50,000 of LTD was converted to capital stock.

7. Also during 19X2, the Hoosier Hotel partially financed the equipment purchase with a long-term loan of $12,000.

Required:

Prepare an SCF for the Hoosier Hotel for 19X2 using the indirect method.

Problem 4.10

The Hawkeye Hotel's balance sheet for December 31, 19X5, is provided below.

Hawkeye Hotel
Balance Sheet
December 31, 19X5

Current Assets		
Cash		$ 12,540
Marketable Securities		100,000
Accounts Receivable		73,811
F&B Inventory		10,833
Prepaid Insurance		4,318
Total Current Assets		201,502
Property and Equipment, at Cost		
Land		262,000
Building		1,572,805
Equipment		213,843
		2,048,648
Less Accumulated Depreciation		303,227
		1,745,421
Total Assets		$1,946,923
Current Liabilities		
Notes Payable		$ –0–
Mortgage Payable – Current		50,000
Accounts Payable		18,776
Accrued Wages		6,843
Total Current Liabilities		75,619
Long-Term Liabilities		
Mortgage Payable		950,695
Owners' Equity		
Common Stock, No Par, Authorized 100,000		
Shares, Issued 75,000 Shares		750,000
Retained Earnings		170,609
Total Liabilities and Owners' Equity		$1,946,923

The Hawkeye Hotel's general ledger as of December 31, 19X6, contained the following accounts:

	DR.	CR.
Cash	$ 19,278	
Accounts receivable	75,000	
Allowance for doubtful accounts		$ 1,211
Food inventory	7,800	
Beverage inventory	4,136	

Prepaid insurance	4,667	
Land	262,000	
Building	1,927,817	
Equipment	241,470	
Accumulated depreciation		411,137
Accounts payable		6,821
Accrued wages		7,953
Notes payable		25,000
Mortgage payable (current)		50,000
Mortgage payable (long-term)		1,105,399
Common stock		750,000
Retained earnings		107,109
Room revenues		1,349,866
Food and beverage revenues		753,722
Telephone revenues		73,936
Other sales		1,006
Interest income		785
Rooms expenses:		
Labor	450,000	
Other	115,037	
Food and beverage expenses:		
Cost of sales	225,000	
Labor	250,000	
Other	149,161	
Telephone expenses:		
Cost of calls	52,470	
Labor	22,000	
Other	2,000	
Administrative & general:		
Labor	100,000	
Other	150,677	
Marketing expense	45,000	
Property operation & maintenance:		
Labor	42,000	
Other	10,000	
Utilities	57,478	
Property taxes	80,000	
Fire insurance expense	31,462	
Interest expense	161,087	
Depreciation expense	110,225	
Gain on sale of equipment		3,000
Income taxes	51,180	
Total	$4,646,945	$4,646,945

Additional information:

1. Equipment costing $6,750 with accumulated depreciation of $2,315 was sold for $7,435.

2. The mortgage payable—current balance of $50,000 at the end of 19X6 was reclassified from noncurrent liabilities during 19X6.

3. An addition to the building during 19X6 cost $355,012.

4. Equipment purchases during 19X6 totaled $34,377.

5. Dividends paid during 19X6 totaled $63,500.

<u>Required:</u>

1. Prepare a comparative balance sheet for the Hawkeye Hotel.
2. Prepare the Hawkeye Hotel's income statement for 19X6 in accordance with the *USASH*.
3. Prepare the SCF for the Hawkeye Hotel for 19X6 using the indirect approach.

5 Ratio Analysis

Financial statements issued by hospitality establishments contain a lot of financial information. A thorough analysis of this information requires more than simply reading the reported facts. Users of financial statements need to be able to interpret the reported facts to discover aspects of the hospitality property's financial situation that could otherwise go unnoticed. This is accomplished through **ratio analysis**, which is the comparison of related facts and figures, most of which appear on the financial statements. A ratio gives mathematical expression to a relationship between two figures and is computed by dividing one figure by the other figure. By bringing the two figures into relation with each other, ratios generate new information. In this way, ratio analysis goes beyond the figures reported in a financial statement and makes them more meaningful, more informative, and more useful. In particular, ratio analysis generates indicators for evaluating different aspects of a financial situation.

Ratio analysis can provide users of financial statements with answers to such questions as:

1. Is there sufficient cash to meet the establishment's obligations for a given time period?

2. Are the profits of the hospitality operation reasonable?

3. Is the level of debt acceptable in comparison with the stockholders' investment?

4. Is the inventory usage adequate?

5. How do the operation's earnings compare with the market price of the hospitality property's stock?

6. Are accounts receivable reasonable in light of credit sales?

7. Is the hospitality establishment able to service its debt?

In this chapter, we will first explain the different kinds of standards against which ratios are compared in order to evaluate the financial condition of a hospitality operation. We will also discuss the variety of functions or purposes that ratio analysis serves in interpreting financial statements and the ways in which different ratios are expressed in order to make sense of the information they provide. Most of this chapter then is devoted to a detailed discussion of the ratios most commonly used in the hospitality industry.

Ratio Standards

Ratio analysis is used to evaluate the favorableness or unfavorableness of various financial conditions. However, the computed ratios alone do not say anything about what is good or bad, acceptable or unacceptable, reasonable or unreasonable. By themselves, ratios are neutral and simply express numerical relationships between related figures. In order to be useful as indicators or measurements of the success or well-being of a hospitality operation, the computed ratios must be compared against some standard. Only then will the ratios become meaningful and provide users of financial statements with a basis for evaluating the financial conditions.

There are basically three different standards that are used to evaluate the ratios computed for a given operation for a given period: ratios from a past period, industry averages, and budgeted ratios. Many ratios can be compared with corresponding ratios calculated for the prior period in order to discover any significant changes. For example, paid occupancy percentage (discussed briefly in Chapter 1 and more fully later in this chapter) for the current year may be compared with paid occupancy percentage of the prior year in order to determine whether the lodging operation is succeeding in selling more of its available rooms this year than it had previously. This comparison may be useful in evaluating the effectiveness of the property's current marketing plans.

Industry averages provide another useful standard against which to compare ratios. After calculating the return on investment (discussed later in this chapter) for a given property, investors may want to compare this with the average return for similar properties in their particular industry segment. This may give investors an indication of the ability of the property's management to use resources effectively to generate profits for the owners in comparison with other operations in the industry. In addition, managers may want to compare the paid occupancy percentage or food cost percentage for their own operation with industry averages in order to evaluate their abilities to compete with other operations in their industry segment. Published sources of average industry ratios are readily available.

While ratios can be compared against results of a prior period and against industry averages, ratios are best compared against planned ratio goals. For example, in order to more effectively control the cost of labor, management may project a goal for the current year's labor cost percentage (also discussed in this chapter) that is slightly lower than the previous year's levels. The expectation of a lower labor cost percentage may reflect management's efforts to improve scheduling procedures and other factors related to the cost of labor. By comparing the actual labor cost percentage with the planned goal, management is able to assess the success of its efforts to control labor cost.

Different evaluations may result from comparing ratios against these different standards. For example, a food cost of 33% for the current period may compare favorably with the prior year's ratio of 34% and with an industry average of 36%, but may be judged unfavorably when compared with the operation's planned goal of 32%. Therefore, care must be taken when evaluating the results of operations using ratio analysis. It is necessary to keep in mind not only which standards are being used to evaluate the ratios, but the purposes of the ratio analysis as well.

Purposes of Ratio Analysis

Managers, creditors, and investors often have different purposes in using ratio analysis to evaluate the information reported in financial statements.

Ratios help managers monitor the operating performances of their operations and evaluate their success in meeting a variety of goals. By tracking a limited number of ratios, hospitality managers are able to maintain a fairly accurate perception of the effectiveness and efficiency of their operations. In a food service operation, most managers compute food cost percentage and labor cost percentage in order to monitor the two largest expenses of their operations. In lodging operations, occupancy percentage is one of the key ratios that managers use on a daily basis. Management often uses ratios to express operational goals. For example, management may establish ratio goals as follows:

- Maintain a 1.25 to 1 current ratio.
- Debt/equity ratio is not to exceed 1 to 1.
- Maintain return on owners' equity of 15%.
- Maintain fixed asset turnover of 1.2 times.

These ratios, and many more, will be fully explained later in this chapter. The point here is to notice that ratios are particularly useful to managers as indicators of how well goals are being achieved. When actual results fall short of goals, ratios help indicate where a problem may be. In the food cost percentage example presented earlier in which an actual ratio of 33% compared unfavorably against the planned 32%, additional research is required to determine the cause(s) of the 1% variation. This 1% difference may be due to cost differences, sales mix differences, or a combination of the two. Only additional analysis will determine the actual cause(s). Ratio analysis can contribute significant information to such an investigation.

Creditors use ratio analysis to evaluate the solvency of hospitality operations and to assess the riskiness of future loans. For example, the relationship of current assets to current liabilities, referred to as the current ratio, may indicate an establishment's ability to pay its upcoming bills. In addition, creditors sometimes use ratios to express requirements for hospitality operations as part of the conditions set forth for certain financial arrangements. For example, as a condition of a loan, a creditor may require an operation to maintain a current ratio of 2 to 1.

Investors and potential investors use ratios to evaluate the performance of a hospitality operation. For example, the dividend payout ratio (dividends paid divided by earnings) indicates the percentage of earnings paid out by the hospitality establishment. Potential investors primarily interested in stock growth may shy away from investing in properties that pay out large dividends.

Ratios are used to communicate financial performance. Different ratios communicate different results. Individually, ratios reveal only part of the overall financial condition of an operation. Collectively, however, ratios are able to communicate a great deal of information that may not be immediately apparent from simply reading the figures reported in financial statements.

What Ratios Express

In order to understand the information communicated by the different kinds of ratios used in ratio analysis, it is necessary to understand the various ways in which ratios express financial information. Different ratios are read in different ways. For example, many ratios are expressed as *percentages*. An illustration is the food cost percentage, which expresses the cost of food sold in terms of a percentage of total food sales. If total food sales for a given year is $430,000, while the cost of food sold is $135,000, then the result of dividing the cost of food sold by the total food sales is .314. Because the food cost percentage is a ratio expressed as a percentage, this figure is multiplied by 100 to yield a 31.4% food cost. Another example is paid occupancy percentage, resulting from rooms sold divided by rooms available for sale. If a lodging property has 100 rooms available for sale and sells only 50 of them, then 50 divided by 100 yields .5, which is then multiplied by 100 to be expressed as a percentage (50%).

Some other ratios are expressed on a *per unit basis*. For example, the average breakfast check is a ratio expressed as a certain sum per breakfast served. It is calculated by dividing the total breakfast sales by the number of guests served during the breakfast period. Thus, on a given day, if 100 guests were served breakfast and the total revenue during the breakfast period amounted to $490, then the average breakfast check would be $4.90 per meal ($490 ÷ 100).

The proper way to express still other ratios is as a *turnover* of so many times. Seat turnover is one such ratio, determined by dividing the number of guests served during a given period by the number of restaurant seats. If the restaurant in the previous example had a seating capacity of 40 seats, then seat turnover for the breakfast period in which it served 100 guests would be 2.5 (100 ÷ 40). This means that, during that breakfast period, the restaurant used its entire seating capacity 2.5 times.

Finally, some ratios are expressed as a *coverage* of so many times. The denominator of such a ratio is always set at 1. The current ratio, determined by dividing current assets by current liabilities, is one of the ratios expressed as a coverage of so many times. For example, if a hospitality operation reported current assets of $120,000 and current liabilities of $100,000 for a given period, then the operation's current ratio at the balance sheet date would be 1.2 to 1 (120,000 ÷ 100,000). This means that the hospitality operation possessed sufficient current assets to cover its current liabilities 1.2 times. Put another way, for every $1 of current liabilities, the operation had $1.20 of current assets.

The proper way to express the various ratios used in ratio analysis depends entirely on the particular ratio and the nature of the significant relationship it expresses between the two facts it relates. The ways in which different ratios are expressed are a function of how we use the information that they provide. As we discuss the ratios commonly used in the hospitality industry, pay attention to how each is expressed.

Classes of Ratios

Ratios are generally classified by the type of information which they provide. Five common ratio groupings are as follows:

1. Liquidity
2. Solvency
3. Activity
4. Profitability
5. Operating

Liquidity ratios reveal the ability of a hospitality establishment to meet its short-term obligations. **Solvency ratios**, on the other hand, measure the extent to which the enterprise has been financed by debt and is able to meet its long-term obligations. **Activity ratios** reflect management's ability to use the property's assets, while several **profitability ratios** show management's overall effectiveness as measured by returns on sales and investments. Finally, **operating ratios** assist in the analysis of hospitality establishment operations.

The classification of certain ratios may vary. For example, some texts classify the inventory turnover ratio as a liquidity ratio, but this text and some others consider it to be an activity ratio. Also, profit margin could be classified as an operating ratio, but it is generally included with the profitability ratios.

Knowing the meaning of a ratio and how it is used is always more important than knowing its classification. We will now turn to an in-depth discussion of individual ratios. For each ratio discussed, we will consider its purpose, the formula by which it is calculated, the sources of data needed for the ratio's calculation, and the interpretation of ratio results from the varying viewpoints of owners, creditors, and management.

Exhibits 5.1 through 5.4, financial statements of the hypothetical Grand Hotel, will be used throughout our discussion of individual ratios.

Liquidity Ratios

The ability of a hospitality establishment to meet its current obligations is important in evaluating its financial position. For example, can the Grand Hotel meet its current debt of $214,000 as it becomes due? Several ratios can be computed that suggest answers to this question.

Exhibit 5.1   Balance Sheets

Balance Sheets
Grand Hotel
December 31, 19X0, 19X1, 19X2

ASSETS	19X0	19X1	19X2
Current Assets:			
Cash	$ 20,000	$ 21,000	$ 24,000
Marketable Securities	60,000	81,000	145,000
Accounts Receivable (net)	100,000	90,000	140,000
Inventories	14,000	17,000	15,000
Prepaid Expenses	13,000	12,000	14,000
Total Current Assets	207,000	221,000	338,000
Investments	43,000	35,000	40,000
Property and Equipment:			
Land	68,500	68,500	68,500
Buildings	810,000	850,000	880,000
Furniture and Equipment	170,000	190,000	208,000
	1,048,500	1,108,500	1,156,500
Less: Accumulated Depreciation	260,000	320,000	381,000
China, glassware, silver, linen, and uniforms	11,500	20,500	22,800
Total Property and Equipment	800,000	809,000	798,300
Total Assets	$1,050,000	$1,065,000	$1,176,300
LIABILITIES AND OWNERS' EQUITY			
Current Liabilities:			
Accounts Payable	$ 60,000	$ 53,500	$ 71,000
Accrued Income Taxes	30,000	32,000	34,000
Accrued Expenses	70,000	85,200	85,000
Current Portion of Long-Term Debt	25,000	21,500	24,000
Total Current Liabilities	185,000	192,200	214,000
Long-Term Debt:			
Mortgage Payable	425,000	410,000	400,000
Deferred Income Taxes	40,000	42,800	45,000
Total Long-Term Debt	465,000	452,800	445,000
Total Liabilities	650,000	645,000	659,000
Owners' Equity:			
Common Stock	55,000	55,000	55,000
Paid-in Capital in Excess of Par	110,000	110,000	110,000
Retained Earnings	235,000	255,000	352,300
Total Owners' Equity	400,000	420,000	517,300
Total Liabilities and Owners' Equity	$1,050,000	$1,065,000	$1,176,300

Exhibit 5.2   Income Statements

Income Statements		
Grand Hotel		
For the years ended December 31, 19X1 and 19X2		
	19X1	**19X2**
Total Revenue	$1,300,000	$1,352,000
Rooms:		
Revenue	$ 780,000	$ 810,000
Payroll and related costs	135,000	145,000
Other Direct Expenses	62,500	60,000
Departmental Income	582,500	605,000
Food and Beverages:		
Revenue	430,000	445,000
Cost of sales	142,000	148,000
Payroll and related costs	175,000	180,000
Other Direct Expenses	43,400	45,000
Departmental Income	69,600	72,000
Telephone:		
Revenue	40,000	42,000
Cost of sales	30,000	31,000
Payroll and related costs	10,000	10,500
Other Direct Expenses	5,000	4,500
Departmental Income	(5,000)	(4,000)
Rentals and Other Income Revenue	50,000	55,000
Total Operated Departments Income	697,100	728,000
Undistributed Operating Expenses:		
Administrative & General	105,000	108,500
Marketing	51,500	55,000
Property Operation & Maintenance	65,250	67,500
Energy Costs	80,250	81,500
Total Undistributed Operating Expenses	302,000	312,500
Income Before Fixed Charges	395,100	415,500
Rent	20,000	20,000
Property Taxes	20,000	24,000
Insurance	5,500	6,000
Interest	54,000	60,000
Depreciation	60,000	61,000
Total Fixed Charges	159,500	171,000
Income Before Income Taxes	235,600	244,500
Income Taxes	94,300	97,800
Net Income	$ 141,300	$ 146,700

Note: Data processing, human resources, and transportation expenses are insignificant and are not shown as separate cost centers.

Exhibit 5.3 Statement of Cash Flows

Statement of Cash Flows
Grand Hotel
For the years ending December 31, 19X1 and 19X2

	19X1	19X2
Cash Flows from Operating Activities:		
Net Income	$141,300	$146,700
Adjustments to reconcile net income to net cash provided by operations:		
Depreciation expense	60,000	61,000
Increase in marketable securities	(21,000)	(64,000)
Inc./Dec. in accounts receivable (net)	10,000	(50,000)
Inc./Dec. in inventories	(3,000)	2,000
Inc./Dec. in prepaid expenses	1,000	(2,000)
Inc./Dec. in accounts payable	(6,500)	17,500
Increase in income taxes	2,000	2,000
Inc./Dec. in accrued expenses	15,200	(200)
Inc./Dec. in deferred taxes	2,800	2,200
Net cash from operating activities	201,800	115,200
Cash Flows from Investing Activities:		
Sale of investments	8,000	–0–
Purchase of buildings	(40,000)	(30,000)
Purchase of furniture and equipment	(20,000)	(18,000)
Purchase of china, etc.	(9,000)	(2,300)
Purchase of investments	–0–	(5,000)
Net cash from investing activities	(61,000)	(55,300)
Cash Flows from Financing Activities:		
Payment of dividends	(121,300)	(49,400)
Payment of long-term debt	(25,000)	(21,500)
Borrowed long-term debt	6,500	14,000
Net cash from financing activities	(139,800)	(56,900)
Net Increase in Cash	$ 1,000	$ 3,000

Additional information:

Investments of $8,000 were sold at cost in 19X1.

Current Ratio   The commonest liquidity ratio is the **current ratio**, which is the ratio of total current assets to total current liabilities and is expressed as a coverage of so many times. Using figures from Exhibit 5.1, the 19X2 current ratio for the Grand Hotel can be calculated as follows:

$$\text{Current Ratio} = \frac{\text{Current Assets}}{\text{Current Liabilities}}$$

Exhibit 5.4 Statement of Retained Earnings and Other Information

Grand Hotel Statement of Retained Earnings and Other Information December 31, 19X1 and 19X2		
	19X1	**19X2**
Retained earnings – beginning of the year	$ 235,000	$ 255,000
Net income	141,300	146,700
Dividends declared	121,300	49,400
Retained earnings – end of the year	$ 255,000	$ 352,300
Other Information		
	19X1	**19X2**
Rooms Sold	20,500	21,000
Paid Guests	23,500	24,000
Rooms Occupied by Two or More People	2,400	2,500
Complimentary Rooms	150*	160*
Shares of Common Stock Outstanding	55,000	55,000
Food Covers	55,500	56,000
Food Sales	$280,000	$300,000
Beverage Sales	$150,000	$145,000

*Assume one guest per complimentary room.

$$= \frac{\$338,000}{\$214,000}$$

$$= \underline{1.58} \text{ times or } 1.58 \text{ to } 1$$

This result shows that for every $1 of current liabilities, the Grand Hotel has $1.58 of current assets. Thus, there is a cushion of $.58 for every dollar of current debt. A considerable shrinkage of inventory and receivables could occur before the Grand Hotel would be unable to pay its current obligations. By comparison, the 19X1 current ratio for the Grand Hotel was 1.15. An increase in the current ratio from 1.15 to 1.58 within one year is considerable and would no doubt please creditors. However, would a current ratio of 1.58 please all interested parties?

Owners/stockholders normally prefer a low current ratio to a high one, because stockholders view investments in most current assets as less productive than investments in noncurrent assets. Since stockholders are primarily concerned with profits, they prefer a relatively low current ratio.

Creditors normally prefer a relatively high current ratio, as this provides assurance that they will receive timely payments. A subset of creditors, lenders of funds, believe adequate liquidity is so important that they often incorporate a minimum working capital requirement or a minimum current ratio in loan agreements. Violation of this loan provision could result in the lender demanding full payment of the loan.

Management is caught in the middle, trying to satisfy both owners and lenders while, at the same time, maintaining adequate working capital and sufficient liquidity to ensure the smooth operation of the hospitality establishment. Management is able to take action affecting the current ratio. In the case of the Grand Hotel, a current ratio of 2 could be achieved by selling $90,000 worth of marketable securities on the last day of 19X2 and paying current creditors.[1] Other possible actions to increase a current ratio include:

- Obtain long-term loans.

- Obtain new owner equity contributions.

- Convert noncurrent assets to cash.

- Defer declaring dividends and leave the cash in the business.

An extremely high current ratio may mean that accounts receivable are too high because of liberal credit policies and/or slow collections, or it may indicate that inventory is excessive. Since ratios are indicators, management must follow through by analyzing possible contributing factors.

Acid-Test Ratio

A more stringent test of liquidity is the **acid-test ratio**. The acid-test ratio measures liquidity by considering only "quick assets"—cash and near-cash assets. Excluded from current assets are inventories and prepaid expenses in determining the total quick assets. In many industries, inventories are significant and their conversion to cash may take several months. The extremes appear evident in the hospitality industry. In some hospitality operations, especially quick-service restaurants, food inventory may be entirely replenished twice a week. On the other hand, the stock of certain alcoholic beverages at some food service operations may be replaced only once in three months.

The difference between the current ratio and the acid-test ratio is a function of the amount of inventory relative to current assets. In some operations, the difference between the current ratio and the acid-test ratio will be minor, while in others, it will be significant. Using relevant figures from Exhibit 5.1, the 19X2 acid-test ratio for the Grand Hotel is computed as follows:

$$\text{Acid-Test Ratio} = \frac{\text{Cash, Marketable Securities, Notes Receivable \& Accounts Receivable}}{\text{Current Liabilities}}$$

$$= \frac{\$309,000}{\$214,000}$$

$$= \underline{\underline{1.44}} \text{ times}$$

The 19X2 acid-test ratio reveals quick assets of $1.44 for every $1.00 of current liabilities. This is an increase of .44 times over the 19X1 acid-test ratio. Although the acid-test ratio was 1.0 for l9Xl, the Grand Hotel was not in difficult financial straits. Many hospitality establishments are able to operate efficiently and effectively with an acid-test ratio of 1 or less, for they have minimal amounts of both inventory and accounts receivable.

The viewpoints of owners, creditors, and managers toward the acid-test ratio parallel those held toward the current ratio. That is, owners of hospitality operations prefer a low ratio (generally less than 1), creditors prefer a high ratio, and management is again caught in the middle.

Operating Cash Flows to Current Liabilities Ratio

A fairly new ratio made possible by the statement of cash flows is **operating cash flows to current liabilities**. The operating cash flows are taken from the statement of cash flows, while current liabilities come from the balance sheet. This measure of liquidity compares the cash flow from the firm's operating activities to its obligation at the balance sheet date that must be paid within twelve months. Using the relevant figures from Exhibits 5.1 and 5.3, the 19X2 operating cash flows to current liabilities ratio is computed as follows:

$$\text{Operating Cash Flows to Current Liabilities Ratio} = \frac{\text{Operating Cash Flows}}{\text{Average Current Liabilities}}$$

$$= \frac{115,200}{.5(\$192,200 + \$214,000)}$$

$$= .567 \text{ or } \underline{56.7\%}$$

The 19X2 ratio of 56.7% shows that only $.567 of cash flow from operations was provided by the Grand Hotel during 19X2 for each $1.00 of current debt at the end of 19X2. The prior year's ratio was 107%. This dramatic change should cause management to consider reasons for the change and be prepared to take appropriate action.

All users of ratios would prefer to see a high operating cash flow to current liabilities, as this suggests operations are providing sufficient cash to pay the firm's current liabilities.

Accounts Receivable Turnover

In hospitality operations that extend credit to guests, accounts receivable is generally the largest current asset. Therefore, in an examination of a property's liquidity, the "quality" of its accounts receivable must be considered.

In the normal operating cycle (discussed in Chapter 2), accounts receivable are converted to cash. The **accounts receivable turnover** measures the speed of the conversion. The faster the accounts receivable are turned over, the more credibility the current and acid-test ratios have in financial analysis.

This ratio is determined by dividing revenue by average accounts receivable. A refinement of this ratio uses only charge sales in the numerator; however, quite often charge sales figures are unavailable to outsiders (stockholders, potential stockholders, and creditors). Regardless of whether revenues or charge sales are used as the numerator, the calculation should be consistent from period to period. Average accounts receivable is the result of dividing the sum of the beginning-of-the-period and end-of-the-period accounts receivable by two. When a hospitality operation has seasonal sales fluctuations, a preferred approach (when computing the *annual* accounts receivable turnover) is to sum the accounts receivable at the end of each month and divide by 12 to determine the average accounts receivable.

Exhibit 5.5 uses relevant figures from Exhibits 5.1 and 5.2 to calculate the accounts receivable turnover for 19X2 of the Grand Hotel. The accounts receivable turnover of 11.76 indicates that the total revenue for 19X2 is 11.76 times the average receivables. This is lower than the 19X1 accounts receivable turnover of the Grand Hotel of 13.68. Management would generally investigate this difference. The investigation may reveal

Exhibit 5.5 Accounts Receivable Turnover

$$\text{Accounts Receivable Turnover} = \frac{\text{Total Revenue}}{\text{Average Accounts Receivable*}}$$

$$= \frac{\$1,352,000}{\$115,000}$$

$$= 11.76 \text{ times}$$

$$\text{*Average Accounts Receivable} = \frac{\text{Accounts Receivable at Beginning and End of Year}}{2}$$

$$= \frac{\$90,000 + \$140,000}{2}$$

$$= \$115,000$$

problems or that changes in the credit policy and/or collection procedures significantly contributed to the difference.

Although the accounts receivable turnover measures the overall rapidity of collections, it fails to address individual accounts. This matter is resolved by preparing an aging of accounts receivable schedule which reflects the status of each account. In an aging schedule, each account is broken down to the period when the charges originated. Like credit sales, this information is generally available only to management. Exhibit 5.6 illustrates an aging of accounts receivable schedule.

Since few hospitality establishments charge interest on their accounts receivable, the opportunity cost of credit sales is the investment dollars that could be generated by investing cash. However, credit terms are extended with the purpose of increasing sales. Therefore, theoretically, credit should be extended to the point where the bad debt and additional collection costs of extending credit to one more guest equal the additional profit earned by extending credit to one more guest.

Owners prefer a high accounts receivable turnover as this reflects a lower investment in nonproductive accounts receivable. However, they understand how a tight credit policy and an overly aggressive collections effort may result in lower sales. Nonetheless, everything else being the same, a high accounts receivable turnover indicates that accounts receivable are being managed well. Suppliers, like owners, prefer a high accounts receivable turnover, because this means that hospitality establishments will have more cash readily available to pay them. Long-term creditors also see a high accounts receivable turnover as a positive reflection of management.

Management desires to maximize the sales of the hospitality operation. Offering credit helps maximize sales. However, management also realizes that offering credit to maximize sales may result in more accounts receivable and in selling to some less creditworthy customers. One result

Exhibit 5.6 Aging of Accounts Receivable Schedule

	Aging of Accounts Receivable Schedule Grand Hotel December 31, 19X2					
		Days Outstanding				
Firm Name	Total	0–30	31–60	61–90	91–120	Over 120 days
Ace Co.	$600	$400	$200	$–0–	$–0–	$–0–
Acem Corp.	400	100	–0–	300	–0–	–0–
Ahern, Jim	100	100	–0–	–0–	–0–	–0–
America, Inc.	1,000	950	–0–	–0–	–0–	50
Armadillo Co.	50	–0–	–0–	–0–	50	–0–
⋮						
Zebra Zoo Equip.	80	80	–0–	–0–	–0–	–0–
Total	$145,000	$115,000	$18,000	$7,000	$4,000	$1,000

of management's decision to offer credit is a lower accounts receivable turnover. On the other hand, while management may see a lower accounts receivable turnover as a consequence of higher sales, it does not lose sight of the fact that it also must maintain the operation's cash flow— that is, it must effectively collect on the credit sales.

Average Collection Period

A variation of the accounts receivable turnover is the **average collection period**, which is calculated by dividing the accounts receivable turnover into 365 (the number of days in a year). This conversion simply translates the turnover into a more understandable result. For the Grand Hotel, the average collection period for 19X2 is as follows:

$$\text{Average Collection Period} = \frac{365}{\text{Accounts Receivable Turnover}}$$

$$= \frac{365}{11.76}$$

$$= \underline{\underline{31}} \text{ days}$$

The average collection period of 31 days means that on an average of every 31 days throughout 19X2, the Grand Hotel was collecting all its accounts receivable. The 31 days is a four-day increase over the 19X1 average collection period of 27 days.

What should be the average collection period? Generally, the time allowed for average payments should not exceed the terms of sale by more than 7 to 10 days. Therefore, if the terms of sale are *n*/30 (entire amount is due in 30 days), the maximum allowable average collection period is 37 to 40 days.

The above discussion assumes that all sales are credit sales. However, many hospitality operations have both cash and credit sales. Therefore, the mix of cash and credit sales must be considered when the accounts

Exhibit 5.7   Working Capital Turnover

$$\text{Working Capital Turnover} = \frac{\text{Revenue}}{\text{Average Working Capital}}$$

$$= \frac{\$1,352,000}{\$76,400^*}$$

$$= 17.70 \text{ times}$$

Working Capital (WC) = Current Assets − Current Liabilities

WC (19X2)	$124,000 =	$338,000 − $214,000
WC (19X1)	28,800 =	221,000 − 192,200

*Average Working Capital = $124,000 + $28,800 divided by 2 = $76,400

receivable turnover ratio uses revenue, rather than credit sales, in the numerator. This is accomplished by allowing for cash sales. For example, if sales are 50% cash and 50% credit, then the maximum allowable average collection period should be adjusted. An adjusted maximum allowable average collection period is calculated by multiplying the maximum allowable average collection period by credit sales as a percentage of total sales.

In the previous example of a maximum allowable collection period of 37 to 40 days and 50% credit sales, the adjusted maximum allowable average collection period is 18.5 to 20 days (37 to 40 days × .5). Generally, only management can make this adjustment, because the mix of sales is unknown by other interested parties.

The average collection period preferred by owners, creditors, and management is similar to their preferences for the accounts receivable turnover, because the average collection period is only a variation of the accounts receivable turnover. Therefore, owners and creditors prefer a lower number of days, while management prefers a higher number of days (as long as cash flow is sufficient).

Working Capital Turnover Ratio

The final liquidity ratio presented here is the **working capital turnover ratio**, which compares working capital (current assets less current liabilities) to revenue. For most businesses, the higher the revenue, the greater the amount of working capital required. Thus, as the revenue rises, working capital is expected to rise also. Exhibit 5.7 uses relevant figures from Exhibits 5.1 and 5.2 to calculate the working capital turnover ratio in 19X2 for the Grand Hotel.

For the Grand Hotel, a working capital turnover of 17.70 means that working capital of $76,400 was "used" 17.70 times during the year. Everything else being the same, the lower the current ratio, the greater the working capital turnover ratio. Therefore, those establishments in segments of the hospitality industry with virtually no credit sales and a low level of inventory will generally have an extremely high working capital ratio.

Owners prefer this ratio to be high, as they prefer a low current ratio, thus low working capital. Creditors prefer a lower working capital turnover ratio than owners, because they prefer a relatively high current ratio. Management's preferences fall between owners and creditors. Management desires to maintain an adequate amount of working capital to cover unexpected problems, yet management also desires to maximize profits by using available funds to make long-term investments.

Solvency Ratios

Solvency ratios measure the degree of debt financing by a hospitality enterprise and are partial indicators of the establishment's ability to meet its long-term debt obligations. These ratios reveal the equity cushion that is available to absorb any operating losses. Primary users of these ratios are outsiders, especially lenders, who generally prefer less risk rather than more risk. High solvency ratios generally suggest that an operation has the ability to weather financial storms.

Owners like to use debt instead of additional equity to increase their return on equity already invested. This process is commonly referred to as **financial leverage.** Financial leverage is used when the return on the investment exceeds the cost of the debt used to finance an investment. When using debt to increase their leverage, owners are, in essence, transferring part of their risk to creditors.

As a further explanation of the concept of leverage, let us consider the following example. Assume that total assets of a lodging facility are $100 and earnings before interest and taxes (EBIT) are $50, and interest is 15% of debt. Further assume that two possible combinations of debt and equity are $80 of debt and $20 of equity, and the reverse ($80 of equity and $20 of debt). Further assume a tax rate of 40%. The return on equity for each of the two combinations is calculated in Exhibit 5.8.

The calculations in Exhibit 5.8 reveal that each $1 invested by stockholders in the high debt/low equity combination earns $1.14, while every $1 invested by stockholders in the low debt/high equity combination earns only $.35.

This class of ratios includes two groups—those based on balance sheet information and those based on income statement information. The first three ratios to be examined (the solvency ratio, the debt-equity ratio, and long-term debt to total capitalization) are based on balance sheet information. The following two ratios, the number of times interest earned ratio and the fixed charge coverage ratio, are based on information from the income statement. The final ratio relates operating cash flows to total liabilities.

Solvency Ratio   A hospitality enterprise is solvent when its assets exceed its liabilities. Therefore, the **solvency ratio** is simply total assets divided by total liabilities. The solvency ratio in 19X2 for the Grand Hotel is determined as follows:

$$\text{Solvency Ratio} = \frac{\text{Total Assets}}{\text{Total Liabilities}}$$

Exhibit 5.8   Return on Equity

	High Debt/ Low Equity	High Equity/ Low Debt
Debt	$80	$20
Equity	$20	$80
EBIT	$50	$50
Interest (15%)	12*	3**
Income before taxes	38	47
Income taxes	−15.20	−18.80
	$22.80	$28.20

Return per $1 of equity:

$$\frac{\text{Net income}}{\text{equity}} = \frac{\$22.80}{\$20} = \$1.14 \qquad \frac{\$28.20}{\$80} = \$.35$$

*Debt times interest rate = interest expense   **$20 × .15 = $3

$80 × .15 = $12

$$= \frac{\$1,176,300}{\$659,000}$$

$$= 1.78 \text{ times}$$

Thus, at the end of 19X2, the Grand Hotel has $1.78 of assets for each $1.00 of liabilities or a cushion of $.78. The Grand Hotel's assets could be discounted substantially ($.78 ÷ $1.78 = 43.8%) and creditors could still be fully paid. The Grand Hotel's solvency ratio at the end of 19X1 was 1.65 times. The 19X2 ratio would be considered more favorable from the perspective of creditors.

The greater the leverage (use of debt to finance the assets) used by the hospitality establishment, the lower its solvency ratio. Owners prefer to use leverage in order to maximize their return on their investments. This occurs as long as the earnings from the creditor-financed investment exceed the cost of the establishment's borrowing. Creditors, on the other hand, prefer a high solvency ratio, as it provides a greater cushion should the establishment experience losses in operations. Managers must satisfy both owners and creditors. Thus, they desire to finance assets so as to maximize the return on owners' investments, while not unduly jeopardizing the establishment's ability to pay creditors.

Debt-Equity Ratio

The **debt-equity ratio**, one of the commonest solvency ratios, compares the hospitality establishment's debt to its net worth (owners' equity). This ratio indicates the establishment's ability to withstand adversity and meet its long-term debt obligations. Figures from Exhibit 5.1 can be used to calculate the Grand Hotel's debt-equity ratio for 19X2:

$$\text{Debt-Equity Ratio} = \frac{\text{Total Liabilities}}{\text{Total Owners' Equity}}$$

$$= \frac{\$659,000}{\$517,300}$$

$$= \underline{\underline{1.27}} \text{ to } 1$$

The Grand Hotel's debt-equity ratio of 1.27 to 1 at the end of 19X2 indicates for each $1 of owners' net worth, the Grand Hotel owed creditors $1.27. The debt-equity ratio for 19X1 for the Grand Hotel was 1.54 to 1. Thus, relative to its net worth, the Grand Hotel reduced its 19X1 debt.

Owners view this ratio similarly to the way they view the solvency ratio. That is, they desire to maximize their return on investment by using leverage. The greater the leverage, the higher the debt-equity ratio. Creditors generally would favor a lower debt-equity ratio because their risk is reduced as net worth increases relative to debt. Management, as with the solvency ratio, prefers a middle position between creditors and owners.

Long-Term Debt to Total Capitalization Ratio

Still another solvency ratio is the calculation of long-term debt as a percentage of the sum of long-term debt and owners' equity, commonly called total capitalization. This ratio is similar to the debt-equity ratio except that current liabilities are excluded in the numerator, and long-term debt is added to the denominator of the debt-equity ratio. Current liabilities are excluded because current assets are normally adequate to cover them, therefore, they are not a long-term concern. Figures from Exhibit 5.1 can be used to calculate the 19X2 long-term debt to total capitalization ratio for the Grand Hotel:

$$\begin{array}{l}\text{Long-Term Debt to} \\ \text{Total Capitalization} \\ \text{Ratio}\end{array} = \frac{\text{Long-Term Debt}}{\text{Long-Term Debt and Owners' Equity}}$$

$$= \frac{\$445,000}{\$962,300}$$

$$= \underline{\underline{46.24\%}}$$

Long-term debt of the Grand Hotel at the end of 19X2 is 46.24% of its total capitalization. This can be compared to 51.88% at the end of 19X1. Creditors would prefer the lower percentage because it would indicate a reduced risk on their part. Owners, on the other hand, would prefer the higher percentage because of their desire for high returns through the use of leverage.

Number of Times Interest Earned Ratio

The **number of times interest earned ratio** is based on financial figures from the income statement and expresses the number of times interest expense can be covered. The greater the number of times interest is earned, the greater the safety afforded the creditors. Since interest is subtracted to determine taxable income, income taxes are added to net income and interest expense (earnings before interest and taxes, abbreviated as EBIT) to form the numerator of the ratio, while interest expense is the denominator. Figures from Exhibit 5.2 can be used to calculate the 19X2 number of times interest earned ratio for the Grand Hotel:

$$\text{Number of Times Interest Earned Ratio} = \frac{\text{EBIT}}{\text{Interest Expense}}$$

$$= \frac{\$304,500}{\$60,000}$$

$$= \underline{\underline{5.08}} \text{ times}$$

The result of 5.08 times shows that the Grand Hotel could cover its interest expense by over five times. The number of times interest earned ratio in 19X1 for the Grand Hotel was 5.36 times. This two-year trend suggests a slightly riskier position from a creditor's viewpoint. However, in general, a number of times interest earned ratio of greater than 4 reflects a sufficient amount of earnings for a hospitality enterprise to cover the interest expense of its existing debt.

All parties (owners, creditors, and management) prefer a relatively high ratio. Owners are generally less concerned about this ratio than creditors, as long as interest obligations are paid on a timely basis and leverage is working to their advantage. Creditors and especially lenders also prefer a relatively high ratio, because this indicates that the establishment is able to meet its interest payments. To the lender, the higher this ratio, the better. Management also prefers a high ratio. However, since an extremely high ratio suggests leverage is probably not being optimized for the owners, management may prefer a lower ratio than do lenders.

The number of times interest earned ratio fails to consider fixed obligations other than interest expense. Many hospitality firms have long-term leases which require periodic payments similar to interest. This limitation of the number of times interest earned ratio is overcome by the fixed charge coverage ratio.

Fixed Charge Coverage Ratio

The **fixed charge coverage ratio** is a variation of the number of times interest earned ratio that considers leases as well as interest expense. Hospitality establishments that have obtained the use of property and equipment through leases may find the fixed charge coverage ratio to be more useful than the number of times interest earned ratio. This ratio is calculated the same as the number of times interest earned ratio, except that lease expense (rent expense) is added to both the numerator and denominator of the equation.

Exhibit 5.9 uses figures from Exhibit 5.2 to calculate the 19X2 fixed charge coverage ratio for the Grand Hotel. The result indicates that earnings prior to lease expense, interest expense, and income taxes cover lease and interest expense 4.06 times. The Grand Hotel's fixed charge coverage ratio for 19X1 was 4.18 times. The change of 0.12 times reflects a minor decrease in the Grand Hotel's ability to cover its fixed costs of interest and lease expense. The viewpoints of owners, creditors, and management are similar to the views they hold regarding changes in the number of times interest earned ratio.

Exhibit 5.9 Fixed Charge Coverage Ratio

$$\text{Fixed Charge Coverage Ratio} = \frac{\text{EBIT} + \text{Lease Expense}}{\text{Interest Expense and Lease Expense}}$$

$$= \frac{\$304,500 + \$20,000}{\$60,000 + \$20,000}$$

$$= \frac{\$324,500}{\$80,000}$$

$$= 4.06 \text{ times}$$

Operating Cash Flows to Total Liabilities Ratio

The final solvency ratio presented in this text uses figures from both the statement of cash flows and the balance sheet by comparing operating cash flows to average total liabilities. Both the debt-equity and long-term debt to total capitalization ratios are based on static numbers from the balance sheet. This ratio overcomes the deficiency of using debt at a point in time by considering cash flow for a period of time.

Figures from Exhibits 5.1 and 5.3 are used to calculate the 19X2 **operating cash flows to total liabilities ratio** for the Grand Hotel as follows:

$$\frac{\text{Operating Cash Flow to}}{\text{Total Liabilities Ratio}} = \frac{\text{Operating Cash Flows}}{\text{Average Total Liabilities}}$$

$$= \frac{\$115,200}{.5(\$645,000 + \$659,000)}$$

$$= .177 \text{ or } 17.7\%$$

The 19X1 operating cash flows to total liabilities ratio is 31.2%; thus, the Grand Hotel's ability to meet its long-term obligations with operating cash flows has deteriorated considerably from 19X1 to 19X2.

All users of financial information prefer this ratio to be relatively high; that is, the cash flow from operations should be high relative to total liabilities, given that the amount of debt used is optimal.

Activity Ratios

Activity ratios measure management's effectiveness in using its resources. Management is entrusted with inventory and fixed assets (and other resources) to generate earnings for owners while providing products and services to guests. Since the fixed assets of most lodging facilities constitute a large percentage of the operation's total assets, it is essential to use these resources effectively. Although inventory is generally not a

Exhibit 5.10 Condensed Food and Beverage Department Statement

Condensed Food and Beverage Department Statement Grand Hotel For the year of 19X2		
	Food	Beverage
Sales	$300,000	$145,000
Cost of sales:		
Beginning inventory	11,000	6,000
Purchases	120,000	28,000
Less: Ending inventory	9,000	6,000
Cost of goods used	122,000	28,000
Less: Employee meals	2,000	0
Cost of goods sold	120,000	28,000
Gross Profit	180,000	117,000
Expenses:		
Payroll and related expenses	135,000	45,000
Other expenses	30,000	15,000
Total expenses	165,000	60,000
Departmental income	$15,000	$57,000

significant portion of total assets, management must adequately control it in order to minimize the cost of sales.

Inventory Turnover

The **inventory turnover** shows how quickly the inventory is being used. All things being the same, generally, the quicker the inventory turnover the better, because inventory can be expensive to maintain. Maintenance costs include storage space, freezers, insurance, personnel expense, recordkeeping, and, of course, the opportunity cost of the funds tied up in inventory. Inventories held by hospitality operations are highly susceptible to theft and must be carefully controlled.

Inventory turnovers should generally be calculated separately for food supplies and for beverages. Some food service operations will calculate several beverage turnovers based on the types of beverages available.

Exhibit 5.10 is a condensed food and beverage department statement of the Grand Hotel with food and beverage operations for 19X2 shown separately. Figures from this statement will be used to illustrate the food and beverage turnover ratios.

Exhibit 5.11 calculates the 19X2 food inventory turnover for the Grand Hotel. The food inventory turned over 12.2 times during 19X2, or approximately once per month. The speed of food inventory turnover generally depends on the type of food service operation. A quick-service restaurant generally experiences a much faster food turnover than does a fine dining establishment. In fact, a quick-service restaurant may have a food inventory turnover in excess of 200 times for a year. A norm used in the hotel industry for hotels that have several different types of restaurants and banquets calls for food inventory to turn over four times per month.

Exhibit 5.11 Food Inventory Turnover

$$\text{Food Inventory Turnover} = \frac{\text{Cost of Food Used}}{\text{Average Food Inventory}^{*}}$$

$$= \frac{\$122{,}000}{\$10{,}000}$$

$$= 12.2 \text{ times}$$

$$^{*}\text{Average Food Inventory} = \frac{\text{Beginning and Ending Inventories}}{2}$$

$$= \frac{\$11{,}000 + \$9{,}000}{2}$$

$$= \$10{,}000$$

Although a high food inventory turnover is desired because it means that the food service establishment is able to operate with a relatively small investment in inventory, too high a turnover may indicate possible stockout problems. Failure to provide desired food items to guests may not only immediately result in disappointed guests, but may also result in negative goodwill if this problem persists. Too low an inventory turnover suggests that food is overstocked, and, in addition to the costs to maintain inventory previously mentioned, the cost of spoilage may become a problem.

Exhibit 5.12 uses figures from Exhibit 5.10 to calculate the 19X2 beverage turnover for the Grand Hotel. The beverage turnover of 4.67 means that the beverage inventory of $6,000 required restocking approximately every 78 days. This is calculated by dividing 365 days in the year by the beverage turnover of 4.67. Not all beverage items are sold evenly; thus, some items would have to be restocked more frequently. A norm used in the hotel industry for hotels having several different types of lounges and banquets calls for beverage inventory to turn over 1.25 times per month or 15 times per year.

All parties (owners, creditors, and management) prefer high inventory turnovers to low ones, as long as stockouts are avoided. Ideally, as the last inventory item is sold, the shelves are being restocked.

Fixed Asset Turnover

The **fixed asset turnover** is determined by dividing average total fixed assets into total revenue for the period. A more precise measurement would be to use only revenues related to fixed asset usage in the numerator. However, revenue by source is not available to many financial analysts, so total revenue is generally used.

This ratio measures management's effectiveness in using fixed assets. A high turnover suggests the hospitality enterprise is using its fixed assets effectively to generate revenues, while a low turnover suggests the

Exhibit 5.12 Beverage Turnover

$$\text{Beverage Turnover} = \frac{\text{Cost of Beverages Used}}{\text{Average Beverage Inventory*}}$$

$$= \frac{\$28,000}{\$6,000}$$

$$= 4.67 \text{ times}$$

$$*\text{Average Beverage Inventory} = \frac{\text{Beginning and Ending Inventories}}{2}$$

$$= \frac{\$6,000 + \$6,000}{2}$$

$$= \$6,000$$

establishment is not making effective use of its fixed assets and should consider disposing of part of them.

A limitation of this ratio is that it places a premium on using older (depreciated) fixed assets, since their book value is low. Further, this ratio is affected by the depreciation method employed by the hospitality operation. For example, an operation using an accelerated method of depreciation will show a higher turnover than an operation using the straight-line depreciation method, all other factors being the same.

Exhibit 5.13 uses figures from Exhibits 5.1 and 5.2 to calculate the 19X2 fixed asset turnover ratio for the Grand Hotel. The fixed asset turnover of 1.68 reveals that revenue was 1.68 times the average total fixed assets. For 19X1, the Grand Hotel's fixed asset turnover was 1.62 times. The change of .06 times, although minor, is viewed as a positive trend.

All parties (owners, creditors, and management) prefer a high fixed asset turnover. Management, however, should resist retaining old and possibly inefficient fixed assets, even though they result in a high fixed asset turnover. The return on assets ratio (discussed under profitability ratios) is a partial check against this practice.

Asset Turnover

Another ratio to measure the efficiency of management's use of assets is the **asset turnover**. It is calculated by dividing total revenue by average total assets. The two previous ratios presented, inventory turnover and fixed assets turnover, concern a large percentage of the total assets. The asset turnover examines the use of total assets in relation to total revenue. Limitations of the fixed asset ratio are also inherent in this ratio to the extent that fixed assets make up total assets. For most hospitality establishments, especially lodging businesses, fixed assets constitute the majority of the operation's total assets.

Exhibit 5.14 uses figures from Exhibits 5.1 and 5.2 to calculate the 19X2 asset turnover ratio for the Grand Hotel. The asset turnover of 1.21

Exhibit 5.13   Fixed Asset Turnover

$$\text{Fixed Asset Turnover} = \frac{\text{Total Revenue}}{\text{Average Fixed Assets*}}$$

$$= \frac{\$1,352,000}{\$803,650}$$

$$= 1.68 \text{ times}$$

$$\text{*Average Fixed Assets} = \frac{\text{Total Fixed Assets at Beginning and End of Year}}{2}$$

$$= \frac{\$809,000 + \$798,300}{2}$$

$$= \$803,650$$

Exhibit 5.14   Asset Turnover

$$\text{Asset Turnover Ratio} = \frac{\text{Total Revenues}}{\text{Average Total Assets*}}$$

$$= \frac{\$1,352,000}{\$1,120,650}$$

$$= 1.21 \text{ times}$$

$$\text{*Average Total Assets} = \frac{\text{Total Assets at Beginning and End of Year}}{2}$$

$$= \frac{\$1,065,000 + \$1,176,300}{2}$$

$$= \$1,120,650$$

indicates that each $1 of assets generated $1.21 of revenue in 19X2. The asset turnover ratio for 19X1 was 1.23. Thus, there was virtually no change for the two years.

As with the fixed asset turnover, all concerned parties (owners, creditors, and management) prefer this ratio to be high, because a high ratio means effective use of assets by management, subject to the limitations of using old (depreciated) assets as discussed previously.

Both the fixed asset turnover and the asset turnover ratios are relatively low for most hospitality segments, especially for hotels and motels. The relatively low ratio is due to the hospitality industry's high dependence on fixed assets and its inability to quickly increase output to meet maximum demand. It is common for many hotels and motels to turn away guests four nights a week due to excessive demand, and operate at an extremely low level of output (less than 50%) the three remaining nights.

Four additional measures of management's ability to efficiently use available assets are paid occupancy percentage, complimentary occupancy, average occupancy per room, and multiple occupancy percentage. Although these ratios are not based on financial information, they are viewed as excellent measures of management's effectiveness in selling space, whether it be rooms in a lodging facility or seats in a food service establishment.

Paid Occupancy Percentage

Paid occupancy is a major indicator of management's success in selling its "product." It refers to the percentage of rooms sold in relation to rooms available for sale in hotels and motels. In food service operations, it is commonly referred to as **seat turnover**, and is calculated by dividing the number of people served by the number of seats available. Seat turnover is commonly calculated by meal period. In most food service facilities, different seat turnovers are experienced for different dining periods. The occupancy percentage for lodging facilities and the seat turnovers for food service facilities are key measures of facility utilization.

Using the "Other Information" listed in Exhibit 5.4, the annual paid occupancy of the Grand Hotel can be determined by dividing total paid rooms occupied by available rooms for sale. If the Grand Hotel had 80 rooms available for sale each day, its paid occupancy percentage for 19X2 is calculated as indicated in Exhibit 5.15.

The Grand Hotel's 19X2 annual paid occupancy percentage of 71.92% was an improvement over the 19X1 annual occupancy percentage of 70.21%, when 20,500 rooms were sold. This percentage does not mean that every day 70.21% of the available rooms were sold, but rather that on the average 70.21% were sold. For example, a hotel experiencing 100% paid occupancy Monday through Thursday and 33% paid occupancy Friday through Sunday would end up with a combined result of 71.29%.

There are many factors affecting paid occupancy rates in the lodging industry, such as location within an area, geographic location, seasonal factors (both weekly and yearly), rate structure, and type of lodging facility, to mention a few.

Complimentary Occupancy

Complimentary occupancy, as stated in the *USASH*, is determined by dividing the number of complimentary rooms for a period by the number of rooms available. Using figures from the "Other Information" section of Exhibit 5.4, the 19X2 complimentary occupancy for the Grand Hotel is calculated as follows:

$$\text{Complimentary Occupancy} = \frac{\text{Complimentary Rooms}}{\text{Rooms Available}}$$

Exhibit 5.15 Paid Occupancy Percentage

$$\text{Paid Occupancy} = \frac{\text{Paid Rooms Occupied}}{\text{Available Rooms}^*}$$

$$= \frac{21{,}000}{29{,}200}$$

$$= 71.92\%$$

$$^*\text{Available Rooms} = \text{Rooms Available per Day} \times 365 \text{ Days}$$

$$= 80 \times 365$$

$$= 29{,}200$$

$$= \frac{160}{29{,}200}$$

$$= .55\%$$

Average Occupancy per Room

Another ratio to measure management's ability to use the lodging facilities is the **average occupancy per room**. This ratio is the result of dividing the number of guests by the number of rooms sold. Generally, as the average occupancy per room increases, the room rate also increases.

Using figures from the "Other Information" section of Exhibit 5.4, the 19X2 average occupancy per room for the Grand Hotel can be calculated as follows:

$$\text{Average Occupancy per Room} = \frac{\text{Number of Guests}}{\text{Number of Rooms Occupied by Guests}}$$

$$= \frac{24{,}160}{21{,}160}$$

$$= 1.14 \text{ Guests}$$

The Grand Hotel's 19X2 average occupancy per room was 1.14 guests. The 19X1 average occupancy per room was slightly higher at 1.15 guests.

The average occupancy per room is generally the highest for resort properties, where it can reach levels in excess of two guests per room, and is lowest for transient lodging facilities.

Multiple Occupancy

Another ratio used to measure multiple occupancy of rooms is **multiple occupancy**. This ratio is similar to the average occupancy per room. It is determined by dividing the number of rooms occupied by more than one guest by the number of rooms occupied by guests.

Using figures from the "Other Information" section of Exhibit 5.4, the multiple occupancy of the Grand Hotel for 19X2 can be calculated as follows:

$$\text{Multiple Occupancy} = \frac{\text{Rooms Occupied by Two or More People}}{\text{Rooms Occupied by Guests}}$$

$$= \frac{2,500}{21,160}$$

$$= \underline{\underline{11.81\%}}$$

The multiple occupancy for the Grand Hotel during 19X2 indicates 11.81% of the rooms sold were occupied by more than one guest. The 19X1 multiple occupancy for the Grand Hotel was 11.62%; therefore, a minor increase in multiple occupancy has occurred.

Owners, creditors, and management all prefer high occupancy ratios—paid occupancy percentage, average occupancy per room, and multiple occupancy. The higher the occupancy ratios, the greater the use of the facilities. These ratios are considered to be prime indicators of a lodging facility's level of operations. Occupancy ratios are generally computed on a daily basis and are recorded on the daily report of operations.

Profitability Ratios

Profitability ratios reflect the results of all areas of management's responsibilities. All the information conveyed by liquidity, solvency, and activity ratios affect the profitability of the hospitality enterprise. The primary purpose of most hospitality operations is the generation of profit. Owners invest for the purpose of increasing their wealth through dividends and through increases in the price of capital stock. Both dividends and stock price are highly dependent upon the profits generated by the operation. Creditors, especially lenders, provide resources for hospitality enterprises to use in the provision of services. Generally, future profits are required to repay these lenders. Managers are also extremely interested in profits because their performance is, to a large degree, measured by the operation's bottom line. Excellent services breed goodwill, repeat customers, and other benefits which ultimately increase the operation's profitability.

The profitability ratios we are about to consider measure management's overall effectiveness as shown by returns on sales (profit margin and operating efficiency ratio), returns on assets (return on assets and net return on assets), return on owners' equity (return on owners' equity and return on common stockholders' equity), and the relationship between net income and the market price of the hospitality establishment's stock (price/earnings ratio).

Profit Margin   Hospitality enterprises are often evaluated in terms of their ability to generate profits on sales. **Profit margin**, a key ratio, is determined by dividing net income by total revenue. It is an overall measurement of management's ability to generate sales and control expenses, thus yielding the bottom line. In this ratio, net income is the income remaining after all expenses have been deducted, both those controllable by management and those directly related to decisions made by the board of directors.

Using figures from Exhibit 5.2, the 19X2 profit margin of the Grand Hotel can be determined as follows:

$$\text{Profit Margin} = \frac{\text{Net Income}}{\text{Total Revenue}}$$

$$= \frac{\$146,700}{\$1,352,000}$$

$$= \underline{\underline{10.85\%}}$$

The Grand Hotel's 19X2 profit margin of 10.85% has remained nearly constant from the 19X1 figure of 10.87%. The 10.85% is quite high compared to a Laventhol & Horwath industry average of approximately 2.7%.[2]

If the profit margin is lower than expected, then expenses and other areas should be reviewed. Poor pricing and low sales volume could be contributing to the low ratio. To identify the problem area, management should analyze both the overall profit margin and the operated departmental margins. If the operated departmental margins are satisfactory, the problem would appear to be with overhead expense.

Operating Efficiency Ratio

The **operating efficiency ratio** (also known as **gross operating profit ratio**) is a better measure of management's performance than the profit margin. This ratio is the result of dividing income before fixed charges by total revenue. Income before fixed charges is the result of subtracting expenses generally controllable by management from revenues. The remaining fixed charges are expenses relating to the capacity of the hospitality firm, including rent, property taxes, insurance, depreciation, and interest expense. Although these expenses are the result of board of directors' decisions and thus beyond the direct control of active management, management can and should review tax assessments and insurance policies and quotations, and make recommendations to the board of directors that can affect the facility's total profitability. In calculating the operating efficiency ratio, income taxes are also excluded, since fixed charges directly affect income taxes.

Using figures from Exhibit 5.2, the 19X2 operating efficiency ratio of the Grand Hotel can be calculated as follows:

$$\frac{\text{Operating Efficiency}}{\text{Ratio}} = \frac{\text{Income Before Fixed Charges}}{\text{Total Revenue}}$$

$$= \frac{\$415,500}{\$1,352,000}$$

$$= \underline{\underline{30.73\%}}$$

The operating efficiency ratio shows that nearly $.31 of each $1 of revenue is available for fixed charges, income taxes, and profits. The Grand Hotel's operating efficiency ratio was 30.39% for 19X1.

The next group of profitability ratios compares profits to either assets or owners' equity. The result in each case is a percentage and is commonly called a return.

Exhibit 5.16 Return on Assets

$$\text{Return on Assets (ROA)} = \frac{\text{Net Income}}{\text{Average Total Assets*}}$$

$$= \frac{\$146,700}{\$1,120,650}$$

$$= \underline{\underline{13.09\%}}$$

$$\text{*Average Total Assets} = \frac{\text{Total Assets at Beginning and End of Year}}{2}$$

$$= \frac{\$1,065,000 + \$1,176,300}{2}$$

$$= \underline{\underline{\$1,120,650}}$$

Return on Assets (ROA)

The **return on assets (ROA)** ratio is a general indicator of the profitability of the hospitality enterprise's assets. Unlike the two preceding profitability ratios drawn only from income statement data, this ratio compares bottom line profits to the total investment, that is, to the total assets. It is calculated by dividing net income by average total assets. This ratio, or a variation of it, is used by several large conglomerates to measure the performances of their subsidiary corporations operating in the hospitality industry.

Using figures from Exhibits 5.1 and 5.2, the Grand Hotel's 19X2 return on assets is calculated in Exhibit 5.16. The Grand Hotel's 19X2 ROA is 13.09%, which means there was 13.09 cents of profit for every dollar of average total assets. The 19X1 ROA was 13.36%. Therefore, there was a slight decline in ROA from 19X1 to 19X2.

A very low ROA may result from inadequate profits or excessive assets. A very high ROA may suggest that older assets require replacement in the near future or that additional assets need to be added to support growth in revenues. The determination of low and high is usually based on industry averages and the hospitality establishment's own ROA profile that is developed over time.

ROA may also be calculated by multiplying the profit margin ratio by the asset turnover ratio:

$$\text{Profit Margin} \times \text{Asset Turnover} = \text{ROA}$$

$$\frac{\text{Net Income}}{\text{Total Revenue}} \times \frac{\text{Total Revenue}}{\text{Average Total Assets}} = \frac{\text{Net Income}}{\text{Average Total Assets}}$$

Gross Return on Assets (GROA)

Calculating the **gross return on assets (GROA)** is a variation of the ROA. This ratio measures the rate of return on assets regardless of financing methods. The calculation of ROA uses net income as its numerator and, therefore, includes the cost of debt-financing of the assets. The computation of the GROA, on the other hand, ignores any debt-financing by using income before interest and income taxes (EBIT) as its numerator. Interest is excluded because it is a financing cost. Income taxes are not considered because interest expense is deductible in calculating the operation's tax liability.

Using figures from Exhibits 5.1 and 5.2, the Grand Hotel's GROA for 19X2 can be calculated as follows:

$$\text{Gross Return on Assets} = \frac{\text{EBIT}}{\text{Average Total Assets}}$$

$$= \frac{\$304,500}{\$1,120,650}$$

$$= \underline{\underline{27.17\%}}$$

The Grand Hotel's GROA of 27.17% indicates a gross return of 27.17 cents for each dollar of average total assets for 19X2. This is a slight decline from 19X1 when GROA was 27.39%.

Return on Owners' Equity

A key profitability ratio is the **return on owners' equity (ROE)**. The ROE ratio compares the profits of the hospitality enterprise to the owners' investment. It is calculated by dividing net income by average owners' equity. Included in the denominator are all capital stock and retained earnings.

Exhibit 5.17 uses relevant figures from Exhibits 5.1 and 5.2 to calculate the 19X2 ROE for the Grand Hotel. In 19X2, for every one dollar of owners' equity, 31.30 cents was earned. The 19X1 ROE for the Grand was even higher at 34.46%. To the owner, this ratio represents the end result of all management's efforts. The ROE reflects management's ability to produce for the owners.

An alternative calculation of ROE considers both ROA and average total assets to average owners' equity. For 19X2, the calculation for the Grand Hotel is as follows:

$$\text{ROE} = \text{ROA} \times \frac{\text{Average Total Assets}}{\text{Average Total Owners' Equity}}$$

$$= 13.09\% \times \frac{\$1,120,650}{\$468,650}$$

$$= \underline{\underline{31.30\%}}$$

Thus, the lower the owners' equity relative to total assets (that is, the greater the financial leverage), the greater the ROE.

Return on Common Stockholders' Equity

A few hospitality enterprises have issued preferred stock in addition to common stock. When preferred stock has been issued, a variation of the ROE is the **return on common stockholders' equity**. It is necessary to compute this ratio only when more than one class of stock has been

Exhibit 5.17 Return on Owners' Equity

$$\text{Return on Owners' Equity (ROE)} = \frac{\text{Net Income}}{\text{Average Owners' Equity}^*}$$

$$= \frac{\$146,700}{\$468,650}$$

$$= 31.30\%$$

$$^*\text{Average Owners' Equity} = \frac{\text{Owners' Equity at Beginning and End of Year}}{2}$$

$$= \frac{\$420,000 + \$517,300}{2}$$

$$= \$468,650$$

issued. Common stockholders are concerned with what is available to them—net income less preferred dividends paid to preferred stockholders. The ROE ratio is adjusted as follows:

$$\frac{\text{Return on Common}}{\text{Stockholder's Equity}} = \frac{\text{Net Income} - \text{Preferred Dividends}}{\text{Average Common Stockholders' Equity}}$$

Since the Grand Hotel has not issued preferred stock, the calculation of this ratio is not further illustrated, because it would be the same as the previously calculated ROE.

The return to common stockholders is enhanced with the issuance of preferred stock when the return on investment from the use of the preferred stockholders' funds exceeds the dividends paid to preferred stockholders. From a common stockholder's viewpoint, any time debt or preferred stock can be issued at a "cost" less than the return from investing these "outside funds," the return to common stockholders is increased.

Earnings Per Share (EPS)

A common profitability ratio shown on hospitality establishments' income statements issued to external users is **earnings per share (EPS)**. The EPS calculation is a function of the capital structure of the hospitality enterprise. If only common stock has been issued (that is, there are no preferred stock or convertible debt or similar dilutive securities), then EPS is determined by dividing net income by the average common shares outstanding. When preferred stock has been issued, preferred dividends are subtracted from net income and the result is divided by the average number of common shares outstanding. If any dilutive securities have been issued, the EPS calculation is much more difficult and is beyond the scope of this text.[3]

Using figures from Exhibits 5.2 and 5.4, the 19X2 EPS for the Grand Hotel can be calculated as follows:

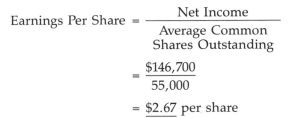

$$\text{Earnings Per Share} = \frac{\text{Net Income}}{\text{Average Common Shares Outstanding}}$$

$$= \frac{\$146,700}{55,000}$$

$$= \underline{\$2.67} \text{ per share}$$

In 19X1, the Grand's EPS was $2.57. Thus, the Grand Hotel's EPS has increased by $.10 from 19X1 to 19X2.

An increase in EPS must be viewed cautiously. The reduction of common stock outstanding by the issuing establishment's purchase of its own stock (treasury stock) will also result in an increased EPS, all other things being equal. Further, EPS is expected to increase as a hospitality enterprise reinvests earnings in its operations because a larger profit can then be generated without a corresponding increase in shares outstanding.

Price Earnings (PE) Ratio

Financial analysts often use the **price earnings (PE) ratio** in presenting investment possibilities in hospitality enterprises. The PE ratio is shown daily in the Wall Street Journal for all stocks listed on the New York and American Stock Exchanges. It is computed by dividing the market price per share by the EPS.

Assume that the market price per share of the Grand Hotel is $25.00 at the end of 19X2. The PE ratio for the Grand Hotel at the end of 19X2 is calculated as follows:

$$\text{Price Earnings Ratio} = \frac{\text{Market Price per Share}}{\text{Earnings per Share}}$$

$$= \frac{\$25}{\$2.67}$$

$$= \underline{9.36}$$

The Grand Hotel's PE ratio of 9.36 indicates that if the 19X2 EPS ratio is maintained, it would take 9.36 years for earnings to equal the market price per share at the end of 19X2.

The PE ratio for different hospitality enterprises may vary significantly. Factors affecting these differences include relative risk, stability of earnings, perceived earnings trend, and perceived growth potential of the stock.

Viewpoints Regarding Profitability Ratios

Owners, creditors, and management obviously prefer high profitability ratios. Owners prefer high profitability ratios because they indicate the return they are receiving from their investments. They will be most concerned about ROE (return on common stockholders' equity if preferred stock has been issued), because ROE measures the precise return on their investments. Although other profitability measures are important to the owner, the ROE is the "bottom line." Other profitability ratios may be relatively low and the ROE may still be excellent. For example, the profit margin could be only 2%, but the ROE could be 20%, based on the following:

Sales	$100
Net Income	$ 2
Owners' Equity	$ 10
Profit Margin	2%
ROE	20%

If the profitability ratios are not as high as other available investments (with similar risks), stockholders may become dissatisfied and eventually move their funds to other investments. This move, if not checked, will result in lower stock prices, and may pose difficulties for the hospitality enterprise when it desires to raise funds externally.

Creditors also prefer high, stable, or even growing profitability ratios. Although they desire stockholders to receive an excellent return (as measured by ROE), they will look more to the ROA ratio because this ratio considers all assets, not simply claims to a portion of the assets as does ROE. A high and growing ROA represents financial safety and, further, indicates competent management. A high ROA also generally means high profits and cash flow, which suggests safety to the creditor and low risk to the lender.

Managers must keep both creditors and owners happy. Therefore, all profitability ratios are especially important to them. Everything else being the same, the higher the profitability ratios, the better. High ratios also indicate that management is performing effectively and efficiently.

Profitability Evaluation of Segments

In chain operations, hotel managers may be evaluated based on the ROA of their individual hotels. A hotel manager may hesitate to replace inefficient equipment with new, more efficient equipment because the replacement may lower income and ROA through an increased asset base and increased depreciation. Rather than using ROA to evaluate the performance of individual hotels, corporate headquarters should consider using **residual income** as an alternative measure. Simply stated, residual income is the excess of a hotel's net income over a minimum return set by the holding company. The minimum return is calculated as a percentage of the hotel's asset base. When residual income is the basis of hotel management performance evaluation, hotel managers are encouraged to maximize residual income rather than ROA.

To illustrate this concept, assume that A&B Corporation owns two hotels—Hotel A and Hotel B—and requires a 10% return on Hotel A's average total assets. Further assume that Hotel A has $5,000,000 of average assets and generates net income of $600,000. The residual income of $100,000 is determined as follows:

Hotel A's net income	$600,000
Less: Minimum required return:	
$5,000,000 × .10	(500,000)
Residual income	$100,000

Now let us assume for purposes of illustration that Hotel B is evaluated on its residual income base, while Hotel A is evaluated on an ROA of 10%. Further assume that each hotel is earning an ROA of 12% prior to

Exhibit 5.18 Investment Evaluations: ROA versus Residual Income

	Current	Proposed	Total
Hotel A			
Net Income	$600,000	$110,000	$710,000
Average Total Assets	$5,000,000	$1,000,000	$6,000,000
ROA	12%	11%	11.83%
Hotel B			
Average Total Assets	$4,000,000	$1,000,000	$5,000,000
Net income	$ 480,000	$ 110,000	$ 590,000
Minimum required return (.10 × average total assets)	(400,000)	(100,000)	(500,000)
Residual income	$ 80,000	$ 10,000	$ 90,000

proposed rooms expansions at the beginning of the year costing $1,000,000 each which are expected to yield $110,000 at each property.

If Hotel A makes the $1,000,000 investment and $110,000 of profits are earned (which is an 11% return), Hotel A's ROA will slip from 12% to 11.83% as shown in Exhibit 5.18. It appears that Hotel A's manager performance is lower. Therefore, since Hotel A's manager is evaluated based on ROA, he/she probably will reject the expansion opportunity, even though overall profits would be increased.

On the other hand, Hotel B's general manager, being evaluated on residual income, would welcome the expansion opportunity since the residual income for Hotel B increases by $10,000 as shown in Exhibit 5.18.

Although residual income appears to resolve the problem of evaluating managers using ROA, its major disadvantage is that it cannot be used to compare the performance of hospitality operations of different sizes.

Operating Ratios

Operating ratios assist management in analyzing the operations of a hospitality establishment. Detailed information necessary for computing these ratios is normally not available to creditors or even owners not actively involved in management. These ratios reflect the actual mix of sales (revenues) and make possible comparisons to sales mix objectives. Further, operating ratios relate expenses to revenues and are useful for control purposes. For example, food cost percentage is calculated and compared to the budgeted food cost percentage to evaluate the overall control of food costs. Any significant deviation is investigated to determine the cause(s) for the variation between actual results and planned goals.

There are literally hundreds of operating ratios that could be calculated. Consider the following:

- Departmental revenues as a percentage of total revenue (sales mix)

- Expenses as a percentage of total revenue

- Departmental expenses as a percentage of departmental revenues

- Revenues per room occupied, meal sold, and so forth

- Annual expenses per room, and so forth

Exhibit 5.19 suggests over 200 useful operating ratios.

This section will consider only some of the most critical ratios, several relating to revenues and several relating to expenses. The revenue ratios include the mix of sales, average room rate, revenue per available room, and average food service check. The expense ratios include food cost percentage, beverage cost percentage, and labor cost percentage.

Mix of Sales   Hospitality establishments, like enterprises in other industries, attempt to generate sales as a means of producing profits. In the lodging segment of the hospitality industry, sales by the rooms department provide a greater contribution toward overhead costs and profits than the same amount of sales in other departments. In a food service operation, the sales mix of entrées yields a given contribution. The same sales total in a different sales mix will yield a different (possibly lower) contribution toward overhead and profits. Therefore, it is essential for management to obtain the desired sales mix. To determine the sales mix, departmental revenues are totaled and percentages of the total revenue are calculated for each operated department.

Using figures from Exhibits 5.2 and 5.4, Exhibit 5.20 shows the 19X2 sales mix for the Grand Hotel. The sales mix of a hospitality operation is best compared with the establishment's objectives as revealed in its budget. A second standard of comparison is the previous period's results. A third involves a comparison with industry averages.

An evaluation of revenue by department is accomplished by determining each department's average sale. For the rooms department, the ratio is the average room rate. For the food service department, it is the average food service check.

Average Room   A key rooms department ratio is the **average room rate**, often called
Rate (ADR)   the **average daily rate** or simply **ADR**. Most hotel and motel managers calculate the ADR even though rates within a property may vary significantly from single rooms to suites, from individual guests to groups and conventions, from weekdays to weekends, and from busy seasons to slack seasons.

Using figures from Exhibits 5.2 and 5.4, the 19X2 ADR for the Grand Hotel can be calculated as follows:

Exhibit 5.19 Selected Operating Ratios Useful in Analysis

CERTAIN OPERATING RATIOS USEFUL IN ANALYSIS	% of Total Revenues	% of Depart. Revenues	% of Depart. Total Cost	% Change from Prior Period	% Change from Budget	Per Available Room	Per Occupied Room	Per Available Seats	Per Cover/Guest	Per Square Foot	Per Full-time Equiv. Employee	% of Total Salaries & Wages	Per Unit Produced or Used
Total Revenues				•	•	•	•			•	•		
Rooms													
Revenue	•			•	•	•	•				•		
Salary, Wages & Burden		•	•	•	•	•	•					•	
Other Expenses		•	•	•	•	•	•						
Departmental Profit		•		•	•	•	•						
Food													
Revenue	•			•	•	•	•	•	•	•			
Cost of Sales		•	•	•	•				•				
Salary, Wages & Burden		•	•	•	•			•	•			•	
Other Expenses		•	•	•	•				•				
Departmental Profit		•		•	•			•	•	•	•		
Beverage													
Revenue	•			•	•	•	•	•	•	•			
Cost of Sales		•	•	•	•								
Salary, Wages & Burden		•	•	•	•			•				•	
Other Expenses		•	•	•	•								
Departmental Profit		•		•	•			•		•	•		
Minor Departments													
Revenue	•			•	•								
Cost of Sales		•		•	•								
Salary, Wages & Burden		•		•	•							•	
Other Expenses		•		•	•								
Departmental Profit		•		•	•								
Administrative & General													
Salary, Wages & Burden	•			•	•	•	•					•	
Other Expenses	•			•	•	•	•						
Departmental Total Cost	•			•	•	•	•						
Marketing													
Salary, Wages & Burden	•			•	•	•	•					•	
Other Expenses	•			•	•	•	•						
Departmental Total Cost	•			•	•	•	•						

(continued)

Exhibit 5.19 *(continued)*

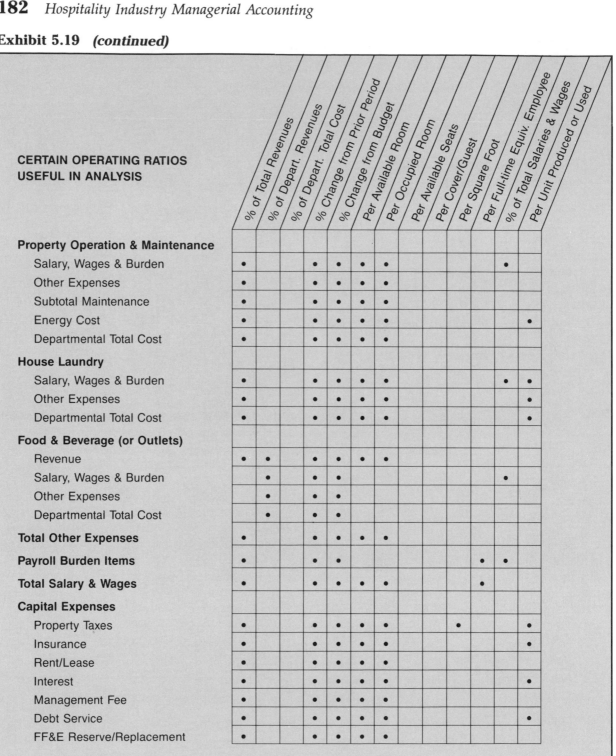

CERTAIN OPERATING RATIOS USEFUL IN ANALYSIS	% of Total Revenues	% of Depart. Revenues	% of Depart. Total Cost	% Change from Prior Period	% Change from Budget	Per Available Room	Per Occupied Room	Per Available Seats	Per Cover/Guest	Per Square Foot	Per Full-time Equiv. Employee	% of Total Salaries & Wages	Per Unit Produced or Used
Property Operation & Maintenance													
Salary, Wages & Burden	•			•	•	•	•				•		
Other Expenses	•			•	•	•	•						
Subtotal Maintenance	•			•	•	•	•						
Energy Cost	•			•	•	•	•						•
Departmental Total Cost	•			•	•	•	•						
House Laundry													
Salary, Wages & Burden	•			•	•	•	•					•	•
Other Expenses	•			•	•	•	•						•
Departmental Total Cost	•			•	•	•	•						•
Food & Beverage (or Outlets)													
Revenue	•	•		•	•	•	•						
Salary, Wages & Burden		•	•	•							•		
Other Expenses		•	•	•									
Departmental Total Cost		•	•	•									
Total Other Expenses	•			•	•	•	•						
Payroll Burden Items	•			•	•					•	•		
Total Salary & Wages	•			•	•	•	•				•		
Capital Expenses													
Property Taxes	•			•	•	•	•			•			•
Insurance	•			•	•	•	•						•
Rent/Lease	•			•	•	•	•						
Interest	•			•	•	•	•						•
Management Fee	•			•	•	•	•						
Debt Service	•			•	•	•	•						•
FF&E Reserve/Replacement	•			•	•	•	•						

Exhibit 5.20 Sales Mix

Departments	Sales	Percentage of Total
Rooms	$ 810,000	59.9%
Food	300,000	22.2
Beverage	145,000	10.7
Telephone	42,000	3.1
Rentals and Other Income	55,000	4.1
Total	$1,352,000	100.0%

$$ADR = \frac{\text{Rooms Revenue}}{\text{Number of Rooms Sold}}$$

$$= \frac{\$810,000}{21,000}$$

$$= \$38.57$$

The ADR for 19X2 is a $.52 improvement over the 19X1 ADR of $38.05 ($780,000 ÷ 20,500 rooms sold). The best standard of comparison to use in evaluating an actual average room rate is the rate budgeted as the goal for the rooms department's operation during the period. This average rate should also be calculated individually for each market segment: business groups, tourists, airline crews, and other categories of guests served.

Revenue per Available Room (REVPAR)

Traditionally, many hoteliers have placed heavy reliance on paid occupancy percentage as a quick indicator of activity and possibly performance. Others have looked at the ADR as an indication of the quality of its operation. However, paid occupancy percentage and average room rate by themselves are somewhat meaningless. A hotel may have a room occupancy of 80%, yet have an ADR of only $40, while a close competitor has a paid occupancy of 70% and an ADR of $60. Which hotel is in the preferable condition?

The combining of paid occupancy percentage and ADR is called **REVPAR** (revenue per available room) and is calculated as follows:

$$REVPAR = \frac{\text{Room Revenue}}{\text{Available Rooms}}$$

OR

$$REVPAR = \text{Paid Occupancy Percentage} \times ADR$$

Using the above example, the hotel with an 80% paid occupancy and the $40 ADR has a REVPAR of $32, while its competitor has a REVPAR of $42 (70% × $60). Everything else being the same for these hotels, one obviously prefers the hotel with the higher REVPAR, not the higher occupancy percentage in this case.

Based on information in Exhibits 5.2, 5.4, and 5.15, the Grand Hotel's

REVPAR for 19X2 is $27.74, while its REVPAR for 19X1 is $26.71. Thus, REVPAR increased by $1.03 in 19X2 over 19X1.

REVPAR is an improvement over simply looking at occupancy percent or ADR separately. Many industry executives prefer this combined statistic.

Average Food Service Check

A key food service ratio is the average food service check. This ratio is determined by dividing total food revenue by the number of food covers sold during the period.

Using figures from Exhibit 5.4, the average food service check for 19X2 for the Grand Hotel can be calculated as follows:

$$\text{Average Food Service Check} = \frac{\text{Total Food Revenue}}{\text{Number of Food Covers}}$$

$$= \frac{\$300,000}{56,000}$$

$$= \underline{\underline{\$5.36}}$$

The $5.36 average food service check in 19X2 is a $.31 increase over the Grand Hotel's average food service check of $5.05 for 19X1 ($280,000 ÷ 55,500 food covers). The average food service check is best compared with the budgeted amount for 19X2. An additional comparison relates this ratio to industry averages.

Additional average checks should be calculated for beverages. Management may even desire to calculate the average check by different dining areas and/or by various meal periods.

Food Cost Percentage

The **food cost percentage** is a key food service ratio that compares the cost of food sold to food sales. Most food service managers rely heavily on this ratio for determining whether food costs are reasonable.

Using figures from Exhibit 5.10, the 19X2 food cost percentage for the Grand Hotel is determined as follows:

$$\text{Food Cost Percentage} = \frac{\text{Cost of Food Sold}}{\text{Food Sales}}$$

$$= \frac{\$120,000}{\$300,000}$$

$$= \underline{\underline{40\%}}$$

The Grand Hotel's 19X2 food cost percentage of 40 indicates that of every $1 of food sales, $.40 goes toward the cost of food sold. This is best compared with the budgeted percentage for the period. A significant difference in either direction should be investigated by management. Management should be just as concerned about a food cost percentage that is significantly lower than the budgeted goal as it is about a food cost percentage that exceeds budgeted standards. A lower food cost percentage may indicate that the quality of food served is lower than desired, or that smaller portions are being served than are specified by the standard recipes. A food cost percentage in excess of the objective may be due to poor portion control, excessive food costs, theft, waste, spoilage, and so on.

Exhibit 5.21 Operated Department Labor Cost Percentages

Labor Cost Percentage	=	$\dfrac{\text{Labor Cost by Departments}}{\text{Department Revenues}}$		

Department	Total Labor Cost	÷	Total Revenue	=	Labor Cost Percentage
Rooms	$145,000		$810,000		17.90%
Food & Beverage	180,000		445,000		40.45%
Telephone	10,500		42,000		25.00%

Beverage Cost Percentage

A key ratio for beverage operations is the **beverage cost percentage**. This ratio results from dividing the cost of beverages sold by beverage sales.

Using figures from Exhibit 5.10, the 19X2 beverage cost percentage for the Grand Hotel can be calculated as follows:

$$\text{Beverage Cost Percentage} = \frac{\text{Cost of Beverages Sold}}{\text{Beverage Sales}}$$

$$= \frac{\$28,000}{\$145,000}$$

$$= \underline{\underline{19.31\%}}$$

The 19X2 beverage cost percentage of 19.31% for the Grand Hotel means that for each $1 of beverage sales, $.19 is spent on the cost of beverages served. As with the food cost percentage ratio, this ratio is best compared with the goal set for that period. Likewise, any significant variances must be investigated to determine the cause(s). Refinements of this ratio would be beverage cost percentage by type of beverage sold and by beverage outlet.

Labor Cost Percentage

The largest expense in hotels, motels, clubs, and many restaurants is labor. Labor expense includes salaries, wages, bonuses, payroll taxes, and fringe benefits. A general **labor cost percentage** is determined by dividing total labor costs by total revenue. This general labor cost percentage is simply a benchmark for making broad comparisons. For control purposes, labor costs must be analyzed on a departmental basis. The rooms department labor cost percentage is determined by dividing rooms department labor cost by room revenue. The food and beverage department labor cost percentage is determined by dividing food and beverage department labor cost by food and beverage revenue. Other operated department labor cost percentages are similarly determined.

Exhibit 5.21 uses figures from Exhibit 5.2 to calculate the 19X2 operated department labor cost percentages for the Grand Hotel. The 19X2 labor cost percentages for the Grand Hotel show the food and beverage department with the highest labor cost percentage at 40.45%. In most lodging firms, this is the case. The standard of comparison for these ratios is the budgeted percentages. Since labor costs are generally the largest expense, they must be tightly controlled. Management must carefully investigate any significant differences between actual and budgeted labor cost percentages.

Ratios for other expenses are usually computed as a percentage of revenues. If the expenses are operated department expenses, then the ratio is computed with the operated department revenues in the denominator and the expense in the numerator. An overhead expense ratio will consist of the overhead expense divided by total revenue. For example, marketing expense percentage is determined by dividing the marketing expense by total revenue. Using figures for the Grand Hotel in 19X2 found in Exhibit 5.2, the marketing expense percentage is 4.07% (marketing expenses of $55,000 ÷ total revenue of $1,352,000).

Limitations of Ratio Analysis

Ratios are extremely useful to owners, creditors, and management in evaluating the financial condition and operations of hospitality establishments. However, ratios are only indicators. Ratios do not resolve problems or even reveal exactly what the problem is. At best, when they vary significantly from past periods, budgeted standards, or industry averages, ratios only indicate that there *may be* a problem. Much more investigation and analysis are required.

Ratios are meaningful when they result from comparing two *related* numbers. Food cost percentage is meaningful because of the direct relationship between food costs and food sales. A goodwill/cash ratio may be somewhat meaningless due to the lack of any direct relationship between goodwill and cash.

Ratios are most useful when compared with a standard. A food cost percentage of 32% has little usefulness until it is compared with a standard such as past performance, industry averages, or the budgeted percentages.

Ratios are often used to compare different hospitality establishments. However, many ratios, especially operating ratios, will not result in meaningful comparisons if the two firms are in completely different segments of the industry. For example, comparing ratios for a luxury hotel to ratios for a quick-service restaurant would serve no meaningful purpose.

In addition, if the accounting procedures used by two separate hospitality establishments differ in several areas, then a comparison of their ratios will likely show differences related to accounting procedures as well as to financial positions or operations.

Finally, financial ratios are generally computed from figures in the financial statements. These figures are based on historical costs. Over time, the effects of inflation render these figures less useful. For example, an ADR of $55 in 19X9 for a given lodging property is not necessarily a better performance than $40 in 19X1; if the inflation rate was greater than 37.5% for the 19X1–19X9 time period, $55 in 19X9 is worth less than $40 in 19X1. Ratios which are most affected by inflation include those which contain property, equipment, or owners' equity in either the numerator or denominator. In addition, depreciation, since it relates to the historical cost of property and equipment, is often "understated," so income figures involving depreciation expense are often "overstated."

Accountants have used some fairly sophisticated techniques, such as restating the financial statements in constant dollars of equal purchasing power, to overcome this limitation in ratio analysis. However, as desirable as this correction is, it is often not used because of the major effort and time required to use it. An alternative approach is to apply an inflation correction factor to ratios that are affected by inflation. For example, using the above ADR example, assume that inflation for the 19X1–19X9 period was 50%. The comparison of ADRs for 19X1 and 19X9 would be as follows:

19X1 (historical)	$40
19X1 (adjusted)	$60*
19X9	$55

*$40 × 150% = $60

Thus, it is clear that the 19X1 ADR is preferred to the 19X9 ADR when inflation is considered.

Even though these limitations are present, a careful use of ratios that acknowledges their shortcomings will result in an enhanced understanding of the financial position and operations of hospitality establishments.

Usefulness of Financial Ratios

Research has been conducted to determine the usefulness of ratios to various users.[4] The following results are based on surveys of hotel general managers (GMs) and financial controllers who were requested to rate individually the usefulness of 45 different ratios to potential users of these ratios. Specifically, they were asked to rate the usefulness of each of these ratios to GMs, corporate executives, owners, and bankers on a scale of most important to least important. The results were then compiled by class of ratios and by users and are summarized as follows:[5]

Class of Ratios	Users			
	GMs	Corporate Executives	Owners	Bankers
Operating	1 (1)	2 (2)	3 (5)	4 (4)
Solvency	4 (5)	3 (3)	1 (2)	1 (1)
Activity	1 (2)	2 (5)	3 (4)	4 (5)
Profitability	4 (3)	2 (1)	1 (1)	3 (2)
Liquidity	3 (4)	1 (4)	2 (3)	4 (3)

The interpretation of the above table is as follows:

- The parenthetic numbers show the relative ranking of usefulness of the classes of ratios to each user group. For example, GMs considered operating ratios most useful (1), followed by activity ratios (2) and so forth.

- The non-parenthetic numbers reveal the relative usefulness of a class of ratios across the various user groups. For example, the survey results suggest operating ratios are considered most useful by general managers, followed by corporate executives, then owners and bankers.

- Owners and bankers are tied in their rating of solvency ratios.

In addition, the survey of GMs revealed that across all user groups the ten most useful ratios were:

1. Profit margin
2. Occupancy percentage—month-to-date
3. Cost of labor percentage
4. Daily occupancy percentage
5. ADR
6. Total revenue percentage change from budget
7. Cost of food sold percentage
8. Cost of beverage sold percentage
9. Room sales to total sales
10. Operating efficiency ratio

Computerization

Liquidity, solvency, activity, profitability, and operating ratios are by-products of the financial statements discussed in earlier chapters. Therefore, computers can automatically calculate and report these important statistics. The speed of the computers will allow these statistics to be created almost at will, assuming the financial data is stored in the computer.

However, many ratios need not be calculated on a daily basis. In fact, if they cover too short a period, they may not provide important information at all. Although it is difficult for many managers to do, it is important that they determine the key ratios to be calculated and the frequency with which they should be provided. If all the ratios were calculated daily, there would be the risk of "information overload." So much information (and so many reams of paper) would be provided that the manager would not have the time—or the desire—to look through it to find the valuable items.

Unlike many other ratios, operating ratios may be very useful when they are prepared frequently. For example, knowing food cost on a daily or weekly basis might be of great assistance to management. If food cost changes significantly for any day, management will want to know it in order to determine the cause(s) so that corrective action can be taken. Computers can play a major role in information gathering and the preparation of operating ratios. For example, when a hotel's night audit is computerized, many of the lodging statistics are a by-product of the process: average daily rate, occupancy percentage, double occupancy percentage, and so forth. These statistics can then be compared with the budget to give management a timely and convenient measure of the operation's success.

In addition, many other operating ratios can be generated quickly and with almost no manual intervention. The following example shows how this might work. Assume that the Grand Hotel has a computerized time clock system. The clocks record the time in and time out for employees as they enter and leave the building. Once a day, a computer in the accounting department receives the previous day's employee data from the clocks and calculates the total time for each employee. Departmental labor costs can then be determined based upon each employee's hourly rate, which is in the payroll system. The computer can even determine overtime, vacation, holiday, and sick pay. It can then report the payroll cost by department and job classification to management. If daily sales are entered into the computer, it would also be possible to track labor cost as a percentage of sales. Similar applications exist for food cost, preventive maintenance, and energy costs.

Summary

Ratio analysis permits investors, creditors, and operators to receive more valuable information from the financial statements than they could receive from reviewing the absolute numbers reported in the documents. Vital relationships can be monitored to determine solvency and risk, performance in comparison with other periods, and dividend payout ratios. A combination of ratios can be used to efficiently and effectively communicate more information than that provided by the statements from which they are calculated.

There are five major classifications of ratios: liquidity, solvency, activity, profitability, and operating. Although there is some overlap among these categories, each has a special area of concern. Exhibit 5.22 lists the 34 ratios presented in this chapter and the formulas by which they are calculated. It is important to be familiar with the types of ratios in each category, to know what each ratio measures, and to be aware of the targets or standards against which they are compared.

For example, a number of liquidity ratios focus on the hospitality establishment's ability to cover its short-term debts. However, each person examining the establishment's financial position will have a desired performance in mind. Creditors desire high liquidity ratios indicating that loans will probably be repaid. Investors, on the other hand, like lower liquidity ratios since current assets are not as profitable as long-term assets. Management reacts to these pressures by trying to please both groups.

The five ratio classifications vary in importance among the three major users of ratios. Creditors focus on solvency, profitability, and liquidity; investors and owners consider these ratios, but highlight the profitability ratios. Management uses all types of ratios, but is especially concerned with operating and activity ratios which can be used in evaluating the results of operations.

It is important to realize that a percentage by itself is not meaningful. It is only useful when it is compared with a standard: an industry average, a ratio from a past period, or a budgeted ratio. It is the comparison against budget ratios that is the most useful for management. Any significant difference should be analyzed to determine its probable cause(s). Once management has fully investigated areas of concern revealed by the ratios, then corrective action can be taken to rectify any problems.

Exhibit 5.22   List of Ratios

Ratio	Formula
1. Current ratio	Current assets/current liabilities
2. Acid-test ratio	Cash, marketable securities, notes and accounts receivable/current liabilities
3. Operating cash flows to current liabilities ratio	Operating cash flows/average current liabilities
4. Accounts receivable turnover	Revenue/average accounts receivable
5. Average collection period	365/accounts receivable turnover
6. Working capital turnover	Revenue/average working capital
7. Solvency ratio	Total assets/total liabilities
8. Debt-equity ratio	Total liabilities/total owners' equity
9. Long-term debt to total capitalization ratio	Long-term debt/long-term debt and owners' equity
10. Number of times interest earned ratio	EBIT/interest expense
11. Fixed charge coverage ratio	EBIT + lease expense/interest expense and lease expense
12. Operating cash flows to total liabilities ratio	Operating cash flows/average total liabilities
13. Inventory turnover:	
Food inventory turnover	Cost of food used/average food inventory
Beverage turnover	Cost of beverages used/average beverage inventory
14. Fixed asset turnover	Total revenue/average fixed assets
15. Asset turnover	Total revenues/average total assets
16. Paid occupancy percentage	Paid rooms occupied/rooms available
17. Complimentary occupancy	Complimentary rooms/rooms available
18. Average occupancy per room	Number of room guests/number of rooms occupied
19. Multiple occupancy percentage	Rooms occupied by two or more people/rooms occupied by guests
20. Profit margin	Net income/total revenue
21. Operating efficiency ratio	Income before fixed charges/total revenue
22. Return on assets	Net income/average total assets
23. Gross return on assets	EBIT/average total assets
24. Return on owners' equity	Net income/average owners' equity
25. Return on common stockholders' equity	Net income – preferred dividend/average common stockholders' equity
26. Earnings per share	Net income/average common shares outstanding
27. Price earnings ratio	Market price per share/earnings per share
28. Mix of sales	Departmental revenues are totaled; percentages of total revenue are calculated for each
29. ADR	Room revenue/number of rooms sold
30. REVPAR	Paid occupancy percentage × ADR
31. Average food service check	Total food revenue/number of food covers
32. Food cost percentage	Cost of food sold/food sales
33. Beverage cost percentage	Cost of beverages sold/beverage sales
34. Labor cost percentage	Labor cost by department/department revenues

Endnotes

1. This may be determined mathematically using the following formula:

    $\dfrac{CA - x}{CL - x} =$ desired current ratio where x indicates the amount of current assets which would be used to retire current liabilities. The calculation for the Grand Hotel is as follows:

    $$\frac{338,000 - x}{214,000 - x} = 2; \qquad x = 90,000; \qquad \frac{248,000}{124,000} = 2 \text{ times}$$

2. The Laventhol & Horwath "profit margin" is based on net income before income taxes rather than net income, and was 2.7% for 1988. See Laventhol & Horwath, *U.S. Lodging Industry 1989* (Philadelphia: Laventhol & Horwath, 1989).

3. The interested student is referred to intermediate accounting texts, most of which contain a full discussion of EPS calculations in various situations.

4. Raymond S. Schmidgall, "Financial Ratios: Perceptions of Lodging Industry General Managers and Financial Executives," *FIU Hospitality Review*, Fall 1989, pp. 1–9.

5. As a note of caution, the research is based on perceptions of lodging general managers and financial controllers and does not necessarily reflect the actual views of corporate executives, owners, and bankers. Nonetheless, the great consistency of answers among all respondents suggests that this information is reliable.

Key Terms

accounts receivable turnover
acid-test ratio
activity ratios
asset turnover
average collection period
average daily rate (ADR)
average occupancy per room ratio
average room rate (ADR)
beverage cost percentage
complimentary occupancy
current ratio
debt-equity ratio
earnings per share (EPS)
financial leverage
fixed asset turnover
fixed charge coverage ratio
food cost percentage
gross operating profit ratio
gross return on assets (GROA)
inventory turnover
labor cost percentage
liquidity ratios
long-term debt to total capitalization ratio

multiple occupancy
number of times interest earned ratio
operating cash flows to current liabilities ratio
operating cash flows to total liabilities ratio
operating efficiency ratio
operating ratios
paid occupancy
price earnings (PE) ratio
profit margin
profitability ratios
ratio analysis
residual income
return on assets (ROA)
return on common stockholders' equity
return on owners' equity (ROE)
REVPAR
seat turnover
solvency ratio
solvency ratios
working capital turnover ratio

Discussion Questions

1. How does ratio analysis benefit creditors?

2. If you were investing in a hotel, which ratios would be most useful? Why?

3. What are the limitations of ratio analysis?

4. How do the three user groups of ratio analysis react to the solvency ratios?

5. What is leverage, and why may owners want to increase it?

6. What do activity ratios highlight?

7. How is the profit margin calculated? How is it used?

8. Which standard is the most effective for comparison with ratios?

9. What does the ratio expression "turnover" mean?

10. Of what value is the food sales/total sales ratio to the manager of a hotel? To a creditor?

Problems

Problem 5.1

Indicate the effects of the transactions listed below on each of the following: total current assets, working capital (CA – CL), and current ratio. Indicate increase with "+," indicate decrease with "–" and indicate no effect or effect cannot be determined with "0." Assume an initial current ratio of greater than 1.0.

	Total Current Assets	Working Capital	Current Ratio
1. Food is sold for cash	_____	_____	_____
2. Equipment is sold at less than its net book value	_____	_____	_____
3. Beverages are sold on account	_____	_____	_____
4. A cash dividend is declared	_____	_____	_____
5. Accrued payroll is paid	_____	_____	_____
6. Treasury stock is purchased	_____	_____	_____
7. A fully depreciated fixed asset is retired	_____	_____	_____
8. Equipment is purchased with long-term notes	_____	_____	_____
9. Utility expenses are paid (they were not previously accrued)	_____	_____	_____
10. A cash dividend is paid	_____	_____	_____

Problem 5.2

The Duke Snyder Motel has operated for several years as you become the new manager. In order to better understand the financial situation, you are to examine the financial statements for the year just ended (19X4) and perform ratio analysis. The motel's balance sheet and condensed income statement are below:

Duke Snyder Motel
Balance Sheet
December 31, 19X4

Assets

Current Assets:	
Cash	$ 95,000
Accounts Receivable	100,000
Inventories	5,000
Total Current Assets	200,000

Property and Equipment:	
Land	60,000
Building (net)	300,000
Furniture & Equipment (net)	80,000
Total Property and Equipment	440,000

Total Assets	$640,000

Liabilities and Owners' Equity

Current Liabilities	$210,000
Long-Term Liabilities:	
Note from Owner	40,000
Mortgage Payable	80,000
Total Liabilities	330,000

Owners' Equity	
Common Stock	100,000
Retained Earnings	210,000
Total Owners' Equity	310,000

Total Liabilities and Owners' Equity	$640,000

Duke Snyder Motel
Condensed Income Statement
For the year ended December 31, 19X4

Sales	$1,500,000
Cost of Goods Sold	200,000
Operating Expenses	800,000
Contribution Margin	500,000
Undistributed Operating Expenses	125,000
Income Before Fixed Charges	375,000
Interest	120,000
Other Fixed Charges	162,000
Income Before Taxes	93,000
Income Tax	27,900
Net Income	$ 65,100

Required:

Calculate the following ratios:

1. Current ratio

2. Acid-test ratio

3. Debt-equity ratio

4. Number of times interest earned ratio

5. Operating efficiency ratio

6. Profit margin

7. Return on owners' equity (assume that the only change in owners' equity during 19X4 is the net income of $65,100)

8. Return on total assets (assume that total assets were $640,000 on January 1, 19X4)

Problem 5.3

The following information applies to the Maris Restaurant:

Cash and marketable securities	$10,000
Property and equipment	$1,500,000
Total sales	$2,000,000
Profit margin	5%
Acid-Test ratio	1.2 to 1
Current ratio	1.5 to 1
ROE	10%
Accounts receivable turnover	20 times

Assume the following:

1. The accounts receivable turnover is based on total sales.

2. Total assets are equal to current assets plus property and equipment.

3. The balances of balance sheet accounts at the beginning of the year are the same as the end of the year.

Required:

Determine the following:

1. Total current assets

2. Total current liabilities

3. Net income

4. Asset turnover

5. Total owners' equity

6. Long-term debt

7. Return on assets

8. Debt-equity ratio

Problem 5.4

The Hodges, a 300-room hotel, has provided you with the following data for the months of June and July:

	June	July
Single rooms sold	2,400	2,418
Double rooms sold	4,200	4,278
Room revenue	$396,000	$399,000
Number of paid guests	9,900	9,910

Required:

1. Compute the following for June and July:
   a. Paid occupancy percentage
   b. Multiple occupancy percentage
   c. Average number of guests per double room sold (assume that only one guest stayed in each single room sold)
   d. Monthly ADR
   e. Monthly REVPAR

2. Was the Hodges' financial performance better in June or July? (Assume that fixed costs were constant and that the variable costs per room sold remained constant. Support your answer with detailed discussion.)

Problem 5.5

The Gibson Hotel is a 250-room facility with several profit centers. The hotel is open throughout the year, and generally about 2% of the rooms are being repaired or renovated at all times; therefore, assume that they are unavailable for sale. During 19X1, the hotel sold 77,800 rooms and experienced an average occupancy per room of 1.32 people. The accounting department has supplied the following information concerning the food department:

Ending Inventory	$35,000
Consumption by Employees (free of charge)	5,000
Cost of Sales	312,000
Food Cost Percentage	40%
Food Inventory Turnover	10 times

Required:

Determine the following:

1. Occupancy rate for 19X1

2. Number of paid guests for 19X1

3. Beginning inventory of food

4. Food sales

5. Multiple occupancy percentage (assume that no more than two persons occupied a double room)

Problem 5.6

Donna Drysdale, co-owner of Drysdale Pizza, provides you with information as follows for 19X3 and 19X4:

	19X3	19X4
Food sales	$800,000	$850,000
Other sales	50,000	60,000
Total sales	850,000	910,000
Cost of food sold	160,000	170,000
Cost of other sales	20,000	24,000
Total cost of sales	180,000	194,000
Gross profit	670,000	716,000
Controllable expenses:		
Salaries and wages	160,000	170,000
Employee benefits	50,000	55,000
Other expenses	150,000	170,000
Income before occupation costs, interest and depreciation	310,000	321,000
Depreciation expense	80,000	80,000
Interest expense	80,000	75,000
Occupation costs	40,000	45,000
Income before income taxes	110,000	121,000
Income taxes	30,000	35,000
Net income	$ 80,000	$ 86,000

Other data:	19X2	19X3	19X4
Rent expense	–	$10,000	$11,000
Food customers served	–	66,667	65,385
Food inventory at year-end	$ 4,800	$ 5,000	$ 5,300
Employee meals*	–	$ 1,500	$ 1,550

*Included as part of employee benefits.

Required:

1. Determine the following for 19X3 and 19X4:

    a. Average food service check
    b. Food cost percentage
    c. Labor cost percentage
    d. Labor cost per customer served
    e. Number of times interest earned
    f. Operating efficiency ratio
    g. Fixed charge coverage ratio
    h. Profit margin

2. Was Drysdale Pizza more efficient in 19X3 or 19X4? Support your answer with figures and discussion.

Problem 5.7

The Kaline Hotel's current assets and current liabilities from the past three years' balance sheets are as follows:

	19X1	19X2	19X3
Current Assets:			
Cash	$15,000	$10,000	$ 8,000
Marketable Securities	30,000	25,000	20,000
Accounts Receivables (net)	70,000	85,000	95,000
Inventory—Food	20,000	22,000	25,000
Prepaid Expenses	10,000	12,000	15,000
Total	$145,000	$154,000	$163,000
Current Liabilities:			
Accounts Payable	$ 60,000	$ 62,000	$ 65,000
Notes Payable	30,000	30,000	30,000
Wages Payable	20,000	22,000	25,000
Taxes Payable	10,000	11,000	12,000
Total	$120,000	$125,000	$132,000
Selected Operations Data:			
Sales (total)	$1,000,000	$1,100,000	$1,200,000
Cost of Food Consumed	150,000	160,000	168,000

Note: Assume that 50% of the sales were on account.

Required:

1. Compute the trend of the following:
   a. Current ratio
   b. Acid-test ratio
   c. Accounts receivable turnover (19X2 and 19X3 only)
   d. Inventory turnover (19X2 and 19X3 only)

2. Based on the above calculated ratios, comment on the liquidity trend of the Kaline Hotel.

Problem 5.8

The Mantle Inn commenced operations on January 1, 19X1, and has been operating for two years. Assume that you are the new Assistant Manager and desire to gain some insight into financial relationships of your new employer. Balance sheets and condensed income statements for the first two years are provided below.

Balance Sheets
Mantle Inn
December 31, 19X1 and 19X2

Assets	19X1	19X2
Current Assets:		
Cash	$ 10,000	$ 15,000
Marketable Securities	–0–	50,000
Accounts Receivable	55,000	60,000
Inventories	10,000	12,000
Total Current Assets	75,000	137,000

Property and Equipment:		
Land	100,000	100,000
Building (net)	1,950,000	1,900,000
Furniture & Equipment (net)	240,000	200,000
Total Property & Equipment	2,290,000	2,200,000
Total Assets	$2,365,000	$2,337,000
Liabilities and Owners' Equity		
Current Liabilities	$ 55,000	$ 60,000
Long-Term Debt	1,300,000	1,250,000
Total Liabilities	1,355,000	1,310,000
Owners' Equity:		
Common Stock	1,000,000	1,000,000
Retained Earnings	10,000	27,000
Total Owners' Equity	1,010,000	1,027,000
Total Liabilities and Owners' Equity	$2,365,000	$2,337,000

Condensed Income Statements
Mantle Inn
For the years ended December 31, 19X1 and 19X2

	19X1	19X2
Sales	$1,200,000	$1,400,000
Operated Department Expense	620,000	700,000
Operated Department Income	580,000	700,000
Undistributed Operating Expenses	380,000	400,000
Total Income Before Fixed Charges	200,000	300,000
Fixed Charges	185,000	200,000
Income Taxes	5,000	45,000
Net Income	$ 10,000	$ 55,000

Required:

1. Calculate the following ratios for both years:
   a. Current ratio
   b. Solvency ratio
   c. Profit margin
   d. Operating efficiency

2. Calculate for 19X2 the following ratios:
   a. Fixed asset turnover ratio
   b. Total assets turnover ratio
   c. Accounts receivable turnover ratio
   d. Number of days accounts receivable outstanding
   e. Return on total assets
   f. Return on owners' equity

Problem 5.9

Musial Enterprises consists of four hotels. The corporation's required annual return for each hotel is 12% of each hotel's average total assets. The net income and average total assets for each hotel are as follows:

	Gibson Hotel	Brock Hotel	Smith Hotel	Carey Hotel
Net income	$ 2,700,000	$ 4,500,000	$ 3,000,000	$ 3,000,000
Average total assets	$20,000,000	$15,000,000	$25,000,000	$18,000,000

Each hotel has the opportunity to expand. The cost of expansion per hotel is $5,000,000, and the expected annual after-tax profit per hotel is $650,000.

Required:

1. Determine the ROA for each hotel before the expansion consideration.

2. If the expansion is based on maintaining or improving a hotel's ROA, which hotels would be expanded? Why?

3. Calculate the residual income for each hotel before and after the proposed expansion.

Problem 5.10

The owner of the Martin Motel and Restaurant has asked you to prepare an income statement and balance sheet based on the following:

1. Accounts receivable = $10,000
2. Accounts payable = $15,000
3. Current assets consist of cash, accounts receivable, and inventory
4. Current liabilities consist of only accounts payable
5. Current ratio = 1.2 to 1
6. Acid-test ratio = .8 to 1
7. Accounts receivable turnover = 30 times (all sales are credit sales)
8. Food inventory turnover = 9.625 times
9. Beverage inventory turnover = 6.3525 times
10. Fixed asset turnover = 13/47 times
11. Depreciation expense = 10% of book value at year-end
12. Long-term debt = 9 times accounts payable
13. Interest rate = 10%
14. Tax rate = 20%
15. Average room rate = $20.00
16. Average food and beverage check = $5.00
17. Size of motel = 25 rooms
18. Occupancy percentage = 80%
19. Number of food and beverage checks = 30,800

20. Undistributed Operating Expenses = 33⅓% of total revenue
21. Food cost percentage = 40%
22. Beverage cost percentage = 22%
23. Food and beverage labor and other cost percentage = 30%
24. Rooms labor and other cost percentage = 40%
25. Food sales = 62½% of total food and beverage sales
26. Debt-equity ratio = 1 to 1
27. Return on owners' equity = 1.330667%

Assume that the balance sheet at the beginning of the year is the same as at the end of the year.

6 Basic Cost Concepts

The word *cost* is used in many different contexts and may convey very different meanings. For example, each of the following expressions uses the term to refer to something different: the cost of a dishwasher was $5,000; the labor cost for the period was $10,000; the cost of damages to the hotel from the hurricane approximated $10,000. In the first expression, cost refers to the purchase price of an asset; one asset (cash) was given in exchange for another asset (the dishwasher). The second expression uses cost to refer to an expense for the period; cash (an asset) was paid to employees for services they provided. In this case, assets were not directly exchanged; rather, cash was paid for labor services rendered by employees to generate revenues and accounts receivables. The accounts receivables, when collected, result in cash. In the third expression, the cost due to the hurricane refers to a loss—a dissipation of assets without the receipt of other assets either directly or indirectly. Obviously, the term cost may have a variety of meanings. In this chapter, we will generally use cost to mean expenses.

Managers must understand many cost concepts, including those in the following questions:

1. What are the hotel's fixed costs?

2. Which costs are relevant to purchasing a new microcomputer?

3. What are the variable costs of serving a steak dinner?

4. What is the opportunity cost of adding 25 rooms to the motel?

5. What is the standard cost of catering a banquet for 500 people?

6. What are the hotel's controllable costs?

7. How are fixed cost portions of mixed costs determined?

8. How are costs allocated to operated departments?

9. Which costs are sunk costs in considering a future purchase?

10. Which costs are relevant to pricing a lobster dinner?

In this chapter, we will discuss a variety of cost concepts. We will consider costs in relation to sales volume and operated departments. We will also discuss the separation of mixed costs into fixed and variable elements, provide a simplified approach to the problem of cost allocation, and consider the concept of relevant costs in decision-making. The Supplemental Reading to this chapter contains a detailed discussion of more advanced approaches to cost allocation, including illustrations of the direct and step methods of cost allocation.

General Nature of Cost

Cost, considered as an expense, is the reduction of an asset, generally for the ultimate purpose of increasing revenues. Costs include cost of food sold, labor expense, supplies expense, utilities expense, marketing expense, rent expense, depreciation expense, insurance expense, and many others. Because the profit margin for most hospitality operations is less than 10%, more than 90% of their revenues (ultimately cash) is used to pay these expenses or costs. From management's viewpoint, there are several different types of costs. It is essential that managers understand both the types of costs and their applications.

Costs in Relation to Sales Volume

One way of viewing costs is to understand how they change with changes in the activity (sales) of the hospitality operation. In this context, costs can be seen as fixed, variable, step, or mixed (partly fixed and partly variable).

Fixed Costs

Fixed costs are those which remain constant in the short run, even when sales volume varies. For example, room sales may increase by 5% or food sales may decline by 10% while, in both cases, the fixed costs remain constant. The graph in Exhibit 6.1 plots costs along the vertical axis and sales volume along the horizontal axis. The graph shows that total fixed costs remain constant even when sales volume increases.

Common examples of fixed costs include salaries, rent expense, insurance expense, property taxes, depreciation expense, and interest expense. Certain fixed costs may be reduced if a lodging facility closes for part of the year. For example, insurance and labor expenses may be avoided during the shut-down. Fixed costs which may be avoided when a company shuts down are called **avoidable costs**.

Fixed costs are often classified as either capacity or discretionary costs. **Capacity fixed costs** relate to the ability to provide goods and services. For a hotel, the capacity fixed costs relate to the ability to provide a number of rooms for sale. The fixed costs include, but are not limited to, depreciation, property taxes, interest, and certain salaries. There is a quality dimension related to capacity fixed costs. For example, if the hotel were to eliminate its swimming pool or air conditioning system, it could still provide the same number of rooms, but at a lower level of service.

Discretionary fixed costs do not affect a lodging establishment's current capacity. They are costs which managers may choose to avoid during the short run, often to meet a budget. However, continued avoidance will generally cause problems for the hospitality operation. Discretionary

Exhibit 6.1   Fixed Costs: Total and Per Unit

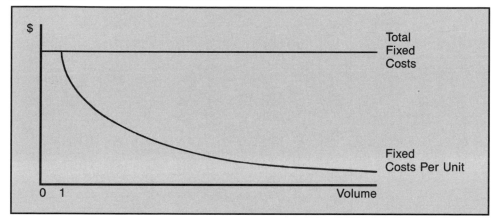

fixed costs include educational seminars for executives, charitable contributions, employee training programs, and advertising. Generally, reducing such costs has no immediate effect on operations. However, if these programs continue to be curtailed, sales and various expenses may be seriously affected. During a financial crisis, discretionary fixed costs are likelier to be cut than fixed capacity costs because they are easier to restore and have less immediate impact.

Fixed costs can also be related to sales volume by determining the average fixed cost per unit sold. For example, if fixed costs total $10,000 for a period in which 2,000 rooms are sold, the average fixed cost per room sold is $5.00 ($10,000 ÷ 2,000 rooms). However, if 3,000 rooms are sold during the period, then the average fixed cost per room sold is $3.33 ($10,000 ÷ 3,000 rooms). As the sales volume increases, the fixed cost per unit decreases. The graph in Exhibit 6.1 also illustrates this relationship.

Although they are constant in the short run, all fixed costs change over longer periods. For example, the monthly lease payment on a machine may increase about once a year. Therefore, from a long-term perspective, all fixed costs may be viewed as variable costs.

Variable Costs

Variable costs change proportionally with the volume of business. For example, if food sales increase by 10%, the cost of food sold may also be expected to increase by 10%. Exhibit 6.2 depicts total variable costs and variable costs per unit as each relates to sales volume. Total variable costs (TVC) are determined by multiplying the variable cost per unit by the number of unit sales. For example, the TVC for a food service operation with a variable cost per meal of $3 and 1,000 projected meal sales would be $3,000.

Theoretically, total variable costs vary with total sales, whereas unit variable costs remain constant. For example, if the cost of food sold is 35%, then the unit cost per $1 of sales is $.35, regardless of sales volume. The graph in Exhibit 6.2 shows that unit variable costs are really fixed—that is, the cost per sales dollar remains constant. In actuality, of course, a business should be able to take advantage of volume discounts as its sales increase beyond some level. When this occurs, the cost of sales should increase at a slower rate than sales.

Exhibit 6.2   Variable Costs: Total and Per Unit

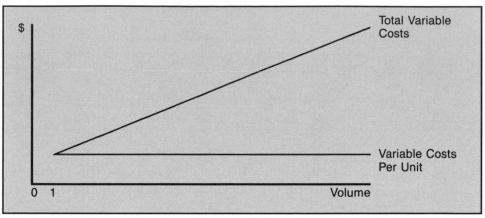

Exhibit 6.3   Step Costs

In truth, few costs, if any, vary in *exact* proportion to total sales. However, several costs come close to meeting this criterion and may be considered variable costs. Examples include the cost of food sold, cost of beverages sold, some labor costs, and supplies used in production and service operations.

Step Costs   **Step costs** are constant within a range of activity but different among ranges of activity. Exhibit 6.3 illustrates this relationship. Supervisor salaries are typical step costs. For example, if a housekeeping supervisor is able to oversee no more than 15 room attendants, then the operation must add another supervisor upon adding the sixteenth room attendant. This new supervisor would be able to supervise an additional 14 room attendants.

Step costs resemble fixed costs when one step includes the operation's probable range of activity. In Exhibit 6.3, for example, range 2 might be a hotel's expected range of activity. In such cases, step costs are considered fixed costs for analytical purposes. When there are many steps and

Exhibit 6.4 Total Mixed Costs

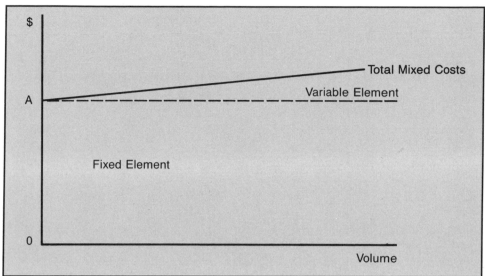

the cost differences between steps are small, then step costs, for analytical purposes, are considered mixed costs (to be discussed next).

Mixed Costs   Many costs are partly fixed and partly variable—that is, they are a mix of both fixed and variable cost elements. These costs are sometimes referred to as semi-variable or semi-fixed. In this text, we will refer to costs that are partly fixed and partly variable as **mixed costs**.

The mixed cost's fixed element is determined independently of sales activity, while the variable element is assumed to vary proportionally with sales volume. As with variable costs, the variable element of mixed costs may not vary in exact proportion to sales activity. However, the assumption of a linear relationship between variable cost elements and sales volume is generally accepted because any difference is usually considered insignificant. However, this assumption is reasonable only across a relevant range of activity. For example, the relevant range for a hotel *may* be paid occupancy levels between 40% and 95%. Outside of this range, the variable cost-sales relationship *may* be different.

The graph in Exhibit 6.4 depicts the two elements (fixed and variable) of mixed costs. The portion of the vertical axis below point A represents fixed costs, while the difference between the slopes of the total mixed costs and fixed cost lines reflects the variable element of total mixed costs. The graph in Exhibit 6.5 shows a decrease in unit mixed costs as sales volume increases. This decrease is not as dramatic as the decrease in fixed costs per sales unit (Exhibit 6.1) because the variable element in mixed costs results increases with each unit sold, therefore increasing total mixed costs.

Several examples of mixed costs, including a brief discussion of their fixed and variable elements, are listed in Exhibit 6.6.

Total mixed costs (TMC) for any cost can be estimated with the following equation:

Exhibit 6.5 Mixed Costs per Sales Unit

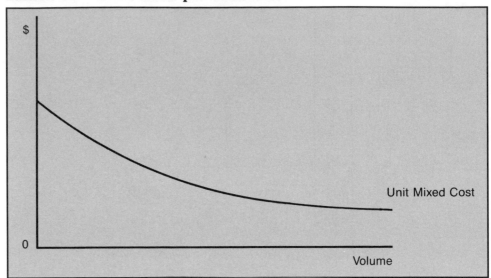

$$TMC = \text{fixed costs} + (\text{variable cost per unit} \times \text{unit sales})$$

Thus, a hotel with a franchise fee of $1,000 per month and $3 per room sold would estimate its franchise fees (a mixed cost) for a month with 3,500 projected room sales as follows:

$$\begin{aligned} \text{Franchise fees} &= \$1,000 + (3,500 \times \$3) \\ &= \underline{\$11,500} \end{aligned}$$

Total Costs   Total costs (TC) for a hospitality establishment consist of the sum of its fixed, variable, step, and mixed costs. If step costs are included in either fixed or mixed costs, the TC may be determined by the following equation:

$$TC = \text{fixed costs} + (\text{variable cost per unit} \times \text{unit sales})$$

An estimation of TC for a rooms-only lodging operation which sells 1,000 rooms and has total fixed costs of $20,000 and variable costs per unit of $20, is $40,000.

$$\begin{aligned} TC &= \$20,000 + (1,000 \times \$20) \\ &= \underline{\$40,000} \end{aligned}$$

Total costs are depicted graphically in Exhibit 6.7.

The equation for TC corresponds to the general equation for a straight line, which is as follows:[1]

$y = a + bx$
where y = value of the dependent variable (total costs)
  a = the constant term (total fixed costs)
  b = slope of the line (variable cost per unit)
  x = the value of the independent variable (units sold)

Exhibit 6.6   Fixed and Variable Elements of Mixed Costs

	Elements	
Mixed Cost	**Fixed**	**Variable**
1. Telephone expense	Cost of system/rental of system	Cost of calls
2. Building lease	Fixed cost per square foot of space rented	Percentage of revenue in addition to fixed amount
3. Automobile lease	Fixed cost/day	Additional charge per mile automobile is driven
4. Executive remuneration	Base pay	Bonuses based on sales
5. Repair and maintenance	Minimum amount required to maintain lodging firm at low occupancy	Additional maintenance required with higher occupancy levels

Exhibit 6.7   Total Costs

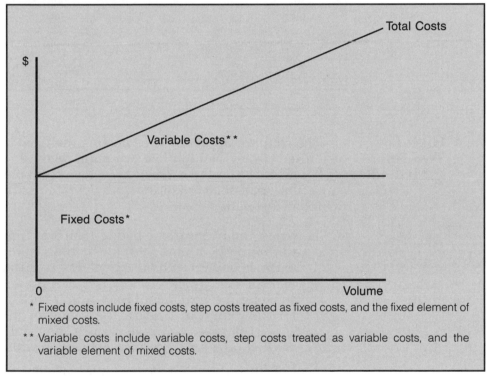

* Fixed costs include fixed costs, step costs treated as fixed costs, and the fixed element of mixed costs.

** Variable costs include variable costs, step costs treated as variable costs, and the variable element of mixed costs.

Determination of Mixed Cost Elements

When making pricing, marketing, and expansion decisions, management needs to estimate the fixed and variable elements of each mixed cost. We will consider three methods of estimating mixed cost elements: the high/low two-point method, the scatter diagram, and regression analysis. The maintenance and repair expense of the hypothetical Mayflower Hotel for 19X1 will be used to illustrate all three methods. Exhibit 6.8 presents the monthly repair and maintenance expense together with rooms sold by month for the Mayflower Hotel.

Exhibit 6.8 Monthly Repair and Maintenance Expenses

	19X1 Monthly Repair and Maintenance Expense Mayflower Hotel	
Month	Repair and Maintenance Expense	Rooms Sold
January	$6,200	1,860
February	6,100	1,820
March	7,000	2,170
April	7,500	2,250
May	8,000	2,480
June	8,500	2,700
July	7,900	2,790
August	8,600	2,800
September	7,000	2,100
October	6,000	1,900
November	6,500	1,800
December	5,900	1,330
Total	$85,200	26,000

High/Low Two-Point Method

The simplest approach to estimating the fixed and variable elements of a mixed cost is the **high/low two-point method**. This approach is simple because it bases the estimation on data from only two periods in the entire time span of an establishment's operations. The method consists of the following eight steps:

1. Select the two extreme periods (such as months) of sales activity (for example, rooms sold) in the time span under consideration (such as one year). If an extreme value is due to an event beyond management's control and does not represent normal operations, consider the next value. For example, if a country club is closed for the month of January, the value for the next lowest month should be used. Extreme values may only be apparent when charted on a *scatter diagram,* which we will discuss shortly.

2. Calculate the differences in total mixed cost and activity for the two periods.

3. Divide the mixed cost difference by the activity difference to determine the variable cost per activity unit (for example, each room sold).

4. Multiply the variable cost per activity unit by the total activity for the period of lowest (or highest) sales to arrive at the total variable cost for the period of lowest (or highest) activity.

5. Subtract the result in Step 4 from the total mixed cost for the period of lowest activity to determine the fixed cost for that period.

6. Check the answer in Step 5 by repeating Steps 4 and 5 for the period with the greatest activity.

7. Multiply the fixed cost per period by the number of periods in the time span to calculate the fixed costs for the entire time period.

8. Subtract the total fixed costs from the total mixed costs to determine the total variable costs.

The high/low two-point method is illustrated below using data from Exhibit 6.8.

1. High month—August
   Low month—December

2.

	Repair and Maintenance Expense	Rooms Sold
August	$8,600	2,800
December	5,900	1,330
Difference	$2,700	1,470

3. Variable Cost per Room Sold $= \dfrac{\text{Mixed Cost Difference}}{\text{Rooms Sold Difference}}$

   $= \dfrac{\$2,700}{1,470}$

   $= \$1.8367$

This result means that for every additional room sold, the hotel will incur repair and maintenance variable costs of $1.8367.

4. Total Variable Cost of Repair and Maintenance Expense for December $=$ December Rooms Sold × Variable Cost

   $= 1,330 \times 1.8367$

   $= \$2,442.81$

5. Total Fixed Cost of Repair and Maintenance Expense for December $=$ Total Repair and Maintenance Cost for December − Variable Repair and Maintenance Cost for December

   $= \$5,900.00 - \$2,442.81$

   $= \$3,457.19$

6. Check results by using the high month, August.

   Variable Cost $= 2,800 \times 1.8367$

   $= \$5,142.76$

   Fixed Costs $= 8,600.00 - 5,142.76$

   $= \$3,457.24$

Compare the result in Step 5 with Step 6 as follows:

Fixed Costs—Step 6	$3,457.24
Fixed Costs—Step 5	− 3,457.19
	.05 (minor difference due to rounding)

7. Calculate total fixed costs for the year.

   Total Fixed Costs = Fixed Costs per Month × 12 Months

   = $3,457.19 × 12

   = $41,486.28

8. Determine total variable costs of repair and maintenance expense for the year.

   Total Variable Costs = Total Mixed Costs − Total Fixed Costs

   = $85,200 − $41,486.28

   = $43,713.72

The high/low two-point method considers only two extreme periods and is a fairly simple way of estimating the variable and fixed elements of mixed costs. This approach assumes that the extreme periods are a fair reflection of the high and low points for the entire year; therefore, the results will be inaccurate to the degree that the two periods fail to represent fairly the high and low points of activity. The scatter diagram, though tedious, is a more accurate approach.

Scatter Diagram

The **scatter diagram** is a detailed approach to determining the fixed and variable elements of a mixed cost. The steps involved in this method are as follows:

1. Prepare a graph with the independent variable (sales volume) on the horizontal axis and the dependent variable (cost) on the vertical axis.

2. Plot data on the graph by periods.

3. Draw a straight line through the points, keeping an equal number of points above and below the line.

4. Extend the line to the vertical axis. The intersection indicates the fixed costs for the period.

5. Multiply the fixed costs for the period by the number of periods to determine the fixed costs for the time span.

6. Total variable costs are determined by subtracting total fixed costs (Step 5) from total mixed costs.

7. Variable costs per sales unit are determined by dividing total variable costs by total units sold.

Exhibit 6.9 Scatter Diagram

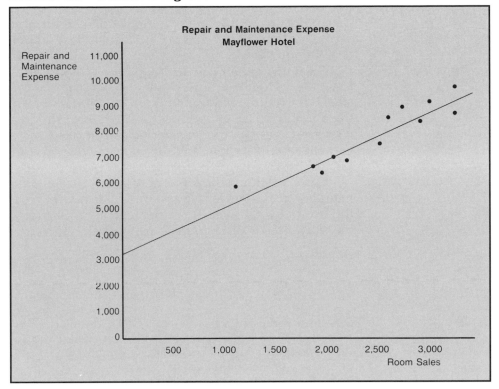

Exhibit 6.9 is a scatter diagram of the maintenance and repair expense of the Mayflower Hotel. The scatter diagram was graphed with rooms sold as the independent variable (horizontal axis) and repair and maintenance expense as the dependent variable (vertical axis). Each monthly repair and maintenance expense was plotted and a straight line was drawn through the points. The line might vary depending on who draws it; however, it should approximate a "best fit." In this case, there are five points above the line, five points below the line, and two points on the line. The line intersects the vertical axis at $3,300. This is the fixed cost approximation per month. The estimated annual fixed costs are $39,600 ($3,300 × 12 months). Therefore, total variable repair and maintenance costs are $45,600, determined by subtracting total fixed costs of $39,600 from total costs of $85,200. Variable repair and maintenance costs per room sold is $1.75, determined by dividing the total variable costs of $45,600 by the number of rooms sold for the year (26,000).

The scatter diagram is an improvement over the high/low two-point approach because it includes data from all periods in the time span under consideration. In our example, the calculations use data from 12 months of a year. However, these calculations are time consuming, and the placement of the straight line between the data points is an approximation rather than a precise measurement. Regression analysis (discussed below) is a still more accurate approach. However, since an assumption when using regression analysis is a linear relationship between the two variables, a scatter diagram is still useful for determining linearity.

Regression analysis is a mathematical approach to fitting a straight line to data points perfectly—that is, the difference in the distances of the data points from the line is minimized. The formulas used in regression analysis allow us to make the calculations without plotting points or drawing lines.

As stated earlier, the formula for a straight line is $y = a + bx$. In our Mayflower Hotel example, y stands for repair and maintenance expense, x stands for rooms sold, a stands for the fixed cost element, and b stands for the variable cost per room sold. Therefore, the total repair and maintenance expense (y) for any period is the fixed cost element (a) plus the variable cost per room sold (b) multiplied by the number of rooms sold (x).

Once we know the monthly fixed cost element of the repair and maintenance expense, we multiply that figure by 12 months to calculate the annual total fixed cost element. The formula for determining the monthly fixed cost element is as follows:

$$\text{Fixed Costs} = \frac{(\Sigma y)(\Sigma x^2) - (\Sigma x)(\Sigma xy)}{n(\Sigma x^2) - (\Sigma x)^2}$$

The formula is explained as follows:

Σ means the "sum of." So, Σx and Σy mean the sum of all x values and the sum of all y values, respectively. Σxy means the sum of all x and y values that are multiplied together.

y stands for the dependent variable.

x stands for the independent variable.

n stands for the number of periods in the time span.

Exhibit 6.10 presents the calculated values for the Mayflower Hotel. Putting these values into the formula reveals that the monthly fixed cost element of repair and maintenance expense is \$2,719.57.[2] Fixed cost per month multiplied by 12 equals the total fixed element of repair and maintenance expense for 19X1 (\$32,634.84).

The total variable costs are determined by subtracting total fixed costs from total costs. Using the total cost figure for the Mayflower Hotel's repair and maintenance expense found in Exhibit 6.8, we can calculate the total variable cost element as follows:

Repair and Maintenance Expense	\$ 85,200.00
Total Fixed Cost Element	– 32,634.84
Total Variable Cost Element	\$ 52,565.16

The variable cost per room sold is determined by solving for the value of b using the formula for a straight line:

$$y = a + bx$$
$$85,200 = 32,634.84 + b(26,000)$$
$$b = \$2.02 \text{ per room sold}$$

These computations, performed manually, are too complex for practical application. Many computers and hand-held financial calculators have programs available to perform these calculations. The user simply enters

Exhibit 6.10 Calculating Values for Fixed Cost Elements

Determination of Repair and Calculation of Values
for Maintenance Fixed Cost Element
Mayflower Hotel

Month	(x) Rooms Sold	(y) Repair and Maintenance Expense	x^2	xy
January	1,860	$ 6,200	3,459,600	11,532,000
February	1,820	6,100	3,312,400	11,102,000
March	2,170	7,000	4,708,900	15,190,000
April	2,250	7,500	5,062,500	16,875,000
May	2,480	8,000	6,150,400	19,840,000
June	2,700	8,500	7,290,000	22,950,000
July	2,790	7,900	7,784,100	22,041,000
August	2,800	8,600	7,840,000	24,080,000
September	2,100	7,000	4,410,000	14,700,000
October	1,900	6,000	3,610,000	11,400,000
November	1,800	6,500	3,240,000	11,700,000
December	1,330	5,900	1,768,900	7,847,000
Totals	26,000	$85,200	58,636,800	189,257,000

the appropriate data. However, because this is so easy, there is a tendency for the user to feed raw data into the calculator or computer and accept the output as truth. The cliché "garbage-in, garbage-out" applies here. The user should select variables that have a logical relationship. For example, repair and maintenance expense and number of meals served may not be a meaningful relationship. If more guests dine in a hotel's restaurant, repair and maintenance expense in food service operations will increase, but dining in the restaurant does not affect repair and maintenance in other departments. Rooms sold, or even number of hotel guests, relates more logically to repair and maintenance expense.

As with the high/low two-point method, values representing abnormal operating conditions should not be included in regression analysis.

Evaluation of the Results   The three methods demonstrated to estimate the fixed and variable elements of the Mayflower Hotel's repair and maintenance expense produced the following results:

	Fixed	Variable	Total
High/low two-point method	$41,486.28	$43,713.72	$85,200
Scatter diagram	39,600.00	45,600.00	85,200
Regression analysis	32,634.84	52,565.16	85,200

The difference between the fixed cost amounts determined by the simplest (the high/low two-point method) and the most complex (regression analysis) methods is $8,851.44. This difference is more than 25% of the figure reached by regression analysis. Regression analysis is the most precise method and easily performed with a financial calculator or a computer. However, the major determination of which method to use is based on cost/benefit considerations.

Fixed Versus Variable Costs

Many goods and services may be purchased on either a fixed or variable cost arrangement. For example, a lease may be either fixed (offered at a fixed price) or variable (offered at a certain percentage of revenues). Management's decision to select a fixed or variable cost arrangement is based on the cost/benefit considerations involved. Under a truly fixed arrangement, the cost remains the same regardless of activity and, therefore, management is able to lock in a maximum amount. Under a variable arrangement, the amount paid depends on the level of activity. The level of activity at which the period cost is the same under either arrangement is called the **indifference point**. An example follows to illustrate this concept.

Assume that a food service operation has the option of signing either an annual fixed lease of $48,000 or a variable lease set at 5% of revenue. The indifference point is $960,000, determined as follows:

$$\text{Variable Cost Percentage} \times \text{Revenue} = \text{Fixed Lease Cost}$$
$$.05(\text{Revenue}) = 48,000$$
$$\text{Revenue} = \frac{48,000}{.05}$$
$$\text{Revenue} = \$960,000$$

When annual revenue is $960,000, the lease expense will be $48,000, regardless of whether the lease arrangement is fixed or variable. Therefore, if annual revenue is expected to exceed $960,000, then management should select a fixed lease in order to minimize its lease expense. On the other hand, if annual revenue is expected to be less than $960,000, a variable lease will minimize lease expense. Exhibit 6.11 is the graphic depiction of this situation. A review of Exhibit 6.11 suggests the following:

1. Using a variable lease results in an excess lease expense at any revenue point to the *right* of the indifference point. For example, using the previous illustration, if revenue is $1,200,000, the lease expense from a variable lease is $60,000, or $12,000 more than for a fixed lease of $48,000 annually.

2. Using a fixed lease results in an excess lease expense at any revenue point to the *left* of the indifference point. For example, using the previous illustration, if revenue is $720,000, the lease expense is still $48,000, or $12,000 more than for a variable lease.

Direct and Indirect Costs

In Chapter 3, certain expenses were called direct while other expenses were implied to be indirect. In that context, we were discussing

Exhibit 6.11   Indifference Point

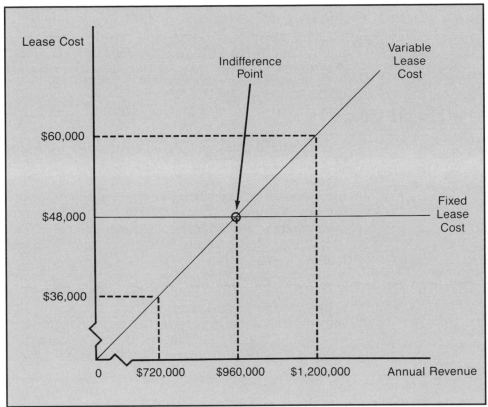

direct and indirect expenses as they pertained to the operated departments (profit centers) within a lodging establishment. In other words, the "objects" of direct/indirect expense were considered to be the operated departments that generate income and incur expenses, such as the rooms department and the food and beverage department. We indicated that direct costs of the rooms department included payroll and related expenses, commissions, contract cleaning, guest transportation, laundry and dry cleaning, linen, operating supplies, reservations, uniforms, and other expenses as well. In this earlier context, we considered the undistributed operating expenses, management fees, fixed charges, and income taxes to be indirect (overhead) expenses.

However, depending on the object of the incurred expenses, many costs may be both direct and indirect. In general, a direct cost is one readily identified with an object, whereas an indirect cost is not readily identified with an object. Therefore, whether a cost is direct or indirect depends upon the context of the discussion and, in particular, on whether the object incurring the cost can be identified in the discussion's context. For instance, when speaking of the service center formed by the general manager's department, the general manager's salary can be ascribed as a direct cost of the service center and can be classified as a subset of administrative and general expense. However, in the context of discussing all operated departments (profit centers) and other service centers (for example, the marketing department), the general manager's salary would be ascribed as an indirect cost of these other departments, because the object of this cost in those departments cannot be directly identified.

This distinction is important because department heads are responsible for the direct costs of their departments since they exercise control over them; however, they are normally not responsible for indirect costs.

Overhead Costs

Overhead costs include all costs other than the direct costs incurred by profit centers. Thus, overhead costs are indirect costs when the cost objectives are the profit centers. Overhead costs include the undistributed operating expenses (administrative and general, data processing, human resources, transportation, marketing, property operation and maintenance, and energy costs), management fees, fixed charges (insurance, rent, depreciation, interest, property taxes, and so forth), and income taxes.

In the discussion of the income statement in Chapter 3, overhead costs were not distributed to the profit centers. This is because these expenses were regarded as indirect costs, not readily ascribed to objects in the operated departments. However, management and the board of directors of a hospitality establishment may want to distribute overhead costs among the profit centers. This process is commonly called **cost allocation**.

Allocation of Overhead Costs

The Supplemental Reading to this chapter discusses and illustrates advanced cost allocation approaches. For our purposes here, however, we will consider a simplified approach that allocates overhead costs using a single allocation base (such as square footage). This method is referred to as the **single allocation base approach (SABA)**. We will illustrate this approach with the hypothetical Walters Motor Inn, whose unallocated income statement for a typical month is shown in Exhibit 6.12.

As the exhibit shows, the monthly net income for the entire operation is $4,500. The rooms and food and beverage departments have generated incomes of $40,000 and $8,500, respectively. The only overhead cost that will not be allocated among departments is income tax. All other costs will be allocated based on square footage. The square footage of the rooms department is 40,000, while the food and beverage department occupies 15,000 square feet. Therefore, 72.73% of the overhead costs will be allocated to the rooms department and 27.27% will be allocated to the food and beverage department.

Exhibit 6.13 illustrates this allocation. Exhibit 6.14 shows the allocated income statement of the Walters Motor Inn. The rooms department's bottom line after cost allocation is $9,453, while the food and beverage department's bottom line is $(2,953).

If an allocation base other than square footage had been used, there would have been different cost allocation amounts and, therefore, different departmental income reported after allocation. For example, the Walters Motor Inn employs 14 people in the rooms department and 20 people in the food and beverage department. If the SABA had used the number of employees in each department as the allocation base, the rooms

Exhibit 6.12   Sample Unallocated Income Statement

Unallocated Income Statement
Walters Motor Inn

	Rooms	Food & Beverage	Total
Revenue	$60,000	$40,000	$100,000
Cost of Sales	0	16,000	16,000
Payroll and Related Expenses	14,000	11,000	25,000
Other Direct Expenses	6,000	4,500	10,500
Total Expenses	20,000	31,500	51,500
Departmental Income	$40,000	$ 8,500	$48,500
Undistributed Operating Expenses:			
Administrative & General			12,000
Marketing			3,000
Property Operation and Maintenance			2,000
Energy Costs			4,000
Total Income Before Fixed Charges			27,500
Insurance			3,000
Depreciation			18,000
			21,000
Income Before Income Taxes			6,500
Income Taxes			2,000
Net Income			$4,500

Note: Data processing, human resources, and transportation expenses are insignificant and are not shown as separate
cost centers.

Exhibit 6.13   Overhead Costs

Overhead Costs
Walters Motor Inn

Overhead Cost Area (2)	Overhead Cost	Percentage		Amount (1)	
		Rooms	Food & Bev.	Rooms	Food & Bev.
A & G	$12,000	72.73%	27.27%	$ 8,728	$ 3,272
Marketing	3,000	72.73	27.27	2,182	818
POM	2,000	72.73	27.27	1,455	545
Energy Costs	4,000	72.73	27.27	2,909	1,091
Insurance	3,000	72.73	27.27	2,182	818
Depreciation	18,000	72.73	27.27	13,091	4,909
Total	$42,000			$30,547	$11,453

(1) All amounts are rounded to the nearest $1.
(2) A & G = administrative & general; POM = property operation and maintenance.

Exhibit 6.14   Sample Allocated Income Statement

Allocated Income Statement
Walters Motor Inn

	Rooms	Food & Beverage	Total
Revenue	$60,000	$40,000	$100,000
Cost of Sales	0	16,000	16,000
Payroll and Related Expenses	14,000	11,000	25,000
Other Direct Expenses	6,000	4,500	10,500
Total Expenses	20,000	31,500	51,500
Departmental Income	40,000	8,500	48,500
Allocated Overhead Costs:			
Administrative & General	8,728	3,272	12,000
Marketing	2,182	818	3,000
Property Operation and Maintenance	1,455	545	2,000
Energy Costs	2,909	1,091	4,000
Insurance	2,182	818	3,000
Depreciation	13,091	4,909	18,000
Total	30,547	11,453	42,000
Income Before Income Taxes	$9,453	$(2,953)	6,500
Income Taxes			2,000
Net Income			$4,500

department would absorb 41.18% of the overhead costs, while the food and beverage department would absorb 58.82%. The Walters Motor Inn allocated income statement, in very abbreviated form, would now appear as follows:

	Rooms	Food & Beverage	Total
Departmental Income	$ 40,000	$ 8,500	$ 48,500
Overhead Costs Allocated	17,296	24,704	42,000
Post Allocation Departmental Income	$ 22,704	$ (16,204)	$ 6,500

The above figures show that a different allocation base results in different allocated amounts and, therefore, in different departmental incomes following allocation. Ideally, costs should be allocated based on their actual usage by the profit centers and the nature of the expense involved. For example, if the hotel is leased on a square footage basis, then square footage is a suitable allocation base for the hotel's rent expense. On the other hand, since the general manager's supervisory role is often his or her primary role in managing the hotel, the general manager's salary may be allocated based on the number of employees supervised or even payroll expense by department.

The above discussion suggests that a different allocation base be used to allocate different overhead costs among departments. This is referred to as the **multiple allocation base approach (MABA)**. MABA is generally preferable to SABA because MABA allocates overhead costs on the basis of an observed relationship between the cost and the profit center. The Supplemental Reading to this chapter contains a discussion of two multiple allocation base approaches.

After Cost Allocation

As Exhibit 6.14 shows, the food and beverage department of the Walters Motor Inn shows a $2,953 loss after cost allocation. Assuming the cost allocation was reasonable, what should be done, if anything? Management should consider at least four factors when deciding what to do about an underperforming department:

1. The underperforming department's income

2. The extent to which the overhead costs allocated to the underperforming department are fixed

3. The extent to which the presence and performance of the department affects other profit centers

4. Operating alternatives for the underperforming department

In our example, management of the Walters Motor Inn might propose closing the food and beverage department; however, this would result in the loss of the department's income of $8,500. Furthermore, assuming that the allocated overhead costs would be incurred anyway, the $11,453 allocated to the food and beverage department would be re-allocated to the rooms department. (To the extent that some of these costs could be avoided, closing down a "losing" department would be favorable to the overall profit picture. However, other factors must be considered.) The Walters Motor Inn would thus incur a $2,000 pre-tax loss by closing the food and beverage department, determined as follows:

Income before income taxes (per Exhibit 6.14)	$ 6,500
Loss of food and beverage department income	(8,500)
Net Result	$(2,000)

Management must also consider the food and beverage department's impact on other profit centers. For example, if the food and beverage department is closed, sales in the rooms department, and thus rooms income, might decrease. The final consideration is how the food and beverage operation is being managed. Perhaps a new menu, renovations, or other changes, might correct the department's performance problems.

Controllable Costs

Managers should generally hold their subordinates responsible only for those costs they can control; to do otherwise may be counterproductive. Controlling costs means using judgment and authority to regulate costs—that is, keeping costs within certain limits rather than eliminating them. **Controllable costs** are costs over which a person is able to exert an influence. For example, the food department manager may be able to influence food usage, personnel preparing and serving food, and supplies used in food production and service. Therefore, cost of food sold, payroll expense, and food and service supplies expense are controllable costs for the food department manager. On the other hand, the food department manager generally has no control over rent paid for the space the restaurant occupies. However, the board of directors may be able to control the rent expense; therefore, from the board's perspective, rent is a controllable expense.

Several costs cannot be easily influenced or changed in the short run; these costs are often considered non-controllable. However, such costs can be regulated over the long run and from this perspective can be viewed as controllable. In general, all costs are controllable given sufficient time and input from a high enough level of management.

The income statement is organized on a responsibility accounting basis. The direct expenses of each profit center are those costs which the respective department heads control. For example, the food and beverage department manager has authority over (and can therefore control) cost of sales, payroll and related expenses, and other direct expenses of the food and beverage department. Exhibit 6.15 is a table listing several costs as they relate to the general manager's ability to control them.

The general manager and department managers should be held accountable for costs they control. First, the controllable fixed costs incurred should be compared to the amounts budgeted for the period. Second, the controllable variable costs should be compared to the product of the variable unit costs times the unit sales. For example, assume that a food and beverage department's costs are budgeted at $2,000 of fixed costs per month and $3 per meal served. Further assume that 3,000 meals were served during the month and that the actual costs incurred were $2,200 for fixed costs and $9,300 for variable costs. A quick review reflects the following:

	Budget	Actual	Difference
Fixed costs	$ 2,000	$2,200	$200
Variable costs	9,000	9,300	300
	$11,000	$11,500	$500

The manager's performance reflects actual costs of $500 in excess of the budget. (In practice, costs and expenses are shown by account, rather than being categorized simply as fixed and variable.)

Differential Costs

In a decision-making situation, costs which differ between two alternatives are called **differential costs**. By focusing on differential costs, decision-makers can narrow the set of cost considerations to those that make a difference between two alternatives. For example, suppose management is considering the installation of a front office computer to replace two obsolete posting machines. In this situation, differential costs include the purchase price of the computer and any other costs associated with the new computer that differ from the costs involved in using the

Exhibit 6.15   The General Manager's Control over Selected Costs

Controllable Costs	Non-controllable Costs
Variable	
Cost of food sold	Rent expense (% of sales)
Cost of beverages sold	
Room supplies	
Food and beverage supplies	
Payroll costs—wages	
Fixed	
Payroll costs—salaries	Depreciation
Professional fees	Property taxes
Liability insurance	Property insurance
	Interest expense
	Rent expense (fixed portion)

existing posting machines. Such costs might include labor, utilities, supplies, and insurance. Costs which remain the same with or without the new computer are non-differential and need not be considered in the decision-making process.

Relevant Costs

Relevant costs are those which must be considered in a decision-making situation. In order for a cost to be relevant, it must be differential, future, and quantifiable. The differential criterion demands that the cost between two or more alternatives be different. The future characteristic demands that the cost must not have already occurred, but must be incurred only after the decision is made. Finally, relevant costs must be quantifiable. The unquantifiable preference for Machine A over Machine B is not a cost consideration in the decision-making process. The following example illustrates the concept of relevant costs.

Happy Harry, owner of Harry's Place, has been approached by a salesperson selling ranges. The salesperson wants to sell Happy Harry a new range and provides the following information:

Cost of new range	= $5,000
Estimated useful life of new range	= 6 years
Annual operating costs:	
Electricity	= $800
Repairs	= $200
Labor	= $10,000
Estimated salvage value after 6 years	= $500

Happy Harry believes his present range, with a major repair job, should last for 6 more years. In order to make a rational and informed decision, Happy Harry compiles the following data on his present range:

Exhibit 6.16   Relevant Costs—Happy Harry's

	Alternatives	
Cost	Buy New	Keep Old
Cost of new range	$5,000	—
Electricity (annually)	800	$ 700
Repairs (annually)	200	500
Salvage value of present range now	300	—
Salvage value of range (end of 6th year)	500	100
Major repair job	—	1,200

Original cost	= $2,000
Estimated cost of required major repair	= $1,200
Estimated salvage value now	= $300
Estimated salvage value after 6 years	= $100
Annual operating costs:	
Electricity	= $700
Repairs	= $500
Labor	= $10,000

The relevant costs are listed in Exhibit 6.16. All of these costs are relevant because they are differential, future, and quantifiable. The original cost of the present range is irrelevant because it is not a future cost (but rather a *sunk cost,* discussed below), and the cost of labor is irrelevant because it is not differential. (The process of selecting an alternative is discussed later in this chapter.)

Sunk Costs

A **sunk cost** is a past cost relating to a past decision. A sunk cost may be differential yet irrelevant because it is not future. In the case of Happy Harry's decision, the original cost of the old range, $2,000, is a sunk cost.

In many decision-making situations, management will review financial records to determine the net book value (cost less accumulated depreciation) of a fixed asset which is to be replaced. This suggests that many managers consider the net book value of a fixed asset (rather than its original cost) the sunk cost. However, in this text, we will consider both the original cost and the net book value sunk costs. The relevant cost in replacing a fixed asset is the asset's current value. The current $300 value of Happy Harry's old range and its projected value of $100 at the end of six years are both relevant costs since they are differential, future, and quantifiable.

Opportunity Costs

The cost of the best foregone opportunity in a decision-making situation is the **opportunity cost**. Opportunity costs are among the relevant cost considerations in decision-making situations. If the decision-making process is rational, then the opportunity cost is less than the value associated with the outcome of the decision. For example, let's assume that $100,000 may be invested in one of three ways:

Investment	Annual Return
XYZ Corporation Bonds	10%
ABC Company Preferred Stock	12%
Uninsured Time Certificate of Deposit	9%

Assume that all three alternatives involve the same amount of risk—that is, the degree of certainty of receiving the specified return is the same for all three investment choices. Further assume that the ability of each investment to be converted into cash is the same for all three alternatives. Everything else being the same, the rational choice is to invest in ABC Company Preferred Stock. The best foregone opportunity is the investment in XYZ Corporation Bonds. Therefore, the opportunity costs associated with making the rational choice amount to $20,000 over two years ($100,000 × 10% × 2). The choice is a rational one because the return on the alternative selected ($24,000 from ABC stock) exceeds the opportunity costs of $20,000. The potential return of 9% on the Uninsured Time Certificate of Deposit is not an opportunity cost because it is not the best foregone opportunity. However, it is a relevant cost because it is future, differential, and quantifiable.

Standard Costs

Standard costs are a forecast of what actual costs should be under projected conditions. These standards may serve as comparisons for control purposes and as evaluations of productivity. Generally, standard costs are established on a unit basis. For example, standard recipe costs consider the planned cost of a food serving such as a dinner or an à la carte item. Assume that the standard recipe cost for a dinner is $4.50. If 100 dinners are served, then the budgeted cost is $450. An actual food cost of $475 reveals a $25 variance. If the variance is significant, it is investigated to determine the probable cause(s) and appropriate corrective action. (The comparison of budgeted and actual costs will be presented in more detail in Chapter 10.)

Decision-Making Situations

Many situations call on management to make decisions using the cost concepts presented in this chapter. Several of these decision-making situations are listed below:

1. Which piece of equipment should be purchased?

2. What prices should be set for the hospitality operation's goods and services?

3. Can the hospitality operation ever afford to sell goods and services below cost?

Exhibit 6.17   Illustration of Relevant Costs in Management Decisions

	Microcomputers	
	#1	#2
Costs – Hardware	$3,450	$4,250
Annual operating costs:		
Electricity	100	100
Supplies	200	200
Maintenance contract	200	100
Repairs (not covered by maintenance contract)	50	50
Software	2,000	1,800

Exhibit 6.18   Cost Analysis Solution

Cost Analysis

	Microcomputers	
Relevant Cost	#1	#2
Hardware	$3,450	$4,250
Operating costs – maintenance contract for 5 years		
$200 × 5	1,000	—
$100 × 5	—	500
Software	2,000	1,800
Total cost	$6,450	$6,550

4. During what time periods of a day should the hospitality establishment remain open?

5. When should a seasonal resort close?

6. Which business segment of the hospitality operation should receive the largest amount of funds?

7. Where should the hospitality enterprise expand?

In attempting to answer these and other cost-related questions, remember that there is no definitive method of evaluating costs. However, when applied correctly, the cost concepts presented in this chapter are useful in clarifying, and thereby helping to resolve, these problems.

Illustration of Relevant Costs in Management Decisions

The selection process used to purchase a microcomputer will illustrate the application of relevant costs to a decision-making situation. Suppose a hotel wants to purchase a new microcomputer to be used by the controller for planning purposes. Even though the controller should become more productive by using the computer, his/her salary will not change because of the purchase. The costs associated with the purchase of either microcomputer #1 or microcomputer #2 are listed in Exhibit 6.17.

Other information to consider includes:

1. Each computer is expected to have a useful life of five years, after which it would be considered completely worthless.
2. The different timing of costs that may be associated with each computer is ignored in this example, as well as any income tax implications. Because these matters affect capital purchases, they will be discussed further in Chapter 13.
3. The controller likes the appearance of computer #2 better; however, he/she is unable to place any value on this preference.
4. The value to the hotel of the controller's increased productivity is the same regardless of which microcomputer is purchased.

The irrelevant costs are the non-differential ones which include electricity, supplies, and repairs. All other costs listed for the two computers are relevant because they are future, differential, and quantifiable. The controller's preference for microcomputer #2 is not directly considered since it has not been quantified. The value of the controller's increased productivity has not been quantified since it is non-differential between the two computers. In either case, the value to the hotel of this increase in productivity is expected to far exceed the cost of either computer.

Exhibit 6.18 presents a cost analysis useful in deciding which computer to purchase. Based on the lowest cost alternative, microcomputer #1 would be selected. If the $100 difference between microcomputers #1 and #2 were considered immaterial, then microcomputer #2 most likely would be purchased due to the controller's unquantified preference for it.

Computerization

Cost analysis is perhaps one of the best uses for the personal computer. With the help of a spreadsheet program, not only can cost analyses be performed, but "what if" situations can be examined. Any of the cost analysis methods described in this chapter can be used. Once the correct formulas are entered into the spreadsheet, it can be used over and over again. With the proper construction of a cost model, month-to-month variances can be determined instantly. Variances can be identified by specific cost (for example, food, room, or maintenance) for further analysis. A spreadsheet program can quickly perform tasks which, if done manually, might take several hours. Even complex calculations like regression analysis can be done in a matter of seconds.

The "what if" calculations allow the manager to analyze costs and revenues under different circumstances. Exhibit 6.19 shows how a manager might use a "what if" model to determine the best rate to charge hotel guests in order to maximize profits. In the example, the manager made the following assumptions:

$$\begin{array}{c} \text{Rooms} \\ \text{Revenues} \end{array} = \begin{array}{c} \text{Available Rooms} \\ \text{for Sale} \end{array} \times \begin{array}{c} \text{Average} \\ \text{Rate} \end{array} \times \begin{array}{c} \text{Projected} \\ \text{Occupancy} \end{array}$$

$$\begin{array}{c} \text{Room} \\ \text{Variable} \\ \text{Expenses} \end{array} = \begin{array}{c} \text{Available Rooms} \\ \text{for Sale} \end{array} \times \begin{array}{c} \text{Projected} \\ \text{Occupancy} \end{array} \times \begin{array}{c} \$8.40 \\ \text{per Room} \end{array}$$

Exhibit 6.19   Computer-Generated Rooms Department Rate Analysis

	ROOM DEPARTMENT RATE ANALYSIS					
AVAILABLE ROOMS FOR SALE	36,500	36,500	36,500	36,500	36,500	36,500
AVERAGE RATE	$40.00	$45.00	$47.50	$50.00	$52.50	$55.00
PROJECTED OCCUPANCY	77.5%	75.0%	72.5%	70.0%	65.0%	60.0%
Room Revenue	$1,131,500	$1,231,875	$1,256,969	$1,277,500	$1,245,563	$1,204,500
Room Variable Expenses	237,615	229,950	222,285	214,620	199,290	183,960
Room Profits	893,885	1,001,925	1,034,684	1,062,880	1,046,273	1,020,540

$$\text{Room Profits} = \text{Rooms Revenues} - \text{Room Variable Expenses}$$

The manager then copied these formulas to see the results in a number of different situations. In this case, the manager projected that, as the room rate increased, the occupancy decreased. However, the lower occupancy is offset by the increased total revenue. In this example, the rate of $50.00 and 70% occupancy maximizes revenues. In addition, in this example, room profits are highest at this level.

"What if" models can be designed to be very sophisticated. For example, in the illustration above, the model could have reflected the effect that the different levels of occupancy would have on food and beverage operations, telephone revenues, gift shop sales, and other profit centers.

Summary

This chapter highlighted the variety of definitions the term *cost* can have in the accounting world. In general, a cost as an expense is the reduction of an asset incurred with the intention of increasing revenues. Such costs include labor costs, cost of food sold, depreciation, and others.

There are many specific types of costs. A fixed cost is one which remains constant over a relevant range of operations for the short term. A variable cost is one which changes directly with the level of activity. Depreciation is usually considered a fixed expense, while cost of food sold is assumed to be variable. Many costs are mixed, a combination of fixed and variable elements. For example, telephone expense can be divided into a fixed portion (the cost of the system) and a variable portion (the cost of making calls). Step costs are constant within a range of activity but vary among ranges of activity.

Three methods of determining the fixed and variable elements of mixed costs were presented in this chapter. The simplest is the high/low two-point method, which examines the cost differences between the periods of lowest and highest activity. A scatter diagram can be used to visualize the relationship between all periods' activities and costs. Regression analysis, the most sophisticated method addressed, uses equations to determine the appropriate fixed-variable relationship.

Several types of costs are important in decision-making situations. Differential costs are useful when comparing two or more options; they are the costs which differ among the options. Relevant costs must be differential costs. In addition, relevant costs must be quantifiable and incurred in the future. Sunk costs are not considered in decision-making situations because they were incurred in the past.

Other costs include controllable costs. Controllable costs are costs which can be regulated. All costs before management fees and fixed charges are generally considered under the general manager's control.

Understanding the relationships among the different types of costs can be very beneficial to a hospitality manager. Different purchase or lease options can be more easily analyzed, operations can be monitored against standards, and costs can be broken into their fixed and variable portions in order to forecast future expenses.

Endnotes

1. This basic equation is most useful for forecasting purposes (the topic of Chapter 9) and for budgeting purposes (the topic of Chapter 10).

2. $$\text{Fixed Cost Element} = \frac{(85,200)(58,636,800) - (26,000)(189,257,000)}{12(58,636,800) - (26,000)(26,000)}$$

$$= \frac{4,995,855,360,000 - 4,920,682,000,000}{703,641,600 - 676,000,000}$$

$$= \frac{75,173,360,000}{27,641,600}$$

$$= \$2,719.57 \text{ per month}$$

Key Terms

avoidable costs
capacity fixed costs
controllable costs
cost allocation
differential costs
discretionary fixed costs
fixed costs
high/low two-point method
indifference point
mixed costs
multiple allocation base approach (MABA)

opportunity cost
overhead costs
regression analysis
relevant costs
scatter diagram
single allocation base approach (SABA)
standard costs
step costs
sunk costs
variable costs

Discussion Questions

1. What are some of the different meanings of *cost*?

2. What is the difference between overhead costs and indirect costs?

3. What is an opportunity cost?

4. Which technique is the most accurate method of determining the fixed and variable elements of a mixed cost? Why?

5. What are the two definitions of sunk costs?

6. Which hotel costs are fixed in the short run? the long run?

7. Why would you consider allocating costs to the profit centers?

8. How are relevant costs defined? What is an irrelevant cost? Give an example.

9. Why are differential costs considered in a decision-making situation?

Problems

Problem 6.1

The following monthly income statement has been prepared by Dwayne Kris, CPA, for Troy Caballo, the owner of the Caballo Inn. As Mr. Caballo's private consultant, you are asked to explain several cost relationships.

Caballo Inn
Income Statement
For the month ended January 31, 19X1

	Net Revenues	Cost of Sales	Payroll and Related Exp.	Other Expenses	Income (Loss)
Rooms	$105,430	$ –0–	$20,000	$ 1,450	$ 83,980
Food	52,400	18,864	15,000	1,000	17,536
Beverage	26,720	6,680	10,000	12,400	(2,360)
Other	4,000	–0–	–0–	–0–	4,000
	$188,550	$25,544	$45,000	$14,850	$103,156

Undistributed Operating Expenses:

Administrative and General	16,720
Data Processing	4,170
Marketing	3,400
Property Operation and Maintenance	5,080
Energy Costs	15,400

Income Before Fixed Charges	58,386
Rent	5,400
Property Taxes	1,220
Insurance	2,000
Interest	3,330
Depreciation	5,500
Income Before Income Taxes	40,936
Income Taxes	15,136
Net Income	$25,800

Required:

1. What are the direct expenses of the rooms department?

2. What is the total of the overhead expenses for the period?

3. Which costs are controllable by the general manager or people under his/her supervision?

4. Which costs are considered fixed?

5. What is the relationship of the cost of sales to sales?

Problem 6.2

Veronica Jackson wants to analyze labor costs in her restaurant operations. She has the operating statistics for the previous year and has asked for your assistance.

	Customers	Labor Costs
January	4,000	$15,500
February	2,400	10,450
March	3,700	18,500
April	4,450	19,000
May	4,400	19,000
June	4,800	20,250
July	5,000	20,500
August	3,900	18,500
September	3,800	18,000
October	3,100	15,500
November	2,900	15,250
December	3,000	16,650

Required:

1. Using the high/low two-point method, determine Ms. Jackson's monthly fixed labor costs.

2. What is the variable labor expense per customer served at Ms. Jackson's restaurant?

Problem 6.3

Tanya Daniels has been successfully operating her restaurant, The Lion's Den, for the past five years. She has to renegotiate her lease and has two options: a $3,000 per month fixed charge or a variable rate of 5% of revenue. She has completed next year's budget to "Income Before Lease Expense" and expects annual sales of $1,000,000.

Required:

1. What is the indifference point (annual sales) for these lease options?
2. Which option should Ms. Daniels choose? Why?

Problem 6.4

The D.K. Pizza House has provided you with the following information on its costs at various levels of monthly sales.

Monthly sales in units	3,000	6,000	9,000
Cost of food sold	$ 4,500	$ 9,000	$13,500
Payroll costs	3,500	5,000	6,500
Supplies	600	1,200	1,800
Utilities	360	420	480
Other operating costs	1,500	3,000	4,500
Building rent	1,000	1,000	1,000
Depreciation	200	200	200
Total	$11,660	$19,820	$27,980

Required:

1. Identify each cost as variable, fixed, or mixed.
2. Develop an equation to estimate total costs at various levels of activity.
3. Project total costs with monthly sales of 8,000.

Problem 6.5

Kent's Inn needs new laundry equipment. Paul Kent, the owner, is faced with the following two alternatives:

	Buy	Lease
Cost of equipment	$20,000	–
Semi-annual equipment rental	–	$ 3,000
Salvage value in five years	1,000	–
Annual costs:		
Labor	15,000	15,000
Supplies	1,000	1,000
Utilities	3,000	3,000
Interest expense	1,500	–
Repairs	200	–

Additional information:

Assume that the laundry equipment has a five-year life.

Required:

1. Which costs are irrelevant?
2. Prepare a five-year cost schedule for each alternative. (Ignore income taxes and the time value of money.)
3. Which alternative do you recommend?

Problem 6.6

Paul Jones is considering replacing Jones & Smith's present dishwasher with a new energy-efficient model. Although the old dishwasher has a present book value of $2,000, its current market value is only $1,500 and, if held for five more years, this would drop to $500. If Paul decides not to buy the new machine, approximately $300 of repairs must be performed now on the present dishwasher. The following is a schedule of expected annual expenses over the next five years for each option:

	Keep Present Dishwasher	Buy New Dishwasher
Maintenance	$ 300	$ 100
Labor	9,000	9,000
Energy	700	500
Water	300	300

The new machine would cost $3,450 and is expected to have a salvage value of $1,000 at the end of five years.

Required:

1. Which costs are sunk?
2. Which costs are irrelevant?
3. Which alternative should Paul choose? Support your decision with numbers.

Problem 6.7

Consider the following monthly income statement for the Double K Hotel:

Double K Hotel
Income Statement

	Rooms	Food & Beverage	Gift Shop	Total
Revenue	$500,000	$500,000	$2,000	$1,002,000
Cost of Sales	–0–	180,000	1,000	181,000
Payroll & Related Expenses	120,000	130,000	400	250,400
Other Direct Expenses	40,000	45,000	100	85,100
Departmental Income	$340,000	$145,000	$ 500	$ 485,500

Undistributed Expenses:	Payroll & Related	Other	Total
Administrative and General	$60,000	$30,000	$90,000
Marketing	45,000	25,000	70,000
Property Operation and Maintenance and Energy Costs	30,000	40,000	70,000
Insurance		10,000	10,000
Depreciation		80,000	80,000
			320,000
Income Before Income Taxes			$165,500
Income Taxes			50,000
Net Income			$115,500

Indirect expenses will be allocated based on the number of employees, who are distributed as follows:

Department	Number of Employees
Rooms	55
Food and Beverage	70
Gift Shop	1/2
Administrative and General	20
Marketing	15
Property Operation & Maintenance and Energy Costs	10

Required:

Prepare a fully-allocated income statement using the single allocation basis approach to cost allocation.

Problem 6.8

The owner of the Double K Hotel in Problem 6.7 would like to develop a fully-allocated income statement using the step method. (The unallocated income statement is presented in Problem 6.7.) Indirect expenses will be allocated on the following bases:

Indirect Expense	Basis
Insurance	Book value of fixed assets
Depreciation	Square footage
Property Operation and Maintenance and Energy Costs	Square footage
Marketing	Ratio of sales
Administrative and General	Number of employees

Additional information:

Department	Book Value of Fixed Assets	Square Footage	Number of Employees
Rooms	$8,000,000	120,000	55
Food and Beverage	3,000,000	20,000	70
Gift Shop	20,000	500	1/2
Administrative and General	400,000	6,000	20

Marketing	200,000	4,000	15
Property Operation and			
Maintenance and Energy Costs	1,500,000	10,000	10

Service department expenses should be allocated in the following order:

1. Administrative and General
2. Property Operation and Maintenance and Energy Costs
3. Marketing

Required:

Prepare a fully-allocated income statement for the Double K Hotel using the step method. Note: The Supplemental Reading to this chapter discusses and illustrates the step method.

Problem 6.9

Sara Rose, owner of Rose Inn, is confused by the fully-allocated financial statements which suggest the Rose Inn's lounge is losing money. As she sees it, there are three alternatives:

1. Continue the lounge operation as is.
2. Close the lounge and convert the space to a small meeting room.
3. Lease the space to Bevco.

The following table summarizes the Rose Inn's fully-allocated monthly income statements:

	Rooms	Food	Lounge	Total
Departmental profit	$150,000	$30,000	$10,000	$190,000
Allocated overhead	100,000	25,000	15,000	140,000
Pre-tax income	$ 50,000	$5,000	$(5,000)	50,000
Income taxes				20,000
Net income				$ 30,000

Additional information:

1. Closing the lounge would reduce overhead costs by $7,000. Leasing the lounge to Bevco would reduce overhead costs by $2,000.
2. The space can be leased to Bevco for 5% of sales. Bevco is a reputable operator, and Sara Rose believes that it will operate the lounge as effectively as Rose Inn has done in the past. Annual forecasted lounge sales are expected to be $150,000.
3. If the lounge is closed, room profits are expected to decrease by 2%, while food department profits are expected to increase by 20%.
4. The cost to convert the lounge for alternative use is assumed to be equal to the market value of the lounge equipment.
5. The lounge space, if used for small meetings, is expected to yield pre-tax profits of $3,000.

Required:

Based on the above information, recommend the best alternative to Sara Rose. Support your solution with numbers.

Problem 6.10

Tammy's Motor Inn has been open for five months, and Tammy Weaver, the general manager, is conducting some cost analyses. She has not yet determined the amount of fixed and variable expenses the inn is incurring. The following is a summary of room sales and expenses incurred each month.

	Number of Rooms	Costs
June	3,488	$122,319
July	3,842	128,940
August	3,584	124,320
September	3,333	119,431
October	3,261	117,642

Required:

1. Using regression analysis, determine the fixed cost per month for Tammy's Motor Inn.

2. What is the variable cost per room?

3. If Tammy's Motor Inn expects to sell 3,666 rooms in January of the next year, what are the fixed costs, total variable costs, and total expenses?

Supplemental Reading
Should overhead costs be allocated?*

One of a Series Sponsored by AH&MA's Financial Management Committee
By A. Neal Geller and Raymond S. Schmidgall

Overhead costs are not allocated to profit centers under the *Uniform System of Accounts for Hotels* (USAH). The most recent USAH briefly discusses methods and bases for allocation but neither prescribes nor illustrates the process. The allocation process is fairly complex, and is not well understood by the lodging industry. This article, therefore, has two purposes:

1) to discuss the advantages and drawbacks of allocation and
2) to illustrate cost allocation.

Cost allocation is the assignment of overhead costs to operated departments according to benefits received, responsibilities, or other logical measures of use. Such overhead costs as the general manager's salary are spread across profit centers such as rooms and food and beverages.

Please refer at this point to the glossary of terms in Exhibit 1.

Advantages of allocation

The major advantage of cost allocation is that it results in better decision-making by the general and departmental managers. These decisions are improved when based on fully allocated income statements:

PRICING. Pricing is best accomplished when the full costs of an operated department are known.

MARKETING. Management can best determine which services to emphasize after the full costs of each operated department are realized.

Dr. A. Neal Geller, *associate professor, School of Hotel Administration, Cornell University, teaches accounting and financial management. His bachelor's and master's degrees are from Cornell, his doctorate, from Syracuse University. Dr. Geller has extensive experience in hotel management, including corporate finance. His consulting work involves financial analysis and planning.*

Dr. Raymond S. Schmidgall *teaches accounting and finance at Michigan State University's department of Hotel, Restaurant and Institutional Management. He is a Certified Public Accountant, a Ph.D. in accounting, a member of AH&MA's Financial Management Committee (as is Neal Geller) and a consultant in accounting and finance.*

CHANGES IN CAPACITY. Expansion or reduction in the capacity of the hotel/motel operation should be based on the profit potential (net of indirect costs) of the operating departments.

STAFFING. More judicious staffing decisions are possible with the full cost of each operated department known to management. In addition, cost allocation provides department heads with more realistic assessments of overhead costs their departments must cover. Without the benefit of fully-allocated income statements, a rooms department manager, for example, may not understand why a 70% contribution from the rooms department is imperative for the firm to realize a profit.

EXHIBIT 1
Glossary of Terms

Cost Center: An area of responsibility for which costs are accumulated; based on costs only and not revenues e.g. the marketing department.

Fixed Charges: Expenses that relate to the capacity of the operation. These include rent, interest, property taxes, insurance, depreciation and amortization. (See page 16, *USAH*)

Indirect Costs: All undistributed operating expenses *and* fixed charges. (See page 16, *USAH*)

Operated Departments: Departments that generate revenue and incur expenses. These include rooms, food & beverage, casino, telephone, etc.

Overhead Costs: Another term commonly used for indirect costs.

Profit Center: Another term commonly used for operated department.

Service Center: A department in a hotel that provides services to other departments. Examples are accounting, payroll, credit, and personnel.

Undistributed Operating Expenses: Operating expenses incurred for the benefit of the operated departments. These traditionally have not been allocated to the operated departments. They include the general categories of administrative and general, marketing, guest entertainment, and property operation, maintenance and energy costs. (See page 16, *USAH*)

Finally, fully-allocated income statements are useful in dealing with government regulations. They provide better information for wage-and-price guidelines, government per-diem rates and general lobbying efforts.

Drawbacks of allocation

The major drawbacks of cost allocation relate primarily to the managers of operated departments and to misunderstandings as to its use. For example:

- Department heads may not understand the process and may resist it.
- Department heads may defer discretionary costs such as repairs, or otherwise strive to achieve short-run profitability at the expense of the long-run profitability of the company.
- Fully-allocated department statements are not appropriate for performance evaluation.

The effects of these drawbacks will be minimized if top-level management will do the following:

1. Explain completely the process of cost allocation and emphasize the benefits to the hotel/motel (or company).
2. Emphasize the importance of management for the long-term rather than focusing all the attention on the current period.
3. Separate department costs in fully-allocated statements between direct and indirect. Further, separate the indirect costs between "controllable by department head"—if any—and "beyond the control of the department head."
4. Stress a team approach to managing the various profit and cost centers of the hotel/motel operation.

Bases of allocation

The USAH contains several suggested bases for cost allocation as you will see in Exhibit 2. A cost allocation base is a factor that determines how much is allocated to a cost objective (department). For example, the rent expense of a hotel may be allocated on the basis of square footage of each department. If the rent expense is $10,000

for the period and the square footage of the rooms and food departments are 18,000 and 6,000 square feet respectively, then 75% ($7,500) would be allocated to the rooms department and 25% ($2,500) to the food department.

It is important to note that the allocation bases should be chosen separately from the allocation method used. While the rent may be allocated to operated departments as shown in the above example, or indirectly through the service centers, the allocation base can be the same. (Again, note Exhibit 2.)

Methods of allocation

The allocation method determines the degree of directness in allocating indirect costs from their cost centers to the profit centers. The three methods listed in USAH are diagrammed and discussed briefly here.

The direct method (see Exhibit 3) results in all indirect costs flowing directly from the cost centers to the profit centers. With this approach, no portion of fixed cost is allocated to service centers. The direct method is simple and easily understood.

The step method (see Exhibit 4) requires a two step allocation process. First, fixed costs are allocated to the profit and service centers. Second, the costs of service centers, including the allocated fixed costs, are allocated to the profit centers. In the second step, the costs of the service centers providing the most services to the other service centers are allocated first.

Once a service center's costs are allocated, no additional costs are allocated to this service center. The step method does not consider the reciprocal provision of services among other service centers. The formula method incorporates this additional refinement. The step method is more realistic than the direct method because it recognizes services provided by some service centers to others.

The formula method also requires two steps in the allocation process (See Exhibit 5). The first step—the allocation of fixed costs—is the same as under the step method. The second step gives full consideration for services rendered by service centers to each other. The second step is generally complex and requires mathematical computations best performed by a computer.

Illustration of allocation

The direct and step methods of cost allocation are illustrated here by using Walters Motor

EXHIBIT 2 Suggested Allocation Bases	
ALLOCATED COSTS	ALLOCATION BASES
Rent	1. Percentage applicable to revenue sources 2. Square feet of area occupied (fixed rent)
Real estate taxes	Square feet of area occupied
Insurance—building and contents	1. Square feet of area occupied 2. Square feet plus investment in furniture and fixtures
Interest	Same as insurance
Depreciation—building	Square feet of area occupied
Depreciation—furniture and fixtures	1. Department asset records 2. Square feet of area occupied
Telephone	Number of extensions
Payroll taxes and employee benefits	1. Number of employees 2. Detailed payroll
Administrative and general:	
Executive office	Number of employees
Accounting and control	1. Accumulated costs 2. Number of employees
Security	Square feet of area occupied
Marketing	Ratio to sales
Energy costs	Cubic feet of area occupied
Property operation and maintenance	1. Job orders 2. Square feet of area occupied

Source: *Uniform System of Accounts for Hotels (Seventh Edition)* p. 127.

Inn. The formula method is not illustrated because it is beyond the scope of this article.

The Walters Motor Inn is a 70-room property with food and beverage operations. It uses the *Uniform System of Accounts for Hotels*. To simplify the illustrations, we have included only three undistributed operating expense categories and two fixed charge categories. The Inn's income statement for March, developed in accordance with the USAH, is shown in Exhibit 6. Note that

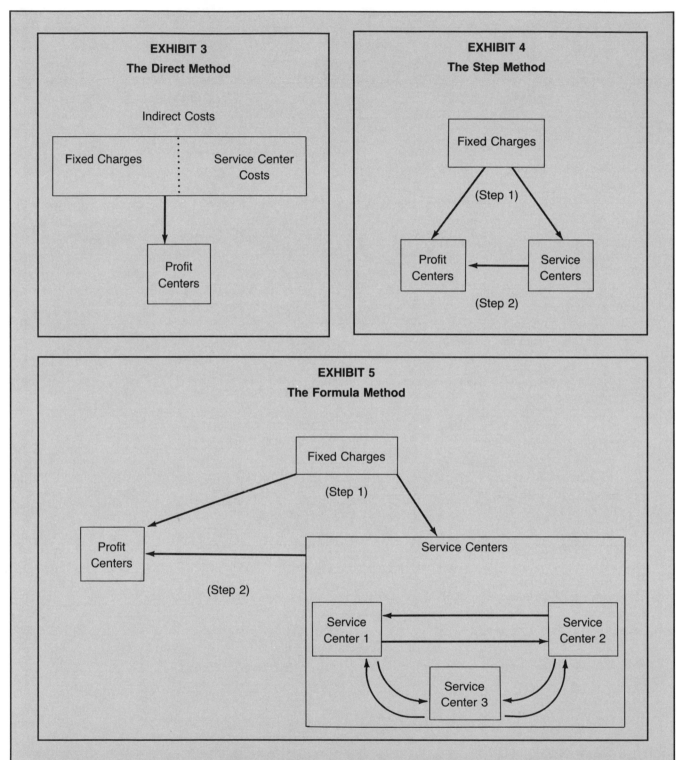

EXHIBIT 3
The Direct Method

Indirect Costs

Fixed Charges : Service Center Costs → Profit Centers

EXHIBIT 4
The Step Method

Fixed Charges → (Step 1) → Profit Centers ← Service Centers (Step 2)

EXHIBIT 5
The Formula Method

Fixed Charges → (Step 1) → Profit Centers / Service Centers

Profit Centers ← (Step 2) Service Centers

Service Center 1, Service Center 2, Service Center 3

the indirect expenses have not been allocated to the profit centers so that the rooms and food and beverage departmental incomes, prior to cost allocation, are $34,000 and $14,500 respectively.

Regardless of the allocation method used, a cost allocation base must be selected for each indirect cost. The indirect expenses and the allocation bases selected for cost allocation of the Walters Motor Inn's indirect expenses are shown in Exhibit 6-A.

The bases selected were chosen on recommendations from the USAH. The notable excep-

EXHIBIT 6

Unallocated Income Statement, Walters Motor Inn for the Month of March

	Rooms	Food & Beverage	Total
Revenue	$50,000	$50,000	$100,000
Cost of Sales	-0-	18,000	18,000
Payroll and Related Expenses	12,000	13,000	25,000
Other Direct Expenses	4,000	4,500	8,500
Total Expenses	16,000	35,500	51,500
Departmental Income (Loss)	$34,000	$14,500	48,500

Undistributed Operating Expenses:	Payable Related	Other	Total
Administrative & General (A & G)	$10,000	$2,000	12,000
Marketing	2,000	1,000	3,000
Property Operation, Maintenance and Energy Costs (POM & EC)	2,000	4,000	6,000
Total Income Before Fixed Charges			27,500
Insurance			3,000
Depreciation			18,000
			21,000
Income Before Income Taxes			6,500
Income Taxes			2,000
Net Income			$ 4,500

EXHIBIT 6-A

Indirect Expenses	Bases
Insurance	Book value of fixed assets (BV-FA)
Depreciation	Square footage (SF)
POM & EC	Square footage (SF)
Marketing	Ratio to sales (RS)
A & G	Number of employees (NE)

EXHIBIT 6-B

Department	Book Value of Fixed Assets	Square Footage	Number of Employees
Rooms	$900,000	40,000	14
Food & Beverage	300,000	15,000	20
A & G	50,000	2,500	4
Marketing	30,000	500	1
POM & EC	220,000	2,000	1

tion is Property Operation & Maintenance and Energy Costs. To simplify the illustrations, these two costs (POM and EC) were combined and allocated using one of the recommended bases for property operation and maintenance. The information required to establish the allocation bases for the Walters Motor Inn is shown in Exhibit 6-B.

Illustration of direct method

The direct method of cost allocation is accomplished by allocating all indirect expenses to the profit centers and then preparing the fully-allocated income statement. For the Walters Motor Inn, four bases of allocation are used.

The base for allocating the Inn's insurance is the book value of fixed assets of the rooms and food and beverage departments. The total book value-fixed assets for the two profit centers is $1.2 million of which $900,000 pertains to the rooms and $300,000 pertains to the food and beverage department. Since the book value-fixed assets of

EXHIBIT 7

Allocation of Costs—Direct Method

Expense to be Allocated	Amount to be Allocated	Allocation Base	Proportion to		Amounts Allocated to	
			Rooms	Food & Beverage	Rooms	Food & Beverage
Insurance	$ 3,000	BV-FA	.7500	.2500	$ 2,250	$ 750
Depreciation	18,000	SF	.7273	.2727	13,091	4,909
POM & EC	6,000	SF	.7273	.2727	4,364	1,636
Marketing	3,000	RS	.5000	.5000	1,500	1,500
A & G	12,000	NE	.4118	.5882	4,942	7,058
TOTAL	$42,000				$26,147	$15,853

EXHIBIT 8

Fully Allocated Income Statement—Walters Motor Inn Direct Method—For the Month of March

	Rooms	Food & Beverage	Total
Revenue	$50,000	$ 50,000	$100,000
Cost of Sales	-0-	18,000	18,000
Payroll and Related Expenses	12,000	13,000	25,000
Other Direct Expenses	4,000	4,500	8,500
	16,000	35,000	51,500
Departmental Income	34,000	14,500	48,500
Allocated Expenses (from Exhibit 7)	26,147	15,853	42,000
Departmental Income (loss) after Allocation	$ 7,853	$ (1,353)	6,500
Income Taxes			2,000
Net Income			$ 4,500

the rooms department is 75% of the combined book value-fixed assets for the two departments ($900,000 divided by $1,200,000), the rooms department is allocated $2,250 of the insurance expenses (.75 x $3,000).

The proportions of other indirect expenses and amounts allocated to the rooms and food and beverage departments were determined in similar fashion using the selected base of allocation as noted previously. Exhibit 7 contains the indirect costs, the amount to be allocated, the allocation base, the proportions to be allocated to rooms and food and beverage, and the amounts allocated to these two departments.

Exhibit 8 contains the fully-allocated income statement. Under this method, the rooms depart-

ment income after allocation is $7,853 while the food and beverage department loss after allocation is ($1,353). Note that income taxes are not allocated to profit centers.

Illustration of step method

The step method of allocation requires two steps:

1. Allocate fixed charges to service centers and profit centers, and,
2. Allocate service center expenses to profit centers.

EXHIBIT 9

Service and Profit Centers	Insurance		Depreciation	
	BV-FA	Proportionate Share of BV-FA	Square Feet	Proportionate Share of Sq. Ft.
Rooms	$ 900,000	.6000	40,000	.6667
Food & Beverage	300,000	.2000	15,000	.2500
A & G	50,000	.0333	2,500	.0417
Marketing	30,000	.0200	500	.0083
POM & EC	220,000	.1467	2,000	.0333
TOTAL	$1,500,000	1.0000	60,000	1.0000

EXHIBIT 10

Step 1: Allocation of Fixed Charges to Profit Centers and Service Centers

Fixed Charge	Total Amount	Allocated to				
		Rooms	F&B	A&G	Marketing	POM&EC
Insurance	$ 3,000	$ 1,800	$ 600	$100	$ 60	$ 440
Depreciation	18,000	12,000	4,500	750	150	600
TOTAL	$21,000	$13,800	$5,100	$850	$210	$1,040

Following these steps, the fully-allocated income statement is prepared.

The bases for allocating indirect expenses of the Walters Motor Inn were the same as used to illustrate allocation by the direct method. The difference under the step method is that part of the indirect expenses was first allocated to service centers. Thus, in determining the proportionate share of a base for each cost objective, one must consider both the amounts pertaining to profit centers and to service centers.

The two fixed charges to be allocated are insurance and depreciation. The ratios used to allocate these expenses were calculated as shown in Exhibit 9. Using the ratios thus calculated, the fixed charges were allocated as shown in Exhibit 10.

In step 2, the service center expenses plus the fixed charges allocated to the service centers were allocated to the profit centers. A portion of these new totals was allocated directly to the profit centers with the remaining portion allocated in an established sequence to the service centers until all indirect expenses were allocated to the two profit centers.

Step 2 of the cost allocation of the Walters Motor Inn was accomplished by allocating Administrative and General expenses, Property Operation/Maintenance expenses, Energy Costs, and Marketing expenses. The order is specified on the basis of service centers serving the largest number of service centers.

The Administrative and General expenses to be allocated in Step 2 total $12,850—$12,000 from the unallocated income statement plus $850 of fixed charges allocated in Step 1. Using the number of employees as the allocation base, the $12,850 was allocated to the two remaining service centers and two profit centers as shown in Exhibit 11.

Property Operation/Maintenance and Energy Costs are allocated next under Step 2. The total to be allocated is $7,397. This is the sum of $6,000 from the unallocated income statement, $1,040 from Step 1, and $357 from Administrative and General. The total was allocated to the marketing department and the two profit centers on

EXHIBIT 11

Department	Number of Employees	Proportioned Share of Total Employees	Amount Allocated
Rooms	14	.3889	$ 4,998
Food & Beverage	20	.5555	7,138
POM & EC	1	.0278	357
Marketing	1	.0278	357
TOTAL	36	1.0000	$12,850

EXHIBIT 12

Department	Square Feet	Proportioned Share of Square Footage	Amount Allocated
Rooms	40,000	.7207	$5,331
Food & Beverage	15,000	.2703	1,999
Marketing	500	.0090	67
TOTAL	55,000	1.0000	$7,397

EXHIBIT 13

Step 2: Allocation of Expenses from Service Centers to Profit Centers

	Service Centers			Profit Centers	
	A&G	POM&EC	Marketing	Rooms	Food & Beverage
Unallocated service center costs	$ 12,000	$ 6,000	$ 3,000	$ -0-	$ -0-
Allocated per Step 1	850	1,040	210	13,800	5,100
Costs to be allocated	12,850	7,040	3,210		
A & G	(12,850)	357	357	4,998	7,138
	$ -0-	7,397			
POM & EC		(7,397)	67	5,331	1,999
		$ -0-	3,634		
Marketing			(3,634)	1,817	1,817
TOTAL		$ -0-	$25,946	$16,054

the basis of square footage. The proportionate share and amounts of Property Operation/Maintenance and Energy Costs were calculated as shown in Exhibit 12.

Lastly, the Marketing expense was allocated to the two profit centers on the basis of ratio to sales. Therefore, the total Marketing expense of $3,634 ($3,000 from the unallocated income state-ment, $210 from Step 1, $357 from Administrative and General, and $67 from Property Operation/Maintenance and Energy Costs) was allocated $1,817 and $1,817 to the food and beverage department. Exhibit 13 shows the step down process (Step 2) of the step method.

The fully-allocated income statement under the step method of cost allocation is shown in

---

EXHIBIT 14

Fully Allocated Income Statement, Walters Motor Inn
Step Method—For the Month of March

	Rooms	Food & Beverage	Total
Revenue	$50,000	$ 50,000	$100,000
	-----------	-----------	------------
Cost of Sales	-0-	$ 18,000	$ 18,000
Payroll and Related Expenses	$12,000	13,000	25,000
Other Direct Expenses	4,000	4,500	8,500
	$16,000	$ 35,500	$ 51,500
Departmental Income	$34,000	$ 14,500	$ 48,500
Allocated Expenses (from Exhibit 10)	25,946	16,054	42,000
Departmental Income (loss) after Allocation	$ 8,054	$(1,554)	6,500
Income Taxes			2,000
Net Income			$ 4,500

Exhibit 14. After cost allocation, the rooms department income is $8,054 while the food and beverage department shows a loss of ($1,554).

Conclusion

The precision offered by the allocation procedures discussed and illustrated here increases from the direct to the step methods. So does the cost of preparation.

The decision to use a more sophisticated cost-allocation method must be made following a cost-benefit analysis. Hotel management must determine the value of the more precise information.

Cost allocation is an attention-getting tool. It should not lead to hasty decisions. The results raise a number of questions for management; among them:

— What action should be taken if the departmental income after allocation is negative?
— Should a department's services be cur-

tailed if a loss is shown after a full allocation?
— Should advertising for a department's services be increased if a loss is shown after full allocation?

Management decisions should be made only after careful cost-benefit analysis. Allocation of indirect costs allows management to make such decisions in a more informed and accurate manner.

REFERENCES

Cost Allocation under the Uniform System of Accounts. Cornell Hotel and Restaurant Quarterly. November, 1980 issue. Cornell University, School of Hotel Administration.

Notes

*This article is reprinted with permission from *Lodging*, July 1981, pp. 36-41.

7 Cost-Volume-Profit Analysis

Cost-volume-profit (CVP) analysis is a set of analytical tools used to determine the revenues required at any desired profit level. Many business people refer to CVP analysis as a **breakeven analysis**. However, the **breakeven point** of a firm is only one point among an infinite number of possible points that can be determined. When properly used, CVP analysis provides useful information about the structure of operations and answers many types of questions such as:

1. What is the breakeven point?

2. What is the profit at any given occupancy percentage above the breakeven point?

3. How will a $50,000 increase in property taxes next year affect the sales breakeven point?

4. How much must rooms sales increase next year to cover the increase in property taxes and/or other expenses and still achieve the desired profit?

5. How many rooms must be sold to achieve a $100,000 profit?

6. What is the effect on profit if prices, variable costs, or fixed costs increase?

This chapter begins with a definition of CVP analysis followed by a clarification of both the assumptions of the CVP model and the limitations of CVP as an analytical tool. Next, we will describe the relationships depicted in the CVP model, namely the relationships among revenues, variable costs, fixed costs, and levels of activity. We will then illustrate CVP analysis by discussing both the simple situation of a single product offering and the more complex multiple product situation. We will also discuss the effects of income taxes within the CVP model and modify the basic model to more adequately reflect cash flow considerations. Finally, we will consider the topic of the relative mix of fixed and variable costs through a discussion of operating leverage.

CVP Analysis Defined

CVP analysis is a management tool that expresses the relationships among various costs, sales volume, and profits in either graphic or equation form. The graphs or equations assist management in making decisions. A simple example may be used to illustrate this process.

Assume that the manager of the Red Cedar Inn, a 10-room motel, would like to know what price must be charged in order to make a profit of $2,000 in a 30-day period. The available information is as follows:

- Variable costs per room sold equal $5.

- If the average price is between $20 and $25, 250 rooms can be sold.

- Fixed costs for a 30-day period are $2,500.

Given these three pieces of information, using CVP analysis the manager is able to calculate that the selling price must average $23 in order to attain the goal of a $2,000 profit in a 30-day period. This selling price is determined on the basis of the CVP model by working through the calculations of the following formula:

$$\frac{\text{Selling}}{\text{Price}} = \frac{\text{Variable Costs}}{\text{per Room}} + \frac{\text{Desired Profit} + \text{Fixed Costs}}{\text{Number of Rooms to be Sold}}$$

$$= 5 + \frac{2,000 + 2,500}{250}$$

$$= 5 + 18$$

$$= \underline{\underline{\$23}}$$

Since the selling price of $23 suggested by the CVP analysis is within the range of $20 to $25 required to sell the specified number of rooms, the manager will be able to reach the desired goal of a $2,000 profit in 30 days by establishing the price at $23. The Red Cedar Inn's summarized operations budget for the 30-day period is as follows:

Room sales (250 × $23)		$5750
Variable costs (250 × $5)	$1250	
Fixed costs	2500	3750
Profit		$2000

CVP Assumptions, Limitations, and Relationships

CVP analysis, like all mathematical models, is based on several assumptions. When these assumptions do not hold in the actual situations to which the model is applied, then the results of CVP analysis will be suspect. The commonest assumptions are as follows:

1. Fixed costs remain fixed during the period being considered. Over time, fixed costs do change. However, it is reasonable to assume that fixed costs remain constant over a short time span.

Exhibit 7.1 Graphic Depiction of Revenue

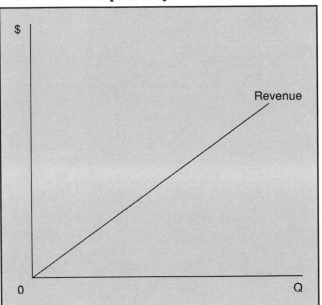

This relationship between fixed costs and levels of sales activity is depicted in Exhibit 6.1 of Chapter 6.

2. Variable costs fluctuate in a linear fashion with revenues during the period under consideration. That is, if revenues increase x%, variable costs also increase x%. This relationship is depicted in Exhibit 6.3 of Chapter 6.

3. Revenues are directly proportional to volume—that is, they are linear. As unit sales increase by x%, revenues increase by x%. This relationship is shown in Exhibit 7.1.

4. Mixed costs can be properly divided into their fixed and variable elements. (Several methods to accomplish this task were presented in Chapter 6.)

5. All costs can be assigned to individual operated departments. This assumption limits the ability of CVP analysis to consider joint costs. These are costs which simultaneously benefit two or more operated departments. Joint costs, or a portion thereof, are not eliminated by discontinuing the offering of services such as food, beverage, telephone, and so forth. Therefore, for the purposes of CVP analysis, joint costs cannot be assigned to individual operated departments. Because of the existence of joint costs, the breakeven point cannot be determined by operated department. However, it can still be determined for the entire operation.

6. The CVP model considers only quantitative factors. Qualitative factors such as employee morale, guest goodwill, and so forth,

Exhibit 7.2   Cost-Volume-Profit Graph

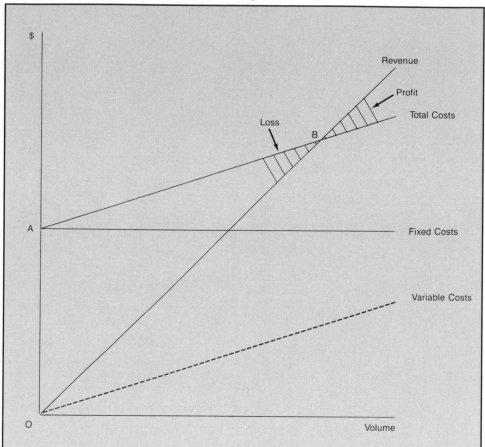

are not considered. Thus, management must carefully consider these qualitative factors before making any final decisions.

The cost-volume-profit relationships depicted in CVP equations and graphs consist of fixed costs, variable costs, and revenues. The relationships of fixed costs, variable costs, and revenues to volume and profits are graphically illustrated by Exhibit 7.2. The CVP graph shows dollars on the vertical axis and volume (rooms sales) on the horizontal axis. The fixed cost line is parallel to the horizontal axis from point A. Thus, the amount of the fixed costs theoretically would equal the loss the hospitality operation would suffer if no sales took place. The variable cost line is the broken straight line from point 0. This suggests that there are no variable costs when there are no sales and the straight line suggests that variable costs change proportionately with sales. The sum of variable costs and fixed costs equals total costs. The total cost line is drawn from Point A parallel to the variable cost line. This suggests that total costs increase only as variable costs increase, and that variable costs increase only from increased sales.

The revenues line commences at point 0 and reflects a linear relationship between revenues and units sold. Point B is the intersection of the total cost line and the revenues line. At point B, revenues equal total costs; this is the breakeven point. The vertical distance between the revenues line and the total cost line to the right of point B represents profit, while the vertical distance between these two lines to the left of Point B represents operating loss.

In this way, the CVP model shows the relationship of profit to sales volume and relates both to costs. As the volume of sales increases and reaches the point where the amount of revenues generated by those sales equals the total costs of generating them, then the hospitality operation arrives at its breakeven point. As the volume of sales increases past the breakeven point, the amount of revenues generated by those sales increases at a faster rate than the costs associated with those sales. Thus, the growing difference between revenues and cost measures the increase of profit in relation to sales volume.

It is important to stress again that the CVP model of the relations of costs, sales volume, and profit is based entirely upon its assumptions about the relationship of costs and revenues to sales volume. Although both costs and revenues are assumed to increase in direct linear proportion to the increase of sales volume, revenues must increase at a faster rate than costs if the business is to succeed; in other words, revenues must exceed variable costs. When this is true, both revenues and costs increase in proportion to sales, but they do so at different rates. It is because of this difference in growth rates of revenues and costs in relation to sales that the total revenue and total cost lines are bound to intersect and reach a balance (breakeven point) as sales increase.

CVP Equation—Single Product

The CVP graph, although appealing in its simplicity, is not sufficiently precise, and it is often time-consuming to manually construct a graph for each question to be solved using CVP analysis. However, computers can produce these graphs quickly and easily. As an alternative, CVP analysis uses a series of equations that express the mathematical relationships depicted in the graphic model.

A CVP equation expresses the cost-volume-profit relationships and is illustrated in Exhibit 7.3. At the breakeven point, net income is zero and the equation is simply shown as follows:

$$0 = SX - VX - F$$

The equation may be rearranged to solve for any one of the four variables as follows:

Equation	Determines
$X = \dfrac{F}{S - V}$	Units sold at breakeven
$F = SX - VX$	Fixed costs at breakeven
$S = \dfrac{F}{X} + V$	Selling price at breakeven

Exhibit 7.3 Cost-Volume-Profit Analysis Equation—Single Product

A CVP analysis equation expresses the cost-volume-profit relationships as follows:

$$I_n = SX - VX - F$$

where: I_n = Net income
  S = Selling price
  X = Units sold
  V = Variable cost per unit
  F = Total fixed cost

therefore: SX = Total revenue
  VX = Total variable costs

$$V = S - \frac{F}{X}$$ Variable cost per unit at breakeven

This CVP equation assumes the sale of a single product such as rooms or meals. Most hospitality firms sell a vast array of goods and services. However, before turning to this more complex situation, let's look at an illustration of this simple CVP analysis equation through the following example.

CVP Illustration— Single Product

The Michael Motel, a 30-room budget motel, has the following cost and price structure:

• Annual fixed costs equal $90,000.

• Average selling price per room is $20.

• Variable cost per room sold equals $8.

What is the number of room sales required for the Michael Motel to break even?

$$X = \frac{F}{S - V}$$ (equation for units sold at breakeven)

$$= \frac{90,000}{20 - 8}$$

$$= \underline{7,500} \text{ rooms}$$

Exhibit 7.4 depicts the breakeven point of the Michael Motel at 7,500 rooms. The total revenue at the breakeven point is shown as $150,000 (the result of multiplying the selling price per room by the number of rooms sold).

What is the occupancy percentage at breakeven for the Michael Motel?

Exhibit 7.4 Breakeven Point—Michael Motel

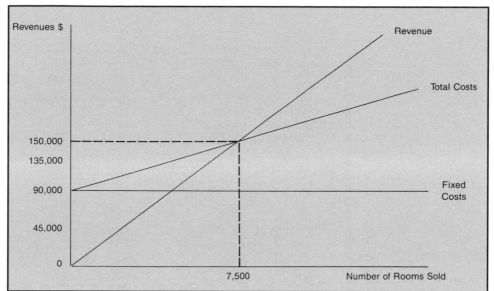

$$\text{Occupancy Percentage} = \frac{\text{Rooms Sold}}{\text{Rooms Available}}$$

$$= \frac{7,500}{365 \times 30}$$

$$= \frac{7,500}{10,950}$$

$$= \underline{\underline{68.49\%}}$$

If the proprietor desires the Michael Motel to earn $12,000 for the year, how many rooms must be sold? This can be determined by modifying the equation for units sold at breakeven.

$$X = \frac{F + I_n}{S - V} \quad \text{(equation for units sold at \$12,000 profit level)}$$

$$= \frac{90,000 + 12,000}{20 - 8}$$

$$= \frac{102,000}{12}$$

$$= \underline{\underline{8,500}} \text{ rooms}$$

Therefore, for $12,000 to be earned in a year, the Michael Motel must sell 1,000 rooms beyond its breakeven point. The profit earned on these additional sales is the result of the selling price less variable cost per room multiplied by the excess rooms (20 − 8 = 12; 12 × 1,000 = $12,000).

The difference between selling price and variable cost per unit is often called **contribution margin (CM)**. In this example, the CM is $12—for

Exhibit 7.5   Net Income—Michael Motel

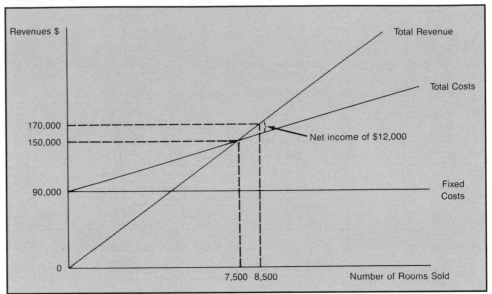

each room sold, $12 is available to cover fixed costs or contribute toward profits. Beyond the breakeven point, 1,000 additional rooms sales result in a $12,000 profit (rooms sales beyond breakeven × CM = profit).

Exhibit 7.5 is a graphic depiction of the $12,000 of net income. When total revenue is $170,000 (8,500 × $20), expenses equal $158,000 (calculated by multiplying $8 by 8,500 and then adding $90,000), resulting in a $12,000 net income. The distance between the total revenue line and the total cost line at the 8,500 rooms point represents the net income of $12,000.

Likewise, if rooms sales are less than the 7,500 breakeven point, $12 (CM) is lost per room not sold. For example, we can calculate the loss for the year if the Michael Motel sells only 6,500 rooms. Based on the above information, the answer should be $12,000 (CM × rooms less than breakeven). Using the general formula, the proof is as follows:

$$
\begin{aligned}
I_n &= SX - VX - F \quad \text{(general formula)} \\
&= 20(6,500) - 8(6,500) - 90,000 \\
&= 130,000 - 52,000 - 90,000 \\
&= -\underline{\underline{\$12,000}}
\end{aligned}
$$

Thus, a loss of $12,000 would be incurred when rooms sales are only 6,500 for the year.

Margin of Safety

The **margin of safety** is the excess of budgeted or actual sales over sales at breakeven. For the Michael Motel above, the level of sales when net income of $12,000 is earned is $170,000. Since the breakeven sales were $150,000, the margin of safety for the Michael Motel when $12,000 of profit is generated is $20,000 and 1,000 rooms as follows:

	Breakeven	Profit of $12,000	Margin of Safety
Sales—$	$150,000	$170,000	$20,000
Sales—Rooms	7,500	8,500	1,000

Sensitivity Analysis

Sensitivity analysis is the study of the sensitivity of the CVP model's dependent variables (such as room sales) to changes in one or more of the model's independent variables (such as variable costs and selling prices). The CVP model shows how the dependent variable will respond to a proposed change.

Again we will use the Michael Motel to illustrate this concept. Assume that the Michael Motel's fixed costs increase by $12,000. How many more rooms must be sold in order to earn $12,000 of net income? (Assume that selling price and variable costs percentage remain constant.)

$$\text{Increased Room Sales} = \frac{\text{Increase in Fixed Costs}}{\text{Contribution Margin}}$$

$$= \frac{12,000}{12}$$

$$= \underline{\underline{1,000}}$$

Thus, a $12,000 increase in fixed costs (the independent variable) will require an increase in room sales of 1,000 units (the dependent variable) to cover the increased fixed costs and still make $12,000 in profits.

The proof is as follows:

Increased sales	
1,000 rooms × $20 =	$20,000
Increased variable costs	
1,000 rooms × $8 =	8,000
Increased fixed costs =	12,000
Bottom line impact	$ –0–

CVP Equation—Multiple Products

Many hospitality operations, especially hotels, sell more than just a single product. In order to determine the operation's breakeven point (or any profit level) using CVP analysis, a different CVP equation is required. This equation is illustrated in Exhibit 7.6.

The **contribution margin ratio (CMR)** results from dividing CM by the selling price. Using the Michael Motel illustration, CMR is determined as follows:

$$\text{CMR} = \frac{\text{CM}}{\text{S}}$$

$$= \frac{20 - 8}{20}$$

Exhibit 7.6   Cost-Volume-Profit Analysis Equation—Multiple Products

$$R = \frac{F + I_n}{CMR_w}$$

where   F = Total fixed costs
I_n = Net income
R = Revenue at desired profit level
CMR_w = Weighted average contribution margin ratio

$$= \frac{12}{20}$$

$$= \underline{\underline{.6}}$$

The CMR means that for every $1 of sales for the Michael Motel, 60% is contributed toward fixed costs and/or profits. However, recall that in a multiple product situation, more than just rooms is being sold. Therefore, the CMR must be a **weighted average CMR (CMR_w)**. That is, an average CMR for all operated departments must be weighted to reflect the relative contribution of each department to the establishment's ability to pay fixed costs and generate profits.

The weighted average CMR can be determined from more than one formula. In the more complex formula, a CMR is determined for each operated department and the weighted average of the various CMRs is determined as illustrated in Exhibit 7.7.

To illustrate the calculation of CMR_w, assume that the Michael Motel adds a coffee shop. Exhibit 7.8 shows a partial income statement for the Michael Motel after the first year the coffee shop has been in operation. Using the equation in Exhibit 7.7, the CMR_w of .5 for the Michael Motel is determined as follows:

$$CMR_w = \frac{R_1}{TR} \times \frac{(R_1 - TV_1)}{R_1} + \frac{R_2}{TR} \times \frac{(R_2 - TV_2)}{R_2}$$

$$= \frac{150,000}{200,000} \times \frac{(150,000 - 60,000)}{150,000} + \frac{50,000}{200,000} \times \frac{(50,000 - 40,000)}{50,000}$$

$$= .75(.6) + .25(.2)$$

$$= .45 + .05$$

$$= \underline{\underline{.5}}$$

Alternatively, the CMR_w can sometimes be determined using a simpler formula using total revenues and total variable costs as follows:

$$CMR_w = \frac{TR - TV}{TR}$$

Exhibit 7.7 Weighted Average Contribution Margin Ratio

$$
\text{CMR}_w = \frac{R_1}{TR} \times \frac{(R_1 - TV_1)}{R_1} + \frac{R_2}{TR} \times \frac{(R_2 - TV_2)}{R_2} + \frac{R_3}{TR} \times \frac{(R_3 - TV_3)}{R_3} +
$$
$$
\cdots + \frac{R_n}{TR} \times \frac{(R_n - TV_n)}{R_n}
$$

where

R_1 = Revenue for operated department 1
R_2 = Revenue for operated department 2
R_3 = Revenue for operated department 3
R_n = Revenue for operated department n
TR = Total revenue
TV_1 = Total variable cost for operated department 1
TV_2 = Total variable cost for operated department 2
TV_3 = Total variable cost for operated department 3
TV_n = Total variable cost for operated department n

Exhibit 7.8 Partial Income Statement—Michael Motel

Operated Department	Revenue	Variable Costs	Contribution Margin
Rooms	$150,000	$ 60,000	$ 90,000
Coffee Shop	50,000	40,000	10,000
	$200,000	$100,000	$100,000

$$
= \frac{200,000 - 100,000}{200,000}
$$
$$
= .5
$$

The simpler formula is easier to use when you know the breakdown of fixed and variable costs for the entire property. However, when calculating the effects of various changes within departments (for example, the sales mix), the formula in Exhibit 7.7 allows you to substitute figures more easily.

To further illustrate the use of the CMR_w formula, assume that forecasted activity at the Michael Motel shows the variable cost percentage dropping to 30%. Since the CMR equals one minus the variable cost percentage, the new rooms department CMR would be .7. Assuming the same sales mix (75% rooms, 25% coffee shop), the formula can be used to revise the CMR_w as follows:

$$\text{Revised CMR}_w = .75\,(.7) + .25\,(.2)$$
$$= .525 + .05$$
$$= \underline{.575}$$

CVP Illustration— Multiple Products

The following series of questions and answers uses the Michael Motel to illustrate how the CVP calculations are used to analyze profit levels, sales mix, and breakeven points in the more complex, and also more typical, situations where hospitality operations sell multiple goods and services. Consider the following information for the Michael Motel:

- Annual fixed costs are $150,000.
- Sales mix is 75% rooms, 25% coffee shop.
- The Rooms Department CMR is .6 and the Coffee Shop CMR is .2.

What is revenue when the Michael Motel breaks even?

$$R = \frac{F}{CMR_w} \quad \text{(equation for revenue at the breakeven point)}$$
$$= \frac{150,000}{.5}$$
$$= \underline{\$300,000}$$

Therefore, the Michael Motel's breakeven point is reached when revenue is $300,000. Since in this application of CVP analysis, multiple units are being sold, the breakeven point is expressed in dollars, not units sold, which is used when analyzing single product/service operations.

What is the Michael Motel's total revenue when a profit of $12,000 is earned?

$$R = \frac{F + I_n}{CMR_w}$$
$$= \frac{150,000 + 12,000}{.5}$$
$$= \underline{\$324,000}$$

In order for the Michael Motel to earn $12,000, its revenue must increase by $24,000 beyond its breakeven sales of $300,000. Alternatively, the additional revenues beyond breakeven could have been determined as follows:

$$\text{Revenue Beyond Breakeven} = \frac{I_n}{CMR_w}$$

$$= \frac{\$12{,}000}{.5}$$

$$= \$24{,}000$$

Failure to reach breakeven sales will result in a loss of $.50 for every $1 of sales that falls short of breakeven. For the Michael Motel, total sales of $280,000 will result in a $10,000 loss determined as follows:

$$I_n = R(CMR_w) - F$$

$$= \$280{,}000 \ (.5) - \$150{,}000$$

$$= \$140{,}000 - \$150{,}000$$

$$= -\$10{,}000$$

Additional Questions and Solutions

If net income is to be $20,000, how much must rooms revenues be, given a ratio of 75% of rooms revenue to total revenue?

$$R = \frac{F + I_n}{CMR_w}$$

$$= \frac{150{,}000 + 20{,}000}{.5}$$

$$= 340{,}000$$

$$\text{Rooms Revenue} = .75R$$

$$= .75(340{,}000)$$

$$= \$255{,}000$$

In this situation, rooms revenue must be $255,000. A total revenue of $340,000 is required to yield a net income of $20,000, and 75% of this total revenue represents the contribution of the rooms department.

If room prices increase by 20% and the number of rooms sold remains constant, what is the revised breakeven point?

In this situation, we can expect that the price change will affect the rooms department's relative contribution to the operation's ability to meet fixed costs or profit goals. Therefore, the CMR_w must first be recalculated. This is accomplished by recalculating the CMR for the rooms department and then determining the revised CMR_w. The 20% room price increase not only increases the CMR for the rooms department, it also changes the sales mix for the Michael Motel.

$$\text{Revised CMR for Rooms} = \frac{150{,}000(1.20) - 60{,}000}{150{,}000(1.20)}$$

$$= \frac{180{,}000 - 60{,}000}{180{,}000}$$

$$= \text{2/3 or .6667}$$

$$\text{Revised CMR}_w = \frac{180,000}{230,000}(.6667) + \frac{50,000}{230,000}(.2)$$

$$= .5652$$

$$\text{Revenue} = \frac{F}{\text{CMR}_w}$$

$$= \frac{150,000}{.5652}$$

$$= \$265,392.78$$

Thus, the effect on breakeven of a 20% rooms price increase is to reduce the amount of revenue needed to break even from $300,000 to $265,392.78.

If the sales mix changes to 60% rooms and 40% food from the prior mix of 75% rooms and 25% food, what happens to the breakeven point?

Again, the CMR_w must first be revised. The revised CMR_w is divided into total fixed costs to yield the new breakeven point.

$$\text{Revised CMR}_w = .6(.6) + .4(.2)$$

$$= .36 + .08$$

$$= .44$$

$$\text{Revenue} = \frac{F}{\text{CMR}_w}$$

$$= \frac{150,000}{.44}$$

$$= \$340,909.09$$

Thus, the changes in sales mix result in a reduction in the weighted average CMR from .50 to .44. This, in turn, results in an increase of $40,909.09 in the amount of revenue needed for the operation to break even.

If fixed costs increase by $20,000 and all other factors remain constant, what is the revised breakeven point? (Assume a CMR_w of .5.)

In this situation, F is simply increased from $150,000 to $170,000. The new total for fixed costs is then divided by the CMR_w of .5 in order to calculate the new breakeven point.

$$\text{Revenue} = \frac{170,000}{.5}$$

$$= \$340,000$$

The breakeven point when revenues equal $340,000 could have been determined by dividing the increased fixed costs of $20,000 by .5 (the CMR_w) and adding the result ($40,000) to the original breakeven revenue of $300,000.

If fixed costs increase by $20,000, variable costs decrease by 5 percentage points, and all other factors remain constant, what is the revised breakeven point?

If variable costs decrease by 5 percentage points, then CMR_w increases by the same 5 percentage points. Thus, the revised CMR_w is .55.

$$\text{Revised } CMR_w = \text{Prior } CMR_w + \text{Variable Cost Decrease}$$
$$= .5 + .05$$
$$= \underline{\underline{.55}}$$

$$\text{Revenue} = \frac{170,000}{.55}$$
$$= \underline{\underline{\$309,090.90}}$$

Income Taxes and CVP Analysis

Up to this point, the CVP model has treated all costs as either fixed or variable in relation to revenues. However, income taxes vary, not with revenues, but with pre-tax income. Rather than simply treating income tax as a variable expense (which it is not), management can adjust the CVP equations to reflect this relationship between income taxes and pre-tax income. The CVP equations reflect this refinement by substituting I_b, the notation for pre-tax income, in place of I_n. When I_n and the tax rate (t) are known, I_b can be determined with the following formula:

$$I_b = \frac{I_n}{1 - t}$$

For example, assume that the Michael Motel desires to earn $12,000 of net income ($I_n$) and its tax rate is 20%. Pre-tax income (I_b) is determined as follows:

$$I_b = \frac{12,000}{1 - .2}$$
$$= \frac{12,000}{.8}$$
$$= \underline{\underline{\$15,000^*}}$$

*Proof:

Pre-tax income	$15,000
Taxes (20%)	− 3,000
Net income	$12,000

The CVP equation is now altered for income taxes as follows:

$$R = \frac{I_b + F}{CMR_w}$$

This revised CVP analysis equation can be illustrated using the Michael Motel. Assume the following situation:

- Desired net income equals $30,000.
- Annual fixed costs equal $150,000.
- Tax rate equals 20%.
- CMR_w equals .5.

From this information, we can calculate the pre-tax income as follows:

$$I_b = \frac{\$30,000}{1 - .2}$$

$$= \$37,500$$

Once we calculate the pre-tax income as $37,500, we can then use the revised CVP equation to arrive at the breakeven point:

$$R = \frac{I_b + F}{CMR_w}$$

$$= \frac{37,500 + 150,000}{.5}$$

$$= \frac{187,500}{.5}$$

$$= \$375,000*$$

*Proof:

Revenue	$375,000
Variable costs (50%)	−187,500
Fixed costs	−150,000
Pre-tax income	37,500
Income taxes	− 7,500
Net income	$30,000

When an enterprise breaks even, its net income and pre-tax income both equal zero. Therefore, the breakeven point for a given operation is the same regardless of the tax rate.

Profit-Volume Graphs

In CVP graphs such as Exhibit 7.2, profits and losses are represented by the vertical difference between the total revenue and total cost lines at any point. When management desires to focus on the impact on profits of changes in sales volume, a **profit-volume graph** is often used, because it more clearly depicts the relationship between volume and profits. In this graph, revenues and costs are not shown.

Exhibit 7.9 is the profit-volume graph (for the Michael Motel) which is used to illustrate the CVP analysis when a firm has multiple products.

Exhibit 7.9   Profit-Volume Graph

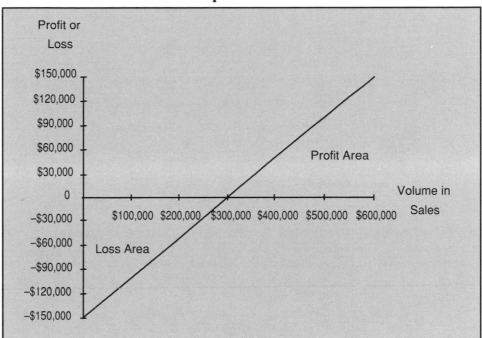

The breakeven point is reached when sales equal $300,000, as calculated above. If sales are $0, then losses are $150,000, which is the total amount of fixed costs. Likewise, if $150,000 of profit is to be earned, then total sales would have to be $600,000. Although the graph shows this result, one must question if this point is outside the Michael Motel's possible range of activity. If rooms revenue is 75% and the selling price per room is $20, then 22,500 would have to be sold, determined as follows:

$$\text{Required Rooms Sales in Units} = \frac{\text{Rooms Revenue}}{\text{Room Selling Price}}$$

$$= \frac{.75(\$600,000)}{\$20}$$

$$= \underline{\underline{22,500}}$$

However, we established earlier in this chapter that the Michael Motel is a 30-room property. The total rooms it could sell in a year is 10,950; thus, 22,500 is beyond its reach. It would have to expand its size or increase its prices to achieve sales of $600,000 and net income of $150,000. The point to remember is: do not blindly use these analytical tools.

Cash Flow CVP Analysis

In addition to applying CVP analysis to evaluate profit levels, sales mixes, and pre-tax incomes, managers and owners are also interested in evaluating various levels of cash flow. They are interested in knowing the amount of revenues required to produce a sufficient flow of cash to reach

Exhibit 7.10 Cash Flow Cost-Volume-Profit Analysis Equation

$$R = \frac{CF_b + F - NCE + NECD}{CMR_w}$$

where

CF_b = Desired cash flow before taxes

F = Fixed costs (including depreciation)

NCE = Non-cash expenses – expenses which do not entail cash payments such as depreciation and amortization.

$NECD$ = Non-expense cash disbursements – cash payments which do not relate directly to expenses

Non-expense cash disbursements are for loan payments excluding interest expense, payments for fixed assets, etc. Payment for accounts payable, payroll payable, etc., are considered to relate "directly" to expense, thus, they would not be included in this figure

such benchmarks as the breakeven point and other cash flow levels. The CVP analysis equations previously demonstrated may be modified to provide answers to these questions. The cash flow CVP equation is illustrated in Exhibit 7.10.

The application of CVP analysis to problems involving cash flow can be illustrated using the Michael Motel in light of the following information:

- Fixed costs equal $150,000.
- Tax rate equals 20%.
- CMR_w equals .5.
- Desired positive cash flow (after taxes) is $30,000.
- Non-cash expenses equal $10,000. (This is depreciation expense for the period.)
- Non-expense cash disbursements equal $20,000.

In this situation, we can calculate the total revenue required to yield the desired positive cash flow (CF_d) of $30,000. But, first, we need to calculate the desired cash flow before taxes:

$$
\begin{aligned}
CF_b &= \frac{CF_d + NECD - NCE}{1 - t} - NECD + NCE \\
&= \frac{30{,}000 + 20{,}000 - 10{,}000}{1 - .2} - 20{,}000 + 10{,}000 \\
&= \frac{40{,}000}{.8} - 10{,}000 \\
&= 50{,}000 - 10{,}000 \\
&= \underline{\$40{,}000}
\end{aligned}
$$

Exhibit 7.11   Cash Flow—Michael Motel

Cash receipts (revenue)	$400,000
Cash disbursements:	
Variable costs	200,000
Fixed costs	140,000*
Non-expenses (reduction in debt)	20,000
Income taxes	10,000**
Positive cash flow	$ 30,000

*Total fixed costs less depreciation equals fixed costs cash disbursements ($150,000 – $10,000 = $140,000).

**Income Taxes = (Revenue – Variable Costs – Fixed Costs) (Tax Rate)
Income Taxes = (400,000 – 200,000 – 150,000) (.2)
Income Taxes = 50,000 (.2)
Income Taxes = $10,000

We can now calculate the total revenue required to yield the desired cash flow before taxes by using the following formula:

$$R = \frac{CF_b + F - NCE + NECD}{CMR_w}$$

$$= \frac{40,000 + 150,000 - 10,000 + 20,000}{.5}$$

$$= \frac{200,000}{.5}$$

$$= \$400,000$$

Therefore, the Michael Motel must have total revenues of $400,000 in order to generate sufficient cash internally to make its payments and to attain the desired positive cash flow level. The proof of our calculations appears in Exhibit 7.11.

Alternatively, the total revenue at which the Michael Motel has breakeven cash flow (that is, CF_d equals 0) can be determined. First, we need to calculate the desired cash flow before taxes as follows:

$$CF_b = \frac{CF_d + NECD - NCE}{1 - t} - NECD + NCE$$

$$= \frac{0 + 20,000 - 10,000}{1 - .2} - 20,000 + 10,000$$

$$= 12,500 - 20,000 + 10,000$$

$$= \$2,500$$

Now we calculate total revenue required to yield a breakeven cash flow as follows:

$$R = \frac{CF_b + F - NCE + NECD}{CMR_w}$$

$$= \frac{2,500 + 150,000 - 10,000 + 20,000}{.5}$$

$$= \frac{\$162,500}{.5}$$

$$= \underline{\underline{\$325,000}}$$

Therefore, the Michael Motel requires revenue of $325,000 to yield sufficient cash so that it does not have to borrow working capital funds. The revenue required for cash flow breakeven of $325,000 is $25,000 greater than the breakeven revenue of $300,000 as computed previously. This difference is due to the excess of the required pre-tax cash flow and NECD over NCE, determined as follows:

$$\text{Difference in revenue} = \frac{CF_b + NECD - NCE}{CMR_w}$$

$$= \frac{2,500 + 20,000 - 10,000}{.5}$$

$$= \underline{\underline{\$25,000}}$$

Comprehensive Problem

The Smith Hotel will be used to more fully illustrate CVP analysis. Exhibit 7.12 contains the income statement according to the *USASH* format for the Smith Hotel for the year ended December 31, 19X1.

For CVP analysis, expenses need to be identified as either variable or fixed. For illustration purposes, the direct expenses of the operated departments for the Smith Hotel are assumed to be variable, while overhead costs (the undistributed operating expenses and fixed charges) are assumed to be fixed costs. Income tax is a function of income before income taxes. These assumptions are shown in Exhibit 7.13.

Given this information, we will now use CVP analysis to calculate each of the following situations for the Smith Hotel:

1. Weighted average contribution margin ratio

2. Breakeven point

3. Total revenue to yield a net income of $500,000

4. Rooms revenues when profit equals $500,000

5. Breakeven point if fixed costs increase by $300,000

6. Breakeven point if fixed costs increase by $300,000 and revenues increase 10% for each department through price increases

Exhibit 7.12 Income Statement—Smith Hotel

Summary Income Statement
Smith Hotel
For the year ended December 31, 19X1

	Revenue	Cost of Sales	Payroll and Related Expenses	Other Expenses	Income (Loss)
Operating Departments:					
Rooms	$4,000,000	$ 0	$ 500,000	$ 300,000	$3,200,000
Food and Beverage	1,800,000	500,000	700,000	200,000	400,000
Telephone	200,000	160,000	30,000	10,000	0
Total	$6,000,000	$660,000	1,230,000	510,000	3,600,000
Undistributed Operating Expenses:					
Administrative and General			100,000	50,000	150,000
Data Processing			50,000	50,000	100,000
Human Resources			30,000	260,000	290,000
Transportation			20,000	40,000	60,000
Marketing			100,000	300,000	400,000
Property Operation and Maintenance			100,000	100,000	200,000
Energy Costs			0	400,000	400,000
Income Before Fixed Charges			$1,630,000	$1,710,000	2,000,000
Rent, Property Taxes and Insurance				$ 200,000	
Interest				1,000,000	
Depreciation				500,000	1,700,000
Income Before Income Taxes					300,000
Income Taxes					60,000
Net Income					$ 240,000

Situation #1: Determine the CMR_w.

From Exhibit 7.13, the CMR_w may be determined as follows:

$$CMR_w = \frac{\text{Contribution Margin*}}{\text{Total Revenue}}$$

$$= \frac{\$3,600,000}{\$6,000,000}$$

$$= \underline{\underline{.6}}$$

*Total operated departments income

Exhibit 7.13   Assumed Relationship of Revenues, Variable Costs, and Contribution Margin—Smith Hotel

	Revenue	Variable Costs	Contribution Margin
	Relationship of Revenues, Variable Costs, and Contribution Margin		
	Smith Hotel		
	For the year ended December 31, 19X1		
Rooms	$4,000,000	$ 800,000	$3,200,000
Food and Beverage	1,800,000	1,400,000	400,000
Telephone	200,000	200,000	0
Total	$6,000,000	$2,400,000	3,600,000
Fixed Costs			3,300,000
Income Before Income Taxes			300,000
Income Taxes			60,000
Net Income			$ 240,000

Situation #2:   Determine the breakeven point.

$$R = \frac{F}{CMR_w}$$

$$= \frac{\$3,300,000}{.6}$$

$$= \$5,500,000$$

Situation #3:   Determine the total revenue required to yield $500,000 of net income. (Assume that the sales mix remains constant.)

First, the effect of income taxes on net income must be accounted for, assuming the Smith Hotel's income tax rate of 20%. The amount of income before income taxes that the hotel must generate in order to achieve the desired net income of $500,000 can be determined as follows:

$$I_b = \frac{I_n}{1 - t}$$

$$= \frac{\$500,000}{1 - .2}$$

$$= \$625,000$$

Second, the total revenue needed to yield this amount of income before income taxes is calculated as follows:

$$R = \frac{I_b + F}{CMR_w}$$

$$= \frac{\$625,000 + \$3,300,000}{.6}$$

$$= \frac{\$3,925,000}{.6}$$

$$= \$6,541,666.67$$

Situation #4: Determine the amount of room revenue when the Smith Hotel makes $500,000 of net income.

First, from the information provided on the Smith Hotel's summary income statement (Exhibit 7.12), we can determine the relative contribution of rooms revenue to total revenue.

$$\frac{\text{Rooms Revenue}}{\text{Total Revenue}} = \frac{\$4,000,000}{\$6,000,000}$$

$$= .6667$$

Second, we can then multiply .6667 by the total revenue and arrive at the required rooms revenue as part of the total revenue for the Smith Hotel to achieve $500,000 of net income.

$$\text{Room Revenue} = \$6,541,666.67 \times .6667$$

$$\text{Room Revenue} = \$4,361,329.17$$

Situation #5: Determine the breakeven point for the Smith Hotel if fixed costs increase by $300,000 and all other things remain constant.

The breakeven point is determined as follows:

$$R = \frac{F}{CMR_w}$$

$$= \frac{\$3,600,000}{.6}$$

$$= \$6,000,000$$

Note the Smith Hotel's breakeven point increases from $5,500,000 to $6,000,000 when its fixed costs increase by $300,000. Alternatively, the new breakeven point could have been determined by dividing the increased fixed costs ($300,000) by the CMR_w and adding the result to the previously calculated breakeven point of $5,500,000 as follows:

$$R = \$5,500,000 + \frac{\$300,000}{.6}$$

$$= \$6,000,000$$

Situation #6: Determine the breakeven point for the Smith Hotel if fixed costs increase by $300,000 and revenues increase 10% for each department through price increases. Assume that all factors remain constant.

First, a revised CMR_w must be determined as follows:

	Total Revenue	Total Contribution Margin
Prior	$6,000,000	$3,600,000
Increase	600,000	600,000
Revised	$6,600,000	$4,200,000

Exhibit 7.14   Cost Structures of Properties A and B

	Property A $	%	Property B $	%
Revenues	$500,000	100%	$500,000	100%
Variable costs	300,000	60	200,000	40
Fixed costs	200,000	40	300,000	60
Net income	$ 0	0%	$ 0	0%

$$\text{Revised CMR}_w = \frac{\text{Revised Total Contribution Margin}}{\text{Revised Total Revenue}}$$

$$= \frac{4,200,000}{6,600,000}$$

$$= \underline{.6364}$$

Then the total fixed costs are increased by $300,000 to $3,600,000, and the breakeven point is determined as follows:

$$R = \frac{F}{\text{CMR}_w}$$

$$= \frac{\$3,600,000}{.6364}$$

$$= \underline{\$5,656,819.61}$$

Operating Leverage

Operating leverage is the extent to which an operation's expenses are fixed rather than variable. If an operation has a high level of fixed costs relative to variable costs, it is said to be highly levered. Being highly levered means a relatively small increase in sales beyond the breakeven point results in a relatively large increase in net income. However, failure to reach the breakeven point results in a relatively large net loss.

If an operation has a high level of variable costs relative to fixed costs, it is said to have low operating leverage. A relatively small increase in sales beyond the breakeven point results in a small increase in net income. On the other hand, failure to reach the breakeven point results in a relatively small net loss.

For example, consider the cost structures of two hospitality operations illustrated in Exhibit 7.14. Note that both properties will break even when their revenues equal $500,000. However, Property A has a CMR of .4, while Property B has a CMR of .6. This reveals that, for each revenue dollar over the shared breakeven point, Property A will earn only $.40 while Property B will earn $.60. On the other hand, for each revenue dollar under the breakeven point, Property A loses only $.40 while Property B loses $.60. Both properties identify the same breakeven point as the difference between revenues and expenses, and, for both properties, the

Exhibit 7.15 Operating Leverages of Properties A and B

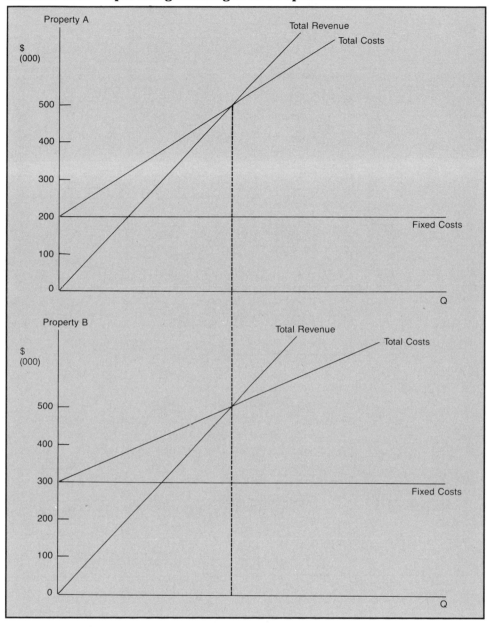

costs of failure equal the rewards of success. They both risk as much as they gain, but for Property B, the stakes are higher. Property B is more highly levered than Property A.

Exhibit 7.15 is a graphical representation of the cost structures of Properties A and B and reflects their identical breakeven points. However, it is the vertical distance between the total revenue and total cost lines that measures the degree of profitability for each property. Since Property B is more highly levered, the distance between the total cost and total revenue lines is greater at all operating levels compared to Property A, except at the breakeven point.

Exhibit 7.16   Profit-Volume Graph for Properties A and B

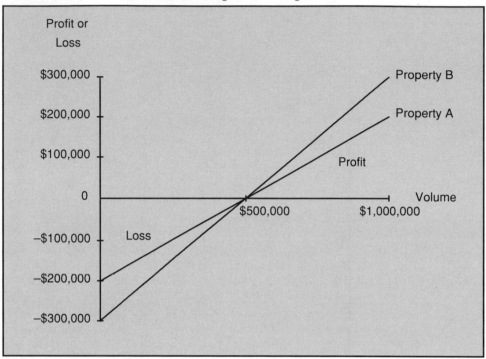

The degree of operating leverage desired by a hospitality property reflects the degree of risk that the operation desires to take. All other things being the same, the more highly levered the operation, the greater the risk. However, the greater the risk, the greater the expected returns, as reflected in Exhibit 7.15. For example, if sales are $300,000 below the breakeven point, Property A loses only $120,000 ($300,000 × .4), while the more highly levered Property B loses $180,000 ($300,000 × .6). However, if sales are $300,000 over the breakeven point for both operations, Property A earns only $120,000 of profit, while Property B generates $180,000 of profit.

Exhibit 7.16 contains the profit-volume graph for Properties A and B. Notice that both properties break even when sales equal $500,000. When sales of $1,000,000 are generated, Property B earns $300,000, while Property A earns only $200,000; however, when sales are zero, Property B loses $300,000, while Property A loses only $200,000.

Computerization

As mentioned in Chapter 6, spreadsheet programs can perform very extensive and sophisticated calculations, including the formulas discussed in this chapter. For example, the breakeven calculation could easily be entered into a spreadsheet and multiple levels of calculations could be performed quickly and accurately. As in the "what if" models in Chapter 6, these formulas can be repeated many times in the same model to determine the optimum solution to a question. In the case of CVP

Exhibit 7.17 Computer-Generated Rooms Department Rate Analysis—Salem Hotel Company

Room Department Rate Analysis Salem Hotel Company						
Available Rooms for Sale	36,500	36,500	36,500	36,500	36,500	36,500
Average Rate	$40.00	$45.00	$47.50	$50.00	$52.50	$55.00
Projected Occupancy	77.5%	75.0%	72.5%	70.0%	65.0%	60.0%
Room Revenue	$1,131,500	$1,231,875	$1,256,969	$1,277,500	$1,245,563	$1,204,500
Room Variable Expense	237,615	229,950	222,285	214,620	199,290	183,960
Room Profits	893,885	1,001,925	1,034,684	1,062,880	1,046,273	1,020,540
F&B Revenues	424,313	410,625	396,938	383,250	355,875	328,500
F&B Variable Expenses	318,234	307,969	297,703	287,438	266,906	246,375
F&B Profits	106,079	102,656	99,235	95,812	88,969	82,125
Total Departmental Profits	999,964	1,104,581	1,133,919	1,158,692	1,135,242	1,102,665
Contribution Margin Ratio	64.3%	67.2%	68.6%	69.8%	70.9%	71.9%
Fixed Expenses	$ 760,000	$ 760,000	$ 760,000	$ 760,000	$ 760,000	$ 760,000
Breakeven Point*	$1,182,461	$1,130,112	$1,108,518	$1,089,305	$1,072,100	$1,056,604

*Breakeven point was calculated by the computer using the formula which divided Fixed Expenses by the quantity (1 – Contribution Margin Ratio).

analysis, the breakeven point could be easily determined, and then the analysis could be conducted to find the revenues which would generate the desired net income.

Multiple-product CVP analysis is also ideally suited to spreadsheet programs. Contribution margins for each profit center can be quickly determined and combined to create a total picture for the business. Exhibit 7.17 shows how this might be done with the Salem Hotel Company. Expanding upon the model shown in Chapter 6, the effects of the lower occupancy also caused a reduction in food and beverage revenues. Food and beverage revenues equal the product of available rooms for sale × projected occupancy × $15 average check. This is based on past performance that suggests an average of $15 dollars of food and beverage sales per room sold. The food and beverage variable expenses equal food and beverage revenue × .75.

With any reduction in business, variable costs would also be reduced. The effect is that profitability peaks at 70% occupancy and the combined contribution margin is 69.8%.

With this information, the breakeven point of the hotel is shown for each of the occupancy, revenue, and expense levels in the analysis. The breakeven point at the maximum profitability level is $1,089,305. Some managers might, however, prefer to operate under the scenario of $55 room rate and 60% occupancy because it has the lowest breakeven point and, all other things being equal, is therefore the least risky option. When the revenue and expense lines in the analysis are changed, the computer automatically calculates the contribution margin and the breakeven point.

In addition, computers can produce CVP graphs to reflect visually the results of CVP analysis. Many users find such graphs to be more understandable than a table of numbers.

Summary

Managers use cost-volume-profit (CVP) analysis as an analytical tool to examine the relationships among costs, revenues, and sales volume. By expressing these relationships in graphic form or by using mathematical equations, management can determine an operation's breakeven point, sales requirements for a specified net income level, and/or the mix of sales within the operation.

In order to use CVP analysis to determine the breakeven point, various relationships must be assumed. First, fixed costs are constant; they will not fluctuate within the range of operating activity being studied. Also, both variable costs and revenues fluctuate linearly with sales volume; that is, a percentage increase in sales volume (for example, rooms sold) will result in the same percentage increase in revenues and variable expenses. In a "shut-down" situation (when sales are zero), there are no variable costs or revenues, but the fixed costs will be at their constant level; therefore, the theoretical bottom line for such a shut-down period will be a net loss equal to the fixed costs of the period.

The breakeven point is defined as the level of sales which generates revenues equal to total (fixed and variable) costs. CVP analysis allows management selling a single product/service (for example, only rooms) to arrive at this breakeven level of revenues with the aid of the equation:

$$X = \frac{F}{S - V}$$

The S − V element of the equation is the contribution margin, which is the amount of money generated by the sale that may be applied to cover fixed cost, or, beyond the breakeven point, to contribute to profit. Therefore, the equation reflects the fixed cost divided by the dollars provided to cover fixed costs per sales unit.

In the more complex situation where more than one good or service is sold, the CVP formula is as follows:

$$R = \frac{F + I_n}{CMR_w}$$

The CMR_w element of the equation reflects the weighted average of the CMRs for the profit centers. The CVP formulas for the multiple products operation may be used to determine breakeven points by substituting 0 for I_n. This formula may further be modified by substituting I_b for I_n to consider the effect of income taxes.

Once the CVP relationship is understood, it can become a vital tool offering aid in a number of situations. It can provide management with benchmark sales levels (such as the breakeven level, the amount needed to provide a specific net income, or the required level to provide for cash needs), prices, or sales mix. It can be used to examine the differences between levels of sales or costs. It can also be used to examine different cost structures, as the effect of differences in the CMR can be seen over different sales levels.

Key Terms

breakeven analysis
breakeven point
contribution margin
contribution margin ratio
cost-volume-profit analysis
margin of safety

operating leverage
profit-volume graph
sensitivity analysis
weighted average contribution
 margin

Discussion Questions

1. What are the assumptions underlying the CVP analysis?

2. What does the term $S - V$ represent in the CVP equation? How does its use differ from that of the CMR?

3. Draw a CVP graph of the following operation: $F = \$10$; $S = \$1$; $V = \$.50$. What is the meaning of the regions (between the total revenue and total cost lines) to the left and right of 20 units sold?

4. What is income before taxes for a hospitality operation which generates no sales during a period?

5. What is the advantage of using CVP equations instead of CVP graphs to express relationships?

6. How does CMR for a single department, or for an enterprise selling only one product/service, differ from a weighted average CMR (CMR_w)? How is CMR_w determined?

7. What part of the CVP equation used to determine the breakeven point must be changed in order to produce the answer in terms of sales dollars versus sales units? Why is this so?

8. What is the sales mix? How does it affect CMR_w?

9. Why should non-cash expenses be subtracted in the CVP formula used to determine the revenue level at the cash flow breakeven point?

10. If, by changing an operation's sales mix, the CMR_w decreases, how is the breakeven level of sales affected?

Problems

Problem 7.1

Keith Jones is considering investing $1,500,000 in a 60-room motel, The Olympia Inn. Based on his market research, he has determined that a reasonable room rate for the region is $39.95. He projects variable costs to be $12.00 per room, and his annual fixed costs are estimated at $400,000.

Required:

1. Determine the number of rooms sales required for The Olympia Inn to break even.

2. Assuming all 60 rooms will be available 365 days during the year, what is The Olympia Inn's projected breakeven occupancy percentage?

3. How many rooms must be sold if Mr. Jones is to make a 15% return on his investment? (Assume that there is no tax effect.)

Problem 7.2

John Rhoades, owner of Rhoades Inn, has requested your assistance in analyzing his 50-room "rooms only" property. He provides you information as follows:

1. The average rooms sales price is $30.

2. Monthly fixed costs equal $20,000.

3. His variable costs per room sold equal $10.

Required:

1. Determine the Rhoades Inn's breakeven point in revenue.

2. If revenues equal $450,000, what is the Rhoades Inn's margin of safety in revenues and rooms sold?

3. If John desires his property to generate a pre-tax profit of $100,000, how many rooms must be sold?

4. What is the occupancy percentage for the Rhoades Inn when pre-tax profit earned is $100,000?

Problem 7.3

Sid Gull, the owner/operator of the Iowa Inn, is interested in determining the level of sales necessary to realize a net income of $500,000 next year. He has compiled records on each department's sales and costs, and assumes that the sales mix will be the same next year. The major department, the rooms department, had sales of $2,500,000, and its contribution margin was $1,750,000. The coffee shop had sales of $750,000 and variable costs of $300,000. The restaurant had sales of $1,200,000 and variable costs of $750,000. Mr. Gull assumes that the fixed costs will be $1,000,000.

Required:

1. What is the CMR_w?

2. What is the required level of total sales to generate $500,000 net income? (Assume that there are no income taxes.)

3. What is the required level of total sales to generate $500,000 net income if the income tax rate is 30%?

Problem 7.4

Dustin Gordon, the executive vice president of COB, is considering expanding the company's operations into the hospitality industry. The company's goals include diversification, but also require an 18% return on their investment after taxes. Mr. Gordon has studied a hotel property which yields the following results:

1. The rooms department generates 80% of the sales and operates with a CMR of .76.

2. The food and beverage department generates the other 20% of sales, and has a CMR of .55.

3. Fixed costs per year are estimated to be $240,000.

4. In order to purchase the hotel, COB would have to invest $1,500,000.

5. COB's tax rate is 30%.

Required:

What level of sales is required before Mr. Gordon would recommend investing in the hotel to COB's board of directors?

Problem 7.5

The condensed income statement reflects variable costs, fixed costs, and revenues of the Château Stacie.

	Revenues	Variable Costs	Department Income
Rooms	$ 900,000	$270,000	$630,000
Food & Beverages	600,000	480,000	120,000
	$1,500,000	$750,000	750,000
Fixed Costs			600,000
Pre-tax Income			150,000
Taxes			45,000
Net Income			$105,000

Required:

1. Compute Château Stacie's breakeven point.

2. If the fixed rent of $100,000 a year is exchanged for a variable lease of 5% of revenue, what is the new breakeven point?

3. Assume (independent of #2) that the management of Château Stacie is considering placing a new promotional food and beverage brochure costing $2,000 in the rooms. The promotion is expected to increase the traffic in the restaurant by 1,000 people whose average check is expected to be $12. Should the promotion be undertaken? Support your response with figures.

4. Determine (independent of #2 and #3) the total food and beverage sales when the Château Stacie earns $500,000 of net income. Assume that room sales equal food and beverage sales in this situation.

Problem 7.6

The Mackinaw and Minier Hotels' summarized operating results are as follows:

	Mackinaw Hotel	Minier Hotel
1. CMR_w	60%	50%
2. Annual fixed costs	$1,200,000	$1,000,000
3. Tax rate	20%	20%

Required:

1. Compute each hotel's breakeven point.

2. Draw a profit-volume chart, including a profit-volume line, for each hotel for sales volumes ranging from $0 to $3,000,000.

3. Which hotel is riskier? Why?

Problem 7.7

The KDJ Inn's summary income statement is as follows:

	Rooms	Food	Total
Revenues	$1,500,000	$500,000	$2,000,000
Variable Costs	300,000	400,000	700,000
Contribution Margin	$1,200,000	$100,000	1,300,000
Fixed Costs			1,000,000*
Pre-tax Income			300,000
Income Taxes			75,000
Net Income			$ 225,000

*Includes lease expense of $480,000.

Required:

1. What is the breakeven point for the KDJ Inn?

2. If the fixed cost lease is traded for a variable lease of 20% of total sales, what is the revised breakeven point for the KDJ Inn?

3. If (independent of #2) the variable costs increase by 10%, by what percentage must sales increase in order for the KDJ Inn to earn its net income of $225,000?

4. If (independent of #2 and #3) the KDJ Inn is to earn net income of $300,000, what must its room sales equal? (Assume that the sales mix remains constant.)

Problem 7.8

Stephanie Miller, an experienced business person and consultant, realizes the importance of cash flow. Therefore, whenever she is requested to provide a client with a breakeven level of sales, she also provides them with a cash flow breakeven analysis. The present owner has provided Ms. Miller with the following information for BMS, Inc.

BMS Inc.
Monthly Condensed Income Statement

Rooms Revenues		$100,000
F&B Revenues		40,000
Total Revenue		140,000
Departmental Expenses		
Rooms	$20,000	
F&B	20,000	
Total Departmental Expense		40,000
Contribution Margin		100,000
Fixed Costs		
Interest Expense	10,000	
Depreciation	20,000	
Other Fixed Costs	50,000	
Total Fixed Costs		80,000
Income Before Tax		20,000
Tax		5,000
Net Income		$15,000

Other Information:

1. Assume the tax rate to be constant over any level of pre-tax income.

2. The monthly mortgage payment is $15,000, of which $10,000 is interest expense.

3. All inventories are purchased on a cash basis and are expensed when purchased since they are insignificant.

4. There is no major change in current assets, other than cash, or current liabilities from month to month.

Required:

You are to assist Ms. Miller in:

1. Determining the level of sales required to provide BMS, Inc. with $40,000 net income.

2. Determining the level of sales required to provide BMS, Inc. with $20,000 positive cash flow for a month.

Problem 7.9

Edwin and Carla's Dude Ranch (ECDR) is a 40-room hotel near Denver with a 30-seat restaurant and stables (a profit center). Edwin and Carla Cass, the owners, are interested in having you use CVP analysis to aid them in determining various sales levels for their resort. The following is a summary of the most recent annual income statement.

Edwin and Carla's Dude Ranch
Condensed Income Statement
For the year ended December 31, 19X5

	Rooms	Food	Stables	Total
Revenues	$500,000	$200,000	$5,000	$705,000
Variable Expenses	150,000	150,000	4,000	304,000
Contribution Margin	$350,000	$50,000	$1,000	401,000
Fixed Expense				151,000
Income Tax				125,000
Net Income				$125,000

Required:

1. What is the food department's CMR?

2. What is the weighted average CMR for ECDR?

3. What is the breakeven point?

4. The Casses wish to increase net income by $30,000 and feel this can be done by increasing room sales *only*. Determine the necessary increase in room sales to meet this requirement.

5. Assume (independent of #4) that revenue from the stables can be increased, but only with a $500 increase in advertising (a fixed cost) for brochures to go in each room. What level of sales from the stables must be generated to cover this cost?

6. Assume that the brochures mentioned in #5 are used as a direct mailing. The cost would now be $1,500 to cover printing and mailing, but sales for each department would increase. Assuming that room sales, food sales, and stable revenue remain at 5 to 2 to .05, how much must revenues increase for net income to remain constant?

Problem 7.10

The condensed income statement of the Green Valley Inn (GVI) is as follows:

	Revenue	Direct Expenses Fixed	Variable	Department Income
Rooms	$2,000,000	$200,000	$200,000	$1,600,000
Food and Beverage	1,000,000	200,000	500,000	300,000
Other	200,000	50,000	100,000	50,000
	$3,200,000	$450,000	$800,000	1,950,000
Other Fixed Costs				1,600,000
Pre-tax Income				350,000
Taxes				70,000
Net Income				$280,000

Required:

1. Compute the GVI's CMR_w.

2. Determine the GVI's breakeven point.

3. Assume that GVI's sales mix changes such that rooms revenue is 45%, food and beverage revenue is 50%, and other revenue is 5%. What is the total amount of sales when the GVI earns $500,000 of net income?

4. Assume that the tremendous growth mentioned in #3 in GVI's food and beverage operations is due to extensive advertising in the local media at the cost of $200,000. What level of food and beverage sales is required to cover this expenditure?

8 Cost Approaches to Pricing

Pricing is one of the most difficult decisions hospitality managers make. If prices are set too high, lower demand may result in reduced sales. When prices are set too low, demand may be high, but lowered sales revenue is likely to result in costs not being covered. Either way, the hospitality operation's profitability may be placed in jeopardy. How can a hospitality manager ensure that prices are neither too high nor too low?

Establishing prices which result in maximized revenues is extremely difficult. Some managers would suggest that the process of setting effective prices involves a bit of luck. Yet, while there may be no completely scientific method guaranteed to determine the best prices to maximize profits, good managers will seek to establish a rational basis for their pricing decisions. General approaches to the pricing problem provide ways of using relevant information and the manager's knowledge of the relationships among sales, costs, and profits to establish a reasonable basis for effective pricing.

Our discussion of cost approaches to pricing in this chapter will answer many of the important questions that come to mind regarding the pricing process, such as the following:

1. Which costs are relevant in the pricing decision?
2. What is the common weakness of informal pricing methods?
3. What are the common cost methods of pricing rooms?
4. What are common methods of pricing food and beverages?
5. How may popularity and profitability be considered in setting food prices?
6. Will departmental revenue maximization result in revenue maximization for the hospitality firm?
7. What is price elasticity of demand?
8. What is integrated pricing?

We will begin this chapter with a discussion of the importance of pricing and the need for profits by both profit-oriented and non-profit-oriented operations. Next, we will explain and illustrate the concept of the price elasticity of demand. We will then consider a variety of approaches to pricing both rooms and meals, discuss the effect of sales mix on profits, and address the topic of integrated pricing.

The Importance of Pricing

A major determinant of a hospitality establishment's profitability is its prices. Whether prices are set too low or too high, the result is the same—a failure to maximize profits. When prices are below what the market is willing to pay, the establishment will realize less revenues than it could generate through its operations. Alternatively, prices set too high will reduce sales and thereby fail to achieve the operation's potential for profit. Management's goal is to set prices which result in profit maximization.

Another factor to consider when setting prices is the "positioning" of the establishment's offerings within the marketplace. Prices set too low may tend to degrade the perceived quality of products, whereas inflated prices may tend to reduce the perceived value of products from the guest's perspective.

Profits should not result simply because revenues happen by chance or luck to exceed expenses. Profits should occur because revenues generated have been carefully calculated to exceed expenses incurred. The emphasis should not be defensive, that is, on keeping costs down to make a profit. Aggressive management should set out to generate sufficient revenues to cover costs. Cost containment is a respectable secondary objective *after* marketing efforts are undertaken to achieve a reasonably high level of sales.

In this chapter, prices will be approached from a cost perspective. However, this is not meant to suggest that non-cost factors such as market demand and competition are irrelevant. In some situations, they may be critical to the pricing decision.

For-profit operations desire to make profits for such reasons as expanding operations, providing owners with a return on capital invested, and increasing the share prices of stock. Many non-profit operations must also make a profit (often called "revenues in excess of expenses") for expanding operations, replacing fixed assets, and upgrading services. Since both types of operations need to generate profits, their approaches to pricing will not necessarily be different. The differences generally relate to costs and type of demand. For example, some non-profit food service operations, including some in the institutional setting, do not have to cover many capital costs such as interest expenses, property taxes, or depreciation. Further, the demand for the products and/or services may be different. The demand for food service in a hospital is quite different from the demand for food service in most hotels or restaurants. Many non-profit operations have less direct competition, so they may have greater leeway in pricing their products and/or services.

The emphasis in this chapter will be on commercial (for-profit) operations. However, since we will be discussing cost-oriented approaches to pricing, our discussion will apply to non-profit operations as well.

Exhibit 8.1   Price Elasticity of Demand Formula

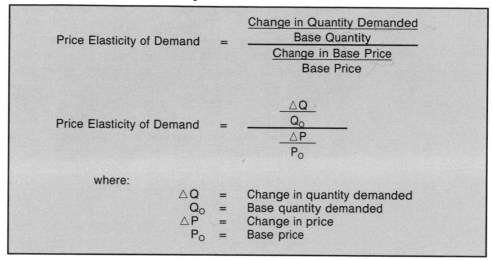

$$\text{Price Elasticity of Demand} = \frac{\dfrac{\text{Change in Quantity Demanded}}{\text{Base Quantity}}}{\dfrac{\text{Change in Base Price}}{\text{Base Price}}}$$

$$\text{Price Elasticity of Demand} = \frac{\dfrac{\Delta Q}{Q_o}}{\dfrac{\Delta P}{P_o}}$$

where:

ΔQ = Change in quantity demanded
Q_o = Base quantity demanded
ΔP = Change in price
P_o = Base price

Price Elasticity of Demand

The concept of the **price elasticity of demand** provides a means for measuring how sensitive demand is to changes in price. In general, as the selling price of a product or service decreases, everything else being the same, more will be sold. When the price of a product is increased, only rarely is more of the product sold, everything else being the same, and even then there may be other factors which account for the increased demand.

The demand for a product or service may be characterized as **elastic** or **inelastic**. Exhibit 8.1 illustrates the price elasticity of demand formula for mathematically determining whether the demand is elastic or inelastic. The base quantity demanded (Q_o) is the number of units sold during a given period before changing prices. The change in quantity demanded (ΔQ) is the change in the number of units sold during the period the prices were changed in comparison to the prior period. The base price (P_o) is the price of the product and/or service for the period prior to the price change. The change in price (ΔP) is the change in price from the base price. Strictly speaking, this equation will virtually always yield a negative number, since it is the result of dividing a negative change in quantity demanded by a positive price change or vice versa. (In other words, as price goes up, quantity demanded goes down and vice versa.) By convention, however, the negative sign is ignored.

If the elasticity of demand exceeds 1, the demand is said to be elastic. That is, demand is sensitive to price changes. With an elastic demand, the percentage change in quantity demanded exceeds the percentage change in price. In other words, any additional revenues generated by the higher price are more than offset by the decrease in demand. When demand is elastic, price and total revenues are inversely related, so a price increase will decrease total revenues.

If elasticity of demand is less than 1, demand is said to be inelastic. That is, a percentage change in price results in a smaller percentage change in quantity demanded. Every operation desires an inelastic demand for its products and/or services. When prices are increased, the percentage reduction in quantity demanded is less than the percentage of the price increase. Therefore, revenues and generally profits increase despite some decrease in the quantity demanded.[1]

Let's look at an example illustrating the calculation of price elasticity of demand. A budget motel sold 1,000 rooms during a recent 30-day period at $20 per room. For the next 30-day period, the price was increased to $22, and 950 rooms were sold. The demand for the budget motel over this time period is considered to be inelastic, since the calculated price elasticity of demand is less than 1. The calculation of price elasticity of demand is as follows:

$$\text{Price Elasticity of Demand} = \frac{50}{1,000} \div \frac{2}{20}$$
$$= .05 \div .1$$
$$= \underline{\underline{.5}}$$

In general, the demand for products and services in the lodging and the commercial food service segments of the hospitality industry is considered to be elastic. Generally, demand will be elastic where competition is high due to the presence of many operations and where the products and/or services offered are fairly standardized. On the other hand, where competition is low or non-existent or where an operation has greatly differentiated its products and/or services, then demand may be inelastic. At the extreme, some resorts, clubs, high-check-average restaurants, and luxury hotels are known to have an inelastic demand for their products and services. Generally, quick-service restaurants and medium and low priced hotels/motels are considered to have elastic demand for their products and services. However, these are generalizations, and there are exceptions.

This analysis of demand/price relationships assumes that other things are the same. However, hospitality operations seldom increase prices without effectively advertising their products in an effort to counter potential decreased demand. Therefore, the concept of the price elasticity of demand tends to be more theoretical than practical in nature.

Informal Pricing Approaches

There are several informal approaches to setting prices for selling food, beverages, and rooms. Since each of these approaches ignores the cost of providing the product, they are only briefly presented here as a point of departure for our discussion of more scientific approaches to setting prices.

Several managers price their products on the basis of what the competition charges. If the competition charges $80 for a room night, or an average of $20 for a dinner, then managers using competitive pricing set those prices as well. When the competition changes its prices, managers using this pricing approach follow suit. A variation of this approach is changing prices when the leading hospitality operation changes its prices.

Although these approaches may seem reasonable when there is much competition in a market, they ignore the many differences that exist among hospitality operations, such as location, product quality, atmosphere, customer goodwill, and so forth. In addition, they ignore the cost of producing the products and services sold. Hospitality operations must consider their own cost structures when making pricing decisions. A dominant operation with a low cost structure may "cause" competitors to go bankrupt if those competitors ignore their own costs and price their products following the competitive approach.

Another informal pricing approach used by some managers is intuition. Intuitive pricing is based on what the manager feels the guest is willing to pay. Generally, managers using this approach rely on their experience regarding guests' reactions to prices. However, as with competitive pricing, intuition ignores costs and may result in a failure not only to generate a reasonable profit, but even to recover costs.

A third approach is psychological pricing. Here, prices are established on the basis of what the guest "expects" to pay. This approach may be used by relatively exclusive locations (such as luxury resorts) and by operators who think that their guests believe "the more paid, the better the product." Although psychological pricing does possess a certain merit, it fails to consider costs and, therefore, may not result in profit maximization.

Finally, the trial and error pricing approach first sets a product price, monitors guests' reactions, and then adjusts the price based on these reactions. This approach appears to consider fully the operation's guests. However, problems with this method include:

- Monitoring guests' reactions may take longer than the manager would like to allow.

- Frequent changes in prices based on guests' reactions may result in price confusion among guests.

- There are many outside, uncontrollable factors that affect guests' purchase decisions. An example illustrates this problem: a 10% price increase in rooms may appear to be too high if occupancy is down by more than 10% over the next 30 days. However, other factors that may be part of the consumer decision include competition, new lodging establishments, weather conditions (especially if the lodging facility is a resort), and so on.

- The trial and error approach fails to consider costs.

Although all of the informal price approaches have some merit, they are most useful only when coupled with the cost approaches we are now going to consider.

Cost Approaches: Four Modifying Factors

Before looking at specific cost approaches to pricing, however, we need to set the stage. When pricing is based on a cost approach, four modifying factors to consider are historical prices, perceived price/value relationships, competition, and price rounding. These price modifiers relate to the pricing of nearly all products and services.

First, prices that have been charged in the past must be considered when pricing the hospitality operation's products. A dramatic change dictated by a cost approach may seem unrealistic to the consumer. For example, if a breakfast meal with a realistic price of $3.49 was mistakenly priced at $1.49 for five years, the food service operation may be "forced" to move slowly from $1.49 to $3.49 by implementing several price increases over a period of time.

Second, the guest must perceive that the product and/or service is reasonably priced in order to feel that he or she is getting a good value. Many guests in the 1990s appear to be more value-conscious than ever. Most are willing to pay prices much higher than a few years ago, but they also demand value for the price paid. The perceived value of a meal includes not only the food and drink but also the atmosphere, location, quality of service, and many other often intangible factors.

Third, the competition cannot be ignored. If an operation's product is viewed as substantially the same as a competitor's, then everything else being equal, the prices would have to be similar. For example, assume that an operation's price calculations for a gourmet burger may suggest a $4.50 selling price; however, if a strong nearby competitor is charging $3.50 for a very similar product, everything else being the same, then competition would appear to force a price reduction. However, remember that it is extremely difficult for *everything* else to be the same: the location is at least slightly different, one burger may be fresher, one may be grilled and the other fried, and so on.

Finally, the price may be modified by price rounding. That is, the item's price will be rounded up to the nearest $.25 or possibly up to $X.95.

Mark-Up Approaches to Pricing

A major method of pricing food and beverages is marking up the cost of the goods sold. The mark-up is designed to cover all non-product costs, such as labor, utilities, supplies, interest expense, taxes, and also to provide the desired profit.

Under the mark-up approaches to pricing are **ingredient mark-up** and **prime ingredient mark-up**. The ingredient mark-up approach considers all product costs. The prime ingredient mark-up considers only the cost of the major ingredient.

The four steps of the ingredient cost approach are as follows:

1. Determine the ingredient costs.
2. Determine the multiple to use in marking up the ingredient costs.
3. Multiply the ingredient costs by the multiple to get the desired price.
4. Determine whether the price seems reasonable based on the market.

The multiple determined in Step 2 is generally based on the desired product cost percentage. For example, if a product cost percentage of 40% is desired, the multiple would be 2.5, determined as follows:

Exhibit 8.2   Chicken Dinner Ingredients and Cost

Ingredient	Cost
Chicken – 2 pieces	$ .59
Baked potato with sour cream	.19
Roll and butter	.09
Vegetable	.15
Salad with dressing	.18
Coffee – refills free	.12
Total cost	$1.32

$$\text{Multiple} = \frac{1}{\text{Desired Product Cost Percentage}}$$

$$= \frac{1}{.4}$$

$$= \underline{\underline{2.5}}$$

The ingredient cost approach can be illustrated using ingredient cost figures for a chicken dinner listed in Exhibit 8.2. Assuming a desired multiple of 3.5, the price of the chicken dinner is determined as follows:

$$\text{Price} = \text{Ingredients' Cost} \times \text{Multiple}$$

$$= \$1.32 \times 3.5$$

$$= \underline{\underline{\$4.62}}$$

If the result appears reasonable based on the market for chicken dinners, then the chicken dinner is sold for about $4.62. (In this instance, price rounding might set the price at $4.75 or $4.95.)

The prime ingredient approach differs only in that the cost of the prime ingredient is marked up rather than the total cost of all ingredients. In addition, the multiple used, all other things being equal, would be greater than the multiple used when considering the total cost of all ingredients. The multiple used would generally be based on experience, that is, what multiple has provided adequate cost coverage and desired profit. Using the same chicken dinner example, the prime ingredient cost is chicken with a cost of $.59. Using an arbitrary multiple of 7.8, the chicken dinner is priced at $4.60, calculated as follows:

$$\text{Price} = \text{Prime Ingredient Cost} \times \text{Multiple}$$

$$= \$.59 \times 7.8$$

$$= \underline{\underline{\$4.60}}$$

If the cost of chicken in the above example increases to $.69 for the dinner portion, then the new price would be $5.38 ($.69 × 7.8). The prime ingredient approach assumes that the costs of all other ingredients change in proportion to the prime ingredient, that is, when the prime ingredient's cost increases 10%, then other ingredients' costs have also increased 10%. When changes in the other ingredients' cost percentage differ from the prime ingredient's, then the product cost percentage will differ from the established goal.

Pricing Rooms

Two well-known cost approaches to pricing rooms are the $1 per $1,000 approach and the Hubbart Formula approach.

$1 per $1,000 Approach

The **$1 per $1,000 approach** sets the price of a room at $1 for each $1,000 of project cost per room. For example, assume that the average project cost of a hotel for each room was $80,000. Using the $1 per $1,000 approach results in a price of $80 per room. Doubles, suites, singles, and so on would be priced differently, but the average would be $80.

This approach fails to consider the current value of facilities when it emphasizes the project cost. A well-maintained hotel worth $100,000 per room today may have been constructed at $20,000 per room 40 years ago. The $1 per $1,000 approach would suggest a price of $20 per room; however, a much higher rate would appear to be appropriate. This approach also fails to consider all the services which guests pay for in a hotel complex, such as food, beverages, telephone, laundry, and so forth. If a hotel is able to earn a positive contribution from these services (and the successful ones do), then the need for higher prices for rooms is reduced.

Hubbart Formula

A more recently developed cost approach is the **Hubbart Formula**, which is a *bottom-up* approach to pricing rooms. In determining the average price per room, this approach considers costs, desired profits, and expected rooms sold. In other words, this approach starts with desired profit, adds income taxes, then adds fixed charges and management fees, followed by operating overhead expenses and direct operating expenses. It is called bottom-up because the first item, net income (profit), is at the bottom of the income statement. The second item, income taxes, is the next item from the bottom of the income statement, and so on. The approach involves the following eight steps:

1. Calculate the desired profit by multiplying the desired rate of return (ROI) by the owners' investment.

2. Calculate pre-tax profits by dividing desired profit (Step 1) by 1 minus tax rate.

3. Calculate fixed charges and management fees. This calculation includes estimating depreciation, interest expense, property taxes, insurance, amortization, rent, and management fees.

4. Calculate undistributed operating expenses. This calculation includes estimating administrative and general, data processing, human resources, transportation, marketing, property operation and maintenance, and energy costs.

5. Estimate non-room operated department income or losses, that is, food and beverage department income, telephone department income or loss, and so forth.

6. Calculate the required rooms department income. The sum of pre-tax profits (Step 2), fixed charges and management fees (Step

3), undistributed operating expense (Step 4), and other operated department losses less other operated department income (Step 5) equals the required rooms department income.

7. Determine the rooms department revenue. The required rooms department income (Step 6) plus rooms department direct expenses of payroll and related expenses plus other direct expenses, equals rooms department revenue.

8. Calculate the average room rate by dividing rooms department revenue (Step 7) by expected rooms to be sold.

Illustration of the Hubbart Formula

The Harkins Hotel, a 200-room hotel, is projected to cost $9,900,000 inclusive of land, building, equipment, and furniture. An additional $100,000 is needed for working capital. The hotel is financed with a loan of $7,500,000 at 12% annual interest with the owners providing cash of $2,500,000. The owners desire a 15% annual return on their investment. A 75% occupancy is estimated; thus, 54,750 rooms will be sold during the year (200 × .75 × 365). The income tax rate is 40%. Additional expenses are estimated as follows:

Property taxes	$ 250,000
Insurance	50,000
Depreciation	300,000
Administrative & general	300,000
Data processing	120,000
Human resources	80,000
Transportation	40,000
Marketing expense	200,000
Property operation and maintenance	200,000
Energy costs	300,000

The other operated departments' income or losses are estimated as follows:

Food and beverage	$ 150,000
Telephone	(50,000)
Rentals and other income	100,000

Rooms department direct expenses are $10 per room sold.

Exhibit 8.3 contains the calculations used in the Hubbart Formula and reveals an average room rate of $67.81.

The formula for calculating room rates for singles and doubles, where the doubles are sold at a differential of y from singles, is shown in Exhibit 8.4. For the Harkins Hotel, a double occupancy rate of 40% and a price differential of $10 would result in the calculation of single and double rates as follows:

$$\text{Doubles sold in one day} = \frac{\text{double occupancy}}{\text{rate}} \times \frac{\text{number}}{\text{of rooms}} \times \frac{\text{occupancy}}{\text{percentage}}$$

$$= .4(200)(.75)$$

$$= \underline{\underline{60}}$$

$$\text{Singles sold in one day} = 150 - 60$$

$$= \underline{\underline{90}}$$

Exhibit 8.3   Calculation of Average Room Rate Using the Hubbart Formula

Item	Calculation	Amount
Desired net income	Owners' Investment × ROI 2,500,000 × .15 = 375,000	$375,000
Pretax income	Pretax income = $\dfrac{\text{net income}}{1-t}$ Pretax income = $\dfrac{375,000}{1-.4}$ Pretax income = $625,000	$625,000
Interest expense	Principal × int. rate × time = int. exp. 7,500,000 × .12 × 1 = 900,000	900,000
Income before interest and taxes		1,525,000
Estimated depreciation, property taxes, and insurance		600,000
Income before fixed charges		2,125,000
Undistributed operating expense		1,240,000
Required operated departments income		3,365,000
Departmental results excluding rooms		
Less: Food and beverage income		(150,000)
Rentals and other income		(100,000)
Plus: Telephone department loss		50,000
Rooms department income		3,165,000
Rooms department direct expense	54,750 × $10 = 547,500	547,500
Rooms revenue		3,712,500
		÷ 54,750
Required average room rate		$67.81

$$90x + 60(x + 10) = (\$67.81)(150)$$
$$90x + 60x + 600 = \$10{,}171.50$$
$$150x = \$9{,}571.50$$
$$x = \frac{\$9{,}571.50}{150}$$
$$x = \$63.81$$

$$\underline{\text{Single Rate}} = \underline{\$63.81}$$

$$\underline{\text{Double Rate}} = \$63.81 + 10.00$$
$$= \underline{\$73.81}$$

Alternatively, the double rate could be set as a percentage of the single rate. When this is the case, the formula is slightly altered as follows:

Exhibit 8.4 Determining Single and Double Room Rates from an Average Room Rate

Singles Sold (x) + Doubles Sold (x + y) = Average Rate (Rooms Sold)

where:

x = Price of singles
y = Price differential between singles and doubles
x + y = Price of doubles

$$(\text{Average rate}) (\text{Rooms sold}) = (\text{doubles sold})(x)(1 + \text{percentage mark-up}) + (\text{singles sold})(x)$$

The percentage mark-up is simply the percentage difference of the double rate over the single rate. To illustrate this approach, we will again use the Harkins Hotel example. Assume a 40% double occupancy and a mark-up of 15%.

$$90x + 60(x)(1.15) = (\$67.81)(150)$$
$$90x + 69x = \$10,171.50$$
$$159x = \$10,171.50$$
$$x = \frac{\$10,171.50}{159}$$
$$x = \$63.97$$

$$\text{Single Rate} = \$63.97$$

$$\text{Double Rate} = 63.97(1.15)$$
$$= \$73.57$$

The Hubbart Formula is most useful in setting target average prices as opposed to actual average prices. A lodging establishment does not generally earn profits in its first two or three years of operation. Thus, the average price determined using this formula is a target price at the point of profitability for the prospective property. As stated previously, even when this approach is used to set room prices, the four modifying factors must be considered. For example, assume that the average target price for a hotel is $75, when the average rate for competitive hotels is only $50. If the proposed hotel would be opening in two years, is the target price too high? By the end of the two years, the competitor's average price with annual 5% price increases would be $55.13, determined as follows:

Current price (1/1/X1)	$50
Increase in room rate after first year (12/31/X1)	
5% × $50	2.50
	52.50
Increase in room rate after second year (12/31/X2)	
5% × $52.50	2.63
	$55.13

Since the proposed hotel would be new, a price premium could be expected; however, a difference of nearly $20, given a competitor's average price of just over $55, would appear to be too much. Therefore, a more reasonable price might be $65, which, after three years of successive price increases of 5% per year, would be increased to just over $75 as follows:

	Annual increase at 5%	Selling Price
Initial room rate		$65.00
At the end of year X3	$3.25	$68.25
At the end of year X4	$3.41	$71.66
At the end of year X5	$3.58	$75.24

Yield Management

For many years, lodging establishments have sold rooms strictly on the basis of room availability. In general, a transient hotel would sell its rooms Monday through Thursday (when it is busiest) at prices close to its targeted rate for each type of guest, while the weekend average room rates would be set at a much lower price. Such hotels sometimes offer weekend packages which include a hotel room and one or more meals to lure guests for the weekend. These approaches can be successful as long as the marginal revenue exceeds the marginal cost; that is, as long as the price exceeds the cost to provide food and services to the hotel guest.

However, in the past few years, hoteliers have become more aggressive in pricing rooms by using a concept popularly referred to as **yield management**. The focus of yield management is selling rooms in a way that maximizes total revenues, rather than trying simply to sell all available rooms. Yield management in substance considers room availability at the time of the advanced sale, compared to typical advanced sales at this time. That is, before selling a room in advance, the hotel considers the probability of being able to sell the room to other market segments that are willing to pay higher rates.

For example, assume for simplicity that the 100-room XYZ Hotel has both business and group rates per room of $80 and $55, respectively. Further assume that the average group takes 20 rooms and is booked three weeks in advance, while the typical business person reserves his/her room seven days in advance. Further assume that, on the average, business people and groups stay two nights.

Given the above information, should a group desiring 20 rooms for April 21 and 22 be sold the rooms at $55 per room on April 1? Assume that 40 rooms have already been sold to business people at $80 per room, and the reservationist believes 55 more rooms could be sold at $80 per person to business people. Based on the information, total room revenue is greater when the sale is *not* made to the group, and the rooms are held for business people. The analysis is as follows:

Alternative #1

Group sales	20 rooms @ $55 =	$1,100
Business sales	80 rooms @ $80 =	6,400
Total		$7,500

Alternative #2

Business sales   95 rooms @ $80 = $7,600

The difference of $100 per night favors Alternative #2. Of course, the illustration is fairly simplistic. Other considerations are the desired stay and income from other services provided by the XYZ Hotel to potential guests.

Bottom-Up Approach to Pricing Meals

A bottom-up approach similar to the Hubbart Formula used to price rooms may be used to determine the average meal price for restaurants. Seven steps for determining the average meal price are as follows:[2]

1. Determine desired net income by multiplying investment by desired return on owners' investment (ROI).

2. Determine pre-tax profit by dividing the desired net income by 1 minus the tax rate.

3. Determine fixed charges.

4. Determine controllable expenses.

5. Determine food revenue by first adding figures from Steps 2–4 and then dividing this sum by 1 minus the desired food cost percentage.

6. Determine meals to be served by multiplying days open by number of seats by seat turnover for the day.

7. Determine price of the average meal by dividing the total food revenue by the estimated number of meals to be served.

To illustrate the average restaurant meal price calculation, Morgans, a 100-seat restaurant, will be used. Information regarding Morgans is found in Exhibit 8.5. Given this information, Exhibit 8.6 shows that the average meal price for Morgans, inclusive of beverage sales, desserts, and so forth, is $18.22. In those calculations, total food revenue is determined by dividing total expenses and net income (prior to cost of food sold) by 1 minus the cost of food sold percentage. If management could turn the seats over faster, everything else being the same, then the average meal price required to provide the owners with the desired 12% return would be reduced. For example, if the seat turnover could be increased to 3, then the average meal price is determined as follows:

$$\text{Average Meal Price} = \frac{\text{Food Revenue}}{\text{Meals Sold}}$$

$$= \frac{1,140,477}{93,900}$$

$$= \$12.15$$

Exhibit 8.5 Essential Factors for Determining the Average Meal Price at Morgans

Item	Amount	Other
Owner's investment	$200,000	Desired ROI = 12%
Funds borrowed	500,000	Interest Rate = 10%
Tax rate	—	30%
Fixed charges (excluding interest)	100,000	Annual amount
Controllable expenses	500,000	Annual amount
Cost of food sold percentage	—	40%
Seat turnover	—	2 times per day
Days open (closed one day per week)	—	313 days

Exhibit 8.6 Calculation of Average Meal Price at Morgans

Item	Calculation	Amount
Desired net income	$200,000 \times .12$	$ 24,000
Pretax profits	$\dfrac{24,000}{1 - .3} = \dfrac{24,000}{.7}$	$ 34,286
Interest	$500,000 \times .10 \times 1$	50,000
Other fixed charges		100,000
Controllable expenses		500,000
Total expenses and net income prior to cost of food sold		$ 684,286
Total food revenue	$\dfrac{684,286}{.6}$	$1,140,477
Meals sold	$313 \times 100 \times 2$	62,600
Average meal price	$\$1,140,477 \div 62,600$	$ 18.22

On the other hand, a less frequent turnover requires a higher average meal price, all other things being the same. For Morgans, a seat turnover of 1.5 requires an average meal price of $24.29.

The entire discussion of the bottom-up approach to pricing meals has centered on average meal prices. Few food service establishments price all meals at one price, or even all meals for a given meal period at one price. However, the average meal price per meal period can be determined as follows:

1. Calculate the revenue per meal period by multiplying the total food revenue by the estimated percentage of that total earned during that meal period.

2. Divide the revenue per meal period by the meals sold per meal period. (Meals sold per meal period is calculated by multiplying the days the food service business is open by the seat turnover by the number of seats.)

Once again, we will use Morgans to illustrate these calculations.

Assume that management estimates the total food revenue to be divided between lunch and dinner revenue as 40% and 60%, respectively. Further assume that the luncheon seat turnover is 1.25 and the dinner seat turnover is .75. Using the total revenue for Morgans as calculated in Exhibit 8.6, the average meal prices by meal period are determined as follows:

Revenue per meal period:
Lunch 40% × $1,140,477 = $ 456,191
Dinner 60% × $1,140,477 = 684,286
Total = $1,140,477

Meals sold per meal period:
Lunch 313 × 100 × 1.25 = 39,125

Dinner 313 × 100 × .75 = 23,475

$$\text{Average meal prices by meal period} = \frac{\text{Meal Period Revenue}}{\text{Meals Sold}}$$

$$\text{Lunch} = \frac{\$456,191}{39,125} = \$11.66$$

$$\text{Dinner} = \frac{\$684,286}{23,475} = \$29.15$$

Food Sales Mix and Gross Profit

Traditionally, restaurateurs have placed heavy emphasis on food cost percentage. The multiple in the mark-up approach used to price meals for many restaurants has been set at 2.5 times, so that a 40% cost of food sold could be achieved. This emphasis resulted in many managers evaluating the profitability of their food service operations by reviewing the food cost percentage. However, the food cost percentage is not the best guide to evaluating food sales, as will be shown below.

Consider a restaurant that may sell one of three alternative sales mixes for the week as listed in Exhibit 8.7. Notice in each sales mix, the same number of meals is served. Exhibit 8.8 shows the total revenue, total cost of food sold, the gross profit, and food cost percentage for each alternative. The selling price and cost per meal remains constant for each menu item across the three alternative sales mixes.

Exhibit 8.9 compares the three alternatives. The sales mix with the lowest total food cost percentage is mix #1 at 39.56%, while mix #3 has the highest at 41.99%, or nearly 2.5% greater than mix #1. If the most desirable mix is based on food cost percentage, then mix #1 is selected. However, under mix #3, the gross profit is $4,670 compared to a low of $4,140 for mix #1. Gross profit generated by mix #3 is $530 more than the profit generated by mix #1. Therefore, all other things being the same, mix #3 is preferred, because a higher gross profit means a higher net income.

Exhibit 8.10 reveals the average gross profit for the three sales mix alternatives. The gross margin reflects the average gross profit per meal sold. The average gross margin under sales mix #3 ($4.67) is $.53 and $.22 higher than under mixes #1 and #2, respectively. Based on these results,

Exhibit 8.7 Sales Mix Alternatives and Number of Meals

| | Sales Mix Alternatives | | |
	#1	#2	#3
Chicken	500	300	200
Fish	200	300	300
Steak	300	400	500
Total	1,000	1,000	1,000

Exhibit 8.8 Profitability of Three Sales Mix Alternatives

	Selling Price	Cost Per Meal	Menu Item Food Cost Percentage	Meals Sold	Revenue	Total Cost of Food	Gross Profit
Alternative #1							
Chicken	$4.95	$1.65	33.33%	500	$2,475	$825	$1,650
Fish	6.95	2.75	39.57	200	1,390	550	840
Steak	9.95	4.45	44.72	300	2,985	1,335	1,650
Total				1,000	$6,850	$2,710	$4,140

$$\text{Food cost \%} = \frac{2,710}{6,850} = 39.56\%$$

	Selling Price	Cost Per Meal	Menu Item Food Cost Percentage	Meals Sold	Revenue	Total Cost of Food	Gross Profit
Alternative #2							
Chicken	$4.95	$1.65	33.33%	300	$1,485	$495	$990
Fish	6.95	2.75	39.57	300	2,085	825	1,260
Steak	9.95	4.45	44.72	400	3,980	1,780	2,200
Total				1,000	$7,550	$3,100	$4,450

$$\text{Food cost \%} = \frac{3,100}{7,550} = 41.06\%$$

	Selling Price	Cost Per Meal	Menu Item Food Cost Percentage	Meals Sold	Revenue	Total Cost of Food	Gross Profit
Alternative #3							
Chicken	$4.95	$1.65	33.33%	200	$990	$330	$660
Fish	6.95	2.75	39.57	300	2,085	825	1,260
Steak	9.95	4.45	44.72	500	4,975	2,225	2,750
Total				1,000	$8,050	$3,380	$4,670

$$\text{Food cost \%} = \frac{3,380}{8,050} = 41.99\%$$

fewer meals could be sold under mixes #2 and #3 than under mix #1, yet the gross profit under mix #1 still would be earned:

$$\frac{\text{Gross Profit of Mix \#1}}{\text{Gross Margin of Other Sales Mix Alternative}}$$

Exhibit 8.9 Comparison of Sales Mix Alternatives

Sales Mix Alternative	Total Revenue	Total Cost of Food	Gross Profit	Food Cost %
1	$6,850	$2,710	$4,140	39.56%
2	7,550	3,100	4,450	41.06
3	8.050	3.380	4.670	41.99

Exhibit 8.10 Average Gross Profit of Sales Mix Alternatives

Sales Mix	Gross Profit	Meals Sold	Gross Margin
1	$4,140	1,000	$4.14
2	4,450	1,000	4.45
3	4,670	1,000	4.67

Mix #2 to Mix #1

$$\frac{\$4,140}{\$4.45} = \underline{\underline{930.34 \text{ meals}}}$$

Thus, under sales mix #2, 930.34 meals sold at an average gross margin of $4.45 yields $4,140 of gross profit, which is the same as that generated under mix #1 when 1,000 meals are sold.

Mix #3 to Mix #1

$$\frac{\$4,140}{\$4.67} = \underline{\underline{886.51 \text{ meals}}}$$

Thus, under sales mix #3, 886.51 meals sold at an average gross margin of $4.67 yields $4,140, the same gross profit as that generated with mix #1 when 1,000 meals are sold.

These results are more clearly reflected in the graph found in Exhibit 8.11. The gross profit is related to meals sold in sales mixes #1 through #3. Gross profit increases progressively from sales mix #1 to sales mix #3. The same gross profit for sales mix #1 can be achieved by sales mixes #2 and #3 with fewer meals sold.

Menu Engineering

A relatively new method of menu analysis and food pricing is called **menu engineering**.[3] This sophisticated and fairly complex approach considers both the profitability and popularity of competing menu items. The emphasis is on gross margin (called *contribution margin* by Kasavana and Smith). For all practical purposes, food cost percentages are ignored. The emphasis on gross margin rather than food cost percentage is based on the fact that managers bank dollars, not percentages.

Exhibit 8.11   Gross Profit Graph of Three Sales Mix Alternatives

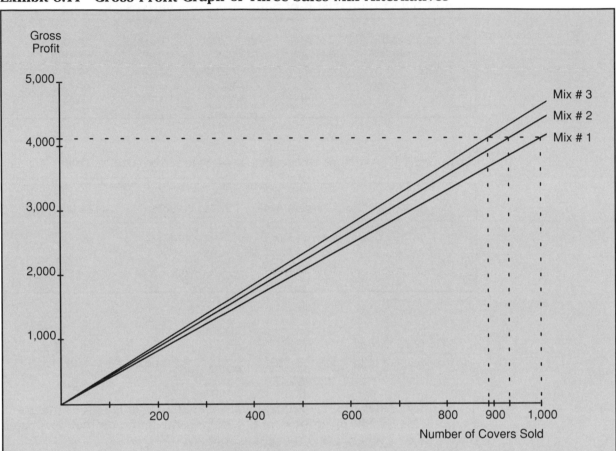

Menu engineering requires the manager to know each menu item's food cost, selling price, and quantity sold over a specific period of time. The menu item's gross margin (selling price minus food cost) is characterized as either high or low in relation to the average gross margin for all competing menu items sold.

For example, if a menu item has a gross margin of $3.00 when the average gross margin for the menu is $3.50, then the menu item is classified as having a low gross margin. If the menu item has a gross margin of $4.50, then it is classified as high for profitability purposes.

Each menu item is further classified by popularity (high or low) based on the item's menu mix percentage, that is, the menu item count for each menu item as a percentage of the total menu items sold. Where n equals the number of competing menu items, the dividing point for determining high and low popularity is calculated as follows:

$$70\% \times \frac{1}{n}$$

Therefore, if there are 10 competing items on a menu, the dividing point is 7%, determined as follows:

$$70\% \times \frac{1}{10} = \underline{.07} \text{ or } \underline{7\%}$$

Exhibit 8.12 Profitability/Popularity Classification of Menu Items

Profitability	Popularity	Classification
High	High	Stars
High	Low	Puzzles
Low	High	Plowhorses
Low	Low	Dogs

Given a ten-item menu, any menu items with unit sales of less than 7% of the total items sold would be classified as having a low popularity, while any equal to, or greater than, 7% would be classified as having high popularity.

The profitability and popularity classifications for each menu item result in four categories of menu items as shown in Exhibit 8.12. In general, stars should be retained, puzzles repositioned, plowhorses repriced, and dogs removed from the menu. (For more discussion of management actions regarding the four classifications, see the Supplemental Reading to this chapter.)

Exhibit 8.13 is a graphic illustration of menu engineering results, which contains menu items in the four classifications. Eight menu items, identified by letters corresponding to the following table, are shown on the graph.

Menu Item	Item Contribution Margin	Number Sold	Classification
A	$5.10	150	Star
B	$6.53	430	Star
C	$4.90	430	Plowhorse
D	$1.50	150	Plowhorse
E	$4.90	130	Dog
F	$1.50	90	Dog
G	$6.53	130	Puzzle
H	$5.10	90	Puzzle

In general, one prefers stars to dogs, puzzles, and plowhorses. However, are stars *always* preferred to puzzles and plowhorses? Specifically, is menu item A preferred to items C and G? Using the information for these menu items, we determine the following:

Menu Item	Classification	Item Contribution Margin	Number Sold	Total Item Contribution Margin
A	Star	$5.10	150	$ 765.00
C	Plowhorse	$4.90	430	$2,107.00
G	Puzzle	$6.53	130	$ 848.90

Menu items C and G provide $2,107 and $848.90 of contribution margin, respectively, compared to only $765 for item A. Thus, in this case, both items C and G (non-star items) are preferred to the star menu item A. Further, as can be seen on Exhibit 8.13, the dog item E, with a total item contribution margin of $637, is nearly as profitable as the star menu item A.

Exhibit 8.13   Graph of Menu Engineering Results

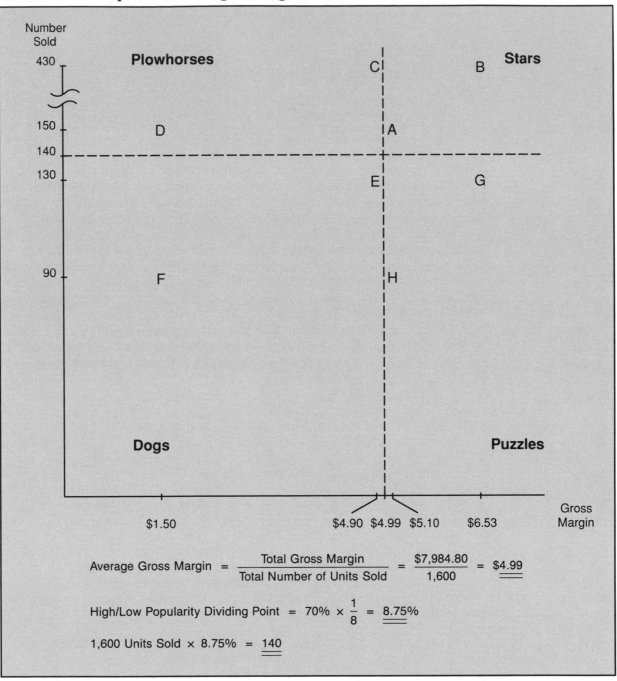

Number
Sold

430 — **Plowhorses**   C¦   B   **Stars**

150 —   D   ¦A
140 — -
130 —   E¦   G

90   —   F   ¦H

                                                                    Gross
                                                                    Margin
        Dogs   **Puzzles**

        $1.50 $4.90 $4.99 $5.10 $6.53

Average Gross Margin $= \dfrac{\text{Total Gross Margin}}{\text{Total Number of Units Sold}} = \dfrac{\$7,984.80}{1,600} = \underline{\underline{\$4.99}}$

High/Low Popularity Dividing Point $= 70\% \times \dfrac{1}{8} = \underline{\underline{8.75\%}}$

1,600 Units Sold $\times$ 8.75% $= \underline{\underline{140}}$

The key to this analysis is not simply to classify menu items, but rather to consider total contribution margin. A menu may be analyzed using menu engineering and revised to eliminate all dogs. However, if the total contribution margin is not increased, little, if anything, has been accomplished.

Exhibit 8.14 is a menu engineering worksheet useful for determining the classification of each menu item. Even when this form is used,

Exhibit 8.14 Menu Engineering Worksheet

Menu Engineering Worksheet

Restaurant: _____

Date: _____

Meal Period: _____

(A) Menu Item Name	(B) Number Sold (MM)	(C) Menu Mix %	(D) Item Food Cost	(E) Item Selling Price	(F) Item CM (E-D)	(G) Menu Costs (D*B)	(H) Menu Revenues (E*B)	(L) Menu CM (F*B)	(P) CM Category	(R) MM% Category	(S) Menu Item Classification

Column Totals: N | | | | | | I | J | M | | |

K = I/J   O = M/N   Q = (100%/items)(70%)

Additional Computations:

BOX = 364 points

however, a graph should be prepared for each menu analyzed to provide a better perspective of the relationships of menu items. A more complete discussion of menu engineering, including a comprehensive example, is contained in the Supplemental Reading to this chapter.

Integrated Pricing

Many businesses in the hospitality industry, especially the lodging sector, have several revenue-producing departments (profit centers). Allowing each profit center to price its products independently may fail to optimize the operation's profits. For example, the swimming pool department manager may decide to institute a direct charge to guests. This new pricing policy may maximize swimming pool revenues, but, at the same time, guests may opt to stay at other hotels where pool privileges are provided at no additional cost. Therefore, revenues for other profit centers such as rooms and food and beverage are lost from guests who select competing hotels because of the new pool charge policy.

Prices for all departments should be established such that they optimize the operation's net income. This will generally result in some profit centers *not* maximizing their revenues and thus their departmental incomes. This **integrated pricing** approach is essential and can only be accomplished by the general manager and profit center managers coordinating their pricing.

Computerization

Many of the pricing methods discussed in this chapter do not require sophisticated mathematical models to determine the desired price. However, even simple tasks can waste valuable time when they must be repeated many times. Because the standard formulas are frequently used, their computerization could benefit managers. This is especially true when management wants to view a number of scenarios in order to determine the best pricing options.

The Hubbart Formula can be translated into a computerized worksheet with relative ease. By entering each of the inputs into the formula separately, as shown in Exhibit 8.15, management can vary assumptions and see the results of "what if" questions. In the past, the number of scenarios considered was seriously limited by the time that a staff member could devote to "number crunching." Now, suggestions can be calculated almost at will.

The personal computer also can be a tool for food and beverage outlets. There are menu engineering packages available which will calculate the contribution margins and menu mix percentages after the user inputs the menu items' sales prices, costs, and demands. Then, they determine the classification of each menu item and print the menu engineering graph for the manager. More sophisticated systems will interface a personal computer with the point-of-sale register and with the inventory information. Having done this, it is possible to generate not only the outputs of menu engineering, but also to gather all of the inputs. When this type of a system is used, management can generate daily sales and cost

Exhibit 8.15 Hubbart Formula Worksheet

INPUTS:	Alternatives				
	1	2	3	4	5
Investment	$2,000,000	$2,000,000	$2,000,000	$2,000,000	$2,000,000
ROI	16.0%	16.0%	16.0%	12.0%	16.0%
Tax Rate	30%	30%	30%	30%	30%
Long-Term Debt	4,000,000	4,000,000	4,000,000	4,000,000	4,000,000
Interest Rate	15.0%	15.0%	15.0%	15.0%	15.0%
Estimated Fixed Charges (excluding interest expense)	60,000	60,000	60,000	60,000	85,000
Undistributed Operating Expenses	600,000	600,000	600,000	600,000	650,000
Departmental Profits					
Food	135,000	135,000	135,000	135,000	135,000
Telephone	10,000	10,000	10,000	10,000	10,000
Rooms Department					
Variable Costs per Room Sold	$15	$15	$15	$15	$18
Number of Rooms	200	200	200	200	200
Occupancy Rate	75%	80%	65%	75%	60%
Hubbart Calculation					
Desired Net Income	$320,000	$320,000	$320,000	$240,000	$320,000
Pretax Income	457,143	457,143	457,143	342,857	457,143
Interest Expense	600,000	600,000	600,000	600,000	600,000
Income Before Fixed Charges	1,117,143	1,117,143	1,117,143	1,002,857	1,142,143
Required Room Dept. Income	1,572,143	1,572,143	1,572,143	1,457,857	1,647,143
Rooms Revenue	2,393,393	2,448,143	2,283,893	2,279,107	2,435,543
Required Average Rate	$43.71	$41.92	$48.13	$41.63	$55.61

reports so that pricing decisions can be made at any time. This is especially useful for restaurants which offer a large number of specials or vary their entrées based on market availability.

Summary

An optimal pricing structure can play a large role in the profitability of a hospitality operation. If rooms are underpriced, profits are lost. If meals are overpriced, demand may decrease, causing a decrease in profits. Management needs to be aware of these effects and set prices accordingly.

The relationship between the percentage change in price and the resulting percentage change in demand is called elasticity. In order to determine the price elasticity of demand for a product, the manager utilizes this formula:

$$\frac{\text{Change in Quantity Demanded}}{\text{Base Quantity}} \div \frac{\text{Change in Price}}{\text{Base Price}}$$

If the result (ignoring the negative sign) is greater than 1, the demand for the product is said to be elastic. In other words, a change in price results in a larger percentage change in the quantity demanded. Raising prices results in reduced revenues. Inelastic demand exists when the change in price is greater than the percentage change in demand, and the formula results in an answer of less than 1. Every manager would prefer to have products with inelastic demand. When this is the case, raising prices results in increased revenues because the percentage decrease in demand is less than the percentage increase in prices.

There are a number of informal pricing methods. Some managers base prices on what the competition charges. Other managers assume that they intuitively know the price the public will accept. Still another method is psychological pricing by which managers determine what they think customers expect to pay.

These methods, although frequently used, fail to examine costs. More technical methods, such as the mark-up and the bottom-up approaches, start with costs and determine prices to ensure that the result is adequate net income.

The mark-up approach begins with the cost and multiplies it by a mark-up based on the desired product cost percentage. There are two variations of this approach. One sets a mark-up factor for the total cost of the meal. The other multiplies only the prime ingredient cost by a factor. The result of either of these approaches should be a price that will not only cover the food cost, but also the labor and other costs.

The Hubbart Formula is a method used to price rooms. It begins with the required return on the investment and adds to it the costs of operation, including taxes, management fees, fixed charges, undistributed operating expenses, and other departmental income. Using this approach, departmental incomes (or losses) from other profit centers are added to (or subtracted from) the total indirect expenses of the hotel to determine the required rooms department income. The direct expenses of the rooms department plus the required rooms department income equal the required rooms department revenue. The average price per room is calculated by dividing the required rooms department revenue by the number of rooms expected to be sold during the period.

The cost approaches appear rigorous and objective; however, they generally are based on estimates. Further, when the proposed price is computed on the basis of one of the cost approaches presented, careful consideration must be given to prices being charged by the competition before the implementation of any price changes. Differences in price must be supported by a different offering, such as a better location, more amenities, and so on. Finally, in a multi-product situation, such as a hotel, prices of the various products, food, beverages, and rooms, must be set on an integrated basis.

Endnotes

1. A third situation occurs when the elasticity of demand is exactly 1. In this case, demand is said to be **unit elastic,** meaning that any percentage change in price is accompanied by the same percentage change in quantity demanded. Total revenues remain constant.

2. Based on terminology used in the *Uniform System of Accounts for Restaurants* (Washington, D.C.: National Restaurant Association, 1983).

3. Michael L. Kasavana and Donald I. Smith, *Menu Engineering—A Practical Guide to Menu Analysis,* Rev. Edition (Okemos, Mich.: Hospitality Publications Inc., 1990).

Key Terms

elastic demand
Hubbart Formula
inelastic demand
ingredient mark-up
integrated pricing
menu engineering

$1 per $1,000 approach
price elasticity of demand
prime ingredient mark-up
unit elastic
yield management

Discussion Questions

1. What are four methods of informal pricing?
2. What disadvantages are inherent with informal pricing?
3. How is the cost mark-up factor often calculated?
4. What is the difference between the mark-up and the prime ingredient mark-up pricing methods?
5. What is price elasticity of demand?
6. What is the philosophy behind bottom-up pricing?
7. What does menu engineering consider in its review of menu items?
8. What is the relation between contribution margins and cost percentages?
9. How is the $1 per $1,000 technique used to price rooms?
10. Which pricing method is the most applicable for restaurants? Why?

Problems

Problem 8.1

Kristy's has been charging an average of $45 for its hotel rooms and has operated at an 80% occupancy. A recent average room price increase to $50 has been proposed. The general manager expects the occupancy to decline to 77% as a result of the price increase.

Required:

1. Compute the price elasticity of demand.
2. How is demand characterized for Kristy's, based on your calculations in #1.

Problem 8.2

Erica's Eatery enjoys a strong market position in a midwestern city. Erica Eastman, the owner, desires to maintain the high quality of service as well as excellent profits. Food items are marked up by a factor of 3.5 and beverages are to have a beverage cost percentage of 20%. Assume that a new item, Chicken Continental, has a $2.25 food cost, and a drink to be tested, the Great Escape, has a beverage cost of $.48.

Required:

Determine the selling price of both the Chicken Continental and the Great Escape by using the mark-up method.

Problem 8.3

Leigh's, a 150-seat casual dining place, is proposed to be built in a southern city. Marie Leigh, the owner, would have to invest $400,000 and borrow $600,000. A reasonable return on equity investment is 15%, and the cost of debt would be 12% annually. The average tax rate would be 40%. Fixed charges excluding interest would total $100,000 a year, while controllable expenses (except for food costs) are expected to total $500,000 annually. The seat turnover is expected to be 2 times per day for 360 days of the year. The food cost percent is expected to be 35%. The income from investments owned by Leigh's is expected to be $10,000 annually.

Required:

1. What should be the average price per meal?
2. Assume that Leigh's is only open for lunch and dinner, that lunch covers are twice dinner covers, and that lunch prices are $4 less than dinner prices. What are the average lunch and dinner prices?

Problem 8.4

Monica's Motel, a 100-room property constructed in 19X1 for $680,000, has just been purchased by a new firm, Lodging Limited, which is reconsidering the motel's pricing structure.

The motel was purchased with $800,000 of long-term debt and $400,000 equity. Lodging Limited is in the 35% tax bracket and requires a 15% return on its equity investment. The accountant for Lodging Limited has estimated annual fixed charges and undistributed operating expenses to be $600,000 and annual rooms department expenses of $125,000 when occupancy is 68%. There are no other operated departments and any other income is deemed immaterial.

Assume that the hotel will operate 365 days during the year and have a 68% room occupancy.

Required:

1. Determine the average room rate by the $1 per $1,000 method.
2. Determine the average room rate by the Hubbart Formula.

Problem 8.5

Josie's Place Inn, a proposed 30-room motel with a fully-equipped restaurant will cost $750,000 to construct. An estimated additional $50,000 will be invested in the business as working capital. Of the total $800,000 investment, $400,000 is to be secured from the Columbo Federal Bank at the rate of 10% interest. The projected occupancy rate is 80% for the year. The owners desire a 15% return on equity after the corporation pays income taxes of 25%. The estimated undistributable expenses, not including income taxes and interest expense, total $480,000. The estimated direct expenses of the rooms department are $7 for each room sold. Consider a year to have 365 days.

Required:

1. Determine the average price of a room using the Hubbart Formula, assuming the contribution from the restaurant department is $0.
2. If the double rooms are sold at a premium of $10 over singles, what is the price of singles and doubles? Assume a double occupancy rate of 40%.
3. If the restaurant generates a department profit of $20,000 per year, how much may average room rates be decreased and still meet the owners' financial goals?

Problem 8.6

The Lynn Inn, a 100-room lodging facility, is proposed for construction in the north central part of the United States. The total cost of construction is $5,000,000. Another $200,000 is required for pre-opening costs and working capital purposes. Pre-opening costs of $100,000 are to be amortized over the first five years of operations. To simplify the problem, depreciation is calculated on a straight line basis over 24 years (assume $200,000 of salvage value).

The owners will borrow $3,000,000 at an annual interest rate of 12%. The owners desire an 18% return on their equity investment. Other unallocable costs except for management fees total $1,500,000 annually. Management fees are based on 3% of room sales.

Assume that telephone department and food service department profits total $0 and $300,000, respectively. Further assume that all room department costs are variable and total 25% of room revenues, and that the Lynn Inn can achieve a 70% occupancy rate for the first year. Finally, assume an average tax rate of 25%.

Required:

1. Determine the average room rate for the Lynn Inn.
2. Assume that telephone department losses total $50,000. How much must the average room rate be modified to cover this loss?
3. Assume (independent of #2) that the Lynn Inn has singles, doubles, and suites. Further, the relationship between sales and prices are as follows:

	Price	Sales Mix
Singles	??	30%
Doubles	$10 premium over single rate	50
Suites	125% of doubles rate	20
		100%

What is the average room rate for suites and doubles?

Problem 8.7

Stan Rey, the manager of Masons, a casual dining facility, has just been exposed to the concept of analyzing a menu based on its gross profits rather than food cost percentage. The four major entrées at Masons and their selling prices (SP) and food costs (FC) are as follows:

	SP	FC	CM
Chicken	$5.95	$1.78	4.17
Fish	$6.95	$2.43	4.52
Pork chops	$8.95	$3.58	5.37
Steak	$11.95	$5.97	5.98

Three alternative sales mixes are as follows:

	Sales Mixes		
	#1	#2	#3
Chicken	400	350	100
Fish	300	300	150
Pork chops	200	200	250
Steak	100	150	500
Total	1,000	1,000	1,000

Required:

1. Compute the total revenue, gross profit, and food cost percentage for each alternative.

2. How many meals would have to be sold for mixes #1 and #2 so that each would provide the gross profit earned with sales mix #3?

3. Which sales mix would you prefer? Why?

Problem 8.8

Barbara Rope, a wealthy investor, is considering investing $2,000,000 in a 300-room hotel. Debt financing would total $8,000,000. She desires to know the average rate her hotel will have to charge, given the following alternatives.

	Alternatives				
	#1	#2	#3	#4	#5
Desired ROI	14%	15%	16%	17%	18%
Interest rate	12%	12%	13%	14%	14%
Tax rate	30%	30%	30%	30%	30%

Estimated annual fixed charges (excluding interest)	$700,000	$700,000	$700,000	$700,000	$700,000
Management fees (% of room sales)	3%	3%	3%	4%	4%
Undistributed operating expense	$3,000,000	$3,000,000	$3,500,000	$3,500,000	$3,500,000
Departmental profits:					
Food	$300,000	$300,000	$400,000	$450,000	$450,000
Telephone	$10,000	$10,000	$10,000	$10,000	$10,000
Variable costs per room sold	$15	$15	$20	$20	$20
Occupancy rate	65%	70%	65%	75%	80%

Required:

Compute the average daily room rate for each alternative. To minimize the calculations, consider using a spreadsheet program.

Problem 8.9

Bobbie's Place has not changed its menu in three years. Recently, the owner, Bobbie Schmidt, read about menu engineering and desires your assistance in analyzing the dinner menu. The seven dinner entrées, their selling prices, costs, and the menu counts for a recent month are as follows:

	Selling Price	Food Cost	Number Sold
Sirloin steak	$ 9.95	$3.00	240
King crab	15.95	6.00	50
Lobster	18.45	8.00	60
Prime rib	14.50	4.25	300
Whitefish	8.75	2.50	80
New York strip	12.45	5.75	180
Chicken à la king	8.50	2.60	280

Required:

1. Complete a menu engineering worksheet using the format of Exhibit 8.14.

2. What recommendations would you offer the owner based on your analysis?

Note: Review of the menu engineering discussion in the Supplemental Reading to this chapter would be helpful in working this problem.

Problem 8.10

The K&S Restaurant desires to analyze its luncheon menu prior to making several changes. The manager, Louis Kass, has provided the following information:

	Selling Price	Food Cost	Number Sold
Hamburger Deluxe	$4.95	$1.50	180
Cheeseburger Deluxe	$5.25	$1.60	120
Turkey Sandwich	$4.25	$1.25	80
Ham & Cheese on Rye	$6.25	$1.70	220
Egg Salad Sandwich	$3.95	$1.10	50
Fishwich	$4.50	$1.30	80
Pizzaburger	$3.00	$ .85	100
Chicken Delight	$6.25	$2.10	140
Taco Salad	$3.25	$ .85	60
Chef Salad	$3.95	$1.25	100

Required:

1. Complete a menu engineering worksheet using the format of Exhibit 8.14. Alternatively, use a computerized menu engineering program.

2. Complete a second menu engineering worksheet after revising the menu as follows:

   A. Drop the poorest performing item (dog) and allocate the units sold of this item to the plowhorses on a pro rata basis.

   B. Lower the prices of puzzle items by 5% and increase sales of each by 10%.

   C. Increase the prices of plowhorses by 5% and decrease sales of each by 5%.

   D. Increase prices of each star to either the next $X.45 or $X.95 and assume that the number sold of each remains constant.

3. Compare the results of menu engineering of #1 and #2 above with regard to the following:

   A. Number of items sold

   B. Total sales

   C. Average contribution margin

   D. Total contribution margin

   E. Number of dogs and stars after each analysis

Supplemental Reading
Menu Engineering*
What to do with plowhorses, stars, puzzles and dogs

By Donald Smith, Director,
Michigan State's School of Hotel, Restaurant & Institutional Management

A menu is a portfolio of items. The way you manage this portfolio determines what your consumer demand and profit contribution margin will be. The key to any menu's success is whether or not it produces more customers and more contribution dollars.

Menu engineering is a tool foodservice operators can use to evaluate one menu against another. It requires that the operator know each menu item's total product cost, selling price, and quantity sold over a specific period of time. A menu item's revenue contribution margin and sales activity is categorized as either relatively high or low. Each menu item is classified and evaluated for both its marketing (popularity) and pricing (profit) success.

By categorizing and classifying menu items through logical mathematical procedures, menu engineering enables the operator to make the right decisions.

Food cost percentages

Most foodservice operators have been conditioned to judge profitability by cost of goods percentages. To establish a total product cost in a foodservice operation, management must know three key pricing factors: standard recipe cost, garnish cost, and supplementary food cost.

Standard recipe cost. The cost of all products used to produce one standard portion of a menu item. For example, New York Strip Steak may be served as a 10 oz. portion of 180A strip loin extra short. At $6 per pound, the cost of the standard 10 oz. portion would be $3.75 ($6 lb./10 oz. equals 5/8 lb. x $6 equals $3.75).

Garnish cost. Products used in garnishing the standard recipe for each item to enhance eye appeal and flavor. For example, parsley, fruit, lobster butter, mushroom caps and onion rings. The New York Strip Steak might be garnished with onion rings and mushroom caps.

Supplementary food cost. Foods that are included with menu items regardless of selection or sales price. Many restaurants offer bread, butter, salad (including salad dressing) and po-tato with all menu items. Supplementary foods can account for a substantial cost factor.

The total product cost for a standard portion of New York Strip Steak might be as follows:

Standard recipe cost	$3.75
Garnish cost	.18
Supplementary food cost	.57
	$4.50

Once management analyzes the total cost of each menu item, the menu's potential cost of goods can be determined. The potential cost of goods is the total cost if all items purchased are sold, and if no foods are incorrectly portioned, stolen, or otherwise wasted. Obviously, potential cost of goods sold and actual costs will vary. Variance—usually from one to three percent—depends on the type of restaurant and the effectiveness of management control. Actual food costs are determined by purchases and inventory at the end of an accounting period.

As a rule of thumb, the variance in potential and actual cost of goods at fast food operations is one half to one percentage point; at table service and specialty restaurants, it is two to two and a half percentage points. Any larger variance should signal management that a problem exists.

To determine each menu item's food cost percentage, the item's total product cost for a standard portion is divided by its selling price. The food cost percentage for the entire menu is determined by dividing the menu's total food cost by total revenues.

Cost percentages, however, should not be the sole means of evaluating food profitability. Illustration 1 ranks the menu items at Johny's Grill, a hypothetical restaurant that we will use as a case study. The menu items are ranked from highest to lowest contribution margin. For our purposes, contribution margin is the amount left over after subtracting the item's total standard portion cost from its selling price.

As you can see, low food cost percentages do not necessarily indicate profitability. The chicken entree has the lowest food cost percentage, 31%, but yields only a $2.74 contribution margin. The lobster tail entree produces the highest contribu-

1. Items Ranked by Contribution Margin

(A) CM Classification	(B) Menu Item	(C) CM	(D) Food Cost %
1. HIGH	Lobster Tail	4.65	41%
2. HIGH	Prime Rib (20 oz.)	4.30	46%
3. HIGH	NY Strip Steak	4.00	41%
4. HIGH	Top Sirloin Steak	3.65	39%
5. LOW	Shrimp	3.05	41%
6. LOW	Red Snapper	3.00	39%
7. LOW	Prime Rib (12 oz.)	3.00	45%
8. LOW	Chicken	2.74	31%
9. LOW	Chopped Sirloin	2.55	41%
10. LOW	Tenderloin Tips	2.45	42%

2. Menu A: When Chicken is Most Popular Item

	Menu Mix	Cost	Income
Chicken	1000	$1500	$ 4,500
Steak	400	1200	2,800
Lobster	300	1350	2,700
	1700	$4050	$10,000

Potential Food Cost: $\dfrac{4050}{10,000} = 40.5\%$

Contribution Margin: $5,950

Average C.M. per Guest: $3.50

3. Menu B: When Steak is Most Popular Item

	Menu Mix	Cost	Income
Chicken	300	$ 450	$ 1,350
Steak	800	2400	5,600
Lobster	600	2700	5,400
	1700	$5550	$12,350

Potential Food Cost: $\dfrac{5550}{12350} = 44.9\%$

Contribution Margin: $6,850

Average C.M. per Guest: $4.03

tion margin—$4.65—and has a food cost percentage of 41%.

Illustrations 2 and 3 show the importance of tracking the effects of varied consumer demand—menu mix—on contribution margin and potential food cost. Each menu contains the same three entrees prepared with similar standard recipe and product costs. The total number of covers sold is the same for each menu—1,700—but the consumer purchase pattern, menu mix, is different.

In Illustration 2, Menu A, the chicken entree is the most popular item. It produces, however, only $4,500 in income when 1,000 covers are sold. Menu A's food cost percentage is 40.5%, its average contribution margin per guest is $3.50, and it generates a total contribution margin of $5,950.

In Illustration 3, Menu B, the steak entree is the most popular item. With only 800 covers sold, it produces income of $5,600. Menu B's food cost percentage is 44.9%, but its average contribution margin per guest is $4.03. It generates a total contribution margin—$6,850—higher than Menu A.

The menu with the lowest cost of goods percentage is the least profitable as a result of menu mix. The more a foodservice operator can shift demand to higher contribution margin items, the greater the menu's total contribution margin will be.

Gathering information

Every attempt to improve your menu begins with a statistical evaluation of your current situation. A foodservice operator's objective is to make the next menu more profitable and appealing to the guest. In order to do this, management must consider:

- The wants and needs of the target market
- What menu items to offer
- How to describe menu items
- How to cost and price each item
- How and where to place each item on the menu
- How to graphically design the complete menu

Management needs accurate information to answer these questions. Hence, the first step in menu engineering is to systematically gather information about each current menu item. This should include standard recipe cost and direct labor cost.

All recipes require lesser or greater time and skill depending on the product recipe and stage of raw or readiness of the ingredients. For our purposes in this article, we will treat direct labor, a semi-variable cost, as a fixed cost. The subject of direct labor input to each menu item will not be discussed.

Using menu engineering

Lets see how menu engineering works in actual practice. Johny's Grill is a table specialty restaurant with ten items on its dinner menu. Illustration 4 shows how menu engineering was used to analyze Johny's menu for a 30-day period.

1. First, the operator lists all menu entrees in column A. Only entree items are listed. Do not list appetizers, desserts or other side items. Do not list alcoholic beverage sales on this list. The ratio of food to beverage sales is a key to successful merchandising in most restaurants. The analysis of beverage sales, however, should be done separately. While we separate purchases for the purposes of our menu analysis, the successful operator is always concerned with the guests' total expenditure.

Daily specials must also be analyzed separately. By listing purchases of daily specials separately, their impact on the menu is more easily identified. If the operator's suggestive selling program is effective, daily specials should become popular with relatively high contribution margins.

2. The total number of purchases for each item is listed in column B, menu mix. All purchases are listed on a per person basis.

3. Each item's sales is divided by the total number of purchases—3,000 in this case—to determine that item's menu mix percentage, column C.

4. In column D, each item's menu mix percentage is categorized as either high or low. Any menu item that is lower than 70% of the menu mix average percentage is considered low. Any item that is 70% or above the average is considered high. On a ten-item menu, for example, each item would theoretically get 10% of the mix. On a 20-item menu the average would be 5%. For Johny's ten-item menu, we multiply 10% times 70% to get the desired menu mix percentage rate of .07, or 7%. Any item 7% or higher is considered high. Any item less than 7% is low.

5. Each item's published menu selling price is listed in column E.

6. Each item's standard food cost is listed in column F. An item's standard portion cost is composed of standard recipe costs, garnish cost, and supplemental food cost. Not all items, however, will have all three cost components.

7. The contribution margin for each item is listed in column G. Contribution margins are determined by subtracting the item's standard food cost (column F) from its selling price (column E).

8. In column H we determine the total menu revenues by multiplying the number of purchases of each item (column B) by its selling price (column E).

9. In column I we determine the total menu food cost by multiplying each item's standard food cost (column F) by the number of items purchased (column B).

10. The total menu contribution margin is listed in column J. This is determined by multiplying each item's contribution margin (column G) times the item's total number of purchases (column B).

11. In column K we list the contribution margin percentage for each item. This is determined by dividing each item's contribution margin by the total menu contribution margin which is the total of column J, $9,644.80.

12. Each item's contribution margin is categorized as either high or low in column L, depending upon whether or not the item exceeds

4. How Menu Engineering Was Used to Analyze a Menu for a 30-Day Period

A Menu Item	B Menu Mix	C MM%	D MM% Category	E Menu Price	F Food Cost	G CM
Shrimp	210	7%	H	$7.95	$4.90	3.05
Chicken	420	14	H	4.95	2.21	2.74
Chopped Sirloin	90	3	L	4.50	1.95	2.55
Prime Rib/12 oz.	600	20	H	7.95	4.95	3.00
Prime Rib/20 oz.	60	2	L	9.95	5.65	4.30
New York Strip	360	12	H	8.50	4.50	4.00
Top Sirloin	510	17	H	7.95	4.30	3.65
Red Snapper	240	8	H	6.95	3.95	3.00
Lobster Tail	150	5	L	9.50	4.95	4.55
Tenderloin Tips	360	12	H	6.45	4.00	2.45
TOTALS	3,000	100%				

Potential Food Cost: 56.17%

the menu's average contribution margin. The menu's average contribution margin is determined by dividing the total contribution margin—$9,664.80—column J, by the total number of items sold, 3,000. The average contribution margin for Johny's Grill is $3.22.

13. We use all the data we have gathered to classify each item into categories in column M. Each menu item is classified as either a Star, Plow Horse, Puzzle, or Dog. These classifications are standard marketing theory terms (see below).

14. In column N we list the decisions made on each item. Should the item be retained, repositioned, replaced, or repriced?

The four key menu categories

When accurate information has been gathered and analyzed for each menu item as we have done in Illustration 4, the items are then categorized for decision making. All menu items can be grouped into four categories: Stars, Plow Horses, Puzzles and Dogs.

Stars. Menu items high in both popularity and contribution margin. Stars are the most popular items on your menu. They may be your signature items.

Plow Horses. Menu items high in popularity but low in contribution margin. Plow horses are demand generators. They may be the lead items on your menu or your signature items. They are

often significant to the restaurant's popularity with price conscious buyers.

Puzzles. Menu items low in popularity but high in contribution margin. In other words, Puzzles yield a high profit per item sold, but they are hard to sell.

Dogs. Menu items low in popularity and low in contribution margin. These are your losers. They are unpopular, and they generate little profit.

How to use the categories

Once you have grouped your menu into the four key categories, you are ready to make decisions. Each category must be analyzed and evaluated separately.

Stars. You must maintain rigid specifications for quality, quantity, and presentation of all Star items. Locate them in a highly visible position on the menu. Test them occasionally for price inelasticity. Are guests willing to pay more for these items, and still buy them in significant quantity? The Super Stars of your menu—highest priced Stars—may be less price sensitive than any other items on the menu. If so, these items may be able to carry a larger portion of any increase in cost of goods and labor.

Plow Horses. These items are often an important reason for a restaurant's popularity. Increase their prices carefully. If Plow Horses are

H Total Menu Revenues	I Menu Food Cost	J Menu CM	K CM%	L CM Category	M Class	N Action Taken
$ 1,669.50	$ 1,029.00	$ 640.50	6.6	L	Plowhorse	Carefully increase price
2,079.00	928.20	1,150.80	11.9	L	Plowhorse	Retain as low price leader
405.00	175.50	229.50	2.4	L	Dog	Eliminate
4,770.00	2,970.00	1,800.00	18.6	L	Plowhorse	Retain
597.00	339.00	258.00	2.7	H	Puzzle	Increase Price
3,060.00	1,620.00	1,440.00	14.9	H	Star	Increase Price
4,054.50	2,193.00	1,861.50	19.3	H	Star	Retain
1,668.00	948.00	720.00	7.4	L	Plowhorse	Increase Price
1,425.00	742.50	682.50	7.1	H	Puzzle	Test by lowering price as special to see if demand increases
2,322.00	1,440.00	882.00	9.1	L	Plowhorse	Increase price in stages
$22,050.00	$12,385.20	$9,664.80	100%			

Average Contribution Margin: $3.22

highly price sensitive, attempt to pass only the cost of goods increase on to the menu price. Or, consider placing the increase on to a Super Star item. Test for a negative effect on demand (elasticity). Make any price increase in stages (from $4.55 to $4.75 then $4.95). If it is necessary to increase prices, pass through only the additional cost. Do not add more. Relocate non-signature and low contribution margin Plow Horses to a lower profile position on the menu. Attempt to shift demand to more profitable items by merchandising and menu positioning. If the item is an image maker or signature item, hold its current price as long as possible in periods of high price sensitivity.

Determine the direct labor cost of each Plow Horse to establish its labor and skill intensiveness. If the item requires high skills or is labor intensive, consider a price increase or substitution. Also, consider reducing the item's standard portion without making the difference noticeable. Merchandise the Plow Horse by packaging it with side items to increase its contribution margin. Another option is to use the item to create a "better value alternative." For example, prime ribs can be sold by the inch, and steaks can be sold by the ounce. This offers guests an opportunity to spend more, and get more value.

Puzzles. Take them off the menu. Particularly if a Puzzle is low in popularity, requires costly or additional inventory, has poor shelf life, requires skilled or labor intensive preparation, and is of inconsistent quality. Another option is to reposition the Puzzle and feature it in a more popular location on the menu. You can try adding value to the item through Table D'Hote packaging. Rename it. A Puzzle's popularity can be affected by what it is called, especially if the name can be made to sound familiar.

Decrease the Puzzle's price. The item may have a contribution margin that is too high and is facing price resistance. Care must be taken, however, not to lower the contribution margin to a point where the Puzzle draws menu share from a Star. Increase the item's price and test for inelasticity. A Puzzle that has relatively high popularity may be inelastic.

Limit the number of Puzzles you allow on your menu. Puzzles can create difficulties in quality consistency, slow production down, and cause inventory and cost problems. You must accurately evaluate the effect Puzzle items have on your image. Do they enhance your image?

Dogs. Eliminate all Dog items if possible. Foodservice operators are often intimidated by influential guests to carry a Dog on the item. The way to solve this problem is to carry the item in inventory (assuming it has a shelf life) but not on the menu. The special guest is offered the opportunity to have the item made to order upon request. Charge extra for this service. Raise the Dog's price to Puzzle status. Some items in the

Dog category may have market potential. These tend to be the more popular Dogs, and may be converted to Puzzles.

Whenever possible, replace Dogs with more popular items. You may have too many items. It is not unusual to discover a number of highly unpopular menu items with little, if any, relation to other more popular and profitable items held in inventory. Do not be afraid to terminate Dogs, especially when demand is not satisfactory.

Developing new menu items

There are three reasons to add new menu items. To increase demand, to increase contribution margins, and to create greater market share for your operation.

Each new menu item should be carefully considered and pre-tested as a special before adding it to the menu. When adding new items, attempt to build off of products already in inventory. Try to develop new items that require low skills, and are not labor intensive. Add items that have the growth potential to become highly popular. Items not easily prepared at home—roasts and fish, for example—have good potential. Make sure food cost for the new item is relatively stable. And finally, aim for items with low food cost and good plate coverage. This will allow you to give the item a lower price and still maintain a high contribution margin.

Increase demand. Add a menu item with already proven popularity to increase frequency or broaden your market. For example, salad bars have high appeal to light eaters, and have proven their effectiveness in both fast food and specialty restaurants. Eggs and omelettes are also items with high popularity. Another way to increase demand is by adding a signature item that cannot be found anywhere else.

Increase contribution margin. Try to add new items with high contribution margins, espe-cially if they do not require additional inventory. For example, 20 oz. prime rib is a particularly good item to add when smaller cuts are already being served.

Signature items. Signature items, like Plow Horses, may be the most important reason for your restaurant's popularity. These are items found only at your operation, the specialty of the house. Properly developed and merchandised, they can create greater market share, and bring prestige and visibility to your operation. Add signature items with the utmost care.

Summary and conclusion

Menu engineering provides management with a tool to evaluate the effectiveness of its current menu, and to make decisions on menu pricing, content and design. It is a step-by-step process that helps management develop a menu with both popularity and profits.

Every attempt to improve your menu must begin with a statistical analysis of your current situation. By categorizing and classifying menu items through logical mathematical procedures, menu engineering enables the operator to make the right decisions.

The key to any menu's success is whether or not it produces more customers and more contribution dollars. A foodservice operator's objective must always be to make the next menu more profitable and appealing to the guest.

Notes

*This article is reprinted with permission from Hospitality Publications, Okemos, Mich., 1982.

9 Forecasting Methods

Every hospitality manager's job includes forecasting, which is the calculation and prediction of future events such as sales for the following day, week, or month. Forecasting is necessary in order to plan the most effective and efficient ways to meet expected sales volume. For example, if the food and beverage manager of a hotel forecasts 500 dinner guests, then food, beverages, and other supplies must be obtained, and the appropriate personnel must be scheduled to prepare and serve the food and beverages to the guests. Generally, the accuracy of sales forecasts is a major determinant of the cost effectiveness of the hospitality operation. For example, if 400 meals are forecast and 500 guests show up, the food and beverage provisions and the number of employees scheduled to work may not be adequate. This may result in poor service and overtime wages. On the other hand, if 600 meals had been forecast, service would probably have been outstanding; however, due to possibly excessive labor costs, efficiency would have been reduced. The general topic of forecasting raises several questions such as:

1. How important is forecasting?
2. Is forecasting limited to financial forecasts?
3. How is forecasting conducted by unit managers in the hospitality industry?
4. How does forecasting enable management to be successful?
5. What are the limitations to forecasting?
6. How does forecasting differ from planning?
7. What is the difference between seasonal and cyclical patterns?
8. How do quantitative and qualitative forecasting methods differ?
9. How is a moving average calculated?
10. When are causal forecasting approaches most useful in the hospitality industry?

This chapter begins by explaining the distinction between implicit and explicit forecasts. A general discussion of forecasting in the hospitality industry is followed by identifying the personnel who are responsible for preparing forecasts. Next, we turn to the nature of forecasting itself, focusing on the underlying patterns of data used in forecasts and providing an overview of various forecasting methods. The problem of selecting a forecasting method appropriate to individual hospitality operations is given special consideration. Finally, we will illustrate the chapter's discussion of forecasting by providing case studies of how forecasts are prepared by three different hospitality operations.

Implicit Versus Explicit Forecasts

Some hospitality managers may insist that they do not believe in forecasting. However, their actions almost always prove otherwise. For example, when the manager decides to replace an inoperative piece of equipment, such as a range, he or she is implicitly forecasting that profits will be higher if a new range is purchased.

This intuitive approach to managing may be useful, since unforeseen events often occur and must be resolved quickly. However, managing in this fashion on a daily basis is less than optimal. It is generally more useful to forecast consciously. Implicit forecasts are unsystematic, imprecise, and difficult to evaluate rationally. Explicit forecasts are systematic, may be reasonably reliable and accurate, and are easier to evaluate rationally.

Forecasting in the Hospitality Industry

A major function of management is planning, and a subset of the planning function is forecasting. Forecasting is generally used to predict what will happen in a given set of circumstances. The forecast gives an idea of expected results if management makes no changes in the way things are done. In planning, forecasts are used to help make decisions about which circumstances will be most desirable for the hospitality operation. Thus, if a forecast shows rooms demand will decrease next month, management should prepare an action plan to prevent rooms sales from declining. After the action plan is completed, a new forecast must be made to reflect the impact of the action plan.

Planning, and thus forecasting, is pervasive in hospitality operations. In a hotel operation, rooms sales and food and beverage sales account for approximately 85% of the total sales activity of a hotel. Many operations, especially food service and lodging chains, forecast sales for several years in long-range budgets. At the other extreme, sales are forecast for months, days, parts of a day, and sometimes even on an hourly basis, since management must plan to service the forecasted sales.

Hospitality establishments also provide estimates of future activity in management reports to stockholders, which include both qualitative and quantitative forecasts. For example, Marriott Corporation included the following in a recent annual report:[1]

> As we enter the 1990s, our clear goal is to enhance Marriott's position as the world's number one company in lodging and contract services.

Exhibit 9.1 Personnel Involved in Making Short-Term Forecasts

	Rooms Forecast	Food & Beverage Forecast	Catering Forecast
Average number of personnel involved	3 people	3 people	2 people
Person responsible for final forecast	General manager (GM) and to a lesser extent the front office manager	Food and beverage director and to a lesser extent the GM	Director of catering and to a lesser extent the food and beverage director

Source: Raymond S. Schmidgall, "While Forecasts Hit Targets, GMs Still Seek Better Guns," *Lodging*, November 1989.

In the 1990s, we believe the best use of our time and resources will be to sharpen our focus on "mega" markets where Marriott has a competitive advantage.

Through development and acquisition, we plan to double the number of our hotels by the mid–1990s.

Personnel Responsible for Forecasting

Forecasting of sales and related expenses is the responsibility not only of the accounting department, but also of management personnel in other departments. For example, the year-ahead forecast should include input from (1) the sales director's forecast of group rooms business, (2) the front office manager's forecast of rooms occupancy from all other sources, (3) a joint forecast of rooms business by the sales director and front office manager, (4) the controller, and (5) the general manager and management team review.

Exhibit 9.1 reveals the results of research regarding the number of people involved in making short-term (3- to 10-day) forecasts. Across all properties surveyed, the range of the number of personnel involved in the three areas shown above was 1–6 people. The larger the property, the greater the number of personnel involved with the forecast. For example, the mega-hotels (1,000 or more rooms) that responded use six people in their rooms forecast, while hotels with fewer than 150 rooms involve an average of two people.

The Nature of Forecasting

It is important to understand the nature and limitations of forecasting. First, forecasting deals with the future. A forecast made today is for activity during a future period, be it tonight's dinner sales or next year's rooms sales. The time period involved is significant. A forecast today for tomorrow's sales is generally much easier than an estimate today of next year's sales. The more removed the forecast period is from the date the forecast is made, the greater the difficulty in making the forecast and the greater the risk that the actual results will differ from the forecast.

Second, forecasting involves uncertainty. If management were certain about what circumstances would exist during the forecasted period, the forecast preparation would be a trivial matter. Virtually all situations faced by managers involve uncertainty; therefore, judgments must be made and information gathered on which to base the forecast. For example, assume that rooms sales for a major hotel must be forecast for one year in advance. The manager (forecaster) may be uncertain about competition, guest demand, room rates, and so forth. Nevertheless, using the best information available and his or her best judgment, he or she forecasts that x rooms at an average room rate of $\$y$ will be sold.

Third, forecasting generally relies on information contained in historical data. Historical activity (for example, past sales) may not be a strong indicator of future activity, but it is considered a reasonable starting point. When historical data appear to be irrelevant to the future time period, the forecasts should be modified appropriately. For example, a successful World's Fair might have a major impact on hotel occupancies for several months. However, in projecting future hotel occupancies after the fair ends, the recent historical information may well be much less relevant.

Fourth, by their nature, forecasts are generally less accurate than desired. However, rather than discarding forecasts due to their inaccuracy, management should consider using more sophisticated forecasting models when their cost is justified, updating forecasts as necessary, and/or planning more carefully based on the forecasted projections.

Naive forecasting models, such as using the most recent value plus $x\%$, may have been adequate in the past for small hospitality operations. However, more sophisticated models may be appropriate for larger properties. Forecasts should be revised as soon as there is a change in the circumstances on which the forecasts were based. For example, an enhanced food and beverage reputation due to favorable publicity may call for reforecasting next month's food and beverage sales.

Finally, management must plan to cover a deviation of an additional $x\%$ from the forecasted levels. Experience may be the best indication of the required planning. For example, if actual sales historically have differed by an additional 10% from projected sales, management should order sufficient provisions and schedule labor to cover such a deviation for the projected activity.

Underlying Pattern of the Data

Many forecasting methods assume that some pattern exists in past data that can be identified and used in making the forecast. The methods to be presented in this chapter make explicit assumptions about the type of underlying pattern. Thus, the forecaster must attempt to match the pattern with the most appropriate forecasting methods. Three types of pattern are trend, seasonal, and cyclical (discussed below and graphed for a hypothetical hotel in Exhibit 9.2).

The **trend pattern** is simply a projection of the long-run estimate of the activity being evaluated. The trend pattern of the data is often shown for several years. The trend of rooms sales in Exhibit 9.2 is an increasing one and could be determined by using methods presented later in this chapter.

Exhibit 9.2   Underlying Patterns of Data for a Hypothetical Hotel

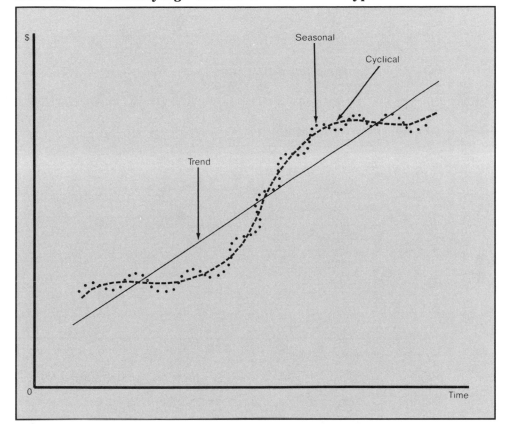

A **seasonal pattern** exists when a series of data fluctuates over time according to some pattern. Business may vary regularly by season of the year, by month, by week, or even by the days of the week. Seasonal patterns exist in the hospitality industry primarily because of forces external to the industry. For example, many summer resort hotels experience high occupancy during the summer months, but are closed during the off-season. The manager of a hospitality operation affected by seasonal business swings must fully appreciate this impact in order to manage efficiently.

The final underlying pattern of data is called cyclical. **Cyclical patterns** are movements about a trend line that generally occur over a period of more than one year. Exhibit 9.2 shows that the cyclical pattern is similar to a seasonal pattern except for the length of the pattern. The cyclical pattern is the most difficult to predict because, unlike a seasonal pattern, it does not necessarily repeat itself at constant intervals. A cyclical pattern can be observed in the annual lodging revenues (constant dollars) as shown in Exhibit 9.3. The graph shows growth of annual revenues from just under $10 billion to nearly $16 billion over 18 years. However, several fairly dramatic declines and increases are reflected.

Finally, random variations are also present in all historical data. By definition, there is no pattern in random variations. They occur for reasons that the hospitality manager cannot anticipate regardless of the

Exhibit 9.3   Annual Lodging Revenues—Constant Dollars

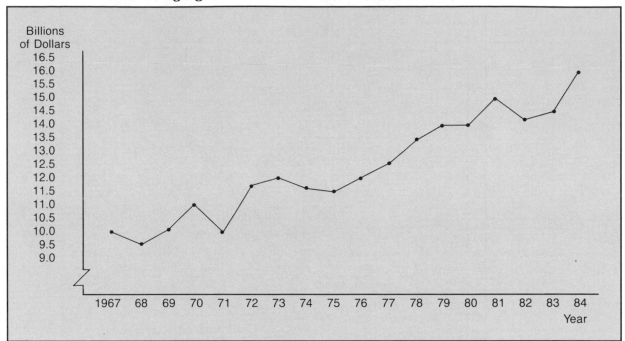

Source: Adapted from the *National Income and Products Accounts of the United States*, U.S. Dept. of Commerce.

forecasting method. Therefore, the actual observed result is a combination of trend and randomness. As long as randomness exists, uncertainty will be present. However, when the forecaster is able to identify the exact pattern of the underlying data, the random deviations are minimized.

Overview of Forecasting Methods

There are numerous ways to forecast, ranging from the simple, unsophisticated method of intuition to complex approaches such as econometric models, where sets of two or more multiple regression equations are used. Forecasting methods may be classified as shown in Exhibit 9.4.

The first breakdown is between informal and formal forecasting methods. Informal methods are based on intuition and lack systematic procedures transferable to other forecasters. Formal forecasting methods outline steps to be followed so they can be applied repeatedly. Formal forecasting methods are divided between **qualitative methods** and **quantitative methods**. The quantitative methods, which will be the thrust of the remainder of this chapter, are further divided between causal and time series approaches.

The **time series approaches** always assume that a pattern recurs over time which, when identified, may be used to forecast values for any subsequent time period. For example, if a seasonal pattern of December hotel occupancies of 30% below the monthly average has been identified, then the estimated hotel occupancy for December of the following year would most likely be 30% below the monthly average for that year.

Exhibit 9.4   Forecasting Methods

Approaches				Brief Description
Informal forecasting				Ad hoc, judgmental or intuitive methods
Formal Forecasting	Quantitative Methods	Causal Methods	**Regression Analysis**	Independent variables are related to the dependent variable using least squares: $y = A + Bx_1 + Cx_2$. Approaches include simple linear regression, multiple linear regression, and nonlinear regression.
			Econometrics	A system of interdependent regression equations describing one or more economic sectors.
		Time Series	**Naive**	Simple rules such as forecast equals last period's actual activity.
			Smoothing	Based on average past values of a time series (moving average) or weighting more recent past values of a time series (exponential smoothing).
			Decomposition	A time series that is broken down into trend, cyclical, seasonality, and randomness.
	Qualitative Methods		**Market Research**	Gathering information from potential customers regarding a "new" product or service.
			Juries of Executive Opinion	Top executives jointly prepare forecasts.
			Salesforce Estimates	A bottom-up approach to aggregating unit managers' forecasts.
			Delphi Method	A formal process conducted with a group of experts to achieve consensus on future events as they affect the company's markets.

Time series approaches assume that the underlying pattern can be identified solely on the basis of historical data from that series. They do not consider the potential effects of certain decisions, such as pricing and advertising, that the manager makes for the future periods. Time series approaches presented in this chapter include naive methods and smoothing methods.

The **causal approaches** assume that the value of a certain variable is a function of other variables. For example, the sales of food and beverages in a hotel are a function, among other things, of hotel occupancy. Thus, a food and beverage sales forecast is based in part on forecasted rooms sales. Causal methods include single and multiple regression methods and econometric models. Only the single regression approach will be presented in this text.[2]

Naive Methods

The simplest time series approach to forecasting is to use the most recently observed value as a forecast. For example, a food service manager's sales projections of $50,000 for the current month may be based upon the $50,000 sales of the previous month. This naive approach to forecasting assumes that there is no seasonality affecting sales. To take seasonality into account, a forecaster might use sales from the same month of the previous year as a base and either add or subtract a certain percentage.

For example, assume that a hotel's January 19X1 rooms sales totaled $150,000. The projection for January 19X2, using an anticipated 10% increase due to expected increased rooms sales and prices, would be $165,000, computed as follows:

$$\text{Base}(1 + 10\%) = \text{Forecast for January 19X2}$$
$$150,000(1.1) = \underline{\$165,000}$$

Although naive methods are based on very simple rules, they may provide reasonably accurate forecasts, especially for estimates of up to one year. In some cases, more sophisticated methods do not sufficiently improve the accuracy of forecasts to justify their use—especially in light of their higher costs.

Moving Averages

In some cases, the major cause of variations among data used in making forecasts is randomness. Since managers do not make business decisions based on randomness that may never again happen, they attempt to remove the random effect by averaging or "smoothing" the data from specified time periods. One such approach to forecasting is the **moving average**, which is expressed mathematically as follows:

$$\text{Moving Average} = \frac{\text{Activity in Previous } n \text{ Periods}}{n}$$

where n is the number of periods in the moving average

This moving average method is illustrated using the contract food service operation at the Bank of Hospitality. Service Company, the contract feeding company, serves lunch five days a week at the Bank of Hospitality, and the manager needs to estimate sales for the thirteenth week. Exhibit 9.5 reveals weekly sales for weeks 1–12. Using a three-week moving average, the estimate for the number of meals to be served during the thirteenth week is 1,025, determined as follows:

$$\text{3-Week Moving Average} = \frac{1,025 + 1,000 + 1,050}{3}$$

Exhibit 9.5 Weekly Meals Served: Bank of Hospitality

Week	Actual Meals Served
1	1,000
2	900
3	950
4	1,050
5	1,025
6	1,000
7	975
8	1,000
9	950
10	1,025
11	1,000
12	1,050

$$= \underline{1,025} \text{ meals}$$

As new weekly results become available, they are used in calculating the average by adding the most recent week and dropping the earliest week. In this way, the calculated average is a "moving" one because it is continually updated to include only the most recent observations for the specified number of time periods. For example, if 950 meals were served during week 13 at the Bank of Hospitality, then the forecast for week 14, using the three-week moving average, would be calculated as follows:

$$\text{Forecast for Week 14} = \frac{\text{Sum Sales for Weeks 11–13}}{3}$$

$$= \frac{1,000 + 1,050 + 950}{3}$$

$$= \underline{1,000} \text{ meals}$$

Alternatively, more weeks could be used to determine the weekly forecast. For example, a 12-week moving average to estimate meals to be sold during the thirteenth week results in a forecast of 994, determined as follows:

$$\text{12-Week Moving Average} = \frac{\text{Actual Weekly Sales for Weeks 1–12}}{12}$$

$$= \frac{11,925}{12}$$

$$= 993.75, \text{ rounded to } \underline{994}$$

It should be noted that the more periods averaged, the less effect the random variations will have on the forecast. This can be seen in the above illustration. The three-week moving average forecast for week 13 was 1,025 meals, compared to the 12-week moving average forecast of 994. In this case, since the actual sales during the thirteenth week turned out to be 950 meals, the 12-week moving average forecast of 994 was more accurate than the forecast based on only three weeks. The increased accuracy is due to minimizing the effect of random variations by using data covering a greater number of time periods.

Although the moving average approach to forecasting is often considered to be more accurate and reliable than the naive methods, there are some disadvantages associated with this approach. One limitation is the need to store and continually update the historical data covering the most recent number of time periods used in calculating the moving average. This requirement would be quite costly for a large retail business, such as Sears or K-Mart, which would have to keep track of sales data for a large number of different items. However, in the hospitality industry the cost of storing and maintaining historical data for moving average forecasts is not unreasonable, since hotels and restaurants sell a comparatively small number of different items.

A more serious limitation is that the moving average method gives equal weight to each of the observations gathered over the specified number of time periods. Many managers would agree that the data from the most recent time periods contain more information about what will happen in the future and, therefore, should be given more weight than the older observations that are calculated into the moving average. The exponential smoothing approach to forecasting not only satisfies this concern to count recent data more heavily than older data, but also eliminates the need for storing all of the historical data covering the specified time period.

Exponential Smoothing

Exponential smoothing is a forecasting method that uses a **smoothing constant** and recent actual and forecasted activity to estimate future activity. This approach has widespread appeal among business forecasters. It essentially says, "If the forecast for a particular period was too high, reduce it for the next period; if it was too low, raise it."

When the exponential smoothing method is used, the hospitality manager requires only three types of data as follows:

1. The forecast from the prior period

2. The actual activity that resulted from this forecasted period

3. A smoothing constant

Both the forecast from the prior period and the actual activity from this period are readily available. The smoothing constant requires the manager to identify what is a good response rate. The smoothing constant should be small if sales have been relatively stable in the past, and large if the product/service is experiencing rapid growth. The smoothing constant is determined using forecasts from two consecutive *previous* periods and the actual demand from the earlier of these two periods as follows:

$$\text{Smoothing Constant} = \frac{\text{Period 2 Forecast} - \text{Period 1 Forecast}}{\text{Period 1 Actual Demand} - \text{Period 1 Forecast}}$$

Once the smoothing constant has been determined, it can be inserted into the general formula for exponential smoothing, which is as follows:

$$\begin{matrix} \text{New} \\ \text{Forecast} \end{matrix} = \begin{matrix} \text{Past} \\ \text{Forecast} \end{matrix} + \begin{matrix} \text{Smoothing} \\ \text{Constant} \end{matrix} \times \left(\begin{matrix} \text{Actual} \\ \text{Demand} \end{matrix} - \begin{matrix} \text{Past} \\ \text{Forecast} \end{matrix} \right)$$

Using the previous illustration with the Bank of Hospitality, the weekly sales will be projected for week 13 using the exponential smoothing method of forecasting. Assume that the forecasted sales for week 12 were 1,020 and that .1 is the smoothing constant. The forecasted sales for week 13 of 1,023 meals is determined as follows:

$$\begin{matrix} \text{Week 13} \\ \text{Forecast} \end{matrix} = \begin{matrix} \text{Week 12} \\ \text{Forecast} \end{matrix} + .1(\text{Week 12 Actual Sales} - \text{Week 12 Forecast})$$

$$= 1,020 + .1(1,050 - 1,020)$$

$$= \underline{\underline{1,023}} \text{ meals}$$

The exponential smoothing method presented in this text is only one of several such approaches.[3] Exponential smoothing techniques are most useful when only short-term forecasts are required, and when reasonably accurate—rather than precise—forecasts are acceptable.

Causal Forecasting Approaches

Causal forecasting approaches include both single and multiple regression as well as econometric models. In this text, we will discuss only single regression analysis.

Regression analysis involves estimating an activity on the basis of other activities or factors that are assumed to be causes or highly reliable indicators of the activity. The activity to be forecasted (such as food sales) is the dependent, unknown variable, while the basis on which the forecast is made (such as room sales and/or advertising expenses) is the independent, known variable. Regression analysis is used to predict the dependent variable given the value of the independent variable.

The level of demand to be estimated is thought to depend upon, or be closely related to, the independent variable. In order to forecast the operation's demand, the closeness of the variables needs to be determined. For example, how closely related are a lodging property's rooms sales to food sales in its restaurant operation?

Two measures of closeness are the **coefficient of correlation** and the **coefficient of determination**. The coefficient of correlation is the measure of the relation between the dependent and independent variables, such as food sales and rooms sales. The formula for determining the coefficient of correlation is as follows:

$$r = \frac{n\Sigma xy - \Sigma x\Sigma y}{\sqrt{[n\Sigma x^2 - (\Sigma x)^2][n\Sigma y^2 - (\Sigma y)^2]}}$$

where x is the independent variable
y is the dependent variable
n is the number of observations
r is a positive relationship value between 0 and 1

The closer the r value is to 1, the stronger the relationship between the dependent and independent variables being measured.

The square of the coefficient of correlation (r^2) is the coefficient of determination. This measure reflects the extent to which the change in the independent variable explains the change in the dependent variable.

Exhibit 9.6   Room Guests and Meals Served

	x Room Guests	y Meals Served
January	4,060	5,200
February	4,100	5,360
March	4,200	5,720
April	4,250	5,430
May	4,200	5,680
June	4,150	5,520
July	4,300	5,800
August	4,350	5,910
September	4,400	6,020
October	4,200	5,840
November	4,080	5,510
December	3,600	5,020

Regression analysis is illustrated using data from the hypothetical Forest Hotel. Exhibit 9.6 contains the number of room guests and meals served in the dining room for 19X1. Using these data, we can develop a regression equation that will allow us to forecast meals to be served based on our knowledge of the number of hotel guests. The regression formula is as follows:

$$y = a + bx$$

where
y = Meals served
a = Meals served to non-hotel registrants
b = Average number of meals served to each hotel guest
x = Number of hotel room guests

Given the data in Exhibit 9.6 and using formulas[4] and a computer spreadsheet program to determine a and b, the regression equation becomes:

$$y = 370 + 1.254(x)$$

This equation indicates that 370 people not registered as guests at the Forest Hotel dine there monthly and, further, that each registered room guest eats 1.254 meals at the hotel each day.

Assuming that the sales forecast for January, 19X2, is 3,000 rooms at an average occupancy per room of 1.5 people, the projected meals to be sold is determined as follows:

$$
\begin{aligned}
\text{Forecasted Meals Sold} &= 370 + 1.254(3000)(1.5) \\
&= 370 + 5,643 \\
&= \underline{\underline{6,013}}
\end{aligned}
$$

The forecasted 6,013 meals to be sold during the first week of January, 19X2, includes 370 meals for diners not registered as guests and 5,643 meals for hotel guests.

The coefficient of correlation (r) measures the relationship between hotel room guests and meals served. The r value for the above example is .8568, which suggests a strong relationship between the two variables.

The coefficient of determination (r^2) for this example is .7341, which means that 73.41% of the change in meals served is explained by the change in hotel room guests.

Regression analysis forecasting used when two or more independent variables are related to the dependent variable is called **multiple regression analysis**. For example, the manager of the food and beverage department at a lodging operation may desire to forecast food sales, which are highly dependent upon the number of room guests and advertising expenditures. Although multiple regression analysis is both interesting and challenging, it is beyond the scope of this text.[5]

The usefulness of these regression analysis techniques is a function of satisfactory dependent and independent variables. That is, the higher the correlation of the dependent and independent variables, the greater the probability regression analysis will yield meaningful forecasts.

Limitations of Quantitative Forecasting Methods

Although time series forecasting and causal forecasting can be quite useful, they have limitations. First, they are virtually useless when data are scarce, such as at the opening of a new hotel or restaurant. In these instances, there is no sales history for the newly opened facility from which to collect the data needed to forecast demand. Secondly, they assume that historical trends will continue into the future and are unable to consider unforeseeable occurrences, such as the energy crisis in the early 1970s and its impact on highway lodging properties.

Qualitative Forecasting Techniques

When the limitations of quantitative approaches significantly affect a hospitality operation, qualitative forecasting methods are useful. These methods emphasize human judgment. Information is gathered in as logical, unbiased, and systematic a way as possible, and then judgment is brought to bear on the activity being forecasted. Qualitative forecasting methods include marketing research, jury of executive opinion, sales force estimates, and the Delphi method.

The marketing research method involves systematically gathering, recording, and analyzing data related to a hospitality operation's marketing of products and services. Large hotel chains generally conduct extensive market research before opening a new property to determine whether there is adequate demand. This market research provides data which can then be used in preparing formal sales forecasts.

The jury of executive opinion technique uses key financial, marketing, and operations executives to estimate sales for the forecast period. Generally, the person using this technique will provide the executives with expected economic conditions and changes in the establishment's services. The executives will then independently make their sales forecasts. The person using this technique will then reconcile differences among the executives' opinions.

The sales force estimates technique is similar to the jury of executive opinion in that opinions of corporate personnel are obtained. However, in this case, the input is from lower echelon personnel who estimate their next year's sales. This approach is sometimes used by multi-unit food service operations. Unit managers are polled, and their immediate superiors review and discuss these estimates with each unit manager. Then, the separate sales estimates are combined to create a sales forecast for the food service operation.

The Delphi technique is used for making forecasts which are generally very futuristic in nature—for example, forecasting expected changes in international travel for the coming decade. This technique involves obtaining opinions from a group of experts to achieve consensus on future events that might affect an operation's markets. Rather than meeting together at one place, the group interacts anonymously. Questionnaires are often used. The responses are then analyzed and resubmitted to the experts for a second round of opinions. This process may continue for several rounds until the researcher is satisfied that consensus regarding the forecast has been achieved.

Selection of a Forecasting Method

The specific forecasting method that a hospitality operation adopts will depend on several factors. The two most important are the method's effectiveness in providing usable projections from available data and the cost of using the method. Different methods will be used for different purposes as suggested throughout this chapter. Small establishments lacking personnel with forecasting skills will probably adopt the less sophisticated, but still highly useful, naive methods. On the other hand, large establishments may find the more sophisticated methods to be the most effective. Although these approaches may appear costlier, they may actually be less costly in the long run for large establishments.

In addition to the effectiveness and cost of different forecasting methods, other relevant factors include:

- Frequency with which forecasts will be updated
- Turnaround required for an updated forecast
- Size and complexity of the hospitality operation
- Forecasting skills of personnel involved in making forecasts
- Purposes for which the forecasts are made

Short-Term Forecasts in the Lodging Industry

Exhibit 9.7 is a summary of lodging industry short-term sales forecasting approaches by three profit centers: rooms, food (restaurants), and catering (banquets). Short-term forecasts in this research refer to forecasts covering from 3 to 10 days.

The major purpose of each short-term forecast is to allow for staffing and, in food and catering, for ordering the food supplies to service the dining guests. A distant last purpose is the motivation of personnel, that is, using the short-term sales forecast as a target.

The methods used by the majority of respondents differ by profit center. Most hotels, especially those with reservation systems, forecast room sales using the room reservations at the time of the forecast plus an estimate for walk-ins. For example, a hotel may show 100 rooms reserved for the following Monday and add the average of walk-ins for the past four Mondays of 15 to equal a rooms sales forecast of 115 rooms. In this

Exhibit 9.7 Summary of Lodging Industry Short-Term Sales Forecasting Approaches by Three Profit Centers

	Rooms	Food	Catering
Major purposes of forecast:	Staffing (98%) Motivating personnel (25%)	Staffing (100%) Order food (72%) Motivating personnel (19%)	Staffing (82%) Order food (72%) Motivating personnel (16%)
Methodology:	Room reservations plus estimated walk-ins (93%)	Prior period sales adjusted based on intuition (46%)	Booked catered events plus estimate of additional sales (90%)
	Prior period sales adjusted based on intuition (7%)	Meal reservations and estimate for walk-ins (28%)	Prior period sales adjusted based on intuition (10%)
		Capture ratios related to the rooms forecast (26%)	
Expression of S-T forecast:	Daily number of rooms sold (80%)	Total covers (79%)	Total sales dollars (70%)
	Daily sales dollars (55%)	Total sales dollars (61%)	Total covers (67%)
	Daily number of rooms by type (35%)	Food covers by meal period (60%)	Sales dollars by catered event (47%)
	Daily sales dollars by type of room (20%)	Sales dollars by meal period (44%)	Covers by catered event (47%)

example, the short-term forecast is a combination of known sales plus a four-week moving average for the walk-ins.

A second approach is adjusting the prior period's sales based on intuitive expectations for the forecast period. Only 7% of the lodging establishments reported using this approach, and the majority of these users (60%) were establishments with fewer than 150 rooms.

The commonest approach used to forecast short-term food sales by hoteliers (46%) is using the prior period's sales figure and adjusting it for expected differences for the forecast period. For example, if 100 covers were served at the prior Monday evening dinner, the hotel's forecast for the coming Monday evening would be 100 plus or minus an adjustment for expected differences. These differences could be based on house guests, local events, weather forecasts, and other similar activities.

Twenty-eight percent of the hotels rely in part on meal reservations and estimated walk-ins, while 26% use **capture ratios**—that is, ratios based on hotel guests or some variation of hotel guests. An example of a capture ratio is a hotel which estimates its dinner covers to be 40 plus one quarter of the estimated house guests for the night. If the estimated house guests total 200, then the dinner covers forecasted equal 90, determined as follows:

Forecasted dinner covers $= a + bx$

where a = estimated covers for walk-ins (non-hotel guests)

$$b = \text{percentage of hotel guests expected to eat dinner}$$

$$x = \text{hotel guest count for evening}$$

$$\text{Forecasted dinner covers} = 40 + .25(200)$$
$$= \underline{\underline{90}}$$

The sales forecasting methods reported for catered events include two alternatives:

- Ninety percent use the booked catered events plus an estimate for additional sales not booked when the forecast is made.

- Ten percent use prior period catered sales adjusted for expected differences.

As Exhibit 9.7 shows, the short-term sales forecast is expressed in a variety of ways. For rooms, the commonest way is rooms sold (80%); for food sales, the commonest is total covers (79%); and for catering sales, the commonest is the total forecasted catering sales dollars (70%), followed closely by total covers (67%). Many hotels express the sales forecasts in more than one way.

Most hoteliers compare their actual results to their short-term sales forecasts in order to determine their forecasting accuracy, so that in the future they can refine their forecasting method and allow for forecasting error in staffing and ordering supplies.

Exhibit 9.8 contains a summary of the accuracy of the short-term sales forecasts for rooms, food, beverage, and catering activities. The rooms and catering sales forecasting appear to be the most accurate, as 40% and 42% respectively are accurate to within plus or minus 2% or less, compared to 27% for restaurant food forecasts and 24% for beverage sales forecasts. At the other extreme, only 7% of the hotels report their actual rooms sold differs by greater than 5% from their sales forecast, compared to 37%, 28%, and 40% for restaurant food, catering, and beverage forecasts, respectively. These results, especially in the restaurant food and beverage areas, clearly suggest there is room for improvement.

Forecasting Cases

To illustrate forecasting in hospitality industry firms, three companies from different segments have contributed overviews of one facet of forecasting at their companies. The case illustration from Canteen Corporation, which serves the business and industry segment of the hospitality industry, was provided by Mr. Donald R. Finger, Director of Corporate Planning at Canteen Corporation. It focuses on forecasting at the unit level for a four-week period. A brief description of the calculation of the sales dollars is included as well as the two major expenses, cost of food sold and labor expense. Included with the case is their food forecast form and a copy of an operations budget for one of their restaurants.

The second case is from Pizza Hut. It was prepared by Pat Johns, Director of Strategic Planning at Pizza Hut Inc. Its focus is their weekly sales forecast. This forecast is prepared by starting with the average of the past three weeks (effectively a three-week moving average). It is then adjusted based on several factors, such as local advertising. A major

Exhibit 9.8   Accuracy of Short-Term Sales Forecasts

Degree of Accuracy of Short-Term Forecast:[1]

	Rooms	Restaurant Food	Beverage	Catering
No difference	2%	1%	0%	5%
± 1.0% or less	20	12	8	15
± 1.1–2%	18	14	16	22
± 2.1–3%	17	18	18	13
± 3.1–5%	36	18	18	17
± > 5%	7	37	40	28
Total	100%	100%	100%	100%

[1]Based on the percentage difference between the short-term forecast and the actual sales.

purpose of this forecast is scheduling labor. Included with the case are several forms, including a labor scheduling grid. This form is used to determine the number and types of personnel required on an hourly basis given the sales forecast.

The Stouffer Hotels and Resorts illustration was provided by Raymond O. Holmes, Vice President/Controller of Stouffer Hotels and Resorts. Its focus is the sales forecast for the annual budget. This case details the various managers' roles in forecasting sales for the annual budget. Forms included are the hotel room forecast and the rooms forecast reconciliation and casualty report. The guidelines for completing these reports are also included to illustrate this facet of budgeting.

The three cases cover three segments of the hospitality industry and three time periods—weekly, monthly (four weeks), and annual. They are just a sampling of budgeting practices in hospitality corporations.

Canteen Corporation— Forecasting by Unit Managers

Canteen Corporation is a major competitor in the growing B&I (business and industry) segment of the hospitality industry. With over 1,800 operating units, sales in excess of $1.5 billion, and 36,000 employees, Canteen operates in all of the 50 states and Canada. Owned by Transworld Holdings, Canteen provides food service at the Kennedy Space Center, Yellowstone National Park and other numerous national and state parks, several stadiums such an Yankee, Oakland, and Kansas City, small and large colleges, elementary schools, correctional facilities, banks, hospitals, and industrial plants.

Forecasting at Canteen is conducted at each management level including unit, district, region, and corporate. Forecasting at the unit level (the focus of this section) includes a profit and loss forecast for the next four periods. Canteen operating quarters are 4-4-5, that is, four weeks, four weeks, and five weeks, followed by another 4-4-5, and so forth. Although forecasting varies by region, division, and operation, it is the responsibility of the unit manager.

A major use of the four-period profit and loss forecast is for control purposes, with the major emphasis on the bottom line. However, in addition, copies are provided to higher level management for their use in monitoring the operating unit's performance. The sales forecast is prepared by considering:

1. Operating days in the period

2. Projected customer count (the past two years of experience are considered with emphasis placed on the more recent year in addition to the present population, for example, student enrollment at the school)

3. Check average (the check average of the prior period is generally used as adjusted for known price increases)

The sales dollars forecast is estimated as follows:

$$\begin{matrix} \text{Operating} \\ \text{Days} \end{matrix} \times \begin{matrix} \text{Projected Customer} \\ \text{Count} \end{matrix} \times \begin{matrix} \text{Check} \\ \text{Average} \end{matrix} = \begin{matrix} \text{Forecasted} \\ \text{Sales} \end{matrix}$$

The two major expenses are cost of food sold and labor expense. Cost of food sold is estimated by multiplying the target food cost percentage by the net sales (gross sales less sales tax). Labor expense is forecasted by multiplying the expected labor hours by the appropriate hourly wages.

Finally, the major measures of performance are (1) the bottom line, (2) cost of food ratio, determined by dividing cost of food by gross sales, and (3) sales per labor hour, determined by dividing gross sales by the total labor hours. A food forecast form used by unit managers is shown in Exhibit 9.9. Exhibit 9.10 is an annual budget for a Canteen Corporation operation.

Pizza Hut—A Case in Forecasting

Pizza Hut is the largest retail distributor of pizza in the world, with a distribution system of over 6,000 units, including 3,200 corporate-owned units and just under 3,000 franchised units. Though this makes the Wichita, Kansas-headquartered Pizza Hut one of the largest multi-unit food chains, it is owned by an even larger firm, Pepsico.

The typical Pizza Hut operation consists of approximately 100 seats, 2,300 square footage, and has 25 employees. Pizza Hut's major items, familiar to most pizza lovers, include deep pan pizza and personal pan pizza.

Forecasting pervades the entire organization. The emphasis here is on the store manager. The major forecasting by a unit manager is the preparation of the weekly sales forecast, which is reviewed and approved by his/her area supervisor. Area supervisors use unit sales forecasts in preparing their area sales forecasts, which then are used by district managers in preparing district forecasts, and so forth. The major uses of the weekly sales forecast by the unit manager are labor scheduling and preparing product ingredients for each day.

The weekly sales forecast is detailed by hour for each day. The manager starts with historical data—the average of the daily-hourly sales for the past three weeks. This historical hourly sales average is adjusted for several factors as follows:

- Advertising in local papers

- Local marketing, such as a Cub Scout troop of 20 boys expected between 6–7 p.m. on Tuesday

- Seasonality—including weather changes, time of year, and holidays

Exhibit 9.9   Food Forecast

	Prior Period		Period #	Period #	Period #	Period #
	Forecast	Actual				
	Amt. / %	Amt. / %	Amt. / %	Amt. / %	Amt. / %	Amt. / %

Operation Number: ___ / ___ / ___ / ___ /

Submitted By: _____ / ___

Operation Name: _____

Approved By: _____ / ___

P / L: _____

Mgmt. Fee: _____

Period: _____

Weekly: _____

*Gross Sales: 0

Net Sales: +   100   100   100   100   100   100

Product Cost: −

Variable Labor: +

   Central Bkpng: +

   Fringe: +

   Sub Total: +

Semi-Var. Labor: +

   DMF: +

   Fringe: +

   Sub Total: +

Total Labor Cost: −

Commission Pd/Rent: −

Repair/Replacemt: −

Depreciation: −

Investment Charge: −

Other Direct: −

O/H & Mgmt. Fee: −

Misc. & Vend Income: +

Profit/Contract: ±

Amount Due−(To)Fm: ±

O/H & Mgmt. Fee: ±

Investment Charge: −

DMT Expense: −

Pretax P/(L):   ±

Total Operating Days:

Partial Shutdown Da:

Hol./Full Shutdown:

Population:

Customer Count/Day:

Participation Rate:

Check Average:

Hourly Hours/Day:

Average Hourly Rate:

*Total Hours/Day:

*SPH:

Event	Date	***Critical Milestones***	Event	Date
_____	___/___		_____	___/___
_____	___/___		_____	___/___

Courtesy of Canteen Corporation.

Exhibit 9.10 Budget Profit and Loss—Final

.0000 Description	Line	January Amt	%	February Amt	%	March Amt	%	April Amt	%	May Amt	%
—SALES—											
Food and Bar Items	010	6.1	105.2	9.0	105.9	10.1	106.3	8.1	106.6	8.5	106.3
Sales Tax	030	0.3-	5.2	0.5-	5.9	0.6-	6.3	0.5-	6.6	0.5-	6.3
Net Sales		5.8	100.0	8.5	100.0	9.5	100.0	7.6	100.0	8.0	100.0
Product Cost	040	3.2	55.2	4.6	54.1	5.3	55.8	4.1	53.9	4.4	55.0
Gross Profit		2.6	44.8	3.9	45.9	4.2	44.2	3.5	46.1	3.6	45.0
—VAR. COSTS - DIR.—											
Labor	050	2.3	39.7	3.5	41.2	3.8	40.0	2.9	38.2	2.9	36.3
Fringe	060	1.3	22.4	1.3	15.3	1.5	15.8	1.2	15.8	1.2	15.0
Total Pers. Cost/Dir		3.6	62.1	4.8	56.5	5.3	55.8	4.1	53.9	4.1	51.3
—SEMI-VAR. COSTS—											
Labor	070	0.0		0.0		0.2	2.1	0.2	2.6	0.2	2.5
Fringe	080	0.0		0.0		0.1	1.1	0.1	1.3	0.1	1.3
Tot. Pers. Cost/Su		0.0		0.0		0.3	3.2	0.3	3.90	0.3	3.8
Total Pers. Costs		3.6	62.1	4.8	56.5	5.6	58.9	4.4	57.9	4.4	55.0
Mds. Equip. Replace	100	0.0		0.0		0.0		0.0		0.0	
Rental Expense	110	0.1	1.7	0.1	1.2	0.1	1.1	0.1	1.3	0.1	1.3
Advertising	130	0.0		0.0		0.0		0.0		0.1	1.3
Outside Services	170	0.2	3.4	0.2	2.4	0.2	2.1	0.1	1.3	0.1	1.3
Other Taxes & Insurance	200	0.0		0.0		0.0		0.0		0.0	
Laundry & Cleaning	210	0.2	3.4	0.3	3.5	0.2	2.1	0.1	1.3	0.3	3.8
Other Direct	230	0.1	1.7	0.1	1.2	0.1	1.1	0.1	1.3	0.0	
Total Semi-Var		0.6	10.3	0.7	8.2	0.9	9.5	0.7	9.2	0.9	11.3
P&L Before Oh/Fee		1.6-	27.6	1.6-	18.8	2.0-	21.1	1.3-	17.1	1.4-	17.5
Overhead & Fee Exp.	240	0.4	6.9	0.5	5.9	0.6	6.3	0.5	6.6	0.5	6.3
Profit/Contract		2.0-	34.5	2.1-	24.7	2.6-	27.4	1.8-	23.7	1.9-	23.8
Prof/Cont Aft Sub5		2.0-	34.5	2.1-	24.7	2.6-	27.4	1.8-	23.7	1.9-	23.8
Amount Due from Acct	280	2.0	34.5	2.1	24.7	2.6	27.4	1.8	23.7	1.9	23.8
Contractual P/L		0.0		0.0		0.0		0.0		0.0	
—INCOME RETAINED—											
Overhead & Fee Inc.	310	0.4	6.9	0.5	5.9	0.6	6.3	0.5	6.6	0.5	6.3
Total Inc. Retained		0.4	6.9	0.5	5.9	0.6	6.3	0.5	6.6	0.5	6.3
—OTHER COSTS—											
Personnel Costs	340	0.3	5.2	0.5	5.9	0.3	3.2	0.2	2.6	0.2	2.5
Inv. & Oh. Chg./Cr.	380	0.1	1.7	0.1	1.2	0.1	1.1	0.1	1.3	0.1	1.3
Computer Exp. Alloc.	400	0.0		0.0		0.0		0.0		0.0	
Total Other Costs		0.4	6.9	0.6	7.1	0.4	4.2	0.3	3.9	0.3	3.8
Pre-Tax Profit		0.0		0.1-	1.2	0.2	2.1	0.2	2.6	0.2	2.5

Courtesy of Canteen Corporation.

- Media advertising
- Trend for the past few weeks

Pizza Hut does not prescribe a formalized approach for adjusting the historical data for the above factors, but allows unit managers to use their judgment.

The forecasting form used by unit managers is titled the Hourly

	June		July		August		September		October		November		December		Total Year	
—FORECAST—	Amt	%	Amt	%	Amt	%	Amt	%	Amt	%	Amt	%	Amt	%	Amt	%
	10.3	106.2	7.7	105.5	4.2	105.0	10.4	106.1	8.6	106.2	8.7	106.1	10.0	106.4	101.7	106.0
	0.6-	6.2	0.4-	5.5	0.2-	5.0	0.6-	6.1	0.5-	6.2	0.5-	6.1	0.6-	6.4	5.8-	6.0
	9.7	100.0	7.3	100.0	4.0	100.0	9.8	100.0	8.1	100.0	8.2	100.0	9.4	100.0	95.9	100.0
	5.3	54.6	4.0	54.8	2.2	55.0	5.4	55.1	4.4	54.3	4.5	54.9	5.1	54.3	52.5	54.7
	4.4	45.4	3.3	45.2	1.8	45.0	4.4	44.9	3.7	45.7	3.7	45.1	4.3	45.7	43.4	45.3
	2.9	29.9	2.3	31.5	1.3	32.5	2.9	29.6	2.4	29.6	2.5	30.5	2.8	29.8	32.5	33.9
	1.4	14.4	1.1	15.1	1.1	27.5	1.4	14.3	1.1	13.6	1.1	13.4	1.4	14.9	15.1	15.7
	4.3	44.3	3.4	46.6	2.4	60.0	4.3	43.9	3.5	43.2	3.6	43.9	4.2	44.7	47.6	49.6
	0.2	2.1	0.2	2.7	0.2	5.0	0.2	2.0	0.2	2.5	0.2	2.4	0.2	2.1	2.0	2.1
	0.0		0.1	1.4	0.0		0.1	1.0	0.0		0.1	1.2	0.0		0.6	.6
	0.2	2.1	0.3	4.1	0.2	5.0	0.3	3.1	0.2	2.5	0.3	3.7	0.2.	2.1	2.6	2.7
	4.5	46.4	3.7	50.7	2.6	65.0	4.6	46.9	3.7	45.7	3.9	47.6	4.4	46.8	50.2	52.3
	0.1	1.0	0.0		0.0		0.1	1.0	0.0		0.1	1.2	0.1	1.1	0.4	.4
	0.1	1.0	0.1	1.4	0.1	2.5	0.1	1.0	0.1	1.2	0.1	1.2	0.1	1.1	1.2	1.3
	0.0		0.0		0.0		0.0		0.0		0.0		0.0		0.1	0.1
	0.3	3.1	0.0		0.1	2.5	0.2	2.0	0.0		0.1	1.2	0.2	2.1	1.7	1.8
	0.0		0.0		0.0		0.1	1.0	0.0		0.0		0.1	1.1	0.2	0.2
	0.0		0.3	4.1	0.2	5.0	0.0		0.3	3.7	0.3	3.7	0.0		2.2	2.3
	0.2	2.1	0.2	2.7	0.2	5.0	0.2	2.0	0.2	2.5	0.0		0.2	2.1	1.6	1.7
	0.9	9.3	0.9	12.3	0.8	20.0	1.0	10.2	0.8	9.9	0.9	11.0	0.9	9.6	10.0	10.4
	0.8-	8.2	1.0-	13.7	1.4-	35.0	0.9-	9.2	0.6-	7.4	0.8-	9.8	0.8-	8.5	14.2-	14.8
	0.6	6.2	0.5	6.8	0.2	5.0	0.6	6.1	0.5	6.2	0.5	6.1	0.6	6.4	6.0	6.3
	1.4-	14.4	1.5-	20.5	1.6-	40.0	1.5-	15.3	1.1-	13.6	1.3-	15.9	1.4-	14.9	20.2-	21.1
	1.4-	14.4	1.5-	20.5	1.6-	40.0	1.5-	15.3	1.1-	13.6	1.3-	15.9	1.4-	14.9	20.2-	21.1
	1.4	14.4	1.5	20.5	1.6	40.0	1.5	15.3	1.1	13.6	1.3	15.9	1.4	14.9	20.2	21.1
	0.0		0.0		0.0		0.0		0.0		0.0		0.0		0.0	
	0.6	6.2	0.5	6.8	0.2	5.0	0.6	6.2	0.5	6.2	0.5	6.1	0.6	6.4	6.0	6.3
	0.6	6.2	0.5	6.8	0.2	5.0	0.6	6.1	0.5	6.2	0.5	6.1	0.6	6.4	6.0	6.3
	0.3	3.1	0.2	2.7	0.2	5.0	0.3	3.1	0.2	2.5	0.2	2.4	0.3	3.2	3.2	3.3
	0.1	1.0	0.1	1.4	0.1	2.5	0.1	1.0	0.0		0.0		0.0		0.9	0.9
	0.0		0.0		0.0		0.0		0.0		0.1	1.2	0.1	1.1	0.2	0.2
	0.4	4.1	0.3	4.1	0.3	7.5	0.4	4.1	0.2	2.5	0.3	3.7	0.4	4.3	4.3	4.5
	0.2	2.1	0.2	2.7	0.1-	2.5	0.2	2.0	0.3	3.7	0.2	2.4	0.2	2.1	1.7	1.8

Reading Sheet (see Exhibit 9.11). After this is completed based on the discussion above, the Daily Labor Worksheet (see Exhibit 9.12) is completed in part by using a labor scheduling grid similar to the illustration in Exhibit 9.13.

For example, assume that a Pizza Hut restaurant has forecast $250 of hourly sales between 6 and 7 p.m. The required staffing includes 10 people based on the labor scheduling grid column 9 as follows: 2—production, 3—service, 1—register/telephone, 1—bus/dishwasher, 1—production leader, 1—host/hostess, and 1—floor manager.

Exhibit 9.11   Hourly Reading Sheet

							HOURLY READING SHEET											
DAY		MARKETING WINDOW: LOCAL PROMOTION.																
Date	Open-12	12-1 PM	1-2 PM	2-3 PM	3-4 PM	4-5 PM	5-6 PM	6-7 PM	7-8 PM	8-9 PM	9-10 PM	10-11 PM	11-12 PM	12-1 AM	PROMO $	TOTAL SALES	COMMENTS

Courtesy of Pizza Hut, Inc.

Forecasting at Stouffer Hotels and Resorts

Stouffer Hotels and Resorts, a subsidiary of The Stouffer Company, a wholly-owned division of Nestle Inc., a Switzerland-based conglomerate, operates 41 hotels. Twenty-three hotels are owned or partially owned and operated, while the other 18 hotels are under management agreements. Collectively, 16,000 rooms are operated by Stouffer Hotels with total revenues in excess of $550,000,000 (1990). Some Stouffer Hotels are The Mayflower in Washington, D.C., Wailea Beach in Maui, Hawaii, Denver Concourse in Denver, Colorado, and Stanford Court in San Francisco, California.

Like most hotel corporations, Stouffer Hotels has major objectives to provide excellent service and achieve reasonable profits. This is achieved, in part, by forecasting and even reforecasting throughout the management organization. At the hotel level, forecasting is used in the preparation of the annual budget, the monthly reforecast, and the 10-day forecast. The annual budget is self-explanatory. The reforecast is management's forecast every month for the following twelve months. Included in the reforecast are occupancy percentages and revenue/expense figures down through net operating profit. The 10-day forecast is oriented to forecasting room and food and beverage sales for the next 10

Exhibit 9.12   Daily Labor Worksheet

DAILY LABOR WORKSHEET   Day:_____ Period _____

RESTAURANT NO.	**PAN DOUGH** • # PPP's _____ x .0225 = _____ • Morning Pan Batches (A.M.) _____ • Afternoon Pan Batches (P.M.) _____	**SPECIAL EVENTS/MARKETING** WK_____ WK_____ WK_____ WK_____	**MARKETING WINDOW** _____

HOUR	6	7	8	9	10	11	12	1	2	3	4	5	6	7	8	9	10	11	12	1	2	Promo $/Hrs	Total Sales/Hrs.
PROJECTED SALES	PPP Hours	Basic Open	A.M. Pan	P.M. Pan															Close All.	Disc Hrs.		
GRID HOURS (DIRECT)		2.5																					
SCHEDULED DIRECT HOURS																				▓▓		

JOB #	IN	OUT	6	7	8	9	10	11	12	1	2	3	4	5	6	7	8	9	10	11	12	1	2	3	IN	OUT	JOB #

Courtesy of Pizza Hut, Inc.

Exhibit 9.13   Personal Pan Pizza Labor Scheduling Grid

PERSONAL PAN PIZZA LABOR SCHEDULING GRID

COLUMN NUMBER	1	2	3	4	5	6	7	8	9	10	11	12	13	14	15	16
PROJECTED HOURLY NET SALES	0 TO 40	41 TO 59	60 TO 84	85 TO 115	116 TO 151	152 TO 174	175 TO 196	197 TO 237	238 TO 288	289 TO 331	332 TO 375	376 TO 436	437 TO 502	503 TO 594	595 TO 633	634 TO 673
PRODUCTION PERSON	0	1	1	1	1	1	1	1	2	2	2	2	2	2	3	3
SERVICE PERSON	1	1	2	2	2	2	3	3	3	4	4	4	4	4	4	5
REGISTER/TELEPHONE	0	0	0	0	1	1	1	1	1	1	2	2	2	3	3	3
BUS/DISHWASHER	0	0	0	0	0	0	0	1	1	1	1	1	2	2	2	2
BEVERAGE PERSON	0	0	0	0	0	0	0	0	0	0	0	1	1	1	1	1
PRODUCTION LEADER	1	1	1	1	1	1	1	1	1	1	1	1	1	1	1	1
HOST/HOSTESS	0	0	0	1	1	1	1	1	1	1	1	1	1	1	1	1
FLOOR MANAGER	0	0	0	0	0	1	1	1	1	1	1	1	1	1	1	1
TOTAL	2	3	4	5	6	7	8	9	10	11	12	13	14	15	16	17

OPENING ALLOWANCE

\# OF 6" PIZZAS PREPPED × .0225 HRS. = LUNCH PREP HOURS

Courtesy of Pizza Hut, Inc.

days to assist department heads in scheduling labor and comparing the actual figures to forecasts.

This case will focus on the sales forecasts as part of the annual budget. The sales forecasts result from a cooperative effort of the Director of Sales or Marketing, General Manager and/or Assistant General Manager, Senior Assistant Manager (Rooms Division Manager), Reservations Manager, Food and Beverage Director, and Controller, who constitute the budget committee.

First, the room sales forecast includes forecast of group business for the next 12 months. The Director of Sales/Marketing considers sales booked and tentative group sales. The definite business is reviewed and reduced by *wash factors*. This is also commonly referred to as *net* figures. These figures are developed by researching the "history" of the booked groups. As an example, if a group signed a contract to block 100 rooms on a Saturday night, but their history at previous locations showed that they only pick up 80 rooms in such situations, a 20% wash or net is subtracted from the total. That reduced figure is then blocked. This protects the hotel from holding unused rooms and allows it to maximize revenues. Other factors to consider include the type of group (association, corporate, and so forth) and the group mix (singles versus doubles).

The next area to forecast is tentative business. Considerations must be made in two areas: (1) What are the chances the business will go definite? (2) What is the wash or net factor, as discussed above?

Lastly, the most important area to consider in forecasting is *booking pace*. This means the ability to foresee how much business will book in the future based on current marketing conditions. To do this, one must analyze historical data. This involves comparing how much business was on the books in a given month or year for a specific time and following the *pick-up* or building of business to the actual date. As an example, if we were doing a forecast in June for December, we would:

1. Go to the previous June and see how much business was already on the books for December.

2. Take December's actual figures at the close of December and subtract the figure found in #1 from it. This provides the booking pace for that month.

3. Use this information in our current year projection and forecast.

Tracking booking pace month-to-month shows patterns in booking pressure which is also helpful.

The Reservations Manager estimates the expected non-group business. Consistent in this forecast are historical data and confirmed reservations. For Reservations Managers to have valid information, they compile anywhere from three to five years of experience showing, by month, how many reservations were booked for future months and how many rooms actually sold for those months. This building process will establish a *lead time factor* which then can be used in developing the pattern of historical information versus actual. This same timing process is followed with the groups so that as the budgeted year approaches, you can compare group room nights booked for the future year versus prior years' results which provides a trend as to whether the hotel is on target or not. In addition to the overall patterns by month, the Reservations Manager would have all this information by day to be able to pinpoint when the hotel will be full. The hotel can then begin developing special promotions to fill in the valley periods.

Also considered by the Reservations Manager in forecasting non-group room sales are weekend packages and any special community events scheduled on particular weekends.

It is important to be aware of local conditions that affect hotel occupancy. These can be city-wide conventions, sporting events, concerts, and any number of other possibilities. Once this is known, the supply/demand principles of rate management can be applied. A calendar of events would be maintained showing special events, group activities, conventions, and so forth to help pinpoint times of potential high occupancy.

The occupancy percentage and average rates are developed by the Director of Sales/Marketing and the Reservations Manager. This is done by scheduling all groups that are definite and tentative, laying in the pick-up groups required and then using historical information for the average number of individual travelers for each day. This base gives the hotel the estimated daily occupancy and average transient rate.

This forecast is compared to the occupancy percentages and average rates which have been established by the General Manager and approved by the Vice President—Operations. Occupancy and average rates are developed from prior years, current economic conditions, and competition. If the numbers prepared by the Director of Sales/Marketing and the Reservations Manager differ, then a review is made of the forecast and appropriate adjustments are made.

After the initial rooms forecast is developed, it is reviewed by the budget committee. Once the room sales forecast is deemed acceptable, the food and beverage sales are forecast.

The food and beverage forecast is prepared by the Food and Beverage Manager and cost analyst based on the room sales forecast and historical information, including covers by occupancy percentage and reviewing group functions which reduce outlet use. Also, they put in the special holiday meals (for example, Thanksgiving buffet).

The food and beverage forecast consists of banquet sales and food and beverage outlet sales. The banquet sales estimates are based on confirmed bookings and business that might be picked up.

The definite banquet business is taken from the catering book. This includes both definite group business and booked local business. Pick-up in food and beverage sales is related to forecasted group room pick-up formulated by the rooms department. Average number of guests per room pick-up is multiplied by the average food and beverage banquet check projected. Banquet sales not associated with room sales should also be considered. These sales are projected based on special community events, holidays (for example, Easter, Mother's Day, Thanksgiving), plus known pick-up from historical records for weddings, birthday parties, and community events.

The food and beverage outlet managers would look at historical information as to covers by day, covers by occupied rooms, taking into consideration banquet activities to reduce the guest base where banquet functions are scheduled. A good system of guest tracking would be able to determine a base of local clientele which would be used as the first step in building the number of covers that could be expected in a food and beverage outlet. This would be done by meal period as shown in the following example.

Outlet covers are derived by meal period: breakfast, lunch, and dinner. These covers are determined based upon the number of guests in the hotel. For example, if the hotel is 80% occupied (400 rooms) on a particular day and there are 1.2 persons per occupied room, there are 480 guests in the hotel. Of these 480 guests, we've forecasted 100 will be attending a banquet breakfast, leaving 380 guests available. From past historical data, we know 30% will have breakfast in Restaurant A. (NOTE: the 30% is weighted for outside business—non-hotel guests.) Our projected number of food covers for Restaurant A, breakfast meal period is 114 (380 x 30%). The average check is determined from prior year trends, that is, last year it was $9.50 and this year prices are increased 8% to $10.26. Note that the previous night occupancies are used for calculating breakfast covers.

After the room sales and food and beverage sales are forecast, other hotel revenues such as telephone and gift shop are estimated, as well as the expenses of hotel operations. The other operated department revenues can be developed from the number of rooms occupied.

Exhibit 9.14   Hotel Room Forecast

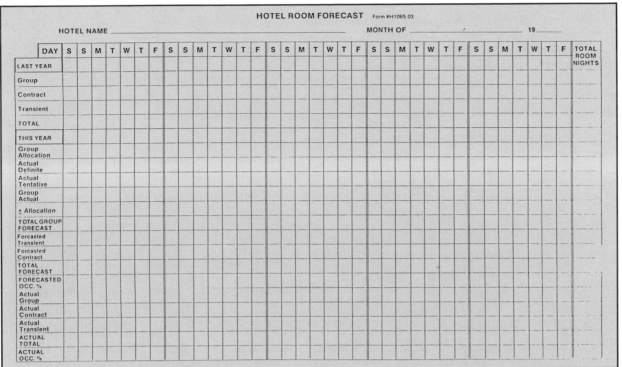

Courtesy of Stouffer Hotels and Resorts.

The hotel room forecast (Exhibit 9.14) and rooms forecast reconciliation and casualty report (Exhibit 9.15) are used as worksheets in the forecasting process. By completing data required on each of these documents, each hotel compiles a 12-month day-by-day forecast as a guideline in order to maximize room revenues and occupancy.

Computerization

Many of the forecasting methods discussed in this chapter would take a great deal of time to calculate manually. However, with the help of a computer and forecasting programs, they can be generated almost immediately. Even general software packages such as electronic spreadsheets can calculate averages and perform trend extrapolation.

Exhibit 9.16 shows how management at the Jefferson Motel forecasts future room sales using moving averages. In order to do this, management first collects historical information—the number of rooms sold and the average rate for the last three weeks' business—and this information is entered into the computer. At this point, the computer generates a forecast for the fourth week's sales by calculating the average of the same day of the week over the previous three weeks. In this case, it was estimated that 93 rooms would be sold on Monday, which is the average of 90, 95, and 93 (rounded to the nearest whole number). This information could be used for labor scheduling or for calculating the forecast of revenues. Average rate is calculated in the same fashion. The forecast of sales is the product of forecast room rate and rooms sold.

Exhibit 9.15 Rooms Forecast Reconciliation and Casualty Report

"Rooms Forecast Reconciliation and Casualty Report"

Hotel: *Solon Hotel (400)*   **Forecast:** _____

Month: *February 1985*   **Actual:** *XX* _____

CRO Status
C = Closed Out
P = Partial Available
A = All available
S = Sell Thru

Day	Date	Opening # Rooms	6 PM Arr.	GTD Arr.	Total Arr.	Due Outs	(6 PM Group Arr.)	(GTD Group Arr.)	R1 # Rooms Tonight	# CXL	% CXL	# 6 PM No-Shows	% 6 PM No-Shows	# GTD No-Shows	% GTD No-Shows	Stay Overs	Unexpected Departures	# Rooms Proj. Tonight	R2 # Rooms to Sell	E.S.P. R1 + R2	CRO Status	# Walk-ins
Sa	2/2	144	15	18	34	96	—	6	81	4	11.8	3	20.0	5	27.8	6	5	70	330	411	A	3
Su	3	73	297	106	133	70	—	51	136	4	3.0	6	22.2	3	2.8	1	4	120	280	416	A	34
Mo	4	154	14	136	150	35	—	39	269	16	10.7	—	—	4	2.9	2	2	249	151	420	A	24
Tu	5	273	19	161	180	81	—	36	372	21	11.7	2	10.5	5	3.1	6	6	344	56	428	A	38
We	6	382	12	175	187	162	—	70	407	24	13.3	5	83.3	3	1.7	7	10	372	28	435	P	6
Th	7	378	17	48	65	126	—	13	317	9	13.9	7	41.2	4	8.3	2	10	289	111	428	A	12
Fr	8	301	32	58	90	203	—	19	188	8	8.9	5	15.6	5	8.6	3	32	141	259	447	A	7
Sa	9	148	42	48	90	108	—	13	130	10	11.1	4	9.5	7	14.6	8	5	112	288	418	A	0
Su	10	112	15	99	114	104	—	53	122	4	3.5	4	26.7	2	2.0	1	2	111	289	411	A	34
Mo	11	145	26	164	190	40	—	65	295	2	1.1	2	7.7	—	—	—	6	285	115	410	A	0
Tu	12	285	12	158	170	106	—	54	349	20	11.8	2	16.7	3	1.9	2	13	313	87	436	A	28
We	13	341	11	167	178	141	—	67	378	20	11.2	4	36.4	3	1.8	4	10	345	55	433	A	14
Th	14	359	10	69	79	177	—	6	261	9	11.4	3	30.0	6	8.7	2	22	223	177	438	A	30
Fr	15	253	47	66	113	246	—	25	120	12	10.6	9	19.1	14	21.2	1	6	80	320	440	A	10
Sa	16	90	57	56	113	46	—	39	157	7	6.2	15	26.3	3	5.4	7	4	135	265	422	A	12
Su	17	147	19	64	83	101	—	50	129	5	6.0	15	23.4	2	3.1	3	11	99	301	430	A	33
Mo	18/H	132	7	135	142	92	—	76	182	6	4.2	6	85.7	2	2.2	1	4	165	235	417	A	40
Tu	19	205	9	107	116	45	—	8	276	14	12.1	4	44.4	12	11.2	2	5	243	157	433	A	30
We	20	273	12	311	323	201	—	228	385	15	4.7	2	16.7	6	1.9	3	15	362	38	423	P	20
Th	21	382	9	36	95	86	—	40	391	9	9.5	2	22.2	4	4.7	7	15	368	32	423	P	11
Fr	22	379	11	22	33	339	—	9	73	7	21.2	6	54.6	4	18.2	—	2	54	346	419	A	16
Sa	23	121	12	41	53	90	—	35	84	—	—	7	58.3	2	4.9	5	3	77	323	407	A	12
Su	24	89	17	85	102	35	—	38	156	1	1.0	6	35.3	2	2.4	—	2	145	255	411	A	3
Mo	25	148	26	122	148	24	—	14	272	21	14.2	4	15.4	5	4.1	1	3	240	160	432	A	28
Tu	26	268	19	171	190	75	—	12	383	22	11.6	2	10.5	9	5.3	4	13	341	59	442	A	41
We	27	382	19	189	208	189	—	69	401	20	9.6	4	21.1	6	3.2	15	36	350	50	451	A	36
Th	28	386	18	103	121	211	—	15	296	19	15.7	5	27.8	7	6.8	5	20	250	150	446	A	31
Fr	3/1	281	15	71	86	236	—	53	131	6	7.0	3	20.0	1	1.4	1	4	118	282	413	A	19

Courtesy of Stouffer Hotels and Resorts.

This worksheet can then be used to compare actual to forecast. For example, although 93 rooms were forecast to be sold on Monday, 95 rooms were actually sold, and management entered the actual results into the computer. When this number was input, the computer generated the variance figure between forecast and actual, and the forecast for the fifth week's rooms sold (the average of the second, third and fourth week's rooms sold). In this manner, management can enter each week's actual figures to calculate the next week's forecast. As a side effect, this also provides management with a record of performance which can be used in future periods as needed.

Exhibit 9.16   Moving Average Forecast Worksheet—Jefferson Motel

Moving Average Forecast Worksheet
Jefferson Motel

ROOMS SOLD DAY	Historical			X X X X X	Forecast Week 4	Actual Week 4	Variance	X X X X X	Forecast Week 5	Actual Week 5	Variance
------	Week 1	Week 2	Week 3								
Monday	90	95	93	X	93	95	2	X	94		
Tuesday	92	90	92	X	91	92	1	X	91		
Wednesday	99	94	95	X	96	94	−1	X	95		
Thursday	89	85	99	X	91	94	3	X	92		
Friday	51	40	44	X	45	40	−5	X	43		
Saturday	33	30	32	X	32	30	−2	X	31		
Sunday	45	50	51	X	49	52	3	X	50		

AVERAGE RATE DAY	Historical			X X X X	Forecast Week 4	Actual Week 4	Variance	X X X X	Forecast Week 5		
------	Week 1	Week 2	Week 3								
Monday	$62.50	$61.50	$63.00	X	$62.33	$61.52	($0.81)	X	$62.28		
Tuesday	62.50	65.00	64.90	X	64.13	62.89	−1.24	X	64.68		
Wednesday	65.00	65.00	65.50	X	65.17	65.70	0.53	X	65.22		
Thursday	62.50	61.00	62.50	X	62.00	62.50	0.50	X	61.83		
Friday	50.00	47.00	43.00	X	46.67	44.44	−2.23	X	45.56		
Saturday	47.80	49.00	40.00	X	45.60	41.25	−4.35	X	44.87		
Sunday	$60.00	$59.80	$62.50	X	$60.77	$65.23	$4.46	X	$61.02		

SALES INFORMATION

DAY	Forecast Week 4	Actual Week 4	Variance	X	Forecast Week 5	Actual Week 5	Variance
------				X			
Monday	$5,776.22	$5,844.40	$68.18	X	$5,826.43		
Tuesday	5,857.51	5,785.88	−71.63	X	5,892.86		
Wednesday	6,256.00	6,175.80	−80.20	X	6,196.11		
Thursday	5,642.00	5,875.00	233.00	X	5,668.06		
Friday	2,100.00	1,777.60	−322.40	X	1,958.89		
Saturday	1,444.00	1,237.50	−206.50	X	1,400.84		
Sunday	$2,957.31	$3,391.96	$434.65	X	$3,044.33		

As an extension of this worksheet, management also has the computer generate a graph of the variance between actual and forecast room sales (see Exhibit 9.17). This very quickly highlights the week's results; although the weekday sales were close to forecast, the weekend sales were significantly below forecast. This graph is used because it quickly alerts managers to potential problems. They can then take timely actions.

Management could also use the computer to generate more sophisticated forecasts. There are programs available which perform linear regression, exponential smoothing, multiple regression, and many other methods mentioned in this chapter.[6]

Exhibit 9.17   Forecast vs. Actual—Jefferson Motel

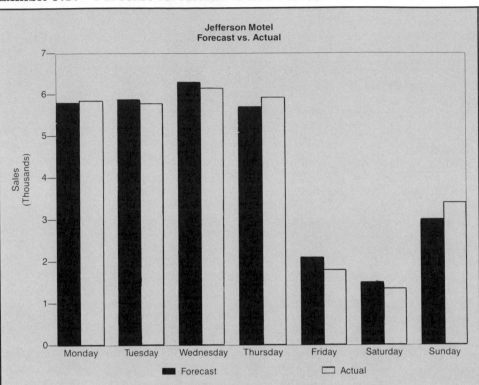

Summary

Forecasting is simply the process of estimating the levels of some future activity such as sales. After an initial sales forecast has been made, the hospitality operation must plan to ensure the desired outcome is achieved.

Forecasts may be implicit or explicit. Implicit forecasts are implied by the expectations reflected by managers' actions when no explicit forecast has been made. In this chapter, we focused on explicit forecasts, that is, on deliberate attempts to estimate levels of future activities. Explicit forecasting techniques provide managers with rational foundations for planning.

Since forecasting deals with the future, it inevitably involves uncertainty. In addition, since forecasts are made on the basis of historical data, they are predicated on the risky assumption that the past will be indicative of the future.

Patterns in existing data include trend, seasonal, and cyclical. A trend is simply the long-run projection of an activity being evaluated. Seasonal patterns exist when a series of data fluctuates according to a seasonal pattern, such as seasons of the year. Cyclical patterns represent movements along a trend line.

Forecasting methods covered in the chapter included both quantitative and qualitative approaches, with the emphasis on the former. Quantitative methods discussed included naive methods, moving averages, exponential smoothing, and regression analysis. Limitations of quantitative methods, such as scarce data and the inability to consider unforeseeable occurrences, sometimes render quantitative methods less useful. When these limitations are significant, qualitative methods may be used. The qualitative methods covered briefly in this chapter included marketing research, jury of executive opinion, sales force estimates, and the Delphi technique.

Finally, forecasting techniques used by unit-level management at three hospitality operations were presented. The three operations—Canteen Corp., Pizza Hut, Inc., and Stouffer Hotels and Resorts—were intentionally selected from three different segments of the hospitality industry: business and industry food service, commercial food service, and hotels, respectively. Although they were chosen to illustrate different applications of forecasting methods, they are not necessarily representative of their respective segments.

Endnotes

1. *Marriott Corporation Annual Report 1989*, pp. 2, 3.

2. The reader interested in pursuing forecasting approaches shown in Exhibit 9.4 which are not discussed in this chapter should see Steven C. Wheelwright and Spyros Makridakis, *Forecasting Methods and Applications* (New York: John Wiley & Sons, 1978).

3. For more information, see Steven C. Wheelwright and Spyros Makridakis, *Forecasting Methods for Management*, 3rd Ed. (New York: John Wiley & Sons, 1980).

4. $$a = \frac{\Sigma x^2 \Sigma y - \Sigma x - \Sigma xy}{n\Sigma x^2 - (\Sigma x)^2}$$

   $$b = \frac{n\Sigma xy - \Sigma x\Sigma y}{n\Sigma x^2 - (\Sigma x)^2}$$

5. The interested reader should see *Forecasting Methods for Management*.

6. For more information on the use of spreadsheet programs for forecasting, see Hugh S. McLaughlin and J. Russell Boulding, *Financial Management with Lotus 1-2-3* (New York: Prentice-Hall, 1986).

Key Terms

capture ratios
causal approaches
coefficient of correlation
coefficient of determination
cyclical pattern
exponential smoothing
moving average
multiple regression analysis

qualitative forecasting methods
quantitative forecasting methods
regression analysis
seasonal pattern
smoothing constant
time series approaches
trend pattern

Discussion Questions

1. What is the difference between implicit and explicit forecasts?

2. How do forecasting and planning differ?

3. What are the purposes and limitations of forecasting?

4. How do cyclical and seasonal patterns of data differ?

5. What are the differences between quantitative and qualitative forecasting methods?

6. How do causal forecasting methods differ from time series methods?

7. How is a moving average calculated?

8. When are exponential smoothing techniques most useful?

9. How can regression analysis be used to forecast food revenues based on occupancy percentage?

Problems

Problem 9.1

Mr. Jim Wheat, manager of the Plains Motel, has decided to forecast monthly room sales for the next three years. The monthly sales for 19X1 were as follows:

January	$194,321	July	$185,197
February	187,296	August	180,200
March	198,431	September	206,711
April	197,911	October	215,840
May	215,640	November	201,612
June	210,411	December	165,411

Jim believes that sales will increase 5% in 19X2, another 5% in 19X3, and another 6% in 19X4.

Required:

Based on the above information, prepare the three-year sales forecast by month for the Plains Motel.

Problem 9.2

Servco operates the hot lunch program at Acres Elementary School. The weekly sales forecast necessary for ordering food provisions and scheduling labor is based on a three-week moving average, that is, Monday's forecast is based on the average sales of the prior three Mondays. The forecast is modified based on a number of factors, including weather. The weather modification is that sales are expected to increase moderately as the school year progresses into cooler weather and to decrease moderately with warmer weather in the spring. In addition, rainy days result in significant increases in sales.

The sales for weeks 4 through 6 were as follows:

	Week 4	Week 5	Week 6
Monday	$450	$460	$475
Tuesday	420	435	440
Wednesday	440	438	520
Thursday	430	445	450
Friday	410	420	435

Required:

Based on the above results, answer the following questions:

1. What type of weather trend do the above figures suggest? Why?
2. Which day did it appear to rain?

Problem 9.3

This problem is a continuation of Problem 9.2. Karin Smith, manager of Servco, desires assistance in preparing the sales forecast for Week 7. To prepare the weekly sales forecast, the days' sales of the prior three weeks are averaged and modified by $\pm\$20$ for expected weather changes. In addition, if a rainy day is expected, an additional $70 of sales is expected.

Required:

Prepare the weekly sales forecast by day for Week 7. Assume that the winter season is approaching, that is, it is expected that Week 7 will be cooler than Week 6. Further, use $450 for sales for Wednesday of Week 6 in place of actual sales of $520. Finally, assume that Monday of Week 7 is expected to be a rainy day.

Problem 9.4

Part I

The Westsider has asked for your assistance in forecasting its room sales and food service sales. To forecast room sales for the week of May 18–24 (Week 4), it considers its group reservations and uses a moving average of the non-group hotel guests rooms sold for the prior three weeks. This moving average then is increased by 2%. Data for the past three weeks are as follows:

| | Non-Group Hotel Guests Rooms | | | Week 4 | | |
	Week 1	Week 2	Week 3	Group Reserva- tions	Non- Group Guests	Total
Sunday	150	160	164	215	_____	_____
Monday	250	270	290	240	_____	_____
Tuesday	245	275	305	250	_____	_____
Wednesday	250	270	260	240	_____	_____
Thursday	240	240	249	200	_____	_____
Friday	120	110	130	50	_____	_____
Saturday	80	90	100	60	_____	_____

Required:

Complete the two right columns above. Round your forecast to the nearest whole number.

Part II

To forecast its food service breakfast sales, the Westsider uses the following formula:

$$y = a + bx_1 + cx_2$$

where x_1 = hotel guests

x_2 = hotel guests at the economy motel adjacent to the Westsider

a = non-hotel (Westsider and the economy motel) guests eating breakfast

b = percentage of hotel guests expected to eat breakfast

c = percentage of economy motel guests that are expected to eat at the Westsider

Additional information is as follows:

1. x_2 = 80
2. b = .8
3. c = .3
4. a = 20

Required:

Forecast breakfast sales for Monday.

Problem 9.5

The Wilderness Inn uses the exponential smoothing method presented in this chapter to forecast total weekly sales. Darlene Jones, the manager, has supplied you with past forecasts and actual sales as follows:

	Forecast	Actual Sales
Week 1	$10,400	$12,400
Week 2	10,800	11,000
Week 3	10,840	10,940
Week 4	10,860	11,360
Week 5	10,960	10,560
Week 6	10,880	11,580

Required:

1. Based on the above information, what is the smoothing constant?

2. Using the smoothing constant (determined in 1), forecast sales for Week 7.

3. Assuming the smoothing constant is .5, what would be the forecasted sales for Week 7?

Problem 9.6

The Evergreen Hotel, a 200-room lodging facility, uses regression analysis to forecast dining room meals. Larry Spruce, the manager, has indicated the regression equations used are as follows:

$$y = 50 + .42x \text{ (breakfast)}$$
$$y = 200 + .21x \text{ (lunch)}$$
$$y = 450 + .35x \text{ (dinner)}$$

where y equals forecasted meals
x equals the number of hotel guests

Further, the average check in the hotel's dining room is expected to be as follows:

breakfast:	$3.25
lunch:	$6.50
dinner:	$12.95

Required:

Forecast daily sales by meal period when the occupancy percentage is expected to be 85% (all rooms are available for sale) and the average occupancy per room is expected to be 1.58.

Problem 9.7

The Brunner forecasts its daily room sales based on the moving average of the prior three weeks' daily sales. Adjustments are made for holidays and seasonal trends as follows:

• If a holiday occurred during the prior three weeks, the day containing the holiday is adjusted by multiplying it by 1.67.

• If a holiday occurs during the forecast week, the forecasted daily sales based on the moving average are reduced by 40%.

• In estimating daily sales for the month of June, the moving average is adjusted upward by 3%.

Room sales for the prior three weeks were as follows:

	May 25–31	June 1–7	June 8–14	June 15–21
Sunday	160	165	168	_____
Monday	180 (holiday)	310	312	_____
Tuesday	300	315	318	_____
Wednesday	310	305	315	_____
Thursday	320	310	315	_____
Friday	180	185	190	_____
Saturday	170	174	177	_____

Required:

Calculate the expected room sales for the week of June 15–21. Round your answer to the nearest whole room. Show all of your work.

Problem 9.8

The Grand Hotel has 300 rooms and is expected to have a 90% occupancy for Monday through Thursday nights, June 16–19, and 50% occupancy the remaining nights of the week. The average occupancy per room of the Grand Hotel is 1.6 on weekends (Friday–Sunday) and 1.4 on weekdays. The expected luncheon average prices are $4.95 for weekdays and $5.95 for weekends. The regression equations to estimate luncheon covers are as follows:

lunch covers for weekdays = $50 + .6(x_1) + .1(x_2)$

lunch covers for weekend days = $150 + .4(x_1) + .2(x_2)$

x_1 = number of lodging guests at the Grand Hotel

x_2 = number of lodging guests at the Fairview Inn, a rooms-only lodging property

The projected room sales and average occupancy for the Fairview Inn for June 15–21 are as follows:

		Room Sales	Average Occupancy/Room
June 15	Sunday	60	1.2
June 16	Monday	80	1.1
June 17	Tuesday	80	1.05
June 18	Wednesday	80	1.05
June 19	Thursday	80	1.1
June 20	Friday	40	1.6
June 21	Saturday	30	2.0

Required:

Forecast the Grand Hotel's luncheon sales in dollars and covers for each day for June 15–21.

Problem 9.9

The Merry Motel uses the moving average approach to forecast its rooms sales for each week and linear regression for forecasting its food sales. The moving average approach utilizes the most recent five weeks of actual data. An adjustment is made for holidays as follows:

- If the holiday occurred during the prior five weeks, the week containing the holiday is adjusted by multiplying it by 110%.

- If the holiday occurs during the forecast week, the forecasted estimate based on the moving average is reduced by 10%.

The rooms sold for the five preceding weeks were as follows:

	Rooms Budgeted	Rooms Sold	Holidays
May 24–31	660	640	Memorial Day May 30
June 1–7	710	700	—
June 8–14	720	710	—
June 15–21	710	720	—
June 22–28	715	710	—
June 29–July 5	?	?	July 4

The average occupancy per room sold is expected to be 1.6 for June 29–July 5.

The regression equations used to forecast the number of meals to be sold are as follows:

Breakfast covers = 50 + .8(number of hotel room guests)
Lunch covers = 150 + .2(number of hotel room guests)
Dinner covers = 60 + .6(number of hotel room guests)

Required:

1. Calculate the expected number of rooms to be sold for the week of June 29–July 5.
2. Calculate the number of meals to be sold for breakfast, lunch, and dinner for the week of June 29–July 5.

Problem 9.10

The Sunset Inn's short-term sales forecast is for seven days. The forecast is prepared on a Friday for the upcoming week (week 5).

The rooms forecast uses reservations to date, and an estimate is made for additional reservations and walk-ins. The forecast for breakfast is a function of the prior night's available house guests, which is the house count less catered breakfast functions.

On Friday the 14th, the reservations for the following week are as follows:

	Group Reservations	Non-Group Reservations
Sunday	50	50
Monday	50	150
Tuesday	100	140
Wednesday	100	130
Thursday	100	120
Friday	20	20
Saturday	20	10

The group business is generally booked at least three weeks in advance with virtually no change. However, business reservations are booked only a few days in advance. Therefore, the additional room sales for non-group reservations are estimated by increasing the non-group reservations by 15% for Sunday, 20% for Monday, 25% for Tuesday, and so on for the remainder of the week.

The forecast for walk-ins is based on a three week moving average for the day to be forecast. Assume that the week to be forecast is Week 5.

	Week 1	Week 2	Week 3	Week 4
Sunday	15	16	14	15
Monday	12	13	11	9
Tuesday	10	14	12	16
Wednesday	8	10	8	12
Thursday	12	14	14	14
Friday	10	11	13	15
Saturday	12	3	5	7

The average daily rate expected for the forecast week is as follows:

	Group	Non-Group	Walk-Ins
Monday–Thursday	$60	$80	$85
Friday–Sunday	40	50	50

The restaurant food forecast for breakfast uses the following equation:

$$bf = a + b(ahg)$$

where bf = forecasted breakfast covers
a = non-hotel guests
b = percentage of available hotel guests dining
ahg = available hotel guests

The breakfast function sheet for the forecast week shows catered events for the following number of hotel guests:

Sunday	50
Monday	100
Tuesday	120
Wednesday	120
Thursday	120
Friday	30
Saturday	30

The number of non-hotel guests expected to eat breakfast each day at the Sunset Inn is estimated as follows:

Monday–Friday	40 each day
Saturday	20
Sunday	10

The percentage of available hotel guests expected to eat breakfast each day and the average food service check for breakfast are as follows:

	% of AHG	Average Food Service Check
Sunday	60%	$4.95
Monday	60%	$4.25
Tuesday	50%	$4.20
Wednesday	50%	$4.25
Thursday	50%	$4.25
Friday	40%	$4.25
Saturday	40%	$5.25

Required:

1. Prepare the rooms sales forecast for Week 5 by day, showing both expected number of room sales and dollar sales by each market segment; that is, group, non-group, and walk-ins.

2. Prepare the breakfast forecast for Week 5 to include both covers and sales dollars by day. For simplicity, assume one person per reservation and per walk-in. Further assume that the number of hotel guests on the Saturday before the Sunday for which we are forecasting is 100.

Supplemental Reading

The ability to forecast, with a reasonable degree of accuracy, the number of rooms that may be occupied and the number of guests to be served in the dining rooms of a hotel for a future period is an important aspect of management. Those two revenue sources make up at least 75 percent to 80 percent of the total, and directly influence a very significant portion of the variable cost of operations. In this article, I will illustrate two methods used in making forecasts: analysis of a time series and regression analysis. Each provides a systematic and disciplined approach to forecasting.

These methods are based upon the generally accepted concept that what has occurred previously under similar circumstances is the best basis for a forecast, provided it is modified by current events and good judgment. The techniques will be used to analyze information through December, 1980 and to forecast results for January-June, 1981. Since the actual results for that period are known, the accuracy of the forecast can be tested.

FORECASTING
Rooms Occupancy and Food Covers by Analyzing Trends

by John D. Lesure, CPA, Laventhol & Horwath

Editor's Note: *This article is sponsored by AH&MA's Financial Management Committee. It is based on an actual experience in forecasting occupancy and covers at a 352-room property operated by a committee member's company. Part I, on forecasting rooms occupancy, appears in this issue; part II, on forecasting covers, in the January 1982 issue.*

Part One

A time series is a set of numbers representing the measurement of activity during time intervals, normally equal in duration. The number of rooms occupied monthly since 1976 in the Suburban Motor Inn shown in Illustration 1 is a time series. This table contains valuable information for the analyst. Since the property contains 352 rooms, it is possible to compute monthly percentages of occupancy from the data and compare those common-sized figures. This can be done by means of a chart (Illustration 2), which shows that there are very wide month-to-month variations. Observation of the numbers and a few calculations also reveals other information:

1. The arithmetic mean (average) of the number of rooms occupied monthly from January, 1976 to May, 1981 was 8,058 or 75.2 percent of rooms available.
2. During the 5-year period, March and June were consistently the best months, with April also showing above average occupancy.

3. The weakest month has been December and in November there has consistently been a sharp drop from the previous month.
4. There are irregular variations. For example, in 1978, rooms occupied in February exceeded the total for January; also, on October 1978, the number fell below the mean for that year although it was well above in 1979 and 1980.
5. The monthly mean of rooms occupied rose in 1977 and 1978 and then dropped in 1979 and 1980.

Thus, the time series shows the following variations for analysis:

1. A trend or tendency to go either up or down over a long range period.
2. Month-to-month differences, some quite sharp, caused by fluctuations in travel patterns and demand, generally called seasonal variations.
3. Irregular surges that may be caused by a variety of outside influences including but not limited to, the economy, gasoline shortages, strikes and bad weather.

By analyzing these factors, we create a basis for forecasting.

Time Series Rooms Occupied Monthly
1976–1981

	1976	1977	1978	1979	1980	TOTAL 1976–1980	1981
January	8,075	8,402	8,555	8,249	7,889	41,170	7,344
February	8,003	8,240	8,870	8,732	8,368	42,213	8,220
March	8,555	9,068	9,166	9,428	9,024	45,241	9,101
April	8,226	8,469	9,039	8,987	8,490	43,211	8,300
May	8,097	8,424	8,697	8,468	8,086	41,772	8,479
June	8,543	8,965	9,082	8,670	8,406	43,666	8,681
July	8,249	8,664	8,642	7,933	7,824	41,312	
August	8,097	8,500	8,664	8,359	8,031	41,651	
September	7,392	7,688	7,931	7,793	7,476	37,780	
October	7,889	8,282	8,271	8,424	8,108	40,974	
November	6,336	6,970	7,054	6,801	6,716	33,877	
December	5,849	6,023	6,034	5,663	5,412	28,981	
TOTAL	93,311	97,695	100,005	97,507	93,830	482,348	50,125
MEAN	7,776	8,141	8,334	8,126	7,819	8,039	8,354

Analysis of the Time Series: Trend

If you hold a ruler on the high or low points of the monthly occupancy ("actual" line) in the chart (Illustration 2) you can see the downward trend. However, the very wide monthly fluctuations tend to obscure the overall tendency, so we prepare a moving average in order to clarify the direction. The "moving average" line on the chart is the moving average percentage of occupancy for the period January, 1979 to May, 1981, and it shows clearly the downward trend in occupancy. Because each point is the arithmetic mean of the occupancies for the previous 12 months, it is called a 12-month moving average. The period can be any suitable length; a 12-month period was selected as being the one that most closely fits the cycles of business in the lodging industry. The 12 month moving average of a series of numbers XI, X2, X3 is obtained by the formula:

$$\frac{X_1 + X_2 \ldots X_{12,}}{12}$$

$$\frac{X_2 + X_3 \ldots X_{13,}}{12}$$

$$\frac{X_3 + X_4 \ldots X_{14,} \ldots}{12}$$

This simply means that the figures for the first 12 months are added and divided by 12 to obtain the starting point. Then as each new monthly figure is added, the occupancy for the same month of the previous year is dropped, and the total divided by 12 to obtain the next mean. The process is continued through the entire series. Illustration 3 shows the 12-month moving average (mean) number of rooms occupied for the period January, 1977 through May, 1981. Since the first 12 months are used to obtain the starting point, the data are lost.

It is clear from the numbers that the trend has been generally downward since January, 1979.

Analysis of the Time Series: Seasonal Index

The seasonal fluctuations can best be illustrated by comparisons with the monthly number of rooms occupied for each year. For example, in 1976 the mean was 7,776 and the number of rooms occupied monthly ranged from only 5,849 in December (25 percent less) to 8,555 in March (10 percent more). Only in October was the number really close to the mean, 1.5 percent more.

A seasonal index expresses the relationship between the number of rooms occupied in one

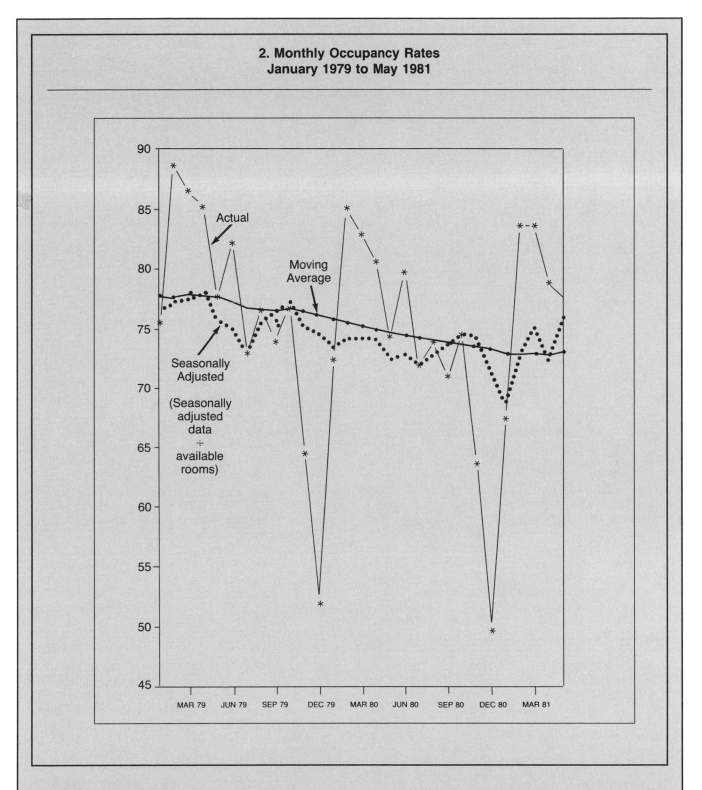

**2. Monthly Occupancy Rates
January 1979 to May 1981**

Actual

Moving
Average

Seasonally
Adjusted

(Seasonally
adjusted
data
÷
available
rooms)

MAR 79   JUN 79   SEP 79   DEC 79   MAR 80   JUN 80   SEP 80   DEC 80   MAR 81

month and the monthly mean for the year. It may be computed in several ways, and Illustration 4 shows one way which consists of the following steps:

1. The number of occupied rooms each month is divided by the arithmetic mean for the year and the ratio is entered in the table. (For example, 8,075 rooms

	1976	1977	1978	1979	1980	1981
			3. Twelve-Month Moving Average			
			Rooms Occupied			
January		7,803	8,154	8,308	8,096	7,774
February		7,823	8,207	8,297	8,065	7,761
March		7,866	8,215	8,319	8,032	7,768
April		7,886	8,262	8,314	7,990	7,752
May		7,913	8,285	8,295	7,958	7,785
June		7,948	8,295	8,261	7,936	7,808
July		7,983	8,293	8,202	7,927	
August		8,017	8,307	8,176	7,900	
September		8,041	8,327	8,165	7,874	
October		8,074	8,326	8,178	7,847	
November		8,127	8,333	8,157	7,840	
December	7,776	8,141	8,334	8,126	7,819	

occupied in January, 1976 divided by the mean of 7,776 equals 1.038.)

2. The arithmetic mean for each month is obtained by adding the ratios for that month for each year and dividing by 5. (i.e. the 5 years considered 1976-1980)

3. Minor adjustments are made to the means for each month so that they total 12.000.

The result of these calculations is a list of monthly ratios that enable us to estimate the number of occupied rooms for a month, if we can forecast the monthly mean for the year. These ratios also enable us to perform another calculation that reveals the cyclical or irregular increases and decreases in monthly occupancy brought about by outside influences. Using the ratios we can "deseasonalize" the original time series leaving numbers that are "seasonally adjusted." In other words, the monthly number of rooms that we would expect to be occupied if there was no seasonal influence. Illustration 5 shows the adjusted data. The number of occupied rooms for each month from January, 1976 to May, 1981 has been divided by the appropriate monthly mean.

(Example: January 1976 = $\frac{8,075}{1.024}$ = 7,886)

Analysis of Time Series: Irregular Index

It is apparent from the table (Illustration 5)

that there is another factor that influences the activity besides the trend and the seasonal changes in demand. This can also be seen in the chart (Illustration 2) by the way the "seasonally adjusted" line moves above and below the trend line, although it follows the generally downward tendency of that line. By removing the seasonal fluctuations from the occupancy ("actual" line), we have smoothed out the sharp fluctuations; if we also remove the trend ("moving average" line) we will have only the irregular increases and decreases left. That is the next step in our analysis and it provides the numbers in the table, Illustration 6.

In order to determine whether or not there are discernable cycles in the irregular increases and decreases, the variances above and below zero are plotted. The result is shown in Illustration 7. By studying the chart and ignoring the minor month-to-month fluctuations, we can discern a cycle that reached a peak in July, 1977, dropped to a low in July, 1979 and has begun to return to reach a point above zero, possibly by July, 1981. It is also apparent that predicting the month-to-month fluctuations would be virtually impossible. However, how important is this index in making a forecast?

In Illustration 6 the arithmetic mean of the monthly irregularities has been computed and in only one case does the ratio show a variation of as much as 1 percent—for December the mean is .989 or −1.1 percent. Further analysis of the chart (Illustration 7) shows that in 3 instances the variance exceeded 5 percent (which could be

4. Seasonal Index

| | \nRatio of Monthly Occupied Rooms To Annual Means | | | | | Monthly |
	1976	1977	1978	1979	1980	Mean
January	1.038	1.032	1.027	1.015	1.009	1.024
February	1.029	1.012	1.064	1.075	1.070	1.050
March	1.100	1.114	1.100	1.160	1.154	1.126
April	1.058	1.040	1.085	1.106	1.086	1.075
May	1.041	1.035	1.044	1.042	1.034	1.039
June	1.099	1.101	1.090	1.067	1.075	1.086
July	1.061	1.064	1.037	976	1.001	1.028
August	1.041	1.044	1.040	1.029	1.027	1.036
September	.951	.944	.952	.959	.956	.952
October	1.015	1.017	.992	1.037	1.037	1.020
November	.815	.856	.846	.837	.859	.843
December	.752	.740	.724	.697	.692	.721

5. Seasonally Adjusted Data
Monthly Occupied Rooms ÷ Seasonal Index (Monthly Mean)

	1976	1977	1978	1979	1980	1981
January	7,886	8,205	8,354	8,056	7,704	7,172
February	7,622	7,848	8,448	8,316	7,970	7,829
March	7,598	8,053	8,140	8,373	8,014	8,083
April	7,652	7,878	8,408	8,360	7,898	7,721
May	7,793	8,108	8,371	8,150	7,782	8,161
June	7,866	8,255	8,363	7,983	7,740	7,994
July	8,024	8,428	8,407	7,717	7,611	
August	7,816	8,205	8,363	8,069	7,752	
September	7,765	8,076	8,331	8,186	7,853	
October	7,734	8,120	8,109	8,259	7,949	
November	7,516	8,268	8,368	8,068	7,976	
December	8,112	8,354	8,369	7,854	7,506	

significant), but that a majority of the points are within 2.5 percent (33 out of 48). In short, the following conclusions can be drawn:

1. In addition to a long-range trend and regular seasonal fluctuations, there is an irregular or cyclical variation.
2. Except that the current tendency of the index shown in Illustration 7 is upward, there is no readily apparent basis for estimating it, other than analysis of a much more extended time series.

4. Although allowance for the irregular variation can be made by using the mean of the monthly ratios for the past 4 years, we can expect fluctuations of as much as 5 percent. However, the chances are better than 2 out of 3 that the variation will not exceed + or 2.5 percent.

We are now in a position to make forecasts of the number of rooms occupied for January through June, 1981 based on the following formula:

6. Computation of Irregular or Cyclical Index

Ratio of Seasonally Adjusted Data to Trend

	1976	1977	1978	1979	1980	Mean
January		1.052	1.025	.970	.952	.999
February		1.003	1.029	1.002	.988	1.006
March		1.024	.991	1.006	.998	1.005
April		.999	1.018	1.006	.988	1.003
May		1.025	1.010	.983	.978	.999
June		1.039	1.008	.966	.975	.997
July		1.056	1.014	.941	.960	.993
August		1.023	1.007	.987	.981	1.000
September		1.004	1.000	1.003	.997	1.001
October		1.006	.974	1.010	1.013	1.001
November		1.017	1.004	.989	1.016	1.007
December	1.043	1.026	1.004	.967	.960	.989

7. Cyclical Variations after "Deseasonalized" Numbers are Divided by Trend

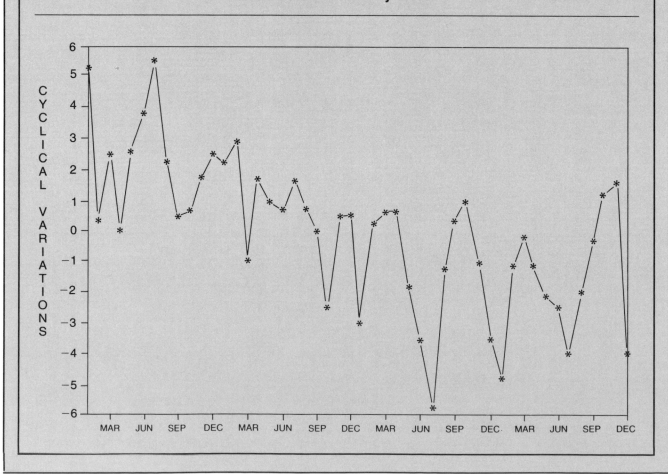

8. Forecast of Rooms Occupied

Month	Trend	×	Seasonal Index	×	Cyclical Index	=	Forecast	Actual	Percentage Variance
January 1981	7,819		1.024		.999		7,999	7,344	8.9 %
February	7,774		1.050		1.006		8,212	8,220	(.1)
March	7,761		1.126		1.005		8,783	9,101	(3.5)
April	7,768		1.075		1.003		8,376	8,300	.9
May	7,752		1.039		.999		8,046	8,479	(5.1)
June	7,785		1.086		.997		8,429	8,681	(2.9)
Total—6 Months							49,845	50,125	(.6)%

Estimate = T (Trend) x S (Seasonal index)
x C (Cyclical or Irregular index)

The trend figure is the most recent point in the 12-month moving average; for January, 1981 that would be December, 1980: 7,819 (Illustration 3). The seasonal index for January is 1.024 (Illustration 4), and the cyclical index is the arithmetic mean for January, .999 (Illustration 6). The appropriate numbers are attained from the tables for the other months and the forecast and comparison with the actual results are shown in Illustration 8. The month-to-month variances are compared with the actual cyclical variations in the following table, together with some explanations for the fluctuations:

Month	Variance in Forecast	Cyclical Variation	Possible Explanation
January, 1981	+8.9	−7.7	Severe storm
February	−.1	+.9	Trips delayed from January
March	−3.5	+4.1	Economic recovery?
April	+.9	−.4	Easter?
May	−5.1	+4.8	Group Business
June	×2.9	+2.4	Lower gasoline prices; supply plentiful

In each case, the variance in the forecast can be nearly completely explained by the cyclical variation and the importance of that index is apparent. Although the estimates are within acceptable limits of the actual results, a much more extensive analysis as a basis for establishing a reliable cyclical index might be justified.

Part Two

In the November issue, I illustrated the forecasting of rooms occupancy by the analysis of a time series (the previous five years) at a 352-room hotel. On the following pages, I illustrate food cover forecasting at the same hotel.

The method used in the food cover forecast is a less time-consuming technique. It is known as linear regression analysis, and relies not only on past experience but assumes a continuing relationship between two variables:

1. number of persons served in the dining rooms (excluding banquets) and
2. number of guests.

Illustration 1 shows the number of persons served in the dining rooms (excluding banquets) and the number of room guests at the 352-room hotel in our case study. Statistics used are for 1979 and 1980.

The Scatter Diagram

In order to determine if there is a relationship between the variables, we prepare a visual presentation called a scatter diagram (Illustration 2). The number of room guests is shown on the X or horizontal axis of the chart and the number of persons served is shown on the Y or vertical axis.

For each monthly relationship we have made a point on the chart. For example, in January 1979 we find the point on the X axis where the number of guests is 11,425 and the point on the Y axis where the number of persons served is 10,125. We then place a point on the chart where a line drawn horizontally from point Y (10,125) will intersect a line drawn vertically from point X (11,425). The same procedure is followed for each pair of variables until all 24 data points have been entered.

It is now apparent that as the number of room guests increases (i.e. moves to the right) the number of persons served also increases (moves upward). Since the points appear to run in a line, the relationship is called linear, and since the number of persons served increases as the number of guests increases, the relationship or correlation is positive. If one variable declined as the other increased, it would be a negative correlation.

The Least Square Line

In order for the chart to be useful, a line must be drawn that comes closest to each of the points in the diagram. That could be done visually by moving a straight edge around on the diagram until there are approximately as many points to the left and above the line as there are to the right and below. However, there is a formula that will enable us to determine where the line should be

---

1. Number of Room Guests and Number of Persons Served in Dining Rooms (Excluding Banquets)

	1979		1980	
	Room Guests	Persons Served In Dining Rooms	Room Guests	Persons Served In Dining Rooms
JANUARY	11,425	10,125	10,518	10,317
FEBRUARY	12,191	10,707	11,402	10,206
MARCH	13,294	11,545	12,368	10,721
APRIL	12,595	11,014	12,126	12,134
MAY	11,733	10,389	11,206	9,905
JUNE	12,093	10,632	12,396	10,668
JULY	10,925	9,745	11,182	9,459
AUGUST	11,600	10,258	11,461	9,113
SEPTEMBER	10,703	9,576	9,846	8,304
OCTOBER	11,703	10,336	10,361	8,825
NOVEMBER	9,130	8,380	9,156	8,811
DECEMBER	7,326	7,009	6,907	6,822

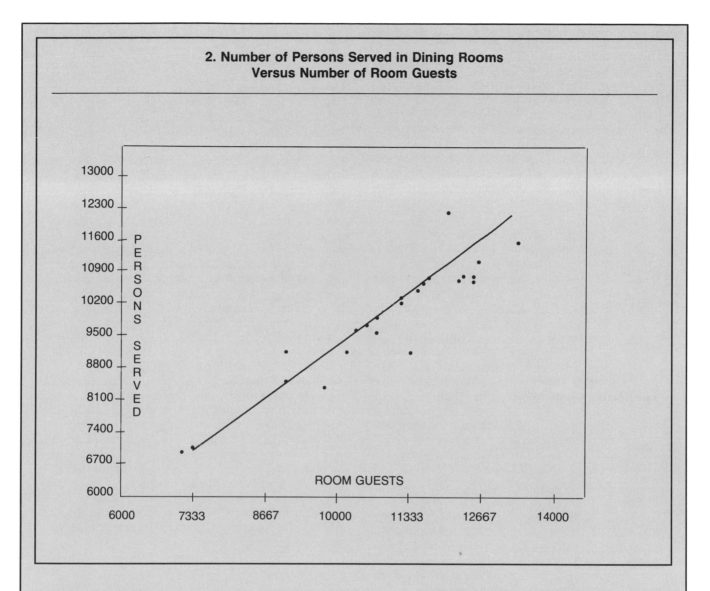

**2. Number of Persons Served in Dining Rooms
Versus Number of Room Guests**

drawn. The formula is based on the concept that the line of "best fit" (i.e. the one coming closest to each point) is the one for which the sum of the squares of all of the distances from the points to the line (called deviations) is the lowest. The distances are squared because the square of a negative deviation (one below and to the right) is a positive number. That line is referred to as the least square line and is determined by the formula:

$$Y = A + B X$$

In our example,

Y = number of persons served in the dining room

A = number of persons served who are not registered in the hotel

B = change in number of persons served for each increase in number of room guests

X = number of room guests

Since we are using one variable (X) to determine another (Y), this is called regression analysis and most programmable calculators have a standard program for a linear regression. We therefore enter the 24 pairs of variables in a calculator which solves the problem as follows:

Y (persons served) = 1,438 + .76 times
X (room guests)

This means that in 1979 and 1980, the number of persons served monthly in the dining rooms consisted of 1,438 non-registered guests plus .76 persons served for each room guest, or stated another way, 76 percent of the room guests had one meal. If we assume that the same relationship will continue in 1981, we can use that formula to estimate the number of persons served each month based upon a forecast of room guests.

The calculator and the linear regression program gives us the following information on the reliability of the relationship between the variables:

- The **coefficient of correlation**, which is the measure of the relationship between the variables is +.93. If all of the points on the scatter diagram fell on the line, the correlation coefficient would be +1 since the relationship is positive. Our "fit" of .93 is very close.
- The **coefficient of determination** is +.86. This is the square of .93 and it represents the extent to which changes in one variable (in this case number of room guests) explain changes in the other (number of persons served). In other words, 86 percent of the variations in the number of persons served in 1979 and 1980 can be explained by changes in the number of room guests during the period.

Since both coefficients are quite high on a scale of 0 to +1, we are confident that the relationship between the variables is a good one, and that the formula can be used in forecasting. We can prove this by testing the accuracy of the formula. We can substitute actual figures from our case study hotel for X (number of room guests in the formula), solve for Y (number of persons served), and see how close the number obtained comes to the actual figures.

The number of room guests at our case study hotel in February 1980 was 11,402. Assume we do not know the actual number of persons served in the dining rooms. What is Y?

$$Y = 1{,}438 + .76 \times 11{,}402$$
$$Y = 10{,}034$$

The actual number of persons served during this month was 10,206. Using the formula, we are able to obtain a forecast for the number of persons served—10,034—that is 99% of the number actual served, for a variation of −.1, proof that the least square line can be used as a basis for estimating.

Using the Formula

Using the least square line is somewhat tedious and only approximate. However, the formula can be used to estimate the number of persons served if we first estimate the number of room guests. We have previously estimated the number of rooms occupied, and we can convert that to the number of guests. In order to do so we need an index which is the ratio of the number of guests for each month divided by the number of rooms occupied for that month. This is also based on past performance and the result of the compilation is shown in Illustration 3. For each month, the total number of guests for the five years 1976-1980 has been divided by the total number of rooms occupied during the same period that was shown in Illustration I in Part I. (November issue)

We can now prepare a forecast for the months of January-June, 1981, based upon our estimates of the number of rooms occupied. The forecast of the number of rooms occupied is first multiplied by the appropriate ratio of guests to rooms and the number of guests is then substituted for X in the formula: $Y = 1{,}438 + .76$ times X in order to compute the number of persons served. The results are shown in Illustration 4 together with the actual number of persons served and the variances. Once again our estimate for the 6 months is quite accurate, although the monthly variances, while tolerable, range up to 8.5 percent.

Conclusions

The detailed analysis of the fluctuations in the demand for rooms and in the number of persons served in the dining rooms provides a basis for estimates of activity in future periods. The basic formulas are reasonably reliable but experience may dictate the use of additional factors. For example, more emphasis might be placed on current trends and market conditions. The results are only as reliable as the data on which they are based and the care with which the information is used. Reliable estimates help department heads plan the use of resources to meet customer demands. However, no formula can substitute for experienced judgment and forecasts should always be subject to the adjustments dictated by changing trends and other circumstances.

3. Number of Room Guests and Ratio of Guests to Rooms Occupied

	1976	1977	1978	1979	1980	Total	Ratio To Rooms Occupied
January	11,150	11,668	11,910	11,425	10,518	56,671	1.3765
February	11,035	11,411	12,410	12,191	11,402	58,449	1.3846
March	11,910	12,724	12,879	13,294	12,368	63,175	1.3964
April	11,389	11,774	12,678	12,595	12,126	60,562	1.4015
May	11,184	11,703	12,135	11,773	11,206	58,001	1.3885
June	11,891	12,560	12,746	12,093	12,396	61,686	1.4127
July	11,425	12,083	12,048	10,925	11,182	57,663	1.3958
August	11,184	11,823	12,083	11,600	11,461	58,151	1.3961
September	10,067	10,536	10,921	10,703	9,846	52,073	1.3603
October	10,855	11,478	11,460	11,703	10,361	55,857	1.3632
November	8,393	9,398	9,531	9,130	9,156	45,608	1.3463
December	7,621	7,897	7,915	7,326	6,907	37,666	1.2997

4. Forecast of Number of Persons Served Compared with Actual

	Rooms Occupied*	Ratio Of Guests	Number Of Guests	Number Of Persons Served** Forecast	Actual	Variance
January, 1981	7,999	1.3765	11,011	9,806	9,035	+8.5%
February	8,212	1.3846	11,371	10,080	10,090	− .1
March	8,783	1.3964	12,265	10,759	11,151	−3.5
April	8,376	1.4015	11,739	10,360	10,186	+1.7
May	8,046	1.3885	11,172	9,929	10,402	−4.6
June	8,429	1.4127	11,908	10,488	10,525	− .4
Total 6 Months				61,422	61,389	− .1%

*From Illustration 8, November issue.
**In main dining room and coffee shop. Does not include banquets.

10 Operations Budgeting

Every rational manager plans for the future. Some plans are formal and others are informal. Budgets are formal plans reduced to dollars. Budgets provide answers to many questions including the following:

1. What are the forecasted revenues for the month?

2. What is the budgeted labor for the year?

3. How many rooms are expected to be sold during any given month, and what is the expected average room rate?

4. What is the budgeted telephone department operating income for the month?

5. What is the estimated depreciation for the year?

6. How close were actual food and beverage revenues to the budgeted amounts for the month?

7. What is the projected net income for the year?

This chapter is divided into two major sections. The first section investigates reasons for budgeting, the process of preparing the operations budget, and the idea of budgeting horizons. The second section focuses on budgetary control and on how hospitality operations use budget reports in the budgetary control process. The Sands Motel, a hypothetical small lodging operation, is used to illustrate both budget preparation and control.

Types of Budgets

Hospitality operations prepare several types of budgets. The **operations budget**, the topic of this chapter, is also referred to as the revenue and expense budget, because it includes management's plans for generating revenues and incurring expenses for a given period. The operations budget includes not only operated department budgets (budgets for rooms, food and beverage, telephone, and other profit centers), but also budgets for service centers such as marketing, accounting, and human resources. In addition, the operations budget includes the planned expenses for depreciation, interest expense, and other fixed charges. Thus, the operations budget is a detailed operating plan by profit centers, cost centers within profit centers (such as the housekeeping department within the rooms department), and service centers. It includes all revenues and all expenses which appear on the income statement and related subsidiary schedules that we discussed in Chapter 3. Annual operating budgets are normally subdivided into monthly periods. Certain information is reduced to a daily basis for management's use in controlling operations. The operations budget enables management to accomplish two of its major functions: planning and control.

Two other types of budget are the cash budget and the capital budget. The cash budget is management's plan for cash receipts and disbursements. We will discuss cash budgeting in Chapter 11 of this text. Capital budgeting pertains to planning for the acquisition of equipment, land, buildings, and other fixed assets. Capital budgeting procedures used by hospitality operations are the topic of Chapter 13.

Budgeting Horizons

The annual operations budget must be subdivided into monthly plans in order for management to use it effectively as an aid in monitoring operations. The monthly plans allow management to measure the operation's overall performance several times throughout the year. Certain elements of the monthly plan are then reduced to weekly and daily bases. For example, many lodging operations have daily revenue plans which differ by property, by day of the week, and by season. The daily revenue is compared to these daily revenue goals on the daily report of operations. Any significant differences (variances) require analysis, determination of causes, and, if necessary, corrective action. (Variance analysis will be discussed later in this chapter.) In addition, every month all revenue and expense amounts are compared to the budgeted amounts, and all significant variances are analyzed and explained.

Alternatives to the monthly breakdown of annual budgets are using thirteen 4-week segments or the 4–4–5 quarterly plan. The 4–4–5 plan consists of two 4-week plans followed by one 5-week which equal the thirteen weeks in a quarter. Four of these quarterly plans serve as the annual operations budget.

Many hospitality organizations also prepare operations budgets on a long-range basis. A common long-range period is five years. A five-year plan consists of five annual plans. The annual plans for the second through fifth years are much less detailed than the current year's annual plan. When long-range budgets are used, the next year's budget serves as a starting point for preparing the operations budget. The long-range budget procedure is used to review and update the next four years and add the fifth year to the plan.

Long-range planning, also referred to as **strategic planning**, is recognized as essential to the controlled growth of major hospitality organizations. It not only considers revenues and expenses (as do annual operating plans), but also evaluates and selects from among major alternatives those which provide long-range direction to the hospitality operation. Major directional considerations may include the following:

- Evaluating whether a proposed acquisition will have a positive effect on existing operations or whether it will hinder or detract from existing operations
- Determining whether the hospitality operation should expand into foreign markets
- Determining whether a quick-service restaurant chain should add breakfast to its existing lunch and dinner offerings
- Considering whether a single-property operation should add rooms or possibly expand to include another property

Reasons for Budgeting

Many small organizations in the hospitality industry have not formalized their operations budgets. Often, the overall goals, sales objectives, expense projections, and the desired bottom line remain "in the head" of the owner/manager. However, there are many reasons every hospitality operation should use formalized budgeting. Several of these are briefly described below:

1. Budgeting requires management to examine alternatives before selecting a particular course of action. For example, there are pricing alternatives for each product and/or service sold. Also, there are many different marketing decisions that must be made, such as where to advertise, how much to advertise, how to promote, when to promote, and so on. There are also several approaches to staffing, each of which will affect the quality of service provided. In nearly every revenue and expense area, several courses of action are available to hospitality operations. Budgeting provides management with an effective means of evaluating these alternatives.

2. Budgeting provides a standard of comparison. At the end of the accounting period, management is able to compare actual operating results to a formal plan. Significant variances may be analyzed to suggest the probable cause(s) which require additional investigation and possibly corrective action. While the preparation of budgets is independent of budgetary control, it is inefficient not to use budgets for control purposes.

3. Budgeting enables management to look forward, especially when strategic planning is concerned. Too often, management is either solving current problems or reviewing the past. Budgeting requires management to anticipate the future. Future considerations may be both external and internal. External considerations include the economy, inflation, and major competition. Internal considerations are primarily the hospitality operation's reactions to external considerations. Hospitality operations should aggressively attempt to shape their environment rather than merely reacting to it.

4. When participative budgeting is practiced, the budget process involves all levels of management. This involvement motivates

the lower level managers because they have real input in the process rather than being forced to adhere to budget numbers that are imposed upon them. Too often, autocratic budgeting approaches result in "unsuccessful" managers who blame the budget preparers (higher level managers) instead of accepting responsibility for poor operating results.

5. The budget process provides a channel of communication whereby the operation's objectives are communicated to the lowest managerial levels. In addition, lower level managers are able to react to these objectives and suggest operational goals such as rooms sold, rooms revenues, rooms labor expense, and so on. When the budget is used as a standard of comparison, the operating results are also communicated to lower level managers. This allows for feedback to these managers. Further, lower level managers are required to explain significant variances—why they exist, what the causes are, and what action is to be taken.

6. Finally, to the degree that prices are a function of costs, the budget process (which provides estimates of future expenses) enables managers to set their prices in relation to their expenses. Price changes can be the result of planning, thereby allowing such changes to be properly implemented. Price changes made on the spur of the moment often result in unprofessional price execution, such as penciled changes on menus, poorly informed service staff who misquote prices, and other similar situations.

Personnel Responsible for Budget Preparation

The complete budget process includes both budget preparation and budgetary control. The major purpose of budgeting is to allow management to accomplish three of its functions: planning, execution, and control.

In most hospitality organizations, the board of directors approves the operating budget, the preparation of which has been delegated to the chief executive officer (CEO). The CEO generally enlists the controller to coordinate the budget preparation process. However, budgeting is not a financial function where bookkeepers, accountants, and the controller have the sole responsibility. The controller facilitates the budget preparation process by initially providing information to operating managers. The major input for the budget should come from operated department (profit center) managers working with their lower level managers and from service department managers.

The controller receives the department managers' operating plans and formulates them into a comprehensive operating budget. This is then reviewed by the CEO and a budget committee (if one exists). If the comprehensive operating budget is satisfactory in meeting financial goals, the CEO and the controller present it to the board of directors. If it is not satisfactory, then the elements requiring change are returned to the appropriate department heads for review and change. This process may repeat several times until a satisfactory budget is prepared.

The final budget should be the result of an overall team effort rather than a decree dictated by the CEO. This participative management approach should result in maximizing departmental managers' motivation.

The Budget Preparation Process

The major elements in the budget preparation process are as follows:

- Financial objectives
- Revenue forecasts
- Expense forecasts
- Net income forecasts

The operations budget process begins with the board of directors establishing financial objectives. A major financial objective set by many organizations, both hospitality and business firms in general, is long-term profit maximization. Long-term profit maximization may mean that the operation does not maximize its profits for the next year. For example, in the next year, profits may be increased by reducing public relations efforts and major maintenance projects; however, in the long run, cuts in these programs may disturb the financial well-being of the hospitality establishment. An alternative objective set by institutional food service operations (for example, hospital food service) is cost containment. Since many of these operations generate limited food service revenues, cost containment is critical to enable these operators to break even.

Another objective may be to provide high quality service, even if it means incurring higher labor costs than allowable to maximize profits. Other objectives set by hospitality organizations have been to be the top establishment in its segment of the hospitality industry, to be the fastest growing establishment, and/or to be recognized as the hospitality operation with the best reputation. Many more objectives could be listed. The critical point is that the board must establish major objectives. These are then communicated to the CEO and are the basis for formulating the operating budget.

When a management company operates a hotel for independent owners, the owners' expectations for both the long and short term must be fully considered. Generally, the owners reserve the right to approve the operating budget. Therefore, failure to consider their views will most likely result in their rejection of the plan, as well as damaged relationships and the need to re-do the budget. Several of the major hotel chains, such as Hilton, Hyatt, and Westin, manage many more hotels than they own. Thus, their management teams at the managed properties must work closely with the owners of each hotel.

Forecasting Revenue

Forecasting revenue is the next step in preparing the operations budget. In order for profit center managers to be able to forecast revenue for their departments, they must be provided with information regarding the economic environment, marketing plans, capital budgeting, and detailed historical financial results of their departments.

Information regarding the economic environment, includes such items as:

- Expected inflation for the next year
- Ability of the operation to pass on cost increases to guests
- Changes in competitive conditions—for example, the emergence of new competitors, the closing of former competitors, and so on
- Expected levels of guest spending for products/services offered by the hospitality operation
- Business travel trends
- Tourist travel trends
- For operations in foreign countries, other factors such as expected wage/price controls and the political environment may need to be considered

In order for this information to be useful, it must be expressed in usable numbers. For example, regarding inflation and the ability of the operation to increase its prices, the information received by department heads may be phrased as follows: inflation is expected to be 6% for the next year and prices of all products and services may be increased by an average maximum of 5%, with a 2.5% increase effective January 1 and July 1.

Marketing plans include, but are not limited to, advertising and promotion plans. What advertising is planned for the upcoming year, and how does it compare with the past? What results are expected from the various advertising campaigns? What promotion will be used and when during the budget year? What results can be expected? Are reduced room prices and complimentary meals part of the weekend promotion? Answers to these questions and many others must be provided in order for managers to be able to prepare their budgets.

Capital budgeting information includes the time of the addition of property and equipment. For an existing property, the completion date of guestroom renovation must be projected in order to effectively estimate room sales. The renovation of a hotel's restaurant, the addition of rooms, and so forth are areas that must be covered before projecting sales and expenses for the upcoming year.

The historical financial information should be detailed by department. The breakdown should be on at least a monthly basis, and in some cases, on a daily basis. Quantities and prices should both be provided. That is, the number of each type of room sold and the average selling price by market segment—business, group, tourist, and contract—should be provided. Generally, financial information for at least the two prior years is provided. The controller should be prepared to provide additional prior information as requested.

Historical financial information often serves as the foundation from which managers build their revenue forecasts. This type of budgeting has been called **incremental budgeting**. For example, rooms revenue of a hotel for 19X1 through 19X4 is shown in Exhibit 10.1. From year 19X1 to 19X4, the amount of revenue increased 10% for each year. Therefore, if future conditions appear to be similar to what they were in prior years,

Exhibit 10.1   Rooms Revenue Increases

		Increase over prior year	
	Amount	**Amount**	**%**
19X1	$1,000,000	—	—
19X2	1,100,000	100,000	10
19X3	1,210,000	110,000	10
19X4	1,331,000	121,000	10

Exhibit 10.2   Rooms Revenue 19X1–19X4

Year	Rooms Sold	Occ. %	Average Room Rates	Rooms Revenues
19X1	25,550	70	$40	$1,022,000
19X2	26,280	72	42	1,103,760
19X3	26,645	73	45	1,199,025
19X4	27,375	75	49	1,341,375

the rooms revenue for 19X5 would be budgeted at $1,464,100, which is a 10% increase over 19X4.

An alternative approach to budgeting revenue based on increasing the current year's revenue by a percentage is to base the revenue projection on unit sales and prices. This approach considers the two variables of unit sales and prices separately. For example, an analysis of the past financial information in Exhibit 10.2 shows that occupancy percentage increased 2% from 19X1 to 19X2, 1% from 19X2 to 19X3, and 2% from 19X3 to 19X4. The average room rates have increased by $2, $3, and $4 over the past three years, respectively. Therefore, assuming the future prospects appear similar, the forecaster may use a 1% increase in occupancy percentage and a $5 increase in average room rate as the basis for forecasting 19X5 rooms revenue. The formula for forecasting rooms revenue is as follows:

$$\frac{Rooms}{Available} \times \frac{Occupancy}{Percentage} \times \frac{Average}{Rate} = \frac{Forecasted}{Rooms\ Revenue}$$

$$36{,}500 \times .76 \times \$54 = \$1{,}497{,}960$$

This simplistic approach to forecasting rooms revenue is meant only to illustrate the process. A more detailed (and proper) approach would include further considerations, such as: different types of rooms available and their rates, different room rates charged to different guests (for example, convention groups, business travelers, and tourists), different rates charged on weeknights versus weekends, and different rates charged based on seasonality (especially for hotels subject to seasonal changes), and so on. In addition, managers of other profit centers, such as food and beverage, telephone, and the gift shop, must forecast their revenue for the year.

Chapter 9 covered sales forecasting and, although much of it related to short-term forecasts, many concepts covered there are relevant to forecasting revenue for the annual budget. In addition to relying on historical information, many hotels, especially convention hotels which have major conventions booked a year or more in advance, are able to rely in part on room reservations in forecasting both room and food and beverage sales. Still, for activities not reserved so far in advance, forecasting must be done using the techniques described in Chapter 9.

Estimating Expenses

The next step in the budget formulation process is estimating expenses. Since expenses are categorized both in relation to operated departments (direct/indirect) and how they react to changes in volume (fixed/variable), the forecasting of expenses is similar to the approach used in forecasting revenue. However, before department heads are able to estimate expenses, they must be provided with information regarding the following:

- Expected cost increases for supplies, food, beverages, and other expenses.

- Labor increases, including the cost of fringe benefits and payroll taxes

Department heads of profit centers estimate their variable expenses in relation to the projected revenues of their departments. For example, historically, the food and beverage department may have incurred food costs at 35% of food sales. For the next year, the food department manager decides to budget at 35%. Therefore, multiplying food sales by 35% results in the projected cost of food sales. Other variable expenses may be estimated similarly.

An alternate way to estimate expense is based on standard amounts. For example, a hotel may have a work standard that requires room attendants to clean two rooms per hour. Given this standard, if 800 rooms sales are budgeted during a month, 400 labor hours would be budgeted for room attendants' labor. If the average hourly wage is $5.50 per hour, $2,200 in wages is budgeted for room attendants for the period. Employee benefits related to room attendants are additional costs that also must be considered.

Another example is guestroom amenities. If the typical amenity package includes soap, mouthwash, shampoo, and so forth and costs $2 per room, then when 800 rooms sales are forecasted, the guest supplies—amenities budget would be $1,600.

Fixed expenses are projected on the basis of experience and expected changes. For example, assume that supervisors in the food department were paid salaries of $85,000 for the past year. Further assume that the new salary level of the supervisors is $90,000 plus another half-time equivalent to be added at a cost of $12,000 for the next year. Thus, the fixed cost of supervisor salaries for the next year is set at $102,000. Other fixed expenses are similarly projected.

The service center department heads also estimate expenses for their departments. The service departments in a hotel comprise the general expense categories of administrative and general, marketing, property operation and maintenance, energy costs, human relations, data processing, and transportation. Service center department heads will estimate their expenses based on experience and expected changes. Generally, the historical amounts are adjusted to reflect higher costs. For example, assume that the accounting department salaries of a hotel for 19X1 were $150,000. Further assume that salary increases for 19X2 are limited to an average of 5%. Therefore, the 19X2 accounting department salaries budget is set at $157,500.

A relatively new budgeting approach, **zero-base budgeting (ZBB)**, is applicable in budgeting for service departments. ZBB, unlike the incremental approach, requires all expenses to be justified. In other words, the assumption is that each department starts with zero dollars (zero base) and must justify all budgeted amounts. Let's look at an example that illustrates the differences between the incremental and ZBB approaches to budgeting.

Assume that the marketing department of a hotel had a total departmental budget of $500,000 in 19X1. In 19X2, cost increases are expected to average 5%, and new advertising in the monthly city magazine is expected to cost $500 per month. Under the incremental approach, the marketing budget would be set at $531,000, determined as follows:

$$\$500,000 + 500(12) + 500,000(.05) = \$531,000$$

Under ZBB, the marketing department would have to justify every dollar budgeted. That is, documentation would be required showing that all budgeted amounts are cost-justified. This means all payroll costs, supplies, advertising, and so forth would have to be shown to yield greater benefits than their cost.

The ZBB approach to budgeting in hotels appears to be limited to the service departments. However, since the total cost of these departments is approximately 25% of the average hotel's total revenue, the total amount can be considerable.

More detailed discussion of ZBB is beyond the scope of this text.[1]

Projecting Fixed Charges

The next step in the budget formulation process is projecting fixed charges. Fixed charges include depreciation, insurance expense, property taxes, rent expense, and similar expenses. These expenses are fixed and are projected on the basis of experience and expected changes for the next year.

For example, assume that interest expense for a hotel was $215,000 for 19X1. Exhibit 10.3 illustrates how the interest expense budget for 19X2 is determined by estimating interest expense based on current and projected borrowings. Based on calculations in Exhibit 10.3, the interest expense budgeted for 19X2 is $170,000.

Even though the above mentioned expenses are considered to be fixed, management and/or the board may be able to affect the fixed amounts for the year. For example, property taxes are generally based on assessed valuation and a property tax rate. A reduction in the assessed valuation will result in a reduction in the hotel's property taxes. Thus, if the property is over-assessed, it should pursue a reduction which, if successful, will lower the property tax expense. Some hotels have been successful in obtaining reductions in their assessments, thus reducing this "fixed" expense for the year.

Exhibit 10.3 Interest Expense Budget 19X2

Debt	Principal	Interest Rate	Time	Amount
Mortgage payment	$500,000	12%	Year	$60,000
Loan from partner A	500,000	18	Year	90,000
Working capital loans	200,000	20	6 mo.	20,000
			Total	$170,000

The final step of the budget formulation process is for the controller to formulate the entire budget based on submissions from operated departments and service departments. The forecasted net income is a result of this process. If this bottom line is acceptable to the board of directors and/or the owners, then the budget formulation is complete. If the bottom line is not acceptable, then department heads are required to rework their budgets to provide a budget acceptable to the board and/or owners. Many changes may be proposed in this "rework" process, such as price changes, marketing changes, and cost reductions, just to mention a few.

Budget Formulation Illustrated

A very simplified lodging example will be used to illustrate the preparation of an operations budget. The Sands Motel is a 20-room lodging facility which does not sell food and beverages. Each room is equipped with a telephone. Thus, the Sands Motel has two profit centers, the rooms department and telephone department. The Sands Motel also has two service centers, administration and a combined maintenance and energy cost department.

The board of directors has established the major financial goal of generating a minimum net income of 15% of sales. The income statements for the past three years are contained in Exhibit 10.4. An analysis of this financial information appears in Exhibit 10.5. Economic environment information relevant to the Sands Motel in 19X4 is summarized as follows:

- No new firms are expected to compete with the Sands Motel.

- Overall consumer demand for motel rooms is expected to remain relatively constant.

- Inflation is expected to be about 5% in the next year.

The major findings and projections for 19X4 are as follows:

Item	Analytical Findings	Projection for 19X4
1. Rooms Revenue		
Paid occupancy	There is no new competition for next year and the Sands has increased its paid occupancy 1 percentage point each year for the last three years. Assume a 1% increase in 19X4.	71%

Exhibit 10.4 Income Statements—Sands Motel

Income Statements
Sands Motel
For the years of 19X1–19X3

	19X1	19X2	19X3
Revenues:			
Rooms	$146,438	$158,634	$171,654
Telephone	2,962	3,466	4,246
Total	149,400	162,100	175,900
Departmental Expenses:			
Rooms:			
Payroll	21,966	23,000	27,465
Laundry	1,464	1,600	1,735
Linen	2,929	3,150	4,324
Commissions	1,470	1,578	1,650
All Other Expenses	1,500	2,380	2,575
Total	29,329	31,708	37,749
Telephone	2,850	3,350	4,285
Total	32,179	35,058	42,034
Departmental Income:			
Rooms	117,109	126,926	133,905
Telephone	112	116	(39)
Total	117,221	127,042	133,866
Undistributed Operating Expenses:			
Administration	27,470	30,105	32,795
Maintenance and Energy Costs	16,952	19,292	21,775
Total	44,422	49,397	54,570
Income Before Fixed Costs	72,799	77,645	79,296
Depreciation	15,000	15,000	15,500
Property Taxes	5,000	5,500	6,000
Insurance	5,000	5,000	5,000
Interest Expense	15,000	16,000	15,000
Income Before Income Taxes	32,799	36,145	37,796
Income Taxes	9,840	10,844	11,339
Net Income	$22,959	$25,301	$26,457

Average Room Rate	This has increased by $2 each year and the Sands Motel has still increased its occupancy percentage. An additional $2 increase appears to be reasonable for 19X4. Note: The $2 increase is 6% of the $33.50 average price for 19X3 and exceeds the expected inflation of 5%.	$35.50
2. Telephone Revenue	This has increased from 2% to 2.5%. A .2% increase appears reasonable for 19X4.	2.7%

Exhibit 10.5   Analysis of Income Statements—Sands Motel

Analysis of Income Statements
Sands Motel
For the years of 19X1–19X3

	19X1	19X2	19X3
Rooms Sold	4,964	5,036	5,124
Occ. %	68	69	70
Average Rate	$29.50	$31.50	$33.50
Rooms Revenue	$146,438	$158,634	$171,654
Telephone revenue as a % of room revenue	2%	2.2%	2.5%
Rooms expenses %			
Payroll	15%	14.5%	16%
Laundry	1	1	1
Linen	2	2	2.5
Commissions	1	1	1
All other expenses	1	1.5	1.5
Total	20%	20%	22%
Administration			
Payroll			
Fixed	$20,000	$22,000	$24,000
Variable	3%	3%	2.5%
Other	2%	2%	2.5%
Maintenance and Energy Costs			
Maintenance			
Fixed	$4,000	$4,500	$5,000
Variable	3%	3%	3%
Energy Costs			
Fixed	$1,000	$1,500	$2,000
Variable	5%	5.2%	5.4%

Fixed Charges

Depreciation – based on cost of fixed assets, expected lives, and straight-line method of depreciation
Property taxes – historically has increased by $500 for 19X1 through 19X3
Insurance – a three-year policy for 19X1-19X3 was quoted at $5,000 per year
Interest expense – based on amount borrowed and prevailing interest rates
Income taxes – based on 30% of income before income taxes

Profit Margin %	15.36%	15.61%	15.04%

3. Rooms Expenses

Payroll	This has fluctuated significantly due to labor unrest. Major pay increases this past year appear to be satisfying the two room attendants and part-time front office personnel. Keep the payroll percentage for 19X4 at 19X3 levels.	16%

Laundry	This has remained constant at 1% of rooms revenue for three years.	1%
Linen	A .5% increase was experienced in 19X3 due to major purchases. The prior 2% appears adequate for 19X4.	2%
Commissions	The average for the past three years has been 1%. Continue to use 1% as an estimate for 19X4.	1%
All Other Expenses	These have stabilized for the past two years at 1.5%. This appears reasonable.	1.5%
4. Telephone Expense	This has nearly equalled telephone revenue each year. A breakeven situation is reasonable for 19X4.	100% of telephone revenue
5. Administration		
Payroll	The fixed portion has increased approximately $2,000 per year from 19X1–19X3. A $3,000 increase is scheduled for 19X4 to reward the general manager. Variable labor (as a percentage of total revenue) is expected to be 3% for 19X4.	$27,000 and 3%
Other	Although this increased to 2.5% in 19X3, it is expected to return to the previous level of 2% in 19X4.	2%
6. Maintenance and Energy Costs		
Maintenance	The fixed portion of part-time workers' pay has increased $500 each year over three years. An increase of $1,000 is scheduled for 19X4. Variable maintenance of 3% appears adequate for 19X4.	$6,000 and 3%
Energy Costs	The fixed portion has increased approximately $500 each year since 19X1. Therefore, the estimated fixed portion should be increased accordingly for 19X4. The variable portion has increased .2% from 19X1–19X3. Energy costs are expected to be moderate in 19X4 and 5.4% appears reasonable.	$2,500 and 5.4%
7. Fixed Charges		
Depreciation	The accountant's calculation of depreciation for 19X4 is $15,000 for existing fixed assets and an additional $700 for a new microcomputer to be purchased in 19X4.	$15,700

Property Taxes	This assessed valuation is expected to increase by 10% for 19X4. The tax rate is not expected to change; therefore, increase property taxes for 19X4 to $6,600.	$6,600
Insurance	The current three-year insurance policy expires on December 31. The new three-year policy requires a $6,000 premium each year.	$6,000
Interest Expense	The flexible interest rate presently at 15% is expected to average 14.5% for 19X4. The average debt outstanding for 19X4 will be $90,000. $90,000 × .145 = $13,050.	$13,050
Income Taxes	Income taxes for 19X1–19X3 were 30% of the income before income taxes. Due to reduced rates, the tax rate for 19X4 will be 25%.	25% of pre-tax income

The operations budget for 19X4 is shown in Exhibit 10.6. The projected 19X4 net income for the Sands Motel of $29,586 is 15.6% of sales, which exceeds the minimum requirement of 15%.

Flexible Budgets

The budgets we have discussed so far have been either fixed or static, in that only one level of activity was planned. However, no matter how sophisticated the budget process, it is improbable that the level of activity budgeted will be realized exactly. Therefore, when a fixed budget is used, variances from several budget line items, specifically for revenues and variable expenses, can almost always be expected. An alternative approach is to budget for several different levels of activity. For example, a hotel may budget at three occupancy levels, such as 69%, 71%, 73%, even though it believes that the level of activity is likeliest to be at the 71% level. With flexible budgeting, revenues and variable expenses change with each level of activity, while fixed expenses remain constant.

Exhibit 10.7 contains three condensed operations budgets for the Sands Motel. The flexible budgeting reflects occupancy at 69%, 71%, and 73%. The static budget for the Sands Motel (Exhibit 10.6) was based on 71% occupancy. The kinds of observations that should be made in relation to flexible budgeting reflected in Exhibit 10.7 include the following:

- Revenues increase/decrease with occupancy.
- Departmental expenses increase/decrease with occupancy.
- Undistributed operating expenses increase/decrease only slightly, since a major portion of these expenses is fixed.
- Fixed expenses remain constant as expected.
- Net income changes with activity, but not as much as revenue.
- Net income as a percentage of total revenue for the three levels of activity is as follows:

Exhibit 10.6 Sample Operations Budget Worksheet

Operations-Budget (Worksheet)
Sands Motel
For the year of 19X4

	Calculation	Amount
Revenue		
Rooms	365 × 20 × .71 × 35.50	$183,996
Telephone	183,996 × .027	4,968
Total		188,964
Departmental Expenses		
Rooms		
Payroll	183,996 × .16	29,439
Laundry	183,996 × .01	1,840
Linen	183,996 × .02	3,680
Commissions	183,996 × .01	1,840
All other expenses	183,996 × .015	2,760
Total		39,559
Telephone	(same as telephone revenue)	4,968
Departmental Income		
Rooms		144,437
Telephone		—0—
Total		144,437
Undistributed Operating Expenses		
Administration	27,000 + .05 (188,964)	36,448
Maintenance and Energy Costs	8,500 + .084 (188,964)	24,373
Total		60,821
Total Income Before Fixed Costs		83,616
Insurance		6,000
Property Taxes		6,600
Depreciation		15,700
Interest Expense		13,050
Income Before Income Taxes		42,266
Income Taxes	42,266 × .30	12,680
Net Income		$29,586

At 69% occupancy:

$$\frac{\text{Net Income}}{\text{Total Revenue}} = \frac{27,237}{183,641} = \underline{14.8\%}$$

At 71% occupancy:

$$\frac{\text{Net Income}}{\text{Total Revenue}} = \frac{29,586}{188,964} = \underline{15.7\%}$$

Exhibit 10.7 Flexible Operations Budget—Sands Motel

		Flexible Operations Budget Sands Motel For the year of 19X4		
		Activity Levels – Occupancy %		
		69%	71%	73%
Revenue				
Rooms		$178,813	$183,996	$189,179
Telephone		4,828	4,968	5,108
Total		183,641	188,964	194,287
Departmental Expenses				
Rooms		38,445	39,559	40,673
Telephone		4,828	4,968	5,108
Total		43,273	44,527	45,781
Departmental Income				
Rooms		140,368	144,437	148,506
Telephone		0	0	0
Total		140,368	144,437	148,506
Undistributed Operating Expenses				
Administration		36,182	36,448	36,714
Maintenance and Energy Costs		23,926	24,373	24,820
Total		60,108	60,821	61,534
Total Income Before Fixed Costs		80,260	83,616	86,972
Insurance		6,000	6,000	6,000
Property Taxes		6,600	6,600	6,600
Depreciation		15,700	15,700	15,700
Interest		13,050	13,050	13,050
Income Before Income Taxes		38,910	42,266	45,622
Income Taxes		11,673	12,680	13,687
Net Income		$27,237	$29,586	$31,935

At 73% occupancy:

$$\frac{\text{Net Income}}{\text{Total Revenue}} = \frac{31,935}{194,287} = \underline{\underline{16.4\%}}$$

Therefore, the minimum required profit margin percentage of 15% can only be realized at the budgeted occupancy levels of 71% and 73%. Since 69% yields less than the targeted 15% profit margin, management may be requested to review the budget at 69% in an attempt to achieve the desired net income.

The flexible budget is relatively easy to prepare using computers. The relationship between revenues and expenses is expressed in formulas, and the computer, with minor human assistance, is able to do the rest. The major benefit of the flexible budget is to provide management and owners with bottom line results for alternative levels of activity. Many activity levels can be projected.

As a note of caution, however, forecasters should realize that different levels of activity will most likely affect prices and possibly related expenses. For example, a room rate of $35.50 was used across the three occupancy levels used in the Sands Motel's flexible operations budget. However, in order to increase occupancy above 73%, an average price reduction may be necessary, and still a greater price reduction may be required beyond 80% or some other higher number.

Budgeting for a New Lodging Property

The preceding discussion covers budgeting for an existing lodging property. However, a hotel in its first year lacks a historical base. How can it prepare its budget?

Certainly one source for budgeting for a hotel's first year is the lodging feasibility study (LFS) that is generally prepared to secure the financing for the property. This study provides a summary of operations including sales, direct expenses of the profit centers, and operating overhead expenses. However, forecasters should not rely totally on these numbers for two major reasons. First, the study is prepared to secure financing, and the figures are not detailed by month, type of market, and so forth. Second, the LFS is prepared before the construction of the hotel, which is probably two years before the opening of the hotel; thus, the figures are somewhat dated. Nonetheless, it is a set of figures with which to start. These numbers should be updated on the basis of current room rates, labor costs, and other expenses.

If a new hotel is part of a chain, cost information of similar properties can be obtained. When used cautiously, this information will be reasonably useful.

Finally, few if any new hotels or restaurants make a bottom line profit their first year. Unexpected expenses arise until the "bugs" are worked out and the market realizes the property exists. Therefore, the initial budget should allow for these higher than normal costs and possibly lower revenues than desired. A critical need is to have sufficient cash to carry the new property to the point of cash breakeven.

Budgetary Control

In order for budgets to be used effectively for control purposes, budget reports must be prepared periodically (generally on a monthly basis) for each level of financial responsibility. In a hotel, this would normally require budget reports for profit, cost, and service centers.[2]

Budget reports may take many forms. Exhibit 10.8, a summary income statement used by The Sheraton Corporation, is prepared monthly and is the summary of the entire hotel operations. It is used by the hotel top management and is also made available to corporate executives and financial analysts. Note not only that absolute dollars are shown for current month and year-to-date, but also that relative percentages to total revenue and individual department expenses as a percentage of departmental revenue are also given. In addition to variances from

Exhibit 10.8   Monthly Summary Income Statement

CURRENT MONTH							YEAR TO DATE					
Actual		Variance From Budget		Variance From Last Year		**Monthly Summary Income Statement**	Actual		Variance From Budget		Variance From Last Year	
$	%	$	%	$	%		$	%	$	%	$	%
	100					Stats – Rooms Available		100				
						Rooms Occupied						
						Average Room Rate						
	100					Total Revenue – Including TVA		100				
	100					Excluding TVA		100				
						Rooms – Revenues						
						Wages & Benefits						
						Other Expenses						
						Departmental Profit						
	100					Food – Revenues		100				
						Cost of Sales						
						Wages – Benefits						
						Other Expenses						
						Departmental Profit						
	100					Beverage – Revenues		100				
						Cost of Sales						
						Wages & Benefits						
						Other Expenses						
						Departmental Profit						
						Food & Beverage Other Income						
						Convention Services Deptl. Profit						
						Total Food & Bev. Profit						
						Minor Operated Departmental Profit						
						Casino Deptl. Profit						
						Rents and Other Income						
						Total Operated Departmental Profit						
						Overhead Departments						
						Administrative & General						
						Marketing						
						Property Operation						
						Total Overhead Departments						
						Gross Operating Profit (Loss)						
						Capital Expenses						
						Taxes						
						Insurance						
						Rent Non-Affiliate						
						Int. & Debt Exp. Non-Affiliate						
						(Int. Income) – Non-Affiliate						
						Other (Adds) & Deductions						
						Total Capital Exp. & Other						
						Cash Earnings (Loss)						
						Depreciation/Replacement Reserve						
						(Deferral) of First Year Loss						
						Amortization 1st Yr. Loss/Pre-Open Exp.						
						Profit: Before Sheraton Charges						
						Rent – Affiliate						
						Int. Exp. (Inc.) Affil. – Net						
						Marketing Fee						
						License Fee						
						Mgmt. Fee – Basic						
						Management Fee – Incentive						
						Total Fees						
						Pretext Profit (Loss) Operations						
						Income Taxes						
						(Gain)/Loss Translation						
						Net Operations						

Courtesy of the Sheraton Corporation

budget on both a dollar basis and a percentage basis, variances from last year's actual are also shown in order to put the budget in perspective and to provide management with trend information.

Exhibit 10.9   Monthly Income Statement—Rooms Department

						Monthly Income Statement						
·········CURRENT MONTH···········						ROOMS DEPARTMENT	···········YEAR TO DATE···········					
Actual		Variance From Budget		Variance From Last Year			Actual		Variance From Budget		Variance From Last Year	
$	%	$	%	$	%		$	%	$	%	$	%
						Revenues						
						Transient – Regular						
						– Group						
						– Airline Crew						
						Extra Room Revenue						
						Total Revenues						
						Expenses						
						Salaries & Wages						
						Benefits						
						Total Wages & Benefits						
						Other Expenses						
						Linen China Glass Silver						
						Contract & Dry Cleaning						
						Operating Supplies						
						Laundry						
						Uniforms						
						Rooms Commission						
						Reservation						
						Miscellaneous						
						Total Other Expenses						
						Total Expenses						
						Departmental Profit						
						Rooms Statistics						
						Total Rooms in Hotel						
						Available for Guest Use						
						Occupied (Overall)						
						Transient – Regular						
						– Group						
						– Comp						
						– Airline Crew						
						Trans Units Occupied						
						Trans Units Double Occupied						
						Average Rate – Overall						
						Transient – Regular						
						– Group						
						– Airline Crew						

Courtesy of the Sheraton Corporation

Exhibit 10.9 is a departmental budget report for the rooms department. It provides a further breakdown of the elements that make up revenues, wages, benefits, and other expenses. It also provides various rooms statistics. This report, which is available to corporate management, also goes to the next level of management below the general manager and controller.

In order for the reports to be useful, they must be timely and relevant. Budget reports issued weeks after the end of the accounting period are too late to allow managers to investigate variances, determine causes, and take timely action. Relevant financial information includes only the revenues and expenses for which the individual department head is held responsible. For example, including allocated overhead expenses such as administrative and general salaries on a rooms department budget report is rather meaningless from a control viewpoint, because the rooms department manager is unable to affect these costs. Further, they detract from the expenses which the rooms department manager can take action to control.

Relevant reporting also requires sufficient detail to allow reasonable judgments regarding budget variances. (Of course, information overload, which generally results in management's failure to act properly) should be avoided.

There are five steps in the budgetary control process:

1. Determination of variances
2. Determination of significant variances
3. Analysis of significant variances
4. Determination of problems
5. Action to correct problems

Determination of Variances

Variances are determined by using the budget report to compare actual results to the budget. The budget report should disclose both monthly variances and year-to-date variances. Variance analysis generally focuses on monthly variances, because the year-to-date variances are essentially the sum of monthly variances.

Exhibit 10.10 is the January 19X4 summary budget report for the Sands Motel. This budget report contains only monthly financial information and not separate year-to-date numbers, as January is the first month of the fiscal year for the Sands Motel.

Variances shown on this report include both dollar variances and percentage variances. The dollar variances result from subtracting the actual results from the budget figures. For example, rooms revenue for the Sands Motel was $14,940, while the budgeted rooms revenue was $15,620, resulting in a difference of $680. The difference is set in parentheses to reflect an unfavorable variance. Dollar variances are considered either favorable or unfavorable based on situations presented in Exhibit 10.11.

Percentage variances are determined by dividing the dollar variance by the budgeted amount. For rooms revenue (Exhibit 10.10), the (4.35%) is the result of dividing $(680) by $15,620.

Variances should be determined for all line items on budget reports along with an indication of whether the variance is favorable or unfavorable. The kind of variance can be indicated by marking it "+" for favorable and "−" for unfavorable, "F" for favorable and "U" for unfavorable, or placing parentheses around unfavorable variances and showing favorable variances without parentheses as shown in Exhibit 10.10. Some enterprises simply asterisk unfavorable variances.

Determination of Significant Variances

Virtually all budgeted revenue and expense items on a budget report will differ from the actual amounts, with the possible exception of fixed

Exhibit 10.10   Summary Budget Report—Sands Motel

	Budget	Actual	Variances $	Variances %
Summary Budget Report				
Sands Motel				
For January 19X4				
Revenue				
Rooms	$15,620	$14,940	$ (680)	(4.35)%
Telephone	429	414	(15)	(3.50)
Total	16,049	15,354	(695)	(4.33)
Departmental Expenses				
Rooms				
Payroll	2,500	2,243	257	10.28
Laundry	156	150	6	3.85
Linen	313	300	13	4.15
Commissions	156	150	6	3.85
All other expenses	234	200	34	14.53
Total	3,359	3,043	316	9.41
Telephone	422	380	42	9.95
Total	3,781	3,423	358	9.47
Departmental Income				
Rooms	12,268	11,911	(357)	(2.91)
Telephone	0	20	20	NA
Total	12,268	11,931	(337)	(2.75)
Undistributed Operating Expenses				
Administration	3,052	2,961	91	2.98
Maintenance and energy costs	2,169	2,220	(51)	(2.35)
Total Income Before Fixed Charges	7,047	6,750	(297)	(4.21)
Insurance	500	500	0	—
Property Taxes	550	550	0	—
Depreciation	1,308	1,308	0	—
Interest Expense	1,087	1,087	0	—
Income Before Income Taxes	3,602	3,305	(297)	(8.25)
Income Taxes	1,081	992	89	8.23
Net Income	$2,521	$2,313	$(208)	(8.25)%

expenses. This is only to be expected, because no budgeting process, however sophisticated, is perfect. However, simply because a variance exists does not mean that management should analyze the variance and follow through with appropriate corrective actions. Only significant variances require this kind of management analysis and action.

Exhibit 10.11   Evaluating Dollar Variance Situations

	Situation	Variance
Revenues	Actual exceeds budget	Favorable
	Budget exceeds actual	Unfavorable
Expenses	Budget exceeds actual	Favorable
	Actual exceeds budget	Unfavorable

Criteria used to determine which variances are significant are called **significance criteria**. They are generally expressed in terms of both dollar and percentage differences. Dollar and percentage differences should be used jointly due to the weakness of each when used separately. Dollar differences fail to recognize the magnitude of the base. For example, a large hotel may have a $1,000 difference in rooms revenue from the budgeted amount. Yet the $1,000 difference based on a budget of $1,000,000 results in a percentage difference of only .1%. Most managers would agree this is insignificant. However, if the rooms revenue budget for the period was $10,000, a $1,000 difference would result in a percentage difference of 10% which most managers would consider significant. This seems to suggest that variances should be considered significant based on the percentage difference. However, the percentage difference also fails at times. For example, assume that the budget for an expense is $10. A dollar difference of $2 results in a 20% percentage difference. The percentage difference appears significant, but generally, little (if any) managerial time should be spent analyzing and investigating a $2 difference.

Therefore, the dollar and percentage differences should be used jointly in determining which variances are significant. The size of the significance criteria will differ among hospitality properties in relation to the size of the operation and the controllability of certain revenue or expense items. In general, the larger the operation, the larger the dollar difference criteria. Also, the greater the control exercised over the item, the smaller the criteria.

For example, a large hospitality operation may set significance criteria as follows:

Revenue	$1,000 and 4%
Variable expense	$500 and 2%
Fixed expense	$50 and 1%

A smaller hospitality operation may set significance criteria as follows:

Revenue	$200 and 4%
Variable expense	$100 and 2%
Fixed expense	$50 and 1%

Notice that the change in criteria, based on size of operation, is generally the dollar difference. Both significance criteria decrease as the item becomes more controllable.

To illustrate the determination of significant variances, the significance criteria above for a small hospitality operation will be applied to the Sands Motel's January 19X4 budget report (see Exhibit 10.10). The following revenue and expense items have significant variances:

1. The unfavorable $680 difference between the budgeted rooms revenue and the actual rooms revenue exceeds the dollar difference criterion of $200, and the unfavorable 4.35% percentage difference exceeds the percentage difference criterion of 4%.

2. The favorable $257 difference between the budgeted rooms payroll expense and the actual rooms payroll expense exceeds the dollar difference criterion of $100, and the favorable 10.28% difference exceeds the percentage difference criterion of 2%.

3. Several rooms expense variances such as laundry, linen, and commissions exceed the percentage difference criterion, but do not exceed the dollar difference criterion, so they are not considered significant; therefore, they will not be subjected to variance analysis.

Variance Analysis

Variance analysis is the process of analyzing variances in order to give management more information about variances. With this additional information, management is better prepared to identify the causes of any variances.

We will look at variance analysis for three general areas—revenue, cost of goods sold, and variable labor. The basic models presented in these areas can be applied to other similar areas. For each area, formulas, a graph, and an example will be provided. In addition, the two significant variances of the Sands Motel, rooms revenue and rooms payroll expense, will be analyzed.

Revenue Variance Analysis

Revenue variances occur because of price and volume differences. Thus, the variances relating to revenue are called *price variance* (PV) and *volume variance* (VV). The formulas for these variances are as follows:

$$\frac{\text{Price}}{\text{Variance}} = \frac{\text{Budgeted}}{\text{Volume}} \times \left(\frac{\text{Actual}}{\text{Price}} - \frac{\text{Budgeted}}{\text{Price}} \right)$$

$$PV = BV(AP - BP)$$

$$\frac{\text{Volume}}{\text{Variance}} = \frac{\text{Budgeted}}{\text{Price}} \times \left(\frac{\text{Actual}}{\text{Volume}} - \frac{\text{Budgeted}}{\text{Volume}} \right)$$

$$VV = BP(AV - BV)$$

A minor variance due to the interrelationship of the price and volume variance is the *price-volume variance* (P-VV), calculated as follows:

$$\frac{\text{Price-Volume}}{\text{Variance}} = \left(\frac{\text{Actual}}{\text{Price}} - \frac{\text{Budgeted}}{\text{Price}} \right) \times \left(\frac{\text{Actual}}{\text{Volume}} - \frac{\text{Budgeted}}{\text{Volume}} \right)$$

$$P\text{-}VV = (AP - BP)(AV - BV)$$

Exhibit 10.12   Rooms Revenue: Budget and Actual—Sample Motel

	Room Nights	Average Price	Total
Budget	400	$20	$8,000
Actual	450	18	8,100
Difference	50	$2	$100(F)

These formulas are illustrated by using the Sample Motel whose budget and actual monthly results for rooms revenue appear in Exhibit 10.12.

The budget variance of $100 is favorable. Variance analysis will be conducted to determine the general cause(s) of this variance—that is, price, volume, or the interrelationship of the two. The price variance for the Sample Motel is determined as follows:

$$
\begin{aligned}
PV &= BV(AP - BP) \\
&= 400(18 - 20) \\
&= 400(-2) \\
&= -\$800 \text{ (U)}
\end{aligned}
$$

The price variance of $800 is unfavorable because the average price charged per room night of $18 was $2 less than the budgeted average price of $20.

The volume variance is computed as follows:

$$
\begin{aligned}
VV &= BP(AV - BV) \\
&= 20(450 - 400) \\
&= 20(50) \\
&= \$1,000 \text{ (F)}
\end{aligned}
$$

The volume variance of $1,000 is favorable, because 50 more rooms per night were sold than planned.

The price-volume variance is determined as follows:

$$
\begin{aligned}
P\text{-}VV &= (AP - BP)(AV - BV) \\
&= (18 - 20)(450 - 400) \\
&= -2(50) \\
&= -\$100 \text{ (U)}
\end{aligned}
$$

The price-volume variance is due to the interrelationship of the volume and price variances. Two dollars per room less than budgeted multiplied by the 50 excess rooms results in an unfavorable $100 price-volume variance.

The sum of the three variances equals the budget variance of $100 for room revenue as follows:

Exhibit 10.13 Revenue Variance Analysis—Sample Motel

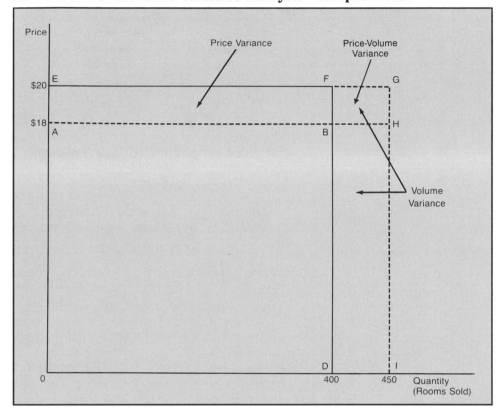

VV	$1,000	(F)
PV	−800	(U)
P-VV	−100	(U)
Total	$ 100	(F)

The price-volume variance in the analysis of revenue variances will be unfavorable when the price and volume variances are different, that is, when one is favorable and the other is unfavorable. When the price and volume variances are the same, that is, either both are favorable or both are unfavorable, then the price-volume variance will be favorable.

Exhibit 10.13 is a graphic depiction of the revenue variance analysis for the Sample Motel. The rectangle OEFD represents the budgeted amount. The rectangle OAHI represents the actual amount of rooms revenue. The price variance is the rectangle AEFB. The volume variance is the rectangle DFGI. The price-volume variance is the rectangle BFGH.

Cost of Goods Sold Analysis

The **cost of goods sold variance** occurs because of differences due to cost and volume. That is, the amount paid for the goods sold (food and/or beverage) differs from the budget, and the total amount sold differs from the budgeted sales. The detailed variances related to the cost of goods are called the *cost variance* (CV), the *volume variance* (VV), and the *cost-volume variance* (C-VV). The formulas for these variances are as follows:

392 Hospitality Industry Managerial Accounting

Exhibit 10.14 Cost of Food Sold: Budget and Actual—Sample Restaurant

	Covers	Average Cost Per Cover	Total Cost
Budget	3,000	$4.00	$12,000
Actual	3,200	4.10	13,120
Difference	200	$ .10	$ 1,120(U)

$$\frac{\text{Cost}}{\text{Variance}} = \frac{\text{Budgeted}}{\text{Volume}} \times \left(\frac{\text{Budgeted}}{\text{Cost}} - \frac{\text{Actual}}{\text{Cost}} \right)$$

$$CV = BV(BC - AC)$$

$$\frac{\text{Volume}}{\text{Variance}} = \frac{\text{Budgeted}}{\text{Cost}} \times \left(\frac{\text{Budgeted}}{\text{Volume}} - \frac{\text{Actual}}{\text{Volume}} \right)$$

$$VV = BC(BV - AV)$$

$$\frac{\text{Cost-Volume}}{\text{Variance}} = \left(\frac{\text{Budgeted}}{\text{Cost}} - \frac{\text{Actual}}{\text{Cost}} \right) \times \left(\frac{\text{Budgeted}}{\text{Volume}} - \frac{\text{Actual}}{\text{Volume}} \right)$$

$$C\text{-}VV = (BC - AC)(BV - AV)$$

The cost-volume variance results from the interrelationship of the cost and volume variances.

The analysis of the cost of goods sold variance formulas is illustrated by using a food service example. The Sample Restaurant, open for dinner only, had cost of food sold results and budgeted amounts for January as shown in Exhibit 10.14. The budget variance of $1,120 is analyzed using variance analysis as follows:

The cost variance is determined as follows:

$$CV = BV(BC - AC)$$
$$= 3,000(4.00 - 4.10)$$
$$= 3,000(-.10)$$
$$= -\$300 \text{ (U)}$$

The cost variance of $300 is unfavorable because the cost per cover of 3,000 covers exceeded budget by $.10.

The volume variance is determined as follows:

$$VV = BC(BV - AV)$$
$$= 4(3,000 - 3,200)$$
$$= 4(-200)$$
$$= -\$800 \text{ (U)}$$

The volume variance of $800 is also unfavorable because excessive volume results in greater costs than budgeted. Remember that this is from an expense perspective. Excessive volume from a revenue perspective is favorable.

The cost-volume variance is determined as follows:

$$C\text{-}VV = (BC - AC)(BV - AV)$$
$$= (4.00 - 4.10)(3{,}000 - 3{,}200)$$
$$= (-.10)(-200)$$
$$= \underline{\$20} \ (U)$$

The cost-volume variance of $20 is also unfavorable, even though the mathematical sign of the result is positive. The cost-volume variance will be unfavorable when the other two variances (cost and volume) are the same, that is, when both are favorable or unfavorable. When the cost and volume variances differ, that is, when one is favorable and the other unfavorable, then the cost-volume variance will be favorable.

The sum of the three variances is $1,120:

Cost Variance	$300 (U)
Volume Variance	800 (U)
Cost-Volume Variance	20 (U)
Total	$1,120 (U)

This sum equals the $1,120 budget variance shown in Exhibit 10.14. These results show that of the total $1,120, only $300 was due to cost overruns. Further investigation should be undertaken to determine why there were excessive food costs of $300. The volume variance of $800 should be more than offset by the favorable volume variance for the Sample Restaurant food revenue. The cost-volume variance of $20 is due to the interrelationship of cost and volume. It is insignificant and requires no additional management attention.

Exhibit 10.15 is a graphic depiction of the cost of food sold variance analysis. The original budget of $12,000 for cost of food sold is represented by the rectangle OABC, while the actual food cost for the period is the rectangle ODFH. Therefore, the difference between these two rectangles is the budget variance. The budget variance is divided among the three variances of cost, volume, and cost-volume. The cost variance is represented by the rectangle ADEB. The volume variance is represented by the rectangle BGHC. The cost-volume variance is represented by the rectangle BEFG.

Variable Labor Variance Analysis

Variable labor expense (as discussed in Chapter 6) is labor expense that varies directly with activity. Variable labor increases as sales increase and decreases as sales decrease. In a lodging operation, the use of room attendants to clean rooms is a clear example of variable labor. Everything else being the same, the more rooms to be cleaned, the more room attendants' hours are necessary to clean the rooms; therefore, the greater the room attendants' wages. In a food service situation, servers' wages are generally treated as variable labor expense. Again, the greater the number of guests to be served food, the greater the number of servers; therefore, the greater the server expense. The remainder of the discussion of labor in this section will pertain to variable labor, which we will simply call labor expense.

Labor expense variances result from three general causes—volume, rate, and efficiency. All budget variances for labor expense may be

Exhibit 10.15   Cost of Food Sold Variance Analysis—Sample Restaurant

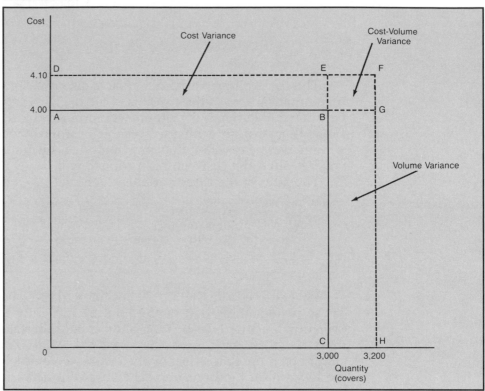

divided among these three areas. *Volume variances* (VV) result when there is a different volume of work than forecasted. *Rate variances* (RV) result when the average wage rate is different than planned. *Efficiency variances* (EV) result when the amount of work performed by the labor force on an hourly basis differs from the forecast. Of course, as with revenue variance analysis and with cost of goods sold variance analysis, there is a variance (called the *rate-time variance*) due to the interelationship of the major elements of the labor budget variance. The formulas for these variances are:

$$VV = BR(BT - ATAO)$$
$$RV = BT(BR - AR)$$
$$EV = BR(ATAO - AT)$$
$$R\text{-}TV = (BT - AT)(BR - AR)$$

where the elements within these formulas are defined as follows:

- BR (Budgeted Rate)—the average wage rates budgeted per hour for labor services.

- BT (Budgeted Time)—hours required to perform work according to the budget. For example, if the work standard for serving meals is 15 customers/hour per server, then servers would require 40 hours (600 ÷ 15) to serve 600 meals.

Exhibit 10.16 Labor Expense: Budget and Actual—Sample Restaurant

	Covers	Time/Cover	Total Time	Hourly Wage	Total
Budget	3,000	4 min.	200 hrs.	$2.50	$500
Actual	3,200	5 min.	266 ⅔	2.40	640
Difference	200	1 min.	66 ⅔ hrs.	$ .10	$140(U)

- ATAO (Allowable Time for Actual Output)—hours allowable to perform work based on the actual output. This is determined in the same way as budgeted time, except that the work is actual versus budget. For example, if 660 meals were actually served, the allowable time given a work standard of 15 meals/hour would be 44 hours (660 ÷ 15).

- AR (Actual Rate)—the actual average wage rate paid per hour for labor services.

- AT (Actual Time)—the number of hours actually worked.

The calculation of these formulas is illustrated in Exhibit 10.16. The work standard for servers of the Sample Restaurant is serving 15 meals per hour. Therefore, on the average, a meal should be served every four minutes (60 ÷ 15).

The volume variance is determined as follows:

$$\begin{aligned} VV &= BR(BT - ATAO) \\ &= 2.50(200 - 213.33^*) \\ &= 2.50(-13.33) \\ &= -\$33.33 \text{ (U)} \end{aligned}$$

*The ATAO of 213.33 is determined by dividing the work standard of 15 covers per hour into the 3,200 covers served.

The volume variance of $33.33 is unfavorable, because more covers were served than budgeted. Normally, the volume variance is beyond the control of the supervisor of personnel to which the labor expense pertains. Therefore, this should be isolated and generally not further pursued from an expense perspective. In addition, an unfavorable volume variance should be more than offset by the volume variance for the related food sales.

The rate variance for the Sample Restaurant is determined as follows:

$$\begin{aligned} RV &= BT(BR - AR) \\ &= 200(\$2.50 - \$2.40) \\ &= 200(\$.10) \\ &= \$20 \text{ (F)} \end{aligned}$$

The rate variance of $20 is favorable because the average pay rate per hour is $.10 per hour less than the budgeted $2.50 per hour. The credit for this is normally given to the labor supervisor responsible for scheduling and managing labor.

The efficiency variance for the Sample Restaurant is determined as follows:

$$EV = BR(ATAO - AT)$$
$$= \$2.50(213.33 - 266.67)$$
$$= \$2.50(-53.34)$$
$$= -\underline{\$133.35} \text{ (U)}$$

The efficiency variance of $133.35 is unfavorable, because an average of one minute more was spent serving a meal than was originally planned. The supervisor must determine why this occurred. It could have been due to new employees who were inefficient due to work overload, or perhaps there were other factors. Once the specific causes are determined, the manager can take corrective action to ensure a future recurrence is avoided.

The rate-time variance is determined as follows:

$$R\text{-}TV = (BT - AT)(BR - AR)$$
$$= (200 - 266.67)(\$2.50 - \$2.40)$$
$$= (-66.67)(\$.10)$$
$$= -\underline{\$6.67} \text{ (F)}$$

The rate-time variance of $6.67 is favorable, even though the negative sign seems to indicate otherwise. This compound variance is favorable when the individual variances within it differ. In this case, the rate variance was favorable; however, the time variance was unfavorable.

The sum of the four variances equals the budget variance of $140 (U) as follows:

Volume Variance	$ 33.33 (U)
Rate Variance	20.00 (F)
Efficiency Variance	133.35 (U)
Rate-time Variance	6.67 (F)
Total	$140.01 (U)

The one cent difference is due to rounding.

Exhibit 10.17 is a graphic depiction of the labor variance analysis of the Sample Restaurant. The budget for labor expense is represented by the rectangle ODEC, while the actual labor expense is represented by the rectangle OAGH. The rate variance is represented by the rectangle ADEB. The volume variance is represented by the rectangle CEIJ. The rectangle JIFH represents the efficiency variance. The rate-time variance is represented by the rectangle BEFG.

Exhibit 10.17 Labor Variance Analysis—Sample Restaurant

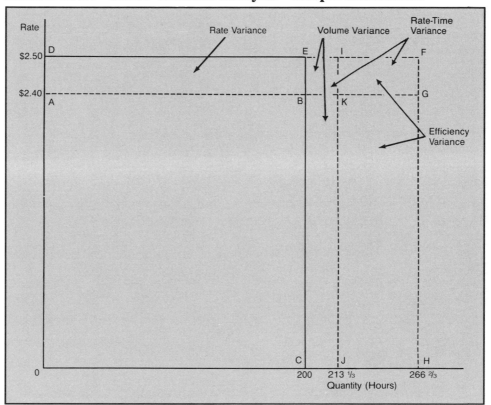

Exhibit 10.18 contains the analysis of the unfavorable rooms revenue variance of $680 identified earlier in the chapter for the Sands Motel. The breakdown is as follows:

Due to unfavorable volume differences	$887.50 (U)
Due to favorable pricing differences	220.00 (F)
Compound variance	12.50 (U)
	$680.00 (U)

Management needs to investigate the causes of the failure to sell 25 additional rooms. This failure was partially offset by a favorable price variance.

If the volume variance was due to controllable causes such as price resistance or rooms being unavailable due to being out-of-order or simply not clean when potential guests desire them, then management action can be taken. If, on the other hand, the causes were beyond management's control, such as weather-related factors, then no specific management action appears to be required.

The other significant variance of the Sands Motel requiring analysis was rooms payroll, which was favorable during January 19X4, at $257. Assume that an analysis of rooms labor reveals the following:

Exhibit 10.18 Rooms Revenue Variance Analysis—Sands Motel

Analysis of Rooms Revenue Variance
Sands Motel
January 19X4

	Room Nights	Price	Total
Budget	440	$35.50	$15,620
Actual	415	36.00	4,940
Difference	25	$ .50	$ 680 (U)

Volume Variance

VV = BP (AV – BV)
VV = 35.50 (415 – 440)
VV = $887.50 (U)

Price Variance

PV = BV (AP – BP)
PV = 440 (36.00 – 35.50)
PV = $220 (F)

Price – Volume Variance

P-VV = (AV – BV) (AP – BP)
P-VV = (415 – 440) (36.00 – 35.50)
P-VV = $12.50(U)

	Budget	Actual	Difference
Room attendants	$ 737	$ 581	$ 156 (F)
Front office	1,763	1,662	101 (F)
	$2,500	$2,243	$ 257 (F)

Since the largest portion relates to room attendants' wages, only this portion is analyzed for illustrative purposes in Exhibit 10.19. The analysis of the $156 variance reveals favorable volume, rate, and efficiency variances.

When analyzing a variable labor variance, pay careful attention to each type of variance. Generally, a volume variance is beyond the scope of the labor supervisor's responsibility. For example, the $156 favorable room attendants' labor variance includes $41.88 of volume variance which is favorable. This results from fewer rooms being sold than budgeted—hardly a reason to praise the supervisor. Likewise, when more rooms are sold than budgeted, the room attendants' labor expense variance would contain an unfavorable volume variance. This portion of the total variance is not the fault of the supervisor and should be excluded when analyzing the budget variance.

Determination of Problems and Management Action

The next step in the budgetary control process is for management to investigate variance analysis results in an effort to determine the cause(s) of the variance. This is needed because the analysis of a revenue variance will reveal differences due to price and/or volume, but not *why* the price

Exhibit 10.19   Rooms Payroll Variance Analysis—Sands Motel

Analysis of Room Payroll Variance
Sands Motel
January 19X4

	Room Nights	Time/ Room	Total Time	Hourly Wages	Total
Budget	440	30 min.	220 hrs.	$3.35	$737
Actual	415	28 min.	193 ⅔	3.00	581
Difference	25	2 min.	26 ⅓	$.35	$156(F)

Volume Variance

$VV = BR (BT - ATAO)$
$VV = 3.35 (220 - 207.5)$
$VV = 3.35 (12.5)$
$VV = \$41.88 \ (F)$

Rate Variance

$RV = BT (BR - AR)$
$RV = 220 (3.35 - 3.00)$
$RV = 220 (.35)$
$RV = \$77 \ (F)$

Efficiency Variance

$EV = BR (ATAO - AT)$
$EV = 3.35 (207.5 - 193.67)$
$EV = 3.35 (13.83)$
$EV = \$46.33 \ (F)$

Rate-Time Variance

$R\text{-}TV = (BT - AT)(BR - AR)$
$R\text{-}TV = (220 - 193.67)(3.35 - 3.00)$
$R\text{-}TV = (26.33)(.35)$
$R\text{-}TV = \$9.22 \ (U)$

Summation of Variances

Volume Variance	$41.88 (F)
Rate Variance	77.00 (F)
Efficiency Variance	46.33 (F)
Rate-Volume Variance	9.22 (U)
	155.99
Rounding Difference	.01
Total	$156.00(F)

and/or volume variances exist. Similarly, the analysis of variable labor expense will reveal differences due to rate, efficiency, and volume but, again, not the exact cause(s) of the variances. Additional investigation by management is required.

For example, assume that the analysis of the room attendants' labor variance reveals that a significant portion of an unfavorable variance is due to rate. Management must investigate the rate variance to determine why the average rate paid was higher than budgeted. An unfavorable labor rate variance may be due to staffing problems, excessive overtime pay, or a combination of these two factors. It may have been due to the scheduling of more higher paid room attendants than originally planned. There may be another reason. Each significant variance requires further management investigation to determine the cause(s).

The final step to complete the budgetary control process is hospitality managers taking action to correct a problem. For example, if a major cause of the rate variance for room attendants is that excessive overtime is paid, this may be controlled by requiring all overtime to be approved a specified number of hours in advance by the next highest management level.

Reforecasting

Regardless of the extensive efforts and the sophisticated methods used in formulating operations budgets, most large hospitality properties reforecast their expected operations as they progress through the budget year. This reforecasting is necessary only when the actual results begin to vary significantly from the budget. Some organizations will start reforecasting at the beginning of the budget year and continue to reforecast every month for the entire year.

Reforecasting at The Sheraton Corporation

For an example, we will look at how The Sheraton Corporation reforecasts. Reforecasting at Sheraton is a continuing process that begins immediately with the new year. It involves a three-step process as follows:

1. Three Month Outlook
2. Advanced Information for Outlook
3. Weekly Activity Report

The Three Month Outlook. Exhibit 10.20 is a short-term forecast used to update the annual budget on an ongoing basis. It is prepared monthly and covers the following 90-day period. The budget continues to be the standard against which goal achievement is measured. The outlook process enables management to evaluate the hotel's immediate future and to react accordingly by determining objectives, making plans, and assigning responsibilities. The general manager should be able to judge the performance of his/her team members relative to their outlook commitments.

The Three Month Outlook blends two types of forecast into its report format:

- Sales forecast (revenues, occupancy, and average rate)
- Profit and loss forecast (complete P & L)

While the general manager is the final approval authority, the hotel controller is responsible for overall coordination of the report preparation.

The Advanced Information for Outlook. Exhibit 10.21 is prepared each month in conjunction with the Three Month Outlook. Its purpose is to provide the home office with a weekly breakout of certain key outlook and budget figures on a month-to-date basis for the following month. The report is the basis for the home office's preparation of a consolidated report each week comparing month-to-date actual results with outlook and budget.

Exhibit 10.20 Three Month Outlook

THREE MONTH OUTLOOK

HOTEL_____ LOCATION_____

Months:			19		19			19		
Report 000.0	OUTLOOK	BUDGET	LAST YEAR	Outlook	Budget	Last Year	Outlook	Budget	Last Year	

Statistics

		OUTLOOK	BUDGET	LAST YEAR	Outlook	Budget	Last Year	Outlook	Budget	Last Year
% Occupancy	%									
Average Room Rate	$									
No. Rooms Occupied										
No. Rooms Available										
Total Revenue (Excl TVA)	$									
Total Revenue (Incl TVA)										

Operated Departments		$	%	$	%	$	%				
Room	–Revenues		100		100		100				
	–Wages & Benefits										
	–Other expenses										
	–Departmental Profit										
Food	–Revenues (Excl. O/L)		100		100		100				
	–Cost of Sales										
	–Wages & Benefits										
	–Other Expenses										
	–Departmental Profit										
Beverage	–Revenues (Excl O/L)		100		100		100				
	–Cost of Sales										
	–Wages & Benefits										
	–Other Expenses										
	–Departmental Profit										
Food & Beverage Other Income											
	–Food & Bev. Dept'l Prof										
Casino Departmental Profit											
Minor Operated Dept. Profit											
Convention Services Dept. Profit											
Rents & Other Income											
Total Operated Departments											
Overhead Departments											
Administrative & General											
Marketing											
Property Operation											
Total Overhead Departments											
Gross Operating Profit											
Taxes											
Insurance											
Rent Non-Affiliate											
Interest & Dept. Exp. Non-Affiliate											
(Interest Income) Non-Affiliate											
Other (Adds) & Deductions											
Cash Earnings (Loss)											
Depreciation/Replacement Reserve											
(Deferral) of First Year Loss											
Amortization of First Year Loss/Pre. Op.											
Profit Before Sheraton Charges											
Rent-Affiliate											
Inf. Exp. (Inc.) Affil.-Net											
Profit Before Sheraton Fees											
Fee	License										
	Management Basic										
	Management Incentive										
	Marketing										
Total Sheraton Fees											
Pretax Profit (Loss) Operations											

	Outlook	Budget	Last Year
Equivalent Full Time Employees			
Salaries & Wages			
Benefits			
Total Compensation			

Joint Ventures			
	Outlook	Budget	Last Year
Joint Venture Pretax Profit			
Partner(s) Equity			
Sheraton Gross Equity Before Deferral/Amort.			
Def./(Amort.) 1st Year Equity Loss			
(Def.)/Amort Fee Income			
Sheraton Net Equity			

International Hotels Only Rate of Exchange
Outlook U.S.
$1.00_____
Budget U.S.
$1.00_____
Last Year U.S.
$1.00_____

Controller _____ Date _____ General Manager _____ Date

Exhibit 10.21   Advanced Information for Outlook/Fiscal Budget

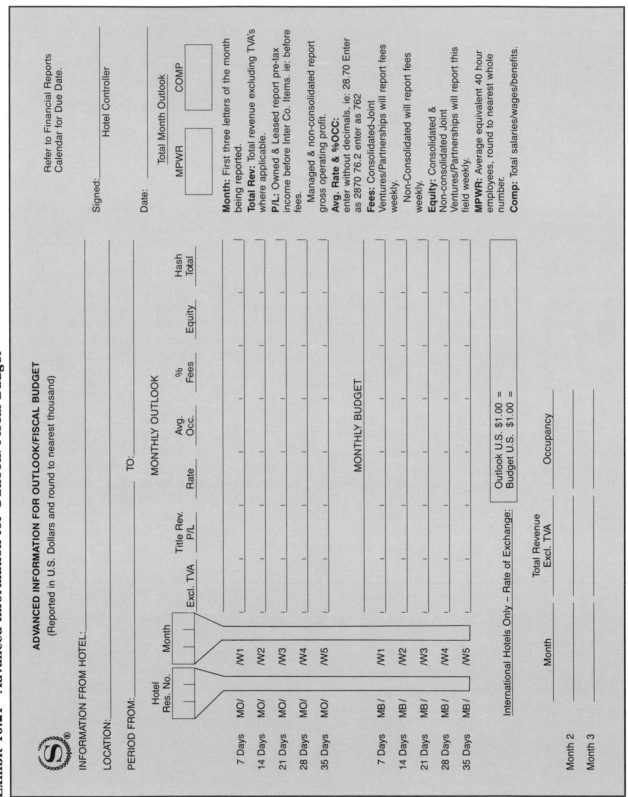

The Weekly Activity Report. Exhibit 10.22 is a calculated estimate of each hotel's key financial results. With the exception of fiscal year beginning and ending dates, the reporting periods cover 7-day time frames from Thursday through Wednesday. The reported information is on a cumulative (month-to-date) basis.

Each hotel uses its Weekly Activity Report as a primary source of financial performance, engaging in a review of its profit and loss (income) statement before the approved information is transmitted to headquarters.

At headquarters, the on-line information enters directly into a computer which generates a report showing actual results with variances to Budget and Outlook.

In addition to the Three Month Outlook, reforecasting is also done on a total year basis at least twice a year for strategic and operating plans.

Budgeting at Multi-Unit Hospitality Enterprises

This chapter has been oriented toward operations budgeting at a single hotel property. However, both lodging and food service chains continue to increase their dominance in their respective hospitality segments. The chains in the food service industry account for more than 50% of the hotel food service sales, and in the lodging industry giants such as Holiday Corporation and Marriott experience over $1 billion in lodging sales annually.

Research on budgeting at multi-unit food service and lodging chains has revealed the following significant results:[3]

1. A majority of companies develop their overall corporate budgets using the bottom-up approach, that is, managers develop individual budgets that are accumulated through successive company layers until an overall corporate budget is proposed. The commonest reasons cited for using the bottom-up approach are (1) the need to increase the feeling of unit-level "ownership" in the budget, and (2) the ability of unit-level personnel to recognize specific problems affecting lower organizational levels.

2. A significant minority develop their budgets at the corporate level and then dictate the budgets to the lower levels in the corporate structure. The major reason cited for the top-down approach is that the sum of the individual restaurant budgets would not meet corporate expectations.

3. Several companies use a combination of the bottom-up/top-down approaches.

4. Whether the budgeting approach is bottom-up or top-down, most companies at the corporate level set financial goals before the budget process begins.

5. The major differences in budgeting by chains versus the single unit organization include:
   - Greater need for coordination
   - Greater volume of information to be processed

Exhibit 10.22 Weekly Activity Report

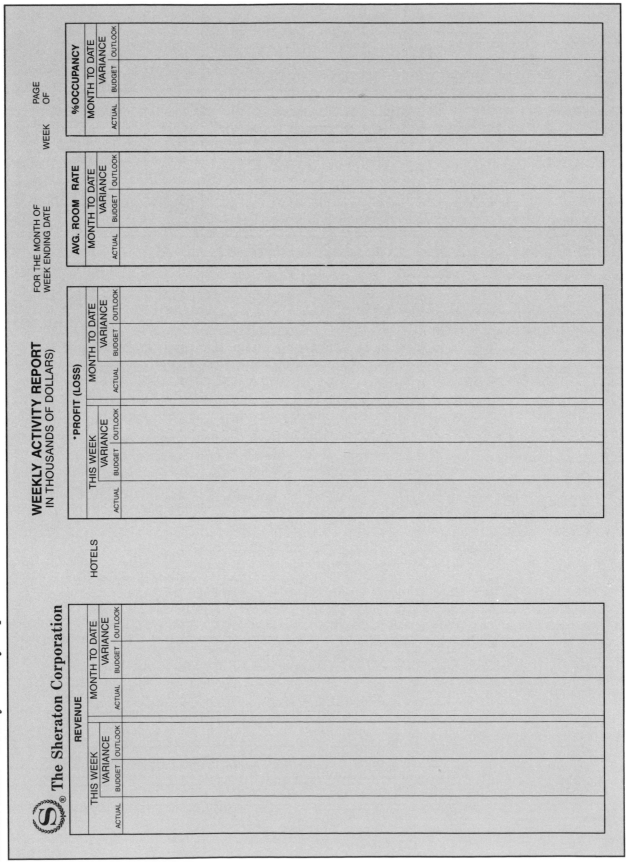

- Use of more sophisticated and frequently computerized procedures
- Greater amount of time required
- Unique procedures to allocate costs between organization levels
- Greater extent of management attention to budget process

6. The percentage of lodging chains which reported allowable variance levels for selected costs is as follows:

	Food Costs	Beverage Costs	Labor Costs	Other Costs
< 1%	5%	5%	6%	6%
1–1.9%	26	28	23	6
2–2.9%	11	11	18	29
3–3.9%	5	6	12	18
4–4.9%	16	11	6	6
> 4.9%	5	6	6	6
No set amount	32	33	29	29
Total	100%	100%	100%	100%

For those lodging chains which set tolerance criteria for variable costs, 1–1.9% was commonest for food costs, beverage costs, and labor costs, while 2–2.9% was commonest for other costs. Food service chains generally have even lower tolerances than do the lodging chains.

Budgeting at The Sheraton Corporation

Budgeting at The Sheraton Corporation involves a three-stage process as follows:

1. Long-range strategic plans
2. Shorter term operating plans
3. Detailed monthly budgets for the following year

The Strategic Plan is done each spring and is a projection of the financial objectives of the corporation over the next five years. It is generally a top-down approach with corporate strategies defined in the areas of marketing, development, and financial performance. The hotels participate individually by providing seven-year summary financial statements to their divisions' offices showing prior year actual, current year budget, forecast, variance, and projected earnings for the next five years (see Exhibit 10.23).

The One Year Operating Plan is done in the fall and is a refinement of Plan Year I of the Strategic Plan. Standardized workpapers are provided to each hotel for use in developing detailed backup for their Plan Year I revenue and expense projections. These workpapers are then subject to review by division operations and support staffs before final acceptance

Exhibit 10.23   Strategic Plan: Comparative Income Statement

Sheraton		STRATEGIC PLAN
Weighted Avg. Exchange Rate–US $1		19 ____ COMPARATIVE INCOME STATEMENT (Round 1c Nearest Thousand)

(HOTEL NAME)

FRS NO ____

(DATE) ____   (REV NO) ____

LINE NO.	Account	PRIOR YEAR ACTUAL 19___	% of Rev	CURRENT YEAR 19___ BUDGET	FORECAST	% of Rev	VARIANCE	PLAN YEAR I 19___	% of Rev	PLAN YEAR II 19___	% of Rev	PLAN YEAR III 19___	% of Rev	PLAN YEAR IV 19___	% of Rev	PLAN YEAR V 19___	% of Rev
1	Total Revenue – Including TVA																
2	Excluding TVA		100			100			100		100		100		100		100
3	Rooms – Revenues		100			100			100		100		100		100		100
4	Wages & Benefits																
5	Other Expenses																
6	Departmental Profit																
7	Food Revenues		100			100			100		100		100		100		100
8	Cost of Sales																
9	Wages–Benefits																
10	Other Expenses																
11	Departmental Profit																
12	Beverage Revenues		100			100			100		100		100		100		100
13	Costs of Sales																
14	Wages & Benefits		100			100			100		100		100		100		100
15	Other Expenses																
16	Departmental Profit																
17	Food & Beverage Other Income																
18	Convention Services Deptl. Profit																
19	Total Food & Bev. Profit																
20	Minor Operated Deptl. Profit																
21	Casino Departmental Profit																
22	Rents and Other Income																
23	Total Operated Deptl. Profit																
24	Overhead Departments																
25	Administrative & General																
26	Marketing																
27	Property Operation																
28	Total Overhead Departments																
29	Gross Operating Profit (Loss)																
30	Capital Expenses																
31	Taxes																
32	Insurance																
33	Rent Non-Affiliate																
34	Int. & Debt Exp. Non-Affiliate																
35	(Int. Income) – Non-Affiliate																
36	Other (Adds) & Deductions																
37	Total Capital Exp. & Other																
38	Cash Earnings (Loss)																
39	Depreciation/Replacement Reserve																
40	(Deferral) of First Year Loss																
41	Amortization 1st Yr. Loss/Pre-Open Exp.																
42	Profit Before Sheraton Charges																
43	Rent – Affiliate																
44	Int. Exp. (Inc.) Affil. – Net																
45	Marketing Fee																
46	License Fee																
47	Mgmt. Fee – Basic																
48	Management Fee – Incentive																
49	Total Fees																
50	Pretax Profit (Loss) Operations																
51	Income Taxes																
52	(Gain)/Loss Translation																
53	Net Operations																
54	Memo Sheraton Gross Equity																
55	Def./(Amort) 1st Yr. Equity Loss																
56	(Def)/Amort. Fee Income																
57	Sheraton Net Equity																
58	Total Salaries, Wages, Benefits																
59	Avg. Equiv. Full-Time Employees																
60	Headcount at 12/31																
61	Overall Occupancy %																
62	Average Rate																
63	No. of Rooms Available																
64	No. of Rooms Occupied																
65	No. of Rooms at Year End																

of the Operating Plan as local management's formal commitment to achieve these goals during the next year.

Upon final acceptance of the hotel's Operating Plan, the Annual Income Statement for Plan Year I automatically becomes the fixed budget against which actual performance will be measured for the next fiscal year. The budget is input into the computer at the corporate headquarters after the hotels break down the annual income statement by month and by departmental components on forms provided for that purpose.

Summary

The budgetary process is valuable to the operation of a hospitality establishment. In order to formulate a budget, the establishment's goals must be stated and each department must look ahead and estimate future performance. As the actual period progresses, management can compare operating results to the budget, and significant differences can be studied. This process forces management to set future goals and to strive to see that they become realized.

In order to formulate a budget, each department estimates its revenues and expenses. This is done by observing past trends and projecting them for another year. The manager must also take into account forces in the economy, new developments in the market, and other significant events which will affect the operation. These projections are then combined to form a budget for the next period's operations. At this point, the budgeted results are compared with the establishment's goals, and the budget is adjusted until these goals are met.

Once completed, the budget becomes a control tool. As the periods progress, management compares the budget with actual performance. The differences between each line item are calculated, and any significant differences are analyzed. Significance depends on both absolute dollar differences and percentage differences. The analysis includes dividing each line item into its components including price and volume for revenues and rate, volume, and efficiency for labor. Management can then address any deficiencies and take corrective action to keep the operations heading toward the defined goals.

Endnotes

1. For more information on zero-base budgeting, see Peter A. Pyrrh, *Zero-Base Budgeting* (New York: John Wiley & Sons, 1973) and Lee M. Kruel, "Zero-Base Budgeting of Hotel Indirect Expense," *The Cornell Hotel & Restaurant Administration Quarterly*, November 1978, pp. 11–14.

2. A *service center* is a department outside the profit centers which provides services to the profit centers or the hotel as a whole—for example, the marketing department. A *cost center* is a department within a profit center for which costs are tracked—for example, housekeeping within the rooms department.

3. Raymond S. Schmidgall and Jack D. Ninemeier. "Foodservice Budgeting: How the Chains Do It," *The Cornell Hotel & Restaurant Administration Quarterly*, February 1986, pp. 51–55. Raymond S. Schmidgall and Jack D. Ninemeier. "Budgeting in Hotel Chains: Coordination and Control," *The Cornell Hotel & Restaurant Administration Quarterly*, May 1987, pp. 79–84.

Key Terms

cost of goods sold variance
incremental budgeting
operations budget
revenue variance
significance criteria

strategic planning
variable labor variance
variance analysis
zero-base budgeting

Discussion Questions

1. What are four future items which should be considered when formulating a budget?

2. How does a budget help an establishment to realize its operating goals?

3. How is the budget formulated?

4. Why should budgets be prepared at various levels of sales?

5. What constitutes a "significant" variance?

6. What does the volume variance highlight for management?

7. Why is an increase in volume favorable in revenue analysis and unfavorable in cost analysis?

8. What does the formula EV = BR(ATAO − AT) calculate?

9. What items should be considered when preparing the rooms revenue section of the budget?

10. What are three possible goals an establishment could set for its operations?

Problems _____

Problem 10.1

Jackie Jackson is the rooms department manager of Waverly Motor Hotel and is preparing a condensed 19X6 annual budget. She has the following information upon which to base her estimates.

- Estimated occupancy percentage: 75%
- Rooms: 100
- Average rate: $50.00
- Labor: Variable: $5.00/room
  Fixed: $100,000 (annual)
- Other operating expenses: $2.50/room

Required:

1. Prepare a condensed budget for the rooms department. (Assume that the hotel is open 365 days a year.)

2. The Waverly's management requires that the department have a departmental profit of at least $1,000,000 and a departmental profit of 75% of revenue. Will Ms. Jackson's condensed budget projections be acceptable to the hotel's management?

Problem 10.2

Barbara Collins is the manager of Shives, a fine dining restaurant, and is preparing next year's budget. She wants to examine three different levels of sales as follows: $700,000, $1,000,000, and $1,300,000. The following information upon which to make the calculations is provided.

- Food cost percentage: 45%
- Labor: Variable: 23%
           Fixed: $80,000
- Other operating expenses: 8%
- Fixed charges: $100,000
- Income taxes: 30% of pre-tax income

Required:

1. Assist her by preparing the condensed operating budget for Shives at the three levels of sales indicated above.

2. Comment briefly regarding the impact of different levels of sales on the restaurant's profits.

Problem 10.3

Jim Small is working on the operations budget for Small's Place for 19X4. The estimated seat turnover by meal period by day is as follows:

	Breakfast	Lunch	Dinner
Mon.–Fri.	1.0	1.5	.75
Sat.	.5	.5	1.5
Sun.	.5	1.5	.5

Small's has 100 seats and its average checks for breakfast, lunch, and dinner for 19X3 were $3.20, $5.20, and $8.80, respectively. Jim Small estimates his enterprise will be able to increase its average prices in 19X4 by 5% over 19X3.

Small's Place has experienced a food cost of 38% in the past. However, by implementing new controls, Jim believes 36% can be achieved in 19X4. Labor is expected to average 30%, while other controllable expenses should total 15% of total sales. Fixed costs are expected to total $100,000, and Small's tax rate is 15%. In addition, investments owned by the restaurant are expected to generate earnings of $10,000.

Assume that 19X4 is leap year and that the first day of the year is Saturday.

Required:

Prepare the operations budget for 19X4 for Small's Place.

Problem 10.4

The Mica Motel (MM), open 365 days a year, consists of an 80-room motel with a 60-seat coffee shop. J.D. Mica provides you with the following information:

1. Of the 80 rooms, 60 are doubles and 20 are singles.

2. The doubles are sold for $22 each and the singles are sold for $18 each.

3. Forecasted occupancy is 84% for doubles and 78% for singles.

4. The average occupancy per room is 1.8. (Only one person stays in a single but two or more may stay in a double for $22/night.)

5. Forty percent of those staying in the singles and 20% of those staying in the doubles eat breakfast in the coffee shop. (There is no walk-in business for breakfast.) The average check is $2.80.

6. The lunch and dinner business have seat turnovers and average checks as follows:

	Lunch		Dinner	
	Turnover	Aver. Ck.	Turnover	Aver. Ck.
Mon.–Fri.	1.25	$4.20	1.0	$10.75
Sat.	.5	4.50	1.0	12.50
Sun.	1.5	5.50	.5	11.25

7. The first day of the year for which you are to prepare the budget is Monday.

8. The food cost percentage is estimated to be 35%.

9. The labor cost percentages are as follows:
   Rooms: 20%
   Food: 32%

10. Other direct expenses of the operated departments are as follows:
    Rooms: 10%
    Food: 12%

11. Undistributed operating expenses include:

    $100,000 of fixed expenses and the remainder is 10% of total revenue

12. Other fixed costs include the following:
    Property taxes $30,000
    Depreciation   60,000
    Interest   50,000

13. The MM's average income tax rate is 30% of income before income taxes.

Required:

Prepare, in reasonable form, the operating budget for the year.

Problem 10.5

For the week of June 6, Melvin Mince, the manager of Melvin's Hotel in northwestern Illinois, budgeted 600 hours for room attendants to clean rooms. This budget was based on a work standard of cleaning one room every 36 minutes. The rooms attendants actually worked 660 hours cleaning 1,050 rooms. The budgeted wage rate for room attendants is $3.40 per hour. The wages paid to room attendants totaled $2,178.00.

Required:

1. What is the amount of the budget variance?
2. What is the amount of the volume variance?
3. What is the amount of the efficiency variance?
4. What is the amount of the rate variance?

Problem 10.6

Harry Booky, the Happy Hotel's accountant, has just finished the hotel's monthly financial statements. He has shown an unfavorable budget variance for room attendants' wages, and the head housekeeper is in the "hot seat." However, since extra rooms were cleaned, the head housekeeper may not be totally responsible for the unfavorable variance. Ms. Edna Degree, the hotel's general manager, has requested that the unfavorable budget variance of $605 be analyzed.

The available information is as follows:

1. Budgeted rooms sales: 6,000
   Budgeted hourly pay rate for room attendants: $4.50
   Work standard: clean 2 rooms per hour

2. Actual results—room sales: 6,400
   Actual average hourly pay rate: $4.55
   Actual hours attendants worked: 3,100

Required:

1. Is the unfavorable budget variance of $605 significant? Why or why not?
2. Compute the volume variance.
3. Compute the rate variance.
4. Compute the efficiency variance.
5. To what degree is the head housekeeper responsible for the unfavorable variance?

Problem 10.7

Stacy Konrad, the manager of the Double K Motel, has done the preliminary budget analysis, but is not sure how to evaluate the results. The following diagram is a depiction of the labor expense for the Double K.

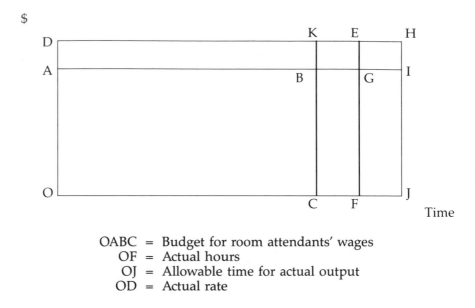

$$
\begin{aligned}
\text{OABC} &= \text{Budget for room attendants' wages} \\
\text{OF} &= \text{Actual hours} \\
\text{OJ} &= \text{Allowable time for actual output} \\
\text{OD} &= \text{Actual rate}
\end{aligned}
$$

Required:

1. Which rectangle represents the rate variance?

2. How is the compound variance represented?

3. Which rectangle represents the volume variance?

4. Which rectangle represents the efficiency variance?

Problem 10.8

Part I

Holly's Hotel budgeted 800 room sales for the week ended March 10. The estimated average price per room was $18.50. The actual average price per room was 10% greater than anticipated, while room sales in units were 10% less than forecasted.

Required:

What is the budget variance for the week? Analyze the budget variance by calculating each revenue variance.

Part II

For the same week, Holly's Hotel's head housekeeper, based on the work standard, budgeted 400 hours for room attendants to clean the rooms sold. The actual hours worked totaled 380. The estimated average wage rate for the attendants is $4.00 per hour. The wages paid totaled $1,444.

Required:

1. Were the room attendants efficient?

2. How much was the price (rate) variance?

3. Based on the above, how would you rate the head housekeeper, considering the dollars spent? Use figures to support your answer.

Problem 10.9

The Armington Café appears to be having some difficulty controlling its food costs. The café's budgeted food cost percentage was 36% based on food sales of $100,000. However, the actual food sales were $110,000, and the actual food cost totaled $40,800. The proprietor, M.D. Schmidt, is concerned about the unfavorable food cost variance of $4,800. The number of covers budgeted and actually served totaled 15,000 and 16,000, respectively. The average food service check was budgeted for $6.6667. The average food service check for the month was $6.875.

Required:

1. Analyze the food revenue variance of $10,000, showing the amounts that relate to volume and price.

2. Analyze the cost of food sold variance and determine the amounts relating to the cost variance, volume variance, and cost-volume variance.

Problem 10.10

R. K. Dwight is interested in long-term operations planning for the rooms department of her hotel, the Dwight Inn. The budget detail for 19X5 is as follows:

	Rooms	Occ. %	ADR	Total
Singles	50	60%	$55	$ 602,250
Doubles	100	75%	$65	1,779,375
Suites	50	80%	$70	1,022,000
			Total	$3,403,625

Payroll costs:
Fixed labor costs (annual) $120,000
Variable labor costs   12% of room sales

Other expenses: (as a percent of room sales)
Commissions   2.0%
Laundry   2.0%
Operating supplies   3.0%
Linen   0.5%
Uniforms   0.5%
All other   1.5%

Assume that the rooms department for years 19X6–19X9 is able to realize occupancy increases of 0.5 percentage points per year for each type of room sales (for example, singles would be 60.5% for 19X6), and that ADR increases of $2 per year can be realized for each type of room. Further assume that variable labor costs increase by 4% each year and fixed labor costs increase by 6% each year. Finally, assume that the other expense percentages are maintained over the five years of 19X5–19X9. Round all figures to the nearest dollar.

Required:

Prepare the five year budget for the rooms department of the Dwight Inn.

11 Cash Management

Cash management refers to the management of a hospitality operation's cash balances (currency and demand deposits), cash flow (cash receipts and disbursements), and short-term investments in securities. Cash management is critical to both large and small hospitality operations. Insufficient cash can quickly lead to bankruptcy. This chapter will address many questions regarding cash management, including the following:

1. What is the difference between income and cash flows?
2. What is contained in a cash budget?
3. How are cash receipts forecasted?
4. How do short-term and long-term cash budgeting approaches differ?
5. What are the relevant factors to consider when investing working capital funds?
6. What are compensating balances?
7. How does a lockbox system speed up cash flow?
8. Why is depreciation expense irrelevant in cash flow considerations?
9. Why are investors interested in cash flow?
10. How are other (non-cash) current assets related to cash flow?

Our discussion of cash management will identify the uses and importance of cash in a hospitality operation. We will consider the distinction between income and cash flows and explain what is meant by negative cash flow. We will discuss basic approaches to using cash budgets for planning purposes. We will also address the major areas of hospitality operations affecting the process of cash budgeting, such as management of working capital including accounts receivable, inventory, and current liabilities. Finally, we will address the special aspects of integrated cash management for multi-unit operations.

Cash and Its Importance

In hospitality establishments, cash consists of petty cash funds, cash on hand for operational purposes, and cash in the bank. Cash on hand includes both house banks and undeposited cash receipts. Cash in the bank includes demand deposits. Some operations also consider time deposits and certificates of deposit as cash. In our discussion, all of these elements will be considered cash.

Petty cash funds are established for making minor cash purchases. These funds are normally maintained on an **imprest basis**—that is, they are replenished by the amount of disbursements since the previous replenishment.

House banks are maintained in order to facilitate cash transactions with guests. Each cash drawer should hold only as much as is needed to transact business. Added together, the house banks in a hotel may total several thousand dollars. Since house banks do not generate earnings, these cash balances should be minimized.

Ideally, the hospitality operation's cash balance in a demand deposit bank account should be zero. That is, daily deposits should equal disbursements from the account. However, cash received and cash disbursed are generally not uniform because the cash receipts for a day seldom equal the cash disbursements for the same day. Therefore, most operations maintain minimum balances in their checking accounts to cover checks drawn. The reason for keeping these cash balances is commonly referred to as a **transaction motive**.

The size of the checking account balance is also influenced by banks. Some banks demand that depositors maintain substantial amounts in their accounts to cover bank services and to serve as compensating balances for bank loans. For example, an operation may receive a loan for $100,000 and be required to maintain a 10% compensating balance. This means $10,000 ($100,000 × 10%) must be maintained in the checking account. Since no interest is earned on the compensating balance, the **effective cost** of the loan is higher than its stated interest rate. The effective cost is determined as follows:

$$\text{Effective Interest Rate} = \frac{\text{Annual Interest on Loan}}{\text{Loan} - \text{Compensating Balance Requirement}}$$

For example, assume that a hotel receives a one-year loan of $100,000 at 10% interest with a compensating balance requirement of $10,000. The effective interest rate is 11.1%, as illustrated below:

$$
\begin{aligned}
\text{Interest} &= \text{Principal} \times \text{Rate} \times \text{Time} \\
&= 100{,}000 \times 10\% \times 1 \text{ year} \\
&= \$10{,}000
\end{aligned}
$$

$$
\begin{aligned}
\text{Effective Interest Rate} &= \frac{\$10{,}000}{100{,}000 - 10{,}000} \\
&= \frac{10{,}000}{90{,}000} \\
&= 11.1\%
\end{aligned}
$$

Aggressive financial managers attempt to keep cash balances as low as possible given in-house cash needs and banking requirements. The cost of maintaining excessive in-house cash or checking accounts is the opportunity cost. The opportunity cost equals the earnings available if the cash were invested. For example, if a hospitality operation has an average annual checking account balance of $40,000 when the bank requires only $25,000, the opportunity cost is the interest that could be earned on $15,000. At an interest rate of 10%, the opportunity cost is $1,500 annually ($15,000 × .1).

Investors also have a keen interest in an operation's cash position. Investors make money in two ways: they receive cash dividends and their wealth increases as the stock prices increase. However, corporations are able to pay cash dividends only as cash is available. Therefore, those investing in corporations for dividends will review financial statements, especially the statement of cash flows, to determine whether the operation has sufficient cash to pay dividends and whether it will be operated in a manner that will allow dividend payments in the future.

Distinction Between Income and Cash Flows

Income flows result from operations generating revenues and incurring expenses. These flows are shown on the income statement and reflect the results of operations. **Cash flows** result from the receipt and disbursement of cash. It is possible for an operation to generate profits (income flow) yet have a negative cash flow (cash disbursements exceed cash receipts).

Exhibit 11.1 illustrates this situation. The statements are simplified statements for illustrative purposes. (Income and cash flow statements are discussed in Chapters 3 and 4.) As the income statement shows, Rambles Restaurant generated net income flows of $15,000; however, cash disbursements exceeded cash receipts by $20,000. In this simplified illustration, the differences in income and cash flows are as follows:

Income Flows	Cash Flows
1. Depreciation $50,000	1. Depreciation has no effect on cash flows.
2. Interest expense $25,000	2. Interest expense is part of the mortgage payment of $50,000. The $25,000 difference between the mortgage payment and the interest expense is the principal reduction portion of the mortgage payment.
3. The purchase of equipment has no direct effect on income flows. The write-off (depreciation) will affect income flows over several years.	3. Payment of $50,000 for equipment purchase (purchased in the last month of the year)
4. Dividends do not affect income flows.	4. Dividends paid of $10,000

Therefore, the $110,000 *cash* outflows listed above (mortgage payment of $50,000, payment of $50,000 for equipment, and dividends of $10,000

Exhibit 11.1   Sample Condensed Income Statement and Cash Flow Statement—Rambles Restaurant

Condensed Income Statement and Cash Flow Statement
Rambles Restaurant
For the year ended December 31, 19X3

Income Statement		Cash Flow Statement	
Sales	$600,000	Cash Receipts:	
Cost of Food Sold	200,000	Cash Sales	$300,000
Payroll Cost	200,000	Collection of Accounts	
Other Operating Expense	100,000	Receivable	300,000
Depreciation	50,000	Total	600,000
Interest	25,000	Cash Disbursements:	
Income Taxes	10,000	Purchases of Food	200,000
		Payment of Payroll	200,000
Net Income	$15,000	Payment of Operating Costs	100,000
		Payment of Income Taxes	10,000
		Payment for Equipment	50,000
		Mortgage Payment	50,000
		Dividends Paid	10,000
		Total	620,000
		Excess Cash Disbursements	$20,000

paid) exceed the sum of the two *income* outflows (depreciation and interest expense) of $75,000. The difference of $35,000 ($110,000 − $75,000) is the same as the difference between the income flows (net income of $15,000) and cash flows (net cash outflow of $20,000). Note that all other cash flows and income flows are the same in this simplified example. In more complex situations, there are usually additional differences between income and cash flows.

A hospitality operation may withstand negative cash flows for short periods of time if cash reserves are adequate to cover the deficits. However, over long periods, negative cash flows will most likely result in failure even if income flows are positive.

Most businesses, including hospitality establishments, have peaks and valleys in their operations. Generally, more cash is required during peak periods because cash is tied up in inventories and especially accounts receivable. Therefore, cash planning is important to ensure sufficient cash at all times. Cash planning is achieved by preparing cash budgets for several months in the future.

Cash Budgeting

Cash budgets are prepared to reflect the estimated cash receipts and cash disbursements for the period. In certain situations, cash may be in short supply and a cash deficit may be projected. If the estimated cash receipts and beginning cash (estimated available cash) are not sufficient to cover projected cash disbursements, management must take action. Even if estimated available cash is greater than projected cash disbursements, the projected cash balance must be reviewed to determine if it is a sufficient buffer for any cash receipt shortfalls and/or unplanned cash disbursements. If the estimated cash balance is insufficient, the operation must plan to increase cash receipts, decrease cash disbursements, or do both. Management actions to cover temporary deficits may include obtaining short-term bank loans, obtaining loans from stockholders, deferring equipment purchases, and deferring dividend payments or a combination of such actions.

If the estimated cash balance at the end of the period appears excessive, then the excess cash should be temporarily invested. The five factors management should consider when investing excess cash are risk, return, liquidity, cost, and size:

- *Risk* refers to the probability of losing the investment. Management should generally take a minimum risk when investing, especially when investing short-run funds. For example, investments in government securities such as Treasury Bills are considered risk-free.

- *Return* refers to the rate of return that can be received on the funds. Generally, the greater the risk and the longer the investment period, the greater the return.

- *Liquidity* refers to the ability to convert the investment to cash. When cash is invested temporarily, it should generally be invested in fairly liquid investments so it can be quickly liquidated as required.

- *Cost* refers to the brokerage cost of investing.

- *Size* refers to the amount of funds available for investing. In general, the more money available for investing, the higher the return.

Because managers need to know in advance whether cash shortages or excesses are likely, they project cash budgets. There are two basic approaches to cash budgeting: the cash receipts and disbursements approach and the adjusted net income approach. The method used depends primarily on the length of time for which the cash budget is prepared.

Cash Receipts and Disbursements Approach

The **cash receipts and disbursements approach** is useful when forecasting cash receipts for periods of up to six months. It shows the direct sources of cash receipts, such as cash sales, collection of accounts receivable, bank loans, sale of capital stock, and so forth. It also reveals the direct uses of cash, such as payment of food purchases, payroll, mortgage payments, and dividend payments. Because the cash receipts and disbursement method reflects the direct sources and uses of cash, it is easy to understand. However, it should generally not be used for periods exceeding six months. Projected figures beyond this point become

Exhibit 11.2 Cash Budget—Cash Receipts and Disbursements Approach

	Cash Budget					
	Cash Receipts and Disbursements Approach					
	For the months of Jan.–June, 19X1					
	January	February	March	April	May	June
Estimated Cash – Beginning	$	$	$	$	$	$
Estimated Cash Receipts:						
Cash Sales						
Collection of Accounts Receivable						
Proceeds from Bank Loans						
Proceeds from Sale of Fixed Assets						
Other						
Total						
Estimated Cash Available						
Estimated Cash Disbursements:						
Inventory						
Payroll						
Operating Expenses						
Taxes						
Insurance						
Mortgage Payments						
Dividends						
Other						
Total						
Estimated Cash Ending						
Minimum Cash Required						
Cash Excess or Shortage	$	$	$	$	$	$

increasingly unreliable, especially when actual operations differ significantly from the operations budget.

Exhibit 11.2 illustrates the basic format of a cash budget based on the cash receipts and disbursements approach. This format consists of two major sections: estimated cash receipts and estimated cash disbursements. Estimated cash receipts are added to the estimated beginning cash to find the estimated cash available for the period. Estimated cash disbursements are subtracted from estimated cash available to determine estimated ending cash. This figure is then compared to the minimum cash required to identify any shortage or excess. (The process of estimating cash receipts and cash disbursements will be presented later in this chapter.)

Exhibit 11.3   Cash Budget—Adjusted Net Income Approach

Cash Budget
Adjusted Net Income Approach
For the year ended December 31, 19X1

Cash – beginning of year		$
Sources of Cash:		
Net income	$	
Add: Income tax expense		
Depreciation		
Amortization		
Other	_____	
Other Sources:		
Proceeds from bank loans		
Sale of fixed assets		
Sale of capital stock		
Other		
Total		_____
Uses of Cash:		
Increase in accounts receivable		
Increase in inventories		
Decrease in current liabilities		
Purchase of fixed assets		
Income taxes paid		
Reduction in long-term debt		
Other		_____
Total		_____
Estimated Cash – end of year		_____
Minimum Cash Requirement		_____
Cash Excess or Shortage		$ _____

Adjusted Net Income Approach

The **adjusted net income approach** is generally preferable for budgeting cash for periods longer than six months. It also reflects the estimated cash balance for management's evaluation. In addition to its usefulness for longer periods of time, it emphasizes external, as opposed to internal, sources of funds. Exhibit 11.3 illustrates the format of a prepared cash budget using the adjusted net income approach.

The adjusted net income method is an indirect approach to cash budgeting because the sources and uses related to operations are indirect rather than direct—for example, direct sources from operations such as cash sales are not shown, nor are direct uses for operations such as disbursements for payroll. This approach has two major sections, sources and uses. The sources section consists of internal and external sources. Internal sources are primarily cash from operations (chiefly reflected by net income plus income tax expense, depreciation, and other expenses that do not require cash). External sources of funds include proceeds from bank loans and the sale of capital stock. The sum of the beginning cash and the sources of cash is the estimated cash available.

The uses of cash are subtracted from cash at the beginning of the year plus sources of cash to find the estimated cash at the end of year. This figure is compared to the minimum cash requirement to determine any excess or shortage.

The adjusted net income approach, much like the statement of cash flows (see Chapter 4), focuses directly on changes in accounts receivable, inventories, and current liabilities. This requires management to consider the amount of cash tied up in accounts receivable and inventory and cash provided by current liabilities. Therefore, this approach encourages closer management review of these working capital accounts.

From a practical viewpoint, both cash budgeting approaches are useful. The cash receipts and disbursements approach should be used for short-term budgets prepared on a monthly or weekly basis. The adjusted net income approach is useful for long-term budgets. Many hospitality establishments prepare cash budgets for long-range periods corresponding to the long-range operations budgets.

Information for Cash Budgeting

The operations budget is the major source of information for preparing a cash budget. For example, estimated cash sales for a period are based on total sales for the period and the estimated percentage of the cash sales.

In addition to the operations budget, the following information is necessary to prepare a cash budget:

- Estimated percentages of cash and credit sales.

- Estimated collection experience for credit sales—that is, when the credit sales will be collected. For example, the collection experience may be 30% during the month of sale, 60% in the following month, and 10% in the second month after the sale.

- Estimated other cash receipts including bank loans, sale of capital stock, and proceeds from sale of fixed assets and investments.

- Estimated payments for inventory items. For example, 10% of purchases may be paid during the month of purchase and 90% paid in the following month.

- Estimated payroll payments. A monthly payroll where all employees are paid on the last day of the month for that month means simply using the payroll expense estimates from the operations budget. Payroll distributed in any other way requires much more calculation.

- The payment schedules for other operating periods. Some operating expenses, such as utilities, are generally paid the month after they are expensed. Operating supplies are often paid for before the recognition of the expense when hospitality operations carry them as "supplies—inventory." Each type of expense must be reviewed to determine when the related cash expenditure is made.

- Capital expenses (such as property taxes and insurance) paid only once or twice a year. In these cases, the payment date, not the

Exhibit 11.4 Operations Budget—The Greenery

Operations Budget The Greenery For the months of March–July, 19X1	March	April	May	June	July
Sales	$63,000	$60,000	$65,000	$70,000	$75,000
Cost of Sales	21,000	20,000	21,700	23,400	25,000
Gross Profit	42,000	40,000	43,300	46,600	50,000
Interest Income	2,000	2,000	2,000	2,000	2,100
Total Income	44,000	42,000	45,300	48,600	52,100
Controllable Expenses					
Salaries and wages	17,000	16,000	18,000	19,000	20,000
Employee benefits	3,000	2,500	3,000	3,000	3,500
Direct operating expenses	3,000	2,500	2,500	2,500	3,000
Marketing	4,000	4,200	4,000	4,500	5,000
Energy Costs	3,000	2,500	2,000	2,000	2,200
Administrative & general	2,000	1,800	1,700	1,800	2,000
Repairs and maintenance	1,000	1,000	1,000	1,000	1,000
Income before Occupation Costs, Interest, and Depreciation	11,000	11,500	13,100	14,800	15,400
Occupation Costs	4,000	4,000	4,000	4,000	4,000
Interest	1,000	1,000	1,000	1,000	1,000
Depreciation	1,700	1,700	1,700	1,700	1,700
Income Before Income Taxes	4,300	4,800	6,400	8,100	8,700
Income Taxes	1,400	1,600	2,100	2,700	2,900
Net Income	$ 2,900	$ 3,200	$ 4,300	$ 5,400	$ 5,800

expense from the operations budget, should be considered.

- A schedule of debt payments (not part of the operations budget). This is required to determine total debt payments.

- Additional information including, but not necessarily limited to, forecasted dividend payments and forecasted fixed asset and investment purchases.

Illustration— Cash Receipts and Disbursements Approach

The Greenery, a hypothetical 100-seat restaurant, will be used to illustrate the cash receipts and disbursements approach to cash budgeting. In this illustration, cash budgets will be prepared for the three-month period of April–June, 19X1. Exhibit 11.4 contains the Greenery's operations budget for March–July, 19X1.

At the Greenery, cash receipts and sales relationships are as follows:

1. Cash sales represent 50% of each month's sales. Therefore, the Greenery's estimated cash receipts from cash sales in April are $30,000 ($60,000 × .5).

2. Charge sales represent the remaining 50%. Twenty percent of the charge sales are collected in the month of sale, while the remaining 80% are collected in the following month. The Greenery's estimated cash receipts from April charge sales total $6,000 ($60,000 × .5 × .2). In addition, March charge sales collected in April yield $25,200 of cash receipts ($63,000 × .5 × .8).

Exhibit 11.5 Estimated Cash Disbursements—The Greenery

Estimated Cash Disbursements in April for Various Controllable Expenses The Greenery			
	From March	For April	Total
Direct Operating Expenses	$1,500	$1,250	$2,750
Energy Costs	1,500	1,250	2,750
Administrative & General	1,000	900	1,900
Repairs & Maintenance	500	500	1,000
Total	$4,500	$3,900	$8,400

3. The Greenery receives cash each month for the projected interest income as shown in Exhibit 11.4. Therefore, the Greenery's cash receipts from interest income total $2,000 for April.

The Greenery's cash disbursements and expenses have the following relationships:

1. Food purchases (cost of sales) are paid during the current month as follows:

   30% of cost of sales of previous month
   70% of cost of sales of current month

   The Greenery's cash disbursements for food during April total $20,300 as follows:

   $$\text{March cost of sales} \times .3 = (\$21,000 \times .3) = \$ 6,300$$
   $$\text{April cost of sales} \ \times .7 = (\$20,000 \times .7) = \underline{\$14,000}$$
   $$\underline{\underline{\$20,300}}$$

2. Salaries, wages, and fringe benefits are paid in the month they are expensed. The April cash disbursements for salaries, wages, and fringe benefits total $18,500.

3. With the exception of marketing, 50% of all remaining controllable expenses are paid in the month expensed. The other 50% are paid in the following month. The Greenery's April cash disbursements of $8,400 for these expenses are shown in Exhibit 11.5.

4. Marketing expense is paid for as follows:
   In January, $24,000 was paid to an advertising agency for $2,000 of advertising for each month of 19X1. The remaining marketing expense (per the operations budget) is paid for during the month it is expensed. Therefore, The Greenery has an actual cash disbursement in April of $2,200 ($4,200 − $2,000) for marketing expense.

5. Occupation costs of $4,000 per month are paid during the month incurred.

6. Interest expense of $1,000 for April is included in the mortgage payment of $2,000 per month.

Exhibit 11.6   Cash Budget—The Greenery

	April	May	June
Cash Budget **The Greenery** **For the months of April–June, 19X1**			
Cash – beginning of the month	$ 5,000	$12,800	$ 20,110
Estimated cash receipts:			
Cash sales	30,000	32,500	35,000
Collection of accounts receivable	31,200	30,500	33,000
Interest received	2,000	2,000	2,000
Total	63,200	65,000	70,000
Estimated available cash	68,200	77,800	90,110
Estimated cash disbursements:			
Food purchases	20,300	21,190	22,890
Salaries, wages, and fringe benefits	18,500	21,000	22,000
Direct operating expenses	2,750	2,500	2,500
Marketing	2,200	2,000	2,500
Energy costs	2,750	2,250	2,000
Administrative & general	1,900	1,750	1,750
Repairs and maintenance	1,000	1,000	1,000
Occupation costs	4,000	4,000	4,000
Mortgage payment	2,000	2,000	2,000
Income taxes	0	0	6,400
Payment of equipment purchase	0	0	5,000
Total	55,400	57,690	72,040
Estimated cash – end of month	$ 12,800	$ 20,110	$ 18,070

7. Depreciation is a write-off of fixed assets and requires no cash flow.

8. Income taxes are paid quarterly. The tax expense for April–June is paid in June.

Other information includes the following:

1. Assume that cash at the beginning of April is $5,000.

2. Equipment costing $5,000 is scheduled for purchase in May and is to be paid for in June.

The Greenery's three-month cash budget for April–June, 19X1, is shown in Exhibit 11.6. Exhibit 11.7 provides explanations for each cash budget line item.

The Greenery has a relatively healthy cash flow, as cash at the beginning of the quarter (April 1) of $5,000 is projected to increase to $18,430 by the end of the quarter (June 30). If the Greenery's management considers cash at the end of any month to be in excess of its cash needs, then it should invest the excess. Many hospitality operations establish a minimum cash balance requirement. Any cash over this amount is available to invest on a temporary basis (if needed for future operations) or paid to the owners. Ideally, the minimum cash balance could be $0 as long as

Exhibit 11.7   Explanation of Cash Budget Line Items—The Greenery

Explanation of Cash Budget Line Items
April – June, 19X1
The Greenery

Monthly Budgets

Line Item	April	May	June
Cash – beginning of the month (BOM)	*$5,000*: based on assumption provided	*$12,800*: cash-EOM, April 19X1	*$20,110*: cash-EOM, May 19X1
Cash sales	*$30,000*: April sales × .5 = 60,000 × .5 = $30,000	*$32,500*: May sales × .5 = 65,000 × .5 = $32,500	*$35,000*: June sales × .5 = 70,000 × .5 = $35,000
Collection of accounts receivable	*$31,200*: April sales × .5 × .2 = 60,000 × .5 × .2 = $6,000; March sales × .5 × .8 = 63,000 × .5 × .8 = $25,200	*$30,500*: May sales × .5 × .2 = 65,000 × .5 × .2 = $6,500; April sales × .5 .8 = 60,000 × .5 × .8 = $24,000	*$33,000*: June sales × .5 × .2 = 70,000 × .5 × .2 = $7,000; May sales x .5 × .8 = 65,000 × .5 × .8 = $26,000
Interest received	*$2,000*	*$2,000*	*$2,000*
Estimated cash available	*$68,200*: cash-BOM + total estimated cash receipts = 5,000 + 63,200 = $68,200	*$77,800*: cash-BOM + total estimated cash receipts = 12,800 + 65,000 = $77,800	*$90,110*: cash-BOM + total estimated cash receipts = 20,110 + 70,000 = $90,110
Food purchases	*$20,300*: March exp. × .3 = 21,000 × .3 = $6,300; April exp. × .7 = 20,000 × .7 = $14,000	*$21,190*: April exp. × .3 = 20,000 × .3 = $6,000; May exp. × .7 = 21,700 × .7 = $15,190	*$22,890*: May exp. × .3 = 21,700 × .3 = $6,510; June exp. × .7 = 23,400 × .7 = $16,380
Salaries, wages, and fringe benefits	*$18,500*: 16,000 + 2,500 = $18,500	*$21,000*: 18,000 + 3,000 = $21,000	*$22,000*: 19,000 + 3,000 = $22,000
Direct operating expenses	*$2,750*: March exp. × .5 = 3,000 × .5 = $1,500; April exp. × .5 = 2,500 × .5 = $1,250	*$2,500*: April exp. × .5 = 2,500 × .5 = $1,250; May exp. × .5 = 2,500 × .5 = $1,250	*$2,500*: May exp. × .5 = 2,500 × .5 = $1,250; June exp. × .5 = 2,500 × .5 = $1,250
Marketing expenses	*$2,200*: April exp. – 2,000 = 4,200 – 2,000 = $2,200	*$2,000*: May exp. – 2,000 = 4,000 – 2,000 = $2,000	*$2,500*: June exp. – 2,000 = 4,500 – 2,000 = $2,500
Energy costs	*$2,750*: March exp. × .5 + April exp. × .5 = (3,000 × .5) + (2,500 × .5) = 1,500 + 1,250 = $2,750	*$2,250*: April exp. × .5 + May exp. × .5 = (2,500 × .5) + (2,000 × .5) = 1,250 + 1,000 = $2,250	*$2,000*: May exp. × .5 + June exp. × .5 = (2,000 × .5) + (2,000 × .5) = 1,000 + 1,000 = $2,000
Administrative & general	*$1,900*: March exp. × .5 + April exp. × .5 = (2,000 × .5) + (1,800 × .5) = 1,000 + 900 = $1,900	*$1,750*: April exp. × .5 + May exp. × .5 = (1,800 × .5) + (1,700 × .5) = 900 + 850 = $1,750	*$1,750*: May exp. × .5 + June exp. × .5 = (1,700 × .5) + (1,800 × .5) = 850 + 900 = $1,750

Exhibit 11.7 *(continued)*

	Monthly Budgets		
Line Item	April	May	June
Repairs and Maintenance	*$1,000*: March exp. × .5 + April exp. × .5 = (1,000 × .5) + (1,000 × .5) = 500 + 500 = $1,000	*$1,000*: April exp. × .5 + May exp. × .5 = (1,000 × .5) + (1,000 × .5) = 500 + 500 = $1,000	*$1,000*: May exp. × .5 + June exp. × .5 = (1,000 × .5) + (1,000 × .5) = 500 + 500 = $1,000
Occupation costs	*$4,000*	*$4,000*	*$4,000*
Mortgage payment	*$2,000*	*$2,000*	*$2,000*
Income taxes	$ 0	$ 0	*$6,400*: April–June exp. = 1,600 + 2,100 + 2,700 = $6,400
Purchase of equipment	$ 0	$ 0	*$5,000*
Estimated cash – EOM	*$12,800*: Est. available cash – est. cash disb. = 68,200 – 55,400 = $12,800	*$20,110*: Est. available cash – est. cash disb. = 77,800 – 57,690 = $20,110	*$18,070*: Est. available cash – est. cash disb. = 90,110 – 72,040 = $18,070

Exhibit 11.8 Projected Cash Available to Invest—The Greenery

Projected Cash Available to Invest The Greenery For the months of April–June, 19X1			
	April	May	June
Cash – BOM	$ 5,000	$ 5,000	$ 5,000
Plus: Total Estimated Cash Receipts	63,200	65,000	70,000
Less: Total Estimated Disbursements	55,400	57,690	72,040
Preliminary Cash EOM	12,800	12,310	2,960
Less: Cash Cushion	5,000	5,000	5,000
Excess Cash for Investing	$ 7,800	$7,310	($2,040)*

*If the excess cash is invested in April and May, The Greenery should prepare to liquidate $2,040 of these investments to maintain the desired cash cushion of $5,000 at the end of June.

daily cash inflow were equal to daily cash outflow. However, this ideal situation is seldom achieved, so a cushion is maintained.

Assume that the Greenery maintains a cash cushion of $5,000 at the end of each month. Exhibit 11.8 presents the projected cash available to invest at the end of each month in the quarter. The Greenery is projected to have excess cash for investing of $7,800 and $7,310 in April and May, respectively. However, in June, temporary investments of $2,040 must be liquidated to provide the $5,000 minimum cash balance at the end of the month.

Exhibit 11.9   Long-Range Operations Budget—The Greenery

Long-Range Operations Budget
The Greenery
For the years of 19X1–19X3

	19X1	19X2	19X3
Sales	$730,000	$850,000	$1,000,000
Cost of sales	240,000	270,000	320,000
Gross profit	490,000	580,000	680,000
Interest income	25,000	30,000	35,000
Total income	515,000	610,000	715,000
Controllable expenses:			
Salaries and wages	200,000	240,000	300,000
Employee benefits	25,000	30,000	35,000
Direct operating expenses	28,000	30,000	32,000
Marketing	40,000	50,000	60,000
Energy costs	30,000	35,000	40,000
Administrative & general	20,000	25,000	30,000
Repairs and maintenance	12,000	14,000	16,000
Total	355,000	424,000	513,000
Income before Occupation Costs, Interest, and Depreciation	160,000	186,000	202,000
Occupation Costs	50,000	50,000	50,000
Interest	15,000	15,000	15,000
Depreciation	20,000	22,000	24,000
Income before income taxes	75,000	99,000	113,000
Income taxes*	25,000	33,000	37,700
Net income	$50,000	$66,000	$75,300

*The income taxes paid each year is the same as the income tax expense in the long-range operations budget.

Illustration—
Adjusted
Net Income
Approach

The adjusted net income approach can be used to prepare the Greenery's long-term cash budgets for 19X1–19X3. Exhibit 11.9 presents the Greenery's operations budgets for 19X1–19X3. Additional information required to prepare cash budgets using the adjusted net income approach is as follows:

1. Equipment acquisitions, which will be purchased with cash, are projected at $10,000 per year for 19X1–19X3.

2. Distributions to owners are projected at 50% of net income.

3. Mortgage payments are estimated to be $30,000 per year for 19X1–19X3, of which 50% is interest expense.

4. The annual change in various current assets and current liabilities is estimated as follows:

	19X1	19X2	19X3
Accounts receivable	+2,000	+3,000	+4,000
Inventory	+1,000	+1,500	+1,500
Current liabilities	+2,000	+3,000	+3,500

Exhibit 11.10   Long-Range Cash Budget—The Greenery

Long-Range Cash Budget
The Greenery
For the years of 19X1–19X3

		19X1	19X2	19X3
Cash – beginning of the year		$ 5,000	$ 24,000	$ 52,500
Sources of cash:				
Net income		50,000	66,000	75,300
Add: Depreciation		20,000	22,000	24,000
Increase in current liabilities		2,000	3,000	3,500
	Total	72,000	91,000	102,800
Uses of cash:				
Increase in accounts receivable		2,000	3,000	4,000
Increase in inventory		1,000	1,500	1,500
Distributions to owners		25,000	33,000	37,650
Purchase of fixed assets		10,000	10,000	10,000
Reduction in long-term debt		15,000	15,000	15,000
	Total	53,000	62,500	68,150
Estimated cash – end of year		$ 24,000	$ 52,500	$ 87,150

The Greenery's long-range cash budget for 19X1–19X3 is shown in Exhibit 11.10. Overall, the cash budget shows a substantial increase in cash—from $5,000 at the beginning of 19X1 to $87,150 at the end of 19X3. This fully considers the distribution of 50% of net income to owners, the cash purchase of $10,000 of equipment each year, and the reduction of long-term debt by $15,000 each year. The Greenery's management must consider the best uses of the excess funds reflected by the cash budget. The factors relevant to short-term investing are also appropriate in a long-term situation, although liquidity is less important.

Float

The use of **float** is another element of cash management. Float is time between the subtraction or addition of cash to the company's books and the actual subtraction or addition to the company's bank account. For example, assume that the Greenery pays a supplier $1,000 on account. When the check is written, the cash is subtracted from the company's cash (general ledger) account. Assume that the check is mailed to the supplier, who receives it three days later. The supplier deposits the check the following day in its own bank, which is different from the Greenery's bank, and two days later the funds are deducted from the Greenery's bank account. The Greenery actually had use of the $1,000 for six days—from the day the check was written and deducted from the books until the day its bank paid the $1,000. This type of float is called **payment float**. The Greenery benefits from payment float, and any reasonable steps to increase payment float are to the Greenery's advantage.

On the other hand, when the Greenery deposits a guest's check into its bank account, it increases its cash account on the books but must wait

Exhibit 11.11   The Effect of Working Capital on Cash

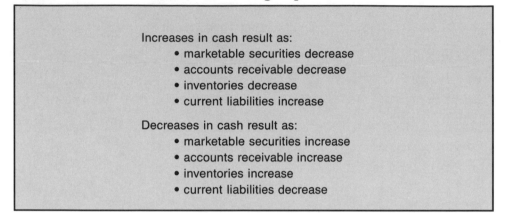

Increases in cash result as:
- marketable securities decrease
- accounts receivable decrease
- inventories decrease
- current liabilities increase

Decreases in cash result as:
- marketable securities increase
- accounts receivable increase
- inventories increase
- current liabilities decrease

to use the funds until its bank has received the funds from the guest's bank. This difference is called **collection float**. The difference between payment float and collection float is **net float**. Since management prefers a positive net float, it should take whatever legal actions it can (referred to as "playing the float") to increase payment float and decrease collection float.

Management of Working Capital

The management of working capital is closely related to the management of cash. **Working capital** (current assets less current liabilities) is directly related to cash; Exhibit 11.11 depicts the effect of working capital on cash. These relationships assume that other activities (such as sales and expenses) remain constant. For example, if marketable securities decrease, cash increases, provided everything else remains the same. Therefore, it is imperative that hospitality managers understand the management of these elements of working capital.

Accounts Receivable

Accounts receivable arise from sales on accounts. Hospitality operations would prefer to transact only cash sales. However, in order to increase sales, credit is often extended to guests. Credit commences when the guest checks into a room without paying for the room. Credit continues until the guest pays the bill—at check-out or after leaving the hotel. Credit should be monitored while the guest stays at the hotel.[1]

Accounts receivable statements should be mailed on a regular basis, usually monthly. A series of collection letters should be used to speed collection of accounts receivable. Delinquent accounts should be turned over to collection agencies only after the hospitality operation has made all reasonable collection efforts. Collection agency fees may range from 30% to 50% of the delinquent amount.

A **lockbox system** speeds the flow of cash from accounts receivable to the bank. This system consists of a post office box from which bank personnel collect all incoming mail and deposit any checks directly in the property's bank account. This process may speed the cash flow from collection of accounts receivable by up to three days by decreasing collection float. In addition, it enhances control over mail cash receipts because company personnel do not have access to this cash. However, the bank does charge for this service, usually by the number of checks handled. If the operation receives many small payments, the cost of a lockbox system may exceed the benefits.

A formula for considering the costs and benefits of a lockbox system provides a breakeven amount. This is the amount of a receivables account which, when invested for the number of days cash flow is speeded up, yields income equal to the added cost of the lockbox system. The formula is as follows:

$$B = \frac{C}{I \times T}$$

where B = Breakeven Amount

C = Bank Charge per Item

I = Daily Interest Rate

T = Change in Time

An example may best illustrate this formula. Assume that a hotel needs to know the breakeven amount for a lockbox system. The bank charges $.20 for each mail receipt processed, funds can be invested at 12% annually, and the lockbox system gets mail cash receipts to the bank two days faster. The breakeven amount per check is $304.14, determined as follows:

$$B = \frac{.20}{\frac{.12}{365} \times 2}$$

$$= \frac{.20}{.0003288 \times 2}$$

$$= \frac{.20}{.0006576}$$

$$= \$304.14$$

This hotel will benefit financially by using a lockbox system for processing mail receipts over $304.14. Therefore, this hotel should instruct its debtors with balances greater than $304.14 to mail their checks to its lockbox, while debtors owing less than $304.14 should send their payments to the hospitality operation for company personnel to process. This assumes that company personnel and related expenses are fixed and will not change by processing more or fewer mail cash receipts.

Accounts receivable, especially city ledger accounts, are monitored by the use of ratio analysis and the preparation of an aging schedule of accounts receivable. Three useful ratios, discussed in Chapter 5, are accounts receivable to sales, accounts receivable turnover, and number of days accounts receivable outstanding, which is a variation of the accounts receivable turnover. These ratios are useful in detecting changes in the overall accounts as they relate to sales.

An aging of accounts receivable (see Exhibit 5.6 in Chapter 5) is useful for monitoring delinquent accounts. Maximum efforts should be exerted to collect the oldest accounts. The aging schedule is also useful for estimating the uncollectible accounts at the end of the accounting period.

Inventory

Inventory is viewed by some as a necessary evil. Hospitality operations must maintain an inventory of food and beverages even though the cost of storing these items is relatively high. The benefit of having food and beverages for sale is obvious, however—they are generally sold at several times their cost.

The non-product costs of maintaining inventory need to be considered so that management will exercise tight control in this area. Several costs directly related to inventory include storage, insurance, and personnel. Inventory requires storage space, and many inventory items must be stored in temperature-controlled environments. Certain inventory items have a limited shelf life; thus, personnel need to monitor these items closely. Inventory must be counted periodically, which also requires personnel and therefore payroll dollars. Overall costs also increase when inventory items spoil and must be discarded. Insurance to cover inventory, although not expensive, is yet another cost. In addition to these costs, there is the opportunity cost of inventory. If funds were not tied up in inventory, they could be invested to provide a return to the hospitality operation. Therefore, management must closely monitor inventory to keep it at a minimum, while still having products available when customers wish to make purchases.

Common means of monitoring inventory include the inventory ratios discussed in Chapter 5. The most commonly used ratio is inventory turnover, calculated by dividing cost of goods used by average inventory. This ratio should be computed not only for food but also for each category of beverages. The results are most meaningful when compared to the planned ratios and to ratios for past periods. These ratios can help management detect unfavorable trends. For example, food inventory turnovers of 2, 1.8, and 1.6 for three successive months suggests a major change in food inventory. Management should determine if the inventory is excessive and take the appropriate action to correct the situation.

Current Liabilities

A large portion of current assets is financed by current liabilities in hospitality operations. The current ratio (computed by dividing current assets by current liabilities) of approximately 1 to 1 for hospitality operations, especially in the lodging sector, reflects this situation. **Trade credit** is free—that is, suppliers do not charge interest to hospitality operations for amounts owed in the normal course of business. Everything else being the same, the longer a property has to pay its bills, the greater its reliance on trade credit to finance its operations.

Current liabilities consist primarily of trade payables, taxes payable, accrued wages, and the current portion of long-term debt. The remainder of this section focuses on trade payables, as the other payables must generally be paid on stipulated dates.

Trade payables resulting from purchases on account generally require payment in 30 days. Sometimes, suppliers offer cash discounts to hospitality operations to encourage their customers to pay their accounts early. For example, a supplier may provide a 2% cash discount if the invoice is paid within ten days of the invoice date. Thus, the terms of sale per the invoice are simply shown as 2/10, *n*/30. The *n*/30 means that if the discounted invoice is not paid within 10 days of the invoice date, then the entire amount (net) is due within 30 days of the invoice date. The effective interest rate of the cash discount is determined as follows:[2]

$$\begin{array}{l}\text{Effective} \\ \text{Interest} \\ \text{Rate}\end{array} = \frac{\text{Cash Discount}}{\begin{array}{c}\text{Invoice Amount} \\ -\text{ Cash Discount}\end{array}} \times \frac{\text{Days in Year}}{\begin{array}{c}\text{Difference between end of discount period} \\ \text{and final due day}\end{array}}$$

The following example illustrates the calculation of the effective interest rate. Assume that a hotel purchases a posting machine for $8,000 and is offered terms of 3/10, *n*/30. The effective interest rate of 56.45% is the result of:

$$\begin{aligned}
\text{Effective Interest Rate} &= \frac{240^*}{8,000 - 240} \times \frac{365}{20} \\
&= \frac{240}{7,760} \times \frac{365}{20} \\
&= .03093 \times 18.25 \\
&= \underline{\underline{56.45\%}}
\end{aligned}$$

$$^*\text{Cash Discount} = \$8,000 \times .03 = \$240$$

Thus, the hotel would be wise to pay the invoice within the cash discount period, even if it had to borrow funds to do so, as long as the interest rate on the loan were less than 56.45%.

Alternatively, assume that the terms of sale are 1/10, *n*/30 and that this hotel must pay interest at an annual rate of 20%.

$$\begin{aligned}
\text{Effective Interest Rate} &= \frac{80}{8,000 - 80} \times \frac{365}{20} \\
&= \frac{80}{7,920} \times \frac{365}{20} \\
&= .0101 \times 18.25 \\
&= \underline{\underline{18.43\%}}
\end{aligned}$$

If the hotel has the cash available and management considers 18.43% to be an attractive return on a short-term investment, the hotel should pay the invoice within the cash discount period. However, if the cash is not available, the hotel should not borrow to pay the invoice, since the effective interest rate of 18.43% is lower than the rate at which the hotel can borrow funds. In this situation, the hotel should not take the cash discount, but rather should pay the full $8,000 30 days after the invoice date.

In general, management should pay bills only when they are due except when cash discounts are available for early payments and they result in lowering costs. The payment of invoices earlier than required results in a higher cost of doing business since the cash expended could have been invested. However, management must consider the intangible factor of supplier relations. Keeping on favorable terms with suppliers is especially advantageous when the hotel or restaurant occasionally needs special favors—such as receiving inventory two days sooner than normally available.

Integrated Cash Management for Multi-Unit Operations

So far, our discussion of cash management could most easily be applied to a single-unit operation. However, for multi-unit operations, an **integrated cash management system** should generally be installed.

An integrated cash management system consists of centralizing cash receipts and especially cash disbursements from the corporate office. Cash receipts, although initially received by the individual unit, are moved quickly to the corporate office. Cash disbursements, for the most part, are made from the corporate bank accounts. For example, payroll checks are prepared at the corporate office. Supplier invoices may also be paid from corporate accounts.

An integrated cash system's primary goal is to minimize the amount of cash the hospitality operation—both the corporate office and the individual facilities—holds. Cash balances at individual units may be reduced by having a centralized cash disbursement system. The checking accounts of individual units become, in essence, cash clearing accounts, maintained at balances just sufficient to facilitate required local disbursements. All excess cash is quickly transferred to the corporate accounts. More cash at the corporate level results in increased financial returns for two reasons. First, a large cash reserve increases the corporation's bargaining power with financial institutions. Second, the corporate office usually staffs more financial experts than individual operations can afford.

An integrated cash management system can pay real dividends. For example, assume that a chain's cash system is able to keep cash in its accounts (available for investment) for two days longer by increasing its net float. The interest earned for a chain with $1 billion of annual sales is $547,945, determined as follows:

$$\text{Interest} = \text{Principal} \times \text{Rate} \times \text{Time}$$
$$= 1,000,000,000 \times .10 \times 2/365$$
$$= \underline{\underline{\$547,945}}$$

An integrated cash management system results in better allocation of funds throughout the operation. When some properties need cash, they receive it from the corporate office rather than a local bank. Some experts suggest that an integrated cash system improves control over collection and disbursement procedures.[3] For example, individual properties may pay invoices before their due dates; however, a centralized system allows for proper monitoring of cash disbursements.

An integrated cash management system uses cash forecasting, including the preparation of cash budgets at both the unit and corporate levels. Both short- and long-term budgets should be prepared at both levels. The centralized system is designed to transfer as much cash as possible to corporate accounts. Some hospitality operations also have their own credit card systems, although most work directly with major credit card companies.

Computerization

Cash management is very important to a business. Management must ensure that there is enough cash to meet the needs of the business, but not too much. Many large companies, including hotel firms, assign people to cash control. However, the typical hotel or restaurant is too small for such an arrangement; the labor cost would exceed the benefits derived.

A computer can help control cash easily and quickly. For example, the cash forecasts shown in Exhibits 11.6 and 11.7 can be computerized and used for weekly, or even daily, analysis. A general cash budget can be developed using the operating budget of the company as a starting point. In fact, because many of the line items in the operating budget affect the cash budget, an already-computerized budget process can be programmed to produce automatically a tentative cash budget for review and modification.

A computerized cash budget can be used for weekly and monthly forecasting of cash needs. The budget can reflect expected cash activity based upon cash incomes and outflows. Cash needed for major expenditures can also be projected in this plan, allowing for the anticipation of unusual items as well as daily transactions. While it might take hours to develop such a plan manually every week, a computer can do it in just a few moments. Assuming basic ratios do not change (such as percentage of cash sales, average check sales, and cost of sales), a cash budget can be quickly developed whenever necessary. This will allow the manager to see what cash is required and decide how to invest any extra cash on hand. Exhibit 11.12 shows how this might be done for a food service operation.

Summary

Cash is a very important asset for hospitality operations. Although it may not earn interest, cash is used to pay debts, make other disbursements, and facilitate guest transactions. Management must try to minimize the operation's cash holdings by investing them in revenue-producing assets while, at the same time, not jeopardizing its operations. This chapter highlighted a number of cash management tools including cash budgets, the treatment of other current assets, and an integrated cash system.

Exhibit 11.12   Computer-Generated Monthly Cash Budget

ABC Restaurant Company Monthly Cash Budget Month of July, 19X1				
	Week 1	Week 2	Week 3	Week 4
Covers Served Restaurant	1,500	1,590	1,350	1,530
Covers Served Banquet	125	333	250	400
Average Price/Cover Rest.	$12.40	$12.40	$12.40	$12.40
Average Price/Cover Banquet	$14.10	$14.10	$14.10	$14.10
Bev. Checks Restaurant	900	954	810	918
Bev. Checks Banquet	38	100	75	120
Average Bev. Sale Restaurant	$ 6.00	$ 6.00	$ 6.00	$ 6.00
Average Bev. Sale Banquet	$ 3.25	$ 3.25	$ 3.25	$ 3.25
Cash – Beginning of Week	$ 1,600	$ 6,784	$12,215	$13,961
Estimated Cash Receipts:				
Cash & Credit Card Sales	24,417	26,695	22,542	25,988
A/R Collections	2,199	3,397	2,966	1,854
Interest on Investments	6	6	6	6
Total Receipts	26,622	30,098	25,514	27,848
Estimated Cash Available	28,222	36,882	37,729	41,809
Estimated Cash Expenditures				
Food Purchases	6,951	8,074	6,740	8,050
Beverage Purchases	1,104	1,210	1,021	1,180
Salaries, Wages, & Benefits	8,507	10,056	8,369	10,089
Direct Operating Expenses	1,346	1,468	1,240	1,429
Marketing & Advertising	300	300	300	300
Administration & General	1,597	1,806	1,531	1,671
Credit Card Commissions	551	601	507	585
Energy Costs	532	602	510	557
Repairs & Maintenance	300	300	300	300
Occupation Costs	250	250	250	250
Mortgage Payment	0	0	0	3,500
Capital Purchases	0	0	3,000	0
Income Tax Allowance	0	0	0	4,625
Total Cash Expenditures	21,438	24,667	23,768	32,536
Estimated Cash – End of Week	$ 6,784	$12,215	$13,961	$ 9,273

Cash budgets are formulated to estimate the operation's future cash position. Two approaches, the cash receipts and disbursements method and the adjusted net income approach, estimate the cash balance at the end of the period and give management the information necessary for planning.

The cash receipts and disbursements method is a direct approach which examines all cash inflows and outflows. Items found in this budget might include the amount of cash sales in the period, collection of accounts receivable, dividends and interest received, the operating expenses which were paid for during the period, and dividends paid. This type of budget is most useful for short-term periods because the estimates upon which it is based are less reliable the further the projections are made into the future.

The adjusted net income approach to cash budgeting is used for periods of over six months. The projected operations for each future year are adjusted to reflect cash flows. This approach also considers any expected changes in current accounts and any capital expenditures. Management should examine excess funds and determine the appropriate way to invest them.

Management must also monitor the activity in other current accounts in order to optimize the operation's liquidity position. Accounts receivable should be analyzed to ensure their timely collection. Inventory is expensive to store but is valuable to operations, so it should also be monitored. This is often done by analyzing the turnover ratio. Current liabilities should be studied with special consideration given to trade discounts. All of these procedures will aid management in cash control and overall operational efficiency.

An integrated cash system can minimize the total cash holdings of a multi-unit corporation. This is accomplished by maintaining a central account to which almost all receipts are deposited and from which almost all disbursements are made. Even when hospitality operations have this central account, it is important for them to make budgets, both for the long- and short-term horizons, and constantly update them as information becomes available.

Endnotes

1. For a thorough discussion of this topic, see Ellis Knotts, "Handling the Credit Function at Small Hotels," *Lodging*, June 1979.

2. Alternatively, the effective interest rate can be calculated without using actual invoice amounts as follows:

$$\text{Effective Interest Rate} = \frac{\text{Percentage Discount}}{100\% - \text{Percentage Discount}} \times \frac{\text{Days in Year}}{\text{Difference between end of discount period and final due day}}$$

3. For a detailed discussion of integrated cash management systems for multi-unit firms, see Laurent P. Caraux and A. Neal Geller, "Cash Management: A Total System Approach for the Hotel Industry," *The Cornell Hotel & Restaurant Administration Quarterly*, November 1977.

Key Terms

adjusted net income approach
cash budgets
cash flows
cash management
cash receipts and disbursements
  approach
collection float
effective cost
float
imprest basis

income flows
integrated cash management
  system
lockbox system
net float
payment float
trade credit
transaction motive
working capital

Discussion Questions

1. What is meant by an *imprest basis*?

2. How is cash used by hospitality operations?

3. What are three items which exemplify the differences between income and cash flows?

4. What are the two different types of cash budget formats? In what circumstances would you use each one?

5. What are five informational items needed to prepare a cash budget using the cash receipts and disbursements approach?

6. What should management consider when investing excess cash?

7. Why must you analyze other current asset accounts when using the adjusted net income approach to cash budgeting?

8. How soon should you turn delinquent accounts receivable over to a collection agency? Why?

9. What is the value of a lockbox system to a hospitality operation?

10. What is an integrated cash management system?

Problems _____

Problem 11.1

Amy Jason is the accountant for the Jason Junction Inn and is unfamiliar with trade discounts. She has just been offered terms of 2/10, *n*/30 and turns to you for help.

Required:

1. Explain what 2/10, *n*/30 means.
2. What is the effective rate of interest under these terms of sale?

Problem 11.2

Warren Peace, owner of the War 'N' Peace Motel, is considering a lockbox system for some of his accounts receivable collections. He can program his computer to send statements with different return addresses depending on the amount of the balance. The bank charges $.25 per item for lockbox service. Warren can invest cash with the bank at an annual interest rate of 9%. He has estimated that using the lockbox would speed up collections by 3 days.

Required:

What is the breakeven amount—that is, the amount at which Warren Peace would be indifferent as to whether a customer sent the check directly to the motel or the post office lockbox?

Problem 11.3

Use the following information to formulate a simplified cash budget for Heidi's Place.

	Dec.	Jan.	Feb.	Mar.
Sales	$40,000	$40,000	$50,000	$75,000
Inventory Purchases	15,000	17,000	18,000	30,000
Other Cash Expenses	15,000	15,000	22,000	37,000
Capital Purchases (With cash)	-0-	-0-	10,000	-0-

Sales: 60% of the sales are cash while the remaining 40% are credit sales. One half of the credit sales are collected in the month of sale and one half in the next month.

Purchases: 80% of the purchases are paid in the month of the purchase while 20% are paid in the next month.

Inventory: Assume that other cash expenses and capital purchases are paid for during the month indicated above (for example, other cash expenses of $15,000 for December were paid in December).

Assume that the beginning cash balance of January 1 is $5,000.

Required:

Prepare a cash budget using the cash receipts and disbursements approach for the months of January–March.

Problem 11.4

Topeka Corporation has just completed a long-range operations budget for 19X1–19X3. They are interested in their ability to buy fixed assets in 19X2 and 19X3 from cash generated by the business. They need tentative cash budgets for 19X1–19X3 to evaluate the situation. The following information is available:

Condensed Operations Budgets
Topeka Corporation
19X1–19X3

	19X1	19X2	19X3
Sales	$5,000,000	$6,000,000	$6,500,000
Operating expenses	4,000,000	5,000,000	6,000,000
Depreciation	500,000	500,000	500,000
Income before taxes	500,000	500,000	-0-
Income tax expense*	200,000	200,000	-0-
Net income	$300,000	$300,000	$ -0-

*The income tax expense is recorded on the books only. The amount paid each year is as follows:

	19X1	19X2	19X3
Income tax liability for each year	$150,000	$150,000	$ 50,000
Increase in accounts receivable	10,000	20,000	10,000
Increase in accounts payable	5,000	15,000	20,000
Increase in inventories	5,000	2,000	1,000
Expected distributions to partners (owners)	100,000	110,000	120,000

Required:

Prepare cash budgets for the Topeka Corporation for 19X1–19X3 using the adjusted net income approach.

Problem 11.5

Eric Smith, the owner and manager of Eric's, has provided the following information about his business for January–March 19X2. The cash balance on January 1, 19X2, is $10,000, and he wants to maintain a minimum balance of $10,000 at the end of each month.

The estimated monthly sales are as follows:

January 19X2	$110,000
February 19X2	130,000
March 19X2	120,000

The sales are 30% cash and 70% credit card. The Smith Express Card is converted to cash each day after the sale; however, the brokerage charge is 4% on gross.

Other expected income is $2,000 from interest to be received in February. In addition, in February, a range with a net book value of $300 is expected to be sold for cash for a $700 gain on the sale.

Food and beverages are paid for the month following the sale, and they average 40% of sales. Sales in December 19X1 totaled $130,000. Employees are paid the last day of the month, and the total compensation is 35% of sales.

Other cash expenses approximate $10,000 per month. In the month of March, $40,000 is expected to be expended on new equipment. Funding for this expenditure comes in part from a long-term loan of $15,000 from the Kansas Bank and Trust.

Required:

Prepare the monthly cash budget for Eric's for January–March 19X2 using the cash receipts and disbursements approach.

Problem 11.6

Beth McNight is the manager of the Night Time Inn and has completed the operating budgets for the next three years as shown below. She is now ready to prepare the cash budget.

Operating Budgets 19X1-19X3			
	19X1	19X2	19X3
Sales	$1,000,000	$1,200,000	$1,500,000
Direct Expenses	450,000	550,000	650,000
Depreciation	200,000	200,000	200,000
Other Fixed Expenses	250,000	250,000	350,000
Income Before Taxes	100,000	200,000	300,000
Income Tax	40,000	100,000	150,000
Net Income	$60,000	$100,000	$150,000

Additional information includes:

A. Dividends paid in a given year are estimated to be 30% of net income for that year.

B. The following is a summary of the only current accounts which are expected to change:

	19X1	19X2	19X3
Accounts Receivable	+10,000	+5,000	+20,000
Accounts Payable	- 5,000	+5,000	+10,000

C. A major piece of equipment which costs $50,000 is scheduled for purchase during 19X3. Beth McNight would like to purchase the machine with company cash rather than borrow the necessary funds.

D. The cash balance at the beginning of 19X1 is $10,000.

E. Assume that the income tax for each year is paid in the year it is shown as expense.

Required:

Prepare cash budgets for 19X1-19X3 for the Night Time Inn using the adjusted net income approach.

Problem 11.7

The Redbird Restaurant's financial information for the months of July–September, 19X2, is as follows:

	Budgeted sales
July	$60,000
August	70,000
September	65,000

In the past, cash and charge sales have been 40% and 60%, respectively, of total sales. Actual sales for May and June totaled $62,000 and $58,000, respectively. Collections on charge sales average 75% in the month following the sale and 25% in the second month after the sale. Food costs average 35% of total revenue. Thirty percent is paid in the month of sale, while the remaining 70% is paid in the following month. Payroll costs are paid at the end of each month and average 30% of total sales.

Other budgeted expenses are as follows:

	July	August	September
Interest—loans	$1,500	$1,495	$1,490
Depreciation	1,000	1,000	1,000
Property taxes	500	500	500
Insurance	400	400	400
Other expenses	2,000	2,000	2,000

The interest is part of Redbird's $2,000 monthly mortgage payment. Property tax payments of $3,000 are made in July and December. The annual insurance premium of $4,800 was paid in January. Other expenses are paid each month as the expense is incurred.

During August, a new cash register is to be purchased for $8,000. The old register will be sold at an expected loss of $500; its net book value at that time will be $1,000. If necessary, the Redbird Restaurant can borrow money from the Illinois State Bank on a six-month note basis—that is, the note and interest would be paid in six months.

The cash balance on July 1, 19X2, is $5,000.

Required:

Prepare the Redbird Restaurant's cash budget for July–September 19X2 using the cash receipts and disbursements approach.

Problem 11.8

Claude Ziggy, owner of Ziggy's Diner, needs your assistance to prepare a cash budget for his restaurant. He estimates cash on July 1 will be $2,400. He wants to maintain a minimum of cash at the end of each month equal to one week's (7 days') disbursements for the next month, not including disbursements related to working capital loans. (Assume that disbursements are made evenly throughout a month.)

Total monthly sales are as follows:

March	$ 50,000
April	120,000
May	120,000
June	150,000
July (estimated)	159,000
August (estimated)	180,000
September (estimated)	142,000
October (estimated)	90,000

The sales are 40% cash and 60% regular credit. Regular credit sales are collected as follows:

Month of sale	10%
Month after sale	60%
Second month after sale	20%
Third month after sale	8%
Bad debts	2%
TOTAL	100%

Interest income of $1,000 is expected in August. In September, the restaurant plans to sell some extra equipment. The chef estimates the equipment will bring

$2,000; the book value of the equipment is $1,000. During September, 1,000 shares of capital stock with $1 par value are to be sold for $5 per share. Cash is to be received in September for the stock sales.

Payments for food are made one month after the sale. The food cost percentage is 35%. Beverages are purchased and paid for one month in advance and the beverage cost percentage is 25%. Beverages sales are 50% of food sales.

Labor is paid during the month wages are earned and represents 40% of total sales. Fixed expenses, except for insurance, depreciation, and property taxes, are $8,000 per month and are paid monthly.

Insurance premiums of $3,000 are paid quarterly in January, April, July, and October of each year. The property taxes of $20,000 for the year are paid in two installments of $10,000 each in July and December. Depreciation expense is $3,000 per month.

The Board of Directors is expected to declare a dividend per share of $.25 in July, payable in August (20,000 shares are outstanding).

In September, the firm plans to acquire fixed assets using cash totaling $20,000. If the firm is to borrow cash to maintain the desired cash balances, it must do so in increments of $1,000. The interest rate is 12% and principal and interest must be paid back in 30 days. (Assume that the funds borrowed, if any, are paid back in the following month.) Assume that a year has 365 days when calculating interest on short-term loans.

Required:

Prepare a monthly cash budget for Ziggy's Diner for July-September using the cash receipts and disbursements approach.

Problem 11.9

The Mackinaw Valley Corporation (MVC) has just purchased a hotel and needs help preparing a cash budget. MVC has provided the following information:

		19X1	19X2	19X3	19X4
A.	Budgeted pre-tax incomes	($100,000)	($60,000)	$40,000	$200,000
B.	Operating expenses— cash	$600,000	$675,000	$700,000	$700,000

C. The hotel and furnishings total $3,500,000 and are depreciated using straight line over a period of 30 years. Assume a salvage value of $500,000.

D. The MVC's tax rate is 30%. Operating losses can be carried forward for up to five years.

E. The property will need $300,000 in renovations in the first year; this expense will be capitalized and depreciated on a straight-line basis over 5 years. Assume that the expenditure is made in 19X1. Further assume that the expense is fully considered in the above budgeted pre-tax incomes.

Required:

1. Prepare a cash budget using the adjusted net income approach. Show only the cash flow excess or deficit for each year.

2. Comment on the opportunities for MVC to pay dividends.

Problem 11.10

The Lakeland Diner has provided the information below for the preparation of its cash budget.

Beginning cash on July 1 is $5,000. The owner of the diner would like to maintain a minimum cash balance at the end of each month equal to one week's (7 days') disbursements for the current month, not including disbursements related to working capital loans. (Assume that disbursements are made evenly throughout a month.)

Monthly total sales are as follows:

March	$ 50,000	September (estimated)	$160,000
April	110,000	October (estimated)	150,000
May	130,000	November (estimated)	130,000
June	150,000	December (estimated)	120,000
July (estimated)	170,000	January (estimated)	100,000
August (estimated)	180,000	February (estimated)	90,000

The sales are 30% cash, 50% credit cards, and 20% regular credit. The diner accepts only MasterCard. Cash is received from MasterCard for each day's sales, and the brokerage charge is 3%. Regular credit sales are collected as follows:

Month of sale	10%
Month after sale	70%
Second month after sale	10%
Third month after sale	9%
Bad debts	1%
Total	100%

Interest income of $3,000 is expected in July. In October, the firm plans to sell some extra equipment. The chef estimates the equipment will bring $5,000. The book value of the equipment is $2,000. During August, 2,000 shares of capital stock with $1 par value are to be sold for $4 per share. Cash is to be received in August for the stock sales. Investment dividends of $8,000 are expected to be received in November.

Payments for food are usually made one month after the sale, and the food cost percentage is 38%. Beverages are usually purchased and paid for one month in advance, and the beverage cost percent is 23%. Beverage sales are 75% of food sales.

Employee wages are paid during the month they are earned and represent 35% of total sales. Other expenses, except insurance, depreciation, and property taxes, are $20,000 per month and are paid on a monthly basis. Insurance premiums of $5,000 are paid quarterly in January, April, July, and October of each year. The property taxes of $30,000 for the year are paid in two installments of $15,000 in July and December. Depreciation expense is $5,000 per month.

The Board of Directors is expected to declare a dividend/share of $.25 in September, payable in October (24,000 shares are outstanding).

In August, the diner plans to acquire fixed assets totaling $20,000 with cash. If the diner is to borrow working capital, it must do so in increments of $1,000. The rate of interest is 12%, and principal and interest must be paid back in 30 days. (Assume that the funds borrowed, if any, are paid back the following month.) For the interest expense calculation, assume that a year has 365 days.

Required:

Prepare the cash budget for the Lakeland Diner for the months of July–December using the cash receipts and disbursements approach.

12 Internal Control

All business operations need strong internal controls to monitor and maintain the quality of goods and services they provide and thereby maximize profits, especially in the long run. Strong internal controls are critical for hospitality operations because (1) many sales transactions involve cash, (2) there are hundreds, and for some operations, thousands of transactions in a day, and (3) many employees handle cash at the front desk, in restaurants, and in beverage operations. However, as we will see in this chapter, internal control includes much more than control over cash and cash sales. This chapter will attempt to answer some of the following questions regarding internal control:

1. What is internal control?

2. What are the major objectives of internal control?

3. What are the differences between accounting and administrative controls?

4. What are the characteristics or principles of internal control?

5. How are internal controls documented?

6. How is flowcharting useful in documenting and monitoring internal control?

7. How does the segregation of duties enhance internal control?

8. What methods of internal control are necessary to safeguard cash?

In this chapter, we will first provide a formal definition and some examples of internal control. Next, several internal control characteristics of hospitality operations are discussed, followed by the basic requirements of internal accounting control for various accounting functions, including cash receipts, cash disbursements, accounts receivable, accounts payable, payroll, inventories, fixed assets, and marketable securities. Next, the implementation and review of internal controls are presented. This is followed by a discussion of internal controls applicable to small operations.

Definition and Objectives of Internal Control

There are many definitions of internal control, but one of the best known was provided by the American Institute of Certified Public Accountants (AICPA). This definition states, "Internal control comprises the plan of organization and all of the coordinate methods and measures adopted within a business to safeguard its assets, check the accuracy and reliability of its accounting data, promote operational efficiency, and encourage adherence to prescribed managerial policies."[1]

According to this definition, internal control consists of the plan of organization and the methods and measures within the operation to accomplish four major objectives. Several methods and measures used by hospitality operations will be discussed later in this chapter. At this point, it is important to realize that each hospitality operation must have a satisfactory plan of organization which should be in writing and which everyone in the operation should understand. Further, the organizational plan should provide for independence among operating, custodial, and accounting functions in order to both prevent fraudulent conversion and assist in providing accurate and reliable accounting data. For example, in a restaurant operation, food should be stored and issued by custodians and requisitioned for use by preparation (operating) personnel. The accounting for the food should be accomplished by accounting personnel. Thus, the storing and issuing, preparation, and accounting functions are separate and independent of each other.

The four AICPA objectives of internal control can be defined as follows:

1. **Safeguard Assets.** As previously defined in this text, assets are resources such as cash, inventory, equipment, buildings, and land. A major objective of internal control is to protect these assets. This objective includes, but is not necessarily limited to, (1) the protection of existing assets from loss such as theft, (2) the maintenance of resources, especially equipment, to ensure efficient utilization, and (3) the safeguarding of resources, especially inventories for resale, to prevent waste and spoilage. This objective is achieved by various control procedures and safeguards which might include the proper use of coolers and freezers for storing food, the use of locks to secure assets, the use of safes or vaults for cash, limiting personnel access to various assets, and segregating the operating, custodial, and accounting functions.

2. **Check Accuracy and Reliability of Accounting Data.** This objective consists of all the checks and balances within the accounting system to ensure the accuracy and reliability of accounting information. Accurate and reliable accounting information must not only be available for reports to owners, governmental agencies, and other outsiders, but is also necessary for management's own use in internal operations. For hospitality establishments, this objective may best be accomplished by adopting a uniform system of accounts. Because accounting information is most useful when received on a timely basis, regular reports for management's use must be prepared promptly.

3. **Promote Operational Efficiency.** Operational efficiency results from providing products and services at a minimum cost. In a hospitality establishment, training programs and proper supervision promote operational efficiency. For example, when room attendants are properly trained and supervised, the cost of cleaning rooms is lower. In addition, the use of mechanical and electronic equipment often improves operational efficiency. Point-of-sale (POS) devices in restaurant operations electronically communicate orders from server stations to preparation areas and often result in greater efficiency. POS devices in lodging operations also automatically post a restaurant sale to a guest's folio. This reduces labor and eliminates the possibility that the guest will check out before all charges have been properly posted to his or her account. Thus, the POS device also safeguards assets.

4. **Encourage Adherence to Prescribed Managerial Policies.** Another major objective of internal control is to ensure that employees follow managerial policies. For example, most operations have a policy that hourly employees must clock in and out themselves—one employee may not clock in another employee. Placing the time clock where managerial personnel can observe employees clocking in and out may encourage workers to adhere to the policy.

These four objectives may seem to conflict at times. For example, procedures to safeguard assets at a hotel may be so detailed that operational efficiency is reduced. Requiring four signatures to obtain a case of steaks from the storeroom may forestall theft, yet it may be so time-consuming that increased labor costs far exceed the potential losses without this elaborate control. Perfect controls, even if possible, generally would not be cost-justified. Management must weigh the cost of the instituting a control against the benefit it would provide. When the proper balance of costs and benefits is achieved, management is performing efficiently.

The four objectives of internal control may be divided between the accounting and administrative functions. The first two objectives, safeguarding assets and ensuring the accuracy and reliability of accounting data, are considered **accounting controls**. The last two objectives, promoting operational efficiency and encouraging adherence to managerial policies, are considered **administrative controls**. Historically, accountants (especially independent external auditors) have focused their attention on internal accounting controls. However, more recently, hospitality establishments are closely reviewing administrative controls, which are more applicable to operations than accounting controls. This focus is necessary if hospitality operations are to achieve their overall objectives of providing appropriate guest service and thereby maximizing their profits.

Internal accounting controls are not only highly desirable, they are also required by law. The Foreign Corrupt Practices Act (FCPA) of 1977, designed to stop illegal payments by publicly held corporations, contains the following provisions covering internal accounting control and recordkeeping:

1. Make and keep books, records, and accounts that, in reasonable

detail, accurately and fairly reflect the transactions and dispositions of the assets of the company.

2. Devise and maintain a system of internal accounting control sufficient to provide reasonable assurances that:

   a. Transactions are executed in accordance with management's general and specific authorization;

   b. Transactions are recorded as necessary: (1) to permit preparation of financial statements in conformity with generally accepted accounting principles or any other criteria applicable to such statements, and (2) to maintain accountability of assets;

   c. Access to assets is permitted only in accordance with management's general and specific authorization; and

   d. The recorded accountability for assets is compared with the existing assets at reasonable intervals, and appropriate action is taken with respect to any differences.

The focus is on accounting controls, not administrative controls. The basic intent of the recordkeeping provision is to provide for reasonably accurate *external* financial reports, while the basic intent of the internal accounting control provision is to signal questionable or illegal payments. The FCPA pertains to those corporations subject to the Securities Acts, essentially corporations and their subsidiaries. Companies violating these provisions may be fined up to $10,000; company personnel may be fined up to $10,000 and imprisoned for up to five years.

Characteristics of Internal Control

The four major objectives of internal control can only be achieved by instituting the many methods and measures of control. For example, to help safeguard assets, an operation might maintain a safe for holding cash overnight. Another procedure to safeguard cash may require that cash receipts be deposited with the bank when they total (for example) $2,000. Before discussing other methods and measures of an internal control system, we will present several general characteristics of such a system. These characteristics include:

- Management leadership
- Organizational structure
- Sound practices
- Competent and trustworthy personnel
- Segregation of duties
- Authorization procedures
- Adequate records
- Procedure manuals
- Physical controls

- Budgets and internal reports
- Independent performance checks

These characteristics are sometimes referred to as elements or principles of internal control. They are essential to all effective internal control systems and apply to any business enterprise.

Management Leadership. Management's leadership is the key to any hospitality operation's system of internal control. The board of directors establishes the operation's highest level policies and management communicates and enforces these policies. These policies should be clearly stated and communicated to all management levels. In addition, the various management levels are responsible for ensuring that the internal control system is adequate. The tone they set in communicating and enforcing policies may determine the degree to which employees will accept them and carry them out. Although there may be exceptions to board and top-level management policies, these exceptions should be minimized so as not to render the policies useless.

Organizational Structure. Only in the smallest hospitality operations is one person able to supervise all employees personally. In most establishments, the organizational structure is divided into the functional areas of marketing/sales, production, accounting/finance, and personnel. The organization chart represents the organizational structure of an operation. (An example of an organization chart for a large lodging establishment was presented in Exhibit 1.6 in Chapter 1). Personnel must know the organization chart and follow the chain of command. Management policies usually prevent employees from circumventing the chain of command by requiring them to discuss any complaints or suggestions with their immediate supervisors or in some cases the human resources department. This approach not only reduces confusion but normally results in greater efficiency. Cases of management fraud constitute an exception to this general rule. In such extreme cases, employees must be able to communicate with the highest levels of management or with internal auditors.

Each position on the organization chart usually has a corresponding written job description. A job description consists of a detailed list of duties for the position. The procedure manual indicates how a job or duty should be performed.

In some hotel chains, the individual hotel controller answers directly to the area controller rather than to the hotel's general manager. Nevertheless, in this situation, the controller and general manager should work as a team, not as adversaries.

Sound Practices. Sound practices are policy measures generally set by the board of directors to create an environment conducive to excellent internal control. Several hospitality operations have adopted the following practices:

- Bonding employees—Employees in a position of trust are covered by fidelity insurance. Some operations carry a blanket bond for minimum coverage on all employees.

- Mandatory vacation policy—Employees are required to take annual vacations. This is rigidly enforced for employees in positions of trust. Other employees then perform the absent employees' duties. If the absent employees have engaged in dishonest practices, the replacements may discover them and management can take action.

- Code of conduct—Recently, some operations have required management personnel to follow a code of management conduct prohibiting illegal acts.

Competent and Trustworthy Personnel. A key characteristic of internal control—perhaps the most important—is personnel. In the hospitality industry, the major difference between competitors is generally the quality of service, which is often a result of staff competency. For example, "service with a smile" may often be more important than the quality of the food served. Personnel must exhibit a caring attitude toward their guests in order for the operation to be successful.

An operation's system of internal control may be rendered useless if personnel are not competent and trustworthy. Generally, systems of internal control are not designed to prevent collusion (two or more people working together to defraud the property). Therefore, the careful selection, training, and supervision of personnel is vital. The operation must hire people with potential and train them properly in the work to be accomplished. This includes not only communicating what the jobs are and how to do them, but following up to make sure that training has been effective. In addition, employees must understand the importance of their jobs in relation to the operation's overall objective.

Finally, employees must be properly rewarded for work performed. This includes not only compensation but also praise for a job well done and promotions when a person is ready and a position is available.

Segregation of Duties. The **segregation of duties** involves assigning different personnel to the functions of accounting, custody of assets, and production. Duties within the accounting function should also be segregated. The major objective of segregating duties is to prevent and detect errors and theft.

To illustrate the segregation of duties, consider the following description of a food service operation. A server takes a guest's order and records it on a guest check. A cook prepares the guest's food order from a copy of the guest check. The food itself was issued from storage by means of a requisition, submitted earlier in the day, based on estimated sales. The guest receives a copy of the guest check and pays the cashier. The cashier records the sale after checking the server's accuracy. In this example, the functions of order taker (sales), cook (production), storekeeper (custody of assets), and cashier (accounting) are separate. In addition to meeting the internal control objective of safeguarding assets by segregating duties, this separation promotes operational efficiency. Additional segregation of duties may further enhance operational efficiency. For example, the production area of a large restaurant may employ many people, including chefs, a garde-manger, a pastry chef, a butcher, a sous chef, and more.

Various tasks within the accounting department are divided among personnel to ensure proper checks and balances. For example, different personnel maintain the general ledger, the city ledger, and the guest ledger. Similarly, the cash reconciliation is prepared by personnel other than those accounting for cash receipts and/or cash disbursements.

Authorization Procedures. Management must properly authorize every business transaction. Management's authorization may be either general or specific. Management provides general authorization for employees to follow in the normal course of performing their jobs. For example, in a food service operation, servers are instructed to sell food and beverage items on the menu at the listed prices. No specific authorization is required to approve a sale in this case. In addition, a guest may pay for purchases with a credit card. If the guest's credit card is satisfactory (current, signed, and so forth), then the cashier may accept it and process the payment without specific authorization.

However, management may also require that certain transactions receive specific authorization. For example, the purchase of fixed assets in excess of a certain amount requires the company president's approval. In this case, the transaction cannot be completed without the president's written authorization.

Adequate Records. Documents for recording transactions are essential to effective internal control. They include such forms as registration cards, folios, guest checks, payroll checks, receiving reports, purchase orders, time cards, and room out-of-order reports. Documents should be designed so that the preparer and ultimate user can understand them. Documents designed for multiple uses will minimize the number of different forms an operation needs. For example, a guest check for a food service operation could be a three-part form with the original copy serving as the customer's bill, the second copy used to communicate the order to production personnel, and the third copy for the server.

Documents are generally pre-numbered to facilitate control. Documents should be prepared when the transaction occurs in order to minimize errors. For example, when a hotel guest charges a meal to his or her room, a voucher is immediately prepared and transferred to the front office. This reduces the chance that the guest will check out without paying the food service charge.

Procedure Manuals. Each job within the hospitality operation can be reduced to writing. The procedure manual should list the details of each position, including how and when to perform each task. The procedure manual encourages consistent job performance, especially for relatively new employees who may be unsure about the details of their jobs. In addition, the procedure manual enables personnel to temporarily fill another position during a regular employee's absence.

Physical Controls. Physical controls are a critical element of safeguarding assets. Physical controls include security devices and measures for protecting assets, such as safes and locked storerooms. In addition, forms and accounting records need to be secured through proper storage and limited access. Mechanical and electronic equipment used to execute and record transactions also helps to safeguard assets. For example, cash registers which limit access to tapes help ensure the prompt and accurate recording of sales transactions in food service and beverage operations.

Budgets and Internal Reports. Budgets and other internal reports are essential elements of a system of internal control. These reports are an important part of an operation's communications system. When budgets are used for control purposes, they help to ensure that management's goals will be attained. If actual performance falls short of the goals, management is informed and able to take corrective action.

Other reports also alert management to operating performance and enable management to take corrective action as necessary. Exhibit 3.2 in Chapter 3 lists 12 such reports including the frequency, content, comparisons, recipients, and purpose of each report. These reports include those prepared daily (daily report of operations), weekly (weekly forecasts), monthly (future bookings reports), and annually (long-range planning).

Independent Performance Checks. This characteristic of internal control is designed to ensure that the other elements of the internal control system are functioning properly. In order for a performance check to be successful, it must be independent—that is, the personnel performing the internal verification must be independent of the personnel responsible for the data being checked. In a number of hospitality operations, the independent performance check is conducted by the internal auditors. In order for the internal audit function to be successful, the auditors must be independent of both operations and accounting and must report directly to top management. (The internal audit function is discussed further in the next section of this chapter.)

Another independent performance check, especially in relation to the accounting function, is the work performed by the independent external auditors. The auditors not only verify financial statements, but also study the internal accounting control system and test it as a basis for how extensive the remaining audit will be. That is, the stronger the system of internal control is, the more reliance can be placed on it. Therefore, all other things being the same, a strong internal control system requires less extensive auditing.

Independent performance checks are the result of the segregation of duties. For example, the preparation of the bank reconciliation by personnel independent of those accounting for cash receipts and disbursements constitutes an independent check.

Internal Auditing

The internal audit function in many lodging and food service chains is a relatively recent development. Some of the 100 largest lodging chains in the United States still do not have a chain-wide internal audit function, although several are in the process of establishing internal audit departments. The Institute of Internal Auditors defines internal auditing as "an independent appraisal activity within an organization for the review of operations as a service to management. It is a managerial control which functions by measuring and evaluating the effectiveness of other controls."[2]

In order for the internal audit function to be effective, it must be independent of the departments and functions that it audits. Since internal

Exhibit 12.1 Responsibilities of the Internal Audit Department

1. Develop a comprehensive long-term audit program.

2. Set policies for the audit activity.

3. Conduct financial audits.

4. Recommend improvements in control to strengthen protection of assets, promote corporate growth, and increase profitability.

5. Examine management's stewardship at all levels for compliance with company policies and procedures.

6. Review operations covering all controls.

7. Monitor the effectiveness of actions taken to correct deficiencies and see that "open" findings are appropriately resolved.

8. Conduct special examinations of sensitive areas.

9. Investigate fraud to discover the modus operandi, the extent of loss, and systems slippages or other deficiencies that warrant redress.

10. Assist the audit committee as needed.

11. Coordinate the work of the internal auditors with that of the independent public accountants.

Source: Paul J. Wendell, Editor, *Corporate Controllers' Manual* (Boston: Warren, Gorham, & Lamont, 1981).

auditors review accounting functions, they should answer to the president of the organization or to the audit committee of the board of directors. However, in many firms, the audit function is part of the accounting department.

The above definition states that the internal audit is a "service to management." The ultimate purpose is to enhance profitability; thus, the internal auditor should be viewed as a partner seeking to assist management. The internal auditor's reports should be constructive and contain explanations and recommendations for improvements. Internal auditors often follow up to ensure that their recommendations are implemented.

The internal audit focuses on both accounting and administrative controls. Like the independent external auditor, the internal auditor is concerned with safeguarding assets and ensuring the reliability of accounting records (and thus the financial statements). However, unlike the external auditor, the internal auditor is concerned with operational efficiency. The internal auditor's review of front office procedures may reveal a more efficient and profitable way to staff the front office. In addition, the internal auditor is concerned with adherence to managerial policies. For example, the internal auditor may investigate whether advance approval of overtime was sought and received as required. The internal auditor may also investigate compliance with a mandatory vacation policy for employees who handle cash.

Exhibit 12.1 lists typical responsibilities of the internal audit department of a large business. Of course, the responsibilities of the internal audit department should be tailored to each operation's needs.

Basics of Internal Accounting Control

This section covers basic requirements of internal accounting control, including several methods of control for the various accounting functions. However, this list of methods is not exhaustive. Each hospitality operation must review these areas and determine control methods best suited to its needs.

Cash Control Cash is the most vulnerable of all assets. It is therefore imperative to have an effective system of internal control over cash. The following list suggests commonly used cash control procedures.

1. All bank accounts and check signers must be authorized by the chief financial officer.

2. All bank accounts should be reconciled monthly, and the bank reconciliation should be reviewed by the controller.

3. The person reconciling bank accounts should receive bank statements (including canceled checks) directly from the bank. Employees who sign checks or have other accounting duties in connection with cash transactions should not reconcile the bank accounts. The reconciliation procedure should include examination of signatures and endorsements and verification of the clerical accuracy of cash receipt and disbursement records. Exhibit 12.2 presents a sample bank reconciliation.

4. The custody of cash should be the responsibility of the general cashier. Another employee should be assigned to account for cash received and review of cash transactions. This segregation of duties provides a check on the cashier's performance.

5. The general cashier must take annual vacations and his or her duties must be assumed by another employee.

6. House banks and petty cash funds should be counted at unannounced intervals by employees independent of the cash control function. Special attention should be given to the propriety of non-cash items such as IOUs and accommodation checks (that is, checks cashed for guests merely to provide them with cash).

7. Disbursements from petty cash funds should be supported by cash register tapes, invoices, or other documents. Such supporting data should be checked when funds are replenished and then canceled to prevent duplicate payment.

Cash Receipts. The following procedures are commonly used for the internal control of cash receipts.

1. Accounting and physical control over cash receipts should be established when the cash is first received, whether at the front desk, at a profit center, or through the mail. For example, incoming mail receipts should be initially listed by an employee independent of both the general cashier and the accounts receivable department. This procedure establishes an independent record

Exhibit 12.2 Bank Reconciliation—Hoosier Hotel

Bank Reconciliation
Hoosier Hotel
December 31, 19X2

Balance per bank statement – 12/31/19X2		$14,622.18
Add: Deposit in Transit		3,641.18
Less: Outstanding checks		
Ck. 4315	$ 18.36	
Ck. 4422	156.14	
Ck. 4429	3,689.18	
Ck. 4440	172.47	
Ck. 4441	396.15	
Ck. 4442	100.00	
Ck. 4443	7.43	
Ck. 4444	799.18	−5,338.91
Other:		
Insufficient funds check received Dec. 31*		+ 324.32
Service charge – December, 19X2**		+ 15.24
Cash balance per books – 12/31/19X2		$13,264.01

Prepared by_____

Approved by_____

*Redeposited January 1, 19X3
**Amount recorded on books in January 19X3, since it was minor in amount.

that later can be checked against daily bank deposits and the general ledger posting to accounts receivable. Initial control of cash received in the hotel or restaurant is accomplished with cash registers and front office accounting machines.

2. Restrictive endorsements, such as "For deposit only to Hoosier Hotel's account," should be placed on checks when first received to guard against the obstruction or illegal diversion of such cash receipts.

3. Employees in the accounts receivable department should not handle checks or currency. Postings to accounts receivable ledger cards should be based on remittance advice or listings of cash receipts.

4. Cash received should be given to the general cashier as soon as is practical. Cash receipts should be deposited daily and intact. They should not be mixed with other cash funds used to pay invoices, incidental expenses, or cash accommodation checks.

5. The general cashier and his or her subordinates should not be responsible for any of the following activities:

    a. Preparation or mailing of city ledger statements

    b. Posting accounts receivable records or balancing detail ledgers with general ledger control accounts

    c. Posting the general ledger

    d. Authorizing rebates, allowances, discounts, or writing off uncollectible accounts

    e. Preparing cash disbursements or reconciling bank accounts

These activities are prohibited in order to reduce the opportunity for the general cashier and his or her subordinates to steal from the operation.

6. General instructions for cashiers often include the following:

    a. The cash drawer must be closed after each sale.

    b. Cashiers must circle and initial any overrings on the tape at the time of occurrence.

    c. Cash registers must be locked and keys removed when unattended.

    d. Cash sales must be rung up when they are made. Sales made on an honor system are prohibited.

    e. Cashiers may not have briefcases, handbags, purses, cosmetic bags, and so forth at cashier stations.

    f. Cashiers should immediately inform the manager if they are experiencing problems with the cash register.

    g. Cashiers should verify the amount of cash banks when they receive and sign for them and should not be allowed to count the banks after that time.

    h. When feasible (or permitted by equipment), items should be rung up separately to allow the cash register to total the sale.

Cash Disbursements. There are several procedures which help to establish a strong system of internal control over cash disbursements.

1. Generally, all disbursements should be made by check. An exception is petty cash disbursements.

2. Checks should be pre-numbered and used in numerical sequence. In addition, it is a good idea to use a check protector (an imprinting device) to enter the amounts on the checks; this deters anyone from altering the amount.

3. Checks drawn in excess of a minimum amount (such as $50) should contain two signatures, while checks under this may require only one signature. Each check signer should carefully review supporting documents to ensure that the documentation has been properly audited and approved. Check signers should not be responsible for preparing checks and should not have custody of blank checks.

4. When a mechanical check signing device is used, only the employee authorized to use it should have the key. The operation should maintain an independent record of the number of checks processed through the device, and that number should be reconciled with the numerical sequence of the checks used.

5. Vouchers, invoices, and other documents supporting cash disbursements should be canceled by stamping them "PAID" when the check is signed. This procedure is designed to prevent duplicate payments should the document become detached from the check copy.

6. Signed checks and disbursement vouchers should not be returned to the check preparer but should be given to an employee independent of this function for immediate mailing.

7. Only authorized check preparers should have access to blank checks. Voided checks should be mutilated to prevent re-use by removing the signature line.

Accounts Receivable

Accounts receivable represent promises to pay the hospitality operation. A critical control in this area is the segregation of duties to prevent accounts receivable employees from pocketing cash received in payment of accounts. Control procedures for accounts receivable include the following:

1. Accounts receivable employees should not handle cash received in payment of accounts. Postings to accounts receivable for cash received should be made from remittance advice or check listings. Control totals for postings should be made independently of accounts receivable employees for posting by the general ledger clerk to the accounts receivable control account.

2. At the end of the month, the total of guest accounts should be reconciled with the independently determined balance in the general ledger control account. These procedures provide protection against manipulation by the accounts receivable employees. The failure to segregate cash handling and accounts receivable may facilitate **lapping**, a common fraudulent practice. Lapping occurs when an accounts receivable clerk steals cash received on an account, then posts cash received the next day on a second account to the first account. For example, assume that Guest A pays $100 on his or her account and the accounts receivable clerk takes the $100. The following day, Guest B pays $150. The accounts receivable clerk takes $50 for personal use and credits Guest A's account for $100. At this point, the accounts receivable clerk has stolen $150. This fraudulent activity may continue for quite some time when there is no segregation of duties or other compensating controls.

3. Non-cash entries to receivable accounts, such as writing off an account as uncollectible, should originate with employees or managers who do not handle cash and are not responsible for maintaining accounts receivable.

4. The credit manager and a member of management should resolve

disputed items. Clerical employees should not routinely adjust accounts receivable.

5. A key feature of control over receivables is an adequate system of internal reporting. Periodically, the accounts receivable should be aged, and special collection efforts should be applied to delinquent accounts. Exhibit 5.6 in Chapter 5 illustrates an aging of accounts receivable. The trend of accounts receivable balances in relation to credit terms should be tracked over time.

6. All collection efforts should be carefully documented, and uncollectible accounts should be written off only with the approval of the controller.[3]

Accounts Payable

There are several internal control procedures for accounts payable. These procedures include the following:

1. Vendors' invoices should be routed directly to the accounts payable department. Purchasing personnel should not handle or approve invoices.

2. Control should be established over vendors' invoices when received. This may be accomplished by the use of a voucher system (see Exhibit 12.3). The voucher system uses pre-numbered vouchers which are prepared from vendors' invoices and recorded in a voucher journal. Invoices should be reviewed for possible cash discounts, and the due dates noted to take advantage of any available discounts.

3. The terms of sale, prices, and list of goods received on vendors' invoices should be checked against purchase orders and receiving reports. All amount extensions and totals should be checked. The person auditing the vendors' invoices should initial these documents.

4. All vouchers, invoices, and supporting documents should be canceled when paid.

5. Only accounting personnel not responsible for the general ledger should maintain the accounts payable subsidiary ledger. The accounts payable subsidiary ledger should be reconciled monthly with the general ledger control account for accounts payable.

6. A monthly trial balance of accounts payable should be prepared for the controller's review. Suppliers should be paid on a timely basis in order to maintain good supplier relationships.

Purchasing and Receiving

This section covers only a few of the major controls of purchasing and receiving.[4] Common control procedures include the following:

1. To the extent practical, the purchasing agent should make all purchases acting upon approved purchase requisitions from department heads.

2. A written purchase order (PO) system should be used. Copies of each PO should be sent to receiving and accounting. In this way, receiving will be aware of materials ordered, while the accounts

Exhibit 12.3   Voucher from Voucher System

Accounts Payable Voucher			Voucher Number	7321						
Pay To: Address:			Date Paid							
			Date Check No.							

DATE	DESCRIPTION	AMOUNT	DISCOUNT % AMOUNT	OTHER DEDUCTIONS FOR	AMOUNT	NET AMOUNT			ACCOUNT	AMOUNT

TOTALS										

ENTERED ON VOUCHER
RECORDED BY _____

PREPARED BY _____

APPROVED FOR PAYMENT BY _____

POSTED BY _____

TOTAL CHARGES _____
LESS DISCOUNT _____
OTHER DEDUCTIONS _____
AMT. OF CHECK _____

AUDITED BY _____

payable department can use the PO to audit the vendor's invoice.

3. A receiving department, separate from the purchasing agent, should receive all incoming goods. All materials received should be carefully checked.

4. The receiving department should prepare a receiving report for each vendor's delivery. A copy of the receiving report should be forwarded to the accounts payable department for verification against the vendor's invoice.

Payroll

Payroll is the largest expense for most hospitality operations. Therefore, controls in this area are critical if the operation is to meet its internal control objectives. Several common control procedures include:

1. Payroll functions should be segregated as follows:

    a. Authorizing of employment and wage rates

    b. Reporting hours worked

    c. Preparing payroll

    d. Signing payroll checks

    e. Distributing paychecks to employees

    f. Reconciling payroll bank accounts

2. Only the personnel department or executives with hiring/ terminating authority should authorize additions to, or terminations from, the staff. Generally, the personnel department

carefully recruits new employees and provides the payroll department with all the relevant information on newly hired employees.

3. Procedures for reporting time worked should be clearly defined. Hourly personnel should use time clocks. Departmental supervisors should approve all hourly employees' time reports.

4. Employees should generally be paid with checks rather than cash. Separate payroll accounts should be maintained. An employee independent of the payroll department should reconcile the payroll bank account.

5. Payroll preparation procedures should include checking the clock card used for the department supervisor's approval and re-checking the hours worked.

6. Payroll sheets and net pay amounts should be checked independently.

7. Personnel independent of the payroll department should distribute paychecks. In addition, department heads should not distribute payroll checks.

8. Undelivered paychecks should be given to the controller or a person designated by the controller. This person should not be from the payroll department. The undelivered paychecks should be held until delivered or voided after a specified number of days.

Inventories

Purchasing and receiving control procedures apply to inventories also. Additional inventory control procedures include the following:

1. Accounting department employees should maintain inventory records. These employees should not have access to inventory, nor should employees with custody of inventory have access to inventory records.

2. Personnel independent of the storage function should periodically take a physical inventory. Accounting personnel should extend the physical inventory and compare it to the book inventory if a perpetual inventory record system is maintained. (*Extending* the physical inventory means listing the proper costs per unit and multiplying the counts of each item by the cost per unit.)

3. Taking physical inventory is best accomplished when:

   a. Like items are grouped together in the storeroom.

   b. Pre-printed inventory forms are used to list all inventory items.

   c. The inventory form is arranged in the same sequence as the inventory items are maintained in the storeroom.

   d. Two individuals conduct the physical inventory; one can count the items while the other records the count. (As noted earlier, the personnel should be independent of the storing function.)

4. The inventory records must be adjusted for any differences between the books and the physical inventory. The inventory adjustment must be approved by an executive such as the controller.

5. Any significant inventory overages or shortages should be investigated, the causes determined, and procedures designed to prevent recurrence of errors.

6. Other operating controls relating to inventory include the following:

    a. Control must be maintained over physical inventories. This is accomplished by storing inventory in the appropriate facilities; for example, food must be stored at proper temperatures.

    b. Daily inventories and usage rates of high priced items should be monitored.

    c. Access to inventory should be restricted to storage employees. Limiting access is accomplished, in part, by securing inventory in locked facilities.

    d. Personnel handling inventory (storage and production personnel) should leave the facilities by an exit easily observed by management.

    e. Records of spoilage, overcooked food, and so forth should be maintained for use in reconciling the physical inventory to the book inventory and for accounting for other discrepancies in food inventory.

Fixed Assets   Fixed assets generally constitute the largest percentage of most hospitality operations' assets. These assets are not liquid; however, controls must still be established to maintain these resources for their intended use—providing services to guests. Several common control procedures are listed below.

1. The board of directors usually issues formal policies establishing which executives and committees have the authority to purchase fixed assets.

2. A work order system should be established for the orderly accumulation of property costs when facilities are acquired. Each approved project is assigned a work order number, and all expenditures are charged to this number as the work progresses.

3. Accounting records maintained under a typical work order system include the following:

    a. An expenditure authorization that defines the project scope, purpose, cost justification, and budgeted amount.

    b. Cost sheets that summarize actual expenditures for comparison to budgeted amounts.

    c. Supporting evidence of costs charged to the project account.

This evidence includes vendors' invoices, material requisitions, and labor time tickets.

4. General ledger control should be established for each principal classification of property cost and each related depreciation accumulation.

5. Physical inventories of fixed assets should be taken periodically by personnel independent of the person with custody of the assets and of the person maintaining the accounting records. The physical inventory should be compared to the equipment listed in the accounting records. Any discrepancies must be resolved and action taken to prevent recurrence of similar errors.

6. The sale, retirement, or scrapping of fixed assets requires formal executive approval. Approval must be from executives not having custody of the fixed asset. Accounting department personnel must determine that retired assets are removed from the books and that proceeds received are properly accounted for.

Marketable Securities

Marketable securities include investments in stocks and bonds of other corporations. Controls over marketable securities often include the following:

1. Accounting department records should identify each marketable security owned by name and certificate number.

2. All marketable security transactions should be approved by the board of directors or a designated committee.

3. Marketable securities should be kept in a safe deposit box to which only the custodian has access.

4. Periodically, independent physical counts of marketable securities should be taken and the count compared to the accounting records.

5. Income from marketable securities recorded in accounting records should be periodically compared to what the investment should be generating. For example, a $100,000 bond at 8% interest should provide $8,000 of interest annually.

Implementation and Review of Internal Controls

Top-level management is responsible for implementing and maintaining the system of internal controls. Since this system is critical to the well-being of the hospitality operation, management must regularly review it to ensure that it is adequate. The internal control system may break down periodically. New personnel may not understand procedures and thus not follow them. For example, a new employee may return disputed statements to the accounts receivable clerk for resolution, reasoning that the clerk can resolve such differences most efficiently.

The internal control system may also need restructuring due to changing business conditions and other circumstances. For example, ten years ago, a hospitality operation may have established a policy stating that cash receipts had to be deposited when they reached $1,000. Due to inflation, the amount might now be raised to $2,000.

An operation's internal controls may be documented and reviewed by flowcharting and by using internal control questionnaires. A **flowchart** diagrams the flow of documents through an organization, indicating the origin, processing, and final deposition of each document. In addition, the flowchart shows the segregation of duties. Exhibit 12.4 is a simplified flowchart of a club operation's payroll system.

Flowcharting is useful because it provides a concise overview of the internal control system. It facilitates review of the internal control system, enabling management to identify weaknesses for corrective action. The Supplemental Reading to this chapter contains a discussion of how analytical flowcharts are prepared.

A second device for studying a hospitality operation's system of internal control is the **internal control questionnaire (ICQ)**. The ICQ uses a series of questions about controls in each accounting area to identify weaknesses. ICQs generally provide complete coverage for each accounting area. However, they do not reveal document flows as do flowcharts. From a practical viewpoint, both flowcharts and ICQs should be used in documenting and reviewing an operation's system of internal control.

Once the review is completed, management must act to strengthen the internal control system. If a system is documented and reviewed without proper follow-up, then the real value of the review process is lost.

Internal Control in Small Operations

Although the hospitality industry has a number of giant firms with system-wide sales exceeding $1 billion, the vast majority of establishments are small. The elaborate control procedures presented thus far are not practical for operations with only a few employees because there are simply not enough people for the proper segregation of duties.

The key person in internal control of a small operation is the owner or manager. Several duties, if performed by the owner or manager, help to offset what might otherwise be weaknesses in the internal control system. These critical duties are outlined below.

1. Cash Receipts

   a. Open all mail and list cash receipts, retaining one copy of the list.

   b. Deposit all cash daily and compare deposit with the cash receipts debit recorded by the bookkeeper.

   c. Reconcile cash receipts with cash register tapes.

2. Cash Disbursements

   a. Sign all checks, carefully review documentation, and cancel all supporting documentation.

   b. Use only pre-numbered checks and account for them as checks are signed.

Exhibit 12.4 Flowchart of a Payroll System

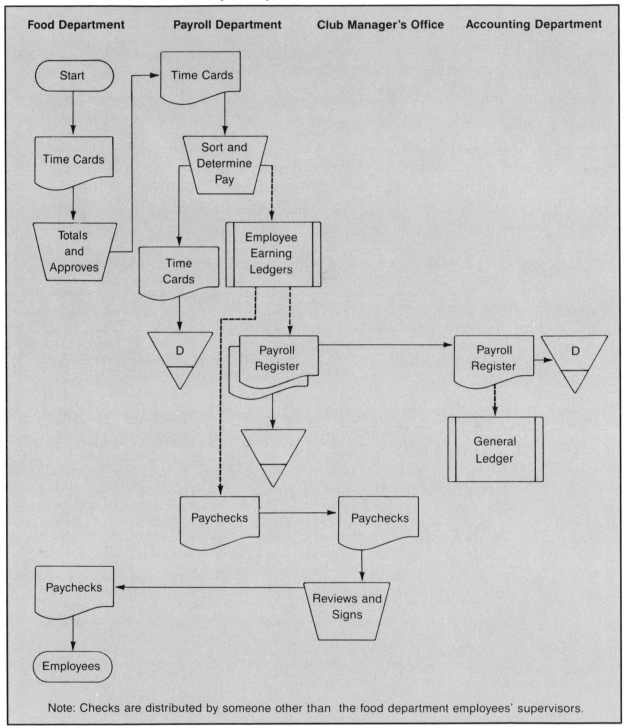

c. Total check disbursements periodically and compare the total to the bookkeeper's cash credit.

d. Prepare the bank reconciliation.

3. Sales

    a. Keep all cash registers locked and remove cash register tapes when not in use.

    b. Compare cash register tape totals with the cash debit for the day and the cash receipts deposited.

4. Payroll

    a. Examine the payroll worksheet (or payroll journal), noting employees' names, authorized gross pay, hours worked, deductions, and net pay. Add the payroll and compare the net pay with the cash credit.

    b. Distribute payroll checks.

5. Accounts Receivable

    a. Review aging of accounts receivable.

    b. Compare statements with individual ledger accounts and mail statements.

    c. Resolve all disputed account balances.

6. Inventories

    a. Periodically supervise or take the physical inventory.

    b. Compare the physical inventory with the perpetual inventory on the books.

    c. Compare cost of goods sold with total sales each month, and investigate any major discrepancies in cost of goods sold percentages.

7. Purchases

    a. Randomly review price quotes for inventory items purchased.

    b. Use a purchase order system and account for all purchase orders.

    c. Randomly compare purchase orders with receiving reports, and vendors' invoices with vendors' statements.

8. General

    a. Review all general journal entries.

    b. Employ a competent, trustworthy bookkeeper.

    c. Engage an independent auditor to conduct an annual audit and to periodically conduct limited surprise audits of cash, inventory, and accounts receivable.

Additional Classification of Controls

At the beginning of this chapter, internal controls were classified as either accounting or administrative controls. Controls may also be classified based on whether they take effect before or after a problem occurs. **Preventive controls** are implemented before a problem occurs. They include such things as the use of locks to safeguard assets, the separation of duties to preclude operating personnel from controlling inventories, and general and specific authorization policies. Preventive controls are less expensive to establish than detective controls. **Detective controls** are designed to discover problems and to monitor preventive controls. Detective controls include external audits, surprise cash internal audits, and bank reconciliations. Detective controls may serve in part as preventive controls; for example, if employees know that audits will be conducted, they will be less likely to take advantage of their access to cash and other assets.

Computerization

Internal controls are an integral part of any accounting system. Computers can help to ensure adherence to the controls established by management.

Accounting software programs can edit data according to the controls. For example, accounts payable programs can verify whether an invoice has already been paid to help prevent duplicate payments. Accounts payable programs may also automatically calculate vendor discounts and verify that a master vendor record has been established before paying the vendor. Similar internal controls can be incorporated into programs for the general ledger, payroll, accounts receivable, fixed assets, and any other accounting functions. If someone attempts to bypass the controls, the computer can record the "error" and report it on an "exceptions report." For example, if the payroll program allows payroll checks to be written for no more than $5,000, an attempt to issue a check for $6,000 will be noted by the computer. Management can then access this information. A good computer control system will allow exceptions only with management override.

Computers can also assist management in internal controls by providing documentation. Word processing is an excellent way to create, revise, and distribute policies, procedures, and other documentation relating to internal controls. This is especially helpful in new operations, where controls are being tested and often revised. In addition, documentation stored on computer can be easily reproduced at a moment's notice. Since computers can store so much information, the operation can keep records of current and past control measures.

Computers can also help managers establish flowcharts and critical paths. For example, there are several flowcharting programs available which can design the exact flowchart for any given set of tasks. In addition, they can lay out a critical path, showing distribution of responsibilities, how long each task should take, and how the individual tasks relate to the entire process. One side benefit of this is a simple review of the separation of duties. A flowchart and critical path provide an overview of who is responsible for specific functions in an accounting office.

The security of the computer system itself can enhance internal controls. Most good data processing systems have a high level of security. They allow users to access specific functions only. For example, with a good security program, someone handling accounts payable would not be able to access payroll. Certain employees might be able to view an accounts payable vendor master record, but not post invoices. System security can also assist in the separation of duties. The system might prevent the person who enters invoices into the accounts payable system from printing the checks.

Summary

Internal control is the overall system of protecting the establishment's assets, ensuring the accuracy and reliability of its accounting records, promoting efficient operations, and encouraging adherence to management policies. An operation must have an adequate internal control system in order to operate profitably in the long run.

There are four main objectives of every internal control system. The first two, checking the accuracy of accounting data and safeguarding assets, are known as accounting controls. These controls ensure that assets are recorded properly and that they are safe from loss through negligence or theft. The other two controls are administrative controls. Promoting operational efficiency means that the operation's products and/or services are produced efficiently. Adherence to managerial policies is important because established rules are only effective if they are followed.

There are several characteristics of a strong internal control system. These characteristics include the physical control of assets, the development of budgets, management leadership, and organizational structure. Competent and trustworthy personnel are necessary for operational efficiency and adequate physical control of the assets.

Management needs to examine every function of the hospitality operation and establish controls for each one. For example, the cash account must have adequate controls because it is highly vulnerable to theft. Management should consider physical controls, segregation of duties, management policies, proper authorization procedures, and adequate performance checks. These characteristics of internal control can help protect the operation's cash.

Management must consider the costs and benefits of internal control policies. A "perfect" system—one that guarantees the safety of assets— would probably be cost-prohibitive. This is especially true for smaller operations that do not have enough personnel to completely segregate duties. In these instances, managers and managing owners must be aware of the available precautions and take an active role in the operation to ensure its success.

Endnotes

1. Committee on Auditing Procedure, *Internal Control—Elements of a Coordinated System and Its Importance to Management and the Independent Public Accountant* (New York: AICPA, 1949), p. 6.

2. "Statement of Responsibilities of the Internal Auditor," *The Internal Auditor,* September/October 1971, p. 12.

3. The reader interested in the detailed procedures of the credit function at hotels should consider an article by Ellis Knotts in *Lodging,* June 1979, entitled "Handling the Credit Function at Small Hotels." This article covers credit extension, credit monitoring, and collection of hotel accounts receivable.

4. The reader interested in a detailed explanation of purchasing and receiving controls should read Chapter 6 of Jack D. Ninemeier's *Planning and Control for Food and Beverage Operations,* 2d ed. (East Lansing, Mich.: Educational Institute of the American Hotel & Motel Association, 1986).

Key Terms

accounting controls	internal control questionnaire (ICQ)
administrative controls	lapping
detective controls	preventive controls
flowchart	segregation of duties

Discussion Questions

1. What is internal control?

2. What are the four AICPA objectives of internal control?

3. What are four characteristics of internal control?

4. Which characteristic of internal control is most important? Why have you chosen this one?

5. Why is the control of cash important to a hospitality operation?

6. What is segregation of duties?

7. How can internal control systems be documented and reviewed?

8. How does flowcharting differ from an internal control questionnaire?

9. How can computers be used to strengthen an enterprise's internal control system?

10. What are three procedures to safeguard inventory?

Problems

Problem 12.1

Several control procedures currently used at the Lions Inn are listed below:

Procedure	Preventive/ Detective	Accounting/ Administrative
1. The Lions Inn uses a cash register.	_____	_____
2. The employee time clock is located just outside the manager's office.	_____	_____

3. An external auditor conducts a surprise cash audit quarterly. _____ _____

4. Only the front office supervisor may approve "room sales allowances." _____ _____

5. Each room attendant's work in cleaning rooms is inspected by a housekeeping supervisor. _____ _____

6. Cash receipts are deposited intact and on a daily basis. _____ _____

7. The internal auditor prepares the monthly bank reconciliation. _____ _____

8. Vegetables are stored in coolers at the proper temperatures. _____ _____

9. Supplier invoices are reconciled to the suppliers' monthly statements. _____ _____

10. Cash drawers must be closed after each sale in all revenue centers. _____ _____

Required:

1. Indicate whether each control is preventive (P) or detective (D) and whether it is an accounting (AC) or administrative (AD) control.

2. If you believe a given control may be both P and D or AC and AD, provide your reasoning.

Problem 12.2

The segregation of duties is a characteristic of an effective internal control system because it helps prevent the fraudulent conversion of assets and increases operational efficiency.

Required:

1. List the minimum number of staff members required to complete a food service transaction which includes: (a) taking an order, (b) preparing the food, (c) serving the food, and (d) collecting the cash. Assume that the major goal is to safeguard assets. At this point, do not concern yourself with operational efficiency.

2. What additional positions are necessary to promote operational efficiency when many guests must be served in a relatively short period of time?

Problem 12.3

At the Divinity Hotel, a 150-room property, the procedure for handling checks returned by the bank marked "insufficient funds" was to carry them as part of the bank balance. That is, when the bank returned a check because payment was refused and charged it to the hotel's account, no entry was made in the books. The returned check was immediately redeposited, and the bank usually collected them. At the end of the month, those checks which had not been collected were treated as reconciling items (NSF checks) by the bookkeeper preparing the bank reconciliation. If the check was later collected, the bookkeeper made no formal entry; however, in preparing the next month's bank reconciliation, the bookkeeper reduced the amount of NSF checks. If the check was still uncollectible after three months, a journal entry was recorded charging "Bad Debt Expense" and crediting "Cash in Bank."

Required:

1. Explain any deficiencies in the Divinity Hotel's cash control system.
2. Provide the manager with suggestions for improving the system.

Problem 12.4

The January 31, 19X2, balance of the Hiatt Hotel's checking account was $10,420.00. The bank statement indicated a balance of $13,424.15 at the same date. Checks written before February 1, 19X2, which had not cleared the bank were as follows:

Check 1059	$ 246.81
Check 1072	$2,621.00
Check 1073	$ 349.06
Check 1074	$ 15.92
Check 1075	$1,123.46
Check 1076	$ 998.43

The bank statement reflected service charges of $32.46, which were not recorded on the books until February 19X2. A check marked "insufficient funds" for $168.24 was returned by the bank on January 31, 19X2, and was redeposited on February 2, 19X2. No entry was recorded on the books when the check was returned or redeposited. On February 1, 19X2, cash receipts of $2,149.83 from business on January 31, 19X2, were deposited in the bank. This cash was recorded as sales during January 19X2.

Required:

Prepare the Hiatt Hotel's bank reconciliation for January 19X2.

Problem 12.5

Sharon Rhoades is owner and manager of Rhoades' Place, a small restaurant. She employs 15 people, including a bookkeeper who handles all the paperwork. Sharon spends little time reviewing financial documents, and lately she is concerned that perhaps too little attention has been paid to the bookkeeper's work. The bookkeeper has worked at Rhoades' Place for several years, and Sharon has trusted the person completely. However, it now seems to Sharon that the payroll costs are increasing more than they should be.

Required:

Assume the role of a consultant and recommend minimum duties that Sharon should perform herself regarding payroll. Explain why each duty is important to safeguard the assets of Rhoades' Place.

Problem 12.6

The Buckeye Motel's books indicated that the general checking account at the end of December 19X1 contained $6,523.34. The bank statement at December 31, 19X1, showed a closing balance of $7,432. Additional information includes:

1. Last month's bank reconciliation showed five outstanding checks:

Check 8923	$100.10
Check 8936	$248.15
Check 8944	$194.21
Check 8945	$648.49
Check 8946	$137.75

2. A comparison of the canceled checks from the bank with the check register revealed five checks written in December 19X1 that had not been paid by the bank:

Check 9164	$384.21
Check 9173	$439.42
Check 9190	$526.14
Check 9191	$422.15
Check 9192	$ 67.42

3. In addition, three checks were canceled in December that had been issued in the prior month:

Check 8944	$194.21
Check 8945	$648.49
Check 8946	$137.75

4. Cash receipts of $1,221.75 recorded on the books on December 31, 19X1, were deposited with the bank on January 2, 19X2.

5. A check for $57.18 received from a guest was returned by the bank on December 31, 19X1, marked "insufficient funds." The check was redeposited on January 2, 19X2. No entry was recorded to reflect the returned check on December 31, 19X1.

Required:

Prepare the Buckeye Motel's December 19X1 bank reconciliation.

Problem 12.7

At the Morehart Motel, a 200-room property, the books and banking had been entrusted to a long-time employee. For nine years no audit was made, but finally a friend of the owners suggested that an audit could not hurt. The audit revealed a cash shortage of over $6,000 for the year in question; since the bookkeeper was not bonded, the owners did not wish to go back further in the records. There was ample evidence in the one year's records to send the bookkeeper to prison.

This employee chose one of the crudest methods of covering the manipulations. He made bank deposits only two or three times a week during the busy season, and each time he stole a few hundred dollars. In the cash receipts journal, he entered the full amount of the cash turned over to him for deposit, but at the same time made an offsetting entry for the shortage in the cash disbursements journal. The latter entries purported to represent checks drawn in payment of food and supply bills and were properly posted to the creditors' accounts in the accounts payable ledger. The auditor promptly discovered the simple manipulation.

Required:

1. Highlight the weaknesses in the internal control system of the Morehart Motel.
2. Offer suggestions to tighten the control.

Problem 12.8

Many of the front office manager's headaches are caused by the skipper—the guest who departs without paying the bill. However, a dishonest employee can cause even more problems by using this situation as a cover-up. Consider the following situation. A guest checks in and is assigned to an $80 room. The clerk forgets to ask for a mailing address. The following day, the guest, hurrying to catch a flight, runs to the cashier's window, throws down $80 in cash, barks "Check me out of 423," and rushes off.

The cashier looks at the bill in the file and notices that the guest left no address. The cashier reasons that the credit department will never track down the guest, so he pockets the $80 and leaves the bill in the file. The next day, room 423 is reported unoccupied. The bill by this time stands at $160 and is charged to "skippers."

Some hotels make no effort to locate skippers; at any rate, such attempts are usually without success. In this case, even finding the guest will not solve the problem; the guest has no receipt to prove his or her claim that the bill was paid.

Required:

What steps could be taken to adequately control cash in this situation?

Problem 12.9

At the Wolverine Inn, salaries and wages were paid semi-monthly by individual checks to the order of each employee. These checks, drawn on a special payroll bank account, were signed jointly by the accountant and the payroll supervisor. Transfers for the total amount of the payroll for the period were made semi-monthly to this special account by a check drawn on the regular bank account. In addition to the amounts periodically transferred, there remained a large balance from the period, representing the uncashed checks.

The Wolverine Inn's accountant had to be absent several days each month. It was her custom to leave a few signed blank checks to be used to pay employees who might quit during her absence.

With an assured minimum balance in the payroll account and the signed blank checks, the payroll supervisor saw an opportunity and seized it. He drew a check to his own order for an amount within the usual minimum balance. Since he always reconciled the monthly bank statements for this account, he was fairly safe from detection.

Required:

1. Which characteristics of internal control were violated in this situation?
2. How could this theft have been prevented?

Problem 12.10

Check-out time at the Wyman Hotel was 2 p.m. Guests checking out after that time were supposed to be charged for an extra day. However, the front office clerks did not post the extra charge on the guest folio until the money was paid. The usual procedure was to collect from those guests who failed to question the charge and then enter the amount on the folio. If the guest objected to the charge, the charge was dropped, as Wyman's management did not want unhappy guests.

One of the cashiers saw the opportunity for some personal gain in this procedure. The cashier would occasionally withhold the money paid by a hotel guest for the extra day, making no charge or credit for it on the guest's folio. The cashier did this only when the guest did not take the receipted statement. The cashier was able to add considerably to his monthly wages until by chance the assistant front office manager noticed his deceptive practices.

Required:

1. List weaknesses in Wyman's procedures for accounting for the extra charges.

2. What corrective action do you recommend?

Supplemental Reading
Computers in Clubs*

By Michael L. Kasavana, Raymond S. Schmidgall and Michael Speer

Club managers are expected to operate their clubs by providing varied services to members. As their jobs have become increasingly demanding, so too have club managers become more involved in analyzing and controlling the business transactions.

In order to properly control the club's operation, an adequate information system is a prerequisite. A useful tool for understanding and analyzing the club's information system is *flowcharting*. Further, the analysis of the club's information system may indicate using a computer will result in more efficient operations.

Flowcharting Defined

Flowcharting is a graphic means of describing an information system. The flowchart consists of symbols which show what happens to documents and communications as they move through a firm's information system. A flowchart consists of four primary elements: (1) Symbols to show predefined items, steps and actions, (2) flow-lines to highlight document and information flows, (3) identification of areas of responsibility of operating departments and (4) written comments and clarifications that complete the flowchart. The primary elements of a flowchart are illustrated in Exhibit 1.

Purposes of Flowcharting

Flowcharting is a technique aimed at illustrating the information and documentation flows of the firm. An alternative method to accomplish this description involves a less efficient tool called a written narrative. A written narrative is a laborious task and does not lend itself easily to system analysis. A detailed flowchart which may cover only a single page might require as many as six to eight pages in an equivalent written narrative.

Michael L. Kasavana, Ph.D., is an associate professor and **Raymond S. Schmidgall, Ph.D., CPA**, is an assistant professor at the School of Hotel, Restaurant and Institutional Management at Michigan State University, East Lansing, Michigan. **Michael Speer, CPA**, is a consultant with the accounting firm of Laventhol & Horwath, Chicago.

The description of an information system serves three major purposes. First, the flowchart provides an excellent means of documenting the system. An outsider such as an auditor or a new employee can quickly obtain an overview of a given process or subsystem by reviewing its flowchart. If changes in an information system are desirable, these changes can most likely be accomplished through a review of the existing system.

The flowchart is also a means of communication. It is a succinct description which tends to minimize misunderstandings associated with the transmission of information within a system. The importance of this communication capability is reinforced in the training and analytical review of present or planned systems.

Additionally, flowcharting provides a basis by which to analyze the information system of an enterprise. The flowchart indicates information flows by area of responsibility and allows for evaluation and delineation by redundant and overlapping functions. This analysis may lead to revisions, thus, strengthening the overall information system.

Types of Flowcharts

There are three types of flowcharts: (1) Analytical, (2) system, and (3) program. The four primary elements of a flowchart discussed above pertain to an *analytical flowchart* which shows the overall information processing function of a club, such as cash disbursements or purchasing.

This flowchart consists of several vertical columns, one for each department, and contains the flow of documents and information among the various departments. Exhibit 1 is an illustration of an analytical flowchart for purchasing supplies. In Exhibit 1, two copies of a purchase requisition are prepared in the food and beverage department. One copy is filed and the original copy is sent to the assistant manager who functions as the purchasing agent for this club. The assistant manager decides on the vendor based on the lowest price quotation per purchase specifications.

A three-part purchase order is prepared with the original being sent to the vendor, the second copy is sent to the receiving department and the third copy is attached with the original copy of the purchase requisition. Then the third copy of the purchase order and the original copy of the purchase requisition are sent to the accounting department, where they are filed alphabetically. A *system flowchart* is primarily concerned with the data processing needs for one specific task application. The three phases of the data processing cycle (input-process-output) are delineated and the various departments involved may be indirectly referenced. Exhibit 2 contains an illustration of a system flowchart for the recording of a food sale and the updating of a member's account.

The third type of flowchart is the *program flowchart* which is even more specific and detailed than the system flowchart. Although the pro-

gram chart details one specific application into a series of substeps, it presents an even more thorough translation or conversion of input data to output information. The program flowchart is based on an analysis of processing steps with no distinction made between departments.

Exhibit 3 depicts the program flowchart for the determination of an employee's net pay. Note that the program flowchart tends to be more detailed and easier to comprehend than does the analytical flowchart. The program flowchart is important to clubs that desire to streamline their operations by avoiding unnecessary or redundant data handling procedures. Since individual applications are isolated, the program flowchart can be used to identify specific weaknesses within club operations.

Exhibit 1

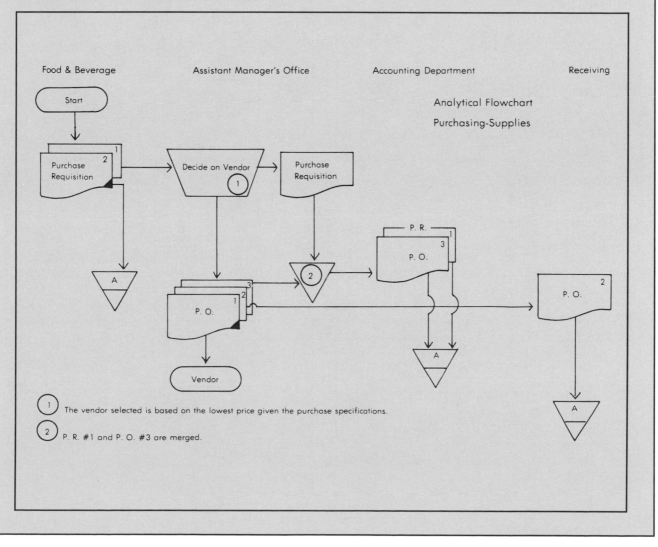

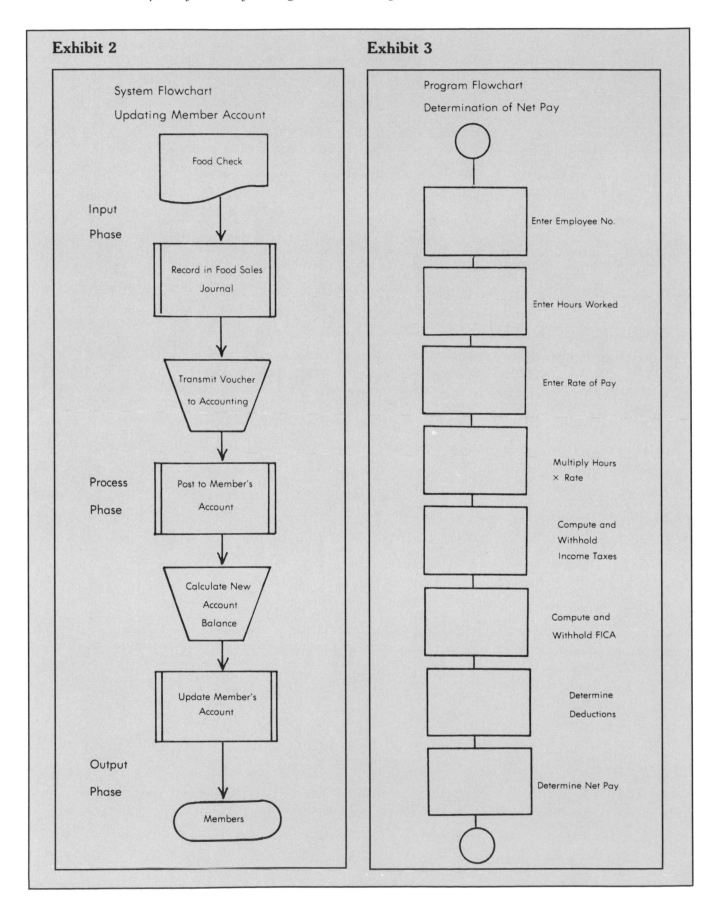

Exhibit 2

System Flowchart

Updating Member Account

Input Phase

Food Check

Record in Food Sales Journal

Transmit Voucher to Accounting

Process Phase

Post to Member's Account

Calculate New Account Balance

Update Member's Account

Output Phase

Members

Exhibit 3

Program Flowchart

Determination of Net Pay

Enter Employee No.

Enter Hours Worked

Enter Rate of Pay

Multiply Hours × Rate

Compute and Withhold Income Taxes

Compute and Withhold FICA

Determine Deductions

Determine Net Pay

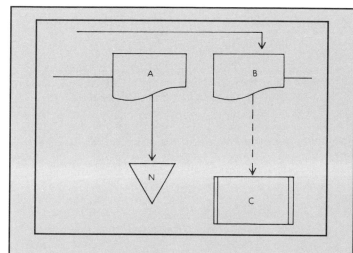

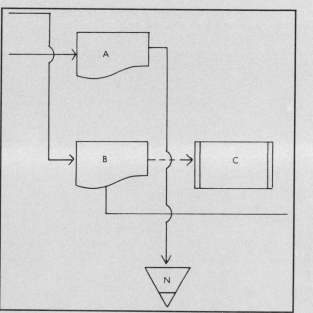

Flowchart Symbols

Standardization in flowcharting symbols results in improved communication of details in an information system. Most of the symbols were established by the United States of America Standards Institute.

The symbols shown are used when preparing analytical flowcharts for nonautomated (non-EDP) information systems. Additional symbols are required when preparing flowcharts for EDP-based information systems.

Flowcharting Techniques

Standardization in flowcharting is not only achieved by using common symbols, but also by drawing flowcharts following established procedures. Several standard techniques are discussed and illustrated below.

* The flowchart should be drawn so that information is shown to move from top to bottom and from left to right. Flowlines should not be slanted.

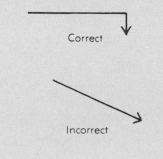

* When drawing flowlines, one should attempt to minimize the crossing of flowlines to reduce confusion. In many situations, various portions of a flowchart can be redrawn to eliminate crossed lines. When crossed lines cannot be avoided, it is desirable to bridge one line over the other.

Two flowcharts shown contain identical document and information flows. However, Flowchart Example 2 is easier to read than Flowchart Example 1.

* The department in which an internal document was created is indicated by darkening of a corner of the document symbol.

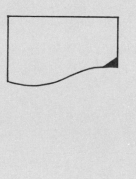

* The method for depicting multiple copies of the same document is illustrated below.

Notice the title is written on the first document and the documents are numbered in the upper right corner.

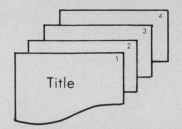

* The flowchart should be divided into columns for each department or function.
* When a document moves from one department to another, the document should be drawn in each department column.
* The type of file should be indicated by placing a letter in the file symbol. The letters indicating various files may be as follows:

Alphabetical	A
Date	D
Numerical	N

Thus a file containing guest records and filed in alphabetical order would be depicted as follows:

* Explanations should be written inside the symbols if there is sufficient space. If additional space is required, an explanation note may be written at the bottom of the column or in a side column. Alternatively, the symbol for annotation of additional information may be used.
* The best flowcharts are generally redrawn, not drawn. Seldom is a reasonably complex flowchart complete, in final form, on the designer's first attempt. Successive attempts will serve to enhance the flowchart's communication ability and clarity.

Flowcharting Illustrated

To illustrate an analytical flowchart, the payroll system for hourly employees of a club will be used. The food manager, who collects employee time cards on Friday of each week, totals the hours, approves the hours totaled and sends the time cards to the payroll clerk. The payroll clerk determines the employee's pay and all the corresponding deductions and withholdings. The employee earnings ledger is updated and the paychecks are prepared by the payroll clerk.

A payroll register is then prepared by the payroll clerk. The payroll clerk sends the original copy of this register to the general ledger clerk. The general ledger clerk uses the payroll register to record wages and taxes payable in the general ledger and then files the register by date. The payroll clerk files both the time cards by date and the duplicate copy of the payroll register by date.

Finally, the paychecks are sent to the club manager for review and signature. After the checks are signed, they are sent to the food manager for distribution to employees.

Exhibit 4 is a flowchart of this payroll system for hourly employees. Note the distinction between the flow of documents and the flow of information. Further, notice that a distinction is shown between the jobs of the payroll clerk and the general ledger clerk in the accounting department.

After the payroll system has been flowcharted, the flowchart should be studied to determine any weaknesses in the system. Any noted weaknesses should result in a subsequent change in the payroll system.

Summary

Flowcharting is a useful tool for analyzing a club's information system. This analysis will generally result in system changes that may involve the acquisition of a computer.

The flowchart is simply a graphic representation of an information system. It shows interrelationships between paper flow and processing by the use of labeled blocks and keyed symbols connected by lines. The flowchart symbols used in the article should be used to enhance communication via flowcharting.

Several flowcharting techniques are presented, which with practice, will allow even beginning flowcharters to prepare clear and concise flowcharts. Finally, flowcharting is illustrated using a club's payroll system.

Exhibit 4

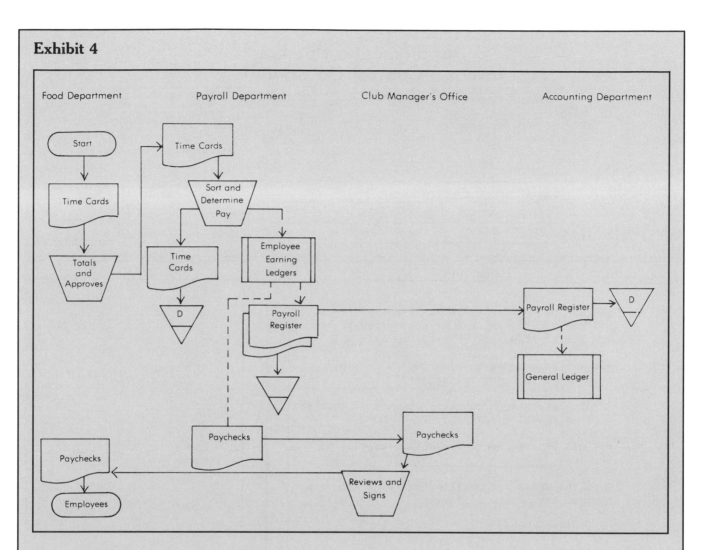

Glossary

Flowchart:

A graphic display of an information system consisting of symbols, flow lines, columns for departments or functions and written comments.

Analytical Flowchart:

A flowchart which shows the overall information processing function of a club, e.g., payroll or purchasing.

System Flowchart:

A flowchart which shows the data processing needs for one specific task application. The input-process-output cycle is shown in this flowchart.

Program Flowchart:

A flowchart detailing one specific application into a series of substeps. It is more detailed than a system flowchart.

Notes

*These articles illustrating flowcharting are reprinted with permission from *Club Management*, January 1982, pp. 20-24, and March 1982, pp. 22-25.

Supplemental Reading
Internal Control Questionnaire
for Financial Reporting: Selected Forms

Reprinted with permission from The Westin Hotels

INTERNAL AUDIT QUESTIONNAIRE

BANK ACCOUNTS

WESTIN HOTELS _____   **Date**

QUESTIONS	YES	NO	COMMENTS
1. Are all bank accounts properly authorized and are persons signing checks authorized to sign, and are their signature cards on file?			
2. Are all bank accounts recorded in control accounts in the general ledger?			
3. Are transfers from one bank account to another under accounting control?			
4. Are all bank accounts reconciled regularly? By whom _____.			

5. Does the person reconciling the bank accounts perform any of the following:
 	
    a. sign checks
 	
    b. make deposits
 	
    c. maintain cash receipts or disbursement records			

6. Are bank statements received direct from the bank in unopened envelopes by the employee preparing the reconciliation.			
7. Does the hotel's reconciliation procedure provide for comparison of checks with cash disbursement record?			
8. Are the bank reconciliations reviewed monthly by the controller?			
9. Are any unreconciled variances carried forward on the bank reconciliations?			

WESTIN HOTELS

INTERNAL AUDIT QUESTIONNAIRE

ACCOUNTS RECEIVABLE

Date

QUESTIONS	YES	NO	COMMENTS
1. Are accounts receivable control accounts balanced with detail daily?			
2. Is a trial balance and aging analysis prepared monthly?			
3. Are past due accounts aged accurately on aging analysis?			
4. Are accounts receivable subsidiary ledgers in agreement with general ledger account 0120-1100 - - Accounts Receivable - Guest and Trade?			
5. Are any accounts not being billed?			
6. Are accounts receivable records given proper fireproof protection and restricted access by authorized persons only?			
7. Is accounts receivable insurance in force? Amounts of Coverage?			
8. Are write-offs strictly controlled and approved by the manager and controller?			
9. Is a dollar control maintained on written off accounts?			
10. Are all accounts and checks aged 120 days (120 days from date of charge) except those where the manager accepts responsibility for collection being submitted to the Seattle Credit Office for collection?			
11. Are city ledger payments opened and a deposit prepared by someone without access to accounts receivable records?			
12. Is the computation of Provision for Doubtful accounts in accordance with Westin policy?			
13. Does the hotel adhere to the Fair Credit Billing Act? (AB 54)			
14. All credit balances, as a result of overpayment, are refunded after five businees days.			
15. Any unclaimed or unidentified credit balances are written off to other income account 7401-0000 Other Income.			

INTERNAL AUDIT QUESTIONNAIRE

ACCOUNTS RECEIVABLE

WESTIN HOTELS

Date

QUESTIONS	YES	NO	COMMENTS
16. All room account charges are billed the second business day following check out.			
17. All credit card charges are billed to the credit card companies the second business day following date of charge.			
18. All tour, convention, banquets, and group business is billed as soon as possible, but not later than five days following such business.			
19. Is interest or a service charge being charged on past due accounts?			

INTERNAL AUDIT QUESTIONNAIRE

CREDIT AND COLLECTION AUDIT PROGRAM

WESTIN HOTELS

Date

QUESTIONS	YES	NO	COMMENTS
1. Does hotel forward all "Notification of Bankruptcy" on a customer's account along with a copy of account to Westin Credit office in Seattle? (U.S. hotels only).			
2. Is a properly completed form CO-7 (Rev. 8/84) prepared for all checks and accounts sent to Westin Credit for collection?			
3. Briefly describe hotel's procedure for handling returned checks.			
4. Is a "credit alert list" prepared by the night audit and is there evidence of review and follow-up?			
5. Does the hotel maintain a monthly log for:			
a. Accounts written off?			
b. Accounts recovered.			
c. Bad Debt Morgue?			
6. All political write-offs have been referred to the Treasurer's office for approval prior to write-off.			

	QUESTIONS	YES	NO	COMMENTS
1.	Does each cashier have his/her own fund for which they are responsible and over which they have sole custody?			
2.	Are properly signed receipts on file for all house funds issued?			
3.	Do receipts for house funds contain provision for recording the deposit box assigned to the cashier for storage of the fund when not in use?			
4.	Are funds checked at intervals as set forth in the company policy by surprise counts made by responsible officials? Show date of last count in comments.			
5.	Do cash count records disclose the inclusion of any questionable items (I.O.U.'s, post-dated checks, returned checks, etc.)?			
6.	Does the total of house funds agree with the balance of General Ledger Account 0100-1100 House Funds?			
7.	Is an over and short record maintained for each cashier and does the record show evidence of regular review by a hotel executive?			
8.	Is the General Cashier's fund maintained on an imprest system?			
9.	Does general cashier balance her bank daily?			
10.	Does the general cashier fund fluctuate?			
11.	Are duplicate keys to cashier banks secure?			
12.	Is general cashier's office secure?			
13.	Are house banks issued by check?			
14.	When house banks are returned, are they deposited to the general bank account through the general cashier's report?			
15.	Is there an alarm control when the general cashier closes for the day?			
16.	Is there TV surveilance of the general cashier's office?			

INTERNAL AUDIT QUESTIONNAIRE

HOUSE BANKS

WESTIN HOTELS

Date

INTERNAL AUDIT QUESTIONNAIRE

CASH RECEIPTS

WESTIN HOTELS

Date

QUESTIONS	YES	NO	COMMENTS
1 Are cash receipts deposited intact daily?			
2 Is the receipt for the bank deposit compared daily with the cash receipts record? By whom and how is it noted?			
3 Is a witness sheet maintained to record the deposit of the cash turn-in envelopes in the drop safe?			
4 Are two persons present when the drop safe is opened and are the contents compared to the entries on the witness sheet?			
5 Are differences between entries on the witness sheet and contents of the drop safe reconciled and verification noted?			
6 Is the general cashier accompanied to and from the drop safe area by a second party?			
7 Is the transporting of the deposit to the bank subject to adequate security measures and is the deposit made by someone other than the person preparing same. (state method)			
8 Is there a clear separation of duties between the persons preparing the deposit, maintaining the cash receipts journal, the disbursements journal, with signatory powers, and preparing the bank reconciliation?			

Deposit prepared by _____

Date of last vacation_____

Position _____

Bank reconciliations completed by

_____

Date of last vacation _____

Position _____

	INTERNAL AUDIT QUESTIONNAIRE			
	CASH RECEIPTS			
WESTIN HOTELS			**Date**	

QUESTIONS	YES	NO	COMMENTS
9 Is a receipt obtained for change requests and due backs? Attach a brief description of the change request and due back system.			
10 Are all checks endorsed with a restrictive endorsement as soon as they are received? (Front Office, Accounts Receivable, Food and Beverage Outlets).			
11 Does the mail opener prepare a list or adding machine tape of city ledger checks prior to sending them to the general cashier.			
12 Are any checks held in Accounts Receivable or by mail opener?			

13   Is a control established over the daily cash receipts prior to their being handled by:
 	
      a. Accounts Receivable
 	
      b. Credit Manager
 	
      c. General Cashier			

14 Are cash receipts for pay station commissions, fat sales, salvage sales, and other miscellaneous revenue properly controlled?			
15 Who replaces the general cashier during vacation or illness?			
16 Are all checks microfilmed prior to deposit to the bank?			
17 If week-end general cashier is normal, is there provision for a night depository?			

13 Capital Budgeting

The hospitality industry, especially the lodging segment, is fixed-asset-intensive. This means that the majority of the assets of hospitality operations are fixed instead of current. This sets hospitality operations apart from many manufacturing firms, where most assets are current. Since establishments in the hospitality industry are so fixed-asset-intensive, capital budgeting becomes an important management concern.

Capital budgeting is the process of determining the amount to spend on fixed assets and which fixed assets to purchase. Capital budgeting addresses such questions as:

1. What piece of equipment among several alternatives should be purchased?

2. Should old equipment be replaced with new?

3. What is meant by the time value of money?

4. How is cash flow computed from an investment?

5. How is payback computed?

6. When is the net present value method preferred to the internal rate of return method?

7. How are alternative investments with different lives considered in the capital budgeting process?

8. Which fixed assets are purchased under capital rationing?

We will begin our consideration of the capital budget by comparing it with the operations budget and by identifying various types of decisions involving capital budgeting. We will then focus on the concept of the time value of money and the computation of cash flow and payback from fixed asset investments. Next, we will explain different models of capital budgets and see how they apply to choices among various kinds of projects. Finally, we will discuss capital rationing and identify special problems with capital budgeting.

Relationship of Capital Budget to Operations Budget

Preparing the operations budget (covered in Chapter 10) is a prerequisite to capital budgeting for equipment. If the operations budget suggests that sales will increase beyond what present equipment is reasonably able to produce, then the present equipment has become functionally obsolete and must be replaced. For example, if a restaurant's budget is based on a realistic assumption that breakfast business will sizably increase, it may be necessary to invest in a large rotary toaster instead of continuing to use a four-piece drop-in toaster.

Capital budgets are prepared not only for the current year, but also are often projected for several years into the future. Construction projects undertaken by some hotel properties may take up to 24 months to complete. Even though capital budgets may be prepared for several years, they must be reviewed annually to consider the impact of changing economic conditions. The capital budget is adjusted as new information becomes available regarding changes in demand for the hospitality operation's goods and services, technological changes, and changes in the cost of providing goods and services. Evaluating past capital budgeting decisions in light of such current information is useful in determining whether those projects should be continued, expanded, reduced in scope, or possibly even terminated. Such current information may also affect the capital budgeting process itself.

Types of Capital Budgeting Decisions

Capital budgeting decisions are made for a variety of reasons. Some are the result of meeting government requirements. For example, the Occupational Safety & Health Administration (OSHA) requires certain safety equipment and guards on meat-cutting equipment. The hospitality operation may spend several hundreds or even thousands of dollars in order to upgrade equipment and meet OSHA's requirements. Regardless of the potential profit or cost savings (if any) from this upgrading of equipment, the government regulation "forces" the hospitality operation to make the expenditure.

A second capital budgeting decision is acquiring a fixed asset to reduce the operation's costs. For example, a lodging operation may have leased vehicles to provide airport transportation. However, to reduce this cost, a van could be purchased.

A third capital budgeting decision is acquiring fixed assets to increase sales. For example, a lodging operation may add a wing of 100 rooms or expand a dining facility from 75 to 150 seats. Another example is a lodging operation determining which franchise is most desirable. As a result of this expansion and/or franchise, both sales and expenses are increased, and, if the proper decision is made, total profits should increase to justify the capital expenditure.

A fourth capital budgeting decision is replacing an existing fixed asset. This replacement may be required because the present fixed asset is fully used up or functionally obsolete, or perhaps the replacement is simply more economical.

All four kinds of capital budgeting decisions require significant expenditures resulting in fixed assets. The return on the expenditures will accrue over an extended period of time. The expenditures should generally be cost justified in the sense that the expected benefits will exceed the cost. The more sophisticated capital budgeting models require a comparison of current cost expenditure for the fixed asset against a future stream of funds. In order to compare current year expenditures to future years' income, the future years' income must be placed on an equal basis. The process for accomplishing this involves the **time value of money**.

Time Value of Money

The saying, "$100 today is worth more than $100 a year from now" is true, in part because $100 today could be invested to provide $100 plus the interest for one year in the future. If the $100 can be invested at 12% annual interest, then the $100 can be worth $112 in one year. This is determined as follows:

$$\text{Principal} + (\text{Principal} \times \text{Time} \times \text{Interest Rate}) = \text{Total}$$

$$100 \quad + \quad (100 \times 1 \times .12) \quad = \underline{\underline{\$112}}$$

Principal is the sum of dollars at the beginning of the investment period ($100 in this case). Time is expressed in years, as long as an annual interest rate is used. The interest rate is expressed in decimal form. The interest of $12 plus the principal of $100 equals the amount available one year hence.

A shorter formula for calculating a future value is as follows:

$$F = A(1 + i)^n$$

$$\text{where } F = \text{Future Value}$$

$$A = \text{Present Amount}$$

$$i = \text{Interest Rate}$$

$$n = \text{Number of Years}$$

One hundred dollars invested at 12% for two years will yield $125.44 determined as follows:

$$F = 100(1 + .12)^2$$

$$= 100(1.2544)$$

$$= \underline{\underline{\$125.44}}$$

An alternative to using this formula to calculate the future value of a present amount is to use a table of future value factors, such as that found in Exhibit 13.1. The future value factors are based on present amounts at the end of each period. For example, the future amount of $100 two years from now at 15% interest is $132.25. This is determined by finding the

Exhibit 13.1   Table of Future Value Factors

Period	1%	2%	3%	4%	5%	6%	7%	8%	9%	10%	12%	14%	15%	16%	18%
1	1.0100	1.0200	1.0300	1.0400	1.0500	1.0600	1.0700	1.0800	1.0900	1.1000	1.1200	1.1400	1.1500	1.1600	1.1800
2	1.0201	1.0404	1.0609	1.0816	1.1025	1.1236	1.1449	1.1664	1.1881	1.2100	1.2544	1.2996	1.3225	1.3456	1.3924
3	1.0303	1.0612	1.0927	1.1249	1.1576	1.1910	1.2250	1.2597	1.2950	1.3310	1.4049	1.4815	1.5209	1.5609	1.6430
4	1.0406	1.0824	1.1255	1.1699	1.2155	1.2625	1.3108	1.3605	1.4116	1.4641	1.5735	1.6890	1.7490	1.8106	1.9388
5	1.0510	1.1041	1.1593	1.2167	1.2763	1.3382	1.4026	1.4693	1.5386	1.6105	1.7623	1.9254	2.0114	2.1003	2.2878
6	1.0615	1.1262	1.1941	1.2653	1.3401	1.4185	1.5007	1.5869	1.6771	1.7716	1.9738	2.1950	2.3131	2.4364	2.6996
7	1.0721	1.1487	1.2299	1.3159	1.4071	1.5036	1.6058	1.7138	1.8280	1.9487	2.2107	2.5023	2.6600	2.8262	3.1855
8	1.0829	1.1717	1.2668	1.3686	1.4775	1.5938	1.7182	1.8509	1.9926	2.1436	2.4760	2.8526	3.0590	3.2784	3.7589
9	1.0937	1.1951	1.3048	1.4233	1.5513	1.6895	1.8385	1.9990	2.1719	2.3579	2.7731	3.2519	3.5179	3.8030	4.4355
10	1.1046	1.2190	1.3439	1.4802	1.6289	1.7908	1.9672	2.1589	2.3674	2.5937	3.1058	3.7072	4.0456	4.4114	5.2338
11	1.1157	1.2434	1.3842	1.5395	1.7103	1.8983	2.1049	2.3316	2.5804	2.8531	3.4785	4.2262	4.6524	5.1173	6.1759
12	1.1268	1.2682	1.4258	1.6010	1.7959	2.0122	2.2522	2.5182	2.8127	3.1384	3.8960	4.8179	5.3502	5.9360	7.2876
13	1.1381	1.2936	1.4685	1.6651	1.8856	2.1329	2.4098	2.7196	3.0658	3.4523	4.3635	5.4924	6.1528	6.8858	8.5994
14	1.1495	1.3195	1.5126	1.7317	1.9799	2.2609	2.5785	2.9372	3.3417	3.7975	4.8871	6.2613	7.0757	7.9875	10.147
15	1.1610	1.3459	1.5580	1.8009	2.0789	2.3966	2.7590	3.1722	3.6425	4.1772	5.4736	7.1379	8.1371	9.2655	11.973
16	1.1726	1.3728	1.6047	1.8730	2.1829	2.5404	2.9522	3.4259	3.9703	4.5950	6.1304	8.1372	9.3576	10.748	14.129
17	1.1843	1.4002	1.6528	1.9479	2.2920	2.6928	3.1588	3.7000	4.3276	5.0545	6.8660	9.2765	10.761	12.467	16.672
18	1.1961	1.4282	1.7024	2.0258	2.4066	2.8543	3.3799	3.9960	4.7171	5.5599	7.6900	10.575	12.375	14.462	19.673
19	1.2081	1.4568	1.7535	2.1068	2.5270	3.0256	3.6165	4.3157	5.1417	6.1159	8.6128	12.055	14.231	16.776	23.214
20	1.2202	1.4859	1.8061	2.1911	2.6533	3.2071	3.8697	4.6610	5.6044	6.7275	9.6463	13.743	16.366	19.460	27.393
21	1.2324	1.5157	1.8603	2.2788	2.7860	3.3996	4.1406	5.0338	6.1088	7.4002	10.803	15.667	18.821	22.574	32.323
22	1.2447	1.5460	1.9161	2.3699	2.9253	3.6035	4.4304	5.4365	6.6586	8.1403	12.100	17.861	21.644	26.186	38.142
23	1.2572	1.5769	1.9736	2.4647	3.0715	3.8197	4.7405	5.8715	7.2579	8.9543	13.552	20.361	24.891	30.376	45.007
24	1.2697	1.6084	2.0328	2.5633	3.2251	4.0489	5.0724	6.3412	7.9111	9.8497	15.178	23.212	28.625	35.236	53.108
25	1.2824	1.6406	2.0938	2.6658	3.3864	4.2919	5.4274	6.8485	8.6231	10.834	17.000	26.461	32.918	40.874	62.668
26	1.2953	1.6734	2.1566	2.7725	3.5557	4.5494	5.8074	7.3964	9.3992	11.918	19.040	30.166	37.856	47.414	73.948
27	1.3082	1.7069	2.2213	2.8834	3.7335	4.8223	6.2139	7.9881	10.245	13.110	21.324	34.389	43.535	55.000	87.259
28	1.3213	1.7410	2.2879	2.9987	3.9201	5.1117	6.6488	8.6271	11.167	14.421	23.883	39.204	50.065	63.800	102.96
29	1.3345	1.7758	2.3566	3.1187	4.1161	5.4184	7.1143	9.3173	12.172	15.863	26.749	44.693	57.575	74.008	121.50
30	1.3478	1.8114	2.4273	3.2434	4.3219	5.7435	7.6123	10.062	13.267	17.449	29.959	50.950	66.211	85.849	143.37
40	1.4889	2.2080	3.2620	4.8010	7.0400	10.285	14.974	21.724	31.409	45.259	93.050	188.88	267.86	378.72	750.37
50	1.6446	2.6916	4.3839	7.1067	11.467	18.420	29.457	46.901	74.357	117.39	289.00	700.23	1083.6	1670.7	3927.3
60	1.8167	3.2810	5.8916	10.519	18.679	32.987	57.946	101.25	176.03	304.48	897.59	2595.9	4383.9	7370.1	20555.

number in the 15% column and the period 2 row (1.3225) and multiplying it by $100.

The present value of a future amount is the present amount which must be invested at x% interest to yield the future amount. For example, what is the present value of $100 one year hence when the interest rate is 12%? The formula to determine the present value of the future amount is as follows:

$$P = F\frac{1}{(1 + i)^n}$$

where P = Present Amount

F = Future Amount

i = Interest Rate

n = Number of Years

Therefore, the present value of $100 one year hence (assuming an interest rate of 12%) is $89.29, determined as follows:

Exhibit 13.2   Table of Present Value Factors

Period	1%	2%	3%	4%	5%	6%	7%	8%	9%	10%	12%	14%	15%	16%	18%
1	.9901	.9804	.9709	.9615	.9524	.9434	.9346	.9259	.9174	.9091	.8929	.8772	.8696	.8621	.8475
2	.9803	.9612	.9426	.9246	.9070	.8900	.8734	.8573	.8417	.8264	.7972	.7695	.7561	.7432	.7182
3	.9706	.9423	.9151	.8890	.8638	.8396	.8163	.7938	.7722	.7513	.7118	.6750	.6575	.6407	.6086
4	.9610	.9238	.8885	.8548	.8227	.7921	.7629	.7350	.7084	.6830	.6355	.5921	.5718	.5523	.5158
5	.9515	.9057	.8626	.8219	.7835	.7473	.7130	.6806	.6499	.6209	.5674	.5194	.4972	.4761	.4371
6	.9420	.8880	.8375	.7903	.7462	.7050	.6663	.6302	.5963	.5645	.5066	.4556	.4323	.4104	.3704
7	.9327	.8706	.8131	.7599	.7107	.6651	.6227	.5835	.5470	.5132	.4523	.3996	.3759	.3538	.3139
8	.9235	.8535	.7894	.7307	.6768	.6274	.5820	.5403	.5019	.4665	.4039	.3506	.3269	.3050	.2660
9	.9143	.8368	.7664	.7026	.6446	.5919	.5439	.5002	.4604	.4241	.3606	.3075	.2843	.2630	.2255
10	.9053	.8203	.7441	.6756	.6139	.5584	.5083	.4632	.4224	.3855	.3220	.2697	.2472	.2267	.1911
11	.8963	.8043	.7224	.6496	.5847	.5268	.4751	.4289	.3875	.3505	.2875	.2366	.2149	.1954	.1619
12	.8874	.7885	.7014	.6246	.5568	.4970	.4440	.3971	.3555	.3186	.2567	.2076	.1869	.1685	.1372
13	.8787	.7730	.6810	.6006	.5303	.4688	.4150	.3677	.3262	.2897	.2292	.1821	.1625	.1452	.1163
14	.8700	.7579	.6611	.5775	.5051	.4423	.3878	.3405	.2992	.2633	.2046	.1597	.1413	.1252	.0985
15	.8613	.7430	.6419	.5553	.4810	.4173	.3624	.3152	.2745	.2394	.1827	.1401	.1229	.1079	.0835
16	.8528	.7284	.6232	.5339	.4581	.3936	.3387	.2919	.2519	.2176	.1631	.1229	.1069	.0930	.0708
17	.8444	.7142	.6050	.5134	.4363	.3714	.3166	.2703	.2311	.1978	.1456	.1078	.0929	.0802	.0600
18	.8360	.7002	.5874	.4936	.4155	.3503	.2959	.2502	.2120	.1799	.1300	.0946	.0808	.0691	.0508
19	.8277	.6864	.5703	.4746	.3957	.3305	.2765	.2317	.1945	.1635	.1161	.0829	.0703	.0596	.0431
20	.8195	.6730	.5537	.4564	.3769	.3118	.2584	.2145	.1784	.1486	.1037	.0728	.0611	.0514	.0365
25	.7798	.6095	.4776	.3751	.2953	.2330	.1842	.1460	.1160	.0923	.0588	.0378	.0304	.0245	.0160
30	.7419	.5521	.4120	.3083	.2314	.1741	.1314	.0994	.0754	.0573	.0334	.0196	.0151	.0116	.0070
40	.6717	.4529	.3066	.2083	.1420	.0972	.0668	.0460	.0318	.0221	.0107	.0053	.0037	.0026	.0013
50	.6080	.3715	.2281	.1407	.0872	.0543	.0339	.0213	.0134	.0085	.0035	.0014	.0009	.0006	.0003
60	.5504	.3048	.1697	.0951	.0535	.0303	.0173	.0099	.0057	.0033	.0011	.0004	.0002	.0001	•

$$P = 100 \frac{1}{(1 + .12)^1}$$

$$= 100(.8929)$$

$$= \underline{\$89.29}$$

The present value of $100 two years hence (assuming an interest rate of 12%) is $79.72 determined as follows:

$$P = 100 \frac{1}{(1 + .12)^2}$$

$$= 100(.7972)$$

$$= \underline{\$79.72}$$

An alternative to using this formula to calculate the present value of a future amount is to use a table of present value factors, such as that found in Exhibit 13.2. The present value factors in Exhibit 13.2 are based on

Exhibit 13.3   Present Value of a $10,000 Five-Year Annuity

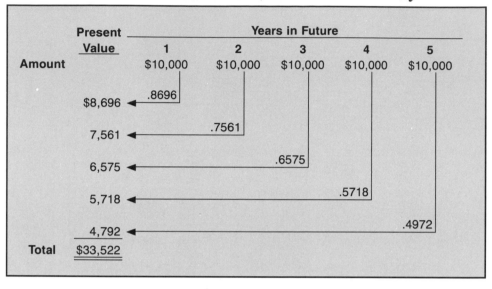

Exhibit 13.4   Shortcut Calculations of the Present Value of a $10,000 Five-Year Annuity

Years Hence	Present Value Factors at 15%
1	.8696
2	.7561
3	.6575
4	.5718
5	+ .4972
	3.3522
3.3522 × 10,000 =	$33,522

future amounts at the end of the period. For example, the present value of $100 a year from now at 15% interest is $86.96. This is determined by finding the number in the 15% column and the period 1 row (0.8696) and multiplying it by $100. The present value of $100 today is simply $100.

Most capital investments provide a stream of receipts for several years. When the amounts are equal at equal intervals, such as the end of each year, the stream is referred to as an **annuity**. Exhibit 13.3 shows the calculation of the present value of an annuity of $10,000 due at the end of each year for five years. The present value factors used in the calculation are from the present value table in Exhibit 13.2.

The present value of an annuity will vary significantly based on the interest rate (also called the **discount rate**) and the timing of the future receipts. Everything else being the same, the higher the discount rate, the

Exhibit 13.5   Table of Present Values of an Annuity

Number of Payments	1%	2%	3%	4%	5%	6%	7%	8%	9%	10%	12%	14%	15%	16%	18%
1	0.9901	0.9804	0.9709	0.9615	0.9524	0.9434	0.9346	0.9259	0.9174	0.9091	0.8929	0.8772	0.8696	0.8621	0.8475
2	1.9704	1.9416	1.9135	1.8861	1.8594	1.8334	1.8080	1.7833	1.7591	1.7355	1.6901	1.6467	1.6257	1.6052	1.5656
3	2.9410	2.8839	2.8286	2.7751	2.7232	2.6730	2.6243	2.5771	2.5313	2.4869	2.4018	2.3216	2.2832	2.2459	2.1743
4	3.9020	3.8077	3.7171	3.6299	3.5460	3.4651	3.3872	3.3121	3.2397	3.1699	3.0373	2.9137	2.8550	2.7982	2.6901
5	4.8534	4.7135	4.5797	4.4518	4.3295	4.2124	4.1002	3.9927	3.8897	3.7908	3.6048	3.4331	3.3522	3.2743	3.1273
6	5.7955	5.6014	5.4172	5.2421	5.0757	4.9173	4.7665	4.6229	4.4859	4.3553	4.1114	3.8887	3.7845	3.6847	3.4976
7	6.7282	6.4720	6.2303	6.0021	5.7864	5.5824	5.3893	5.2064	5.0330	4.8684	4.5638	4.2883	4.1604	4.0386	3.8115
8	7.6517	7.3255	7.0197	6.7327	6.4632	6.2098	5.9713	5.7466	5.5348	5.3349	4.9676	4.6389	4.4873	4.3436	4.0776
9	8.5660	8.1622	7.7861	7.4353	7.1078	6.8017	6.5152	6.2469	5.9952	5.7590	5.3282	4.9464	4.7716	4.6065	4.3030
10	9.4713	8.9826	8.5302	8.1109	7.7217	7.3601	7.0236	6.7101	6.4177	6.1446	5.6502	5.2161	5.0188	4.8332	4.4941
11	10.3676	9.7868	9.2526	8.7605	8.3064	7.8869	7.4987	7.1390	6.8052	6.4951	5.9377	5.4527	5.2337	5.0286	4.6560
12	11.2551	10.5753	9.9540	9.3851	8.8633	8.3838	7.9427	7.5361	7.1607	6.8137	6.1944	5.6603	5.4206	5.1971	4.7932
13	12.1337	11.3484	10.6350	9.9856	9.3936	8.8527	8.3577	7.9038	7.4869	7.1034	6.4235	5.8424	5.5831	5.3423	4.9095
14	13.0037	12.1062	11.2961	20.5631	9.8986	9.2950	8.7455	8.2442	7.7862	7.3667	6.6282	6.0021	5.7245	5.4675	5.0081
15	13.8651	12.8493	11.9379	11.1184	10.3797	9.7122	9.1079	8.5595	8.0607	7.6061	6.8109	6.1422	5.8474	5.5755	5.0916
16	14.7179	13.5777	12.5611	11.6523	10.8378	10.1059	9.4468	8.8514	8.3126	7.8237	6.9740	6.2651	5.9542	5.6685	5.1624
17	15.5623	14.2919	13.1661	12.1657	11.2741	10.4773	9.7632	9.1216	8.5436	8.0216	7.1196	6.3729	6.0472	5.7487	5.2223
18	16.3983	14.9920	13.7535	12.6593	11.6896	10.8276	10.0591	9.3719	8.7556	8.2014	7.2497	6.4674	6.1280	5.8178	5.2732
19	17.2260	15.6785	14.3238	13.1339	12.0853	11.1581	10.3356	9.6036	8.9501	8.3649	7.3658	6.5504	6.1982	5.8775	5.3162
20	18.0456	16.3514	14.8775	13.5903	12.4622	11.4699	10.5940	9.8181	9.1285	8.5136	7.4694	6.6231	6.2593	5.9288	5.3527
25	22.0232	19.5235	17.4131	15.6221	14.0939	12.7834	11.6536	10.6748	9.8226	9.0770	7.8431	6.8729	6.4641	6.0971	5.4669
30	25.8077	22.3965	19.6004	17.2920	15.3725	13.7648	12.4090	11.2578	10.2737	9.4269	8.0552	7.0027	6.5660	6.1772	5.5168
40	32.8347	27.3555	23.1148	19.7928	17.1591	15.0463	13.3317	11.9246	10.7574	9.7791	8.2438	7.1050	6.6418	6.2335	5.5482
50	39.1961	31.4236	25.7298	21.4822	18.2559	15.7619	13.8007	12.2335	10.9617	9.9148	8.3045	7.1327	6.6605	6.2463	5.5541
60	44.9550	34.7609	27.6756	22.6235	18.9293	16.1614	14.0392	12.3766	11.0480	9.9672	8.3240	7.1401	6.6651	6.2482	5.5553

lower the present value. Likewise, everything else being the same, the more distant the receipt, the smaller the present value.

An alternative to multiplying each future amount by the present value factor from the present value table in Exhibit 13.2 is to sum the present factors and make one multiplication. This is illustrated in Exhibit 13.4. Thus, the $33,522 calculated in Exhibit 13.4 equals the calculation performed in Exhibit 13.3. Rather than using the present values from Exhibit 13.2, present values of an annuity are provided in Exhibit 13.5. As a check on your understanding of the present value of an annuity table, locate the present value factor for five years and 15%. As you would expect, it is 3.3522. Thus, the present value of an annuity table is nothing more than a summation of present value factors from Exhibit 13.2. However, this table of present values of an annuity will save much time, especially when streams of receipts for several years must be calculated.

A problem which calls for the use of both present value factors (Exhibit 13.2) and present value of an annuity factors (Exhibit 13.5) is presented in Exhibit 13.6. This problem is solved by treating the stream of receipts as a $10,000 annuity and two separate payments of $5,000 and $10,000 due at the end of years two and four, respectively.

Cash Flow in Capital Budgeting

In most capital budgeting decisions, an investment results only when the future cash flow from the investment justifies the expenditure.

Exhibit 13.6 Present Value of a Stream of Unequal Future Receipts

Problem:

Determine the present value of receipts from an investment using a 15% discount factor which provides the following stream of income.

Years Hence	Amount
0	$10,000
1	10,000
2	15,000
3	10,000
4	20,000
5	10,000

Solution:

Years Hence	Amount	Annuity	Excess of Annuity
0	$10,000	$10,000	$ 0
1	10,000	10,000	0
2	15,000	10,000	5000
3	10,000	10,000	0
4	20,000	10,000	10,000
5	10,000	10,000	0

Calculation:

Present Value of amount due today	=	$10,000
Present Value of the $10,000 annuity for 5 years 10,000 × 3.3522	=	33,522
Present Value of $5,000 due 2 years hence 5000 × .7561	=	3,781
Present Value of $10,000 due 4 years hence 10,000 × .5718	=	5,718
TOTAL		$53,021

Therefore, the concern is with the cash flow from the proposed investment. From the hospitality operation's perspective, the incremental cash flow is the focus rather than the operation's cash flow. **Incremental cash flow** is simply the change in the cash flow of the operation resulting from the investment. Cash flow relating to an investment includes the following:

- Investment initial cost (cash outflow)

- Investment revenues (cash inflow)

- Investment expenses except depreciation (cash outflow)

Depreciation expense results from writing off the cost of the investment; however, it is not a cash outflow and, therefore, does not affect the capital budgeting decision. It is used in determining the income taxes

Exhibit 13.7 Cash Flows from Game Room—Hampton Hotel

Cost of machines	$21,000
Life of machines	3 years
Tax rate	40%
Salvage value of machines	—0—
Annual revenues	$25,000
Related annual expenses excluding depreciation and income taxes	$10,000
Method of depreciation	Straight-line

Cash Flow Calculation

	Years		
	1	2	3
Revenues	$25,000	$25,000	$25,000
Expenses except for depreciation and income taxes	10,000	10,000	10,000
Income taxes	2,720(1)	2,720(1)	2,720(1)
Cash flow	$12,280	$12,280	$12,280

Net cash flow is determined as follows:

Cash flows from above 12,280 × 3 =	$36,840
Cost of machines	21,000
Net Cash Flow	$15,840

(1) Income taxes:

Predepreciation income	$15,000
Less: depreciation	7,000(2)
Taxable income	8,000
Tax rate	× .34
Income taxes	$ 2,720

$$(2)\ \text{Annual depreciation} = \frac{\text{Cost} - \text{Salvage Value}}{\text{Life}} = \frac{21,000 - 0}{3} = \underline{\$7,000}$$

relating to the investment since the IRS allows depreciation to be deducted in computing taxable income.

Exhibit 13.7 illustrates the relevant cash flows of a proposed investment of the hypothetical Hampton Hotel. The Hampton Hotel is considering installing a game room. Since space is available with only minor modifications, the focus is on the cost of machines and related future revenues and expenses. Depreciation of $7,000 per year is used only in determining the pre-tax income from the investment. The cash flow generated by the investment in game machines is $36,840 for three years, resulting in an incremental net cash flow of $15,840 after the cost of the machines is subtracted. The means of financing the game machines is not

Exhibit 13.8 Proposed Investment in Pizza Equipment—Hampton Hotel

Investment		Accept/Reject Criteria		
Cost of Equipment	$48,000	ARR	=	40%
Installation costs	2,000	Payback	=	3 years
		IRR	=	15%
Total	$50,000	NPV	=	0

Depreciation Consideration		Depreciation Percentages	
Salvage Value	$—0—	Year	
Life for tax purposes 5 years		1	15%
		2	22%
		3	21%
		4	21%
		5	21%

Estimated Project Revenue and Expense

	YEARS				
	1	2	3	4	5
Project Revenues	$100,000	$120,000	$140,000	$160,000	$180,000
Project Expenses:					
Labor	25,500	26,200	33,900	37,100	40,300
Cost of product	25,000	30,000	35,000	40,000	45,000
Supplies	5,000	6,000	7,000	8,000	9,000
Utilities	4,000	4,800	5,600	6,400	7,200
Depreciation	7,500	11,000	10,500	10,500	10,500
Other operating expenses	11,000	12,000	14,000	16,000	18,000
Income taxes	11,000	15,000	17,000	21,000	25,000
Project Income	$11,000	$15,000	$17,000	$21,000	$25,000

Total Project Income for Years 1–5 = $89,000

Cash Flow:					
Investment profit	$11,000	$15,000	$17,000	$21,000	$25,000
Add: Depreciation	7,500	11,000	10,500	10,500	10,500
Total	$18,500	$26,000	$27,500	$31,500	$35,500

considered. In capital budgeting models, the discount rate includes the interest cost, if any.

Capital Budgeting Models

Managers in hospitality operations use several different models in making capital budgeting decisions. The models vary from simple to sophisticated. The simple models are **accounting rate of return (ARR)** and **payback**, while more sophisticated models, which require the discounting of future cash flows, are **net present value (NPV)** and **internal rate of return (IRR)**. The advantages and disadvantages of each model will now be addressed and illustrated using the investment data in Exhibit 13.8.

Accounting Rate of Return

The ARR model considers the average annual project income (project revenues less project expenses generated by the investment) and the average investment. The calculation of ARR is simply:

$$ARR = \frac{\text{Average Annual Project Income}}{\text{Average Investment}}$$

The average annual project income is the total project income over its life divided by the number of years. Average investment is project cost less salvage value divided by two. The proposed investment is accepted if the ARR exceeds the minimum ARR required. For example, if the minimum acceptable ARR is 40%, a 52% ARR results in project acceptance.

The ARR model can be illustrated by using the Hampton Hotel's proposed investment in pizza equipment illustrated in Exhibit 13.8. The total project income over the five-year period is $89,000, which results in an average annual project income of $17,800. The average investment is $25,000, determined as follows:

$$\text{Average Investment} = \frac{\text{Project Cost} - \text{Salvage}}{2}$$

$$= \frac{50,000 - 0}{2}$$

$$= \underline{\underline{\$25,000}}$$

The ARR of 71.2% is determined as follows:

$$ARR = \frac{\text{Average Annual Project Income}}{\text{Average Investment}}$$

$$= \frac{17,800}{25,000}$$

$$= \underline{\underline{71.2\%}}$$

Since the project ARR of 71.2% exceeds the required minimum of 40%, if the Hampton Hotel used this capital budgeting model, management would invest in the pizza equipment.

Some managers consider ARR to be useful because it relies on accounting income and, thus, it is easy to calculate and easy to understand. However, these advantages are more than offset by its disadvantages: ARR fails to consider cash flows or the time value of money.

Payback

The payback model compares annual cash flows to the project cost to determine a payback period as follows:

$$\text{Payback Period} = \frac{\text{Project Cost}}{\text{Annual Cash Flows}}$$

If the calculated payback period is equal to or less than the payback objective, then the project is accepted. The payback model is reasonably popular in the hospitality industry because it is conceptually simple. Management simply sets the payback period at the determined length of time required for the operation to get its money back from the project. Also, the payback model is often used as a screening device in conjunction with more sophisticated models, especially in high risk situations. Some operations will not consider evaluating proposed projects using the NPV or IRR approaches unless their initial review using the payback model suggests that the proposed project is viable.

The payback period is determined as follows:

1. Set the project cost equal to project cash flows for years 1 through n, where n is the last year (or portion thereof) required for project cash flows to equal the project cost.

2. The payback period equals the number of years of project cash flows required to equal the project cost.

Using figures from Exhibit 13.8, the payback period for the Hampton Hotel's proposed investment in pizza equipment can be calculated as follows:

$$\text{Project Cost} = \text{Project Cash Flows for Years 1, 2, and .2 of year 3}$$

$$\$50,000 = \$18,500 + \$26,000 + \$5,500$$

$$\$50,000 = \$50,000$$

The final $5,500 of project cash flows is .2 of the third year's project cash flows of $27,500. Therefore, the payback period is 2.2 years. Since the payback period of 2.2 years is less than the accept/reject criterion of 3 years as stated in Exhibit 13.8, based on the payback model, the Hampton Hotel would invest in the proposed pizza project.

Disadvantages to the payback model that require careful consideration are that it fails to consider either the time value of money or the project flows after the payback period. The latter disadvantage is readily apparent when comparing two mutually exclusive projects (A and B) as shown in Exhibit 13.9. Based on the payback method, project A would be accepted rather than project B, because the payback period of 2.33 years for project A is less than 2.6 years for project B. However, the excess cash flow is $10,000 larger for project B. The calculation of the present value of all cash flows of $10,986 and $15,833 for projects A and B, respectively, is convincing. If this is not readily clear, it will be as we now turn to consider the net present value model.

Net Present Value Model

Both the NPV and IRR models overcome the weaknesses of the previous models in that they consider the time value of money. The net present value approach discounts cash flows to their present value. The net present value is calculated by subtracting the project cost from the present value of the discounted cash flow stream. The project is accepted

Exhibit 13.9 Comparison of Two Mutually Exclusive Projects—Payback Model

Years Hence	Project Cost Cash Flows	
	Project A	Project B
0	$10,000	$10,000
1	5,000	3,000
2	4,000	4,000
3	3,000	5,000
4	2,000	6,000
5	1,000	7,000
Payback Period	2.33 years	2.60 years
Excess Cash Flow: Cash flow generated beyond payback period	$5,000	$15,000
Present value of all cash discounted at 15%	$10,986	$15,833

if the NPV is equal to or greater than zero. If the capital budgeting decision considers mutually exclusive alternatives, the alternative with the highest NPV is accepted and other alternatives are rejected.

The advantage of the NPV model over the two models presented previously is the consideration of cash flows and the time value of money. Some managers have suggested that a disadvantage of the NPV model is its complexity. This argument may have been convincing to hospitality operations in the past, but as the hospitality industry continues to mature, the best methods of capital budgeting must be used if decision-making is to be optimized.

Using the Hampton Hotel's proposed investment in pizza equipment (Exhibit 13.8) and assuming a discount rate of 15%, Exhibit 13.10 shows the net present value to be $39,491. Therefore, based on the NPV model, the Hampton Hotel should make the proposed investment, because NPV is positive.

Internal Rate of Return

The IRR model is a capital budgeting approach that considers cash flows and the time value of money and determines the rate of return earned by a proposed project. In determining IRR, the net present value of cash flows is set at zero and the discount rate is determined. The formula is as follows:

$$0 = \frac{CF_1}{1 + r} + \frac{CF_2}{(1 + r)^2} + \ldots + \frac{CF_n}{(1 + r)^n} - PC$$

where CF = Cash Flow

r = Internal Rate of Return

PC = Project Cost

Assume that a proposed project costs $6,850 and is expected to yield a cash flow stream of $3,000 for three years. The internal rate of return is 15%, determined as follows:

Exhibit 13.10 Illustration of NPV—Proposed Investment in Pizza Equipment by Hampton Hotel

Years Hence	Cash Flow	P.V. Factor (15%)	Present Value of Cash Flow
0	$(50,000)	1.0000	$(50,000)
1	18,500	.8696	16,088
2	26,000	.7561	19,659
3	27,500	.6575	18,081
4	31,500	.5718	18,012
5	35,500	.4972	17,651
		Net Present Value	$39,491

$$0 = \frac{3,000}{1.15} + \frac{3,000}{(1.15)^2} + \frac{3,000}{(1.15)^3} - 6,850$$

$$0 = 2,609 + 2,268 + 1,973 - 6,850$$

$$0 = \underline{\underline{0}}$$

Using the IRR model, a project is accepted if the IRR is equal to, or greater than, the established minimum IRR, which is commonly called **hurdle rate** by hospitality financial managers.

Like the NPV model, the IRR model is superior to the ARR and pay-back approaches because it considers the time value of money. The IRR is also superior to the ARR model because it considers cash flows. When there is a capital budgeting decision involving mutually exclusive projects, results from the IRR model may conflict with the NPV approach. This conflict may occur because of the IRR's assumption that all project cash flows are reinvested at the internal rate of return. Since operations normally invest in the most profitable projects first, one should not assume that other projects would result in the same return. This conflict will be discussed in greater detail later in this chapter.

The IRR model is illustrated using the Hampton Hotel's proposed investment in pizza equipment. Although the brief illustration of IRR above may have appeared simple, in practice, manual calculations are by trial and error. Various discount rates are tried until the approximate net present value is found to be zero. The manual approach is illustrated in Exhibit 13.11. Alternatively, the IRR can be quickly and easily determined using a computer.

The exact IRR lies between 41% and 42%. Interpolation would result in approximate determination of 41.5%. Since the IRR of 41.5% exceeds the target of 15%, using this capital budgeting model, the Hampton Hotel should invest in the proposed pizza equipment.

Comparison of NPV and IRR Models

As discussed previously, the NPV and IRR models are preferred to the simplistic ARR and payback models. However, which is preferred, NPV or IRR? The NPV and IRR models, when applied in most situations, provide the same solution whether the situation considers a single

Exhibit 13.11 Illustration of IRR—Proposed Investment in Pizza Equipment by Hampton Hotel

Years Hence	Cash Flow	41% PV Factor (1)	41% PV Cash Flow	42% PV Factor (1)	42% PV Cash Flow
0	$(50,000)	1.000	$(50,000)	1.000	$(50,000)
1	18,500	.7092	13,120	.7042	13,028
2	26,000	.5030	13,078	.4960	12,896
3	27,500	.3568	9,812	.3493	9,606
4	31,500	.2530	7,970	.2459	7,746
5	35,500	.1749	6,369	.1732	6,149
		Total	$ 349		$ (575)

(1) PV factors determined by the formula:

$$\frac{1}{(1+r)^1}, \quad \frac{1}{(1+r)^2}, \quad \frac{1}{(1+r)^3}, \quad \frac{1}{(1+r)^4} \quad \text{and} \quad \frac{1}{(1+r)^5}$$

PV factor for 1 year at 41% is determined by dividing 1 by $(1.41)^1$ to equal .7092

project or mutually exclusive projects. However, in some of the latter situations, the NPV could suggest one project while the IRR model suggests a different project. This outcome results from the assumed reinvestment rates of each model. The NPV model assumes reinvestment at the discount rate used (15% in the Hampton Hotel problem), while the IRR model assumes reinvestment at the computed IRR (41.5% in the Hampton Hotel problem). Even if the superior projects are first selected, it is doubtful that reinvestment would be at the calculated IRR. Reinvestment will likelier be at a lower rate. Therefore, when mutually exclusive projects are considered, the NPV approach is more useful.

The NPV is generally easier to compute than the IRR. However, computers and calculators have reduced the laborious calculations of the IRR model. On the other hand, many industry financial managers prefer the IRR model because the results are easier to interpret.

Mutually Exclusive Projects with Different Lives

To this point in our discussion, mutually exclusive projects have been assumed to have the same useful life. In reality, many mutually exclusive projects do not have equal lives. In such situations, three approaches to decision-making are as follows:

1. Assume that the shorter-lived project is followed with another project and that the combined lives of the two projects equal the life of the mutually exclusive longer-lived project.

2. Assume that the longer-lived project is disposed of at the end of the shorter-lived project's life.

Exhibit 13.12   Comparison of Machine Acquisitions with Different Lives—Approach #1

	Cash Flows		
	Alternative A	Alternative B	
Years Hence	**Machine A (1)**	**Machine B (2)**	**Machine C (3)**
0	$(15,000)	$(6,000)	
1	3,000	3,000	
2	3,000	3,000	
3	3,000	3,000	
4	3,000	3,000	
5	3,000	3,000	$(11,000)
6	3,000		3,000
7	3,000		3,000
8	3,000		3,000
9	3,000		3,000
10	3,000		3,000

NPV – Alternative A

NPV = 3000 (5.0188) – 15,000

NPV = 15,056 – 15,000

NPV = $56

NPV – Alternative B

NPV = 3000 (5.0188) – 6000 – 11,000 (.4972)

NPV = 15,056 – 6,000 – 5,469

NPV = $3,587

(1) Machine A costs $15,000 and provides a project cash flow of $3,000 per year for its ten-year life.

(2) Machine B costs $6,000 and provides a project cash flow of $3,000 per year for its five-year life of years 1 through 5.

(3) Machine C (purchased to replace Machine B) costs $11,000 at the end of year five and provides project cash flow of $3,000 per year for its five-year life of years 6 through 10.

3. Ignore the differences in lives of the two mutually exclusive projects.

The third approach is reasonable only if the lives are both long and the differences are inconsequential. For example, a difference of one year for proposed projects with fourteen- and fifteen-year lives may be immaterial.

The first approach is illustrated in Exhibit 13.12. In this example, a hotel is considering whether to replace its laundry washer with Machine A, which has a ten-year life, or with Machine B, which has a five-year life and no salvage value. At the end of Machine B's life, Machine C, which will have a five-year life, will be acquired. In addition, Machines A and C have no salvage value. Thus, the life of Machine A (ten years) equals the combined lives of Machines B and C. The capital budgeting model and discount rate used are NPV and 15%, respectively. The results suggest that Machine B be purchased now followed by Machine C at the end of year five.

The second approach, that of assuming the longer-lived project is disposed of at the end of the short-lived project's life, is illustrated in Exhibit 13.13. The same situation is assumed as in Exhibit 13.12 except the comparison is only for five years as Machine B is totally used at the end of year five. In addition, at the end of year five, Machine A is assumed to have a salvage value of $7,000. The NPV of Machines A and B are −$1,463

Exhibit 13.13 Comparison of Machine Acquisitions with Different Lives—Approach #2

Machine A costs $15,000 and provides project cash flow of $3,000 per year for five years and then may be sold for $7,000. Machine B costs $6,000 and provides project cash flow of $3,000 per year for five years. At the end of five years, the machine is worthless.

	Cash Flows	
Years Hence	**Machine A**	**Machine B**
0	$(15,000)	$(6,000)
1	3,000	3,000
2	3,000	3,000
3	3,000	3,000
4	3,000	3,000
5	10,000	3,000

NPV – Machine A

NPV = 3,000 (3.3522) + 7,000 (.4972) – 15,000
NPV = 10,057 + 3,480 – 15,000
NPV = 13,537 – 15,000
NPV = –$1,463

NPV – Machine B

NPV = 3,000 (3.3522) – 6,000
NPV = 10,057 – 6,000
NPV = $4,057

and $4,057, respectively. Therefore, based on the available information, Machine B would be purchased.

Capital Rationing

Up to this point, no limit on projects has been discussed as long as the project returns exceeded the reject criteria. In reality, there are often limited funds available. For example, a parent corporation may limit funds provided to a subsidiary corporation, or a corporation may limit funds provided to a division. This concept of limiting funds for capital purposes, regardless of the expected profitability of the projects, is called **capital rationing**. Under capital rationing, the combination of projects with the highest net present value should be selected.

Exhibit 13.14 considers five proposed projects and calculates several possible combinations and their NPVs. In this illustration, projects B and C are considered to be mutually exclusive, and only $150,000 is available for capital projects.

The optimum combination is projects A, B, and E, because this yields the highest combined NPV. Other feasible combinations result in a lower NPV. In the several combinations where all funds would not be spent on projects, excess funds would be invested at the going interest rate; however, the present value of the return on the excess funds would be the amount invested, thus there would be no related NPV on these excess funds. (This assumes that the going interest rate is equal to the discount rate.)

Exhibit 13.14   Capital Rationing—Five Proposed Projects

Project	Project Cost	NPV
A	$ 60,000	$30,000
B	70,000	20,000
C	50,000	15,000
D	100,000	40,000
E	20,000	10,000

Combination	Total Investment	Total NPV
A, B, & E	$150,000	$60,000
A, C, & E	130,000	55,000
A & B	130,000	50,000
A & C	110,000	45,000
C & D	150,000	55,000
D & E	120,000	50,000

Use of Capital Budgeting Models in the Lodging Industry

A recent survey of the 150 largest lodging chains revealed that 74% of the respondents use IRR, while 66%, 55%, and 32% use payback, NPV, and ARR, respectively.[1] These results differ significantly from a similar survey in 1980 which showed that only 33% of hospitality businesses used IRR, while 71% and 36% used payback and NPV, respectively.[2] The more recent survey did not request reasons for the changes, but it seems likely that computer usage is a major reason. Calculations of NPV and IRR are virtually child's play for the computer.

Computerization

Spreadsheet programs on personal computers have automated many of the calculations discussed in this chapter. The internal rate of return and net present value calculations have been simplified into short computer instructions which execute the calculations automatically. For example, using *Lotus 1-2-3*, the "functions" typed to calculate the three formulas mentioned above are:

Internal Rate of Return = @IRR(i, V1 . . . Vn)

i = Guess at a rate of return

V1 . . . Vn = Range of cash flows, starting with the first and ending with the last

Net Present Value = @NPV(i, V1 . . . Vn)

i = Interest rate to be used

V1 . . . Vn = Range of cash flows, starting with the first and ending with the last

Exhibit 13.15 Computer-Generated Telephone Investment Analysis

Washington Hotel Company
Telephone Investment Analysis

	Year:				
	19X1	**19X2**	**19X3**	**19X4**	**19X5**
Proposed Telephone System 1					
Investment = $70,000					
Cash Savings:					
Long Distance Charges	$45,000	$46,350	$47,741	$49,173	$50,648
Yearly Maintenance	10,800	11,340	11,907	12,502	13,127
Depreciation	20,000	20,000	20,000	20,000	20,000
Total Pretax Savings	75,800	77,690	79,648	81,675	83,775
Plus Salvage Value					7,300
Net Pretax Cash Savings	75,800	77,690	79,648	81,675	91,075
Less Taxes @ 34%	(25,772)	(26,415)	(27,080)	(27,770)	(30,966)
Net Aftertax Savings	50,028	51,275	52,568	53,905	60,109
Less Depreciation Savings	20,000	20,000	20,000	20,000	20,000
Net Aftertax Cash Flow	$30,028	$31,275	$32,568	$33,905	$40,109
Net Present Value at 12%:	$49,231				
Proposed Telephone System 2					
Investment = $75,000					
Cost Savings:					
Long Distance Charges	$48,000	$49,440	$50,923	$52,451	$54,024
Yearly Maintenance	8,400	8,820	9,261	9.724	10,210
Depreciation	15,000	15,000	15,000	15,000	15,000
Total Pretax Savings	71,400	73,260	75,184	77,175	79,234
Plus Salvage Value					5,000
Net Pretax Cash Savings	71,400	73,260	75,184	77,175	84,234
Less Taxes @ 34%	(24,276)	(24,908)	(25,563)	(26,240)	(28,640)
Net Aftertax Savings	47,124	48,352	49,621	50,935	55,594
Less Depreciation Savings	15,000	15,000	15,000	15,000	15,000
Net Aftertax Cash Flow	$32,124	$33,352	$34,621	$35,935	$40,594
Net Present Value at 12%:	$55,784				

Net Present Value Information

Cash Flows:

Option 1:	($70,000)	$30,028	$31,275	$32,568	$33,905	$40,109
Option 2:	($75,000)	$32,124	$33,352	$34,621	$35,935	$40,594

Internal Rate of Return:

Option 1:	36.36%	Choose Option:	2
Option 2:	39.58%		

Exhibit 13.15 is an example of how some of these functions could be used. The first section examines two telephone systems by looking at their estimated cash savings due to decreased expenses over the system presently in use. The lower section demonstrates how a spreadsheet can compare various investments. It shows the two options' internal rates of return and states which option should be chosen.

There are two basic advantages to using a spreadsheet program to perform these calculations. First, once the format of the model is set, it can be used repeatedly. This ensures consistency in the evaluation of all projects. The model represents a standard methodology for determining which investments provide the best returns. Second, it is very quick and accurate. The actual calculation by a computer takes only a few seconds and it is correct every time (assuming the formulas and data have been entered correctly). The computer allows more efficient use of management time, which should be spent evaluating projects, not calculating numbers.

Summary

Managers must carefully consider many necessary additions or changes in fixed assets in order to operate their businesses effectively. Projects are evaluated based on their costs and corresponding revenues. Projects which generate the most money for the firm should be accepted and the others should be rejected. This process is called capital budgeting.

Capital budgeting is appropriate in a number of decision-making processes. It can be used when purchasing equipment to meet government standards or to replace existing equipment. It is also valuable when considering the purchase of equipment which could either increase the operation's revenues or decrease its costs. In each of these cases, budgeting is performed to determine if the revenues (or cost savings) generated by the equipment are greater than the corresponding expenditures, or to decide which option is best for the operation. By using capital budgeting models, management actively works to maximize the operation's profits.

Four capital budgeting approaches were examined in this chapter: accounting rate of return, payback, net present value, and internal rate of return. ARR is defined as the average annual project income divided by the average investment. Although it is a simple method, it does have a number of deficiencies and is, therefore, not used frequently. The payback method is also simple and is used more than the ARR in the hospitality industry. It examines the cash flows generated by the equipment and determines the number of years of cash flows required to recover the investment. The NPV approach looks at the cash flows relating to the project and discounts them to their present value. A project with NPV equal to, or greater than, zero is accepted. The final approach discussed, IRR, examines the cash flows to determine the rate of return the investment generates. In other words, it sets the project NPV equal to zero and calculates the discount rate.

The NPV and IRR methods are more complex than the ARR and payback approaches, but they also provide more valuable results. They both examine cash flows and recognize the time value of money. The major difference between the two is that IRR somewhat unrealistically assumes that the project cash flows will be reinvested in projects which generate the same return. Thus, when mutually exclusive projects are analyzed, the NPV method is preferred over the IRR.

Endnotes

1. Raymond S. Schmidgall and James W. Damitio, "Capital Budgeting Practices by Major Lodging Chains in 1990," unpublished paper.
2. James J. Eyster, Jr., and A. Neal Geller, "The Capital-Investment Decision: Techniques Used in the Hospitality Industry," *The Cornell Hotel and Restaurant Management Quarterly*, May 1981, pp. 69–73.

Key Terms

accounting rate of return	incremental cash flow
annuity	internal rate of return
capital rationing	net present value
discount rate	payback
hurdle rate	time value of money

Discussion Questions

1. What is capital budgeting?

2. What are four situations which might require capital budgeting?

3. Why is one dollar today worth more than one dollar a year from now?

4. How is the payback method of capital budgeting performed?

5. What is project cash flow?

6. What are the disadvantages of using the payback method of capital budgeting?

7. How can two mutually exclusive projects with different lengths of lives be analyzed?

8. What role does the accept/reject criterion play in the NPV and IRR methods of capital budgeting?

9. Which method of capital budgeting is the most effective? Explain your choice.

10. What is capital rationing?

Problems

Problem 13.1

Phil Rail, owner of the Rail Haven Motel, desires to know how much money must be invested in order to accumulate a total of $100,000 ten years hence. The options are as follows:

1. X amount is invested today at an annual interest rate of 12%.

2. X amount is invested today at a semi-annual interest rate of 6%.

3. *X* amount is invested today and at the beginning of each of years 2–10. The annual interest rate is 12%.

4. *X* amount is invested today and at the beginning of each year for years 2–5. In addition, $25,000 is invested at the beginning of year 6. The annual interest rate is 12%.

Required:

Determine the amount of *x* for each alternative.

Problem 13.2

James Wayne, proprietor of the Wayne Country Inn, desires to know the present value of various streams of dollars. Today is the beginning of year one. Assume an annual discount rate of 12% for all alternatives. The streams are as follows:

1. Ten thousand dollars received at the beginning of each year for ten years.

2. One hundred thousand dollars received at the end of the tenth year.

3. Ten thousand dollars received at the end of each year for ten years.

4. Twelve thousand dollars received at the end of each year for the first five years and eight thousand dollars received at the beginning of each year for the last five years.

Required:

Determine the present value of each stream of dollars for the four scenarios.

Problem 13.3

Martice Smith and Associates is considering investing $5,000,000 in a new motel and has predicted the following income stream over its 10-year life.

YEAR	NET INCOME
1	$ (245,000)
2	(115,600)
3	18,400
4	276,320
5	455,000
6	1,066,700
7	1,150,000
8	1,069,300
9	1,055,700
10	1,000,250

The motel is expected to have no salvage value at the end of its 10-year life.

Required:

1. Using the ARR method, what is the rate of return for this project?

2. If Martice Smith and Associates requires 35% return on its investment, should this motel be purchased?

Problem 13.4

Carol Rollins, owner of Carollins, is considering buying an energy efficient oven for her restaurant. However, she is concerned that the cost savings adequately offset the purchase price; she would prefer the project to have no more than a 2.5 year payback period. She is basing her decision on the following information:

Project Cost: $23,500
Cost Savings:

	Years				
	1	2	3	4	5
Energy	$2,000	$2,500	$3,000	$3,000	$3,000
Maintenance	3,000	3,000	2,000	1,000	1,000
TOTAL	$5,000	$5,500	$5,000	$4,000	$4,000

Required:

1. Determine if Ms. Rollins should invest in this oven.
2. If there was an estimated cash savings of $4,500 for each year, would this oven be purchased, based on the payback criterion?

Problem 13.5

Susie Reed, owner of the Wild Life, an amusement park, is contemplating purchasing a new roller coaster/water combination ride for $1,500,000. She has determined that it would increase park revenues by $300,000 a year because of its originality, but it will cost approximately $70,000 a year to operate.

Assume a 15% discount rate and a 10-year life for the equipment.

Required:

Use the NPV model to determine if the equipment should be purchased.

Problem 13.6

The Jonathan Club is considering adding pizza to its menu. However, a conveyor oven will have to be purchased which will cost $20,000. It has an estimated seven-year life and Jon Jones, the manager, has determined that the club could sell approximately $50,000 worth of pizzas each year with a food cost of 35%, labor cost of 30% and other negligible operating costs. At the end of seven years, the conveyor oven should be able to bring $2,000 at an auction.

Assume that the Club requires a 15% return on investment.

Required:

Use the IRR method to determine if the machine should be purchased.

Problem 13.7

Jason and Jamie Hills, owners of the Hills Hotel, are considering upgrading their front office equipment by purchasing a new front office machine. The annual operating costs for front office machines are as follows:

COST	PRESENT MACHINE	PROPOSED MACHINE
Labor	$15,000	$12,000
Maintenance	500	200
Utilities	500	600
Insurance	60	100

The present machine has a present market value of $3,000 and will be useful for the next five years, but be worth $-0- at the end of five years. The proposed machine will cost $15,000.

To simplify the problem, assume that both machines would be depreciated by using the straight-line method of depreciation. Further assume a discount rate of 12% and a tax rate of 30%. Further assume that the proposed machine will be worth $5,000 at the end of year five.

Required:

Using the NPV model, should the new machine be purchased? Show all your work.

Problem 13.8

Leta O'Donnel, a wealthy Midwesterner, is considering the purchase of the Fairview Hotel for $20,000,000. The expected pre-depreciation earnings for years 1–10 are as follows:

Years	Pre-Depreciation Income
1	$ (500,000)
2	(100,000)
3	400,000
4	1,000,000
5	3,000,000
6	5,000,000
7	5,000,000
8	5,000,000
9	5,000,000
10	5,000,000

Assume that the hotel can be sold at the end of year 10 for $15,000,000.

For depreciation purposes, the depreciation methods and purchase cost of the Fairview Hotel are allocated as follows:

Land	10%	(no depreciation)
Equipment	20%	(DDB; 10 years)
Building	70%	(SL; $5,000,000 salvage value; 30 years)
	100%	

Further assume an average income tax rate of 30% and that all net operating losses are carried forward for up to five years.

Required:

1. Assuming a discount rate of 12%, determine the net present value of this investment.

2. Determine the IRR of this investment.

3. Explain why the Fairview Hotel should or should not be purchased.

Problem 13.9

The Holt Company is considering selling one of its buildings and leasing it back for the remaining five years of the building's life. The building is to be demolished in five years to make way for a new highway. The restaurant's earnings before depreciation, interest, property taxes, insurance, and income tax for each of the next five years are estimated as follows:

Year 1	Year 2	Year 3	Year 4	Year 5
$121,000	$125,000	$131,000	$133,000	$135,000

If the building is not sold and leased back, the building depreciation, property taxes, insurance, and interest expense figures for the five years would be the following:

	Year 1	Year 2	Year 3	Year 4	Year 5
Depreciation	$10,000	$8,000	$6,000	$4,000	$2,000
Interest	?	?	?	?	?
Property taxes	3,000	3,200	3,400	3,600	3,800
Insurance	3,000	3,000	3,000	3,000	3,000

The depreciation expense over the next five years will result in a zero net book value at the end of year 5. Interest expense pertains to a mortgage of $10,000 with principal repayments of $2,000 at the end of each year. The interest rate is 10%. The Holt Company's average tax rate is 33%. The local government will pay only $20,000 for the land and building at the end of five years.

If the building is sold now, the price would be $50,000. Assume that a capital gains tax rate on gain on the sale is 25% and that any tax due will be paid at the time of the sale. The building could be leased back at $12,000 per year.

Required:

Use the net present value model to determine whether the building should be sold and leased back. Assume a discount rate of 12%.

Problem 13.10

Daniel David, president of the Grand Rabbits Corporation, is considering two investment projects. Only one of the two will be selected this year. Information regarding each project is as follows:

Investment Project #1: Renovate an existing motel for $1,000,000. After tax, cash flows are expected to be $200,000 per year for 20 years.

Investment Project #2: Build a new motel for $4,000,000. After tax, annual cash flows are expected as follows:

Year	
1	$(200,000)
2	(50,000)
3	200,000
4	600,000
5–20	1,100,000

Assume a discount rate of 12%.

Required:

1. Based on the NPV model, which of the two projects should be selected?
2. Based on the IRR model, which of the two projects should be selected?

14 Lease Accounting

Leasing entitles someone to use equipment, land, or buildings without buying them. Leasing often provides a way to use resources when purchasing them is not possible or desirable. For example, a food service chain may lease space in a shopping mall because that space is not for sale. A hotel may lease equipment for a single day for a special function. This chapter will address several questions about lease accounting, including the following:

1. What are the advantages and disadvantages of leasing resources?
2. What are executory costs in relation to leases?
3. How are leases classified for accounting purposes?
4. What are the criteria for capitalizing leases?
5. How are leasehold improvements amortized?
6. What is a triple-net lease?
7. What is an incremental interest rate?
8. What is a sale and leaseback?
9. How are financial ratios affected by the accounting for leases?
10. What are several common provisions of lease agreements?

In this chapter, we will first consider the various uses of leases in the hospitality industry. We will discuss some of their advantages and disadvantages, as well as some provisions common to all leases. We will then focus on the differences between operating leases and capital leases and present guidelines for accounting for the different types of leasing arrangements. Finally, we will investigate the effects that leases may have on a hospitality operation's financial statements and ratios.

Leases and Their Uses

A **lease** is an agreement conveying the right to use resources (equipment, buildings, and/or land) for specified purposes and a limited time. From an operational perspective, the resource is available for use;

operating personnel generally have little concern whether the company owns or leases it. Lease agreements govern the parties to the lease, usually the lessor and the lessee. The **lessor** owns the property and conveys the right of its use to the **lessee** in exchange for periodic cash payments called **rent**.

Leasing is popular in the United States with businesses in general and with the hospitality industry in particular. For example, restaurants may lease space in shopping malls, lodging companies may lease hotels, and gambling casinos may lease slot machines.

Historically, several hotel companies have leased many of their hotels from real estate and insurance companies. The **variable lease** was a common lease arrangement used by Holiday Corporation during the 1950s and 1960s. Holiday Corporation (the lessee) paid the lessors a percentage of rooms, food, and beverage revenues. For example, a 25–5–5 lease resulted in the lessee paying the lessor 25% of rooms revenue, 5% of food revenue, and 5% of beverage revenue. Since these rental payments were based on revenues and since the lessee corporation paid all operational expenses before generating any profits, the lessee shouldered much of the hotel property's financial risk.

The leasing of hotels is less popular today. Few hotel companies have signed new property leases in the 1980s and 1990s. Instead, they manage hotels under **management contract** arrangements. Under these contracts, the hotel owners make substantial payments from the hotel's gross revenues to the hotel management companies, much like the hotel companies used to pay lessors for leased properties.[1]

Many hotels continue to lease equipment ranging from telephone systems to computers to vehicles. Many food service corporations lease both their buildings and equipment. In part, the extent of leasing by hospitality companies is revealed in footnotes to their annual financial statements. Marriott Corporation owns both lodging and food service chains. In its 1989 annual financial statements, Marriott Corporation reported $719,000,000 in rent expenses for all its leases. This amounted to nearly 10% of its total revenues for 1989. The lease footnote from Marriott's 1989 annual report is shown in Exhibit 14.1.

Advantages and Disadvantages of Leases

The following list presents some of the advantages of leasing.

- Leasing conserves working capital because it requires little or no cash deposit; cash equal to 20% to 40% of the purchase price is required when purchasing property and equipment. Therefore, for the cash-strapped operation, leasing may be the only way to obtain the desired property or equipment.

- Leasing often involves less red tape than buying with external financing. Although a lease agreement must be prepared, it usually is less complicated than the many documents required to make a purchase, especially when financing is involved.

- Leasing allows more frequent equipment changes, especially when equipment becomes functionally obsolete. However, the lessee cannot expect this flexibility to be cost-free. The greater the probability of technological obsolescence, the greater the lease payment (all other things being the same).

Exhibit 14.1 Marriott Corporation: Lease Footnote

LEASES

Fiscal Year	Capital Leases	Operating Leases
	(in millions)	
1990	$ 17	$ 156
1991	12	146
1992	9	140
1993	8	133
1994	7	119
Thereafter	51	1,061
Total minimum lease payments	104	$1,755
Less amount representing interest	(40)	
Present value of minimum lease payments	$ 64	

Many of the leases included above involve facilities used in the fast food and family restaurant businesses (reported as discontinued operations). Most leases contain one or more renewal options, generally for five or 10-year periods. Future rentals on leases have not been reduced by minimum sublease rentals of $87 million payable to the company under noncancelable subleases.

Rent expense for continuing operations consists of:

	1989	1988	1987
	(in millions)		
Minimum rentals on operating leases	$119	$105	$ 98
Additional rentals based on sales	43	42	42
Payments to owners of managed and leased hotels based primarily on profits	557	538	431
	$719	$685	$571

Source: *Marriott Corporation 1989 Annual Report.*

- Leasing allows the lessee to receive tax benefits which otherwise may not be available. For example, an unprofitable operation may not be able to take advantage of tax credits available to purchasers of certain equipment. However, a lessor, who can use the tax credits, may pass on part of the tax credit in the form of lower rental payments to the lessee.

- Leasing generally places less restrictive contracts on a lessee than financial institutions often place on long-term borrowers.

- Leasing has less negative impact on financial ratios, especially when the leases are not capitalized. Property acquired for use through an operational lease is not shown on the balance sheet. Future rent obligations also do not appear on the balance sheet, although some footnote disclosure may be required. For this reason, leases are often referred to as **off-balance-sheet financing**.

- Operating leases may allow an operation to obtain resources without following a capital budget.

Therefore, in many cases, leasing may be a lower overall cost alternative for many hospitality operations. However, there are also disadvantages of leasing, such as the following:

- Any residual value of the leased property benefits the lessor unless the lessee has the opportunity to acquire the leased property at the end of the lease.

- The cost of leasing in some situations is ultimately higher than purchasing. This is especially true when there are only a limited number of less-than-competitive lessors.

- Disposal of a financial lease before the end of the lease period often results in additional costs.

The above list of advantages and disadvantages is not exhaustive.[2]

Provisions of Lease Contracts

Each lease is a unique product of negotiations between the lessor and lessee which meets the specific needs of each party. However, all lease contracts normally contain certain provisions. The following list presents some of these common provisions.

1. Term of lease—The term of a lease may be as short as a few hours (usually for a piece of equipment) or as long as several decades (as is common with real estate).

2. Purpose of lease—This provision generally limits the lessee to using the property for certain purposes. For example, a restaurant lease may state, "The lessee shall use the leased premises as a restaurant and for no other purpose without first having obtained the written consent of the lessor."

3. Rental payments—The lease specifies the amount of rental payment and when it is due. It also indicates any adjustments; for example, adjustments for inflation are often based on the consumer price index for a given city. **Contingent rent** is also specified. For example, a lease may stipulate that contingent rent equal to 3% of all annual food and beverage sales in excess of $700,000 is due the fifteenth day of the first month after the end of the fiscal year.

4. Renewal options—Many leases contain a clause giving the lessee the option to renew the lease. For example, a lease may provide "an option to renew this lease for an additional five-year period on the expiration of the leasing term upon giving lessor written notice 90 days before the expiration of the lease."

5. Obligations for property taxes, insurance, and maintenance— Leases, especially long-term leases, specify who shall pay the **executory costs**—that is, the property taxes, insurance, and maintenance costs—on the leased property. A lease in which the lessee is obligated to pay these costs in addition to the direct lease payments is commonly called a **triple-net lease**.

6. Other common lease provisions include:

- The lessor's right to inspect the lessee's books, especially when part of the lease payment is tied to sales or some other operational figure.

- The lessor's obligations to restore facilities damaged by fire, tornadoes, and similar natural phenomena.

- The lessee's opportunity to sublease the property.

- The lessee's opportunity to make payments for which the lessor is responsible, such as loan payments to preclude default on the lessor's financing of the leased property.

- Security deposits, if any, required of the lessee.

- Indemnity clauses protecting the lessor.

The Supplemental Reading for this chapter contains a sample lease. Although it serves only as an example and is not intended to be representative of all hotel leases, the reader will note that it contains several of the above-mentioned provisions.

Lease Accounting

Historically, leases were accounted for simply as executory contracts—that is, the rental expense was generally recognized with the passage of time. Leases were not capitalized as assets, nor were liabilities recognized for the lessee's obligations under lease contracts. However, as leases have become more sophisticated and economically similar to sale/purchase transactions, many accountants have argued for a change in lease accounting.

The Accounting Principles Board, the past accounting rule-making body, issued four opinions regarding lease accounting. The Financial Accounting Standards Board (FASB), the present rule-making body, has issued more than ten statements relating to lease accounting. A major result of these rules is that many long-term leases are now capitalized—that is, they are recorded as fixed assets with recognition of a liability.

Most of the remainder of this chapter presents lease accounting guidelines for lessees. Lease accounting for lessors is beyond the scope of this text. Our discussion is meant to cover the major elements of lease accounting and is certainly not exhaustive. The student interested in further study of lease accounting should consult an intermediate accounting text and/or FASB statements.[3]

Classification of Leases

In general, lessees classify leases for accounting purposes as either operating leases or capital leases. At the extremes, operating leases differ substantially from capital leases. **Operating leases** are normally (but not always) of relatively short duration, and the lessor retains the responsibility for executory costs. They can usually be canceled easily. **Capital leases** are of relatively long duration, and the lessee often assumes responsibility for executory costs. In addition, they are generally non-cancelable or at least costly to cancel. Capital leases are capitalized, while operating leases are not.

The FASB has established four capitalization criteria for determining the status of non-cancelable leases. If a non-cancelable lease meets any one of the four criteria, the lessee must classify and account for the lease as a capital lease. Non-cancelable leases not meeting any of the four criteria may be accounted for as operating leases. The FASB criteria are reproduced below:[4]

1. The property is transferred to the lessee by the end of the lease term, hereafter referred to as **title transfer provision**.

2. The lease contains a bargain purchase option, hereafter referred to as **bargain purchase provision**.

3. The lease term is equal to 75% or more of the estimated economic life of the leased property, hereafter referred to as **economic life provision**.

4. The present value of minimum lease payments (excluding executory costs) equals or exceeds 90% of the excess of fair market value of the leased property over any investment tax credit retained by the lessor, hereafter referred to as **value recovery provision**.

The bargain purchase option (criterion #2) means that the purchase price at the end of the lease period is substantially less than the leased property's expected market value at the date the option is to be exercised. The bargain price is generally considered substantially less than the market value only if the difference, for all practical purposes, ensures that the bargain purchase option will be exercised. The "economic life" (criterion #3) refers to the useful life of the leased property. The following list explains several terms in the value recovery provision (criterion #4):

- *Present value* refers to determining present value as discussed in Chapter 13.

- *Minimum lease payments* consist of minimum rental payments during the lease term and any bargain purchase option. If no bargain purchase option exists, the minimum lease payments include any guaranteed residual value by the lessee or any amount payable by the lessee for failure to renew the lease. Minimum lease payments do not include contingent rent (such as a percentage of sales). Executory costs are also excluded in determining minimum rental payments when the lease specifies that lease payments include these costs.

- *Fair market value* represents the amount the leased item would cost if it were purchased rather than leased.

- *Investment tax credit* is a credit which the federal government used to allow against the federal income tax liability of the hospitality operation. When it was allowed, up to 10% of the cost of qualifying equipment could typically be taken as a credit. The credit generally applied to personal property (such as equipment), but not to real property (such as land and buildings). Investment tax credits are no longer allowed by current tax laws; however, if they are reinstated, they would be treated as indicated by criterion #4. Note that, when there is no investment tax credit, criterion #4 in effect states that if the present value of minimum lease payments (excluding executory costs) equals or exceeds 90% *of the fair market value* of the leased property, the lease must be capitalized.

- *Residual value* refers to the estimated market value of the leased item at the end of the lease term. When the residual value is guaranteed by the lessee, then the lessee is ultimately liable to the lessor for the residual value.

Accounting for Operating Leases

Operating leases are accounted for as simple rental agreements—that is, the expense is generally recognized when the rent is paid. For example, if a restaurant company leases space in a shopping mall for $5,000 per month and pays rent on the first day of each month, the monthly rental payment would be recorded as follows:

Rent Expense	$5,000	
Cash		$5,000

When rent is paid in advance, it should be recorded in a prepaid rent account. For example, if the restaurant company had paid three months' rent in advance, the proper entry would be:

Rent Expense	$ 5,000	
Prepaid Rent	10,000	
Cash		$15,000

This accounting entry recognizes rent expense for the current month and delays recognition of rent for the following two months (based on the matching principle—see Chapter 1).

In the event rent is paid for a period beyond twelve months from the balance sheet date, the rental payment should be recorded as "deferred rent" and shown as a deferred charge on the balance sheet. Any rent paid for future periods is recognized during the period to which it relates by an adjusting entry. In the example above, the adjusting entry to recognize the second month's rent would be:

Rent Expense	$5,000	
Prepaid Rent		$5,000

Accounting for Capital Leases

A capital lease is similar to the purchase of a fixed asset. Therefore, the accounting for capital leases recognizes an asset and applicable liabilities. The amount to be recorded as an asset and a liability is the present value of minimum lease payments, as defined earlier in relation to the fourth capitalization criterion. The lease payments are discounted using the lessee's incremental borrowing rate, or, if known, the lessor's implicit rate of interest in the lease *if* it is lower than the lessee's incremental borrowing rate. The former is used oftener because the lessee does not usually know the lessor's implicit interest rate in the lease. The lessee's **incremental borrowing rate** is the rate of interest the lessee would have to pay if financing the purchase of the leased item.

Executory costs included with the lease payments must be excluded in determining the present value of minimum lease payments. However, a bargain purchase option or a lessee's guaranteed residual value must be included. For example, a lease agreement may require a monthly payment of $1,000, of which $200 is for maintenance. This $200 for maintenance is excluded in determining the present value of minimum lease payments. On the other hand, if the lessee guarantees a residual value of $2,000 for the leased item the present value of $2,000 should be included in determining the present value of minimum lease payments.

When the lessee makes subsequent lease payments, the lease obligation is reduced by the difference between the lease payment (excluding executory costs) and the interest on the lease obligation. The interest is calculated by using the effective interest method, which results in a constant rate of interest throughout the lease term. This is accomplished by multiplying the interest rate used in discounting the minimum lease payments by the lease obligation for the lease period. For example, assume that a lease payment is $5,000 for the month, including $500 for property taxes, and the lease obligation for the period is $480,000. Further assume that the lessee's incremental borrowing rate is 10%. The entry to record the lease payment is as follows:

Property tax expense	$ 500	
Interest expense	4,000	
Lease obligations	500	
Cash		$5,000

The interest expense of $4,000 is determined as follows:

$$\text{Interest} = \frac{\text{Lease}}{\text{Obligation}} \times \frac{\text{Incremental}}{\text{Borrowing Rate}} \times \frac{\text{Time}}{\text{(in Years)}}$$

$$= 480,000 \times .10 \times \frac{1}{12}$$

$$= \underline{\$4,000}$$

Therefore, the lease obligation is debited by $500, determined as follows:

$$\frac{\text{Reduction in}}{\text{Lease Obligation}} = \frac{\text{Lease}}{\text{Payment}} - \frac{\text{Executory}}{\text{Costs}} - \frac{\text{Interest}}{\text{Expense}}$$

$$= 5,000 - 500 - 4,000$$

$$= \underline{\$500}$$

Illustration of Accounting for Capital Leases

The Chambers Hotel signs a lease agreement with a major computer manufacturer for the use of a front office computer. Provisions of the lease agreement and other relevant facts for classifying the lease are as follows:

1. The term of the lease is five years, commencing on January 1, 19X1. The lease is non-cancelable.

2. Annual payments of $55,000 are due at the beginning of each year.

3. The leased computer has a fair market value of $200,000 at January 1, 19X1.

4. The estimated economic life of the computer is seven years, and there is no expected residual value.

5. The Chambers Hotel is to pay all executory costs directly except for annual maintenance costs of $10,000 which are included in the annual lease payments.

6. The lease contains no renewal or bargain purchase options, and the equipment reverts to the lessor at the end of the lease period.

7. The Chambers Hotel's incremental borrowing rate is 12%.

8. The Chambers Hotel depreciates its own computer equipment on a straight-line basis.

9. The lessor's implicit rate of return on leasing the computer to the Chambers Hotel is unknown.

10. There are no tax credits applicable to this situation.

The Chambers Hotel must determine whether the lease should be capitalized by comparing the lease provisions to the FASB lease capitalization criteria. Exhibit 14.2 illustrates this comparison. As the exhibit indicates, the lease should be capitalized, based on criterion #4, because the present value of lease payments, excluding executory costs, exceeds 90% of the fair market value of the leased equipment. The calculations are presented below.

Fair market value of leased equipment	$200,000
90% factor	$\times$ .9
	180,000
Present value of lease payments (see Exhibit 14.3)	181,678
Excess of lease payments	$ 1,678

The journal entry to record the capitalization of the leased equipment accompanied by the first payment of $55,000 is as follows:

Leased equipment under capital leases	$181,678	
Prepaid maintenance	10,000	
Cash		$ 55,000
Obligations under capital leases		136,678

Exhibit 14.2 FASB Lease Capitalization Criteria

FASB Lease Capitalization Criteria
and the lease of computer equipment
by the Chambers Hotel

Lease Capitalization Criteria	Computer Lease Provisions		Capitalize Yes/No
1. Title transfer provision	Item 6 states the "equipment reverts to the lessor at the end of the lease."		No
2. Bargain purchase provision	Item 6 states the lease contains no bargain purchase options		No
3. Economic life provision	$\frac{\text{Life of lease}}{\text{Useful life of equipment}} = 5/7 = 71.4\%$ 71.4% < 75%		No
4. Value recovery provision	45,000 (4.0373)* = 200,000 (.9) = excess of PV of lease payments over 90% of FMV is	$181,678** (180,000) $1,678	Yes

*For the derivation of this factor, see Exhibit 14.3.
**This amount is actually $181,678.50; however, the detail of cents is droped here and throughout the rest of htis illustration.

Exhibit 14.3   Present Value of Five Lease Payments – Chambers Hotel

Annual lease payments	$ 55,000
Less: Amount for executory costs	10,000
Net lease payment	45,000
Present value of an annuity for 4 payments at 12% (3.0373) Plus present value factor for the initial (undiscounted) payment (1.0000) = 4.0373	x 4.0373 $181,678

This single entry consists of the capitalization of the lease at $181,678 (the present value of the five lease payments), the recognition of the related liability at $136,678, and the initial payment of $55,000, of which $10,000 relates to maintenance and the remaining $45,000 to the lease.

The single entry could have also been recognized in two parts:

(1) Capitalization of lease

Leased equipment under capital leases	$181,678	
Obligations under capital leases		$181,678

This entry simply records the present value of the five lease payments.

(2) Lease payment

Obligations under capital leases	$45,000	
Prepaid maintenance	10,000	
Cash		$55,000

This entry records the initial cash payment, the $10,000 executory payment, and the reduction in the "obligation" account.

The prepaid maintenance would be written off throughout the year by a monthly entry of $833 ($1/12$ of the annual payment):

Maintenance expense	$833	
Prepaid maintenance		$833

Future payments will result in the recognition of interest expense, the reduction of the obligation under capital leases, and prepayment of maintenance for the next year. In practice, at year-end (December 31, 19X1), interest expense would be accrued by debiting interest expense by $16,401 and crediting accrued interest by $16,401 because of the matching principle.

The Chambers Hotel would record its second lease payment on January 1, 19X2, as follows:

Interest expense	$16,401	
Obligations under capital leases	28,599	
Prepaid maintenance	10,000	
Cash		$55,000

The interest expense of $16,401 results from multiplying the $136,678, recorded as "Obligations under capital leases" throughout the year, by the Chambers Hotel's incremental borrowing rate of 12%. The reduction in the liability "Obligations under capital leases" of $28,599 is the difference between the *net* lease payment of $45,000 and the interest expense of $16,401. Exhibit 14.4 shows the amortization of the $136,678 lease obligation over the term of the lease.

The leased equipment should be depreciated over its lease term of five years. The annual entry for depreciation expense (based on straight-line) would be as follows:

Depreciation expense	$36,336	
Accumulated depreciation—capital leases		$36,336

This entry assumes a zero salvage value because the equipment reverts to the lessor at the end of the lease term. At the end of the five-year term, the leased equipment is returned to the lessor and the two accounts, "Leased equipment under capital leases" and "Accumulated depreciation—capital leases," each at $181,678, are reduced to zero:

Exhibit 14.4 Lessee's Amortization of Obligation under Capital Leases—Chambers Hotel

Date of Payment	(1) Annual Lease Payment	(2) Interest Expense[1]	(3) Reduction in Liability[2]	(4) Balance of Liability Account[3]
1/1/X1				$136,678
1/1/X2	$ 45,000	$16,401	$ 28,599	108,079
1/1/X3	45,000	12,969	32,031	76,048
1/1/X4	45,000	9,126	35,874	40,174
1/1/X5	45,000	4,826*	40,174	$ –0–
	$180,000	$43,322	$136,678	

*Rounding error of less than $5.

Note: The total annual lease payments ($180,000) less the balance of the obligation at January 1, 19X1 ($136,678) equals the interest expense of $43,322.

[1]Interest expense is calculated by multiplying the annual interest rate (12%) by the prior balance of the liability account.

[2]The reduction in the liability is computed by subtracting the interest expense (column 2) from the annual lease payment (column 1).

[3]The balance of liability account (column 4) is reduced each year by the amount in column 3.

Accumulated depreciation – capital leases	$181,678	
Leased equipment under capital leases		$181,678

Throughout the five-year period, the following expenses related to the leased item were incurred:

Maintenance – $10,000/year	$50,000
Depreciation – the capitalized cost of the lease	181,678
Interest expense – the sum of the five net lease payments less the capitalized cost of the lease ($225,000 – $181,678):	43,322
Total Expense	$275,000

Notice that the total expense equals the five annual payments of $55,000.

Leasehold Improvements

Buildings which are leased for several years, such as restaurants in shopping malls, often require extensive improvements before the commencement of operations. Often, the space leased is not capitalized since none of the capitalization criteria is met. However, any improvements to the space must be capitalized as **leasehold improvements**. For example, the cost of walls, ceilings, carpeting, and lighting installed in leased space is capitalized. The leasehold improvement is recognized as an intangible asset, and the cost must be amortized against revenue over the life of the lease or the life of the leasehold improvement, whichever is shorter. For example, assume that the Chambers Hotel leased three acres of adjoining land for parking facilities and the land was improved by adding storm sewers, sidewalks, lighting, and pavement at the cost of $200,000. Further assume that the life of the improvement is 10 years, while the land was leased for 30 years. The annual amortization of the leasehold improvement would be $1/10$ of the cost—$20,000 per year for 10 years. This expense is generally recognized monthly ($1/12$ of annual amortization) as follows:

Amortization of leasehold improvement	$1,667	
Leasehold improvement		$1,667

Sale and Leasebacks

Sale and leasebacks are transactions whereby an owner of real estate agrees to sell the real estate to an investor and then lease it back. The original owner's use of the property continues without interruption. The property is sold to the investor (lessor) at market value and then leased back to the seller (lessee) for an amount equal to the investor's cost plus a reasonable return.

The major reason for sale and leaseback transactions is to raise capital which was previously tied up in the property. The investors in these transactions are usually looking for a financial return, as they have no interest in managing hospitality operations.

The lessee should account for the lease based on the FASB's four criteria for classifying leases. If the seller (lessee) makes a profit from the sale of the now leased assets, such profit should generally be deferred and amortized over the lease term. Losses should be recognized in their entirety when the sale and leaseback agreement is signed. The student interested in a more detailed discussion of this topic is encouraged to consult an intermediate accounting text.

Leases and Their Effect on Financial Ratios

Whether a leased item is accounted for as a capital lease or an operating lease can have a major impact on the financial statements, especially the balance sheet. Therefore, several financial ratios are also affected. Property leased under an operating lease is not shown on the balance sheet, while property leased under a capital lease is shown. The balance sheet disclosure of capital leases includes both assets and liabilities. Therefore, most financial ratios involving noncurrent assets and long-term liabilities are affected by how leases are accounted for. Four financial ratios affected by capitalizing leases are shown in Exhibit 14.5.

In general, capitalizing leases negatively affects these ratios—that is, the ratios suggest a less desirable financial situation than they would if the leases had been accounted for as operating leases. For example, if a lease is capitalized, the assets and liabilities increase. This means the net

Exhibit 14.5   Financial Ratios Most Affected by Lease Accounting

Ratio	Ratio Formula	How capital lease affects ratio
1. Asset turnover	revenue ÷ average total assets	Capitalizing leases results in increasing the average total assets, therefore reducing the asset turnover ratio.
2. Return on assets	net income ÷ average total assets	Increased average total assets will also reduce the return on assets.
3. Debt-equity ratio	total debt ÷ total equity	Capitalizing leases results in increasing the total debt, therefore increasing the debt-equity ratio.
4. Number of times interest earned ratio	earnings before interest and taxes ÷ interest expense	Capitalizing leases results in increased interest expenses, therefore reducing this ratio.

income must also increase in order to maintain a constant return on assets. Thus, many hospitality operations prefer not to capitalize leases. They often negotiate lease provisions so that the lease does not qualify as a capital lease under any of the FASB's four capitalization criteria.

Summary

Leasing is a special type of financing used by many hospitality businesses. By entering into a lease agreement, the lessee acquires the right to use specific resources for a limited time and a specific purpose. The advantages for the lessee include the conservation of working capital, the benefits of tax deductions which might not otherwise be available, and, in some cases (when the lease is accounted for as an operating lease), a favorable effect on the balance sheet ratios. In exchange for these advantages, the lessee must make some sacrifices. In many instances, the residual value of the property remains with the lessor, there may be substantial penalties for termination of the lease contract, and the cost of leasing may be higher than purchasing the leased item. The operator contemplating a lease arrangement must weigh the advantages and disadvantages before entering into the contract. In many cases in the hospitality industry, the lease contract proves advantageous.

There are many aspects common to most leases. Provisions contained in most lease contracts include the length and purpose of the contract, the specific rent payments, any lessee obligations, and renewal options.

When deciding between leasing and purchasing an asset, many businesses consider how the agreement will affect the financial statements. Depending upon its terms, a lease will either be capitalized (recorded on the balance sheet as an asset and liability) or treated as an operational lease (expensed as the payments are made). If capitalized, certain financial ratios can be negatively affected. Some managers avoid capital leases because of this effect.

In addition to accounting for the initial lease, leasehold improvements must be recorded and subsequently amortized over either the life of the lease or the life of the improvement, whichever is shorter.

Management should study all the variations of the lease agreement before signing any contract. Establishments judged solely on their financial ratios will probably be more interested in whether a lease is capitalized. Other establishments may value the difference between the total lease payments and the benefits of having a present cash flow.

Historically, leases have been a popular way to finance assets. The trend indicates that leases will continue as viable means of hospitality financing, especially for equipment.

Endnotes

1. The reader interested in studying management contracts is referred to James J. Eyster's *The Negotiation and Administration of Hotel Management Contracts*, 2d ed. (Ithaca, N.Y.: School of Hotel Administration, Cornell University, 1980).

2. For more detail on this topic, see Pietrat Elgers and John J. Clark, *The Lease-Buy Decision* (New York: The Free Press, 1980) and T. M. Clarke, *Leasing* (London: McGraw-Hill, 1978).

3. Consider Lanny G. Chastien, Richard E. Flaherty, and Melvin C. O'Connor's *Intermediate Accounting*, 3d ed. (New York: McGraw-Hill, 1989).

4. FASB Financial Accounting Standard #13, *Accounting for Leases*, 1976.

Key Terms

bargain purchase provision	management contract
capital lease	off-balance-sheet financing
contingent rent	operating lease
economic life provision	rent
executory costs	residual value
incremental borrowing rate	sale and leaseback
lease	title transfer provision
leasehold improvements	triple-net lease
lessee	value recovery provision
lessor	variable lease

Discussion Questions

1. What are three major advantages to the lessee of lease financing?

2. What are some provisions common to most leases?

3. What are the FASB's four criteria for determining if a lease is a capital or an operating lease?

4. If a hotel operation enters into a capital lease agreement, what effect will it have on the debt-equity ratio?

5. What major effects do capital leases (compared to operating leases) have on an operation's balance sheet?

6. What are leasehold improvements?

7. What is a sale and leaseback agreement?

8. What are lease executory costs and how do they influence the determination of whether a lessee should capitalize a lease?

9. What is meant by guaranteed residual value? How does it affect the present value of lease payments?

10. At what value is a capitalized lease recorded?

Problems

Problem 14.1

Jimmy Ko, proprietor of Jimmy's Place, has recently leased a computer which does not meet any of the FASB's accounting requirements for capitalizing the lease. The three-year lease contract requires Jimmy to make an original payment of $4,000 on July 1, 19X1, for the first and last month's rent expense of $2,000 each.

On August 1, 19X1, Jimmy is required to make the next month's payment of $2,000. Jimmy's Place maintains its books on a strict accrual accounting basis.

Required:

1. Prepare the journal entry to record the original payment for July 1, 19X1.

2. Prepare the adjusting journal entry for July 31, 19X1.

3. Prepare the journal entry for the August 1, 19X1 payment.

Problem 14.2

Fidencio Lopez, owner of Fido's Pizzeria, has just signed a lease contract for several major machines (ovens and so forth). The lease required an initial payment of $10,000 when the lease was signed and five future payments of $10,000 each at one-year intervals. The restaurant's incremental interest rate is 12%. Mr. Lopez's accountant has determined that the lease must be capitalized.

Required:

1. Determine the amount of the capitalized lease.

2. Prepare an amortization table for the liability related to the capitalized lease. (Use the format provided in Exhibit 14.4.)

Problem 14.3

Bob and Audrey Read are the owners/operators of Resort Kove, a small hotel in central Ohio. On July 1, 19X1, they entered into a lease arrangement with Larose Leasing for a wide screen TV for the beverage operation. The lease provides for the equipment to become the property of Resort Kove at the end of the five-year lease period. The lease payments are $4,161 annually, payable at the beginning of each year. Assume that the Reads' average rate of borrowing is 10%, while their incremental rate is 12%. The first year's payment is made on July 1, 19X1.

Required:

1. Prepare the journal entry to record the capitalization of the lease and the first lease payment.

2. Prepare the journal entry for July 1, 19X2, to record the second annual payment.

Problem 14.4

On January 1, 19X1, Brian's Bungalow leased a 100-room motel property for 25 years. The estimated life of the property is 35 years. The lease is not capitalized since it does not meet any of the FASB's requirements. The business also leased a posting machine on July 1, 19X2, for a five-year period. The machine's life is seven years, and the equipment reverts to the lessor at the end of five years. The cost of the posting machine, if purchased, would be $6,000; annual lease payments are $1,525, payable at the beginning of each year. Brian's has an incremental borrowing rate of 12%, and the present value of $1 for four periods is 3.0373.

The rooms are to be renovated effective July 1, 19X2, at a cost of $2,000 per room. The life of the renovation is estimated at 30 years.

Required:

1. Should the lease of the posting machine be capitalized? If so, at what amount?

2. Should the renovation be capitalized? If so, at what amount?

3. If the renovation is capitalized, what is the annual amortization?

Problem 14.5

The Irish Inn is contemplating the purchase or lease of a new dryer. Tip O'Reilly, owner of the Irish Inn, believes that the lease would not be capitalized and thus his financial ratios would not be adversely affected by the lease. He has asked you to examine the proposed arrangement, which is as follows:

Term of Lease:	6 years
Estimated life of dryer:	9 years
Average cost of debt:	11%
Incremental cost of debt:	12%
Lease payments due:	
—first payment due at signing (January 1, 19X1)	
—next five payments annually beginning January 1, 19X2	
Annual lease payment:	$1,000
First lease payment:	$1,000
Fair market value:	$4,500

There is also no option to buy at the end of lease; the dryer reverts to lessor at the end of the lease period.

Required:

1. Is the owner correct in his belief that the lease would not be capitalized? Show all your work in arriving at your decision.

2. What is the present value of the lease payment stream?

3. Prepare the journal entry to record the lease assuming it will be capitalized.

4. What is the amount of interest for 19X1?

5. What is the amount of interest over the life of the lease (19X1–19X5)?

Problem 14.6

Alfredo Salvador is contemplating the purchase or lease of a new computer for his hotel. The proposed lease arrangement is as follows:

Term of lease:	5 years
Estimated life of computer:	10 years
Average cost of debt:	10%
Incremental cost of debt:	9%
Lease payments due:	
—first payment due at signing (January 1, 19X1)	
—next four payments annually beginning January 1, 19X2	
Annual lease payment:	$10,000
Fair market value:	$50,000
Lessee's guarantee of residual value:	$5,000

Required:

1. Determine the present value of the payment stream.

2. Prepare the journal entry to record the initial lease payment and capitalization (if necessary) of the lease.

3. Prepare the journal entry to record the second lease payment.

Problem 14.7

On January 1, 19X5, the Clairemount Hotel plans to sign a five-year lease for its telephone system. Provisions of the lease are as follows:

1. The lease is non-cancelable.

2. Annual payments beginning on January 1, 19X5, are $35,000 each for five years.

3. The telephone system has a fair market value of $140,000 at January 1, 19X5.

4. The estimated useful life of the system is seven years.

5. Included in the $35,000 annual payment is $5,000 for maintenance costs.

6. The Clairemount Hotel's average and incremental interest rates are 12% and 11%, respectively. The lessor's implicit interest rate is 10%.

7. The Clairemount Hotel agrees to guarantee a residual value of $10,000.

Required:

1. Determine the present value of the lessee's payments related to the lease.

2. Should the lease be capitalized? Explain your position.

Problem 14.8

The Koelling Hotel has just signed a lease with IRC, Inc. for a new front office computer. Lease provisions and other relevant information are as follows:

1. The lease term is five years starting on January 1, 19X2.
2. Annual payments are $60,000 starting on January 1, 19X2.
3. The fair market value of the computer at January 1, 19X2, is $225,000.
4. The estimated economic life of the computer is seven years.
5. The lease payments include $10,000 for maintenance and $3,000 for insurance.
6. The Koelling Hotel's incremental borrowing rate is 10%, while IRC's implicit rate of return on leasing the computer is 12%.

Assume that the lease is capitalized.

Required:

1. Provide the journal entry to record the first lease payment and the lease.
2. Provide the journal entry to record the second payment.
3. Calculate the total interest expense over the five years.

Problem 14.9

Robert Traub, owner/manager of Traub's Place, has just signed a seven-year lease for kitchen equipment. Details are as follows:

1. The estimated life of the equipment is ten years.
2. Semi-annual lease payments commencing with the signing of the lease on January 1, 19X3, are $10,000.
3. Each lease payment includes executory costs of $500.
4. Traub's incremental interest rate is 10%, while its average interest rate is 9%.
5. Traub's guarantees a residual value of $10,000.
6. The fair market value of the leased equipment is $90,000.

Assume that the lease is capitalized.

Required:

1. Record the initial lease payment and the lease.
2. Prepare an amortization schedule for the lease liability.

Problem 14.10

The King's Inn's financial situation at the end of 19X3 and 19X4 is summarized below:

	19X3	19X4
Total property and equipment (fixed assets)	$5,800,000	$6,000,000
Total assets	$6,500,000	$6,750,000
Interest expense (for the year)	$600,000	$625,000
Income taxes (for the year)	$400,000	$420,000
Net income (for the year)	$500,000	$550,000

On January 1, 19X4, the King's Inn leased adjoining sporting facilities for its guests' use. The lease was negotiated so that it was not capitalized. However, *if* any of the capitalization criteria had been met, the above accounts would have been affected at the end of 19X4 as follows:

Total property and equipment—increase by $850,000
Total assets—increase by $850,000
Interest expense for 19X4—increase by $100,000

Note: Income taxes and net income would not be affected as rent expense (for operating leases) would equal the depreciation and interest expense (for the capitalized lease).

Required:

1. Calculate the following ratios given that the King's Inn did *not* capitalize the lease of the sporting facilities:

    a. Return on fixed assets
    b. Return on total assets
    c. Number of times interest earned

2. Calculate the same ratios listed in #1 for the King's Inn assuming that the lease was capitalized.

3. Based on your calculations, was the King's Inn wise in negotiating an operating lease? Why?

Appendix
Sample Lease

Lease Intended for Security

This **LEASE INTENDED FOR SECURITY** ("Lease") dated as of _____, is between _____ a Delaware corporation, with its principal office at _____ ("Lessor") and _____, a _____, with its principal office at _____ ("Lessee").

Lessor agrees to acquire and to lease and to sell to Lessee and Lessee agrees to hire and purchase from Lessor certain personal property (the "Units" and individually a "Unit") described in the Schedule (the "Schedule") attached hereto and made a part hereof, upon the terms and conditions hereinafter set forth:

Section 1. Procurement, Delivery and Acceptance.

1.1 Lessee has ordered or shall order the Units pursuant to one or more purchase orders or other contracts of sale ("Purchase Agreements" and individually a "Purchase Agreement") from one or more vendors ("Vendors" and individually a "Vendor"). Prior to the earlier of the time that title to any Unit has been transferred by the applicable Vendor or the "Delivery Date" (as hereinafter defined) Lessee shall assign to Lessor all the right, title and interest of Lessee in and to the applicable Purchase Agreement insofar as it relates to such Unit by execution and delivery to Lessor of a Purchase Agreement Assignment substantially in the form of Exhibit A hereto. The Delivery Date of each Unit shall be the date on which the Unit is first placed in service by Lessee. Lessor agrees to accept the assignment and, subject to the conditions of Section 1.2, assume the obligations of Lessee under the Purchase Agreement to purchase and pay for such Unit, but no other duties or obligations of Lessee thereunder; provided, however, that Lessee shall remain liable to Vendor in respect of its duties and obligations in accordance with the Purchase Agreement. Lessee represents and warrants in connection with the assignment of any Purchase Agreement that (a) Lessee has the right to assign the Purchase Agreement as set forth herein, (b) the right, title and interest of Lessee in the Purchase Agreement so assigned shall be free from all claims, liens, security interests and encumbrances, (c) Lessee will warrant and defend the assignment against lawful claims and demands of all persons and (d) the Purchase Agreement contains no conditions under which Vendor may reclaim title to any Unit after delivery, acceptance and payment therefor.

1.2 The obligation of Lessor to pay for each Unit is subject to the following conditions:

(a) Lessee shall have accepted such Unit on the Delivery Date thereof:

(b) the Delivery Date for such Unit shall be during the Utilization Period set forth in the Schedule; and

(c) there shall exist, as of the Delivery Date of such Unit no Event of Default nor any event which with notice or lapse of time or both, would become an Event of Default.

If any of the foregoing conditions have not been met with respect to any Unit, Lessor shall assign, transfer and set over unto Lessee all the right, title and interest of Lessor in and to such Unit and the Purchase Agreement insofar as it relates to such Unit.

1.3 Lessee shall execute and deliver to Lessor, within 15 days of the Delivery Date of each Unit accepted by Lessee, an Acceptance Supplement in the form of Exhibit B hereto, confirming the Delivery Date of such Unit and the acceptance of such Unit as of the Delivery Date. Each Acceptance Supplement shall be accompanied by the invoice relating to any Unit covered by such Acceptance Supplement if it has been received. If the invoice has not been received, Lessee shall, within 5 days of its receipt (unless otherwise specified by Lessor), forward it to Lessor.

1.4 As soon as possible, but no later than the first assignment by Lessee of a Purchase Agreement hereunder, Lessee shall deliver to Lessor in form and substance satisfactory to Lessor:

(a) a certificate evidencing Lessee's authority to enter into and perform its obligations under this Lease;

(b) a certificate as to the incumbency of the person or persons authorized to execute and deliver this Lease and any other agreements or documents required hereunder, including the signatures of such persons;

(c) certificates of insurance, loss payable endorsements or other evidence acceptable to Lessor that Lessee has complied with the provisions of Section 7 of this Lease;

(d) as to any Unit which will be installed or affixed on any real property, a Consent to Removal in the form of Exhibit C hereto; and

(e) such other documents as may be reasonably requested by Lessor.

Section 2. Term, Rent and Payment.

2.1 The term of this Lease as to each Unit shall commence on the Delivery Date in respect thereof and continue as specified in the Schedule.

2.2 Lessee shall pay to Lessor rental for each Unit in the amounts and at the times set forth in the Schedule.

2.3 Rent and all other sums due Lessor hereunder shall be paid at the principal office of Lessor set forth above.

2.4 This Lease is a net lease and Lessee shall not be entitled to any abatement or reduction of rent or any setoff against rent, whether arising by reason of any past, present or future claims of any nature by Lessee against Lessor or otherwise. Except as otherwise expressly provided herein, this Lease shall not terminate, nor shall the obligations of Lessor or Lessee be otherwise affected by reason of any defect in, damage to, loss of possession or use or destruction of any Unit, however caused, by the attachment of any lien, encumbrance, security interest or other right or claim of any third party to any Unit, by any prohibition or restriction of or interference with Lessee's use of the Unit by any person or entity, or by the insolvency of or the commencement by or against Lessee of any bankrupty, reorganization or similar proceeding, or for any other cause, whether similar or dissimilar to the foregoing, any present or future law to the contrary notwithstanding. It is the intention of the parties that all rent and other amounts payable by Lessee hereunder shall be payable in all events in the manner and at the times herein provided unless Lessee's obligations in respect thereof have been terminated pursuant to the express provisions of this Lease.

Section 3. Warranties.

LESSEE ACKNOWLEDGES AND AGREES THAT (a) EACH UNIT IS OF A SIZE, DESIGN, CAPACITY AND MANUFACTURE SELECTED BY LESSEE, (b) LESSEE IS SATISFIED THAT THE SAME IS SUITABLE FOR ITS PURPOSES, (c) LESSOR IS NOT A MANUFACTURER THEREOF NOR A DEALER IN PROPERTY OF SUCH KIND AND (d) LESSOR HAS NOT MADE, AND DOES NOT HEREBY MAKE, ANY REPRESENTATION OR WARRANTY OR COVENANT WITH RESPECT TO THE TITLE, MERCHANTABILITY, CONDITION, QUALITY, DESCRIPTION, DURABILITY OR SUITABILITY OF ANY SUCH UNIT IN ANY RESPECT OR IN CONNECTION WITH OR FOR THE PURPOSES AND USES OF LESSEE. Lessor hereby assigns to Lessee, to the extent assignable, any warranties, covenants and representations of Vendor with respect to any Unit, provided that any action taken by Lessee by reason thereof shall be at the expense of Lessee and shall be consistent with Lessee's obligations pursuant to Section 2 hereunder.

Section 4. Possession, Use and Maintenance.

4.1 Lessee shall not (a) use, operate, maintain or store any Unit improperly, carelessly or in violation of any applicable law or regulation of any governmental authority, (b) abandon any Unit, (c) sublease any Unit or permit the use thereof by anyone other than Lessee without the prior written consent of Lessor, which consent shall not be unreasonably withheld, (d) permit any Unit to be removed from the location specified in the Schedule without the prior written consent of Lessor, (e) affix or place any Unit to or on any other personal property or to or on any real property without first obtaining and delivering to Lessor such waivers as Lessor may reasonably require to assure Lessor's legal title and security interest and right to remove such Unit free from any lien, encumbrance or right of distraint, or any other claim which may be asserted by any third party, or (f) sell, assign or transfer, or directly or indirectly create, incur or suffer to exist any lien, claim, security interest or encumbrance of any kind on any of its rights hereunder or in any Unit.

4.2 Lessee shall at its expense at all times during the term of this Lease maintain the Units in good operating order, repair, condition and appearance.

4.3 Lessee shall not alter any Unit or affix or place any accessory, equipment or device on any Unit, if such alteration or addition would impair the originally intended function or use or reduce the value of any such Unit. All repairs, parts, supplies, accessories, equipment and devices furnished, affixed or installed to or on any Unit, excluding temporary replacements, shall thereupon become subject to the security interest of Lessor. If no Event of Default has occurred and is continuing, Lessee may remove at its expense any such accessories, equipment and devices at the expiration of the term of this Lease with respect to such Unit, provided such parts, accessories, equipment or devices are readily removable and provided that such removal will not impair the originally intended function or use of such Unit.

4.4 If Lessor supplies Lessee with labels, plates or other markings, stating that the Units are leased from Lessor, Lessee shall affix and keep the same upon a prominent place on the Units during the term of this Lease.

4.5 Upon prior notice to Lessee, Lessor shall have the right at all reasonable times to inspect any Unit and observe its use.

Section 5. General Tax Indemnity.

5.1 Lessee agrees to pay or reimburse Lessor for, and to indemnify and hold Lessor harmless from, all fees (including, but not limited to, license, documentation, recording or registration fees), and all sales, use, gross receipts, personal property, occupational, value added or other taxes, levies, imposts, duties, assessments, charges or withholdings of any nature whatsoever, together with any penalties, fines or additions to tax, or interest thereon (all of the foregoing being hereafter referred to as "Impositions"), arising at any time prior to or during the term of this Lease, or upon any termination of this Lease or upon the return of the Units to Lessor, and levied or imposed upon Lessor, directly or otherwise, by any federal, state or local government or taxing authority in the United States or by any foreign country or foreign or international taxing authority upon or with respect to (a) any Unit, (b) the exportation, importation, registration, purchase, ownership, delivery, leasing, possession, use, operation, storage, maintenance, repair, return, sale, transfer of title or other disposition thereof, (c) the rentals, receipts, or earnings arising from any Unit, or (d) this Lease or any payment made hereunder, excluding, however, taxes measured by Lessor's net income imposed or levied by the United States or any state thereof

but not excluding any such net income taxes which by the terms of the statute imposing such tax expressly relieve Lessee or Lessor from the payment of any Impositions which Lessee would otherwise have been obligated to pay, reimburse or indemnify.

5.2 Lessee agrees to pay on or before the time or times prescribed by law any Impositions (except any Impositions excluded by Section 5.1) provided, however, that Lessee shall be under no obligation to pay any such Imposition so long as Lessee is contesting such Imposition in good faith and by appropriate legal proceedings and the nonpayment thereof does not, in the opinion of Lessor, adversely affect the title, property, use, disposition or other rights of Lessor with respect to the Units. If any Impositions (except any Impositions excluded by Section 5.1) shall have been charged or levied against Lessor directly and paid by Lessor, Lessee shall reimburse Lessor on presentation of an invoice therefor.

5.3 If Lessor shall not be entitled to a corresponding and equal deduction with respect to any Imposition which Lessee is required to pay or reimburse under Sections 5.1 or 5.2 and which payment or reimbursement constitutes income to Lessor, then Lessee shall also pay to Lessor the amount of any Impositions which Lessor is obligated to pay in respect of (a) such payment or reimbursement by Lessee and (b) any payment by Lessee made pursuant to this Section 5.3.

5.4 Lessee shall prepare and file, in a manner satisfactory to Lessor, any reports or returns which may be required with respect to the Units.

Section 6. Risk of Loss; Waiver and Indemnity.

6.1 In the event that any Unit shall be or become worn out, lost, stolen, destroyed or irreparably damaged, from any cause whatsoever, or taken or requisitioned by condemnation or otherwise (any such occurrence being hereinafter called a "Casualty Occurrence") prior to or during the term of this Lease as to such Unit, Lessee shall give Lessor prompt notice thereof. On the first rental payment date following such Casualty Occurrence or, if there is no such rental payment date, 30 days after such Casualty Occurrence, Lessee shall pay to Lessor an amount equal to the then "Balance Due" (as hereinafter defined) for such Unit. The Balance due for each Unit is the sum of

    (a)   any and all amounts with respect to such Unit which under the terms of this

Lease may be then due or which may have accrued to such payment date (computing the rental for any number of days less than a full rental period by a fraction of which the numerator is such number of days and the denominator is the total number of days in such full rental period); plus

(b) before the Base Date for such Unit as set forth in the Schedule, the amount Lessor is obligated to pay for such Unit, and thereafter, the sum of (i) the present value, as of such payment date, of the entire unpaid balance of all rental for such Unit which would otherwise have accrued hereunder from such payment date to the end of the term of this Lease as to such Unit, and (ii) the present value, as of such payment date, of the amount of the mandatory or optional payment required or permitted to be paid by Lessee to Lessor at the end of the term of this Lease in accordance with the Schedule. Such present values are to be computed in each case by discounting at the Implicit Interest Rate set forth in the Schedule.

Upon the making of such payment by Lessee in respect of any Unit, the rental for such Unit shall cease to accrue, the term of this Lease as to such Unit shall terminate and Lessee shall be entitled to possession of such Unit. Provided that Lessor has received the Balance Due for such Unit, Lessee shall be entitled to the proceeds of any recovery in respect of such Unit from insurance or otherwise, and Lessor, subject to the rights of any insurer insuring the Units as provided herein, shall execute and deliver, to Lessee, or to its assignee or nominee, a bill of sale (without representations or warranties except that such Unit is free and clear of all claims, liens, security interests and other encumbrances by or in favor of any person claiming by, through or under Lessor) for such Unit, and such other documents as may be required to release such Unit from the terms of this Lease and to transfer title thereto to Lessee or such assignee or nominee, in such form as may reasonably be requested by Lessee, all at Lessee's expense. Except as hereinabove in this Section 6.1 provided, Lessee shall not be released from its obligations hereunder in the event of, and shall bear the risk of, any Casualty Occurrence to any Unit prior to or during the term of this Lease with respect to such Unit.

6.2 Lessee hereby waives and releases any claim now or hereafter existing against Lessor on account of, and agrees to indemnify, reimburse and hold Lessor harmless from, any and all claims (including, but not limited to, claims relating to patent infringement and claims based upon strict liability in tort), losses, liabilities, demands, suits, judgments or causes of action, and all legal proceedings, and any costs or expenses in connection therewith, including allocated charges, costs and expenses of the Legal Department of Bank of America National Trust and Savings Association and any other attorneys' fees and expenses incurred by Lessor, which may result from or arise in any manner out of the delivery, condition, use or operation of any Unit prior to or during the term of this Lease as to such Unit, or which may be attributable to any defect in any Unit, arising from the material or any article used therein or from the design, testing or use thereof, or from any maintenance, service, repair, overhaul or testing of any Unit regardless of when such defect shall be discovered, whether or not such Unit is in the possession of Lessee and no matter where it is located.

Section 7. Insurance.

Lessee, at its own cost and expense, shall keep each Unit insured against all risks, in no event for less than the amount set forth in Section 6.1 (b) with respect to such Unit, and shall maintain public liability insurance against such risks and for such amounts as Lessor may require. All such insurance shall be in such form and with such companies as Lessor shall approve, shall specify Lessor and Lessee as insureds and shall provide that such insurance may not be cancellable as to Lessor or altered in any way which would affect the interest of Lessor, without at least ten days prior written notice to Lessor. All liability insurance shall be primary, without right of contribution from any other insurance carried by Lessor. All insurance covering loss or damage to the Units shall contain a "breach of warranty" provision satisfactory to Lessor and shall provide that all amounts payable by reason of loss or damage to the Units shall be payable solely to Lessor.

Section 8. Default.

8.1 The following shall constitute events of default ("Events of Default") hereunder:

(a) Lessee shall fail to make any payments to Lessor when due hereunder;

(b) Any representation or warranty of Lessee contained herein or in any document furnished to Lessor in connection herewith shall be incorrect or misleading in any material respect when made;

(c) Lessee shall fail to observe or perform any other covenant, agreement or warranty made by Lessee hereunder and such failure shall continue for _____ days after written notice thereof to Lessee;

(d) Any default shall occur under any other agreement between Lessee and Lessor or under any agreement between Lessee and any affiliate of Lessor;

(e) Lessee shall make an assignment for the benefit of creditors or shall file any petition or action under any bankruptcy, reorganization, insolvency or moratorium law, or any other law or laws for the relief of, or relating to, debtors; or

(f) Any involuntary petition shall be filed under any bankruptcy statute against Lessee, or any receiver, trustee, custodian or similar official shall be appointed to take possession of the properties of Lessee, unless such petition or appointment is set aside or withdrawn or ceases to be in effect within sixty days from the date of said filing or appointment.

8.2 If any Event of Default shall occur, Lessor, at its option, may,

(a) proceed by appropriate court action or actions either at law or in equity, to enforce performance by Lessee of the applicable covenants of this Lease or to recover damages for the breach thereof; or

(b) by notice in writing to Lessee terminate this Lease, but Lessee shall remain liable as hereinafter provided; Lessor may, at its option, do any one or more of the following: (i) declare the aggregate Balance Due with respect to the Units immediately due and payable and recover any damages and expense in addition thereto which Lessor shall have sustained by reason of the breach of any covenant, representation or warranty contained in this Lease other than for the payment of rental; (ii) enforce the security interest given hereunder pursuant to the Uniform Commercial Code or any other law; (iv) require Lessee to return the Units as provided in Section 9 hereof.

8.3 Lessor shall have any and all rights given to a secured party by law, and may, but is not required to, sell the Units in one or more sales. Lessor may purchase at such sale. Lessee acknowledges that sales for cash or on credit to a wholesaler, retailer or user of the Units, or at public or private auction, are all commercially reasonable. The proceeds of such sale shall be applied in the following order: First, to the reasonable expenses of retaking, holding, preparing for sale and selling, including the allocated charges, costs and expenses of the Legal Department of _____ and any other attorneys' fees and expenses incurred by Lessor; Second, to the amounts, except those specified below, which under the terms of this Lease are due or have accrued; Third, to late charges; and Fourth, to the aggregate Balance Due. Any surplus shall be paid to the person or persons entitled thereto. If there is a deficiency, Lessee will promptly pay the same to Lessor.

8.4 Lessee agrees to pay all allocated charges, costs and expenses of the Legal Department of _____ and any other attorneys' fees, expenses or out-of-pocket costs incurred by Lessor in enforcing this Lease.

8.5 The remedies hereunder provided in favor of Lessor shall not be deemed exclusive, but shall be cumulative, and shall be in addition to all other remedies in its favor existing at law or in equity.

8.6 If Lessee fails to perform any of its agreements contained herein, Lessor may perform such agreement, and expenses incurred by Lessor in connection with such performance shall be payable by Lessee upon demand.

Section 9. Return of Units.

If Lessor shall rightfully demand possession of any Unit pursuant to this Lease or otherwise, Lessee, at its expense, shall forthwith deliver possession of such Unit to Lessor, at the option of Lessor (a) by delivering such Unit, appropriately protected and in the condition required by Section 4 of this Lease, to Lessor at such place as may be specified by Lessor within the county in which the Unit was originally delivered or, if the Unit has been moved to another county in accordance with this Lease, within such other county, or (b) by loading such Unit, appropriately protected and in the condition required by Section 4 of this Lease, on board such carrier as Lessor shall specify and shipping the same, freight collect, to the destination designated by Lessor.

Section 10. Assignment.

All or any of the right, title or interest of Lessor in and to this Lease and the rights, benefits and advantages of Lessor hereunder, including the rights to receive payment of rental or any other payment hereunder, and title to the Units, may be assigned or transferred by Lessor at any time. Any such assignment or transfer shall be subject and subordinate to the terms and provisions of this Lease and the rights and interests of Lessee hereunder. No assignment of this Lease or any right or obligation hereunder may be made by Lessee or any assignee of Lessee without the prior written consent of Lessor.

Section 11. Ownership, Security Interest and Further Assurances.

Unless assigned by Lessor, or applicable law otherwise provides, title to and ownership of the Units shall remain in Lessor as security for the obligations of Lessee hereunder until Lessee has fulfilled all of its obligations hereunder. Lessee hereby grants to Lessor a continuing security interest in the Units to secure the payment of all sums due hereunder and agrees, at its expense, to do any further act and execute, acknowledge, deliver, file, register and record any further documents which Lessor may reasonably request in order to protect Lessor's title to and security interest in the Units and Lessor's rights and benefits under this Lease.

Section 12. Late Payments.

Lessee shall pay to Lessor, on demand, interest at the rate set forth in the Schedule on the amount of any payment not made when due hereunder from the date due until payment is made.

Section 13. Effect of Waiver.

No delay or omission to exercise any right,

power or remedy accruing to Lessor upon any breach or default of Lessee hereunder shall impair any such right, power or remedy nor shall it be construed to be a waiver of such breach or default, or an acquiescence therein or of or in any similar breach or default thereafter occurring, nor shall any waiver of any single breach or default be deemed a waiver of any other breach or default theretofore or thereafter occuring. Any waiver, permit, consent or approval of any kind or character on the part of Lessor of any breach or default under this Lease must be in writing specifically set forth.

Section 14. Survival of Covenants.

All covenants of Lessee under Sections 1, 2, 4, 5, 6, 8, 9, and 12 shall survive the expiration or termination of this Lease to the extent required for their full observance and performance.

Section 15. Applicable Law.

This Lease shall be governed by and construed under the laws of California.

Section 16. Effect and Modification of Lease.

This Lease exclusively and completely states the rights of Lessor and Lessee with respect to the leasing of the Units and supersedes all prior agreements, oral or written, with respect thereto. No variation or modification of this Lease shall be valid unless in writing.

Section 17. Financial Information.

Lessee shall keep its books and records in accordance with generally accepted accounting principles and practices consistently applied and shall deliver to Lessor its annual audited financial statements and such other unaudited quarterly financial statements as may be reasonably requested by Lessor. Credit information relating to Lessee may be disseminated among Lessor and any of its affiliates.

Section 18. Notices.

All demands, notices and other communications hereunder shall be in writing and shall be deemed to have been duly given when personally delivered or when deposited in the mail, first class postage prepaid, or delivered to a telegraph office, charges prepaid, addressd to each party at the address set forth below the signature of such party on the signature page, or at such other address as may hereafter be furnished in writing by either party to the other.

Section 19. Counterparts.

Two counterparts of this Lease have been executed by the parties hereto. One counterpart has been prominently marked "Lessor's Copy." One counterpart has been prominently marked "Lessee's Copy." Only the counterpart marked "Lessor's Copy" shall evidence a monetary obligation of Lessee.

IN WITNESS WHEREOF, the parties hereto have executed this Lease as of the day and year first above written.

By_____   By_____

Title_____   Title_____

By_____   By_____

Title_____   Title_____

Address:_____   Address:_____

SCHEDULE TO LEASE INTENDED FOR SECURITY
DATED AS OF _____, 19____
BETWEEN _____ AND ____

A. Description of Units.

Telephone System.

B. Purchase Price.

Purchase Price with respect to each Unit shall mean the amount Lessor is obligated to pay for such Unit. Without the prior written consent of Lessor, the sum of the Purchase Prices of all Units leased hereunder shall not exceed $500,000.

C. Term.

The lease term for each Unit shall consist of an Interim Term followed immediately by a Base Term. The Interim Term for each Unit shall commence on the Delivery Date in respect thereof and shall continue until the Base Date for such Unit. The Base Term for each Unit shall commence on the Base Date for such Unit and shall continue for eighty four (84) months. The Base Date for each Unit shall be the first day of the month following the respective Delivery Date.

D. Rental.

Supplemental Rental: Lessor agrees to advance funds for the purchase of the Units prior to the Delivery Date of such Units, provided with respect to each advance, Lessee executes and delivers to Lessor, no later than ten days prior to the date of such advance, a Request for Advance substantially in the form attached hereto as Exhibit D. With respect to each such advance, Supplemental Rental shall accrue from the date of such advance to, but not including, the Delivery Date of the Units for which such advance was made at a rate per annum equal to one hundred twenty percent (120%) of Bank of _____ "Prime Rate" (the rate of interest publicly announced from time to time by Bank of _____, as its Prime Rate, with any change in the Prime Rate to take effect on the day specified in the public announcement of such change), computed on the funds so advanced and based on a year of 365/366 days and actual days elapsed. Supplemental Rental for such Units shall be payable when billed by Lessor.

If Lessee shall fail to accept, pursuant to Section 1.2 of the Lease, any Unit for which Lessor shall have advanced funds as set forth above, Lessee shall, on demand of Lessor, purchase any such Unit from Lessor for the amount of the funds advanced by Lessor or which Lessor may be obligated to advance and any other costs or obligations incurred by Lessor in connection therewith, plus all accrued and unpaid rentals at the rate set forth above with respect to such Unit to the date of purchase of such Unit by Lessee from Lessor.

Interim Rental: For each day of the Interim Term, Lessee shall pay rental for each Unit equal to 0.0638% of the Purchase Price of such Unit actually paid on or before such day, payable when billed by Lessor.

Base Rental: During the Base Term, Lessee shall pay rental for each Unit, in consecutive monthly installments commencing on the Base Date for such Unit. Each rental payment for each Unit shall be in an amount equal to 1.914% of the Purchase Price of such Unit.

E. Utilization Period.

All Delivery Dates for Units leased hereunder must occur between December 1, 1982 and January 31, 1983, inclusive.

F. Interest on Late Payments.

The interest rate on late payments shall be 19% per annum.

G. Location.

The Units shall be located in _____.

H. Implicit Interest Rate.

The Implicit Interest Rate is 15.27% per annum compounded Monthly.

I. Commitment Fee.

Lessee shall pay to Lessor a non-refundable commitment fee of 1% of $500,000 on the date of execution of this Lease.

J. Purchase Provision.

At the end of the lease term for a Unit, as set forth in this Schedule, provided that this Lease has not been earlier terminated with respect to such Unit, Lessee shall purchase such Unit for a price equal to 1% of the original Purchase Price of such Unit.

Upon Lessee's payment of the Purchase Price, Lessor shall execute and deliver, to Lessee or its assignee or nominee, a bill of sale (without representations or warranties except that such Unit is free and clear of all claims, liens, security interests and other encumbrances by or in favor of any person claiming by, through or under Lessor) for such Unit, and such other documents as may be required to release such Unit from the terms and scope of this Lease and to transfer title thereto to Lessee or such assignee or nominee, in such form as may reasonably be requested by Lessee, all at Lessee's expense.

15 Income Taxes

In 1789, Benjamin Franklin wrote, "But in this world nothing can be said to be certain, except death and taxes."[1] Most businesses and individuals view taxes similarly—as a necessary evil. Most also try to pay as little tax as legally possible. Hospitality managers must attempt to minimize the operation's income taxes in order to increase the owners' financial returns. Questions about taxes addressed in this chapter include the following:

1. Are taxes a major consideration when purchasing capital assets?

2. What is the difference between income exclusion and deductions?

3. How do tax deductions differ from tax credits?

4. How do tax avoidance and tax evasion differ?

5. What are the advantages of a sole proprietorship form of organization?

6. What is double taxation?

7. How can double taxation be avoided by a corporate form of organization?

8. What is a limited partnership and what are its advantages over a general partnership?

9. Which federal tax forms does each type of organization file?

This chapter begins with a discussion of the effect of taxes on business decisions. It presents a brief history and explanation of the objectives of federal income taxes. Next, tax basics for the individual taxpayer are covered. Tax avoidance and tax evasion are discussed, followed by an overview, including the tax advantages and disadvantages, of the various forms of business organization. We then discuss cash versus accrual accounting and accounting income versus taxable income. Finally, state, municipal, and property taxes are discussed briefly.

The purpose of this chapter is not to explain all of the ramifications of the various tax laws, most of which are very complex. Rather, this chapter attempts to illustrate the importance of taxes in a hospitality operation's economic decisions.

Tax Considerations in Economic Decisions

Taxes are an important consideration in most major financial decisions. For example, the purchase of furniture and equipment may be delayed because a new tax incentive will take effect the following year. This is not to suggest that an investment in fixed assets should be delayed simply because of a tax advantage. Other business goals may indicate that the purchase should be made immediately. However, when current business objectives allow a choice of timing, management should plan acquisitions to gain tax advantages which will lower the net cost of acquiring the asset and result in greater net income. Similarly, the disposition of marketable securities, investments, fixed assets, or even an entire business should be considered with the tax effects of the proposed transaction in mind.

Because federal, state, and city taxes may consume over 50% of a business's earnings, management must be ever vigilant to the effect that tax rules may have on business decisions. One major purpose of hospitality associations such as the American Hotel & Motel Association and the National Restaurant Association is to lobby for tax legislation most beneficial to the hospitality industry.

History and Objectives of Federal Income Taxes

Although the United States government first used an income tax to raise revenue during the Civil War, it was not until 1913 that the Sixteenth Amendment established the constitutionality of such a tax and cleared the way for federal income tax as we know it today. Since 1913, Congress has made amendments to the original law and charged the Treasury Department with its enforcement through the Internal Revenue Service (IRS), a branch of the Treasury Department.

Until the late 1960s, major tax law changes were infrequent, often seven to ten years apart. In recent years, however, significant changes have been made to the Internal Revenue Code nearly every year. The most recent major tax law was the Tax Reform Act of 1986. The law and its accompanying explanations are over 1,500 pages long.

The primary objective of income taxes is to raise revenue necessary for the operation of the federal government. This goal has been expanded at various times to include stimulating certain aspects of the economy and accomplishing various social goals.

Tax Basics

Taxes are levied on individuals and corporations. The income of a sole proprietorship must be reported on the proprietor's individual tax return. Similarly, partnerships are not generally taxed, but their partners are. That is, partnerships must report their incomes to their partners, who must include their share of partnership income on their individual returns. Although corporations are separate legal entities in themselves, they are ultimately owned by individual investors. Therefore, corporate tax decisions are often based on the impact they may have on the individual investors. For example, the use of an accelerated method of depreciation reduces taxable income, which in turn reduces taxes and the cash paid in taxes. This allows more cash to be invested or more cash dividends to be paid to investors.

In other words, all of these forms of business organization ultimately affect individual tax returns. Thus, a brief discussion of individual income taxes is warranted.

The individual income tax return is Form 1040 (shown later in Exhibit 15.3). In 1989, individuals with gross income above a certain amount had to file Form 1040 or one of its variations, Form 1040A or Form 1040EZ. An individual's tax is determined as follows:

	Income
	Income
Less:	Adjustments to Income
Equals:	Adjusted Gross Income (AGI)
Less:	Deductions
Less:	Amount for Exemptions
Equals:	Taxable Income
Times:	Tax rate
Equals:	Federal Income Tax
Less:	Tax Credits
Plus:	Other Federal Taxes
Equals:	Total Tax

In addition to Form 1040, several schedules, as appropriate, must be filed. For example, Schedule C summarizes a sole proprietor's business for the year. Discussing all of the numerous schedules is beyond the scope of this text. All IRS offices provide all federal tax schedules and materials explaining these schedules.

The following brief discussion covers the major elements of the Form 1040.

Income, Income Exclusions, and Adjustments

Income on Form 1040 includes, but is not limited to, wages, salaries, and tips (as reported on Form W-2), as well as interest and dividend income, business income or loss from a sole proprietorship, capital gains or losses, rents, royalties, partnership income or loss, and S Corporation income or loss (S Corporations are defined later in this chapter).

Certain non-taxable income (such as interest from state and local government bonds), often referred to as **income exclusions**, is reported on the individual's tax return but excluded from income for tax purposes.

Gross income less adjustments to gross income equals adjusted gross income (AGI). Adjustments to gross income include, but are not limited to, individual retirement account deductions and some other retirement investments.

Deductions, Exemptions, and Taxable Income

Individual taxpayers should itemize **tax deductions** if their total deductions exceed the standardized deduction. For example, in 1989, it was beneficial for married taxpayers (if neither were 65 or older or were blind) filing jointly to itemize if their deductions exceeded $5,200. Itemized deductions include medical and dental expenses in excess of 7.5% of AGI, other taxes (such as state and local income taxes) paid during the tax year, real estate taxes, home mortgage interest expense, contributions to charitable organizations, limited amounts for casualty and theft losses, and the portion of certain summed miscellaneous deductions (such as union and professional dues and tax preparation fees) which exceed 2% of AGI.

In 1989, $2,000 was allowed for each exemption. In general, a taxpayer is allowed one exemption for himself or herself and one for each dependent.

Taxes and Credits

Income taxes are calculated on the basis of taxable income. The current tax rate system for individuals is graduated, with rates ranging from 15% to 33%. In addition, the tax code provides for minimum taxes (the *alternative minimum tax*) for certain individuals who would otherwise not have to pay income taxes. Income taxes less credits plus other applicable taxes equal the total taxes due.

In contrast to tax deductions, which are deducted from AGI to determine taxable income, **tax credits** are deducted directly from taxes due. Credits deductible from income taxes include credit for child and dependent care expenses and foreign tax credit.

Other taxes which must be added to the income taxes due include self-employment tax, commonly known as social security for the sole proprietor, and social security taxes on tip income not reported to the employer.

The tax code is quite complex, as are the many forms and schedules required to complete some individual tax returns. Individuals with complicated returns should consider obtaining assistance from a tax expert.

A Tax Illustration

Warren and Beth Schmidt have two children and own Snicker's Restaurant, an unincorporated business. Exhibit 15.1 presents a summary income statement of their restaurant operation, managed by Warren. Beth earns $15,000 as a part-time education specialist at the local community college. Her W-2 shows $1,500 withheld for federal income taxes. Exhibit 15.2 shows the Schmidts' other income, adjustments to income, deductions, and other taxes. Exhibits 15.3 through 15.5 illustrate the Schmidts' Form 1040, Schedule A, and Schedule C, respectively. Schedule SE—Computation of Social Security Self-Employment Tax and Form 4562—Depreciation must also be filed with the Schmidts' return. These schedules are not included as exhibits here, but their results appear as appropriate on the exhibits; for example, the total depreciation of $30,000 from Form 4562 is shown on line 13 of Schedule C (Exhibit 15.5).

Notice that income from the restaurant, shown on Schedule C, is entered on Form 1040, line 12. Further, note that a refund of $992 is due the Schmidts.

Tax Avoidance

Tax avoidance—that is, planning a transaction to mitigate the tax impact or to avoid the application of taxes completely—is entirely legal and should be aggressively pursued. Judge Learned Hand stated it well:

Over and over again courts have said there is nothing sinister in so arranging one's affairs as to keep taxes as low as possible. Everybody

Exhibit 15.1 Summary Income Statement—Snicker's Restaurant

Summary Income Statement
Snicker's Restaurant
For the year ended December 31, 1989

Sales		$750,000
Cost of Sales		300,000
Gross Profit		450,000
Controllable Expenses:		
Payroll	$200,000	
Employee Benefits	18,000	
Laundry	5,000	
Supplies	10,000	
Utilities	30,000	
Advertising	12,000	
Car Expenses	8,000	
Legal and Professional	8,000	
Office Expense	3,000	
Telephone	3,000	
Travel	5,000	
Dues and Publications	1,000	
Profit Sharing Plans	8,000	
Repairs and Maintenance	10,000	321,000
Income Before Occupation Costs		129,000
Rent		20,000
Property Taxes		6,000
Insurance		6,000
Interest		10,000
Depreciation		30,000
Income Before Taxes		$57,000

does so, rich or poor; and all do right, for nobody owes any public duty to pay more than the law demands: taxes are enforced extractions, not voluntary contributions. To demand more in the name of morals is mere cant.[2]

Management can and should conduct the hospitality operation's business so as to achieve the lowest possible tax cost within the constraints of other business considerations and the prevailing tax laws and regulations. Good tax planning is simply good business management.

For example, consider the purchase or sale of a hospitality establishment. An incorporated seller must decide whether to sell the stock of the company or its assets. Assuming a gain on the transaction, the after-tax differences between these two alternatives can be dramatic. Even in a situation generating an overall loss, tax recognition of gain may be required on certain elements of the transaction if the decision was to sell assets rather than stock.

Exhibit 15.2 Information about the Schmidt Family Income

Other Income:	
Interest income of $250	
Adjustments:	
An IRA of $2,000 (for Warren Schmidt)	
An IRA of $2,000 (for Beth Schmidt)	
Deductions:	
Medical –	
Prescribed drugs	$ 250
Doctor bills, etc.	3,000
Taxes –	
Property taxes – house	$3,000
State income taxes	2,000
Intangibles tax*	500
Interest –	
Mortgage on house	$7,000
Credit cards	1,000
Contributions – $3,100 to Evangel Center	$3,500
Professional dues – Beth Schmidt	$ 200
Tax return preparation fee for 1988 tax return	$ 300
Other Taxes:	
Self-employment tax	$6,250**
Federal taxes paid during year by Warren	$15,000

*A state tax on marketable securities and contracts

**Per Schedule SE (not included)

Conversely, a buyer will be reluctant to acquire the stock of a corporation if the tax basis of the corporation's assets is substantially below the selling price of the stock. In this situation, the buyer's goal is generally to acquire the assets of the corporation at their fair market value in order to preserve this higher base for future depreciation purposes. Even if the stock must be acquired, it is usually possible to effect a tax reorganization to realize a step-up in tax basis.

The point of all this is that, with proper tax planning, tax laws frequently allow both buyer and seller to realize most of their opposing goals. This fairly complex example also illustrates the need for most investors to consult tax experts in order to minimize their taxes. Recognizing these opportunities for tax planning and avoiding excessive or burdensome taxes is perfectly legal and represents a key management responsibility.

In contrast to tax avoidance, **tax evasion** is the fraudulent denial or concealment of a current or future tax liability, such as under-reporting income or claiming unsubstantiated or excessive deductions. For example, a business which intentionally fails to report or under-reports revenues, dividends, interest, fees, or profits from business transactions is guilty of tax evasion. Similarly, tax evasion occurs when non-deductible expenses (such as personal expenses or costs related to personal use of

Exhibit 15.3 Schmidt Family Income Tax Return

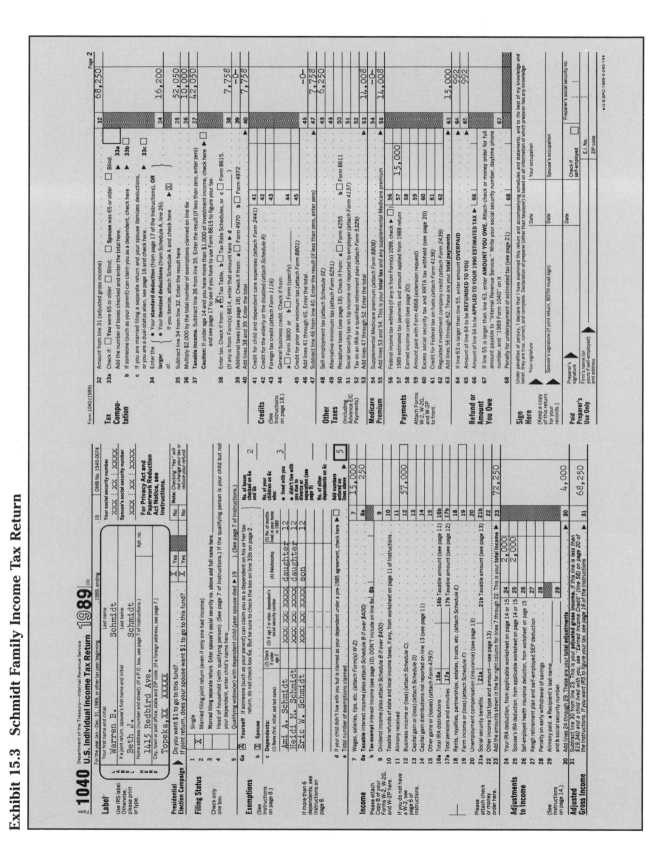

Exhibit 15.4   Schedule A: The Schmidts' Itemized Deductions

SCHEDULES A&B (Form 1040) Department of the Treasury Internal Revenue Service (O)	Schedule A—Itemized Deductions (Schedule B is on back) ▶ Attach to Form 1040. ▶ See Instructions for Schedules A and B (Form 1040).	OMB No. 1545-0074 1989 Attachment Sequence No. 07

Name(s) shown on Form 1040: **Warren B. and Beth J. Schmidt**   Your social security number: xxx xx xxxx

Medical and Dental Expenses (Do not include expenses reimbursed or paid by others.) (See Instructions on page 23.)	1a Prescription medicines and drugs, insulin, doctors, dentists, nurses, hospitals, medical insurance premiums you paid, etc . .	1a	3,250
	b Other. (List—include hearing aids, dentures, eyeglasses, transportation and lodging, etc.) ▶ _____	1b	
	2 Add the amounts on lines 1a and 1b. Enter the total here . . .	2	3,250
	3 Multiply the amount on Form 1040, line 32, by 7.5% (.075) . .	3	5,119
	4 Subtract line 3 from line 2. If zero or less, enter -0-. **Total** medical and dental . . ▶	4	-0-
Taxes You Paid (See Instructions on page 24.)	5 State and local income taxes	5	2,000
	6 Real estate taxes	6	3,000
	7 Other taxes. (List—include personal property taxes.) ▶ _____ Intangibles tax	7	500
	8 Add the amounts on lines 5 through 7. Enter the total here. **Total** taxes . . ▶	8	5,500
Interest You Paid (See Instructions on page 24.)	9a Deductible home mortgage interest (from Form 1098) that you paid to financial institutions. Report deductible points on line 10.	9a	7,000
	b Other deductible home mortgage interest. (If paid to an individual, show that person's name and address.) ▶ _____	9b	
	10 Deductible points. (See Instructions for special rules.)	10	
	11 Deductible investment interest. (See page 25.)	11	
	12a Personal interest you paid. (See page 25.) . . [12a 1,000]		
	b Multiply the amount on line 12a by 20% (.20). Enter the result .	12b	200
	13 Add the amounts on lines 9a through 11, and 12b. Enter here. **Total** interest ▶	13	7,200
Gifts to Charity (See Instructions on page 25.)	14 Contributions by cash or check. (If you gave $3,000 or more to any one organization, show to whom you gave and how much you gave.) ▶ Evangel Center-$3,100	14	3,500
	15 Other than cash or check. (You must attach Form 8283 if over $500.)	15	
	16 Carryover from prior year	16	
	17 Add the amounts on lines 14 through 16. Enter the total here. **Total** contributions . ▶	17	3,500
Casualty and Theft Losses	18 Casualty or theft loss(es) (attach Form 4684). (See page 26 of the Instructions.) . . . . ▶	18	
Moving Expenses	19 Moving expenses (attach Form 3903 or 3903F). (See page 26 of the Instructions.) . . . . ▶	19	
Job Expenses and Most Other Miscellaneous Deductions (See page 26 for expenses to deduct here.)	20 Unreimbursed employee expenses—job travel, union dues, job education, etc. (You MUST attach Form 2106 in some cases. See Instructions.) ▶ Professional dues-$200	20	200
	21 Other expenses (investment, tax preparation, safe deposit box, etc.). List type and amount ▶ _____ Tax preparation-$300	21	300
	22 Add the amounts on lines 20 and 21. Enter the total.	22	500
	23 Multiply the amount on Form 1040, line 32, by 2% (.02). Enter the result here	23	1,365
	24 Subtract line 23 from line 22. Enter the result. If zero or less, enter -0- . . . . . ▶	24	-0-
Other Miscellaneous Deductions	25 Other (from list on page 26 of Instructions). List type and amount ▶ _____	25	
Total Itemized Deductions	26 Add the amounts on lines 4, 8, 13, 17, 18, 19, 24, and 25. Enter the total here. Then enter on Form 1040, line 34, the LARGER of this total or your standard deduction from page 17 of the Instructions . . . . ▶	26	16,200

For Paperwork Reduction Act Notice, see Form 1040 Instructions.   Schedule A (Form 1040) 1989

business property) are intentionally deducted on tax returns as business expenses. Activities of this nature are illegal and untenable for the management of any business.

Forms of Business Organization

The importance of addressing tax questions early is perhaps best illustrated by looking at a new business. One of the basic decisions a

Exhibit 15.5 Schedule C: The Schmidts' Profit or Loss from Business

SCHEDULE C (Form 1040)	Profit or Loss From Business (Sole Proprietorship)	OMB No. 1545-0074
Department of the Treasury Internal Revenue Service (X)	Partnerships, Joint Ventures, Etc., Must File Form 1065. ▶ Attach to Form 1040 or Form 1041. ▶ See Instructions for Schedule C (Form 1040).	1989 Attachment Sequence No. 09

Name of proprietor: Warren B. Schmidt

Social security number (SSN): xxx xx xxxx

A Principal business or profession, including product or service (see Instructions): Foodservice sales

B Principal business code (from page 2) ▶ 3 0 7 9

C Business name and address ▶ Snickers Restaurant, 1950 Main St., Topeka, XX XXXXX

D Employer ID number (Not SSN):

E Method(s) used to value closing inventory: (1) X Cost (2) ☐ Lower of cost or market (3) ☐ Other (attach explanation) (4) ☐ Does not apply (if checked, skip line G)

F Accounting method: (1) X Cash (2) ☐ Accrual (3) ☐ Other (specify) ▶ ....

	Yes	No
G Was there any change in determining quantities, costs, or valuations between opening and closing inventory? (If "Yes," attach explanation.)		X
H Are you deducting expenses for business use of your home? (If "Yes," see Instructions for limitations.)		X
I Did you "materially participate" in the operation of this business during 1989? (If "No," see Instructions for limitations on losses.)	X	

J If this schedule includes a loss, credit, deduction, income, or other tax benefit relating to a tax shelter required to be registered, check here ▶ ☐. If you checked this box, you MUST attach **Form 8271.**

Part I Income

1 Gross receipts or sales	1	750,000
2 Returns and allowances	2	—0—
3 Subtract line 2 from line 1. Enter the result here	3	750,000
4 Cost of goods sold and/or operations (from line 39 on page 2)	4	300,000
5 Subtract line 4 from line 3 and enter the **gross profit** here	5	450,000
6 Other income, including Federal and state gasoline or fuel tax credit or refund (see Instructions)	6	—0—
7 Add lines 5 and 6. This is your **gross income** ▶	7	450,000

Part II Expenses

8 Advertising	8	12,000	22 Repairs	22	10,000
9 Bad debts from sales or services (see Instructions)	9		23 Supplies (not included in Part III)	23	10,000
10 Car and truck expenses	10	8,000	24 Taxes	24	6,000
11 Commissions	11		25 Travel, meals, and entertainment:		
12 Depletion	12		a Travel	25a	5,000
13 Depreciation and section 179 deduction from **Form 4562** (not included in Part III)	13	30,000	b Meals and entertainment		
			c Enter 20% of line 25b subject to limitations (see Instructions)		
14 Employee benefit programs (other than on line 20)	14	18,000	d Subtract line 25c from line 25b	25d	—0—
15 Freight (not included in Part III)	15		26 Utilities (see Instructions)	26	33,000
16 Insurance (other than health)	16	6,000	27 Wages (less jobs credit)	27	200,000
17 Interest:			28 Other expenses (list type and amount):		
a Mortgage (paid to banks, etc.)	17a	10,000	Dues and publications—$1,000		
b Other	17b		Laundry—$5,000		
18 Legal and professional services	18	8,000			
19 Office expense	19	3,000			
20 Pension and profit-sharing plans	20	8,000			
21 Rent or lease:					
a Machinery and equipment	21a				
b Other business property	21b	20,000		28	6,000

29 Add amounts in columns for lines 8 through 28. These are your **total expenses** ▶	29	393,000
30 Net profit or (loss). Subtract line 29 from line 7. If a profit, enter here and on Form 1040, line 12, and on Schedule SE, line 2. If a loss, you MUST go on to line 31. (Fiduciaries, see Instructions.)	30	57,000

31 If you have a loss, you MUST check the box that describes your investment in this activity (see Instructions). If you checked 31a, enter the loss on Form 1040, line 12, and Schedule SE, line 2. If you checked 31b, you MUST attach **Form 6198.**
31a ☐ All investment is at risk.
31b ☐ Some investment is not at risk.

For Paperwork Reduction Act Notice, see Form 1040 Instructions.   Schedule C (Form 1040) 1989

business person must make is determining the legal form of operation: sole proprietorship, partnership, corporation, or one of their hybrid forms such as limited partnership and S Corporation.

Each of these entities offers tax advantages and disadvantages. Tax considerations, however, are only one factor in such a decision. There are practical business and legal considerations, as well as governmental regulatory requirements. The following sections briefly discuss the forms of business organization and the major advantages and limitations of each. Exhibit 15.6 presents an outline of this information.

Exhibit 15.6   Operating Forms for the Hospitality Business

	Sole Proprietorship	Partnership		Corporation	
		General	Limited	Regular	S Corporation
Instrument of Creation	None (assumed name state-ment may be required)	Agreement – oral or written	Certificate of limited partnership	Articles of incorporation	Articles of incorporation, file election with IRS
Organizational Documents	None	Partnership Agreement	Certificate of limited partnership agreement	Articles of incorporation, bylaws, minutes	Articles of incorporation, bylaws, minutes
Type of Tax Return	Schedule C for Form 1040	Form 1065	Form 1065	Form 1120	Form 1120S
Tax Rates	Individual	Individual	Individual	Corporate	Individual
Limited Liability	No	No	Yes – Limited Partners; No – General Partners	Yes	Yes
Recognition of Losses	Owner	Partners	Partners	Corporation	Shareholders

Sole Proprietorship

The **sole proprietorship** is the commonest form of organization in the hospitality industry. As the name implies, the business is owned by a single individual. This form of organization is popular because it is easy to form. Establishing a sole proprietorship may only require filing an assumed business name statement with the proper authorities (such as the county government) and filing a Schedule C on the owner's federal, state, and local tax returns.

The following list indicates some advantages of the sole proprietorship form of organization.

1. Proprietorship eliminates double taxation (defined later under corporate disadvantages). Income is reported only on the owner's individual tax return.

2. Expected losses during start-up and the early years can offset the owner's other income. Losses that exceed the owner's other income may result in net operating losses that can be used to recover some or all of the owner's taxes for the previous year(s).

3. Business tax credits retain their character—that is, if they are tax credits to the business, they are tax credits to be used directly by the owner.

4. The owner maintains complete control over the business by being the sole owner.

Several disadvantages may discourage a hospitality business owner from operating as a sole proprietor. These disadvantages include:

1. Hospitality operations may be risky. The sole proprietor does not enjoy the limited liability available with some other organizational forms; that is, he or she is personally liable for the obligations of the business. However, adequate insurance can at least partially alleviate this problem.

2. Most fringe benefits are severely limited or completely disallowed as deducted tax expenses if they are for the benefit of the sole proprietor. For example, only 25% of the cost of medical insurance for the sole proprietor can be included as a deductible tax expense.

3. The transfer of a portion of the ownership interest in a sole proprietorship requires a change to either partnership or corporate form. In addition, the continuity of the business is not assured at the death of the owner. By contrast, a corporation is legally separate from its owners.

4. The sole proprietor is generally unable to raise large amounts of capital, while a corporation may be able to issue stock or sell bonds.

The sole proprietorship may be an ideal form of organization if the anticipated risk is minimal and is covered by insurance, if the owner is either unable or unwilling to maintain the necessary organizational documents and tax returns of more complicated business entities, and if the business does not require extensive borrowing.

Partnerships   The **partnership** consists of two or more owners joined together, but not incorporated, for the purpose of operating a business. A partnership offers most of the tax and other advantages and disadvantages of a sole proprietorship. The advantages include the following:

1. More than one owner results in greater financial strength. The added capital can provide greater resources for expansion of the business.

2. Partnership arrangements allow flexibility in the allocation of profits, losses, and certain tax benefits among the owners. Such allocations must be reasonable and justified as having economic substance in order to satisfy the IRS.

3. Profits, losses, and tax credits pass through the partnership entity to the owners' individual returns, thus preventing double taxation.

4. Control of the business resides with the partners.

Major disadvantages of the partnership include the following:

1. Partners are taxed on their share of the profits, regardless of whether the partnership actually provides a cash distribution to the partners.

2. Partners may become frustrated in sharing the decision-making process. They may hold different opinions, and, theoretically, each has an equal right to manage the business.

3. Partners generally have unlimited legal liability for the obligations of the business. This can be a significant factor when uninsurable business risks exist. This disadvantage may be partially overcome by the use of a limited partnership form of organization.

Limited Partnerships

A **limited partnership** is a partnership of two or more individuals having at least one **general partner** (a partner with unlimited liability) and at least one **limited partner**. Unlike a general partnership agreement (which can be oral), the limited partnership agreement must be in writing, and the **certificate of limited partnership** must be filed with the proper governmental authorities. Most states regulate the public sale of limited partnership interests. The process of filing documents with the Securities and Exchange Commission to sell limited partnership interests may result in sizable legal fees and other costs. Smaller private issues (issues not generally available to the general public) generally seek an exemption from registration.

The major distinguishing feature of limited partnerships is the limited liability afforded to limited partners: their liabilities are limited to their investments. However, limited partners cannot actively participate in controlling or managing the business. If they do, they will generally lose their limited liability status in any legal matters.

In recent years, the limited partnership has become an attractive financing vehicle for the expansion of hospitality operations. Limited partnerships have been formed for specific projects, with the hospitality establishment acting as the general partner and investors as the limited partners. The limited partnership enables the hospitality establishment to obtain needed capital and still maintain control over operations.

The basic tax advantages available to general partners are also available to limited partners. In addition to limited liability, another advantage available to limited partners (but not to general partners) is that, within certain limits, the limited partners' interests may be assigned without prior approval of the general partners.

Corporations

A **corporation** is a legal entity created by a state or another political authority. The corporation receives a charter or articles of incorporation and has the following general characteristics:

1. An exclusive name
2. Continued existence independent of its stockholders
3. Paid-in capital represented by transferred shares of capital stock
4. Limited liability for its owners
5. Overall control vested in its directors

While hospitality businesses organized as sole proprietorships

Exhibit 15.7 Illustration of Double Taxation

	Dollars	Percentage
Corporate Pre-tax Income over $100,000	$100,000	100.00%
Less: Corporate Tax (39%)	39,000	39.00
Dividend Distribution	61,000	61.00
Less: Individual Income Taxes (33%)	20,130	20.13
After-Tax Benefit to Stockholder	$ 40,870	40.87%

account for the largest number of businesses, hospitality corporations account for the greatest volume in terms of sales, assets, profits, and employees. In a recent year, revenues from corporate lodging businesses totaled nearly two-thirds of the total lodging revenues across the United States.[3] Several hospitality corporations, such as Holiday Corporation, Marriott Corporation, and McDonald's Corporation have annual sales in excess of $2 billion. The major advantages of the corporate form over other forms of business organization include the following:

1. Its shareholders' liability is normally limited to their investments.

2. Owners are taxed only on distributed profits.

3. Employees can be motivated by equity participation (such as stock bonus plans and stock options) and by certain tax-favored fringe benefits.

4. Equity capital can be raised by selling capital stock to the public.

5. A corporation can use its stock to acquire other companies and thereby offer the sellers a tax-free exchange.

6. Tax rates are often lower for small corporations than for individuals.

7. There is free transferability of capital stock by owners.

8. The corporation exists independently of the owners.

As with the other forms of business organization, there are disadvantages of the corporate form. Some of these include the following:

1. **Double taxation**—corporate profits are taxed twice. First, they are taxed on the corporation's own income tax. Then, any profits paid out as dividends are considered taxable income to the individual stockholders. Exhibit 15.7 illustrates that the effective tax rate on the second $100,000 of corporate pre-tax income could be as high as 59% (based on 1989 tax rates). The calculations assume that the individual stockholder/taxpayer's marginal tax rate is 33% and that all after-tax profits are distributed. Thus, the corporate tax of 39% plus the individual tax of 20% (33% of 61%) equals 59%, the

effective tax rate. If this business had been unincorporated, the maximum effective tax rate would have been only 33%.

2. The highest corporate tax rates are higher than the highest individual tax rates (39% compared to 33%).

3. The corporation cannot pass on tax advantages (such as operating losses and tax credits) which might be more advantageous to the owners than to the corporation.

S Corporation

Some of the tax drawbacks of the corporate form of organization can be overcome by filing as an **S Corporation** (the *S* merely refers to subchapter S of the code). In essence, this filing allows the corporation to be taxed like a partnership.

The philosophy behind the S Corporation provisions of the Internal Revenue Code is that a firm should be able to select its form of organization free of tax considerations. The S Corporation is a hybrid form allowing limited liability for owners but avoiding the corporate "curses" of double taxation and higher corporate tax rates.

To qualify as an S Corporation, the corporation must meet several tests, including, but not limited to, (1) having 35 or fewer stockholders, (2) being a domestic corporation that is not a member of a controlled group, and (3) having only one class of stock.

This form of organization can be very useful when corporate losses are anticipated and owners have taxable income that can absorb the losses. It can also be very useful when corporations are profitable without having uses for extra capital; since profits are passed through to stockholders, they are not taxed as accumulated earnings.

Minimizing Taxes

As pointed out earlier, all taxpayers wish to pay as little tax as possible. An example will illustrate how a business can accomplish this end. The owners/managers of a corporation may receive compensation in the form of fringe benefits, salary, and dividends; this package should be structured to minimize taxes. Consider the taxability of these three compensation elements to both the corporation and the sole stockholder:

	C Corporation	Owner/Manager
Fringe benefits	Deductible	Non-taxable
Salary	Deductible	Taxable
Dividends	Non-deductible	Taxable

Certain fringe benefits, such as health insurance, are a tax-deductible expense for a **C Corporation** (the term often used in tax literature to refer to all non–S Corporations) and are not taxable to the recipient, in this case the owner/manager. On the other hand, the corporation may deduct salaries in determining its federal income taxes, but the owner/manager must pay taxes on his/her own salary. Dividends are not a deductible expense to the corporation, and they are taxable to the owner/manager.

To further illustrate these concepts, consider George Brown, the sole stockholder of Brown's Eatery, an incorporated restaurant business.

George has invested $200,000 in the business. In 19X1, he received a salary of $100,000 and the business had net income of $100,000. George received no fringe benefits or dividends.

For the purpose of simplicity, assume a corporate tax rate of 20% on the first $200,000 of taxable income and an individual tax rate of 25% on the first $100,000 of earnings. George Brown and Brown's Eatery paid taxes in 19X1 totaling $45,000, determined as follows:

Taxpayer	Taxable Income	Tax Rate	Taxes
Brown's Eatery	$100,000	20%	$20,000
George Brown	100,000	25%	25,000
		Total	$45,000

In this case, the IRS may rule that part of George Brown's salary is dividends, especially if his salary is considered unreasonably high. Assume that they rule $20,000 of his salary to be dividends. The total taxes increase by $4,000 to $49,000—the salary deduction of $20,000 denied to the corporation times the corporation's tax rate of 20%.

The IRS considers the following factors in determining whether salaries are reasonable:

- The amounts being paid by corporations of similar size in the same industry

- The economic conditions and salary levels in the geographic region in which the corporation operates

- The nature of the shareholder/employee responsibilities and the amount of time the shareholder/employee devotes to the business

- The shareholder/employee's qualifications in terms of education and experience

The owner/manager must formally document the basis of a relatively large salary; that is, he or she must explain the duties and functions performed to justify the salary. The corporation's board of directors should approve the owner/manager's salary.

In this example, we initially assumed that George did not receive any fringe benefits. Suppose that George's effective salary of $80,000 is reduced to $70,000 and he receives $10,000 in fringe benefits (such as health and life insurance). Assume that these fringe benefits are 100% deductible by the corporation and non-taxable to George. The taxes paid by George and his corporation now total $44,500, determined as follows:

Taxpayer	Taxable Income	Tax Rate	Taxes
Brown's Eatery	$110,000*	20%	$22,000
George Brown	90,000**	25%	22,500
		Total	$44,500

*original net income	$100,000
salary declared by IRS as dividends	20,000
cost of fringe benefits	(10,000)
Total	$110,000

**salary	$70,000
dividends	20,000
Total	$90,000

The total tax bill is $4,500 less than it would be if Brown's Eatery provided George with no fringe benefits. The $4,500 reduction is, in effect, the combined tax rates multiplied by the cost of the fringe benefits:

$$(.20 + .25)\$10,000 = \underline{\$4,500}$$

Thus, to minimize taxes, the preferred order is fringe benefits, salary, and dividends. However, just as the IRS is vigilant to determine that salaries are reasonable and do not include dividends, the IRS also has rules regarding fringe benefits. Certain fringe benefits are taxable, such as the premiums paid on life insurance policies when the insurance coverage exceeds $50,000 and the insured is the owner of the policy. The IRS treats the premium on the excess coverage as taxable income to the benefiting employee.

It might appear at this point that a small C Corporation is better off not declaring dividends above a required minimum which satisfies the IRS. However, if corporations accumulate earnings in order to avoid double taxation, they may be subject to an **accumulated earnings tax**. The current rate is 28% on accumulated earnings in excess of $250,000. Specifics of this tax are beyond the scope of this text; however, the tax can be avoided by showing a reasonable need for accumulating earnings (such as business expansion).

How would George Brown's taxes changes if he had filed as an S Corporation? This example assumes that the fringe benefits under an S Corporation would be non-taxable, as they were for the C Corporation. The restaurant's taxable income of $110,000 would be passed directly to George for tax purposes. Therefore, his 19X1 taxes would have been $50,000, determined as follows:

George's salary	$ 90,000
Brown's Eatery income taxable to George	110,000
Total taxable income	200,000
George's tax rate	× .25
Total taxes	$ 50,000

Thus, the S Corporation form of organization costs George an extra $5,500. This result is due entirely to the 5% difference in the Eatery's tax rate of 20% as a C Corporation and George's tax rate of 25%.

The tax rates vary for C Corporations and individuals. The top rates are higher for corporations than individuals, as discussed before. However, at lower taxable income levels, individual rates exceed corporate rates. Thus, based on the assumed rates used in our illustration, the C Corporation is better than the S Corporation for Brown's Eatery.

The 1989 federal tax rate schedules for individuals and corporations were as follows:

Individual (Married filing joint)

Taxable Income	Tax Rate
$0–30,950	15%
$30,950.01–74,850	$4,642.50 + 28% of the amount over $30,950
$74,850.01–155,320	$16,934.50 + 33% of the amount over $74,850
over $155,320	varies

Corporation

Taxable Income	Tax Rate
$0–50,000	15%
$50,000.01–75,000	$7,500 + 25% of the amount over $50,000
$75,000.01–100,000	$13,750 + 34% of the amount over $75,000
$100,000.01–335,000	$22,250 + 39% of the amount over $100,000
over $335,000	$113,900 + 34% of the amount over $335,000

For example, $100,000 of taxable income to a married individual filing a joint return results in federal income taxes of $25,234.00.

First	$ 30,950	×	.15	= $	4,642.50
Next	43,900	×	.28	=	12,292.00
Next	25,150	×	.33	=	8,299.50
Total	$100,000				$25,234.00

Thus, the effective average rate is 25.23%.

For a C Corporation, the first $100,000 is taxed as follows:

First	$ 50,000	×	.15	=	$ 7,500
Next	25,000	×	.25	=	6,250
Next	25,000	×	.34	=	8,500
Total	$100,000				$ 22,250

Thus, the effective average rate is 22.25%.

Accounting Methods

There are different accounting methods available. After the legal form of operation has been chosen, management must determine which accounting method best reflects the type of business and provides optimum ability to minimize or postpone taxes. Minimizing or postponing taxes is achieved by effectively timing the recognition of income and deduction of expenses.

Cash Method Versus Accrual Method

Tax laws require the taxpayer to use the method of accounting which most clearly reflects income. The accrual method of accounting is appropriate for taxpayers with significant inventories. Further, the use of the accrual method of accounting is required if the taxpayer is a corporation or a partnership with a C Corporation as a partner. However, if the business is small (average annual sales of $5,000,000 or less), the cash method of accounting may be used for tax purposes. Under this method, items of income and expense are generally reported for tax purposes when cash is actually received or paid out.

Even under the cash method, there are exceptions. For example, fixed assets must generally be depreciated over the life of the asset rather than being deducted as an expense in the year paid. Exhibit 15.3 shows that Snicker's Restaurant was accounted for on a cash basis. For tax purposes, food inventories were $–0– as shown on Schedule C; however, there was depreciation of $30,000 for 1989.

A cash-basis taxpayer has some flexibility in reporting income and expenses. The timing of income collection, or the payment of expenses, can be controlled to some extent, particularly near year-end.

The accrual method of accounting reports income when it is earned, rather than when the cash is collected. It reflects expenses when they are incurred, rather than when they are paid. As is the case with many areas of tax law, there are exceptions to the general rule. Under the accrual method, some items of income (such as advance rentals) are taxed when collected rather than when earned. Similarly, an expense item must be fixed and determinable before it can be deducted for tax purposes. Estimated expenses, while generally acceptable for financial accounting, may not be deducted for tax reporting until all factors which affect the expense item have become fixed and determinable.

Installment Sales Method

For financial accounting purposes, when goods or property is sold on the installment method (that is, the sales price is received in periodic payments over time), the entire sales price is recognized at the time of sale, and the entire cost of goods sold deducted as an expense of sale. Tax reporting, however, allows recognizing the profit on sales made on the installment method on a pro rated basis as cash is received. This method is frequently chosen upon the sale of a business such as a hotel or restaurant.

Accounting Income Versus Taxable Income

Thus far, the importance of tax planning for a transaction at an early stage of its development has been emphasized. In addition, several options for selecting the legal entity within which to conduct a business have been presented. After the form of organization is selected, the method of accounting (cash versus accrual) most suitable for mitigating the tax costs of operation is chosen. All of these choices are made with the overall business objectives of the operation in mind.

These choices can result in differences between the amount and timing of income or expenses reported in financial statements and the amounts reported on the tax return. Other tax requirements or choices can cause further differences in the amount or timing of the reporting of income and expense.

Accelerated Depreciation

Tax legislation in 1981 and 1982 liberalized tax depreciation rules with enactment of an Accelerated Cost Recovery System (ACRS) which provided for faster recovery (depreciation) of capital expenditures. The 1986 tax law significantly tightened the tax rules for depreciating real estate, but retained the liberal rules for depreciating personal property such as

Exhibit 15.8   Depreciation of Equipment for Tax and Financial Reporting Purposes

Year	MACRS Recovery[1]	Straight-Line Recovery[2]	Difference
19X1	$ 200,000	$ 100,000	$ 100,000
19X2	320,000	100,000	220,000
19X3	192,000	100,000	92,000
19X4	115,200	100,000	15,200
19X5	115,200	100,000	15,200
19X6	57,600	100,000	(42,400)
19X7	0	100,000	(100,000)
19X8	0	100,000	(100,000)
19X9	0	100,000	(100,000)
19X0	0	100,000	(100,000)
Total	$1,000,000	$1,000,000	$0

[1]The MACRS for 5-year tax life is calculated using the double declining method and the half-year convention; that is, one half of a year's depreciation is taken in the year of the purchase (19X1) and one half in 19X6.

1st year	–	20.00%
2nd year	–	32.00
3rd year	–	19.20
4th year	–	11.52
5th year	–	11.52
6th year	–	5.76
Total		100.00%

[2]Assuming a zero salvage value. Annual depreciation is determined by dividing the cost ($1,000,000) by the life (10 years) to equal the annual depreciation ($100,000).

equipment and furniture. Since 1986, the depreciation rules have been based on the **Modified Accelerated Cost Recovery System (MACRS)**.

In financial accounting, a building may be depreciated over 30 years or more. MACRS currently allows, for tax purposes, recovery over 31.5 years. Similarly, furniture and equipment may be depreciated over seven to ten years (or more) for financial accounting purposes, while the same items are depreciated for tax purposes over five years under MACRS. Thus, the timing of reporting net income for financial purposes can be significantly different from that for taxable income.

This situation will be reversed in the later years of an asset's life; the deduction for depreciation, especially with furniture and equipment, will be greater for financial accounting than for tax accounting. At the end of the asset's life, the deduction for depreciation will be the same in total for both financial reporting and tax accounting. The difference is in the timing of the deduction.

Exhibit 15.8 uses a purchase of $1,000,000 worth of equipment to illustrate the difference between MACRS recovery expense and depreciation using the straight-line method. For tax purposes, the MACRS allows the cost of the equipment to be recovered over five years, while for financial reporting purposes, the hospitality operation chooses to depreciate the equipment over ten years using the straight-line method. In the first five years, MACRS results in $442,400 more expense (cost recovery) than the straight-line method, while the reverse results in the last five years.

Pre-Opening Expenses

For many years, hospitality firms were able to deduct, for tax purposes, many expenses as they were incurred before formally opening a new hotel, even if such expenses were deferred for financial reporting purposes. This was especially true if the operation was not the first hotel in the business. The current tax law disallows immediate write-off and requires pre-opening expenses to be amortized over a five-year period beginning with the month the hotel or restaurant opens for business.

First-Year Losses

First-year losses of a hospitality operation are usually capitalized as a deferred charge and amortized over several years for financial accounting purposes. However, for tax purposes, such costs are generally deductible as incurred, so taxable income is lower than financial accounting income, improving the first-year cash flow by deferring taxes. This situation reverses after the first year. As the first-year losses are amortized for financial accounting with no offsetting amortization for tax accounting, the result is a higher taxable income than book income and a corresponding higher tax payment.

Loss Carrybacks and Carryforwards

A final example of the differences between financial and tax accounting is the treatment of operating losses sustained by a business. Current tax laws allow a net operating loss to be carried back and applied as a deduction against prior taxable income, resulting in a refund of taxes previously paid. Losses may be carried back three years and carried forward fifteen years.

For financial accounting purposes, an operating loss will generally flow through to reported earnings. In certain situations, the tax benefit may then reduce this pre-tax book loss by up to the amount of previously paid taxes. Financial accounting rules permit the recording of a tax benefit on an operating loss if it can be carried back and used against taxable income for the previous year. For example, assume that an enterprise incurs a $100,000 pre-tax loss which can be carried back against prior years' taxable income. Further assume that $30,000 of previously paid taxes can be recovered. The pre-tax loss is then reduced by the $30,000 recovery.

State and Municipal Taxes

Until recently, managers paid little attention to state and local taxes because rates were low and the amounts involved did not warrant serious study. This has changed in recent years as state and local governments have been increasing tax rates and seeking new ways to generate tax revenues. Today's manager should realize that state and local taxes also require planning to reduce the overall tax burden.

The financial manager of a multi-state operation should be aware that the manner in which business is conducted in a state determines whether and how the business is subject to that state's tax laws. Early tax planning is as important here as it is in all areas of tax planning.

Planning is also important in a multi-corporate form of business when one corporate unit is profitable and a second is unprofitable. The manager should investigate whether state tax laws allow consolidation of operations to offset the income of one corporation with the loss of another, minimizing the total tax burden. If state laws do not permit consolidation and the mix of profit and loss is expected to continue for some time, the manager should consider whether a corporate reorganization is desirable. A reorganization which merged the loss operation into the profitable one would achieve the same tax results as filing a consolidated return. Of course, in this situation, other business objectives should also be weighed.

Property Taxes

Taxes levied on real estate and personal property such as furniture, fixtures, and equipment are commonly called **property taxes**. In recent years, property taxes for hotels have approximated 3% of gross revenues, which may seem insignificant. However, a .5% reduction for a hotel with $20,000,000 in sales would save the business $100,000.

Property taxes are generally levied at the local level. The tax is a result of the assessed value of the property and the tax rate. Property taxes differ by state and locality; for example, the general property tax formula in Michigan is:

$$\text{Property Taxes} = \frac{\text{Assessed Valuation}}{1,000} \times \text{Tax Rate}$$

In this formula, the **assessed valuation** is the value the tax assessor places on the property to be taxed. The tax rate is stated in *mills*, which is tax dollars per $1,000 of assessed valuation. Assume that Rocky's Hotel had an assessed valuation of $10,000,000 and a tax rate of 60 mills. The annual property tax would be calculated as follows:

$$\begin{aligned}
\text{Property Taxes} &= \frac{10,000,000}{1,000} \times 60 \\
&= 10,000 \times 60 \\
&= \$600,000
\end{aligned}$$

Although property taxes are normally viewed as a fixed cost (that is, not controllable by management), management should challenge any assessed valuation considered to be excessive. For example, in Michigan the assessed valuation is by law 50% of market value. Assume that Rocky's Hotel had recently been purchased for $18,000,000. Based on Michigan law, the assessed valuation for Rocky's Hotel should be reduced to $9,000,000, which is 50% of the market price. The $1,000,000 assessed valuation reduction, given the tax rate of 60 mills, reduces property taxes by $60,000 annually.

Summary

Governments levy income taxes to raise the revenue they need to provide their constituents with services and to achieve a variety of social goals. Both individuals and businesses pay taxes. Most financial business decisions have tax implications. Therefore, hospitality managers must understand taxes in order to make sound decisions.

Federal income taxes are based on a self-reporting system, whereby the taxpayer prepares the appropriate tax forms. For the individual, tax considerations include income, adjustments to income, deductions, exemptions, credits, other taxes, and taxes paid. Form 1040, Form 1040A, or Form 1040EZ must be filed by all qualifying taxpayers.

Tax avoidance refers to legally paying the least amount of tax. Tax evasion is the illegal attempt to pay less or no tax. Hospitality managers should strive for tax avoidance.

One major tax consideration is the form of organization a business selects. The major forms are the sole proprietorship, the partnership, and the corporation, while hybrid forms include the limited partnership and the S Corporation. Each form offers advantages and disadvantages. The disadvantage of individual unlimited liability can be overcome by incorporating; however, incorporation results in double taxation. Avoiding double taxation and unlimited liability can be achieved by filing as an S Corporation; however, S Corporations are limited to one type of stock and 35 or fewer stockholders. An operation should consider the size, goals, and riskiness of its business, then select a form which minimizes the disadvantages and maximizes the advantages.

Just as there are different business forms, there are different accounting methods. Businesses must decide whether cash accounting or accrual accounting better meets their needs. There are also differences between accounting for financial purposes and accounting for tax purposes. These differences may involve the treatments of depreciation, pre-opening expenses, first-year losses, and loss carrybacks and carryforwards.

State, municipal, and property taxes all deserve the manager's attention. These taxes, which used to be negligible, have been growing. Although property taxes are thought of as fixed expenses, attentive managers may be able to successfully challenge assessed valuations and reduce the property tax burden.

Endnotes

1. Letter to Jean Baptiste Le Roy, 13 Nov. 1789.

2. Commissioner v. Newman (CA-2), 47–1 USTC 99175, 159 Fed.(2d)848.

3. Albert J. Gomes, *Hospitality in Transition* (New York: American Hotel & Motel Association, 1985).

Key Terms

accumulated earnings tax	certificate of limited partnership
assessed valuation	corporation
C Corporation	double taxation

general partner
income exclusions
limited partner
limited partnership
loss carrybacks
loss carryforwards
Modified Accelerated Cost
   Recovery System (MACRS)

partnership
property taxes
S Corporation
sole proprietorship
tax avoidance
tax credits
tax deductions
tax evasion

Discussion Questions

1. What are five types of income that must be reported on an individual's tax return?

2. How do tax deductions differ from tax credits?

3. What are the major advantages of a sole proprietorship?

4. What are the major advantages of a corporation?

5. How may the disadvantage of unlimited liability be overcome in selecting a form of organization?

6. Why are limited partnerships so useful in raising capital funds for hospitality operations?

7. How does accelerated depreciation (as opposed to straight-line depreciation) save profitable hospitality businesses tax dollars?

8. What are two limitations to S Corporations?

9. What is double taxation?

10. Under what circumstances is the sole proprietorship form best?

Problems

Problem 15.1

Leslie Boyer is considering opening a franchised quick-service restaurant (QSR). He believes that in a typical year he will gross nearly $1,200,000 and net $100,000 before income taxes. Angela, his wife, is expected to have taxable income of $100,000 from her apartment rentals. Her business is not incorporated. Leslie wants to avoid double taxation but also wants to limit his liability.

Required

1. What form of organization do you suggest?

2. How might Leslie overcome the liability problem without incorporating?

Problem 15.2

Based on the information in the previous problem, calculate income taxes for the Boyers (ignore exemptions and deductions) and their businesses in the following situations:

1. Assume that the Boyers' average tax rate is 25% and that both the QSR and the real estate business are unincorporated.

2. Assume that the Boyers' average tax rate is 25%, the average corporate rate is 20%, and the QSR is incorporated.

3. Assume the same situation as in B above and that the QSR pays Leslie $50,000 in dividends that are taxed at the Boyers' average tax rate.

4. Assume that the Boyers' average tax rate is 25%, the average corporate rate is 20%, and the QSR is incorporated but is treated as an S Corporation for tax purposes.

Problem 15.3

Jerome Woods, owner of Woods Place, wants to know the potential tax liability of his restaurant given various levels of taxable income and different forms of organization. Assume that Woods Place potentially generates pre-tax income at three levels:

Low level	$50,000
Medium level	$80,000
High level	$150,000

Required:

1. Using the 1989 tax rates, calculate the income tax liability if Woods Place is incorporated and files its tax returns as a C Corporation.

2. Using the 1989 tax rates for a married individual filing jointly, calculate the income tax liability for Jerome Woods, assuming Woods Place is unincorporated. (Ignore Jerome's deductions and exemptions.)

Problem 15.4

Nicole Bustle is earning a mint selling real estate. During the past five years, she has had average annual taxable income of $200,000. Her husband, Richie, would like to open a 100-unit motor hotel. The feasibility study conducted for the lodging facility suggests losses of $150,000, $100,000, and $50,000 for the first three years, respectively. The following three years, the motor hotel is expected to generate pre-tax profits of $100,000 per year. Assume that the Bustles' average tax rate is 28%. Further assume that the average corporate tax rate is 20% and that corporate tax losses can be carried forward for up to five years.

Required:

Based on the above information, how should Richie Bustle organize his motor hotel business? Note: consider providing "tax savings" to support your answer.

Problem 15.5

J. Deere Restaurants, Inc., must decide whether to use the cash or accrual method of accounting for tax purposes. The chairperson, John Deere, has provided you with the following information:

	Basis	
	Cash	Accrual
Sales	$1,000,000	$1,100,000
Cost of Sales	350,000	325,000
Labor	300,000	310,000
Other Expenses (excluding taxes)	200,000	190,000

John believes that the approach which minimizes taxes for the first year is the preferred method. Assume that the taxes for J. Deere Restaurants, Inc., will be based on the following tax structure:

Taxable Income	Tax Rate
$0–50,000	15%
$50,000.01–75,000	$7,500 + 25% of the amount over $50,000
$75,000.01–100,000	$13,750 + 34% of the amount over $75,000
$100,000.01–335,000	$22,250 + 39% of the amount over $100,000
over $335,000	$113,900 + 34% of the amount over $335,000

Required:

Determine which method J. Deere Restaurants, Inc., should use.

Problem 15.6

The Waterloo Inn is an unincorporated lodging facility owned by James Waters. During 19X1, the inn provided its owner with $55,000 in net income. In addition, James received $1,000 in interest and dividend income for 19X1. James's deductions and exemptions for 19X1 are as follows:

Exemptions: his wife, Sally, and their two children, Lisa and Dianne. Assume that $2,000 is allowed for each exemption.

Deductions:	Home mortgage interest	$7,000
	Real estate taxes	3,000
	Contributions	5,000

Since the above deductions exceed the standard deduction, James will itemize deductions.

James also must pay self-employment taxes of 15.3% on his first $51,300 of earned income. He has paid estimated federal income taxes and self-employment taxes of $20,000 during 19X1.

Required:

1. Compute James Waters' self-employment taxes for 19X1.

2. Compute his federal income taxes for 19X1. Assume that Sally and James are filing a joint return and that their average tax rate is 28%. (Hint: use Exhibits 15.3 through 15.5 as a guide for determining parts 2 and 3 of this problem.)

3. Determine how much Mr. Waters owes or has coming from the federal government for 19X1.

Problem 15.7

The Celtic Corporation has purchased $2,000,000 worth of equipment for its hotels in the current year. The President, Fred Boston, has heard that using the MACRS recovery offers cash savings over the straight-line method. The equipment could be depreciated over five years for tax purposes using the recovery rates shown in Exhibit 15.8. It could also be depreciated over ten years using the straight-line method and have zero salvage value. The marginal tax rate for the Celtic Corporation is 30%. Taxes saved due to the difference between MACRS and straight-line depreciation are invested at the end of each year at 10% interest compounded annually.

Required:

1. Determine the amount of the "tax savings fund" from taxes saved and interest earned over the first five years. Use the half-year conversion for depreciation as shown in Exhibit 15.8.

2. Calculate the interest earned over the ten-year period. Assume that for the sixth through tenth years the taxes paid due to excess straight-line depreciation over MACRS comes at the end of each year from the "tax savings fund."

Problem 15.8

George Borchgrevink, the owner of Borch's Motel, has recently learned about the concept of double taxation. He wants to know how much tax he and his incorporated motel would pay in each of the following situations.

1. Borch's Motel earns pre-tax income of $100,000 after paying George a salary of $50,000 during 19X1. Borch's Motel also pays George $50,000 in dividends during 19X1.

2. Borch's Motel earns pre-tax income of $80,000 after paying George a salary of $70,000 during 19X1. Borch's Motel also pays George $30,000 in dividends during 19X1.

3. Borch's Motel earns pre-tax income of $60,000 after paying George a salary of $90,000 during 19X1. Borch's Motel also pays George $10,000 in dividends during 19X1.

Required:

1. Ignoring George's deductions and exemptions, calculate the total income taxes paid by George and his corporation for each of the above situations, using an average corporate tax rate of 20% and an average individual tax rate of 25%.

2. Ignoring George's deductions and exemptions, calculate the total income taxes paid by George and his corporation for each of the above situations, using an average corporate tax rate of 25% and an average individual tax rate of 20%.

Problem 15.9

Zera Adams owns a very successful food service chain. The chain is incorporated and generates net income of $300,000 each year. Her salary is $40,000 a year and she receives no fringe benefits. The food service chain pays her dividends equal to 40% of its net income each year. Zera's average tax rate is 28%. The corporate income tax rates are as follows:

Taxable Income	Tax Rate
$0–50,000	15%
$50,000.01–75,000	$7,500 + 25% of the amount over $50,000
over $75,000	$13,750 + 34% of the amount over $75,000

Zera is an excellent owner/manager, but does not know much about taxes. At a recent conference for entrepreneurs, she heard about S Corporations, double taxation, excessive salary being considered dividends, and other related matters. She is the sole owner of her business and insists the business retain its corporate form; however, she wants to minimize taxes.

Required:

1. Based on the above information, calculate the income taxes paid by the corporation and Zera (ignore deductions and exemptions in calculating her personal income taxes).

2. How would you advise Zera to minimize her taxes? Consider that the minimum dividends would have to be 12% of net income and the maximum salary could be $100,000. The maximum fringe benefits would cost $20,000. Assume that these fringe benefits are deductible to the corporation and nontaxable to zero. She still wants to receive salary, dividends, and fringe benefits totaling $160,000.

3. Based on your advice, what would be the tax reduction?

Problem 15.10

Gayle Koelling owns and manages the unincorporated Christmas Inn. She and her husband Melvin file a joint return. Their tax situation for 19X2 is as follows:

A.	Income	
	Income from the Christmas Inn	$60,000
	Interest income	600
	Dividend income	2,000
	Capital gain from sale of investment	10,000
	Melvin's salary	75,000
B.	Adjustments to Income	
	Keogh retirement plan investment	$10,000
C.	Exemptions	
	Four (two children) at $2,000 each	
D.	Itemized Deductions (Schedule A)	
	Medical	$3,000

Property taxes	4,000
State income taxes	4,000
Intangibles tax	300
Home mortgage interest	6,000
Personal interest	1,500
Charitable contributions	8,000

E. Tax Rate

Average federal income tax rate—25%

Self employment tax rate—15.3% on the first $51,300 of earned income

Note: Social security taxes were properly withheld from Melvin's paychecks. Self-employment taxes need to be calculated for Gayle.

F. Tax Payments
- Melvin's employer withheld $10,000 of federal income tax during 19X2.
- Gayle paid estimated taxes of $20,000 during 19X2.

Required:

Calculate the amount of federal taxes due or to be refunded to the Koellings for 19X2. Note: Follow Schedule A (Exhibit 15.4) to determine the deductibility of the Koellings' itemized deductions in determining their taxable income.

Appendix A
Uniform Systems Schedules

ROOMS—SCHEDULE 1

	Current Period
REVENUE	
Transient—Regular	$
Transient—Group	
Permanent	
Other	_____
Total Revenue	
ALLOWANCES	_____
NET REVENUE	_____
EXPENSES	
Salaries and Wages	
Employee Benefits	_____
Total Payroll and Related Expenses	_____
Other Expenses	
Commissions	
Contract Cleaning	
Guest Transportation	
Laundry and Dry Cleaning	
Linen	
Operating Supplies	
Reservations	
Uniforms	
Other	_____
Total Other Expenses	_____
DEPARTMENTAL INCOME (LOSS)	$_____

FOOD AND BEVERAGE—SCHEDULE 2

	Current Period		
	Food	Beverage	Total
REVENUE	$_____	$_____	$_____
ALLOWANCES	_____	_____	_____
NET REVENUE	_____	_____	_____
COST OF FOOD AND BEVERAGE SALES			
Cost of Food and Beverage Consumed			
Less: Cost of Employee Meals	_____	_____	_____
Net Cost of Food and Beverage Sales	_____	_____	_____
OTHER INCOME			
Meeting Room Rentals			
Cover Charges			
Miscellaneous Banquet Income			
Miscellaneous Other Income			
Other Cost of Sales	_____	_____	_____
Net Other Income	_____	_____	_____
GROSS PROFIT (LOSS)	$_____	$_____	$_____
EXPENSES			
Salaries and Wages	$_____	$_____	$_____
Employee Benefits	_____	_____	_____
Total Payroll and Related Expenses	$_____	$_____	$_____
Other Expenses			
China, Glassware, Silver, and Linen			
Contract Cleaning			
Kitchen Fuel			
Laundry and Dry Cleaning			
Licenses			
Music and Entertainment			
Operating Supplies			
Uniforms			
Other			_____
Total Other Expenses			_____
DEPARTMENTAL INCOME (LOSS)			$_____

TELEPHONE—SCHEDULE 3

	Current Period
REVENUE	
Local	$
Long-Distance	
Service Charges	
Pay Station	
Total Revenue	
ALLOWANCES	
NET REVENUE	
COST OF CALLS	
Local	
Long-Distance	
Total Cost of Calls	
GROSS PROFIT (LOSS)	
EXPENSES	
Salaries and Wages	
Employee Benefits	
Total Payroll and Related Expenses	
Other Expenses	
Printing and Stationery	
Uniforms	
Other	
Total Other Expenses	
DEPARTMENTAL INCOME (LOSS)	$

GIFT SHOP—SCHEDULE 4

	Current Period
REVENUE	$
ALLOWANCES	
NET REVENUE	
COST OF MERCHANDISE SOLD	
GROSS PROFIT (LOSS)	
EXPENSES	
Salaries and Wages	
Employee Benefits	
Total Payroll and Related Expenses	
Other Expenses	
Operating Supplies	
Uniforms	
Other	
Total Other Expenses	
DEPARTMENTAL INCOME (LOSS)	$

GARAGE AND PARKING—SCHEDULE 5

	Current Period
REVENUE	
Parking and Storage	$
Merchandise	
Other	
Total Revenue	
ALLOWANCES	
NET REVENUE	
COST OF MERCHANDISE SOLD	
GROSS PROFIT (LOSS)	
EXPENSES	
Salaries and Wages	
Employee Benefits	
Total Payroll and Related Expenses	
Other Expenses	
Licenses	
Management Fee	
Operating Supplies	
Uniforms	
Other	
Total Other Expenses	
DEPARTMENTAL INCOME (LOSS)	$

OTHER OPERATED DEPARTMENTS—SCHEDULE __

	Current Period
REVENUE	
Services	$
Sales of Merchandise	
Total Revenue	
ALLOWANCES	
NET REVENUE	
COST OF MERCHANDISE SOLD	
GROSS PROFIT (LOSS)	
EXPENSES	
Salaries and Wages	
Employee Benefits	
Total Payroll and Related Expenses	
Other Expenses	
China and Glassware	
Contract Services	
Laundry	
Linen	
Operating Supplies	
Uniforms	
Other	
Total Other Expenses	
DEPARTMENTAL INCOME (LOSS)	$

RENTALS AND OTHER INCOME—SCHEDULE 6

	Current Period
SPACE RENTALS	
Clubs	$
Offices	
Stores	
Other	
Total Rentals	_____
CONCESSIONS	
Total Concessions	_____
COMMISSIONS	
Laundry	
Valet	
Games and Vending Machines	
In-house Movies	
Other	
Total Commissions	_____
CASH DISCOUNTS EARNED	
ELECTRONIC GAMES AND PINBALL MACHINES	
FORFEITED ADVANCE DEPOSITS	
INTEREST INCOME	
SALVAGE	
VENDING MACHINES	
OTHER	_____
TOTAL RENTALS AND OTHER INCOME	$ _____

ADMINISTRATIVE AND GENERAL—SCHEDULE 7

	Current Period
SALARIES AND WAGES	$
EMPLOYEE BENEFITS	
Total Payroll and Related Expenses	
OTHER EXPENSES	
Credit Card Commissions	
Data Processing	
Dues and Subscriptions	
Human Resources	
Insurance—General	
Operating Supplies	
Postage and Telegrams	
Professional Fees	
Provision for Doubtful Accounts	
Travel and Entertainment	
Other	
Total Other Expenses	
TOTAL ADMINISTRATIVE AND GENERAL EXPENSES	$

DATA PROCESSING—SCHEDULE 8

	Current Period
SALARIES AND WAGES	$
EMPLOYEE BENEFITS	
Total Payroll and Related Expenses	
OTHER EXPENSES	
Dues and Subscriptions	
Training	
Maintenance	
Hardware	
Software	
Operating Supplies	
Service Bureau Fees	
Other	
Total Other Expenses	
TOTAL DATA PROCESSING EXPENSES	$

HUMAN RESOURCES—SCHEDULE 9

	Current Period
SALARIES AND WAGES	$
EMPLOYEE BENEFITS	
Total Payroll and Related Expenses	
OTHER EXPENSES	
Dues and Subscriptions	
Employee Housing	
Employee Relations	
Medical Expenses	
Operating Supplies	
Recruitment	
Relocation	
Training	
Transportation	
Other	
Total Other Expenses	
TOTAL HUMAN RESOURCES EXPENSES	$

TRANSPORTATION—SCHEDULE 10

	Current Period
SALARIES AND WAGES	$
EMPLOYEE BENEFITS	
Total Payroll and Related Expenses	
OTHER EXPENSES	
Fuel and Oil	
Insurance	
Operating Supplies	
Repairs and Maintenance	
Uniforms	
Other	
Total Other Expenses	
TOTAL TRANSPORTATION EXPENSES	$

MARKETING—SCHEDULE 11

	Current Period
SALES	
Salaries and Wages	$
Employee Benefits	
Total Payroll and Related Expenses	
Other Expenses	
Total Sales	
RESERVATIONS	
Salaries and Wages	
Employee Benefits	
Total Payroll and Related Expenses	
Other Expenses	
Total Reservations	
ADVERTISING AND MERCHANDISING	
Direct Mail	
In-house Graphics	
Outdoor	
Point-of-Sale Material	
Print	
Radio and Television	
Selling Aids	
Other	
Total Advertising and Merchandising	
FEES AND COMMISSIONS	
Agency Fees	
Franchise Fees	
Other	
Total Fees and Commissions	
MISCELLANEOUS MARKETING EXPENSES	
TOTAL OTHER EXPENSES	
TOTAL MARKETING EXPENSES	$

PROPERTY OPERATION AND MAINTENANCE—SCHEDULE 12

	Current Period
SALARIES AND WAGES	$
EMPLOYEE BENEFITS	
Total Payroll and Related Expenses	
OTHER EXPENSES	
Building Supplies	
Electrical and Mechanical Equipment	
Engineering Supplies	
Furniture, Fixtures, Equipment, and Decor	
Grounds and Landscaping	
Operating Supplies	
Removal of Waste Matter	
Swimming Pool	
Uniforms	
Other	
Total Other Expenses	
TOTAL PROPERTY OPERATION AND MAINTENANCE	$

ENERGY COSTS—SCHEDULE 13

	Current Period
Electric Current	$
Fuel	
Steam	
Water	_____
TOTAL ENERGY COSTS	$

FIXED CHARGES—SCHEDULE 14

RENT, PROPERTY TAXES, AND INSURANCE

	Current Period
RENT	
Land and Buildings	$
Data Processing Equipment	
Telephone Equipment	
Other Equipment	
Total	_____
TAXES OTHER THAN INCOME AND PAYROLL	
Real Estate Taxes	
Personal Property Taxes	
Utility Taxes	
Business and Occupation Taxes	
Other	_____
Total	_____
INSURANCE ON BUILDING AND CONTENTS	_____
TOTAL RENT, PROPERTY TAXES, AND INSURANCE	$

INTEREST EXPENSE

	Current Period
Mortgages	$
Notes Payable	
Interest on Capital Leases	
Other Long-Term Debt	
Amortization of Deferred Financing Costs	
Other	_____
Total	$

DEPRECIATION AND AMORTIZATION

	Current Period
Buildings and Improvements	$
Leaseholds and Leasehold Improvements	
Furnishings and Equipment	
Capital Leases	
Preopening Expenses	
Other	_____
Total	$
GAIN OR LOSS ON SALE OF PROPERTY	$

INCOME TAXES—SCHEDULE 15

	Current Period
FEDERAL	
Current	$
Deferred	
Total	
STATE	
Current	
Deferred	
Total	
OTHER	
Current	
Deferred	
Total	
TOTAL FEDERAL AND STATE INCOME TAXES	$

SALARIES AND WAGES—SCHEDULE 16

	Current Period	
	Number of Employees	Amount
ROOMS		
Management		$
Front Office		
Housekeeping		
Service		
Security		
Total (Schedule 1)		$
FOOD AND BEVERAGE		
Management		$
Kitchen		
Service		
Other		
Total (Schedule 2)		$
TELEPHONE (Schedule 3)		$
GIFT SHOP (Schedule 4)		$
GARAGE AND PARKING (Schedule 5)		$
OTHER OPERATED DEPARTMENTS (Schedule _)		$
ADMINISTRATIVE AND GENERAL		
Manager's Office		$
Accounting Office		
Credit Office		
Front Office Bookkeeping		
Night Auditors		
Receiving Clerks		
Timekeepers		
Total (Schedule 7)		$
DATA PROCESSING (Schedule 8)		$
HUMAN RESOURCES (Schedule 9)		$
TRANSPORTATION (Schedule 10)		$
MARKETING (Schedule 11)		$
PROPERTY OPERATION AND MAINTENANCE		
Management		$
Engineers		
Grounds		
Office and Storeroom		
Other		
Total (Schedule 12)		$
HOUSE LAUNDRY		
Managers and Assistants		$
Finishing		
Washing		
Other		
Total (Schedule 18)		$
TOTAL SALARIES AND WAGES		$

PAYROLL TAXES AND EMPLOYEE BENEFITS—SCHEDULE 17

		Current Period
PAYROLL TAXES		
Federal Retirement		$
Federal Unemployment		
State Unemployment		
Total Payroll Taxes		
EMPLOYEE BENEFITS		
Nonunion Insurance		
Nonunion Pension		
Profit Sharing		
Union Insurance		
Union Pension		
Workers' Compensation Insurance		
Other		
Total Employee Benefits		
TOTAL PAYROLL TAXES AND EMPLOYEE BENEFITS		$
CHARGED TO DEPARTMENTS		
Rooms	Schedule 1	$
Food and Beverage	Schedule 2	
Telephone	Schedule 3	
Gift Shop	Schedule 4	
Garage and Parking	Schedule 5	
Other Operated Departments	Schedule _	
Administrative and General	Schedule 7	
Data Processing	Schedule 8	
Human Resources	Schedule 9	
Transportation	Schedule 10	
Marketing	Schedule 11	
Property Operation and Maintenance	Schedule 12	
House Laundry	Schedule 18	
TOTAL PAYROLL TAXES AND EMPLOYEE BENEFITS		$

HOUSE LAUNDRY—SCHEDULE 18

	Current Period
SALARIES AND WAGES	$
EMPLOYEE BENEFITS	
Total Payroll and Related Expenses	
OTHER EXPENSES	
Cleaning Supplies	
Laundry Supplies	
Printing and Stationery	
Uniforms	
Other	
Total Other Expenses	
CREDITS	
Cost of Guest Laundry	
Cost of Concessionaires' Laundry	
Total Credits	
COST OF HOUSE LAUNDRY	$
CHARGED TO DEPARTMENTS	
Rooms Schedule 1	$
Food and Beverage Schedule 2	
Other Departments Schedule _	
Total	$

Appendix B
Essentials of Computer Systems

The introduction of a computer system can significantly change the way hospitality business is charted and conducted. Every business collects and analyzes data about its operations. A computer system enables management to speed up the process by which useful information is made available to decision makers. In addition, a computer system can streamline the process of collecting and recording data and expand the ways in which information is organized and reported.

How much does a manager need to know about a computer to operate one? About as much as a motorist needs to know about auto mechanics to drive a car. The automobile responds to the driver's "commands." As long as the driver understands what the vehicle will do when the lever is pulled, the accelerator pushed, the wheel turned, etc., the car ought to perform correctly. In addition, if the motorist knows some basics of auto mechanics and some emergency maintenance techniques, the car ought to perform better and longer. In the same way, if a manager understands how the computer responds to commands and some basics about its operation, it can be an effective tool in managing information needs. While all businesses use some information system, a computerized system enables management to achieve its goals much more easily.

This appendix outlines the basics of computer operation by examining general information concepts and needs, computer hardware and software, data security, and human factors involved in computerizing functions within a hospitality operation.

Data and Information

Hospitality managers are bombarded with facts—data—throughout the day. These isolated bits of data are meaningless until they are related to each other—processed—in a way that converts them into useful information. When the collection of facts bombarding hospitality managers daily is analyzed and organized into information, they can provide significant insights and guide decisions affecting the operation. The objective of all information systems, including computerized ones, is to transform this data into information—and to do so on a timely basis so that the results are still useful to the manager.

There are three distinct types of data. One type is called "alpha" because it consists of only letters of the alphabet. For example, the name of a menu item, a server, or a hotel guest are all types of alpha data. A second kind of data is called "numeric" because it consists of only numbers. Menu prices, room numbers, guest check serial numbers, and occupancy percentages are all numeric data. The third form of data is termed "alphanumeric" since it involves both letters and numbers in the same data entry. A hotel's street address, a menu item description, and personnel records are examples of hospitality alphanumerics.

Why is information so important to the hospitality operation? What does it do? First, information provides knowledge related to operations, service, labor, finance, and other areas of concern. Second, information reduces uncertainty with respect to decision making. Third, information presents feedback which enables corrective action. A survey of customers leaving a restaurant, for example, may offer management information about the business, reduce uncertainty about guest satisfaction, and provide important operational feedback. Information, one of an operation's most valuable resources, is the outcome of data processing.

Data Processing

Regardless of the degree of automation, all businesses use some form of data processing. Data processing is primarily concerned with the transformation of raw, isolated facts (data) into comprehensive, useful information. This occurs constantly—not only in business but everyday life as well. Everyone processes data. For example, when people receive their paychecks, they might consider all of the items they would like to purchase, what the cost of those purchases is, and the difference between the check and total purchases. If the paycheck is larger than the expenditures, a person might decide to place the extra in a savings account. If, on the other hand, expenditures are greater than the paycheck, the person has to reconsider the purchase options—or, perhaps, decide to take out a loan. A collection of data (purchase costs and paycheck amount) has been processed (totaled and compared) and, thus, transformed into information (deficit or surplus) useful in making decisions (what to buy). This conversion is accomplished through procedures referred to as input, process, and output. In the above situation, the paycheck and the purchase options are inputs; the calculation of the different expenditures is the processing; and the deficit or surplus is the output. It is the sequential combination of these factors that compose the basic data processing cycle.

Data Processing Cycle

During input, data are captured and coded to simplify subsequent processing functions. During processing, input data is mathematically manipulated or logically arranged to generate meaningful output. The output, then, can be stored (saved for future reference) and/or reported for immediate use. The basic data processing cycle is presented in Exhibit B-1.

The data processing cycle occurs almost constantly and is not limited to computer applications. Standard recipes, used to convert raw ingredients into menu items, can be seen as data processing techniques. Ingredients and their corresponding quantities are typical (alphanumeric) inputs to recipe production. During processing, by following the recipe's instructions the desired recipe output—a number of standard portions per batch—will result.

Objectives of Data Processing

The objectives of data processing include minimizing turnaround time (elapsed time from input to output), and minimizing the number of times the same piece of data is handled. An efficiently designed data processing system provides managers with rapid access to the information they need to make timely and effective decisions. Inquiry and search procedures should be performed within an acceptable response time. For example, if a front desk clerk needs to find out in which room a guest is registered, the answer should be generated quickly. Also, a busy food and beverage manager, who wants to spot check inventory of the most expensive ingredients immediately following a meal period, would appreciate the speed and accuracy of an effective data processing design. Computer systems are able to minimize turnaround time for almost all data processing tasks.

Reducing the number of times data must be rehandled enhances both the speed and the accuracy of data processing tasks. Consider the

Exhibit B-1   Data Processing Cycle

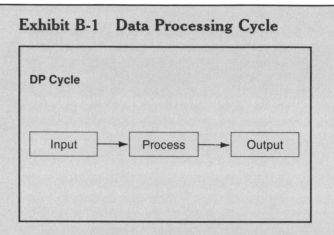

difference between a manual accounting system and a computerized one. In the manual system, an invoice received is first recorded in a journal. Next, the amount is carried over to a ledger. Amounts in the ledger are then used to calculate the financial statements. During any of these steps it is possible for a bookkeeper to write the wrong number, write a number's digits in the wrong order (transpose them), calculate a total incorrectly, etc. In the computerized system, however, the invoice amount is entered only once. The amount can then be accessed by the programs which prepare the journal, ledger, and financial statements. Therefore, if the number is entered correctly, all of the subsequent statements will be correct. If it is entered incorrectly, but the mistake corrected, the correction automatically flows from the journal through to the financial statements. With electronic data processing, there are fewer opportunities for the types of errors to occur that happen when the same data must be rehandled for a variety of different tasks. And, if there is an error, electronic data processing can perform again all the affected tasks almost instantaneously once the error is corrected. The speed, accuracy, and efficiency required for an effective information system are often best achieved through electronic data processing.

Electronic Data Processing

The difference between data processing (DP) and electronic data processing (EDP) lies in the automation of the process and the addition of a memory unit. Electronic data processing employs a computer system for its base of operation. The automation of input, process, and output components results in faster and more efficient opera-

Exhibit B-2   Electronic Data Processing Cycle

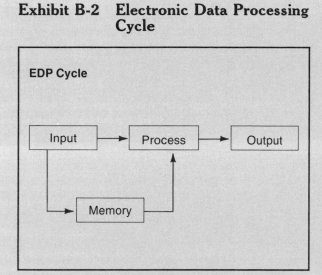

EDP Cycle

Exhibit B-3   Computer Hardware Components

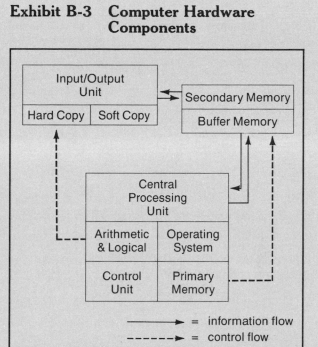

tions. The inclusion of a memory unit enables storage of instructions and data for more reliable and thorough analysis. Exhibit B-2 shows how the addition of memory affects the data processing cycle. This cycle is referred to as the EDP cycle.

What is a Computer? A computer is a managerial tool capable of processing large quantities of data very rapidly and accurately. It can perform arithmetic (addition, subtraction, multiplication, and division) and logical (ranking, sorting, and assembling) operations. The advantages of a computer include: speed, accuracy, retention, and control. Computers process data much more quickly than any other method while maintaining an incredible level of precision. In addition, they are capable of storing and retrieving tremendous amounts of information, and bringing discipline to and controlling procedures otherwise overlooked.

Computer systems are composed of a variety of component parts. It is important that these components be well understood in order to ensure optimal system design and operation. Managers who understand the functions of each component and are comfortable with the computer's operations are more in control of this valuable tool. This knowledge enables them to more effectively verbalize needs or requests when they decide which computer system best suits their operation or when they want to expand the data processing functions their system already performs.

A knowledge of computer jargon (frequently termed "computerese") is extremely helpful in expressing the functions desired from a computer system and in understanding the functioning of the system itself. This section introduces many of these computer terms by explaining the concepts of hardware, software, communication devices, information security, and the human factors involved in computing.

Hardware

The physical equipment found in a computer system is called hardware. Computer hardware is visible, movable, and easy to distinguish. In order to have a computer system, three components are required: the input/output unit, the secondary memory unit, and the central processing unit. Exhibit B-3 shows how these three components are related and indicates their major elements.

The input/output (I/O) unit allows the user to interact with the system. The user can input data and receive output information through a variety of electronic devices. The most common I/O device at work in the hospitality industry is the CRT. (CRT is the acronym for cathode ray tube; that term is very infrequently used now.) The CRT unit is composed of a television-like video screen and a typewriter keyboard. As data is entered through the keyboard, it is displayed on the screen. The CRT operator can edit and verify the on-screen input prior to transmitting it for processing.

Another popular I/O device is the teletype terminal (TTY). The teletype is less expensive than the CRT and does not include a video display component. Instead, input is entered over the keyboard and printed on a roll of paper. As the operator enters data into the system, a printed report can be made at the TTY console. The entered data is then communicated to a remote unit for processing. After processing, the information is relayed back to the TTY and printed on paper. For example, the housekeeping department of a hotel might use TTYs to communicate with the front desk and keep them up-to-date on room status. In this case, the housekeeping department needs some record of the messages sent, but does not require all the capabilities of a CRT. Therefore, the extra cost for a CRT is not justified.

Other types of I/O equipment include keyboard and operator display units such as electronic cash registers (ECR) and line printing terminals. A hotel's food and beverage operation might use ECRs to communicate with the front office. In a computerized hotel system, restaurant charges can be entered into a point-of-sale device in the restaurant and transmitted to the front office where guest folios are automatically updated with the charges.

One important difference between I/O devices is the type of output they produce. CRTs display output on a monitor for the user to examine; this type of output is referred to as "soft copy" because it cannot be handled by the operator or removed from the computer. Printers, however, generate a paper copy of the output which is called a "hard copy." Many systems are designed so that they can produce both types of output. For example, a computer at a hotel's front desk might have a CRT which the clerk can use to view a soft copy of guest folios during check-in and check-out times. However, when the guest checks out, a hard copy of the folio will be generated from a printer so that the guest can keep a copy. Obviously, output displayed on a screen (CRT) is much more temporary and its use more constricted than output printed on paper. Generally hospitality managers obtain essential reports in hard copy form, allowing storage outside the computer and providing a base for information backup.

The central processing unit (CPU) is the most important and expensive hardware component found within a computer system. It is the "brains" of the system and is responsible for controlling all other system components. As shown in Exhibit B-3, the CPU is composed of four subunits. The first subunit is the arithmetic and logical unit (ALU) which performs all the mathematical, sorting, and processing functions.

A second subunit, referred to as the control unit, is responsible for determining which devices in the computer system are accessible to and/or by the CPU. If a device is capable of interacting directly with the CPU, it is said to be "on-line"; "off-line" describes the condition in which there is no established connection between a system device and the CPU. It is interesting to note that although computer devices may be switched on (powered-up) they are not necessarily on-line. For example, when a printer is connected to a computer and turned on, the operator can switch the printer to either on-line or off-line status. The printer will respond to commands from the CPU only when it is on-line.

The third subunit of the CPU is the operating system (OS). The operating system is responsible for orchestrating the hardware and the software within the system. It establishes the system's priorities and directs its resources to effectively accomplish desired tasks. This concept is discussed in greater depth later in this appendix.

The final subunit of the CPU is the primary memory unit which contains permanent programs designed into the system by the manufacturer. The CPU comes equipped with its own set of commands and instructions. These commands are the most basic ones recognized by the computer. To ensure they are not altered by the user, these programs are stored within the computer in a read-only memory (ROM) format. This means that the computer can "read" or understand the information stored in these memory chips, but no one can "write" or save anything in this area of the computer's memory. Since the primary memory is composed of a limited syntax (vocabulary), the computer only recognizes its own preprogrammed commands. If a user tries to enter a different command, the computer will not recognize the input and will respond by reporting that a "syntax error" has occurred. For example, some personal computers will start a program's operation if the user types "GO"; others require the user to type "RUN." If the user types the wrong command, the computer will respond with a message such as "UNDEFINED COMMAND" to alert the user to the problem. Since these commands are specified by the computer manufacturer, different machines utilize different commands. This is why software designed for one brand of computer will not work on other brands; since the primary memories are different, some of the commands are not recognized by the other brands.

Another type of memory, the secondary memory unit, is used to store data and programs needed by the user. Types of secondary memory include diskettes and cassettes. Diskettes are small magnetic plates enclosed in protective coverings. They are frequently referred to as "floppy disks" because they are very flexible. The computer is able to transfer ("write") data from its working memory to the diskette by adjusting its magnetic surface. Once encoded on the diskette, the data can be permanently stored; the user can remove the diskette from the computer and access the data it contains at some other time or with some other (compatible) computer. The computer retrieves ("reads") data from diskettes by scanning the magnetic surface and translating the electronic code into a form the computer can understand. Cassettes are similar to diskettes in that they store data on a magnetic surface. However, they are made of long tape and are read much like an audio cassette tape.

Information in secondary memory can be accessed in either a sequential or random manner. Secondary memory units that are accessed sequentially depend on magnetic tape as their storage media. Their operation is similar to a tape recorder; if someone wants to know what was recorded five minutes ago, the tape must be rewound and played forward while the listener searches for the desired recording. Similarly, computer systems with sequentially accessed secondary memory units record and retrieve transactions in the order in which they are entered. This is not a feasible storage medium for most hospitality applications. Guests do not enter and leave food service operations in exact sequences. Employees do not sign in and out in ascending order by identification number; nor do inventory items become depleted in any specific order. The best secondary memory approach for the hospitality industry involves random access media.

Disks and diskettes are two types of secondary storage media that provide random access memory (RAM) appropriate for hospitality applications. Disks are either installed as a permanent part of the computer (these are called "hard disks" or "fixed disks" when installed in personal computers) or, in large computer systems, can be "loaded"—attached—to disk drives as needed. Data can be stored on the disk in any order, and the disk drive unit remembers where each piece of data is placed. By definition, any data stored on RAM media should be accessible in the identical amount of time, regardless of whether it was placed there one second, week, month, or year ago. Random access memory works especially well in hospitality operations since their clientele, menu items, inventory items, check ins, and so on, occur in random fashion.

Another important component of secondary memory is referred to as buffer memory. Buffer memory is a temporary storage area that stores data which cannot yet be placed into the permanent portion of the memory unit. For example, a restaurant employing remote kitchen printers uses buffer memory to receive orders entered through precheck terminals and awaiting printing at a work station. Since the terminals process and transmit their data at extremely high speeds and kitchen printers tend to be relatively slow devices, an order entered but not immediately printed might risk being lost. The buffer memory (also called a network controller) receives order entry data and holds that data until the appropriate printer becomes available. Other examples of buffer memory use include the intermediate computations in a complex program, and programs known as "scratch pads" which allow the operator to use the computer as a calendar or calculator without interrupting the operations in session at the time. Buffer memory is an important part of the secondary memory unit and one that should not be overlooked.

Although every computer must have each of the three components mentioned, the size and capacity of various computers varies greatly. When computers were first invented, they filled large rooms with electronic tubes and required specific atmosphere control. There are still computers that large; however, they are capable of doing more than all of the original ones combined. Now it is possible to get the same sophistication that the first computers offered in a hand held calculator. This is possible because the electronic tubes mentioned above have been replaced with magnetic chips, no larger than one's fingernail, which can hold as much information as hundreds of tubes. Because of this great size reduction, many small hospitality operations find that their needs can be met by a minicomputer, or even by a microcomputer which is better known as a "personal computer." This term is used for the smallest computers on the market. Despite their small size, they contain the same types of components as the larger machines and may also have additional options such as hard disks, color monitors, graphics printers, and so on.

The major advantages of microcomputers include their low price (a complete system can be purchased for less than $2,500) and the large amount of software available to operate on them. Their major disadvantage, however, is their limited storage capacity—in both secondary and internal memory areas. As a result of this limited memory capacity, some of the more sophisticated programs a hospitality operation may want to use will not run on a microcomputer. If this is the case, the hospitality operation may want to use a minicomputer. Although the difference between mini and microcomputers is becoming increasingly difficult to spot, minicomputers generally have much larger memory capacities. Hospitality operations needing a computer with even larger internal memory capacity and external storage media are more likely to choose a mainframe computer. Mainframe computers are the largest computer systems currently available and can be programmed to handle the extensive amounts of data that a large hospitality operation is likely to generate.

Software

The instructions within a computer system are called software. Software basically tells the hardware what to do, how to do it, and when to do it. To enable rapid data processing, these directives must be written in a language the computer is programmed to understand. There are two basic types of computer languages—high level and low level languages. High level languages (e.g., BASIC, COBOL, FORTRAN, C, and others) are the most sophisticated because a relatively simple command gets the computer to perform complex procedures that involve a number of different operations. For example, some computer languages recognize the word "SORT" and respond to this command by taking a list of separate items and arranging them in some predetermined fashion. High level languages are easy for a novice programmer to work with because they are similar to the user's own spoken language.

At its most basic level, however, a computer is really only able to distinguish between positive or negative electronic charges. This means that a computer is not able to understand the commands of a high level language directly; it must first interpret or compile them into a form that the computer can understand. All computers have low level languages programmed into them because it is at this most basic level that its opera-

tions are carried out. Low level languages are usually referred to as machine languages because they do not require interpreting or compiling before the machines can understand them. The computer can directly distinguish their instructions. There are a variety of low level machine languages, and which language a given computer utilizes depends on the type of compiler or interpreter it has available. These languages are very complex and require a skilled programmer for their development. In general, programs written in machine languages cost more to develop but operate faster than their high level language equivalents.

There are basically two different types of computer software: system software and application software. System software is developed and installed by the system's manufacturer. Its primary purpose is diagnostics, error detection, and error correction. The display of a syntax error message, for example, is not left to the user to program into the system. It comes preprogrammed by the manufacturer as part of the system's software package. System software aids the system in start-up and in establishing continuous operation.

Application software, on the other hand, is purchased separately from the computer and provides programs that allow the computer to perform specific tasks. Although the computer will run without application software, it will not be able to perform those tasks for which it was purchased. For example, application software is required in order for the computer to accomplish the necessary functions involved in maintaining a data base or generating reports. Therefore, when purchasing a computer system, choosing application software is more important than the choice of computer hardware. The user first needs to determine what functions or tasks the system will be required to perform and what application software will best accomplish those tasks. Only then is the user in a position to decide which computer hardware is needed to run the required software. Not all application software is available for every computer brand, and the compatibility of software and hardware is a critical factor in purchase decisions. By focusing first on which application software will best meet the needs of the hospitality operation, managers can ensure that the computer system they purchase accomplishes all the desired tasks.

The design of application software incorporates a plan to achieve a particular purpose. This plan is referred to as an "algorithm," which means "formula," and involves a logical procedure beginning with input data and concluding with output information. An algorithm must be reliable and accurate. Consider the calculation of a food cost percentage. The basic formula is: food cost divided by food revenues. The application software must be capable of computing food cost based upon clearly defined relationships (beginning inventory plus purchases minus ending inventory) and charting food revenues (number of items sold at various selling prices). The actual division of costs by revenues completes the algorithm function.

There are two levels of application software; some software is very application-specific while others can be used for many tasks. For example, a restaurant manager can purchase a software package designed to perform menu engineering. This type of application software performs all of the necessary calculations involved in menu engineering and prints a graph displaying the results. This software has one specific purpose and requires no additional programming by the manager to perform that task; all that is required is input data for the program to work with. On the other hand, a spreadsheet program can be used for a number of different applications. Although the manager needs to program the spreadsheet to accomplish desired tasks, it can perform many different kinds of mathematical calculations, including menu engineering. It can also produce graphs and generate a variety of different reports. Spreadsheets were discussed in Chapter 5. Other types of application software capable of performing a variety of tasks include word processing packages and data base programs.

Word processing packages allow computers to function as advanced typewriters. Users can type on the keyboard while everything is displayed on the computer's monitor and stored in the CPU's temporary memory. Editing is fairly simple because the computer updates the temporary memory whenever changes are made. For example, lines can be added and inserted into the text, words deleted, spelling errors corrected, and whole blocks of text moved from one place to another. In addition, some word processing packages assist writers by checking for spelling errors, providing a built-in thesaurus, and performing some mathematical functions. At any time, the text entered with a word processor can be stored on a secondary memory device, such as a diskette, and be accessed later for further additions or editing. This makes it simpler to write long works at different times. It also makes it possible to type form letters, or other documents that are used repeatedly, only once and to make

any necessary changes or additions prior to printing. Other available features include certain kinds of data base management useful in accomplishing a variety of tasks that involve inserting variable information into prepared documents. For example, a list of guests and their addresses can be stored in a data base and merged with the prepared document to create "personalized" letters sent to each guest for marketing purposes. The letter is only typed once but, as a copy is printed for each guest, the guest's name and address appears in the salutation.

Data base packages are software programs which allow users to store facts about their businesses for future use. The data base provides a means of organizing related facts and arranging them in ways that facilitate searches, updates, and reports. Each fact in a data base is stored in a separate "field," and the fields are arranged in groups so that related facts are stored together in a "record." The data base as a whole is a collection of different records. For example, an inventory data base might be set up for inventory control. This data base would contain one record for each inventory item, and each record would contain a number of fields such as the item's name, number, reorder quantity, number on hand, price per inventory quantity, and so on. The user can then arrange this data for any number of applications: inventory check sheets could be generated to assist in physical inventory, variance analysis could be performed on the difference between actual quantity on hand versus the target amount recorded by the computer, the total value of inventory could be calculated, and so on.

At present, the major disadvantage in data base packages seems to be the sophistication the user needs in order to initially establish the data base. Many data base packages involve a complex set of commands used to define fields and establish records, but an experienced (or patient) user can organize a large amount of information. Once the data base is designed, the main advantage is that the data it contains needs only to be entered and stored once. It can then be accessed by many programs for a variety of purposes. This not only saves storage space, but, more importantly, limits the number of times that data must be updated and ensures that all applications using the data base work with the most current information.

Additional concerns in application software development are program design, file structure, screen formats, and printed formats. Program design deals with the collection of input data, internal manipulation of data, and output routines, while file structure deals with the way data is stored. Although both of these concepts are very important for actually programming software, the typical user need not be expert in either. Users are concerned, however, with ensuring that screen display formats and printed reports are conducive to the ways they will use information. Two additional concepts of importance to users in selecting application software are how "interactive" the programs are and whether they provide "integrated" file structures.

Interactive vs. noninteractive: An interactive program is one in which the system prompts the user to respond to a predetermined sequence of inquiries. As the user responds, the next inquiry in the series is presented. Interactive software is very popular among hospitality operations because it is easier to use and helps ensure that all required information is collected and entered into the computer system. This is important when, for example, a hotel desk clerk is prompted by the computer for information about guests during check-in times. Another advantage of interactive systems is that they can generate reports at any time. This provides an effective means to ensure that data is processed and available to managers in time to be useful in decision making.

Noninteractive systems do not involve a user/system dialogue. Instead, the program reserves specific line numbers for exact data input. Program execution is faster in a noninteractive system since there is no waiting for user response. However, accompanying this gain in execution speed is the loss of on-line editing and the ability to generate reports as needed. Noninteractive programs also demand more sophisticated users, since the data must be entered in the correct order and format without prompting from the computer.

Integrated file structure: Integrated approaches to file storage help achieve data processing objectives because they require a minimum of data handling and operate at high speeds. This is because an integrated software system allows several programs to use the same data base. If the files are integrated, two programs using the identical data only require a single file. For example, data concerning the menu sales mix is essential to calculating both food service revenues and standard food costs. A restaurant employing an electronic cash register (ECR) with the ability to calculate and store menu counts captures this data at the time of a sale. Since menu item prices are also normally stored in an ECR, a revenue report can be generated without any further data entry by the user. Similarly, an ECR with a recipe costing module can use the identical menu sales mix data to produce food cost reports. However, if the restaurant does not have an ECR, menu sales mix data must be collected from an analysis of guest checks and then entered into an adding machine or nonintegrated computer program to produce revenue information. Similarly, in order to calculate standard or ideal food costs without an ECR, the standard recipe cost for each menu item must first be determined and then menu sales mix data entered for a second time into the adding machine or nonintegrated computer program. The advantages of integrated software over nonintegrated software include speed and data integrity (since data is only stored once, it is possible to update it for ALL applications, not just for one). These make integrated software the preferred approach for hospitality industry applications.

Screen and report formats are important concerns to the users of an application program. While the issues of interactive versus noninteractive, and integrated versus nonintegrated software are important, the true value of a program lies in the comprehensibility and usefulness of its output. Screen displays must allow for easy reading and eye comfort. Cluttered, jumbled, or unclear screens are not as powerful as those possessing good spacing and legible information. In addition, screens which make use of color monitor capabilities are often very helpful to inexperienced users whose eyes can readily follow the color differences.

Similarly, reports should be formatted to take full advantage of the printer's capability. The production of a series of standard sized pages is by far superior to a continuous roll of 2½ wide cash register receipt paper. One of the frequent criticisms of computers is that they produce large volumes of irrelevant information. Streamlining (producing only the reports requested by the user) is becoming the trend for application software developers. It is imperative, therefore, that information needs are determined prior to software selection so that only the information needed by the operation is generated.

Operating System

Hardware describes the equipment within a computer system. Software refers to the instructions that direct the operations of the hardware. How do the hardware and software work together? How are priorities established within the

Exhibit B-4   The Role of the Operating System

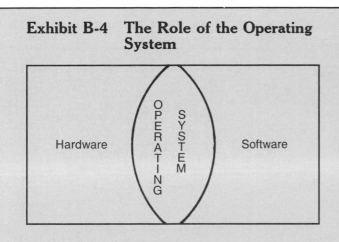

system? The answer to these and related questions lies in the area of the operating system.

The operating system (a portion of which is sometimes called "firmware") is a major component in any computer system application and often differentiates one computer from another. It interfaces hardware and software while maintaining system priorities as shown in Exhibit B-4.

Although it is difficult to imagine how a computer searches for data items, it is similar to the way the human thought process would guide a search for an individual whose address is known. To accomplish this mission, the searcher must evaluate several options about where to go and how to get there, make numerous decisions along the way, and forego alternate activities in the process. Similarly, a computer's operating system directs the computer system's functioning to find the answer to a manager's request for data. The request for the search is made from within an application software program, but it is the computer's operating system that directs the effort and secures the needed data.

Configurations and Networks

When a hospitality operation decides which computer system to purchase, it is important that it match the system with its needs. We have seen that the first consideration is choosing appropriate software to perform the desired tasks and then determining which hardware is needed to run the software. However, the size of the operation and the number of departments needing access to the computer are also significant factors in choosing a computer system. If the business is relatively small, a personal computer which contains a CPU, memory unit, and input/output device may be sufficient. However, if there are a number of distinct groups of people who need to use the computer, more than one CPU and/or input/output device may be required. It is possible to attach these devices to CPUs in various ways so that they meet the user's needs while avoiding spending unnecessary funds on additional hardware.

The design and layout of computer hardware is described as its configuration. How a system is configured affects the communication among its component parts. There are three distinct configuration designs: integrated configuration, distributed configuration, and combined configuration. Each hardware design must address the locations and interactions of the three required pieces of equipment: I/O unit, memory unit, and CPU.

An integrated configuration is characterized by a single central processing unit and a central data base. While the I/O units may be distributed throughout the hospitality establishment, both the CPU used for data processing and the memory unit used for data storage must be in a central location. Since the integrated configuration is dependent on a single CPU and centralized data base, errors there can render the system inoperable and/or result in a permanent loss of stored data. Exhibit B-5 represents one example of an integrated configuration. Note that I/O terminals all communicate with the CPU and that the CPU and memory unit work closely together.

The distributed configuration is very different from the integrated scheme. Instead of one large system, it is a series of smaller systems. Each of the workstation locations possesses a complete computer system, not just an input/output device. The presence of an I/O, memory unit, and CPU at each location provides a multiprocessor environment (many individual computers at different locations) with remote data storage facilities. Since each user group has their own computer there is more specialized application capability (use and storage). The individual stations can be connected—interfaced—to form a local area network (LAN). The LAN facilitates system-wide communication, data sharing, and device sharing. An individual system encountering operational problems would not affect the operation of the other systems in the network. Exhibit B-6 contains a schematic of a distributed configuration.

A combined configuration has some of the characteristics of both integrated and distributed configurations. The interconnection of a personal computer (PC) to an integrated configuration is perhaps the best illustration of the advantages available through combined configurations.

Exhibit B-5   Integrated Configuration

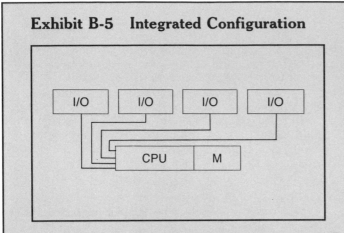

Exhibit B-6   Distributed Configuration

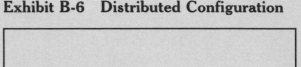

While the PC is distributed in nature (it possesses its own I/O, memory unit, and CPU) its connection to the integrated scheme allows for significant application flexibility not otherwise available. The transfer of data files from the data base of the integrated configuration to the PC enables detailed analysis on that file without affecting the ongoing workings of the integrated design. For example, suppose the integrated configuration depicted in Exhibit B-7 is an electronic cash register system in a hotel with a central data base and a PC in the back office. After transferring the data involving the day's sales, the PC can produce analytical reports without interfering with the ongoing work of the point-of-sale terminals distributed throughout the hotel. The combined configuration is an important arrangement used in the hospitality industry.

The advantages and disadvantages of each system should be considered before purchasing one. The major differences between the different configurations are speed and cost. The CPU is the most expensive component in a computer system; therefore, the more CPUs a configuration requires, the greater its cost. The tradeoff, however, is that the closer the CPU is to the I/O devices, and the fewer I/O devices making demands on it, the faster it will operate. Therefore, the use of different CPU outlets should be studied and evaluated.

The different types of configuration mentioned all make use of links between hardware components. The links, known as networks, allow computers to "talk" to each other. Depending on user needs, the networks can be established to link computers at the same location (in-house), at service bureaus, or at various sites. In-house systems involve the placement of all hardware and software on the user's premises. Service bureaus feature hardware and software at

someone else's premises with the hospitality operation paying for contract applications. For example, some operations use service bureaus to prepare payroll checks. In order to do this, the user inputs the hours worked on the operation's own computer, and "logs on" to the service bureau by making a telephone connection with it. The service bureau then takes the hours worked from the user's computer, combines this with the master payroll file stored at the service bureau, and runs the payroll software. Shared systems support multiple users by distributing portions of the system's hardware and software capability among participant properties. An example of this is a reservation system which allows a reservation for any hotel to be placed at any other hotel in the system.

When computers are located on the same premises, cables can link them together, but when computers are located at different sites, the telephone is used to allow them to communicate with each other. However, computers communicate with one another by relaying digital signals between components, while telephones transmit and receive analog signals. Since computers and telephones communicate using different types of signals, a device called a modem is used to translate analog signals to digital, and vice versa. The word "modem" comes from a combination of the two words *mo*dulate and *dem*odulate. Modulate means to code one type of signal to another; in this case it means to translate the sending computer's digital signals to analog ones. Demodulate refers to the decoding that takes place at the receiving computer which returns the communication to digital signals.

In addition to modems, computers need communication software in order to "talk" to each other. This software regulates the transfer of information by coordinating various factors, such

Exhibit B-7 Combined Configuration

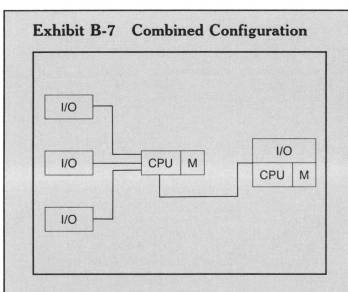

as what type of data will be transferred and how and how quickly the transfer will occur (baud rate). Once both the sending and receiving computers are ready for the transfer to take place, large amounts of information can be easily exchanged using relatively safe and rapid telecommunications techniques.

Data Security

Data security encompasses two major areas of concern for management: energy backup systems and information protection. Although management often focuses on the dangers involved in a power failure, information security can pose a much more serious threat to a hospitality operation. Consider the consequences of payroll information becoming unexpectedly available to employees, the competition gaining access to the guest history files, or the loss of the general ledger files. However, with proper care, both the energy and information problems can be avoided.

The loss or fluctuation of electrical power can lead to problems in computing. Unfortunately, power failures lead to other major problems for a hospitality operation as well; a blackout resulting in a loss of production or storage equipment can be much more traumatic than the temporary absence of a computer. The risks involved in many energy-related computer problems can be significantly reduced by using an uninterruptible power supply (UPS). The UPS is equipped with a battery pack and is placed on the computer's power line so that any fluctuation or degradation in the quality of power coming to the computer will trigger the battery pack which compensates for any energy deficiencies. This provides the computer with a continually stable energy source. In addition, many systems automatically recharge the batteries whenever the normal power source is in operation. When these preventive measures are taken, concerns about energy supply interruptions can be reduced.

Information security is much more complicated than energy backup procedures and should involve the following strategic considerations:

1. Functional division of duties. In the past, separation of duties involved, for example, ensuring that the person who received cash did not record it. In a computerized environment, this type of separation is often not possible or cost justified. It is important, however, to consider separating programmers from operators so that the system is not easily manipulated by dishonest employees.
2. Recovery. There are procedures to minimize the damage that may result from the loss of data. These will be discussed later in this section.
3. Avoidance. Security is enhanced by protecting assets from potential threats. This includes not only keeping the computer room and data files locked, but also ensuring that important files are kept in fire-proof areas, that the equipment is protected from environmental dangers, and so on.
4. Unauthorized access prevention. Unauthorized use of the computer can be avoided by restricting access to the computer through passwords, locked systems, file access codes, etc.
5. Detection and correction. If a problem is detected early, its impact on operations can be minimized and it will be easier to correct. One method of ensuring the early detection of problems related to data security is the use of error logs. Many computer systems generate error logs every time an unusual request is made to the system; this log may be examined by supervisors who can deal promptly with any potential problem.

If these factors are considered when planning and designing a system, they should protect the operation from unauthorized acquisition, modifi-

Exhibit B-8   Information Backup Strategies

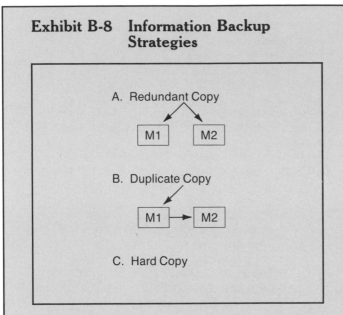

cation, or destruction of information. They are (notice the first letter of each strategy) set up to prevent FRAUD!

Contingency planning is perhaps one of the most overlooked aspects of computer usage. A preventive maintenance program is essential to ensure against downtime. All components must be kept clean and operational to achieve optimal system productivity. There must also be a predetermined emergency maintenance plan. In case of a crisis, what steps can be taken? For example, in addition to energy backup, there should be plans for hardware backup, spare parts, or loaner equipment.

Backup procedures should not be left to emergency situations. Information backup should be a standard operating procedure to ensure that no data is lost at any time. There are basically three ways to back up information: redundant copy, duplicate copy, and hard copy. Exhibit B-8 illustrates these three strategies. While many computer manufacturers advocate using at least two of the three methods, management must ensure that at least one method is regularly used.

Redundant copy is not a very popular backup technique in the hospitality industry because it requires two memory units working simultaneously. As transactions occur, they are written to both memory devices. Assuming that a food service system employs a disk drive as a base for its secondary memory unit, a second disk drive is required; as data entry takes place, data is

sent to both drives for recording on their respective disks.

This presents an expensive hardware configuration and requires more attention than either of the alternative backup methods. It is analogous to recording a theatrical performance on two tape recorders simultaneously. Many people feel it is more efficient to concentrate on producing one superior recording and duplicating it at a later point in time; two recordings are still obtained, but through duplication, not redundancy.

Duplicate copying is the most popular and efficient means to accomplish information backup. The computer system writes to only one memory unit so a second disk drive is not needed. A copy of the single drive can then be made on any type of secondary storage. Because magnetic tape is comparatively inexpensive, but not as well suited as a main secondary memory medium (due to its sequential access characteristics), some operators use it to back up their disk packs. In other words, at the end of the day, the disk pack is duplicated onto magnetic tape for backup purposes. Since the backup tape is stored and used only in case of a disk error, its sequential access method does not severely reduce the operation's ability to maintain efficient computer operations.

Hard copy backup should only be used in conjunction with redundant or duplicate copy procedures. The operator who relies solely on hard copy (printed) information backup will encounter an avalanche of work should data files need to be reconstructed. All information stored in hard copy must be manually re-entered to recreate the system's data base. By itself, hard copy is not a desirable method. When used to supplement one of the other two approaches, however, it provides a means for troubleshooting missing or incorrect transactional recordings. Should a mishap occur that affects only a small section of the disk, that area of the disk can be compared with the most current hard copy to identify problem areas. The duplicate copy disk could then be used to correct those problematic portions of the system's data base discovered through hard copy comparison.

Human Factors

Although it is the last concept presented in this section, human factors are, perhaps, the most critical in ensuring successful computer use. None of the advantages afforded by computers materialize unless the people using the system are properly trained. In addition to training, there is no substitute for current, accurate system documentation. In effect, the overall performance of the entire computer system hinges on the human engineering aspect of computer use.

Training is an ongoing process which prepares both new and present employees to use the system. Whether during conversion to a new computer system or during new employee orientation, hands-on training is the most successful teaching method. There is no better way to become familiar with computer operations than through experience using the system. Training, however, does not have to take place at the hospitality establishment where it may impede daily operations. Many computer vendors have test sites available where employees can be trained to operate computers. However, they should be avoided when vendor trainers use different equipment from that purchased by the hospitality operation. Training personnel on different equipment from that used in their actual positions could cause them to become confused, disoriented, and less confident in their abilities to use the on-site system. By employing the on-site system (perhaps with the software operating in a training mode) users gain a sense of confidence and competence which is difficult to duplicate elsewhere.

Documentation is a complete record of the software the operation will use. It is an important part of the human factor of computing because it facilitates the training process, explains the operation of the computer, and details the procedures required by application software. Good documentation provides flow charts of how the programs work and interact with each other. If the documentation includes an accurate listing of the program code, the software may be customized to better fit the operation's needs and future modifications may be made more easily. In addition, the documentation should include complete operation instructions to ensure not only that the programs are used correctly, but also that infrequently used options

are not forgotten over time. Finally, the documentation should include users' manuals which highlight all of the features of a specific application software program including input specifications, processing routines, and output format options. These manuals are available from software vendors when requested.

In addition to training and documentation, another important human factor concerns the impact the computer system has on employees. If the employees want to guarantee a system's failure, they certainly can. If, on the other hand, they have a positive attitude, the implementation of a new computer system will be smoother and easier. One strategy for converting to a computerized system is to transfer all applications to the computer simultaneously—to go "cold turkey." However, the most successful approach to implementing a new system appears to be through parallel conversion. In parallel conversion, functions are transferred to the computer system on an application-by-application basis. As new application software is purchased for the system and as employees are trained in its use, more and more operational functions can be computerized. For example, a hotel might convert the accounting functions first. Later, the front desk could be computerized, and finally the food and beverage operations. This allows each department to train its employees, test the software, and verify results independently. Parallel conversions should not be unnecessarily drawn out, but should provide a comfort level for everyone involved.

Finally, perhaps the most important human factor in computerization concerns the ways in which computerized data processing and computer-generated reports are used by managers in their decision-making processes. Remember that the computer is a managerial tool. It cannot do everything. It can only take user-specified input and generate output according to the dictates of its preprogrammed procedures. Its output is only as good as its input, and it cannot make decisions!

Glossary

A

ACCELERATED DEPRECIATION

Methods of depreciation that result in higher depreciation charges in the first year and gradually decline over the life of fixed assets.

ACCOUNT

Record containing information regarding a particular type of business transaction.

ACCOUNT FORMAT

A possible arrangement of a balance sheet which lists the asset accounts on the left side of the page and the liability and owners' equity accounts on the right side. Compare Report Format.

ACCOUNTING

Process of identifying, measuring, and communicating economic information (see accrual and cash basis).

ACCOUNTING CONTROLS

Controls for safeguarding assets and ensuring the accuracy and reliability of accounting data. Compare Administrative Controls.

ACCOUNTING CYCLE

Sequence of principal accounting procedures of a fiscal period; analyzing transactions, journal entry, posting to ledger, trial balance, adjustments, preparation of periodic financial statements, account closing, post-closing trial balance.

ACCOUNTING EQUATION

The accounting equation is assets = liabilities + proprietorship. Also referred to as the fundamental accounting equation.

ACCOUNTING PRINCIPLES

The basis for accounting methods and procedures.

ACCOUNTING RATE OF RETURN (ARR)

An approach to evaluating capital budgeting decisions based on the average annual project income (project revenues less project expenses) divided by the average investment.

ACCOUNTING SYSTEM

Subsystem of the information system providing financial reporting for external purposes.

ACCOUNTS PAYABLE

Liabilities incurred for merchandise, equipment, or other goods and services connected with the operation of the property that have been purchased on account.

ACCOUNTS RECEIVABLE

Obligations owed to the organization from sales made on credit.

ACCOUNTS RECEIVABLE TURNOVER

A measure of the rapidity of conversion of accounts receivable into cash; calculated by dividing revenue by average accounts receivable.

ACCRUAL BASIS ACCOUNTING

System of reporting revenues and expenses in the period in which they are considered to have been earned or incurred, regardless of the actual time of collection or payment.

ACCRUED EXPENSE ACCOUNT

Account of expenses that have been incurred but have not yet been paid.

ACCUMULATED DEPRECIATION

A contra-asset account used for accumulating depreciation charges for various fixed assets.

ACCUMULATED EARNINGS TAX

A tax designed to prevent corporations from accumulating earnings in order to avoid double taxation. The tax can be avoided by showing a reasonable need for accumulating earnings (such as business expansion).

ACID-TEST RATIO

Ratio of total cash and near-cash current assets to total current liabilities.

ACTIVITY RATIOS

A group of ratios which reflect management's ability to use the property's assets and resources.

ADJUSTED FORECAST

The preliminary forecast regulated by "other" facts such as conventions, special entertainment events, weather, holidays, and so on.

ADJUSTED NET INCOME APPROACH

One of two basic approaches to cash budgeting. It is generally preferable for budgeting cash for periods longer than six months. Compare Cash Receipts and Disbursements Approach.

ADJUSTING ENTRIES

Entries required at the end of an accounting period to record internal transactions.

ADMINISTRATIVE CONTROLS

Controls for promoting operational efficiency and encouraging adherence to managerial policies. Compare Accounting Controls.

AGING OF ACCOUNTS SCHEDULE

An accounts receivable report reflecting the status of individual accounts and indicating when the charges originated.

ALLOWANCE JOURNAL

Accounting record that serves to reduce or reverse a sale when allowance is given.

AMORTIZATION

The process of writing-off an intangible asset against revenue over its life.

ANNUITY

Refers to the stream of funds provided by a capital investment when the amounts provided are equal at equal intervals (such as the end of each year).

ASSESSED VALUATION

With regard to property taxes, the value the tax assessor places on the property to be taxed.

ASSET

Resource available for use by the business, i.e., anything owned by the business that has monetary value.

ASSET TURNOVER

An activity ratio. Total revenues divided by average total assets.

AUDITING

The process of verifying accounting records and financial reports prepared from accounting records.

AVERAGE COLLECTION PERIOD

The average number of days it takes a hospitality operation to collect all its accounts receivable; calculated by dividing the accounts receivable turnover into 365 (the number of days in a year).

AVERAGE DAILY RATE (ADR)

A key rooms department operating ratio. Rooms revenue divided by number of rooms sold. Also called average room rate.

AVERAGE OCCUPANCY PER ROOM RATIO

An activity ratio measuring management's ability to use the lodging facilities. The number of guests divided by the number of rooms sold.

AVERAGE ROOM RATE

See Average Daily Rate.

AVOIDABLE COSTS

Costs that are not incurred when a hospitality operation shuts down (e.g., when a resort hotel closes for part of the year).

B

BAD DEBTS

An expense incurred due to failure to collect accounts receivable.

BALANCE

The difference between the total debits and total credits of an account.

BALANCE SHEET

Statement of the financial position of the hospitality establishment at a given date, giving the account balances for assets, liabilities, and ownership equity.

BANK

Fixed sum of money provided to an employee who handles cash.

BANK STATEMENT

Record of transactions and account balance, prepared by the bank, to be compared with cash balance as shown in accounting records.

BARGAIN PURCHASE PROVISION

One of four Financial Accounting Standards Board capitalization criteria for determining the status of non-cancelable leases. Under this provision, if a lease has a bargain purchase option, the lessee must classify and account for the lease as a capital lease. A bargain purchase option gives the lessee the option to purchase the leased property at the end of the lease at a price substantially lower than the leased property's expected market value at the date the option is to be exercised.

BEGINNING INVENTORY

Goods available for sale on the first day of the accounting period.

BEVERAGE COST PERCENTAGE

A ratio comparing the cost of beverages sold to beverage sales; calculated by dividing the cost of beverages sold by beverage sales.

BILLING CLERK

Person responsible for charging to guests all vouchers representing food, beverages, room service, and merchandise purchases.

BIN CARD

A perpetual inventory record used in the control of food and beverage products.

BOOKKEEPING

The recording, summarizing, and classifying aspects of accounting.

BOOK VALUE

The difference between the cost of a fixed asset and the related accumulated depreciation. This is also referred to as net book value.

BOTTOM-UP PRICING

Methods for establishing retail prices of goods and services that begin with the desired profit and add all incurred expenses (direct and indirect) to determine the selling price.

BREAKEVEN ANALYSIS

See Cost-Volume-Profit Analysis.

BREAKEVEN POINT

The level of sales volume at which total revenues equal total costs.

BUSINESS ENTITY

The concept that requires that a business maintain its own set of accounts that are separate from other financial interests of its owners.

BUSINESS TRANSACTION

An event or condition that must be recorded.

C

CAPACITY COSTS

Fixed charges relating to the physical plant or the capacity to provide goods and services to guests.

CAPITAL BUDGET

Management's detailed plan for the acquisition of equipment, land, buildings, and other fixed assets.

CAPITAL LEASE

A classification of lease agreements which are of relatively long duration, generally noncancellable, and in which the lessee assumes responsibility for executory costs. For accounting purposes, capital leases are capitalized in a way similar to the purchase of a fixed asset (i.e., recorded as an asset with recognition of a liability).

CAPITAL RATIONING

An approach to capital budgeting used to evaluate combinations of projects according to their net present value (NPV).

CAPITAL STOCK

Shares of ownership of a corporation.

CAPTURE RATIOS

Ratios based on hotel guests or some variation of hotel guests. For example, a hotel may estimate its dinner covers to be 40 plus one quarter of the estimated house guests for the night.

CASH

A category of current assets consisting of cash in house banks, cash in checking and savings accounts, and certificates of deposit. Cash is shown on the balance sheet at its stated value.

CASH BASIS ACCOUNTING

Reporting of revenues and expenses at the time they are collected or paid.

CASH BUDGET

Management's detailed plan for cash receipts and disbursements.

CASH DISBURSEMENTS AND ACCOUNTS PAYABLE JOURNAL

Accounting record of expense transactions and other cash disbursements.

CASH EQUIVALENTS

Short-term, highly liquid investments such as U.S. Treasury Bills and money market accounts.

CASH FLOW

A stream of receipts (inflows) and disbursements (outflows) resulting from operational activities or investments.

CASHIER

Person responsible for handling all cash transactions made in the front office.

CASH MANAGEMENT

The management of a hospitality operation's cash balances (currency and demand deposits), cash flow (cash receipts and disbursements), and short-term investments in securities.

CASH RECEIPTS AND DISBURSEMENTS APPROACH

One of two basic approaches to cash budgeting. It is useful when forecasting cash receipts for periods of up to six months. It shows the direct sources of cash receipts and the direct uses of cash. Compare Adjusted Net Income Approach.

CASH RECEIPTS AND DISBURSEMENTS JOURNAL

Accounting record of each element of a cash transaction; includes guest identification and room number.

CAUSAL APPROACHES TO FORECASTING

Forecasts made on the assumption that the future value of one variable is a function of other variables.

C CORPORATION

The term often used in tax literature to refer to all non-S Corporations.

CERTIFICATE OF LIMITED PARTNERSHIP

A document which must be filed with the proper governmental authorities. Unlike a general partnership agreement (which can be oral), the limited partnership agreement must be in writing.

CERTIFIED PUBLIC ACCOUNTANTS (CPA)

Public accountants who have been licensed to engage in public practice.

CHART OF ACCOUNTS

Listing of general ledger accounts by type of account including account number and account title.

CITY LEDGER

Subsidiary ledger listing accounts receivable of guests who have checked out—also all other receivables.

CLEARING ACCOUNT

Account used to temporarily store information as part of an accounting procedure.

CLOCK CARDS

Cards used in a time clock to record time spent on the job by employees.

CLOSING ENTRIES

Journal entries prepared at the end of the period (normally yearly) to close the temporary proprietorship accounts.

COEFFICIENT OF CORRELATION

A mathematical measure of the relation between the dependent variable and independent variables used in causal forecasting methods.

COEFFICIENT OF DETERMINATION

A measure that reflects the extent to which the change in the independent variable explains the change in the dependent variable. The square of the coefficient of correlation.

COLLECTION FLOAT

The time between when a hospitality business deposits a guest's check (increasing its cash account on the books) and when the business can use the funds (that is, when the bank receives the funds from the guest's bank).

COLLUSION

Two or more people working together to defraud the hospitality property.

COMMON-SIZE BALANCE SHEETS

Balance sheets used in vertical analysis whose information has been reduced to percentages to facilitate comparisons.

COMMON-SIZE INCOME STATEMENTS

Income statements used in vertical analysis whose information has been reduced to percentages to facilitate comparisons.

COMMON-SIZE STATEMENTS

Financial statements used in vertical analysis whose information has been reduced to percentages to facilitate comparisons.

COMMON STOCK

Capital stock of a corporation that generally allows its holders to have voting rights.

COMPARATIVE BALANCE SHEETS

Balance sheets from two or more successive periods used in horizontal analysis.

COMPARATIVE INCOME STATEMENTS

Horizontal analysis of income statements for two accounting periods in terms of both absolute and relative variances for each line item.

COMPARATIVE STATEMENTS

The horizontal analysis of financial statements from the current and previous periods in terms of both absolute and relative variances for each line item.

COMPENSATING BALANCES

A minimum balance for demand deposit accounts required by commercial banks as part of the conditions for a loan agreement.

COMPLIMENTARY OCCUPANCY

The number of complimentary rooms for a period divided by the number of rooms available.

CONSERVATISM

The concept that requires accounting procedures that recognize expenses as soon as possible, but delay the recognition of revenues until they are ensured. For example nonrefundable deposits for future services should be recognized as a liability until the service is actually performed.

CONSISTENCY

The concept that requires that once an accounting method has been adopted, it should be followed from period to period in the future unless a change in accounting methods is warranted and disclosed.

CONSOLIDATED FINANCIAL STATEMENTS

The combined financial statements of a parent corporation and its subsidiary corporations.

CONTINGENT RENT

Rent based on specified variables, such as a percentage of revenues above a given amount.

CONTINUITY OF THE BUSINESS UNIT

The assumption in preparing the accounting records and reports that the business will continue indefinitely and that liquidation is not in prospect—in other words, the business is a going concern.

CONTRIBUTION MARGIN

Sales less cost of sales for either an entire operating department or for a given product; represents the amount of sales revenue that is contributed toward fixed costs and/or profits.

CONTRIBUTION MARGIN RATIO

The contribution margin divided by the selling price. Represents the percentage of sales revenue that is contributed toward fixed costs and/or profits.

CONTROL CYCLE

The never-ending process of planning, assessing results, comparing, correcting, improving, and evaluating.

CONTROLLABLE COSTS

Costs over which a manager is able to exercise judgment and hence be able to keep within predefined boundaries or limits.

CONTROLLER

A chief executive position within the organization of a corporation responsible for all accounting functions within the organization. (In some firms, this person is called a comptroller.)

CORPORATION

A form of business organization that provides a separate legal entity apart from its owners.

COST

An expense; a reduction of an asset—generally for the purpose of increasing revenues.

COST ACCOUNTING

The branch of accounting dealing with the recording, classification, allocation, and reporting of current and prospective costs.

COST ALLOCATION

The process of distributing expenses among various departments.

COST/BENEFIT ANALYSIS

The process of reviewing an investment proposal; listing the expenses and the perceived returns and using this enumeration as a basis for deciding whether to accept the proposal or not.

COST CENTER

Any segment of the company whose expenses can be accumulated into meaningful classifications of data to provide information to management.

COST JUSTIFICATION

The process of justifying expenditures by providing documentation showing that the expected return on investment exceeds the expense incurred.

COST OF GOODS SOLD

Expense incurred in procuring the goods (rather than the services) that are to be resold in the operation of business.

COST OF GOODS SOLD VARIANCE

A group of variances used to examine differences between budgeted and actual amounts paid for goods sold and the total amount sold.

COST PRINCIPLE

The concept that requires recording the value of transactions for accounting purposes at the actual transaction price (cost).

COST-VOLUME-PROFIT (CVP) ANALYSIS

A set of analytical tools used by managers to examine the relationships among various costs, revenues, and sales volume in either graphic or equation form allowing one to determine the revenue required at any desired profit level. Also called breakeven analysis.

CREDIT

Decrease in an asset or increase in a liability or capital—entered on the right side of an account; such amounts are said to be credited to the account.

CREDIT MEMORANDUM

A written statement prepared by the purchaser and signed by the purveyor attesting to the fact that the delivered merchandise did not conform with that ordered.

CURRENT ASSETS

Resources of cash and items that will be converted to cash or used in generating income within a year through normal business operations.

CURRENT LIABILITIES

Obligations that are due within a year.

CURRENT RATIO

Ratio of total current assets to total current liabilities expressed as a coverage of so many times; calculated by dividing current assets by current liabilities.

CYCLICAL PATTERN

A pattern of data (e.g., sales activity) that fluctuates around a trend line according to some regular time period.

D

DAILY REPORT OF OPERATIONS

A frequent major report prepared for management.

DEBIT

Increase in an asset or decrease in a liability or capital—entered on the left side of an account; such amounts are said to be debited or charged to the account.

DEBT-EQUITY RATIO

Compares the debt of a hospitality operation to its net worth (owners' equity) and indicates the operation's ability to withstand adversity and meet its long-term obligations; calculated by dividing total liabilities by total owners' equity.

DECLINING BALANCE DEPRECIATION METHOD

Method of distributing depreciation expense based on a declining percentage rate, providing for a larger depreciation expense in the early years.

DEDUCTIONS

Amounts subtracted from gross income to determine taxable income in accordance with prevailing tax laws.

DEFERRED EXPENSE

Postponement of the recognition of an expense already paid.

DELPHI TECHNIQUE

An approach to forecasting future events that involves achieving a consensus of opinion among experts who interact anonymously with each other in the process of exchanging views and information.

DEMAND

The quantity of any amount of goods which consumers will purchase at a particular price.

DEMAND DEPOSIT

A checking account with a commercial bank.

DEPARTMENTAL INCOME

The difference between an operating department's revenue and direct expenses.

DEPARTMENTAL INCOME STATEMENTS

Supplements to the summary income statement that provide management with detailed financial information by operating department and service centers; also referred to as schedules.

DEPARTMENTAL OPERATING INCOME OR LOSS

Revenue less direct operating expenses equals departmental operating income for each profit center in a hospitality establishment.

DEPARTMENTAL SCHEDULES

See Departmental Income Statements.

DEPRECIATION

Portion of the cost of a fixed asset recognized as an expense for each accounting period; the asset will be used in generating revenues.

DETECTIVE CONTROLS

Controls designed to discover problems and to monitor preventive controls. Detective controls include external audits, surprise cash internal audits, and bank reconciliations.

DIFFERENTIAL COSTS

Costs which differ between two alternatives.

DIRECT EXPENSES

Expenses related directly to the department incurring them and consisting of cost of sales, payroll and related expenses, and other expenses.

DIRECT METHOD

With regard to the statement of cash flows, one of two methods for converting net income to net cash flow from operations. This method shows cash receipts from sales and cash disbursements for expenses and requires that each item on the income statement be converted from an accrual basis to a cash basis. Compare Indirect Method.

DIRECTS

Products received by the hospitality operation which go directly to production areas and/or do not enter inventory records.

DISBURSEMENT VOUCHER

Form used as a means of recording the liability and authorization for payment.

DISCOUNT RATE

The interest rate.

DISCRETIONARY FIXED COSTS

Costs which managers may (in the short run) choose to avoid. These costs do not affect an establishment's capacity.

DIVIDEND

A distribution of earnings to owners of a corporation's stock.

DIVIDEND PAYOUT RATIO

Indicates the percentage of earnings paid out by the hospitality establishment to stockholders; calculated by dividing dividends paid by earnings.

DOUBLE ENTRY SYSTEM

System of recording any business transaction equally to debits and credits.

DOUBLE TAXATION

Occurs when both corporate profits and dividends paid to stockholders are taxed.

DOUBTFUL ACCOUNTS

Accounts receivable that may not be collected.

DRAWING ACCOUNT

An account in which withdrawals of cash by the owner of a business organized as a sole proprietorship are recorded.

E

EARNINGS PER SHARE (EPS)

A ratio providing a general indicator of the profitability of a hospitality operation by comparing net income to the average common shares outstanding. If preferred stock has been issued for the operation, then preferred dividends are subtracted from net income before calculating EPS.

ECONOMIC LIFE PROVISION

One of four Financial Accounting Standards Board capitalization criteria for determining the status of noncancelable leases. If the lease term is equal to 75% or more of the estimated economic life of the leased property, the lessee must classify and account for the lease as a capital lease.

EFFECTIVE COST

The true cost when all elements are considered.

ELASTIC DEMAND

A situation in which the percentage change in quantity demanded exceeds the percentage change in price. In other words, price and total revenues are inversely related, so a price increase will decrease total revenues.

EMPLOYEE'S EARNINGS RECORD

A record for each employee to record gross pay, taxes withheld, deductions, and net pay.

ENDING INVENTORY

Goods available for sale on the last day of the accounting period.

EXECUTORY COSTS

Obligations for property taxes, insurance, and maintenance of leased property.

EXPENSE

Cost incurred in providing the goods and services offered.

EXPONENTIAL SMOOTHING

A forecasting method that uses a smoothing constant (between 0 and 1), along with recent actual and forecasted data, to reflect the relative stability or growth of the activity being forecasted.

F

FEDERAL INCOME TAX

The income taxes calculated on the firm's taxable income according to the federal tax laws.

FEDERAL INCOME TAX WITHHELD

Taxes withheld from employees' gross pay that must be paid to the federal government.

FINANCIAL ACCOUNTING

A branch of accounting dealing with the recording, classifying, and summarizing of transactions involving revenues, expenses, assets, and liabilities.

FINANCIAL ACCOUNTING STANDARDS BOARD

The private sector group that promulgates accounting standards.

FINANCIAL AUDIT

An independent, external audit.

FINANCIAL EXPENSE

Expense associated with owning or renting the property, interest expense, and income taxes.

FINANCIAL LEVERAGE

The use of debt in place of equity dollars to finance operations and increase the return on the equity dollars already invested.

FINANCIAL POSITION

The position of a firm at the end of the accounting period as shown by the balance sheet.

FINANCIAL STATEMENT

Formal medium for communicating accounting information, e.g., balance sheet, income statement, statement of retained earnings.

FIRST-IN, FIRST-OUT (FIFO) METHOD OF INVENTORY VALUATION

Costs charged against revenue in the order in which they were incurred.

FIXED ASSETS

Long-lived assets of a firm that are tangible, e.g., land, equipment, buildings.

FIXED ASSET TURNOVER

A ratio measuring management's effectiveness in using fixed assets to generate revenue; calculated by dividing average total fixed assets into total revenue generated for the period.

FIXED CHARGE COVERAGE RATIO

A variation of the number of times interest earned ratio that considers leases as well as interest expense. Lease expenses and earnings before interest and income taxes divided by interest expense and lease expense.

FIXED CHARGES

A category of expense reported on the income statement that relate to decisions outside the area of control of operating management and consisting of rent, property taxes, insurance, interest, management fees, and depreciation and amortization.

FIXED COSTS

Costs which remain constant in the short run even though sales volume varies; examples of fixed costs include salaries, rent expense, insurance expense, and so on.

FLOAT

The time between the subtraction or addition of cash to the company's books and the actual subtraction or addition to the company's bank account.

FLOWCHART

A visual representation of the movement of information and documents within a hospitality operation.

FLUCTUATION EXPLANATION

A document providing detail not available on the balance sheet which explains drastic changes in balance sheet items.

FOOD AND BEVERAGE MANAGER

Person who plans, directs, organizes, and controls all phases of the food and beverage departments of a food service facility.

FOOD COST PERCENTAGE

A ratio comparing the cost of food sold to food sales; calculated by dividing the wholesale dollar amount of total sales by the retail dollar amount of total sales.

FOOD TRANSFERS

The wholesale cost of food that is used in departments other than the kitchen.

FOOTING

Totaling of columns.

FORECAST

A prediction of future events.

FRONT OFFICE

Point of contact between guests and representatives of management; location where accommodations are arranged and guests' accounts are maintained during their stay.

FULL DISCLOSURE

The concept that requires that financial statements must provide information on all the significant facts that have a bearing on their interpretation. Types of disclosures include the accounting methods used, changes in the accounting methods, contingent liabilities, events occurring subsequent to the financial statement date, and unusual and nonrecurring items.

FUNDAMENTAL ACCOUNTING EQUATION

Assets equal liabilities plus owners' equity. This equation is a balance to be tested and proven, not a formula to be calculated.

FUNDS

Defined as either cash, working capital, or all financial resources for the purpose of reporting changes on the Statement of Changes in Financial Position.

G

GARDE MANGER

Person in charge of cold meat production area in a food service operation.

GENERAL JOURNAL

Record of all accounting transactions.

GENERAL LEDGER

Principal ledger containing all of the balance sheet and income statement accounts.

GENERALLY ACCEPTED ACCOUNTING PRINCIPLES

Accounting principles which have become accepted over time through common usage and also through the work of major accounting bodies. They provide a uniform basis for preparing financial statements.

GENERAL PARTNER

The member(s) of a limited partnership with unlimited liability for the debts of the partnership.

GOING CONCERN

The concept that requires the preparation of accounting records and reports under the assumption that the business will continue indefinitely and that liquidation is not in prospect; also referred to as continuity of the business unit.

GROSS OPERATING PROFIT RATIO

See Operating Efficiency Ratio.

GROSS RETURN ON ASSETS (GROA)

Measures the rate of return on assets regardless of financing methods. Earnings before interest and income taxes divided by average total assets.

GUEST FOLIO

Form containing current guests' statements.

GUEST LEDGER

Subsidiary ledger listing accounts receivable of current guests.

GUEST SERVICES PERSONNEL

Employees who provide mail, key, message, and information services for guests.

H

HEAT, LIGHT, AND POWER

In the past, utility costs of a firm were referred to as heat, light, and power.

HIGH/LOW TWO POINT METHOD

The simplest approach to estimating the fixed and variable elements of a mixed cost. It bases the estimation on data from two extreme periods.

HORIZONTAL ANALYSIS

Comparing financial statements for two or more accounting periods in terms of both absolute and relative variances for each line item.

HOUSE PROFIT

Amount left after the common operating expenses have been deducted from revenue; used to cover the fixed capital expenses and provide a net profit.

HUBBART FORMULA

A bottom-up approach to pricing rooms. In determining the average price per room, this approach considers costs, desired profits, and expected rooms sold.

HURDLE RATE

The established minimum internal rate of return which must be met or exceeded for a project to be accepted under the internal rate of return model of capital budgeting.

I

IMPREST BASIS

Method of maintaining funds by replenishing the amount of disbursements since the previous replenishment.

INCOME AND EXPENSE SUMMARY

A temporary account into which revenue and expense accounts are closed at the end of the accounting period.

INCOME EXCLUSION

Income that is reported on federal tax returns but not subject to taxation; exclusions from income shown on tax forms include amounts for dividends and a portion of long-term capital gains.

INCOME FLOW

Flow which results from operations generating revenues and incurring expenses. These flows are shown on the income statement and reflect the results of operations. Compare Cash Flow.

INCOME STATEMENT

Report on the profitability of operations, including revenues earned and expenses incurred in generating the revenues for the period of time covered by the statement.

INCREMENTAL BORROWING RATE

The rate of interest a lessee would have to pay if financing the purchase of the item to be leased.

INCREMENTAL BUDGETING

Forecasting budgets based on historical financial information.

INCREMENTAL CASH FLOW

The change in cash flow of an operation that results from an investment.

INDIFFERENCE POINT

The level of activity at which the period cost is the same under either a fixed or a variable cost arrangement.

INDIRECT METHOD

With regard to the statement of cash flows, one of two methods for converting net income to net cash flow from operations. This method starts with net income and then adjusts for noncash items included on the income statement.

INELASTIC DEMAND

A desirable situation in which a percentage change in price results in a smaller percentage change in quantity demanded. In other words, price and total revenues are directly related, so a price increase will increase total revenues, despite some decline in quantity demanded.

INFORMATION SYSTEM

All the activities involved in obtaining the information necessary to operate a hotel or motel smoothly and efficiently.

INGREDIENT MARK-UP

See Mark-Up.

INTEGRATED CASH MANAGEMENT SYSTEM

A cash management system for multi-unit operations. It consists of centralizing cash receipts and especially cash disbursements from the corporate office.

INTEGRATED PRICING

An approach to pricing in a hospitality operation having several revenue producing departments that sets prices for goods and/or services in each profit center so as to optimize the operation's net income.

INTEREST EXPENSE

The charge for borrowing money. It is calculated by multiplying the principal times the interest rate times the fraction or more of a year the money is borrowed.

INTERIM STATEMENT

Statement prepared in the periods between annual reports.

INTERNAL CONTROL

The organizational plan, methods, and measures adopted by a hospitality operation to safeguard its assets, check the accuracy and reliability of accounting information, promote operational efficiency, and ensure adherence to the operation's policies and procedures.

INTERNAL CONTROL QUESTIONNAIRE

A second device for studying a hospitality operation's system of internal control. The ICQ uses a series of questions about controls in each accounting area to identify weaknesses.

INTERNAL RATE OF RETURN (IRR)

An approach to evaluating capital budgeting decisions based on the rate of return generated by the investment.

INVENTORY

Food, beverages, and supplies (See Beginning Inventory and Ending Inventory).

INVENTORY TURNOVER

A ratio showing how quickly a hospitality operation's inventory is moving from storage to productive use; calculated by dividing the cost of products (e.g., food or beverages) used by the average product (e.g., food or beverages) inventory.

INVENTORY VALUATION

(See Weighted Average; First-In, First-Out; Last-In, First-Out).

INVOICE

Statement containing the names and addresses of both the buyer and the seller, the date of the transaction, the terms, the methods of shipment, quantities, descriptions, and prices of the goods.

ISSUING

A distribution of food and beverages from the storeroom to authorized individuals who requisition these items.

ISSUING CLERK

A person who is responsible for the issuing function.

J

JOB DESCRIPTION

A written, detailed list of duties and expectations for each employee position within the hospitality operation.

JOINT COSTS

Costs which, when incurred, simultaneously benefit two or more operating departments.

JOURNAL

Accounting record of business transactions (See Allowance journal, Cash disbursements and accounts payable journal, Cash receipts and disbursements journal, General journal, Payroll journal, Sales journal, and Special journal).

JOURNALIZE

To record a transaction in a journal.

JURY OF OPINION

A consensus of views among knowledgeable individuals used in making decisions or forecasts.

L

LABOR COST

The dollar amount paid to all employees, excluding administrative personnel, during an accounting period which can be daily, weekly, monthly, etc.

LABOR COST PERCENTAGE

A ratio comparing the labor expense for each department by the total revenue generated by the department; total labor cost by department divided by department revenues.

LAPPING

A type of theft which occurs when an accounts receivable clerk steals cash received on an account, then posts cash received the next day on a second account to the first account.

LAST-IN, FIRST-OUT (LIFO) METHOD OF INVENTORY VALUATION

Most recent costs incurred charged against revenue.

LEASE

An agreement conveying the right to use resources (equipment, buildings, and/or land) for specified purposes for limited periods of time. The lessor owns the property and conveys the right of its use to the lessee in exchange for periodic cash payments called rent.

LEASEBACK

See Sale and Leaseback.

LEASEHOLD IMPROVEMENTS

Renovations or remodeling performed on leased buildings or space prior to the commencement of operations. For accounting purposes, all leasehold improvements are capitalized (i.e., recorded as an asset with recognition of a liability).

LEDGER

Group of related accounts that comprise a complete unit (See General Ledger, Subsidiary Ledger, Guest Ledger, and City Ledger).

LESSEE

Party which makes periodic cash payments called rent to a lessor in exchange for the right to use property.

LESSOR

Party which owns property and conveys the right of its use to the lessee in exchange for periodic cash payments called rent.

LEVERAGE

See Financial Leverage.

LIABILITIES

Obligations of a business—largely indebtedness related to the expenses incurred in the process of generating income (See Current and Long-Term Liabilities)

LIMITED PARTNER

The member(s) of a limited partnership having limited liability. Limited partners may not actively participate in managing the business.

LIMITED PARTNERSHIP

A form of organization consisting of a partnership between two or more individuals having at least one general partner and one limited partner in which the latter's liabilities are limited to investments.

LINE POSITIONS

Positions within the "chain of command" in a hospitality operation that are directly responsible for all decisions involved in using the hospitality operation's resources to generate revenue and attain other goals of their departments.

LIQUIDITY

The ability of a hospitality operation to meet its short-term (current) obligations by maintaining sufficient cash and/or investments easily convertible to cash.

LIQUIDITY RATIOS

A group of ratios which reveal the ability of a hospitality establishment to meet its short-term obligations.

LOCKBOX SYSTEM

A system used to speed the flow of cash from accounts receivable to the hospitality operation's bank accounts consisting of a post office box from which bank personnel collect all incoming mail and deposit any checks directly in the operation's account with the bank.

LONG-TERM ASSETS (FIXED ASSETS)

Investments or resources of the hotel or motel that will be used to generate income for periods longer than a year. Also called long-lived assets.

LONG-TERM DEBT TO TOTAL CAPITALIZATION RATIO

A solvency ratio showing long-term debt as a percentage of the sum of long-term debt and owners' equity. Long-term debt divided by long-term debt and owners' equity.

LONG-TERM LIABILITIES

Obligations at the balance sheet date which are expected to be paid beyond the next 12 months, or if paid in the next year, they will be paid from restricted funds; also called noncurrent liabilities.

LOSS CARRYBACK

The application of a net operating loss as a deduction against prior years' taxable income, resulting in a refund of taxes previously paid.

LOSS CARRYFORWARD

The application of a prior year's net operating loss as a deduction against subsequent taxable income.

M

MACRS

See Modified Accelerated Cost Recovery System.

MANAGEMENT CONTRACT

Contracts under which hotel owners make substantial payments from the hotel's gross revenues to hotel management companies.

MANAGEMENT FEES

The cost of using an independent management company to operate the hospitality establishment.

MANAGERIAL ACCOUNTING

The branch of accounting designed to provide information to various management levels for the enhancement of controls; includes the preparation of performance reports that compare actual results to budgeted standards.

MARGIN OF SAFETY

The excess of budgeted or actual sales over sales at breakeven.

MARKETABLE SECURITIES

Current assets in the form of investments in stocks and bonds of other corporations.

MARKETING RESEARCH

The systematic gathering, recording, and analyzing of data related to the marketing of goods and services.

MARK-UP

An approach to pricing of goods and services which determines retail prices by adding a certain percentage to the cost of goods sold. The mark-up is designed to cover all non-product costs (e.g., labor, utilities, supplies, interest expense, taxes, etc.) and also cover the desired profit. Ingredient mark-up is based on all ingredients. Prime ingredient mark-up bases the mark-up solely on the cost of the main ingredient.

MATCHING PRINCIPLE

The concept that requires recording expenses in the same period as the revenues to which they relate.

MATERIALITY

The concept that requires that events be recognized and recorded by accounting procedures if "it makes a difference" as determined by some relative standard of comparison. For example, materiality may be established by a rule of thumb which states that an item is recognized if it exceeds X% or more of total assets or income.

MENU ENGINEERING

A method of menu analysis and food pricing that considers both the profitability and popularity of competing menu items.

MIXED COSTS

Costs that are a mixture of both fixed and variable costs; (See Fixed Costs and Variable Costs).

MODIFIED ACCELERATED COST RECOVERY SYSTEM

The legal basis for depreciation rules since 1986.

MORTGAGE

Security on a loan that gives the creditor a lien on property owned by a debtor.

MOVING AVERAGES

Averaging data from specified time periods in a continually updating manner such that as new results become available, they are used in the average by adding the most recent value and dropping the earliest value.

MULTIPLE ALLOCATION BASE APPROACH (MABA)

The use of different allocation bases to allocate different overhead costs among departments. Compare Single Allocation Base Approach.

MULTIPLE OCCUPANCY

The number of rooms occupied by more than one guest divided by the number of rooms occupied by guests.

MULTIPLE REGRESSION ANALYSIS

Regression analysis forecasting used when two or more independent variables are related to the dependent variable.

N

NEGATIVE CASH FLOW

The condition in which cash disbursements exceed cash receipts.

NET BOOK VALUE

The cost of a fixed asset less accumulated depreciation.

NET FLOAT

The difference between payment float and collection float.

NET INCOME

The bottom line on an income statement when revenues exceed expenses.

NET LOSS

The bottom line on an income statement when expenses exceed revenues.

NET PRESENT VALUE (NPV)

An approach to evaluating capital budgeting decisions based on discounting the cash flows relating to the project to their present value; calculated by subtracting the project cost from the present value of the discounted cash flow stream.

NET WORTH

The claims of the owners to assets of a firm. Also, assets less liabilities equal net worth.

NIGHT AUDITOR

Person responsible for posting late charges or credits to guests' accounts; also for checking accounts to see whether or not the day's postings are accurate and in agreement with supporting records.

NONCURRENT RECEIVABLES

Accounts and notes receivable which are not expected to be collected within one year from the balance sheet date.

NOTES PAYABLE

A written promise by a borrower to pay money to a lender on demand or at a definite time.

NUMBER OF TIMES INTEREST EARNED RATIO

A solvency ratio. Expresses the number of times interest expense can be covered. Earnings before interest and taxes divided by interest expense.

O

OBJECTIVE EVIDENCE

The preferred basis of accounting transactions and the resulting accounting records.

OCCUPANCY PERCENTAGE

A ratio indicating management's success in selling its "product"; for hotels or motels, it is referred to as the occupancy rate and is calculated by dividing the number of rooms sold by the number of rooms available; for food service operations, it is referred to as seat turnover and is calculated by dividing the number of people served by the number of seats available.

OFF-BALANCE-SHEET FINANCING

Term sometimes applied to leasing, because property acquired for use through an operational lease is not shown on the balance sheet. Future rent obligations also do not appear on the balance sheet, although some footnote disclosure may be required.

$1 PER $1,000 APPROACH

An approach to rooms pricing that sets the price of a room at $1 for each $1,000 of project cost per room. This approach fails to consider the current value of facilities when it emphasizes the project cost.

OPERATING CASH FLOWS TO CURRENT LIABILITIES RATIO

A fairly new liquidity ratio made possible by the statement of cash flows which compares the cash flow from the firm's operating activities to its obligation at the balance sheet date that must be paid within twelve months. Operating cash flows divided by average current liabilities.

OPERATING CASH FLOWS TO TOTAL LIABILITIES RATIO

A solvency ratio which uses figures from both the statement of cash flows and the balance sheet. Operating cash flows divided by average total liabilities.

OPERATING EFFICIENCY RATIO

A measure of management's ability to generate sales and control expenses; calculated by dividing income before fixed charges by total revenue. Also called gross operating profit ratio.

OPERATING EXPENSE

Cost incurred in providing the goods and services offered by hotels and motels.

OPERATING LEASE

A classification of lease agreements which are usually of relatively short duration, easily cancelled, and in which the lessor retains responsibility for executory costs. For accounting purposes, operating leases are not capitalized, but simply recognized as an expense when rent is paid.

OPERATING LEVERAGE

The extent to which an operation's expenses are fixed rather than variable; an operation that substitutes fixed costs for variable costs is said to be highly levered.

OPERATING RATIOS

A group of ratios which assist in the analysis of hospitality establishment operations.

OPERATING STATEMENTS

Monthly report to management providing detailed financial information reflecting budgeted standards and actual results of the activities of each operating department for the most recent period, the same period a year ago, and year-to-date numbers for both the current and the past year.

OPERATIONS BUDGET

Management's detailed plans for generating revenue and incurring expenses for each department within the hospitality operation; also referred to as the revenue and expense budget.

OPPORTUNITY COSTS

Costs of the best foregone opportunity in a decision-making situation involving several alternatives.

ORGANIZATIONAL CHART

A visual representation of the hierarchical structure of positions within a hospitality operation showing the different layers of management and the chain of command.

ORGANIZATIONAL COSTS

The costs to incorporate a business.

OVERHEAD COSTS

All expenses other than the direct costs of profit centers; examples include undistributed operating expenses, management fees, fixed charges, and income taxes.

OWNERS' EQUITY

Financial interest of the owners of a business—assets minus liabilities.

P

PAID-IN CAPITAL

The capital acquired from stockholders of the corporation.

PAID OCCUPANCY

A measure of management's ability to efficiently use available assets. The number of rooms sold divided by the number of rooms available for sale.

PAR STOCK

That amount of inventory required to satisfy the normal demand for a certain item during a given period of time.

PARTNERSHIP

A form of business organization involving two or more owners that is not incorporated.

PAYBACK

An approach to evaluating capital budgeting decisions based on the number of years of annual cash flow generated by the fixed asset purchase required to recover the investment.

PAYMENT FLOAT

The time between when a hospitality business writes a check (decreasing its cash account on the books) and when the funds are actually deducted from the business's bank account.

PAYROLL JOURNAL

Journal providing a means to record checks, total payroll expense, liabilities for amounts deducted, and the net disbursement.

PAYROLL SUMMARY REPORT

Form that can be used in place of a payroll journal to record payroll expense, liabilities for amounts deducted, and net wage and salary disbursements.

PERMANENT OWNERS' EQUITY ACCOUNTS

A classification of owners' equity accounts that are not closed at the end of an accounting period; e.g., accounts for recording capital stock and retained earnings.

PERPETUAL INVENTORY RECORD

Record of inventory kept up-to-date by entering all additions to and subtractions from stock.

PHYSICAL INVENTORY

Detailed listing of the merchandise on hand at a specific time.

PORTION

A standard quantity of food or beverage served for one person.

PORTION COST

The wholesale price associated with all ingredients required to produce one standard portion.

POST

Transfer data entry in the journal to the appropriate account.

PRECHECK REGISTER

A cash register without an operating cash drawer used in revenue control systems to record and transfer sales information.

PREFERRED STOCK

Stock issued by a corporation which provides preferential treatment on dividends, but may not give the stockholder the privilege of voting.

PREPAID EXPENSES

Expenditures made for expense items prior to the period the expense is incurred.

PREPARATION

The procedure whereby pre-prepared raw food items are processed and made ready for service to the final consumer.

PREVENTIVE CONTROLS

Controls implemented before a problem occurs. They include such things as the use of locks to safeguard assets, the separation of duties to preclude operating personnel from controlling inventories, and general and specific authorization policies.

PRICE EARNINGS (PE) RATIO

A profitability ratio used by financial analysts when presenting investment possibilities. The market price per share divided by the earnings per share.

PRICE ELASTICITY OF DEMAND

An expression of the relationship between a change in price and the resulting change in demand.

PRICE QUOTATION SHEET

A standardized sheet that facilitates a competitive buying procedure which remains in conformance with established standard specifications.

PRICING POLICY

A standard procedure that the firm follows in determining the retail sales value of its product(s).

PRIME INGREDIENT MARK-UP

See Mark-Up.

PROCEDURE MANUAL

A written, detailed description of what tasks, jobs, or duties within a hospitality operation are to be performed, including when, by whom, and how they are to be performed.

PROFITABILITY RATIOS

A group of ratios which reflect the results of all areas of management's responsibilities.

PROFIT CENTER

A revenue producing department within a hospitality operation.

PROFIT MARGIN

An overall measure of management's ability to generate sales and control expenses; calculated by dividing net income by total revenue.

PROFIT-VOLUME GRAPH

A graph that focuses on the impact on profits of changes in sales volume. In this graph, revenues and costs are not shown.

PROPERTY AND EQUIPMENT

Fixed assets including land, buildings, furniture, equipment, construction in progress, leasehold improvements, and property such as china, glassware, silver, linens, uniforms, etc.

PROPERTY TAXES

Taxes levied on real estate and personal property such as furniture, fixtures, and equipment.

PURCHASED GOODWILL

The excess of a hospitality operation's purchase price over the dollars assigned to its individual assets.

PURCHASE ORDER

Order for material sent by the purchasing department.

PURCHASE REQUISITION

A form used to request the purchasing department to purchase merchandise or other property.

PURCHASING

The acquisition of merchandise by the payment of money or its equivalent.

PURCHASING AGENT

A staff position within a hospitality operation providing assistance in the selection and procurement of products (e.g., food and beverages) by gathering product information, screening potential suppliers, and offering recommendations about products to be used and purchase specifications to be developed.

PURVEYOR

A firm which provides or supplies merchandise to customer firms.

Q

QUALITATIVE FORECASTING METHODS

Forecasting methods that emphasize human judgment.

QUANTITATIVE FORECASTING METHODS

Causal and time series approaches to forecasting.

QUICK ASSETS

Current assets consisting of cash or near-cash and excluding inventories and prepaid expenses.

R

RATIO

The mathematical expression of a significant relationship between two related numbers that results from dividing one by the other.

RATIO ANALYSIS

The comparison of related facts and figures.

RECEIVING

To accept delivery of merchandise that has been ordered or is expected by the firm and to record such transactions.

RECEIVING CLERK

A person who performs the receiving function.

RECEIVING REPORT

Report on items received, prepared at time of delivery.

REGRESSION ANALYSIS

A mathematical approach to fitting a straight line to data points such that the differences in the distances of the data points from the line are minimized.

RELEVANT COSTS

Costs which must be considered in a decision-making situation; relevant costs must be differential, future, and quantifiable.

RENT

Cash payments made by a lessee to a lessor.

REPORT FORMAT

A possible arrangement of a balance sheet which lists the assets first, followed by liabilities and owners' equity. Compare Account Format.

REQUISITION

Written order to withdraw items from stock.

RESIDUAL INCOME

The excess of a hotel's net income over an established minimum return.

RESIDUAL VALUE

With regard to leasing, the estimated market value of a leased item at the end of the lease term.

RESORT HOTELS

Lodging properties which cater primarily to non-business travelers and tourists.

RESPONSIBILITY ACCOUNTING

The organization of accounting information (as on an income statement) which focuses attention on departmental results such as the rooms and food and beverage departments.

RESTRICTED CASH

Cash that has been deposited in separate accounts, often for the purpose of retiring long-term debt.

RETAINED EARNINGS

An account for recording undistributed earnings of a corporation.

RETURN ON ASSETS (ROA)

A ratio providing a general indicator of the profitability of a hospitality operation by comparing net income to total investment; calculated by dividing net income by average total assets.

RETURN ON COMMON STOCKHOLDERS' EQUITY

A variation of ROE which is used when preferred stock has been issued. Net income less preferred dividends paid to preferred stockholders divided by average common stockholders' equity.

RETURN ON INVESTMENT (ROI)

The gain associated with the employment of capital.

RETURN ON OWNERS' EQUITY (ROE)

A ratio providing a general indicator of the profitability of a hospitality operation by comparing net income to the owners' investment; calculated by dividing net income by average owners' equity.

REVENUES

Amounts charged to customers in exchange for goods and services.

REVENUE VARIANCE

A group of variances used to examine differences between budgeted and actual prices and volumes.

REVERSING ENTRY

Entry that is the exact reverse of the adjusting entry to which it relates.

REVPAR

Revenue per available room. A combination of paid occupancy percentage and average daily rate. Room revenues divided by available revenues or, alternatively, paid occupancy percentage times average daily rate.

S

SALE AND LEASEBACK

A transaction whereby an owner of real estate agrees with an investor to sell the real estate to the investor and simultaneously rent it back for a future period of time, allowing uninterrupted use of the property while providing the operation with capital that was previously tied up in the property.

SALES HISTORY

The gathering and recording of historical sales data.

SALES JOURNAL

Journal used for posting all sales transactions.

SALES MIX

The combination of products, services, and prices offered by a hospitality operation.

SALVAGE VALUE

Estimated market value of an asset at the time it is to be retired from use.

SCATTER DIAGRAM

A graphic approach to determining the fixed and variable elements of a mixed cost.

S CORPORATION

A hybrid form of organization that allows corporations to be taxed in the same manner as a partnership.

SEASONALITY

Regular variations in levels of activity experienced by hospitality operations over periods of time that may include fluctuations throughout the day, week, month, or year.

SEASONAL PATTERN

A pattern of data (e.g., sales activity) that shows regular fluctuations according to some time period (daily, weekly, monthly, yearly).

SEAT TURNOVER

An activity ratio measuring the rate at which people are served. The number of people served divided by the number of seats available.

SEGREGATION OF DUTIES

An element of internal control systems in which different personnel are assigned the different functions of accounting, custody of assets, and production; the purpose is to prevent and detect errors and/or theft.

SENSITIVITY ANALYSIS

The study of the sensitivity of the CVP model's dependent variables (such as room sales) to changes in one or more of the model's independent variables (such as variable costs and selling prices).

SERVICE BAR

An area that provides beverages exclusively for dining patrons.

SERVICE CENTERS

Departments within a hospitality operation that are not directly involved in generating revenue but that provide supporting services to revenue generating departments within the operation.

SIGNIFICANCE CRITERIA

Criteria used to determine which variances are significant. Generally expressed in terms of both dollar and percentage differences.

SINGLE ALLOCATION BASE APPROACH (SABA)

The allocation of overhead costs among departments using a single allocation base (such as departmental square footage). Compare Multiple Allocation Base Approach.

SMOOTHING CONSTANT

A value used in the exponential smoothing forecasting method. Determined using forecasts from two consecutive previous periods and the actual demand from the earlier of these two periods.

SOLE PROPRIETORSHIP

An unincorporated business organized by one person.

SOLVENCY

The extent to which a hospitality operation is financed by debt and is able to meet its long-term obligations. An operation is solvent when its assets exceed its liabilities.

SOLVENCY RATIO

A measure of the extent to which an operation is financed by debt and is able to meet its long-term obligations; calculated by dividing total assets by total liabilities.

SOLVENCY RATIOS

A group of ratios which measure the extent to which the enterprise has been financed by debt and is able to meet its long-term obligations.

SPECIAL INVENTORY

Any counting of stock that is performed at an irregular time for certain extraordinary purposes.

SPECIAL JOURNAL

Journal used to accelerate the recording of specific kinds of accounting transactions.

SPOT CHECK

A random examination of any particular operating procedure.

STAFFING

Selecting and training a body of persons who are then charged with carrying out the work of a firm.

STAFF ORGANIZATION

A group of assistants to a manager, supervisor, or department head; also, a group of advisors and technical specialists who are charged with aiding the operating departments of a firm.

STAFF POSITIONS

Positions within the organizational structure of a hospitality operation that are responsible for providing expert advice and information to assist management in making decisions. Staff specialists collect information and provide advice, but do not make decisions for line managers.

STAFF SPECIALIST

An advisor or technical expert whose function is to assist operating management.

STANDARD COSTS

Forecasts of what actual costs should be under projected conditions; standard costs serve as a standard of comparison for control purposes or for evaluations of productivity.

STANDARD PURCHASE SPECIFICATIONS

Detailed descriptions setting forth the quality, size, and weight factors desired for particular items.

STANDARD RECIPE

A regulated formula for preparing any particular type of retail food or beverage item.

STATEMENT OF CASH FLOWS

Explains the change in cash for the accounting period by showing the effects on cash of a business's operating, investing, and financing activities for the accounting period.

STATEMENT OF CHANGES IN FINANCIAL POSITION

A basic financial statement that shows sources and uses of funds for an accounting period.

STEP COSTS

Costs which are constant within a range of activity, but different among ranges of activity.

STOCKHOLDERS' EQUITY

The difference between assets and liabilities of a corporation.

STORES

Products received by the hospitality operation that are moved into storage areas and entered in inventory records.

STORING

The process of stocking a place with supplies of food, beverage, and other items that are required for future use.

STRAIGHT-LINE DEPRECIATION

Method of distributing depreciation expense evenly throughout the estimated life of the asset.

STRATEGIC PLANNING

Another name for long-range planning. It not only considers revenues and expenses, but also evaluates and selects from among major alternatives those which provide long-range direction to the hospitality operation.

SUBSIDIARY LEDGER

Special ledger that provides more detailed information about an account; controlled by the general ledger—used when there are several accounts with a common characteristic.

SUMMARY INCOME STATEMENT

Income statements lacking the detail of supporting schedules, intended for external users.

SUM-OF-THE-YEARS'-DIGITS DEPRECIATION METHOD

Method of distributing depreciation expense, with a more rapid depreciation in early years, by estimating the number of years of useful life, adding the digits, and then dividing the sum by the number of years remaining to determine the depreciation rate for the current year.

SUNK COSTS

Past costs relating to a past decision; e.g., the net book value of an fixed asset.

T

TAX ACCOUNTING

The branch of accounting dealing with the preparation and filing of tax forms with the various governmental agencies.

TAX AVOIDANCE

Planning transactions to mitigate the impact of taxes or avoid the application of taxes in such a manner as to achieve the lowest possible tax cost within the constraints of other business considerations and the prevailing tax laws and regulations.

TAX CREDITS

Amounts that are subtracted directly from income taxes calculated on taxable income in accordance with prevailing tax laws.

TAX DEDUCTIONS

Amounts that are deducted from taxable income in accordance with prevailing tax laws.

TAX EVASION

The fraudulent denial or concealment of a current or future tax liability such as the underreporting of income and claiming unsubstantiated or excessive income deductions.

TEMPORARY OWNERS' EQUITY ACCOUNTS

A classification of owners' equity accounts that are closed out at the end of each fiscal year; e.g., all revenue and expense accounts.

TIME SERIES FORECASTS

Forecasts made on the assumption that an underlying pattern is recurring over time.

TIME VALUE OF MONEY

The process of placing future years' income on an equal basis with current year expenditures in order to facilitate comparison.

TITLE TRANSFER PROVISION

One of four Financial Accounting Standards Board capitalization criteria for determining the status of noncancelable leases. If the property is transferred to the lessee by the end of the lease term, the lessee must classify and account for the lease as a capital lease.

TOLERANCE

An allowable variation between the standard and the actual.

TOTAL CAPITALIZATION

The sum of a hospitality operation's long-term debt and owners' equity.

TRADE CREDIT

Term for credit offered by suppliers who do not charge interest to hospitality operations for amounts owed in the normal course of business.

TRANSACTION ANALYSIS

Process of analyzing a transaction into the appropriate accounts; entering debits and credits equally in the accounting record.

TRANSACTION MOTIVE

The rationale for maintaining adequate balances in checking accounts to meet checks drawn on those accounts.

TRANSIENT HOTELS

Lodging operations that cater primarily to business people; transient hotels tend to be busiest Monday through Thursday.

TREASURY STOCK

Capital stock of a corporation that the corporation has repurchased for future issuance.

TREND PATTERN

A pattern of data (e.g., sales activity) characterized by a general direction whose long-run estimate is projected into the future.

TRIAL BALANCE

Listing and totaling of all the general ledger accounts on a worksheet.

TRIPLE NET LEASE

A form of lease agreement in which the lessee is obligated to pay property taxes, insurance, and maintenance on the leased property.

U

UNDISTRIBUTED OPERATING EXPENSES

Expenses not directly related to income generating departments and consisting of administrative and general expenses, data processing, human resources, transportation, marketing, property operation and maintenance, and energy expenses.

UNIFORM SYSTEM OF ACCOUNTS

Standardized accounting systems prepared by various segments of the hospitality industry offering detailed information about accounts, classifications, formats, the different kinds, contents, and uses of financial statements and reports, and other useful information.

UNIT ELASTIC

Elasticity of demand is exactly 1. Any percentage change in price is accompanied by the same percentage change in quantity demanded. Total revenues remain constant.

UNIT OF MEASUREMENT PRINCIPLE

The accounting principle that the monetary values stated in financial statements should represent a stable unit of value so that meaningful comparisons of current and past periods are possible.

V

VALUE RECOVERY PROVISION

One of four Financial Accounting Standards Board capitalization criteria for determining the status of non-cancelable leases. If the present value of minimum lease payments (excluding executory costs) equals or exceeds 90% of the excess of fair market value of the leased property over any applicable investment tax credit retained by the lessor, the lessee must classify and account for the lease as a capital lease.

VARIABLE COSTS

Costs which change proportionately with sales volume.

VARIABLE LABOR VARIANCE

A group of variances used to examine differences between budgeted and actual variable labor expense.

VARIABLE LEASE

A form of leasing agreement in which rental payments are based upon revenues.

VARIANCE ANALYSIS

Process of identifying and investigating causes of significant differences (variances) between budgeted plans and actual results.

VENDOR

A firm that sells wholesale merchandise (See Purveyor).

VERTICAL ANALYSIS

Analyzing individual financial statements reducing financial information to percents by having total assets equal 100% while individual asset categories equal percentages of the 100% and by having total liabilities and owners' equity equal 100% while individual categories of liabilities equal percentages of the 100%.

VOUCHER

Document used for posting a transaction to a guest account.

W

WEIGHTED AVERAGE CONTRIBUTION MARGIN RATIO

In a multiple product situation, an average contribution margin for all operated departments that is weighted to reflect the relative contribution of each department to the establishment's ability to pay fixed costs and generate profits.

WEIGHTED AVERAGE METHOD OF INVENTORY VALUATION

Total cost of a particular commodity available for sale divided by the total number of units of that commodity, resulting in the unit cost to be charged against revenue earned by sale of that commodity.

WORKING CAPITAL

Current assets minus current liabilities.

WORKING CAPITAL TURNOVER RATIO

A liquidity ratio which compares working capital (current assets less current liabilities) to revenue.

WORKSHEET

Working paper used as a preliminary to the preparation of financial statements.

Y

YIELD MANAGEMENT

Selling rooms in a way that maximizes total revenues. Before selling a room in advance, the hotel considers the probability of being able to sell the room to other market segments that are willing to pay higher rates.

Z

ZERO BASE BUDGETING

An approach to preparing budgets that requires the justification of all expenses; this approach assumes that each department starts with zero dollars and must justify all budgeted amounts.

Index

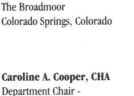

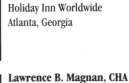

Educational Institute Fellows

Respected industry experts who serve as advisors to the Board of Trustees